CCH® AnswerConn

Tax Cuts and Jobs Act Impact

Guide to Choice of Entity

Robert W. Jamison, CPA, Ph.D
Lori B. Miller, JD, LL.M

Wolters Kluwer

This publication is designed to provide accurate and authoritative information in regard to the subject matter covered. It is sold with the understanding that the publisher is not engaged in rendering legal, accounting, or other professional service. If legal advice or other expert assistance is required, the services of a competent professional person should be sought.

ISBN: 978-0-8080-4990-6

© 2019 CCH Incorporated and its affiliates.
All rights reserved.
2700 Lake Cook Road
Riverwoods, IL 60015
800 344 3734
CCHCPELink.com

No claim is made to original government works; however, within this Product or Publication, the following are subject to CCH Incorporated's copyright: (1) the gathering, compilation, and arrangement of such government materials; (2) the magnetic translation and digital conversion of data, if applicable; (3) the historical, statutory and other notes and references; and (4) the commentary and other materials.

Printed in the United States of America.

FSC
www.fsc.org
MIX
From responsible sources
FSC® C099992

About the Author

Robert W. Jamison, CPA, Ph.D., resides in Leesburg, Virginia. He is a Professor Emeritus of Accounting at Indiana University, Purdue University Indianapolis (IUPUI). In addition to *S Corporation Taxation*, published annually by Wolters Kluwer, Dr. Jamison has been the author of several courses published by the AICPA, various universities' extensions and state CPA societies. His professional experience has included employment with universities, and national and local CPA firms. His articles have appeared in the *Journal of Passthrough Entities, The Tax Adviser, Journal of S Corporation Taxation, The Journal of Accountancy, Practical Tax Strategies*, and various other publications. Professor Jamison has taught many professional education programs for national and local accounting firms and has developed material used in their continuing education programs. He has been a lecturer in AICPA and state CPA societies' programs and has developed and presented training material for several large accounting firms. He is also author of the *TCJA Impact: Guide to Pass-Through Entities, TCJA Impact: Guide to Small Business*, and a coauthor of the 2019 *Multistate Tax Guide to Pass-Through Entities*, published annually by Wolters Kluwer. He is a contributing author to *National Income Tax Workshop*, published annually by Land Grant Universities Tax Education Foundation.

Lori B. Miller, JD, LL.M in taxation, is an attorney in Whitefish, Montana. She is also licensed to practice in California and Washington. Her legal practice emphasizes tax law, estate planning, and business law. She is the lead editor of the *2018 National Income Tax Workbook*.

Contents

CHAPTER 1: Introduction

    ¶1.01   Effects of the Act 1

CHAPTER 2: Entities Analyzed in This Guide

    ¶2.01   Background 3
    ¶2.02   Influence of the Income Tax 4
    ¶2.03   Newer Entities and Adaptations 4
    ¶2.04   Entities Recognized in the Tax Law 5
    ¶2.05   Treatment of the Limited Liability Company 6
    ¶2.06   Summary of State Law and Tax Entities 6

CHAPTER 3: Principal Factors Influencing Choice of Entity

    ¶3.01   Tax and Nontax Factors 7

CHAPTER 4: Tax Rates

    ¶4.01   Individual Rates 9
    ¶4.02   C Corporation Rates 11
    ¶4.03   Disregarded Entity and Partnership Rates 13
    ¶4.04   S Corporation and Shareholder Rates 16

CHAPTER 5: Relationship of Owners to Business Entity

    ¶5.01   Widely-Held Businesses 21
    ¶5.02   Closely-Held Businesses 22
    ¶5.03   The Wharton Study 23

CHAPTER 6: Ownership of Real Estate by the Closely-Held Business

    ¶6.01   Transferring Property to a Corporation 25
    ¶6.02   Transferring Property from a Corporation 29
    ¶6.03   Transfers at Death 30
    ¶6.04   Rent by the Investors to the Business Entity 31

CHAPTER 7: Exit Strategies

¶7.01 Asset Transfers 35
¶7.02 Entity Transfers 44
¶7.03 Classification of Stock Deal as Asset Deal for Tax Purposes 52
¶7.04 Other Considerations 58

CHAPTER 8: Entity Changes

¶8.01 Disregarded Entities and Partnerships 61
¶8.02 Partnerships and Corporations 63
¶8.03 S Corporation Revocations and Terminations 65

CHAPTER 9: Fringe Benefits

¶9.01 Health and Accident Insurance 69
¶9.02 Other Fringe Benefits 73

CHAPTER 10: Conclusion: Tax Rates, Distributions and Entity Choice

¶10.01 In General 81
¶10.02 Not Eligible for Section 199A Deduction
and Subject to Self-Employment Tax 83
¶10.03 Eligible for Section 199A Deduction
and Subject to Self-Employment Tax 85
¶10.04 Not Eligible for Section 199A Deduction and
Not Subject to Self-Employment Tax 87
¶10.05 Eligible for Section 199A Deduction and
Not Subject to Self-Employment Tax 90

APPENDIX: Selected Code Sections Affected by the Tax Cuts and Jobs Act 93

Chapter 1

Introduction

¶1.01 Effects of the Act

The Tax Cuts and Jobs Act of 2017 (TCJA) became law on December 22, 2017. [P.L. 115-97] This law made significant changes to the taxation of corporations, individuals and pass-through entities. The principal purposes of this legislation were twofold:

- To change the U.S. corporate tax system from a worldwide approach to a territorial model; and
- To reduce the corporate tax rates.

The TCJA accomplished both principal objectives, at least to a degree.

- The rates of tax on C corporations were changed from a graduated scale of 15% to 35% in 2017 to a flat 21% rate in 2018.
- Taxation of international operations has been changed from a worldwide "long-arm" structure to a modified territorial system.

Individuals' tax rates were also reduced, although not to the degree that the reduction applied to corporations. The top rate on individuals, which was 39.6 percent for 2017, became 37 percent in 2018. Beginning in 2018, there is also a new deduction for individuals whose income is from an unincorporated business. This deduction, known as the qualified business income (QBI) deduction, or the Section 199A deduction, is a purely paper deduction, which requires no economic outlay.

The apparent disparity between the top corporate rate and the top individual rate has led many business owners to the conclusion that they are better off with a C corporation than a pass-through entity or proprietorship. There are certainly situations in which this strategy works well. However, in other cases, the advantage of a single tax entity still outweighs the immediate apparent savings from the rate differential.

Chapter 2 discusses the different legal entities, along with the default tax status and available elective tax forms for each. Chapter 3 lists some of the principal factors involving the choice of entity. Chapter 4 discusses the tax rates in detail, along with a special deduction that applies to individuals. This deduction, known as the QBI deduction or Section 199A deduction, mitigates the disparity between the tax burdens of the C corporation and individuals.

Chapter 5 describes some divergent relationships between ownership and the business per se. It discusses some of the strategies appropriate to widely-held businesses, those applicable to owners who have little or no involvement in the day to day operations of the business, and to those businesses which provide the substantial or sole source of income and wealth to their owners.

As Chapter 6 demonstrates, many businesses prefer to separate real estate from other assets and operations. This Chapter discusses several reasons why it is often preferable to hold the real estate in an unincorporated entity.

Chapter 7 compares the tax effects of sales of different business entities. Although a sale might not be imminent, when owners choose a tax form it is important to keep the tax consequences of the sales of different business forms in mind when acquiring or establishing a business, as well as when evaluating the advisability of retaining or changing the tax form of an existing entity.

Chapter 8 delves into the means and consequences of changing from one tax form to another. In general, it is relatively easy to switch between C and S corporation status. However, changing from corporate status to that of an unincorporated entity may be expensive, even prohibitively so. Accordingly, the decision to incorporate may be irreversible as a practical matter.

Chapter 9 focuses on medical insurance provided by the business, along with a brief discussion of other fringe benefits. Although the C corporation holds an advantage over the S corporation or the unincorporated entity, there are compensating factors that make the pass-through entities reasonably competitive in providing health insurance. For other benefits, the C corporation has the decided advantage.

Chapter 10 compares the C corporation, the S corporation and the unincorporated entity over various income levels and varying levels of distributions.

As this Guide indicates, there is no "one size fits all" approach to selecting a business entity. Each entrepreneur, investor and tax professional must consider conflicting objectives, and select the entity, or group of entities, that will provide the best results given the foreseeable tradeoffs.

Chapter 2
Entities Analyzed in This Guide

This Guide discusses the C corporation the S corporation, the partnership and the proprietorship. It confines the discussion to businesses that are engaged in business and investment operations within the United States. The discussions of international operations are covered in *TCJA Impact: Guide to International Tax*.

¶2.01 Background

Historically, business entities were structured as proprietorships, partnerships or corporations. In many respects, the choices were quite simple. A proprietorship existed when a person operated a business with no other equity owners and did not incorporate. Although the proprietor would not be protected from the liabilities of the business, in many cases this was not an issue of major concern. In some other cases, the proprietor had no choice. For example, until the 1970s most states prohibited professional practices, such as medicine, law and accountancy, from using the corporate form.

In the renaissance period, Venetian merchants discovered that they could accomplish more by pooling resources. Thus, were born two of the modern business concepts: the partnership and double-entry accounting.

Around the time of the American revolution, the concept of a corporation came to fruition in the United States although this business form had previously been used in Great Britain. Banks and other industries were early users of the corporate form. As the need to raise capital grew during the industrial revolution, the business form which shielded the owners from personal liability and allowed centralized management, become more popular.

In the income tax arena, the corporation became subject to a generalized federal income tax in 1909. Four years later, after the passage of the 16th Amendment to the U.S. constitution, all taxpayers became subject to the income tax. Beginning with the Revenue Act of 1913, the federal taxing statutes recognized the status of partnerships as being aggregations of the business activities of their owners. Accordingly, the income tax was imposed on the owners, rather than the partnership entity.

After World War II, economists and Congress began to study the concept of "tax neutrality," a theory that federal income tax treatment should not be a major determinant in the selection of a business entity. One significant result of this theory was the enactment of Subchapter S in 1958, which allowed certain closely-held corporations to shift the burden of the federal income tax to their shareholders. Later evidence of tax neutrality was the issuance of the entity classification regulations in 1996, also known as the "check the box" election. This election allows an unincorporated entity to select a corporate tax form, either as a C corporation or possibly as an S corporation

If a business did not incorporate and had two or more equity members, it would be a partnership. Generally, partners were not protected from the liabilities of the business, but, again, there may have been no choice, or the likelihood of business liabilities beyond acceptable or insurable amounts may not have been a realistic worry.

Incorporation was the choice when the owners desired limited liability and centralized governance. Various states developed laws concerning creditor protection, as well as the rights and responsibilities of shareholders. Exchanges were able to list corporate securities because of the investor protections and the body of common law that surrounded these entities.

¶2.02 Influence of the Income Tax

When the income tax came into being early in the 20th century, the choice of business organization had some new consequences. Congress decided that corporations should be subject to tax on their own income and shareholders should be subject to tax when they received dividends. In contrast, proprietorships, which were not treated as separate entities under any laws, were not taxed separately, and the proprietor combined business income with his or her other taxable income and deductions. Congress decided that partnerships should not be subject to the income tax at the entity level. Instead, partnerships must allocate income and other tax items among the partners, who report them on their own tax returns. For federal income tax purposes, the partnership is termed a "flow-through," or "pass-through" or "conduit" entity.

¶2.03 Newer Entities and Adaptations

As the complexities of modern law and business practices evolved, there have been adaptations and new additions to the menu of available entities.

In the late 1950s, Congress created a tax election for certain closely-held corporations whereby they could elect to be conduits and pass income and losses through to their shareholders in a manner similar to a proprietorship (if there is only one shareholder) or partnership (if there are two or more shareholders). After considerable modifications to the tax law, these corporations are now known as "S corporations," and have become the most popular of all entities, as evidenced by the types of business returns filed over the last several years. [*See* IRS Statistics of Income from the early 1990s to date]

Professional Corporations. In the late 1960s and early 1970s, many taxpayers tried to adopt the corporate form for more entities (in complete contrast to later movements). The rationale was that professional persons were doomed to the status of self-employment and were ineligible for retirement and fringe benefit plans that provided some major tax advantages to employees. Hence, the professional corporation concept was adopted by various states; in general, a professional corporation is a cross between the historic commercial corporation and the partnership or proprietorship. An owner may be protected from the debts of the business, except to the extent they result from his or her own malpractice or other tortious act.

Limited Liability Companies. Later in the 1970s, the emphasis switched to creating more single tax entities. The state of Wyoming was seeking a vehicle to attract more investors in Wyoming resources and developed the limited liability company (LLC). At first, this entity had governance and other relationships among the owners and entity that were almost identical to a partnership, but all members were protected by unlimited liability for business debts. The objective was to provide investor protection, along with taxation as a conduit, without the restrictions applicable to S corporations.

¶2.04 Entities Recognized in the Tax Law

From its inception, the Internal Revenue Code of 1954 (now the Internal Revenue Code of 1986) has recognized only two business entities: the partnership [Code Sec. 7701(a)(2)] and the corporation. [Code Sec. 7701(a)(3)] Thus, there was no statutory classification for an organization that did not fit exactly into one of these two categories. The IRS agonized for years over whether to treat the limited liability company as a corporation or as a partnership, and generally ruled that the classification depended on the presence or absence of certain corporate attributes.

As the IRS was debating the tax treatment of these entities, the states had come up with a new twist to the limited liability company. Most of the states allowed single owner (called single member) limited liability companies by the mid-1990s. The IRS could not classify these as partnerships, since a partnership must have two or more owners. On the other hand, it made little sense to arbitrarily treat all single-member limited liability companies as corporations, especially if the organization lacked corporate attributes.

¶2.05 Treatment of the Limited Liability Company

In late 1996, the IRS adopted a common-sense approach to the classification of unincorporated entities. The general rule, for an entity with more than one owner, is that it is a partnership, although it can elect to be treated as a corporation for federal income tax purposes. A single member limited liability company is disregarded entirely as a separate entity, unless it elects to be a corporation for federal tax purposes. [Reg. §301.7701-3(b)(1)]

¶2.06 Summary of State Law and Tax Entities

Under current rules, there are a variety of organizations that states charter as business entities, and several of these may have more than one tax classification. Moreover, the tax classification may or may not be self-evident from the state classification. Figure 1 compares the state classification with the federal tax treatments of the most common domestic business entities.

Figure 1. Classification of Domestic Business Entities

State Law	Federal Tax Default	Federal Tax Elections
Proprietorship (dba or business license)	Nonentity: Combine with owner	None
Commercial corporation	C corporation	S corporation *
Professional corporation	C corporation	S corporation *
General partnership	Partnership	C corporation # S corporation # *
Limited partnership	Partnership	C corporation # S corporation # *
Limited liability partnership	Partnership	C corporation # S corporation # *
Limited liability company-single member	Disregarded entity (Proprietorship, branch or division)	C corporation # S corporation # *
Limited liability company-multiple members	Partnership	C corporation # S corporation # *

* Must meet the S corporation eligibility requirements of Code Sec. 1361 and file an election per Code Sec. 1362. Some states require a separate election and/or eligibility.
\# Must elect status under the "check the box" Reg. §301.7701-3.

Chapter 3

Principal Factors Influencing Choice of Entity

¶3.01 Tax and Nontax Factors

This Guide focuses on the tax aspects of entity choice. However, there may be some nontax factors that influence the selection. For example, a person who receives shares in a corporation will hold all of the rights of a shareholder, subject to state law and binding shareholder agreements. A person who receives an interest in a partnership or limited liability company may be treated as a full-fledged member, if the agreement so provides, often subject to approval by other partners or members. If the agreement allows the other partners or members the right to deny a transferee full membership rights, then the transferee may have only a charging order, or interest as an assignee. This interest would treat the holder as a partner for federal income tax purposes, but not for any other purposes. In some cases, attorneys believe that this is an advantage of the limited liability company over the corporation.

> **Comment.** Business owners and tax professionals must always consider state, local and federal nontax laws when selecting an entity. There is no substitute for competent counsel, both in tax and nontax matters.

Some of the tax factors, which are the focal points of this Guide, include:

- Tax rates;
- Exit strategies;
- Relationship of the owners to the entity;
- Compensation and fringe benefit rules;
- Distributions of cash or property;
- Ownership of real estate and other valuable, nondepreciating property; and
- Permanence or reversibility of status.

The most important factor is the relationship of the owner, or owners, to the business in question. The considerations will be different for businesses that have many detached investors and for those that have only a few, or even one, owner.

Chapter 4

Tax Rates

The direct payors of the U.S. income tax are individuals, estates, trusts and C corporations. For over 30 years, both individuals and corporations were subject to graduated rate schedules. From 2010 through 2017, the individual top individual rate was 39.6 percent and the top corporate rate was 35 percent. These rates were sufficiently close that the rate schedule, per se, was not a major determinant of the entity choice.

For calendar tax years after December 31, 2017, the Tax Cuts and Jobs Act of 2017 (TCJA), Pub. L. No. 115-97, reduces the C corporation tax rate from a graduated rate between 15% and 35% to a flat 21% rate. [Code Sec. 11(b)] For certain non-C corporation trades or businesses, the TCJA adds a new deduction for qualified business income. [Code Sec. 199A] These changes substantially impact a taxpayer's overall tax rate and choice of business entity.

The C corporation is subject to tax on its own income. [Code Sec. 11] The corporation does not deduct any payments of dividends to its shareholders. Hence, the term "double tax," since the shareholders must include dividends in gross income.

However, the double tax is subject to mitigating provisions. A C corporation that receives a dividend from another C corporation is allowed a special deduction that reduces the effective rate of tax to somewhere between 10.5 and zero percent of tax. Individuals, estates and trusts are subject to special rates of tax on "qualified dividends." The rates on these dividends range from zero to 15 to 20 percent, depending on the recipient's tax bracket. [Code Sec. 1(h)] A dividend may also be subject to the Net Investment Income Tax (NIIT) if the recipient has sufficient adjusted gross income. [Code Sec. 1411]

¶4.01 Individual Rates

For taxable years beginning after 2017, individuals are subject to a seven-bracket rate schedule, ranging from 10% to 37%. [Code Sec. 1(j)] However, these tax rates do not apply uniformly. There are four filing statuses. Married filing separately has the steepest graduation and reaches the 37% bracket at $300,000 of taxable income. Unmarried individuals and heads of households reach the top level at $500,000, and married taxpayers filing joint returns are subject to lower rates on taxable income of $600,000 or less.

Children with unearned income are subject to steeply graduated rates until they reach age 18. [Code Sec. 1(g), 1(j)(4)] There are other complications. Three separate rate schedules apply to capital gains. These gains are subject to 0% or 15% for taxpayers whose income does not exceed the level at which the top bracket applies to ordinary income. After that level is reached, a capital gain is taxed at 20%, unless it results from unrecaptured Section 1250 gain, gain from a collectible, or the included portion of gain from Section 1202 stock. Those rates are 25% and 28% respectively. Certain "qualified" dividends paid by U.S. corporations or from U.S. source income also qualify for the 0%, 15% and 20% capital gain rates.

Individuals are also subject to taxes other than income tax. The alternative minimum tax (AMT), with a top rate of 28%, applies to individuals with significant tax adjustments and preferences. The TCJA eliminated the principal adjustments that created this tax for many middle-income individuals. The removal of the personal exemption deduction and the limitation of the state and local tax deduction will undoubtedly cause fewer individuals to be subject to this tax in 2018 than was the case in 2017. Moreover, an increased exemption threshold means that married taxpayers filing joint returns will need at least $1,000,000 of alternative minimum taxable income before they start to lose the exemption. For other persons, the full exemption applies until alternative minimum taxable income exceeds $500,000. However, the AMT still applies to some individuals.

An individual who is an employee is subject to FICA and Medicare tax on wages received. [Code Sec. 3121] Self-employed persons are subject to self-employment tax on many types of trade or business income. [Code Sec. 1401] The TCJA did not amend the rules regarding these tax rates and levels of income.

Code Sec. 1411 imposes a net investment income tax (NIIT) on higher-income taxpayers. The tax is 3.8% of unearned income when the taxpayer's adjusted gross income exceeds a threshold amount ($250,000 for married taxpayers filing joint returns and $200,000 for all other individuals). This tax is imposed in addition to the income tax and the self-employment tax. Although there was talk of eliminating this tax in early 2017, there was no removal of, or adjustments to, this tax in the TCJA. This tax does not apply to C corporations. It does apply to estates and trusts that have investment income if taxable income is in the 37% bracket ($12,500 in 2018).

A single item of income may be subject to both the income tax and the self-employment tax or the income tax and the NII tax. No item of income is subject to both the self-employment tax (or FICA tax) and the NII tax.

¶4.02 C Corporation Rates

The flat 21% C corporation income tax rate may result in a lower tax than the individual tax rate on income from a disregarded entity or a pass-through entity. However, the income tax and net investment income tax (NIIT) on C corporation distributions may increase a C corporation shareholder's overall tax rate. If a C corporation distributes its income, the shareholders may have to pay income tax and NIIT on the dividends, and the advantage of the lower C corporation tax rate may be reduced or even eliminated.

C Corporation Distributions. In general, C corporations that retain most of their income will pay less tax than other types of entities. If the business distributes all or a substantial portion of its income, pass-through entity status will generally result in less tax than a C corporation.

A C corporation that makes no distributions will pay a flat 21% on its income. Typically, the 21% rate is lower than the marginal individual income tax rates unless the owners are in the 10% (up to $19,050 for taxpayers filing jointly in 2018) or 12% brackets (over $19,050 but not over $77,400 for joint filers in 2018).

For 2019, the marginal rate for married taxpayers filing jointly exceeds 21% when taxable income exceeds $79,850, but the average rate of tax reaches 21% when taxable income is $339,700. Thus, a taxpayer filing jointly will typically pay less tax using a non–C corporation business form unless income is more than $339,700 and the C corporation makes no distributions.

A C corporation that distributes income to its shareholders will pay the flat 21% tax on its income, and in addition, its shareholders are taxed on the distribution up to a 20% maximum qualified dividend rate. Thus, a C corporation shareholder who is taxed at the maximum qualified dividend rate will be subject to a combined 39.8% (21.00% + 23.80% x 79.00% = 39.80%) tax rate, which exceeds the maximum 37% tax rate on individuals. Because of this double tax, C corporation tax benefits decrease as the distribution percentage rises.

> **Comment.** S corporations, disregarded entities, and partnerships are not affected by a distribution because the income is taxable to the owner regardless of the amount distributed, and distributions are typically not subject to income tax. Since the distributions are not subject to income tax they are also exempt from NIIT.

Net Investment Income Tax. Generally, C corporation distributions are passive income, and subject to the NIIT. On the contrary, distributions from an S corporation are typically non-passive income and are not subject to the NIIT. Thus, for a higher-income taxpayer, C corporation dividends will be subject to an additional 3.8% NIIT.

Other Corporate Taxes. Before 2018, C corporations were generally subject to the alternative minimum tax. There was an important exception, which relieved any corporations with gross receipts of no more than $5,000,000 from this tax. After 2017, all C corporations are exempt from this tax.

However, there are two other taxes that can apply to C corporations. The personal holding company tax applies to corporations that receive a majority of their income from passive sources and certain personal services. [Code Secs. 541–543] They must also be closely-held corporations. [Code Sec. 545] If they do not distribute income as dividends, they must pay a 20% tax on the retained income. [Code Sec. 541] This tax applies to relatively few corporations, given the nature and percentages of income retained. The personal holding company tax applies in addition to the regular income tax in these cases. Therefore, the combined tax on accumulated personal holding company income is 36.8% (21% + (20% x 79%)). The remaining 63.2% of income is subject to tax as a dividend if it is ever distributed.

If a C corporation is not a personal holding company, another tax on accumulated income may apply to the C corporation if it retains income beyond the reasonable needs of the business. The accumulated earnings tax applies to any C corporation, regardless of its income sources or ownership. If a C corporation accumulates income in excess of $250,000 and cannot document that the accumulations are related to the reasonable needs of the business, the accumulated earnings tax is 20% of the accumulation. [Code Sec. 531] Accumulations are presumed to exceed the reasonable needs of the business unless the corporation has "specific, definite, and feasible plans for the use of such accumulation." [Reg. §1.537-1(b)]

As tempting as it might be to subject income to the 21% tax rate, the imposition of the personal holding company tax or the accumulated earnings tax can turn this apparent saving into a costly mistake. The tax imposed on the corporation will be approximately the same as that imposed on the owner of a pass-through entity. Moreover, the earnings will still be locked into the corporation and the owners will undergo a third round of tax. The effective overall rate is the same as that imposed on undistributed personal holding company income.

Example 1. Lotax, Inc. was an S corporation through 2017. In 2018, Lotax revoked its S election in order to take advantage of the lower tax rate. In 2018, Lotax's taxable income was $100,000. Lotax made no distribution in 2018. When the IRS examined the return, it determined that the accumulations were beyond the reasonable needs, and it assessed the accumulated earnings tax. Since the income was typical and there were no specific plans documenting business needs, the sole shareholder decided to withdraw the earnings. The sole shareholder was in the top individual income tax bracket for the year of the distribution. After all of the taxes were paid, the cash left was only $48,158, for an effective overall tax rate of approximately 52%.

	Tax Rate	Amount
Income, pre-tax		$100,000
Income Tax	0.21	(21,000)
After Income Tax		79,000
Accumulated Earnings Tax	0.2	(15,800)
After Accumulated Earnings Tax		63,200
Dividend Tax	0.238	(15,042)
Income Left After Tax		$48,158

If Lotax had remained an S corporation the tax rate would have been lower and the after-tax cash considerably higher. If the income did not qualify for the QBI deduction the tax on the $100,000 would have been $37,000 and the after-tax cash available to the shareholder would have been $63,000. If the income qualified for the Section 199A deduction, the tax would have been only $29,600, leaving the shareholder with $70,400 available cash.

¶4.03 Disregarded Entity and Partnership Rates

Unlike a C corporation that generates tax at the entity and shareholder levels, owners of a disregarded entity or partnership are taxed on income from the business at the owner level. Each partner in a partnership and owner of a disregarded entity includes his or her share of the entity's income or loss on his or her tax return regardless of whether the income is distributed to the owner. If the business is subject to self-employment (SE) tax, the owner also pays SE tax on almost all the income.

Certain trades or businesses operated as a disregarded entity or partnership are eligible for the new Code Sec. 199A qualified business income (QBI) deduction. If the business is not subject to SE tax, for example, a real estate rental activity, a disregarded entity or partnership may be preferable to a C corporation that is ineligible for the QBI deduction, or an S corporation that pays wages that do not constitute QBI.

Self-Employment Tax. The self-employment (SE) tax rate is 15.3%. The rate consists of two parts: 12.4% for Social Security (old-age, survivors, and disability insurance) and 2.9% for Medicare (hospital insurance). The Social Security program limits the amount of earnings subject to Social Security tax for a given year. For 2019, this contribution and benefit base is $128,400. Thus, there is no Social Security tax for earnings over $132,900. There is no limit on earnings subject to the Medicare tax and higher-income taxpayers pay an additional Medicare tax. Generally, the amount subject to SE tax is 92.35% of net earnings from self-employment.

An owner of a disregarded entity or a partner in a partnership must pay SE tax if net earnings from self-employment are $400 or more. However, several types of income are typically not subject to SE tax, such as salaries, rental income received by an investor (not a real estate dealer) who does not provide substantial services to tenants or materially participate in farm management or production, and an S corporation owner's share of taxable income. Self-employed taxpayers can deduct one-half of SE tax paid.

If all the business income is subject to SE tax, the disregarded entity or partnership is subject to more tax than the C corporation (with no distributions) at almost all income ranges. For example, if the taxpayer has $10,000 SE income and $10,000 taxable income less one-half of the SE tax, the taxpayer's overall tax rate (excluding the QBI deduction and the standard deduction) is approximately 23% [($1,413 SE tax + $929 (tax on $10,000 − $707 one-half SE tax)) ÷ $10,000].

If the business intends to distribute a substantial portion of its income, a pass-through entity will usually generate less tax than a C corporation. An S corporation shareholder will pay less overall SE/employment tax than a partner in a partnership or an owner of a disregarded entity because the shareholder does not pay SE tax on the taxable income of the corporation.

QBI Deduction. The taxpayer's choice of business entity may increase or decrease the QBI deduction. C corporations do not qualify for the QBI deduction. Thus, with the QBI deduction, the point where the individual tax rate exceeds the corporate tax rate increases. For disregarded entity and pass-through entity owners, the QBI deduction effectively reduces the individual income tax rates (but not the SE tax rate) by 20%. For example, the 10% rate becomes 8%, and the 37% rate becomes 29.6%.

The QBI deduction is applied at the owner level, and is limited by the owner's income, and potentially by the owner's share of the entity's W-2 wages and its unadjusted basis in assets (the W-2 wage limit). The QBI deduction is limited to the lesser of 20% of QBI or 20% of the taxpayer's taxable income before the QBI deduction. QBI does not include wages, salaries, and guaranteed payments for services. [Code Sec. 199A(c)(4)] The deduction may be further reduced or eliminated by the W-2 wage limit.

The W-2 wage limit does not apply if the taxpayer's taxable income is equal to or below a threshold amount. The limit phases in if the taxpayer's income is over the threshold amount but less than the threshold amount plus $50,000 ($100,000 for married filing jointly). The limit is fully phased in for a taxpayer whose income exceeds the threshold plus $50,000 ($100,000 for married filing jointly). In 2018, the threshold is $157,500 ($315,000 for married filing jointly). This amount is indexed for inflation in tax years after 2018. The thresholds for 2019 are $321,400 for married filing joint returns, $160,725 for married filing separate returns, and $160,700 for single and head of household returns.

A disregarded entity and a partnership do not typically pay wages to their owners. Partnerships may make guaranteed payments to partners who provide services to the partnership. However, partnerships are not required to make guaranteed payments, and payments are not subject to the reasonable compensation standard that applies to S corporation payments. Guaranteed payments to a partner are taxed as ordinary income to the partner receiving the payment. However, they are not QBI [Code Sec. 199A(c)(4)(B)] and are not wages for purposes of the W-2 wage limit.

Thus, the QBI deduction for a disregarded entity may be higher than the deduction for a partnership that makes guaranteed payments, because guaranteed payments do not constitute QBI. Similarly, at some income levels, the QBI deduction for a disregarded entity may be higher than the deduction for an S corporation that must pay wages to its shareholders.

> **Comment.** While reasonable compensation and Code Sections 707(a) and 707(c) payments are not included in the owner's QBI, they are an item of QBI if they are properly allocable to the partnership's trade or business and are otherwise deductible for federal income tax purposes. [Prop. Reg. §§1.199A-3(b)(2)(ii)(I) and (J)] This means that wages and salary paid to a shareholder-employee of an S corporation and guaranteed payments paid to a partner will reduce QBI at the entity level.

Once the owner's taxable income exceeds the QBI threshold, the deduction for a disregarded entity owner or partner may begin to decrease if the deduction is limited by the lack of W-2 wages and depreciable property. Above the phase-in range, the W-2 wage limit applies in full, and there may be no deduction.

Figure 1 shows the phase-in of the W-2 wage limit for a disregarded entity that pays no wages and has no depreciable assets. The phase-in begins at $180,000 pre-tax income (when taxable income begins to exceed the $157,500 threshold). The limit is fully phased in and there is no QBI deduction at $240,000 of pre-tax income (when taxable income exceeds the $157,500 threshold plus $50,000).

Figure 1. Phase-in of W-2 Wage Limitation for Disregarded Entity (2018 Rates and Threshold)

Pre-tax Income	QBI Deduction	Owner Income Tax	Owner SE Tax	Total Tax
180,000	31,526	24,554	20,742	45,296
190,000	30,404	27,191	21,010	48,201
200,000	24,111	31,070	21,278	52,348
210,000	17,029	36,153	21,546	57,699
220,000	9,158	41,829	21,814	63,643
230,000	498	47,951	22,081	70,032
240,000	0	51,578	22,349	73,927

¶4.04 S Corporation and Shareholder Rates

Shareholders of S corporations report the income and losses of the corporation on their individual tax returns (regardless of whether the income is distributed to the shareholders) and are taxed at their individual income tax rates. This allows S corporations to avoid double taxation on the corporate income. However, S corporations may be responsible for an entity-level tax on certain built-in gains and passive income.

Corporate Level S Corporation Taxes. From 1987 through 2017, there were special burdens associated with the built-in gains tax and passive investment income tax for former C corporations. In addition to requiring immediate double taxation on the items that were subject to these taxes, the rates were set at the top corporate rate, which had been 35% since 1993. This created an instant tax increase for corporations in low to moderate income tax brackets that converted from C to S status.

Example 2. Lowco was a C corporation that used the cash method of accounting. For the recent years before 2017, Lowco's taxable income averaged around $100,000 per year. At the beginning of 2017, Lowco's net accounts receivable were approximately $50,000. If Lowco had continued as a C corporation, in 2017, the accounts receivable would have contributed around $10,000 to its tax liability for the year. However, if Lowco converted to S corporation status for 2017 these receivables would likely have been recognized built-in gains, with a resultant 35% tax at the corporate level.

The Tax Cuts and Jobs Act of 2017 mitigated this result by enacting the flat 21% rate discussed at ¶4.02, above. Therefore, the rate differential is gone.

Example 3. Assume that Lowco, from Example 2 faced the same situation in 2018. If Lowco remained a C corporation, the tax resulting from $50,000 of income attributable to the opening accounts receivable would be $10,500 (21% of $50,000). If Lowco converted to S status, the built-in gain tax resulting from the accounts receivable would also be $10,500.

Employment and Self-Employment Taxes. Whereas a disregarded entity or partnership may be subject to SE tax on almost 100% of its income, an S corporation pays its shareholders a salary and its taxable income is not subject to SE tax. An S corporation must pay its shareholder-employees reasonable compensation. If the salary paid to an S corporation shareholder is not reasonable, the IRS can recharacterize a shareholder distribution as wages that are subject to payroll and withholding tax.

QBI does not include reasonable compensation paid by an S corporation. If an S corporation fails to pay a reasonable wage to its shareholder-employees, the shareholder-employees cannot include an amount equal to reasonable compensation in QBI. [Prop. Reg. §1.199A-3(b)(2)(ii)(H)]

Example 4. Zeke owns all of the stock in Zerocomp Corporation, an S corporation. In the current year, Zerocomp's taxable income is $220,000, after deducting $15,000 of compensation it paid to Zeke. Zerocomp has no other employees. Zerocomp is taking a most dangerous position, unless it can demonstrate that the value of Zeke's services does not exceed $15,000. Assume that the IRS adjusts Zeke's compensation to $115,000. Zerocomp must pay the additional FICA and Medicare taxes on $100,000. In addition, Zeke's QBI from Zerocomp is only $120,000, rather than the $220,000 he initially claimed.

Although the S corporation shareholder's FICA burden may be less than a partner or proprietor's SE tax, below the QBI threshold, the shareholder's QBI deduction may be lower because the wages do not constitute QBI. Above the threshold, the wages may prevent application of the W-2 wage limit and increase the QBI deduction.

Employment Tax. An S corporation and a partnership are both pass-through entities for income tax purposes. Generally, they do not pay income tax at the entity level (although certain taxes may apply to S corporations with C corporation history). Unlike the owner of a partnership who pays income tax and SE tax on almost all his or her share of the partnership income, the wage or salary paid by an S corporation to its shareholder-employees is subject to income and employment tax and the net income (regardless of whether the corporation retains or distributes the income) is subject to only income tax. Thus, if all the business income is subject to SE tax, the disregarded entity or partnership is subject to more SE/employment tax than the S corporation at almost all income ranges.

The employment tax on the shareholder's salary decreases the tax savings of an S corporation, but the S corporation still typically provides a tax savings over the partnership or disregarded entity. However, as the income that is subject to SE/employment tax reaches the Social Security wage contribution base ($128,400 for 2018), the tax savings of an S corporation levels off.

QBI Deduction. An S corporation may produce less tax than that of an unincorporated entity for its shareholders, but it can also decrease the QBI deduction. An S corporation must pay a wage or salary to its shareholder-employees. Payment of wages converts a portion of the income from QBI to income that does not qualify for the QBI deduction, since wages cannot be QBI. However, depending on the salary that the S corporation pays, the loss of a portion of the QBI deduction by an S corporation does not usually offset the cost of additional SE tax.

For a taxpayer with income that exceeds the QBI threshold, the wages paid limit application of the W-2 wage limit and allow the shareholders to claim more of the deduction.

Figure 2 compares the QBI deduction for an S corporation that pays a salary that is 75% of its pre-tax income. While the payment of wages prevents application of the W-2 wage limit when taxable income exceeds the threshold, wages are not QBI and the payment of wages reduces the QBI deduction at income levels at or below the threshold.

¶4.04

Figure 2. Comparison of QBI Deduction for Disregarded Entity and S Corporation (2018 Rates and Threshold)

Pre-tax Income	QBI Deduction – Disregarded Entity	QBI Deduction – S Corporation
$ 10,000	$ 0	$ 0
20,000	1,317	770
30,000	3,176	1,156
40,000	5,035	1,541
50,000	6,893	1,926
60,000	8,752	2,311
70,000	10,611	2,697
80,000	12,470	3,082
90,000	14,328	3,467
100,000	16,187	3,852
110,000	18,046	4,238
120,000	19,904	4,623
130,000	21,763	5,008
140,000	23,633	5,393
150,000	25,606	5,779
160,000	27,579	6,164
170,000	29,553	6,549
180,000	31,526	7,016
190,000	30,404	7,495
200,000	24,111	7,973
210,000	17,029	8,451
220,000	9,158	8,929
230,000	498	9,408
240,000	0	9,886
250,000	0	10,364
260,000	0	10,842
270,000	0	11,318
280,000	0	11,790
290,000	0	12,261
300,000	0	12,733

Even though the QBI deduction may be lower, the overall tax savings of an S corporation may be higher than a disregarded entity or partnership at some income levels. Figure 3 compares the total tax on a disregarded entity and an S corporation that pays a salary that is 75% of its pre-tax income.

¶4.04

Figure 3. Comparison of Total Tax on Disregarded Entity and S Corporation (2018 Rates and Threshold)

Pre-tax Income	Total Tax – Disregarded Entity	Total Tax – S Corporation
$ 10,000	$ 1,413	$ 1,148
20,000	3,353	2,903
30,000	5,573	5,067
40,000	7,878	7,299
50,000	10,183	9,532
60,000	12,489	12,119
70,000	15,168	15,255
80,000	18,217	18,392
90,000	21,265	21,529
100,000	24,314	24,665
110,000	27,363	27,901
120,000	30,410	31,218
130,000	33,550	34,535
140,000	36,648	37,852
150,000	38,810	41,170
160,000	40,973	44,487
170,000	43,134	47,805
180,000	45,296	50,382
190,000	48,201	53,096
200,000	52,348	56,327
210,000	57,699	59,556
220,000	63,643	62,786
230,000	70,032	66,015
240,000	73,927	69,472
250,000	77,648	72,983
260,000	81,369	76,496
270,000	85,091	80,027
280,000	88,811	83,597
290,000	92,532	87,167
300,000	96,253	90,737

If the S corporation pays a lower salary, the tax savings of the S corporation increases. An S corporation that pays a salary that is 2/7 of its pre-tax income will prevent application of the W-2 wage limit and generate less overall tax than a partnership or a disregarded entity at all income levels. However, especially at modest income levels, 2/7 of the income may not be sufficient compensation for the S corporation shareholder-employee.

¶4.04

Chapter 5

Relationship of Owners to Business Entity

Perhaps the most important factor in the selection of a business entity form is the relationship of the entity to the owners of the majority of the entity. A widely-held business, where the majority of the owners have little or no involvement in the day to day business operations, has different considerations from the closely-held business, where persons who control the business are deeply involved in its operations.

¶5.01 Widely-Held Businesses

In the case of widely-held enterprises, the majority of the owners may have no involvement in the day-to-day operations of the business. In many cases, they have little knowledge of the business operations of the entity. They may have purchased stock on a broker's recommendation either because the dividend payout is expected to be good, the stock is expected to appreciate in value, or both. They have no knowledge as to the identity of their fellow owners. If they did, it would probably not affect their investment decisions.

Most of the entities that cater to this type of investor are C corporations, for which there is no limit as to the number or tax status of the owners. The C corporation pays tax on its own income, and the tax rate is a flat 21%. Thus, the tax for corporations is not as high as the tax on upper bracket individuals' incomes. The investor is taxable on the dividends actually received, unless the investor is a governmental unit or tax-exempt entity. The tax rate on dividends received from U.S. corporations by U.S. persons is lower than the rate on most other types of income. For individuals, the top income tax rate on most domestic dividends is 20%, as opposed to the top rate of 37% on other types of income. For individuals, there is also a 3.8% Net Investment Income Tax that is imposed on dividends if the individual is in a middle or top bracket, setting the effective rate at slightly less than 24%. A domestic corporation that receives a dividend from another domestic corporation is entitled to a 50% dividends-received deduction. This has the effect of reducing the effective tax rate on dividend income to 10.5% for corporations.

There are some publicly traded partnerships (PTPs), largely in the investment fund area, including hedge funds. These entities have the ability to pass through capital gains and losses to the investors and avoid double taxation. However, there are limited sources of income for which a publicly traded entity may be classified as a partnership for federal income tax purposes.

A PTP is a partnership with interests traded on an established securities market or secondary market. [Code Sec. 7704(b)] A PTP is treated as a corporation unless 90% or more of its gross income is "passive-type" income. [Code Sec. 7704(a)] This passive type income is limited to the following: [Code Sec. 7704(d)]

- Interest;
- Dividends;
- Real property rent;
- Gain from the sale or other disposition of real property;
- Income and gains from natural resources;
- Any gain from the sale or disposition of a capital asset used for the production of qualifying income; and
- In certain cases, income and gains from commodities or futures, forwards, and options with respect to commodities.

¶5.02 Closely-Held Businesses

When effective ownership of a business is concentrated in the hands of a few persons, and the business is expected to provide a substantial portion of the owners' livelihoods, some considerations apply here that do not apply to a widely-held business.

The double taxation of C corporations and shareholders, as well as the restriction of loss deductions to the C corporation's own taxable income may impede the flow of capital between the owners and the entity. Accordingly, many closely-held businesses choose to be S corporations or partnerships, with the single tax model. With these entities, there is usually no corporate income tax imposed on the entity. Instead, the tax on the entity's income is borne by the owners. As a corollary, the owners are able to withdraw most of the entity's income without being subject to a second round of tax.

¶5.03 The Wharton Study

On June 12, 2018, the University of Pennsylvania Wharton School of Business published the results of a study predicting a "mass conversion" of pass-through entities to the C corporation form. [http://budgetmodel.wharton.upenn.edu/issues/2018/6/12/projecting-the-mass-conversion-from-pass-through-entities-to-c-corporations] This study predicted that 235,780 business owners will make that change, as a result of the enactment of the Tax Cuts and Jobs Act of 2017. The researchers reasoned that the combined rate of 21% on the C corporation's income, plus the maximum rate of 23.8% on the dividends to the shareholders (including the qualified dividend rate of 20% and the net investment income tax of 3.8%) would cause the total tax rate on the income to be less than that imposed on the owner of a pass-through entity.

The Wharton study ignores some crucial variables. Although it compiles different results for businesses that retain all of their income and businesses that retain none, it does not test any retentions or distributions between those extremes. The Wharton study assumes that all owners of a pass-through entity are subject to the NII tax, although the owners who materially participate in the entity's business are exempt from this tax. Moreover, the Wharton study disregards the effects of the self-employment tax and FICA tax on the entity selection decision.

This study predicts that 235,780 business owners will make that change. However, in 2017, 8,889,031 entities filed partnership or S corporation returns. [Internal Revenue Service Data Book 2017, Publication 55B, Washington, DC, issued March 2018: Table 2, p. 4. Number of Returns Filed, by Type of Return, Fiscal Years 2016 and 2017: Table 2, p. 4] Thus, the "massive conversion" that Wharton predicts should move approximately 2.65% of the pass-through entities to C corporation status, not to mention the millions of individuals who will still report income from single-member limited liability companies on Schedule C, Schedule E and Schedule F.

The typical profile of the owner in the Wharton study is a "physician, attorney or investor" with income of $2,500,000 or more. This is a strange grouping, to say the least. The objectives of investors, who may be balancing immediate cash returns and retention for growth are completely different from those of professionals, whose financial objectives generally leave as little as possible inside the entity.

As Chapter 10 of this material indicates, the pass-through entity is usually a much better option for owners who intend to withdraw a substantial portion of the earnings of the business. As Chapter 7 discusses, the pass-through entity is often superior to the C corporation when the existing owners decide to sell all or a substantial portion of the business to new owners. Moreover, it is nearly always desirable to keep real estate used in the business outside of a corporate shell. Since the Wharton study seems to include none of these factors in reaching its conclusions, the study may be little more than another academic paper, which lends itself well to discussion among scholars, but has limited relevance to real-world problems.

One situation in which the Wharton study seems to have some truth is in the world of widely-held investment companies. In February 2018, Ares Management announced that it would convert from limited partnership to C corporation status. Much of Ares's income is from management fees, which are taxed as ordinary income. Without the conversion, the income would have been taxable at the partners' rates, which would be as high as 40.8% (37% income tax plus 3.8% for individual partners, 21% for C corporation partners). With the conversion, the rate becomes 21% on all income, distributed or not. The investors' tax becomes 23.8% for individuals and 10.5% (after the dividends-received deduction) for corporate investors. Depending on the amount distributed, there could be a slightly higher or considerably lower tax rate overall due to the change in corporate status.

In May 2018, the global investment services firm KKR (Kohlberg Kravis Roberts & Co. L.P.) announced it was converting from partnership to C corporation status. KKR has thousands of investors and is subject to taxes in many industrialized countries. As a partnership, KKR was required to send Schedules K-1 to each of its partners, some of whom may have only held interests for a few days, or even hours, in a taxable year. Under post 2017 law, KKR would be subject to the Centralized Partnership Audit Regime (CPAR), which would have caused administrative nightmares. Many of KKR's investors were in the top income tax brackets. Others, including foreign entities and tax-exempt organizations, needed to set up "blocker" U.S. C corporations to hold their interests in KKR, in order to protect themselves from IRS audits, which could have opened all of their financial dealings to examination. These U.S. C corporations are subject to a 50% deduction on much of the dividend income. Thus, for these investors, KKR's conversion may put them in much more favorable situations than they would have been in if KKR had remained a partnership.

However, for smaller organizations without all of these issues, the switch to C corporation status may not be a wise move. Owners may not all be in the top tax bracket. Income may not be subject to NII tax. The owners may have longer term commitments to the business, in which case the investment in the company is not merely a marketable security held as a portfolio investment. Finally, the decision to adopt C corporation status is irreversible for all practical tax purposes.

Chapter 6

Ownership of Real Estate by the Closely-Held Business

It is often advisable for a closely-held business to keep real estate in an entity separate from the core business. Some of the reasons for doing so include keeping assets separate from the claims of possible creditors or lawsuits. For example, a professional partnership or corporation may be subject to a catastrophic judgment. If the office building is property of the corporation, the persons to whom judgments have been awarded may have an automatic claim to the real estate. If the real estate is held outside the entity, the creditors may not have such an easy claim.

¶6.01 Transferring Property to a Corporation

This chapter focuses on the federal income tax aspects of real estate ownership. It does not deal with any nontax problems. One simple example of tax aspects of real estate ownership concerns the freezing of basis when real estate is owned by a corporation. It is easy and inexpensive to transfer property into a corporation. If the persons, or group of persons acting in concert, transfer property into a corporation in exchange for stock, and the same persons own 80% or more of the stock after the transfer, there is typically no immediate income tax as result of the transfer. [Code Sec. 351; *see* Chapter 8, describing the conversion of business forms]

> **Example 1.** Allen owns a warehouse building and land that he uses in his business and transfers this property to the corporation. The adjusted basis and fair market value are:
>
> | Property | Adjusted Basis | Fair Market Value |
> | --- | --- | --- |
> | Building | $275,000 | $800,000 |
> | Land | 175,000 | 400,000 |
> | Total | $450,000 | $1,200,000 |

Assuming there are no liabilities associated with this property, and that Allen owns 100% of the stock in the corporation, there would be no gain recognized on the transfer. The corporation's basis in the property would be the same as Allen's basis had been before the transfer. Allen's stock basis would be $450,000, although the fair market value of the stock would be $1,200,000. In essence, Allen has shifted the pre-transfer appreciation to the corporation. If the corporation has an S election in effect, there is no change in the ultimate taxability of any sale of the property as long as Allen owns 100% of the stock. However, Allen, or any subsequent shareholder, cannot remove the property from the corporation without recognizing any gain, measured by the difference between the fair market value of the property at the time of the removal and the property's basis at that time, after adjustment for subsequent depreciation and other items.

Effect of Liabilities on the Transfer of Real Estate. In many cases, real estate may be heavily mortgaged. The owners may have claimed depreciation, including cost-segregated rapid depreciation on some of the elements of a building. They may have held the building for many years. They may have used the land and building as security for refinancing in times when the values of the property have risen considerably above their initial acquisition costs. When real estate is subject to liabilities, there may be some special hazards in the transfer of property to a corporation, even when the transfer would otherwise meet the tax-free exchange criteria of Code Section 351. The problem comes when the corporation assumes liabilities from the shareholder or takes the property subject to the liabilities. In general, the corporation's relief of shareholder liabilities does not cause the transfer to be taxable, although it reduces the shareholder's basis, compared to what it would have been without the liabilities. [Code Sec. 357(a)]

Example 2. Assume that the land and building in Example 1 were subject to a mortgage of $300,000. The mortgage provided purchase money for Allen's acquisition of the property several years ago. The corporation took over the mortgage, since it was necessary to do so to transfer the property. This liability transfer does not cause any of Allen's gain to be taxable at the time of the transfer. However, Allen's stock basis becomes $150,000, which is the excess of his $450,000 basis over the liabilities of which he was relieved. The fair market value of his stock is $900,000 ($1,200,000 - $300,000 of liabilities assumed). The corporation's basis in the property is $450,000, in total.

¶6.01

If there is a tax avoidance motive, or lack of a business purpose, to the transfer of any of the liabilities, all of the liabilities taken by the corporation from that shareholder are treated as boot and may cause recognition of gain. [Code Sec. 357(b)]

Example 3. Assume the same facts in Example 2 except that Allen had refinanced the property one year before the transfer. Allen had used $30,000 of the refinancing to pay some personal bills and, with the remainder, refinanced the purchase money mortgage. At the time of the transfer to the corporation. the refinanced mortgage had an outstanding principal balance of $180,000. Although this liability does not exceed Allen's basis in the transferred property, it must be treated as additional consideration, or "boot," paid by the corporation to acquire the stock. Allen must recognize gain to the lesser extent of the gain realized or the boot received. The gain realized is calculated as:

Fair market value of stock	$1,020,000	
Liability relief	$180,000	
Total		$1,200,000
Adjusted basis:		
Building	$275,000	
Land	175,000	
Total		(450,000)
Gain realized		$750,000

Since the boot received is $180,000 less than the gain realized, Allen must recognize $180,000 of gain on the transfer. His basis in the stock becomes:

Basis of property transferred	$450,000
Plus gain recognized	180,000
Less liabilities transferred	(180,000)
Basis of stock	$450,000

Allen recognizes gain as if he had sold the property. Thus, he must apportion the gain between the land and the building in proportion to the relative fair market value of each. [Rev. Rul. 68-55, 1968-1 CB 140]

¶6.01

Property	Fair Market Value	Percent of value
Building	$800,000	66.67
Land	400,000	33.33
Total	$1,200,000	100.00

Property	Percent of value	Allocation to boot
Building	66.67	$120,000
Land	33.33	60,000
Total	100.00	$180,000

Unfortunately for Allen, the gain on the building is ordinary income, since it is depreciable property to the corporation and Allen owns more than 50% of the stock. [Code Sec. 1239] The gain on the land is Section 1231 gain. The corporation calculates its basis in the property as:

Property	Allen's basis	Gain recognized	Corporation's basis
Building	$275,000	$120,000	$395,000
Land	175,000	60,000	235,000
Total	$450,000	$180,000	$630,000

If the shareholder transfers property subject to liabilities and there is a valid business purpose for the transfer, there still may be gain recognized by the shareholder. This occurs when the liabilities exceed the adjusted basis of the property.

Comment. This chapter deals with real estate. However, the rules apply to transfers of all property. A likely occurrence of recognized gain exists where the property is depreciable personal property and rapid deductions such as bonus depreciation and Section 179 have reduced the basis, but there is still a substantial principal balance on purchase money debt.

Example 4. Assume the same facts as in Example 1 except that the mortgage on the land and building was $500,000 on the date of the transfer. There was a valid business purpose for the debt, and no tax avoidance motive for the transfer of the debt to the corporation. However, the liabilities exceed Allen's adjusted basis by $50,000.

Allen must recognize $50,000 of gain, which he would allocate in the same manner as he did in Example 3. The corporation would allocate its basis to the assets in the same manner as in Example 3.

¶6.02 Transferring Property from a Corporation

The major disadvantages of real estate ownership by a corporation occur when there is any intention of transferring the property back to the owner or disposing of the property to new owners. There are also tax problems to be encountered on the sale of all or part of the business when the corporation owns real estate. Moreover, especially in a family-owned business, the succession plan for retirement or death of a member in an older generation may be best served by having the real estate outside a corporate shell.

For instance, a senior member of a family-owned corporation may want to transfer ownership to a member of the younger generation during his or her lifetime. One means for accomplishing this goal is to use a stock redemption. However, a stock redemption must be treated as a dividend (from a C corporation or an S corporation with substantial accumulated earnings and profits and little AAA (Accumulated Adjustments Account). This equity account is the maximum amount available for distributions to shareholders, before any distributions are treated as dividends.) In order to avoid dividend treatment where family members continue to hold a majority of the stock of the corporation, it is necessary to effect a complete termination of a shareholder's interest in the corporation. [Code Sec. 302(b)(3)] This rule requires that a shareholder surrender all stock, employment, directorship and other connections with the corporation, except for lending and rental arrangements.

Example 5. Newton is the majority shareholder of Thunder Corporation. His daughters Pauline and Debbie have assumed most of the day to day management of the corporation. Newton is planning to retire. The fair market value of his stock is $1,800,000. Pauline and Debbie each own 5% of the stock. Pauline and Debbie would like to use a leverage buyout to redeem Newton's stock and become the sole owners of the corporation. Newton is amenable to this idea. Neither daughter has the funds to acquire Newton's stock. Thunder has limited liquid assets but has a land and building worth $1,000,000 and adjusted basis of $200,000. If the corporation did not own the land and building, the value of Newton's stock would be $800,000. If Thunder did not own the real estate, the corporation would not need to compensate Newton for the building when it redeemed his stock. However, if Thunder owns the real estate it must include this value in the value of Newton's stock.

Distribution of noncash property from a corporation to a shareholder has one of two consequences to the distributing corporation. If the property has appreciated in value, the corporation must recognize gain as if the property had been sold to the shareholder. [Code Sec. 311(b)] If the property has adjusted basis greater than its fair market value at the time of the distribution, the corporation recognizes no loss. [Code Sec. 311(a)] If the distribution is made by a C corporation, the gain is includible in the corporation's income and is ultimately taxable at the corporate rate of 21%. However, the shareholder must also report the value as a dividend or an amount received in exchange for stock, as the case may be. In case of a dividend, the amount taken into account is the fair market value of the property received. [Code Sec. 301(b)(1)] If the distribution is in redemption of stock and the transaction qualifies as an exchange, the amount realized is also the fair market value of the property. [Code Sec. 1001(b)] The same rule applies to property received by the shareholder in a complete liquidation. [Code Sec. 331]

In case of a dividend or gain from the sale of stock in a C corporation, the income is subject to the Net Investment Income Tax. [Code Sec. 1411] The shareholder's participation or lack thereof in the corporation's business activities has no bearing on this tax.

If the corporation is an S corporation at the time of the transfer, it is subject to the same gain recognition and loss nonrecognition rules as a C corporation. Gains will generally flow through to the shareholders unless the property was held by the corporation while it was a C corporation before the S election took effect. In that case any gain attributable to C corporation years will be subject to the built-in gains tax to the corporation if the distribution occurs within five years of the effective date of the S election.

> **Example 6.** Thunder, from Example 5, may consider transferring the land and building to Newton rather than using liquid assets and incurring liabilities. However, the distribution would cause Thunder to recognize gain on the land and building. The gain would be the difference between the fair market value of that land and building and their combined adjusted basis at the time of the distribution.

¶6.03 Transfers at Death

Another reason for keeping land and buildings out of closely-held corporations is the treatment of transfers at death. When a shareholder dies, the stock owned at the time of death takes a new basis to the estate or other successor. In general, the basis becomes the fair market value at the date of the decedent's death. [Code Sec. 1014] When the property held by the decedent is stock in a corporation, the stock gets a new basis at the time of death, but the property inside the corporation is unaffected.

> **Example 7.** Assume that Newton, from Example 5, held his stock until he died. At that time Pauline and Debbie each received half of the stock. The value of Newton's stock was $1,800,000. Within the corporation the value of the real estate was $1,000,000 and the value of the other assets was $800,000. The other assets were primarily cash, FIFO inventory and accrual method accounts receivable. The basis in these assets, other than the real estate was approximately the same as its fair market value. However, the basis of the real estate was only $200,000.
>
> After Newton's death, the basis of the stock to each of his daughters becomes $900,000 each ($1,800,000 total). If Newton had held the property outside the corporation the basis of the land and building would step up from $200,000 to $1,000,000.

¶6.04 Rent by the Investors to the Business Entity

Conceptually, an integrated business may have several different facets and the owners may wear several hats. Although at least a portion of any owner's role will be some form of equity investment, some other business relationships are likely. In the closely-held business, one or more owners are likely to be employed (or active partners) in the business. Regardless of the business form, owners may be creditors, landlords or both.

It is a fairly widespread and well-advised business structure to have an owner or multiple owners of the business hold real estate separately and rent it to the business.

If the operating business is a proprietorship or partnership for tax purposes and the percentage ownership in the operating business and the real estate are in identical proportions, there is limited income tax saving potential. However, since real estate rent is not subject to self-employment tax, separating the real estate from the operating business can result in some savings.

> **Example 8.** Sally and Andy are equal members in SA, LLC, which operates a professional photography studio and art gallery. The company has a prime location near offices and shopping malls. The company's gross revenues are approximately $800,000 per year. Expenses of operating the business, other than those related to the

land and building, are approximately $300,000 per year. Expenses of the building, including taxes, insurance, maintenance, interest and depreciation, average $80,000 per year. The building has a fair rental value of $150,000 per year.

If Sally and Andy operate the business as one entity, the income will be:

Gross income	$800,000
Operating expenses	(300,000)
Property expenses	(80,000)
Net taxable income	$420,000

Sally and Andy will each have $210,000 subject to income and self-employment tax. In contrast, if they operate the property as a separate business and charge fair market rent the tax results will be:

Gross income	$800,000
Operating expenses	(300,000)
Rent expense	(120,000)
Net taxable income	$380,000

Sally and Andy will each have $190,000 subject to self-employment tax. The $40,000 net income from the rental will not be subject to self-employment tax.

The rental of property from an organization under common control is often termed "self-rental." It is also popular when the operating business is a C corporation or S corporation. This business structure allows owners to shift money out of the corporation in a manner that is fully deductible by the corporation and is not subject to FICA or self-employment tax by the business or the owners. However, there are some cautions to be observed.

First, the passive activity loss rules address the potential opportunity to convert income from an active trade or business into passive activity income. Under the self-rental rule, net income from the rental of property to a trade or business in which the property owner materially participates cannot be classified as passive. [Reg. §1.469-2(f)(6)] However, any net loss from a self-rental is passive. [*See* Carlos v. Comm'r, 123 T.C. No. 16 (2004)] In the context of the QBI deduction, a self-rental arrangement may allow the rent to be treated as QBI. However, if the business is a specified service trade or business (SSTB) there are rules that limit the ability to treat the income from a self-rental activity as QBI. If there is more than 50% common ownership, the rent income is prorated between the SSTB and the other tenants. [Reg. §1.199A-5(c)(2)(ii)]

Chapter 7

Exit Strategies

When entrepreneurs and investors are forming a business, or where either is considering material changes in the ownership or operations, the parties should be looking ahead at the eventual disposition of the business. As is the case with any tax situation, the view should be to maximize after-tax considerations to the owners, given what their desires might be.

When it is time to dispose of a going business, there are two basic ways to accomplish this. With an asset deal, the purchaser acquires the assets of the business and whatever liabilities are necessary to affect the exchange. The other form is an entity transfer, whereby the buyer acquires the seller's interest in the entity, such as a partnership interest, an interest in a limited liability company or stock in a corporation.

In general, purchasers prefer to acquire assets. The nontax reasons for this preference deal mainly with the risk of hidden liabilities. The tax reasons include a fresh-start basis for acquired assets. This may be especially important with the availability of bonus depreciation for used property, a rule added by the TCJA. Other tax reasons include the opportunity to shed all prior tax history and elections.

¶7.01 Asset Transfers

In an asset deal, the seller must recognize gain or loss on each of the assets sold. In the case where the business being acquired is a going concern, both the buyer and seller must use the residual method of accounting for the assets. [Code Sec. 1060] The process is a step allocation to seven classes of assets. [Reg. §§1.1060-1, 1.338-6(b)] At each step, the amount allocated is the total consideration (less any consideration allocated to a senior class) or the identifiable fair market value of the asset within the class, whichever is less. The classes in order of seniority are: [Reg. §1.338-6(b)(2)]

Class	Description
I	Cash and demand deposits
II	CDs, government, and marketable securities
III	Accounts receivable incurred in the ordinary course of business
IV	Inventory
V	All assets not included in other classes.
VI	Intangible assets, other than goodwill and going-concern value
VII	Goodwill and going-concern value

The following examples will illustrate the effects of choice of entity on the tax consequences of the purchase and sale of a going concern. In some circumstances, the C corporation and S corporation yield similar results, principally from the purchaser's perspective. From the seller's perspective, it is difficult to visualize any situation where the C corporation yields superior results to the S corporation.

Sellers' Tax Consequences. The owners of the business whose assets are being sold may have significantly differing after tax yields, depending on the tax classification of the entity whose assets are being sold. In these examples, it is assumed that the owners will take all of the cash from the asset sale, rather than leaving it in any business entity.

C Corporation Asset Sale Illustrated. An example of the C corporation asset sale is shown below.

Example 1. Jeannie, Paul, and Caroline were all equal shareholders in Bull's Eye, Inc. Bull's Eye's balance sheet showed the following as of the current date:

Assets	Adjusted Basis	Fair Market Value
Cash	$20,000	$20,000
Equipment	80,000	240,000
Land & Building	200,000	600,000
Goodwill		440,000
Total	$300,000	$1,300,000
Liabilities	$210,000	$210,000
AAA	80,000	
Common stock	10,000	1,090,000
Total	$300,000	$1,300,000

¶7.01

Marksman, a C corporation owned by Victor, Sally and Sandy, all of whom were unrelated to Jeannie, Paul, or Caroline, offered $1,300,000 for all of Bull's Eye's assets. Bull's Eye's basis in its assets was $300,000. The terms were $210,000 in liability assumption and $1,090,000 in cash.

Jeannie, Paul, and Caroline each had $100,000 basis in their stock. They decided to structure the deal as an asset sale.

Using the residual method, Bull's Eye would allocate the amount realized and the resultant gain or loss on each class of assets.

Class	Assets	Allocation	Basis	Gain
I	Cash	$20,000	$20,000	$0
II	N/A			
III	N/A			
IV	N/A			
V	Equipment, Land & Building	840,000	280,000	560,000
VI	N/A			
VII	Goodwill	440,000	0	440,000
Total		$1,300,000	$300,000	$1,000,000

If Bull's Eye is a C corporation, the gain would be taxable to the corporation, resulting in federal income tax of $210,000. That would leave $880,000 ($1,090,000 - 210,000) of cash to distribute to the three shareholders. That distribution and the resultant tax, would leave each shareholder with $247,320 in cash, after tax, assuming that each shareholder is in the top tax bracket. The NII tax would also apply to the gains even if the shareholders materially participated in Bull's Eye's business operations. The computations for the after-tax cash are:

C corporation	Tax Rate	Amount
Cash		$1,090,000
Corporate Tax	0.21	(210,000)
After Tax		880,000
Per shareholder		293,333
Basis		(100,000)
Gain		193,333
CG + NII Tax	0.238	(46,013)
Cash in pocket		$247,320
Total for all shareholders		$741,960

¶7.01

Marksman acquires a cost basis in each asset. Marksman acquires none of Bull's Eye's tax attributes, such as earnings and profits, AAA, elections, etc. Marksman would be able to claim a tax benefit for each of the depreciable assets. The equipment, valued at $240,000, would likely qualify for bonus depreciation. The building would be subject to 39-year straight line MACRS, and the goodwill allowance would be 180-month straight line.

S Corporation Asset Sale Illustrated. Structurally the sale of S corporation assets is similar to the sale of C corporation assets. However, the single tax imposed on S corporation earnings and gains generally yields the sellers more after-tax assets.

Example 2. Assume the same facts in Example 1 except that Bull's Eye was an S corporation. Also assume, for reasons that will become apparent in Example 4, that Bull's Eye had been an S corporation for at least five years preceding the sale.

The gains pass through to the shareholders and are taxable at the individual rates. Further assume that all of the gain on the equipment is depreciation recapture. Fifty percent of the gain on the land and building is taxable at the 25% rate. The goodwill is self-generated and has never been depreciated. The remaining gain is Section 1231 gain, taxable at the rate of 20%. Therefore, there is a blended rate of 22.5% on the gain from the land and building. The rate of tax on the goodwill is 20%. All of the shareholders materially participate in Bull's Eye's activities so there is no NII tax.

S Corporation

Assets	Gain	Per shareholder	Tax rate	Tax
Cash	$0			$0
Equipment, Land & Building	160,000	$53,333	37.00%	19,733
Land & Building	400,000	133,333	22.50%	30,000
Goodwill	440,000	146,667	20.00%	29,333
Tax on each shareholder	$1,000,000	$333,333		$79,067

The after-tax cash to each shareholder is:

Cash to each shareholder ($1,090,000 /3)	$363,333
Tax for each shareholder	(79,067)
Cash in pocket	$284,267
Total for all shareholders	$852,801

Example 3. Comparing the after-tax results of Example 1 and Example 2, The tax savings of an asset sale by an S corporation are approximately 13% greater than a sale of assets by a C corporation.

C corporation	$247,320
S corporation	$284,267
S corporation savings	$36,947
Percent savings	13%

This example demonstrates a key advantage of the S corporation over the C corporation. Although the year-to-year taxes may be similar, or even lower for the C corporation during the operational years, the consequences may be dramatically different when the time comes to sell the business.

S Corporation Recently Converted from C Corporation Status. In some cases it may be possible to operate a business as a C corporation and then convert to S corporation status shortly before the sale. In that case, the corporation needs to be aware of the built-in gains tax, which can impose double taxation on certain S corporation income for up to five years after the S election takes effect. [Code Sec. 1374]

The built-in gains tax applies to any gains or income that were unrealized (according to the historical cost accounting model or the tax accounting method) while the corporation was a C corporation. After 2017, the rate of this tax is 21%. This tax reduces the flow of gain through to the shareholders.

Example 4. Assume the same facts in Example 1 except that Bull's Eye was a C corporation until immediately before the sale to Marksman. Jeannie, Paul, and Caroline had structured the sale to take place on the first day of a taxable year and made an S election to take effect on that day. Since all of the gains are subject to the built-in gains tax, the cash to the shareholders would be the same as in Example 1. However, the tax on ordinary income, due to the depreciation recapture on the equipment, would result in a greater tax than the shareholder's tax on the distribution, even without the NII tax.

¶7.01

Assets	Gain	BIG Tax	Taxable to shareholders
Equipment, Land & Building	$160,000	($33,600)	$126,400
Land & Building	400,000	(84,000)	316,000
Goodwill	440,000	(92,400)	347,600
	$1,000,000	($210,000)	

Assets	Gain per shareholder	Shareholder tax rate	Shareholder tax rate
Equipment, Land & Building	$42,133	37.00%	$15,589
Land & Building	105,333	22.50%	23,700
Goodwill	115,867	20.00%	23,173
	$263,333		$62,463

The after-tax cash to each shareholder would be:

Cash	$1,090,000
Corporate Tax (BIG)	(210,000)
After Tax	880,000
Per shareholder	293,333
Shareholder tax	(62,463)
Cash in pocket	$230,871
Total for all shareholders	$692,613

As Example 4 illustrates, converting from a C corporation to an S corporation shortly before an asset sale may not be a wise tax strategy. In fact, many C corporations that are contemplating asset sales make an S election with the intention of waiting at least five years before the sale.

Comment. If a corporation makes an S election and an opportunity for an asset sale arises shortly thereafter, the corporation may want to consider revoking its S election. This revocation is a corporate action that requires consent of the holders of more than 50% of the outstanding shares. [Code Sec. 1362(d)(1)] There is no requirement that an S election needs to stay in effect for any period of time.

Asset Sale by Partnership. There is only a single level of tax on an unincorporated entity. The sellers would generally recognize the same amounts of gain as was the case with the S corporation, if it is not subject to the built-in gains tax. However, there can be some significant differences between the incidence of tax on the sale of assets by a partnership. The primary cause is that not all gains and losses are allocated in proportion to partners' capital accounts. In contrast, an S corporation must allocate all gains and losses proportionately to each share of stock.

Partnerships may have voluntary special allocations, if the results have substantial economic effect or are in accordance with each partner's interest in the partnership. [Code Sec. 704(b)] In addition, a partnership may have mandatory special allocations of gain or loss on property that was contributed by partners. In this case, the contributing partner must be allocated the amount of gain or loss that would have been taxable if the property had been sold in a taxable transaction at the time it was contributed to the partnership. [Code Sec. 704(c)]

Example 5. Assume the same facts in Example 1 except that Bull's Eye is a limited liability company taxed as a partnership. Assume that Caroline had contributed the land and building in exchange for an interest in the company. At the time of the contribution, the land and building have a basis of $220,000 and a fair market value of $520,000. Fifty percent of the difference between fair market value and basis was due to depreciation on the building. Therefore, if she had sold the building in a taxable sale, 50% of her gain would have been taxed at 25% and the remaining 50% at 20%, resulting in a blended rate of 22.5%. None of the other property had been contributed by any member. There are no special allocations of any item of income or loss according to the operating ("partnership") agreement. However, the company must allocate $300,000 of the gain on the land and building to Caroline.

The gain computation is:

	Gain	Pre-contribution gain	Remaining gain
Equipment	$160,000		$160,000
Land & Building	400,000	$300,000	100,000
Goodwill	440,000		440,000
Total	$1,000,000	$300,000	$700,000

The company allocates the gain to the members.

	Caroline	Jeanne	Paul
Equipment	$53,333	$53,333	$53,333
Land & Building	333,333	33,333	33,333
Goodwill	146,667	146,667	146,667
Total	$533,333	$233,333	$233,333

The tax to each member is:

	Tax rate	Caroline	Jeanne	Paul
Equipment	37.00%	$19,733	$19,733	$19,733
Land & Building	22.50%	75,000	7,500	7,500
Goodwill	20.00%	29,333	29,333	29,333
Total		$124,067	$56,567	$56,567

Resulting in after-tax cash to the members:

	Caroline	Jeanne	Paul
Cash	$363,333	$363,333	$363,333
Tax	(124,067)	(56,567)	(56,567)
Cash in pocket	$239,267	$306,767	$306,767
Total			$852,800

In addition to the income tax, there might be self-employment tax imposed on the sale of cash method accounts receivable or property such as inventory, held for sale in the ordinary course of the partnership's trade or business. There is no self-employment income to any shareholder when a C corporation or S corporation sells its assets.

Comparison of Sellers' After-Tax Returns. The examples in this part of the chapter demonstrate that the best tax results to the seller in an asset sale occur with pass-through entities. The C corporation would be the least expensive on the asset sale, *per se*, but the disadvantage is the second round of tax when the shareholders want to withdraw the proceeds. Figure 1 shows the after-tax amount, and ranking of the entity choices, from the seller's perspective.

Figure 1. After Tax Cash from Asset Sales Compared

Entity	After-tax to owners	Rank	Reference
Historic S corporation	852,800	1	Example 2
Partnership	852,800	1	Example 5
C corporation	741,960	3	Example 1
Converted S corporation (formerly C corporation within the last five years)	692,612	4	Example 4

The worst option is the S corporation where the sale takes place immediately after conversion from C corporation status. The imposition of the built-in gains tax places the corporation in the same position that it would have been in if it had not converted to S corporation status. However, the shareholders were in a worse position than they were with the C corporation, due to the pass through of some of the gains at ordinary income rates, rather than the 23.8 percent rate imposed on the dividend from a C corporation.

Purchaser's Tax Consequences. In a completely taxable transaction, the purchaser will take a cost basis in each of the assets, after applying the residual method. When the purchaser pays an amount in excess of the identifiable values of the assets, the excess is shifted towards goodwill. Thus, there is no opportunity to step up the basis of tangible assets above the agreed value.

The buyer is indifferent to the tax status of the seller of the assets. There is no holdover effect to the tax basis of any of the assets acquired. The buyer has a cost basis in each asset acquired, following the allocation rules of Code Section 1060.

From the buyer's perspective, any expenses of the purchase are added to goodwill. This usually means that the buyer can deduct these expenses by claiming amortization of an intangible asset under Code Section 197.

Example 6. Marksman, the purchaser mentioned in Example 1, allocates the $1,300,000 purchase price as follows:

Assets	New basis
Cash	$20,000
Equipment	240,000
Land & Building	600,000
Goodwill	440,000
Total	$1,300,000

Assuming that Marksman had no relationship to Bull's Eye or to any two of its shareholders, Marksman should be able to claim bonus depreciation on most or all of the equipment basis. Marksman would begin a new 39-year life on the building and start the 180-month amortization period on the goodwill.

Comment. Both bonus depreciation and goodwill amortization are subject to some caveats. For bonus depreciation, the property must either be new property or acquired from unrelated parties. [Code Sec. 168(k)(2)(A)(ii)] The goodwill would not be amortizable if a related party held the property before August 10, 1993. [Code Sec. 197(f)(9)]

¶7.02 Entity Transfers

Many transfers of businesses are structured as stock or other entity sales. There are certain advantages of this form of transaction from the buyer's perspective. For instance, the existing entity may have service contracts and other agreements that would need to be renegotiated. Vehicles, real estate and other property may need to be retitled. Sales tax on the disposition of individual assets may apply, unless the deal falls within the governing states' bulk sale exceptions.

However, the buyer is taking on risks, for example, for unpaid liabilities, tax audits, unknown claims, any lawsuit potential resulting from prior acts of the entity, etc. Moreover, for income tax purposes, the buyer is acquiring a nondepreciable asset. The buyer may get a tax benefit from the assets inside the entity if the entity is a pass-through entity, or if the entity is a C corporation and files a consolidated return with the buyer, which must also be a C corporation. For these reasons the buyer usually prefers an asset purchase from a tax point of view.

The seller usually has an adverse interest in the form of the sale, especially if the entity in question is a corporation. The sale results in capital gain to the seller (with some exceptions for the sale of an interest in a partnership), and the seller may be relieved from risks associated with prior liabilities, both known and unknown, at the time of sale. Buyers usually demand indemnification from the seller, which may take the form of contingent payments, claw backs and other monetary remedies to shift some of the ongoing risk back to the sellers. The efficacy of these measures is the domain of business attorneys, who are invaluable parties to these transactions, from the points of view of both parties.

To analyze the entity transfer, it makes sense to compare the purchaser's situation in an entity purchase with that of its position in an asset purchase. As the following examples will show, an informed and well-advised purchaser is likely to discount the price significantly to reflect the loss of tax benefits.

> **Comment.** A purchaser of an entity may also discount the price to reflect some of the nontax risks, such as unsettled or unknown liabilities. This analysis does not incorporate any nontax factors in setting the hypothetical price.

In some cases, the discount for an entity purchase may depend in part on the purchasing entity's tax characteristics. The following analysis demonstrates some of the variables for a C corporation and for a pass-through entity owned by one or more individuals.

Buyers' Tax Consequences. The buyer's tax consequences depend in part on the nature of the entity being sold. From the buyer's perspective, the most desirable tax form of the entity is unincorporated status, either a proprietorship or partnership. The entity must not have made an election to be treated as a C or S corporation because this election will transform the entity for tax purposes. It is important to note that the entity classification will not disappear merely due to new ownership. [Reg. §301.7701-3(d)(f)(1)]

Purchase of Unincorporated Entity. If there is a single owner of an LLC, the entity is nonexistent for tax purposes. Therefore, the only possible tax treatment is a purchase of all of the assets, subject to all of the liabilities. If there are multiple owners, and the entity has not elected to be a corporation, there are two possible situations, both described in Revenue Ruling 99-6: [1999-1 CB 432]

1. One of the current members has purchased all of the interests of the other members. In this case the continuing member treats the portion of the assets purchased from the other members as newly acquired property with a cost basis and new holding period. The portion of the assets attributable to the member's prior percentage interest is treated as having been received from the partnership in a liquidating distribution. Accordingly, basis and holding period of each of these assets would carry over from the partnership on this portion of the assets.
2. The purchaser was not a member of the partnership prior to the transaction. In this case the new owner is treated as having purchased all of the assets with a cost basis and holding period beginning at the time of the transaction.

Example 7. Refer to Example 5, where Bull's Eye was a three-member limited liability company taxed as a partnership. Marksman would be treated as acquiring the assets. The basis in each asset would be as follows:

Assets	New basis
Cash	$20,000
Equipment	240,000
Land & Building	600,000
Goodwill	440,000
Total	$1,300,000

This is the same result to Marksman as was the actual asset purchase, shown in Example 6.

Thus, when the entity being sold is not a corporation for income tax purposes, the purchaser is indifferent whether the sale takes the form of an asset acquisition or an entity acquisition, from an income tax point of view. Of course, the usual nontax disadvantages of potential liabilities follow the entity acquisition, as do the nontax advantages such as the continuity of contracts.

If there are multiple purchasers, the partnership would stay in existence. In general, there would be no adjustment to the inside basis of the partnership assets. [Code Sec. 743(a)] However, the partnership can easily remedy this imbalance if the partnership has a Section 754 election in place for the year.

Comment. In partnership taxable years beginning before 2018, a partnership would terminate if there was a sale of 50% or more of the interests in the partnership and capital within a 12-month period. [Code Sec. 708(b)(1)(B)] This rule was repealed as part of the Tax Cuts and Jobs Act of 2017. As of early 2019, Regulations Section 1.708-1(b)(2) still contains this rule, but it is no longer valid for post-2017 taxable years. This termination, often termed a *technical termination*, erased all partnership elections, including a prior Section 754 election. However, since there is no technical termination in the year of the sale beginning after 2017, all of the prior elections, including a Section 754 election, remain in effect after the sale.

The partnership must file a Section 754 election with the partnership tax return for the first year in which it is to take effect. [Reg. §1.754-1(b)(1)] The partnership return must be filed timely, including extensions. There is no prescribed form, but a written statement must be included with the return. The election is binding on all future years. It may only be revoked with the permission of the IRS.

Section 743(b) governs the basis adjustment following a sale of partnership interests or the death of the partner. The adjustments required by Section 743(b) are dichotomous. The basis adjustments are made by the partnership, rather than by the individual partner. The adjustments can only benefit the partner who has acquired the partnership interest.

The Section 743(b) adjustments focus on the change in outside basis from the former partner to the new partner. If the new partner's basis exceeds that of the former partner, the partnership adjusts the basis of its assets upwards, so that the new partner's share of inside basis is the same as his or her share of outside basis. Conversely, if the new partner's outside basis is less than the outside basis of the former partner, the partnership must reduce the basis of its assets, so that inside and outside basis to the new partner are equalized.

Example 8. Again, refer to Example 5, where Bull's Eye was a three-member limited liability company taxed as a partnership. Assume that Victor, Sally and Sandy, the three shareholders of Marksman, decide to purchase Bull's Eye as equal partners. On one single day, Victor purchases Caroline's entire interest, Sally purchases Jeanne's entire interest and Sandy purchases Paul's entire interest. Each pays $363,333 in cash, for a total of $1,090,000. The three new members assume all of the three prior members' obligations on the $210,000 debts of the business. With no Section 754 election in effect, the company would not be able to claim any tax benefit, such as depreciation or amortization on the portion of the value of the assets that contributed to the gain recognized by the sellers, as calculated in Example 10. However, if Bull's Eye had a Section 754 election in effect, each purchasing member would receive a special allocation of basis of the company's assets. This adjustment would allow each incoming member to claim his or her share of the depreciation, or basis at time of sale, of all of the partnership assets. In this example, the basis adjustments would give tax results approximating an asset sale.

Section 734(b) governs the basis adjustment after certain distributions when a partnership has a Section 754 election in effect. The basis adjustments under Section 734(b) reflect gain or loss or change in basis resulting from a distribution. Unlike the adjustments under Section 743(b), these adjustments are applied to the common basis of the assets, and all partners benefit (or pay, in the form of reduced basis).

Purchase of Corporate Stock. In contrast to the purchase of interests in a unincorporated entity, the purchase of stock in a corporation does not equate to the purchase of assets, unless there are some special elections under Sections 338 or 336. These are discussed below.

In many cases, the purchaser would benefit from a basis adjustment on an asset, either on the sale of the asset or on the depreciation of the asset. If the purchaser is a C corporation and operates the newly acquired corporation as a subsidiary, it will probably be filing a consolidated return. In essence, the tax benefits of the subsidiary's assets become the parent corporation's deductions. In many cases, especially in the closely-held business environment, the purchaser or purchasers will operate the newly acquired corporation as an S corporation. In this case, the corporation's deductions have a direct impact on the shareholders' taxable incomes.

It might be helpful to turn to the continuing example to illustrate the difference in tax benefits to the purchaser between the asset deal and the stock deal.

¶7.02

Example 9. Refer to Example 1, where Bull's Eye was a C corporation. If Marksman purchases all of the stock, and files a consolidated return with Bull's Eye, the equipment will not be eligible for bonus depreciation. Moreover, its depreciation deductions are calculated on the historic basis. Thus, Marksman will lose the tax benefit of the difference between the fair market value and the historic basis of the equipment. Similarly there is no increase in the basis of the land, building or goodwill, and Marksman will not be able to benefit from depreciation on these assets, except to the extent that Bull's Eye would have been allowed deductions. An approximation of the lost tax benefits at the time of purchase is as follows:

Assets	Asset deal	Stock deal	Difference
Cash	$20,000	$20,000	$0
Equipment	240,000	80,000	160,000
Land & Building	600,000	200,000	400,000
Goodwill	440,000	0	440,000

Assuming a discount rate of 6%, an immediate deduction of the increased equipment basis, a 39-year deduction of the excess building basis and 15-year amortization of the goodwill, it is possible to approximate the net present value for the difference between the asset purchase and the stock purchase.

	Amount	Discount factor	Net Present Value
Equipment	160,000	immediate	160,000
Land & Building	400,000	39 years @6%	153,324
Goodwill	440,000	15 years @6%	264,675
Total			577,999
Tax at 21%			121,380

This is certainly a rough calculation, which assumes that Bull's Eye will hold all of these assets throughout their depreciable life. The discount rate may not be appropriate, and the analysis assumes that there will be no second level of tax due to the distribution of cash or other property to the ultimate shareholders. However, it provides a formula to analyze the tax cost of a stock purchase as compared to an asset purchase.

¶7.02

Sellers' Tax Consequences. The tax consequences to the sellers resulting from an entity sale depend upon the classification of the entity being sold. Sale of the unincorporated entity closely resembles the asset sale in terms of the tax liability and after-tax cash in pocket. In contrast, the sale of corporate stock has significant differences in terms of tax liability and after-tax cash to the selling shareholders.

Sale of Unincorporated Entity. An apparent disadvantage to the unincorporated entity is that a portion of the gain recognized may be ordinary income. [Code Sec. 751(a)] However, there are certain tradeoffs involved that may negate this seeming disadvantage.

In general, the sale of an interest in a partnership produces capital gain or loss. [Code Sec. 741] This capital gain is generally subject to the maximum rate of 20%. If the partnership has any collectibles, which would be subject to the 28% capital gain tax rate, or unrecaptured Section 1250 gain at the time of the sale (25% rate applies) the partnership must allocate those tax attributes to the partners who are selling their interests. [Reg. §1.1(h)-1(b)(1)]

To the extent that a partner sells its share of unrealized receivables and inventory items, the amount realized attributable to those assets is treated as if the partner had sold those assets directly to the purchaser. [Code Sec. 751(a)] These terms require special attention in the area of partnership taxation, where the definitions differ from common business usage. As the term suggests, unrealized receivables include cash method accounts payable, net of cash method accounts payable. However, this term also includes depreciation recapture that would have been recognized if the partner had sold Code Section 1245 or 1250 assets in a transaction that produced ordinary income. [Code Sec. 751(c)] Inventory items also have an unusual definition for purposes of partnership sales and distributions. In addition to property held for sale in the ordinary course of business, the term also includes any property which would result in ordinary income or loss if sold by the partnership. [Code Sec. 751(d)] To add to the confusion, inventory items include unrealized receivables, although there is no double counting of income.

Example 10. As Example 7 indicated there is no appreciable difference from Marksman's point of view between the asset sale and the entity sale when Bull's Eye is an unincorporated entity. Accordingly, Marksman would be willing to pay the same amount for the purchase of assets and the purchase of the entity.

Turning back to Example 5, some additional observations are in order. First, the company has no accounts receivable. It has no inventory. However, the gain attributable to the equipment is an unrealized receivable. The building has been depreciated using the straight-line method. Accordingly, the gain attributable to the building is not an unrealized receivable, but the gain attributable to prior depreciation is unrecaptured Section 1250 gain. The goodwill has never been depreciated. Therefore, the value of this asset is not an unrealized receivable. After classifying these assets, each of the members must determine his or her share of unrealized receivables.

Partnership sale		Unrealized receivables & inventory items	Per member
Sale price	*	240,000	80,000
Basis	*	80,000	26,667
Gain, ordinary income			53,333
Remaining sale price	*	1,060,000	353,333
Basis	*		73,333
Gain, capital *			280,000

* $200,000 of the total gain is unrecaptured Section 1250 gain, allocated $150,000 to Caroline, $25,000 to Paul and $25,000 to Jeannie. Caroline had contributed the land and building when the fair market value exceeded her basis by $300,000. Fifty percent of this was due to depreciation allowed on the building.

Applying a tax rate of 37% to the ordinary income, 25% to the unrecaptured Section 1250 gain and 20% to the remaining capital gain determines the income tax liability of each member.

	Caroline	Jeannie	Paul
Gain, ordinary income	$53,333	$53,333	$53,333
Unrecaptured Section 1250 gain	150,000	25,000	25,000
Remaining capital gain	130,000	255,000	255,000
Tax			
Ordinary 37%	$19,733	$19,733	$19,733
Unrecaptured Section 1250 gain 25%	37,500	6,250	6,250
Remaining capital gain 20%	26,000	51,000	51,000
Total tax	$83,233	$76,983	$76,983

Taking the taxes into account, it is possible to determine the after-tax results to each member.

¶7.02

	Caroline	Jeannie	Paul
Cash $1,090,000 / 3	$363,333	$363,333	$363,333
Tax	(83,233)	(76,983)	(76,983)
Cash in pocket	280,100	286,350	286,350
Total, all members	$852,800		

In this example, the after-tax proceeds to the members are the same as the year after the asset sale, as shown in Example 5. This is not always the case, especially when there is a difference between the inside basis and outside basis of one or more of the members.

Sale of C Corporation Stock. In contrast to the sale of equity interests in an unincorporated entity, there is no ordinary income component of corporate stock. There are only slight differences between the treatment of the sale of C corporation stock and S corporation stock.

The seller of C corporation stock recognizes capital gain, all of which is subject to the maximum rate of 20% if the holding period exceeds one year at the time of the sale. All of the gain is also subject to the NIIT if the seller's adjusted gross income exceeds $200,000 ($250,000 for married taxpayers filing jointly). [Code Sec. 1411(c)(1)(A)(iii)] The composition of the corporation's assets and the degree of shareholder participation have no effect on the NII tax.

The S corporation sale also results in capital gain unless the corporation has deducted certain development costs related to mineral, oil or gas resources. A shareholder must treat his or her share of these items as ordinary income. [Reg. §1.1254-4] If the corporation has any unrealized gain on collectibles, the shareholder's gain on the stock sale, to the extent of his or her allocable portion of collectibles gain, is taxable at 28%. In contrast to the sale of a partnership interest, there is no "look through" of any unrecaptured Section 1250 gain on the sale of the shareholder's stock. [Reg. §1.1(h)-1(b)(1)] Therefore, except for the recapture of mineral development costs and the allocable share of gain attributable to collectibles, all of the shareholder's gain is treated as capital gain subject to the 20% maximum rate, assuming that the shareholder has held the stock for more than one year. If the shareholder has not materially participated in the corporation's business activity, all of the gain is subject to NII tax. If the shareholder has materially participated in the year of the sale, there is no net investment income except to the extent of the shareholder's portion of unrealized gain on the corporation's investment assets (if any). [Code Sec. 1411(c)(4)(A)]

Example 11. Bull's Eye is an S corporation and the deal will be a stock acquisition by Marksman. Due to the loss of tax benefits and other risks associated with the asset purchase, Marksman reduces the purchase price from $1,300,000 to $1,000,000, less the liabilities of $210,000. The three shareholders, having received no other offers, sell their shares. The after-tax return for each shareholder is as follows:

Value		$1,000,000
Liabilities		(210,000)
Net to shareholders		790,000
Cash to each shareholder		263,333
Less basis in stock		(100,000)
Gain		163,333
Tax	23.8%	(38,873)
Cash in pocket		$224,460

Comparing this to the asset sale, from Example 1, where each shareholder's after-tax yield was $247,320, it is apparent that a discount demanded by a buyer to reflect the lack of tax benefits resulting from a stock purchase can put the seller at a disadvantage vis-à-vis an asset sale.

An S corporation stock sale would likely be subject to the same discount demand from the purchaser as a C corporation stock sale. The principal difference is that there might be some characterization as ordinary income if the corporation owns mineral properties or if the corporation has appreciated collectible capital assets. There might also be reduced or eliminated NII tax if the selling shareholder materially participated in the corporation's business. As was the case with the sale of stock in a C corporation, a selling shareholder could expect to receive less cash from a stock sale than from an asst sale if the corporation owned assets with tax benefits attached, such as depreciable assets or property held for resale.

¶7.03 Classification of Stock Deal as Asset Deal for Tax Purposes

The comparisons of asset sales and stock sales may put the parties at a disadvantage if the business arrangements are such that an asset sale is not feasible. There are some valuable techniques available to mitigate these problems. Figure 2 gives a brief overview of these methods.

Figure 2. Techniques Available to Treat Corporate Entity Deal as Asset Deal

Technique	Target must be	Acquiror must be
Section 338(g) election	S corporation or C corporation	S corporation or C corporation, unrelated to seller(s)
Section 338(h)(10) election	S corporation or subsidiary of consolidated parent	S corporation or C corporation, unrelated to seller(s)
Section 336(e) election	S corporation or subsidiary of consolidated parent	Any person, entity or combination, unrelated to seller(s)

Section 338 Elections: Qualified Stock Acquisitions. A Section 338 election is only available to a corporation that purchases at least 80% of the stock of another corporation. Section 338 treats a newly acquired corporation as if it sold all of its assets for the fair market value of each on the acquisition date. This may be accomplished by a mere election and does not require an actual liquidation of the acquired corporation. A "new" corporation (for tax purposes only) springs into existence at the beginning of the next day.

There are two variations on this election:

- Section 338(g) treats a subsidiary corporation as if it sold all of its assets on the acquisition date, immediately after the stock transfer.
- Section 338(h)(10) treats a subsidiary corporation as if it sold all of its assets on the acquisition date, immediately before the stock transfer.

Section 338 General Rules. The buyer must be a corporation. This procedural rule is rigid, but fairly easy to circumvent. If individuals want to acquire a corporation and make a Section 338 election, they need to set up another corporation to be the actual purchaser.

The purchasing corporation may be a C corporation or an S corporation. The buying corporation must acquire at least 80% of the stock within a 12-month period, and none of the acquisitions may be from persons or other entities considered related to the corporation. The relationships generally exclude a corporation and a person who owns less than 50% of the stock. The acquiring corporation must make the election no later than the fifteenth day of the ninth month after the purchaser acquires the stock that puts it over the 80% threshold.

In either case, the corporation is deemed to sell all of its assets at the **adjusted deemed sales price (ADSP)**, which approximates fair market value. [Code Sec. 338(a)(1)] The "old" corporation then terminates its existence for income tax purposes. All of its tax attributes, including elections, tax year, basis, earnings and profits, etc. disappear. Immediately thereafter, a

¶7.03

"new" corporation appears and buys all of the assets that the old one had sold. [Code Sec. 338(a)(2)] The purchase price is the adjusted grossed up basis (AGUB) extrapolating the price paid for the stock (if less than 100%) and adding liabilities assumed, including any tax liability resulting from the deemed sale. When the gain on the deemed sale results in tax liability to the acquired corporation, it is necessary to calculate the value using a simultaneous equation, since the tax liability will vary according to the sales price and the sales price will vary according to the tax liability.

Section 338(g) Illustrated. From the seller's point of view, there are no consequences to a Section 338(g) deal, since this election is made entirely by the purchaser. However, this election may result in immediate tax liability coupled with long-term tax benefits. Unless some unusual factors are present, this election is rarely beneficial.

Example 12. Refer to Example 11. Assume that Marksman made a Section 338(g) election for this acquisition. Marksman paid $790,000 for the stock. This amount, plus the liabilities of $210,000, results in a $1,000,000 value of the assets. However, liabilities must also include the income tax on the gain, at 21%. The simultaneous equations yield the following value:

	Basis	Value	Gain
Cash	$20,000	$20,000	$0
Equipment	80,000	240,000	160,000
Land & Building	200,000	600,000	400,000
Goodwill	0	326,076	326,076
Total	$300,000	$1,186,076	$886,076
Tax	21%		186,076
Aggregate Deemed Sale Price			$1,186,076

The balance sheet of Bull's Eye, immediately after the election, is:

Cash	$20,000
Equipment	240,000
Land & Building	600,000
Goodwill	326,076
Total	$1,186,076
Liabilities	
Existing	$210,000
Tax	186,076
Stock	790,000
Total	$1,186,076

¶7.03

Now that Marksman owns 100% of the stock, it can file consolidated returns with Bull's Eye. It may choose to liquidate Bull's Eye under Sections 332 and 337, where neither Marksman nor Bull's Eye recognizes any gain or loss. Under either of these options, the group will get the full tax benefit from the price deemed paid for the assets. However, it will cost $186,076 to qualify for this benefit. Thus, Marksman is unlikely to make a Section 338(g) election.

The major problem with the Section 338(g) election is that there is no tax benefit from gains recognized by the selling shareholders. Thus, there is a steep tax burden when both the stock sale and the deemed asset sale are taxable.

Example 13. When Caroline, Jeannie and Paul sold their stock, each shareholder's tax liability was $38,873, as shown in Example 11. Thus, the total shareholder tax was $116,619. The corporation's tax resulting from the Section 338(g) election was $186,076, as shown in Example 12. The total tax paid to transfer ownership and tax benefits was $302,695.

Comment. This example illustrates why the Section 338(g) election often provides a disadvantage. If the corporation being acquired was a foreign corporation, not presently subject to U.S. tax, but will be subject to U.S. tax in the future, the election might make sense. If the acquired corporation has both appreciated assets and net operating loss carryforwards there may be no immediate tax liability resulting from the deemed sale. If neither of these situations is present, the Section 338(g) election is not likely to be useful.

Section 338(h)(10) Illustrated. The Section 338(h)(10) election is a more popular election than the Section 338(g) election. The benefit to this election is that the seller recognizes gain as if the assets had been sold. The "new" acquired corporation assigns an approximate fair market value to all of the assets without a second round of tax. However, this election has its complications. For the Section 338(h)(10) election, the target must be able to pass through all of its gains and losses to the seller or sellers. A stand-alone corporation cannot pass through its tax items, and thus may not be the subject of a Section 338(h)(10) election. Accordingly, the only qualified targets are S corporations, whose income passes through to shareholders, or consolidated subsidiaries, whose income is included on the seller's consolidated return for the year of the stock sale.

¶7.03

Example 14. Now assume that Bull's Eye was an S corporation. Marksman purchased all the stock from the three shareholders on a single day. The sellers and Marksman filed a joint Section 338(h)(10) election. Although the actual form of the transaction is a stock purchase, the results are the same as an asset deal. The three shareholders recognized gains as if Bull's Eye had sold all of its assets, and then distributed the proceeds to the three shareholders on the date of the sale. The next day, Bull's Eye has no tax history and the basis of the assets is the adjusted grossed up basis, which is essentially the same as the purchase price of the assets, including Bull's Eye's liabilities.

If Marksman is an S corporation it can operate Bull's Eye as a C corporation subsidiary. However, since it owns 100% of the stock it can elect to treat Bull's Eye as a Qualified Subchapter S Subsidiary. With this election, Bull's Eye is disregarded for tax purposes, and all of the assets, liabilities, income, losses, gains and deductions are treated as originating with Marksman. Marksman can now claim bonus depreciation on the equipment, MACRS depreciation on the full cost of the building and 180-month amortization of the goodwill. The sellers have the same cash in pocket as they did in Example 2.

Section 336(e) Election: Qualified Stock Dispositions. Section 336(e) allows a parent corporation that sells a consolidated subsidiary to treat the stock sale as an asset sale. In substance, the rules are similar to those applicable to a Section 338(h)(10) deal, except that the seller unilaterally makes the election. Thus, the parties must use the residual method for allocation of the consideration — "old" target sells all of its assets at fair market value, and "new" target acquires all of the assets at adjusted-grossed up basis (AGUB).

The target is treated as having sold all of its assets at the Adjusted Deemed Asset Disposition Price (ADADP). When there is a disposition of all of the corporation's outstanding stock within the disposition period, the ADADP is merely the amount realized for the stock plus liabilities of the corporation. [Reg. §1.336-3(b)(1)]

When there is less than 100% of the stock disposed of in that period, the ADADP is the grossed up amount realized. This is generally the fair market value of the stock on the date of each disposition divided by the percentage disposed of in the disposition period. [Reg. §1.336-3(c)(1)]

Although the target corporation is not deemed liquidated in a Section 336(e) transaction, it does acquire a fresh start basis in all of its assets. The aggregate basis is equal to the AGUB, in the same manner as in a Section 338(h)(10) deemed asset purchase. [Reg. §1.336-2(b)(1)(ii)]

There are differences between the rules under Section 338(h)(10) and Section 336(e). Some of the important distinctions are:

- Section 338 requires a qualified stock "purchase" by a corporation, whereas Section 336(e) requires a "qualified stock disposition" (QSD) by a consolidated parent corporation or by S corporation shareholders.
- The seller makes a unilateral election to apply the rules.
- Although the target must be a corporation, the purchaser can be any entity or group.
- The Section 336(e) rules accommodate certain dividend distributions and spinoff transactions.
- There is no deemed liquidation of the target in a Section 336(e) disposition, although most of the corporate and shareholder level prior tax attributes disappear.
- "Creeping," or staggered dispositions are permissible for an S corporation target in a Section 336(e) disposition. If acquirers are eligible to be S corporation shareholders, the target's S election may be preserved during the phases of the disposition.
- If acquirers are eligible to be S corporation shareholders, the target may be an S corporation after the transfer in a Section 336(e) disposition.
- In a Section 336(e) disposition there is no close of the target corporation's taxable year.

Example 15. Assume that Marksman's three shareholders want to purchase all of Bull's Eye's stock and hold it as individuals. If Bull's Eye is a stand-alone C corporation, they will be bound by the results of a stock purchase, with the same consequences as in Example 11. If Bull's Eye is an S corporation, they may be able to treat the stock purchase as an asset purchase.

They cannot join with the sellers in a Section 338(h)(10) election, since the purchaser must be a corporation. However, they can accomplish the same result in one of two ways:

1. They can set up a new corporation ("Newco") by transferring all of the cash for the purchase of Bull's Eye in exchange for the Newco stock. Newco could purchase all of the stock from the Bull's Eye shareholders. Newco could join with the shareholders in a Section 338(h)(10) election. Newco could operate Bull's Eye as a C corporation, although this is not the most popular option with closely-held businesses. If the three new shareholders

¶7.03

elected to treat Newco as an S corporation, Newco could make a QSub election for Bull's Eye, in which case Newco would be treated as the same entity as Bull's Eye.

2. The selling shareholders may make a Section 336(e) election. This would cause the sale to be treated as an asset purchase by the new shareholders. This is most likely a simpler option than the first choice but accomplishes the same results.

In order for either of these strategies to succeed, Bull's Eye must be an S corporation immediately before the deal goes through. Either of these approaches accomplishes the nontax objective of the stock transfer. Either of these methods subjects the deal to a single level of tax on the selling shareholders and none on Bull's Eye. Either of these methods gives Marksman a fresh asset basis and eliminates Bull's Eye's tax history. Thus, for tax purposes, either of these methods produces a result equivalent to the asset sale, demonstrated in Example 3 or Example 4 above.

Summary of the Acquisition Methods and Entity Classification. As the foregoing examples demonstrate, the C corporation is at a disadvantage as compared to the pass-through entities at the time of the sale of the business. This can be especially important when there are highly appreciated assets. Moreover, as these examples indicate, when the purchaser is allowed to claim a new basis on depreciable personal property, as was the case in these examples, there may be an opportunity to claim bonus depreciation. The tax effect of the immediate deduction may provide some cash flow to provide an acceleration of the net present value of the benefits from the acquisition. Another significant asset in these examples was goodwill. This can be the most significant asset in a service business, such as a professional practice. The single level of tax on the sale of this valuable asset should be a consideration when the owners are deciding on the business form, and this determination should be made long before the sale takes place.

¶7.04 Other Considerations

Pass-through entity status is generally preferable to the C corporation form for purchase and sale of a business. However, there are advantages that might be available to a C corporation. Two significant C corporation advantages are:

- The ability to postpone gain on the sale of stock to employees via an Employee Stock Ownership Plan (ESOP)
- The ability to postpone or even exclude gain on the sale of Section 1202 stock.

Employee Stock Ownership Plan Rules. An ESOP is a qualified defined contribution retirement savings plan that is either a stock bonus plan, or a combination stock bonus and money purchase plan that invests primarily in employer securities. [Code Sec. 4975(e)(7)] ESOPs provide corporate employers and their employees the tax benefits of a qualified retirement plan and a financing vehicle for generating capital through their ability to borrow to acquire employer securities.

A shareholder who has held stock in the corporation for at least three years may elect to defer gain on the sale of stock to the ESOP. [Code Sec. 1042(a)] After the sale, the plan must hold at least 30 percent of the stock in the corporation. The shareholder must use the proceeds of the sale to acquire stock or securities in one or more domestic operating corporations within one year of the sale.

An ESOP may own stock in a C corporation or in an S corporation. Ownership of stock in an S corporation provides an unusual advantage in that neither the corporation nor the shareholder is subject to income tax. The incidence of taxation occurs when participants retire and receive their distributions from the plan. However, sale of S corporation stock to an ESOP does not qualify the seller for gain deferral. [Code Sec. 1042(c)(1)(A)] Therefore, it is not unusual for controlling shareholders in a closely-held corporation to sell stock to the ESOP, followed by an S corporation election after the ESOP owns the stock.

Interests in a limited liability company do not constitute securities within the meaning of the ESOP rules. Therefore, an unincorporated entity must incorporate in order for ownership to be eligible for ESOPs. Incorporation is not necessary to make an association election under the regulations discussed in Chapter 8, but interests in an unincorporated entity do not constitute securities, which are the required investments for ESOPs. Moreover, if an ESOP-owned corporation converts to LLC status, the ESOP becomes disqualified, even if the business elects to be classified as a corporation. [K.H. Company, LLC Employee Stock Ownership Plan v. Comm'r, TC Memo 2014-31]

Small Business (Section 1202) Corporation Stock. Code Section 1202 allows investors to exclude a portion of the gain from the disposition of certain small business stock. For stock acquired after August 11, 1993 and before February 18, 2009, the exclusion is 50% of the eligible gain.

[Code Sec. 1202(a)(1)] For stock acquired between February 18, 2009 and September 27, 2010, the exclusion is 75% of the eligible gain. [Code Sec. 1202(a)(3)] All of the eligible gain is excluded if the shareholder acquired the stock after September 27, 2010. [Code Sec. 1202(a)(4)]

The principal limitation of Section 1202 is that the gain in any one year cannot exceed the greater of $1,000,000 or ten times the basis of the stock. [Code Sec. 1202(b)] To qualify for the exclusion, the shareholder must have acquired the stock directly from the corporation in exchange for money, property or services. [Code Sec. 1202(c)(1)(B)]

The corporation may have no more than $50,000,000 of aggregate assets at the time of (and immediately after) the issue of the qualified small business stock. In general, the corporation must use substantially all of its assets in the conduct of an active trade or business. [Code Sec. 1202(c)(2)] Certain professional services, rents, and some other sources of income are not treated as an active trade or business for purposes of this Section. [Code Sec. 1202(e)(3)]

To exclude the gain, the shareholder must have held the stock for more than five years at the time of sale. [Code Sec. 1202(g)(2)(A)] However, if the shareholder does not meet this requirement but holds the stock for more than six months at the time of sale, the seller may defer the gain by investing in other qualified small business stock within 60 days after the sale. [Code Sec. 1045(a)]

None of these rules apply to sales of S corporation stock. Moreover, there are no equivalent rules relating to dispositions of interests in unincorporated entities.

¶7.04

Chapter 8
Entity Changes

Business or tax considerations may necessitate a change in the type of taxpayer entity. This chapter reviews the consequences of a change from an entity taxed as a partnership to an entity that is disregarded as separate from its owner (a disregarded entity), and a change to a partnership from a disregarded entity. It explains how a partnership or multimember LLC can change to a corporation by a transfer, merger, or entity classification election, and the tax implications of that change. This chapter also reviews how an S corporation can convert to a C corporation by revocation or termination of its subchapter S election.

¶8.01 Disregarded Entities and Partnerships

By default, a multimember LLC is taxed as a partnership, and an LLC that has only one member is treated as a disregarded entity. [Reg. §301.7701-3(b)] A multimember LLC may become a single-member LLC if for example, the members sell all the LLC interests to a single member. A single-member LLC may become a multimember LLC if, for example, the company issues membership interests to additional owners, or if the single member sells part of his or her interest in the company.

> **Comment.** If a partnership is reduced to only one partner, the partnership terminates and becomes a sole proprietorship. Under prior law, a partnership was also treated as terminated if, within any 12-month period, there was a sale or exchange of 50% or more of the total interest in partnership capital and profits. Effective for partnership tax years beginning after December 31, 2017, the Tax Cuts and Jobs Act of 2017 repeals the Code Section 708(b)(1)(B) rule providing for technical terminations of partnerships. The provision does not change the present-law rule of Code Section 708(b)(1)(A) that a partnership terminates when the operations of the partnership

are discontinued and the partners cease to carry on any part of the business, financial operation, or venture of the partnership.

Partnership Conversion to Disregarded Entity. When a multimember LLC taxed as a partnership converts to a single-member LLC taxed as a disregarded entity, the LLC is deemed to have made a liquidating distribution of assets to its members. In the case of a proportionate partnership distribution to a partner, the partner recognizes gain only to the extent that any money distributed exceeds the adjusted basis of the partner's interest in the partnership immediately before the distribution. [Code Sec. 731(a)(1)] If a partnership distributes only cash and/or unrealized receivables and inventory in liquidation of a partner's interest in a partnership, the partner recognizes loss to the extent of the excess of the adjusted basis of the partner's interest in the partnership over the sum of money distributed and the basis to the distributee of the unrealized receivables and inventory. [Code Sec. 731(a)(2)]

Thus, if one member of a two-member LLC taxed as a partnership sells his or her entire interest to the other member, the partnership terminates under Code Section 708(b)(1)(A). The selling member must report gain or loss, if any, resulting from the sale of his or her interest in accordance with Code Section 741. The company is deemed to have made a liquidating distribution of all of its assets to the members, and, after the distribution, the purchasing member is treated as acquiring the assets deemed to have been distributed to the selling member in the liquidation of the selling member's interest.

The purchasing member's basis in the assets attributable to the selling member's interest equals the purchase price for that interest. The purchasing member is deemed to receive a distribution of those assets attributable to his or her former interest in the company. He or she must recognize gain or loss, if any, on the deemed distribution of the assets to the extent required by Code Section 731(a).

Disregarded Entity Conversion to Partnership. A single-member LLC that is treated as a disregarded entity may become a multimember LLC that is classified as a partnership if another taxpayer makes a contribution to the company in exchange for an ownership interest. It may also convert to a partnership classification if the existing member sells part of his or her interest.

Generally, a partnership and its partners do not recognize any gain upon a contribution of property to the partnership in exchange for an interest in the partnership. [Code Sec. 721(a)] The basis of the partnership interest acquired by a contribution of property, including money, to the partnership is the amount of the money contributed plus the adjusted basis of the contributed property at the time of the contribution, increased by the amount

¶8.01

of gain, if any, recognized under Code Section 721(b) by the contributing partner. [Code Sec. 722]

Thus, if a new member contributes cash to a single-member LLC in exchange for the issuance of a 50% interest in the LLC, the LLC is converted from a disregarded entity to a partnership. The new member is typically treated as having made a contribution to the LLC in exchange for the LLC interest. The initial member is treated as contributing all of the LLC's assets to the new company in exchange for an interest in the new company.

Under Code Section 721(a), the members do not recognize gain or loss because of the conversion of the disregarded entity to a partnership. The new member's basis is equal to his or her contribution to the LLC. The initial member's basis is equal to the initial member's basis in the LLC assets deemed contributed to the partnership. [Rev. Rul. 99-5, 1996-6 IRB 8, Scenario 2]

If, instead, the sole member of a single-member LLC sells a 50% interest in the company, the sale of the ownership interest in the LLC is treated as the purchase of a 50% interest in each of the LLC's assets, which are treated as held directly by the sole member. Immediately after the purchase, the two members are treated as contributing their respective interests in those assets to a partnership in exchange for ownership interests in the new partnership. The selling member must recognize gain or loss from the deemed sale of the 50% interest in each asset of the LLC. [Code Sec. 1001]

Under Code Section 721(a), the members do not recognize any gain or loss on the conversion of the disregarded entity to a partnership. Under Code Section 722, the purchasing member's basis in the partnership interest is equal to the amount he or she paid for the assets that he or she is deemed to contribute to the newly created partnership. The seller's basis in the partnership interest is equal to the basis in his or her 50% share of the assets of the old LLC. [Rev. Rul. 99-5, 1996-6 IRB 8, Scenario 1]

> **Comment.** If a domestic partnership converts to a domestic multimember LLC that is classified as a partnership, then, in most cases, there is no gain or loss to the partners or the partnership. The tax year of the converting domestic partnership does not close and the resulting domestic LLC does not have to obtain a new employer identification number. [Rev. Rul. 95-37, 1995-1 CB 130]

¶8.02 Partnerships and Corporations

A partnership or multimember LLC can change to a corporation by a transfer of assets to a new corporation, merger with a corporation, or by making an election to be classified as a corporation.

Transfer from Partnership to New Corporation. The transfer of assets from a partnership (including a multimember LLC) to a new corporation can take one of three forms described in Rev. Rul. 84-111. [1984-2 CB 88] It can be an assets-over transfer, an assets-up transfer, or an interest-over transfer.

First, the LLC can contribute all of its assets and liabilities to a corporation in exchange for stock and the assumption of liabilities and then distribute the stock to its members who become shareholders in the corporation (the assets-over form of incorporating). The LLC generally does not recognize gain or loss when it transfers its assets and liabilities to the corporation in exchange for its stock. The members have a basis in the stock that is equal to their adjusted basis in the LLC.

Second, the LLC can distribute all its assets and liabilities to it members, who contribute them to the new corporation in exchange for stock in the new corporation (the assets-up form of incorporating). The basis in the assets distributed to the members equals their adjusted basis less any money distributed. The members generally do not recognize gain or loss on the contribution to the new corporation in exchange for stock and the assumption of the liabilities.

Third, the LLC members can contribute all of their LLC interests to a corporation in exchange for its stock (the interests-over form of incorporating). The members generally recognize no gain or loss on the exchange of their LLC interests for stock. Their basis in the stock equals their basis in the transferred LLC interests reduced by the liabilities that the corporation assumes.

Merger or Formless Conversion. Most states allow an unincorporated entity to merge into a corporation. The corporation may already be in existence or may be a newly created entity. The former members' ownership rights are preserved as shares of stock in the corporation.

In many states there is a simpler method known as a statutory conversion or a formless conversion. The unincorporated entity receives a corporate charter from the state without transferring any assets or issuing any stock. The owners' former interests become shares of stock under state law.

The merger of a partnership into the corporation or the formless conversion of an unincorporated entity (classified as a partnership) to a corporation is treated as an assets-over transaction. The entity is deemed to contribute all its assets and liabilities to the corporation in exchange for the corporate stock. Then the entity is deemed to liquidate, distributing the stock to its partners. [Rev. Rul. 2004-59, 2004-24 IRB 1050]

Entity Classification Election. The easiest way to convert a multimember LLC (or partnership) to corporate status for tax purposes is to make an entity classification election under Regulation Section 301.7701-3 (the "check-the-box" regulation). The partnership retains its current form for nontax purposes but is treated as a corporation for tax purposes.

To make the election, the LLC must file Form 8832, *Entity Classification Election*. Generally, an election specifying an eligible entity's classification cannot take effect more than 75 days before the date the election is filed, and it cannot take effect more than 12 months after the date the election is filed.

If the LLC wants to convert to an S corporation, it must file Form 2553, *Election by a Small Business Corporation*. Form 2553 is generally due by the fifteenth day of the third month of the tax year for which it is to take effect. A C corporation can file the election in the tax year before the tax year for which it is to take effect.

> **Comment.** There are relief provisions for entities that do not timely file Form 8832 but file the form within three years and 75 days of the requested effective date. [Rev. Proc. 2009-41, 2009-39 IRB 439] Similar rules apply to relief for late-filed S corporation elections. [Rev. Proc. 2013-30, 2013-36 IRB 173]

An election to change classification from a partnership to a corporation is treated in the same way as a merger or formless conversion of a partnership to a corporation. Thus, the election is treated as an assets-over transaction. [Rev. Rul. 2004-59, 2004-24 IR. 1050] The partnership is deemed to have contributed all of its assets and liabilities to the corporation in exchange for stock, followed by a deemed liquidation of the partnership and distribution of the stock to its partners.

> **Comment.** Incorporation of a multimember LLC (or partnership) by a transfer of assets, merger or formless conversion, or entity classification election is typically tax-deferred. However, in limited circumstances, contribution of liabilities can result in gain. If liabilities are contributed to avoid tax, or have no legitimate business purpose, the liabilities assumed by the corporation are treated as money paid for the contributed property. [Code Sec. 357(b)] In addition, a shareholder may recognize gain if the adjusted basis in the assets transferred is less than the liabilities that the corporation assumes from that shareholder. [Code Sec. 357(c)]

¶8.03 S Corporation Revocations and Terminations

An S corporation can revoke its S election at any time. Revocation terminates the election, at which time the entity becomes a C corporation. The election may also be terminated for failure to qualify as a small business corporation. When a corporation's S election terminates, the corporation becomes a C corporation. A corporation is generally prohibited from re-electing S corporation status within five years of the termination of its S election.

Revocation or termination of S corporation status is generally not a taxable event and the corporation and the shareholders do not recognize any gain or loss because of the revocation or termination. However, if the revocation or termination results in a change in accounting method, Code Section 481(a) requires adjustments to accounts receivable, accounts payable, inventory, and other items to prevent amounts from being duplicated or omitted. New rules apply to adjustments for an eligible terminated S corporation.

Revocation of S Election. To revoke its S election, the corporation files a statement with the IRS service center where the S election was filed indicating the effective date of the revocation. The statement must indicate the number of shares issued and outstanding (including nonvoting stock) and it must be signed by any person authorized to sign the corporation's income tax returns. The corporation must attach a statement of consent that is signed by the holders of more than 50% of the stock (including nonvoting stock) on the date that the revocation is filed. [Reg. §1.1362-6(a)(3)(i)]

If the corporation files the revocation statement and the required consent within two months and 15 days of the beginning of the tax year, and the corporation does not specify another effective date, the revocation is retroactive to the first day of the corporation's tax year. An S corporation may also specify any date for revocation that is on or after the filing date of the revocation.

If the revocation date is not at the beginning of a tax year, the corporation must file two tax returns for one year. The period from the beginning of the tax year through the last day of S corporation status is the S short year. [Code Sec. 1362(e)(1)(A)] The period beginning with the first day after the S short year and ending with the last day of the tax year is the C short year. [Code Sec. 1362(e)(1)(B)]

Termination of S Election. An S corporation election terminates when a corporation ceases to meet the definition of a small business corporation. This can happen if there is an ineligible shareholder, too many shareholders, or a second class of stock. It can also happen if the corporation has accumulated earnings and profits from C corporation years and its gross receipts from passive investment income exceed 25% of its total gross receipts for three consecutive years.

S Corporation Re-election. There is a general prohibition against making a new S corporation election if the corporation terminated an S election within five years. [Code Sec. 1362(g)] Thus, if a corporation decides to terminate its S status and become a C corporation, it must remain a C corporation for at least five years. If the corporation then decides to reelect S status, it may be subject to tax at the entity level (such as the built-in gains tax). [Code Sec. 1374]

The IRS can reduce the period to one year. The IRS will allow an early reelection if there was a change in ownership of more than 50% of the corporation's shares since termination of the prior election, and the prior termination was beyond the control of the current shareholders.

Section 481(a) Adjustments. Effective December 22, 2017, any Section 481(a) adjustment of an eligible terminated S corporation attributable to the revocation of its S corporation election is taken into account ratably during the six-tax-year period beginning with the year of change. Thus, if an eligible S corporation revokes its election, and it must change from the cash method to an accrual method, it can take any increased tax into account over a six-year period.

An eligible terminated S corporation is any C corporation that is an S corporation before December 22, 2017, during the two-year period beginning on December 22, 2017, and revokes its S corporation election under Code Section 1362(a), and all of the owners on the date that the S corporation election is revoked are the same owners (and in identical proportions) as the owners on December 22, 2017.

Revenue Procedure 2018-44 provides that an eligible terminated S corporation, as defined in Code Section 481(d)(2), that is required to change from the overall cash method to an overall accrual method of accounting as a result of a revocation of its S corporation election, and that makes this method change for the C corporation's first tax year after such revocation, takes into account the resulting Section 481(a) adjustment ratably during the six-year period beginning with the year of change. In addition, an eligible terminated S corporation that can continue to use the cash method after the revocation of its S corporation election and that changes to an overall accrual method for the C corporation's first tax year after the revocation, may elect to take into account the resulting Section 481(a) adjustment ratably during the six-year period beginning with the year of change. [Rev. Proc. 2018-44, 2018-37 IRB 426]

Chapter 9

Fringe Benefits

Businesses can typically deduct the cost of fringe benefits provided to employees and employees can typically exclude fringe benefits from gross income. However, the choice of business entity may impact when a service provider must include those benefits in income. Medical insurance is probably the most important benefit and the bulk of this chapter is devoted to this topic. However, there are some other fringe benefits, discussed briefly at the end of the chapter.

¶9.01 Health and Accident Insurance

Employers can typically pay health and accident insurance premiums for their employees and deduct the cost of the premiums. An employee can exclude the value of the coverage from gross income. [Code Sec. 106(a)] The employee has no gross income when the insurance company pays benefits to the extent the payments are used for medical care. [Code Sec. 105(b)]

C Corporations. The C corporation is the entity that provides the most taxpayer-friendly treatment of fringe benefits. This entity respects the separation of the employer from the employee. Thus, when the tax law refers to an "employer" or an "employee," there is little ambiguity as to who is who when the employer is a C corporation. For most purposes, a shareholder-employee of a C corporation, even one who owns all of the stock, is treated as an employee. Thus, many additional fringe benefits paid by the company on behalf of the shareholder-employee are excluded from gross income.

> **Example 1.** Ozzie owns all of the equity in Ozco. If Ozco is a C corporation and Ozzie is an employee, Ozco may pay health insurance premiums on behalf of Ozzie. Ozco will be entitled to a deduction for these premiums as an ordinary and necessary business expense, assuming that the amounts are not excessive. Moreover, if Ozzie is

a bona fide employee, he excludes the insurance coverage from his gross income. The corporate deduction and shareholder-employee exclusion provide a double tax benefit.

Proprietorships. A self-employed taxpayer falls outside of the common law definition of employee. [Code Sec. 105(g)] Thus, without special provisions to the contrary, a self-employed person would not be eligible for any treatment as an employee with respect to his or her trade or business. There are some rules that expand the definition of employee to include a self-employed person. However, these are specific to certain benefits, such as retirement plans, and there is no such rule applicable to health insurance.

Although a self-employed person may not exclude the cost of health insurance, there is a deduction allowed on Schedule 1 of Form 1040 as an adjustment to gross income. [Code Sec. 162(l)] This deduction is not as advantageous as an exclusion, for three reasons.

1. First, if the self-employed person or the person's spouse is eligible to participate in another employer's subsidized plan, the deduction is not permitted.
2. Second, the deduction does not reduce self-employment income.
3. Third, the deduction is limited to net earned income from the business, so that in a year of very low income, the deduction may be less than the cost of the insurance, and in a loss year, there is no deduction for the cost of medical insurance.

The earned income is generally the Schedule C income, less the 50% Schedule 1 deduction for self-employment tax. [Code Secs. 162(l)(2), 401(c), 164(f)]

Example 2. Assume that Ozzie is a sole proprietor and pays for his health insurance from his business account. He may not deduct the cost of the health insurance as a business expense but may be able to claim a deduction on his form 1040 Schedule 1. His deduction cannot exceed his earned income from the business, so if the proprietorship is not having a profitable year, Ozzie would be entitled to little or no deduction. In addition, he may not claim a deduction if he is eligible to participate in a subsidized plan maintained by another employer. Moreover, he may not claim a deduction for this insurance above adjusted gross income if his wife is eligible to participate in a health insurance plan sponsored by her employer. The proprietorship offers a single tax benefit, but not the double tax benefit of the C corporation.

¶9.01

Partnerships. A partnership may provide health insurance to its employees and claim the deduction as an ordinary necessary trade or business expense. An employee may exclude the value of the premiums paid by the employer, as well as the benefits paid by the policy for medical expenses. However, that exclusion is dependent upon a person's status as an employee of the partnership.

Under the general principles of common law and tax law, a partner may not be an employee of a partnership in which he or she holds a direct interest. [Rev. Rul. 69-184, 1969-1 CB 1256] Instead, a partner is treated as a self-employed person with respect to his or her distributive share of the partnership's trade or business income. [Code Sec. 1402(a)] This treatment extends to a guaranteed payment from the partnership for services or capital provided by the partner to the partnership. [Reg. §1.1402(a)-1(b)]

The IRS has ruled explicitly that health insurance provided by a partnership to a partner is to be treated as a guaranteed payment and is subject to income tax and self-employment tax. [Rev. Rul. 91-26, 1991-1 CB 184] The partnership can deduct the guaranteed payment. A partner is not an employee for purposes of the Section 106 exclusion and the partner must include the payment in gross income.

Example 3. Assume that Ozzie is a 50% partner in the Lacey partnership. The partnership provides a health insurance policy for Ozzie. He may not exclude the premiums on this policy since he cannot be an employee of Lacey. Lacey must report the cost of the premiums as a guaranteed payment. Thus, the partnership claims a deduction for the entire cost, but Ozzie must report it as income from the partnership. Assuming that the guaranteed payment relates to a trade or business, this guaranteed payment constitutes self-employment income. Ozzie may claim a health insurance deduction on Form 1040, Schedule 1, but this deduction would be limited to all of his self-employment income from Lacey, including any other guaranteed payments, and distributive shares in partnership income. In other words, if he should have a loss from Lacey, including the guaranteed payment, he would not be able to claim an adjusted gross income deduction for this income.

S Corporations. Under Code Section 1372, for purposes of certain employee fringe benefits, an S corporation is treated as a partnership and any person who directly or indirectly owns more than 2% of the stock in the S corporation (at any time during the year), or stock with more than 2% of the voting power (a 2% shareholder) is treated as a partner in a partnership. The 2% shareholder is treated as self-employed, and not as an employee of the S corporation, solely for purposes of determining the exclusion of employee fringe benefits provided by the S corporation. Thus, many fringe benefits are not available to such 2% shareholder-employees, partners, and sole proprietors on a tax-favored basis.

Section 1372 applies to S corporations and "2% shareholders." Therefore, persons who do not own more than 2% of the stock in the corporation are treated in the same manner as C corporation employees. However, in determining 2% ownership, the constructive stock ownership rules of Code Section 318 apply. Thus, a shareholder is treated as owning any shares belonging to his or her spouse, parents, children or grandchildren, as well as any stock for which he or she holds an option to purchase. [Code Sec. 318(a)(1), (4)] A beneficiary of a trust would be treated as the owner of the trust's shares to the extent of the beneficiary's actuarial percentage interest in trust property. [Code Sec. 318(a)(2)] Thus, virtually every family member of a shareholder who is employed by the corporation is subject to the limitations on the exclusion of fringe benefits.

The premiums paid or furnished by an S corporation on behalf of its 2% shareholder-employees as consideration for services rendered are treated, for income tax purposes, like partnership guaranteed payments. The S corporation can deduct the cost of the insurance premiums and the payments are included in the shareholder's gross income.

The premiums are included in the 2% S corporation shareholder's wages for purposes of income tax withholding. However, the S corporation does not have to withhold, and the corporation does not have to pay, social security or Medicare tax on the value of the health and accident insurance provided to a 2% shareholder if it is provided under an accident or health insurance plan for employees that meet the exclusion in Code Section 3121(a)(2)(B).

Code Section 162(l)(1)(A) allows an individual who is an employee to take a deduction for amounts paid during the tax year for insurance that constitutes medical care for the taxpayer, his or her spouse, and dependents. The deduction is not allowed to the extent that the amount of the deduction exceeds the earned income derived by the taxpayer from the trade or business with respect to which the plan providing the medical care coverage is established. Also, the deduction is not allowed for amounts during a month in which the taxpayer is eligible to participate in any subsidized health plan maintained by an employer of the taxpayer or his or her spouse.

For purposes of the deduction, an employee is any individual who has earned income for the tax year, and it includes a partner and sole proprietor.

[Code Sec. 401(c)(1)] A 2% S corporation shareholder can claim the deduction for self-employed health insurance costs. To qualify for the deduction, the S corporation must make the payments directly and report the payments on the shareholder-employee's Form W-2, or the shareholder-employee must pay the premiums and furnish proof of payment to the corporation. The corporation must reimburse the shareholder and report the reimbursement on the shareholder-employee's Form W-2. [Notice 2008-1, 2008-1 CB 251]

In addition, the shareholder must report the premium payments or reimbursements from the S corporation as gross income on his or her individual income tax return. If the accident and health insurance premiums are not paid or reimbursed by the S corporation and included in the 2% shareholder-employee's gross income, a plan providing medical care coverage for the 2% shareholder-employee is not established by the S corporation and the 2% shareholder-employee cannot claim the deduction under Code Section 162(l).

> **Example 4.** Assume that Lacey from Example 3 is an S corporation and Ozzie owns 50% of the stock. Ozzie is also an employee. Lacey pays medial insurance premiums for Ozzie's benefit. Lacey deducts these payments as compensation to Ozzie. Lacey includes the value of the premiums paid on Ozzie's Form W-2 for the year. However, this income is not subject to employer or employee FICA. As long as Ozzie's other salary payments are at least as much as the medical insurance, Ozzie may claim a deduction on Schedule 1 of his Form 1040.

¶9.02 Other Fringe Benefits

Most of the other significant fringe benefits are best used by a C corporation. However, some of these are subject to some nondiscrimination requirements that prevent the C corporation from providing the bulk of the benefits to owners and other highly compensated persons.

Medical Expense Reimbursement Plans. An employer can reimburse an employee for medical expenses that are not covered by insurance, including some over-the-counter medications and these payments are typically excluded from the employee's income. A 2% S corporation shareholder, partner, or sole proprietor is not considered an employee for purposes of an uninsured or self-insured medical reimbursement plan. [Code Sec. 105(g)] Thus, any amounts provided to the owner under a medical reimbursement plan must be treated as compensation.

Cafeteria Plans. A cafeteria plan provides participants with an opportunity to receive certain qualified benefits on a pre-tax basis. All participants in a cafeteria plan must be current or former employees. [Code Sec. 125(d)(1)(A)] Self-employed taxpayers are not treated as employees. Thus, 2% shareholders of S corporations, partners, and sole proprietors may not participate in these plans.

Health Savings Accounts. A health savings account (HSA) is a tax-exempt account that is set up to pay certain medical expenses. Only a person who is covered by a high-deductible health plan (HDHP) can establish an HSA. For 2018, the contribution limit is $3,450 for self-only coverage and $6,900 for family coverage, which includes all other coverage. HSA-eligible individuals over 55 years of age can contribute an extra $1,000 each year.

An employer may make deductible contributions to an HSA on behalf of one or more employees. The employer's contributions reduce the amount that the employee can contribute to his or her HSA. Employer contributions are treated as employer-provided coverage for medical expenses under an accident or health plan excluded from an eligible employee's gross income [Code Sec. 106(d)] and the contributions for the employee are not subject to social security or Medicare tax. Distributions from the plan are not taxable if they are used to pay the plan owner's medical expenses during his or her lifetime or up to one year after death. The employee cannot deduct employer contributions on his or her federal income tax return as HSA contributions or as medical expense deductions under Code Section 213. [Notice 2004-2, Q&A 19, 2004-2 IRB 269]

A partnership may contribute to a partner's HSA. However, contributions by a partnership to a bona fide partner's HSA are not contributions by an employer to the HSA of an employee. If a partnership's contributions to a partner's HSA are treated as distributions to the partner under Code Section 731, the contributions are not deductible by the partnership and do not affect the distributive shares of partnership income and deductions. The contributions are reported as distributions of money but are not included in the partner's net earnings from self-employment. An eligible partner can deduct the amount of the contributions made to the partner's HSA as an adjustment to gross income.

If, instead, the partnership's contributions to a partner's HSA are treated as guaranteed payments for services rendered to the partnership, they are deductible by the partnership and includible in the partner's gross income. Because the contributions are guaranteed payments derived from the partnership's trade or business, and are for services rendered to the partnership, the contributions are included in the partner's net earnings from self-employment under Code Section 1402(a). An eligible partner can deduct the amount of the contributions made to the partner's HSA as an adjustment to gross income.

An S corporation may contribute to the HSA of a 2% shareholder-employee. Contributions by an S corporation to an HSA of a 2% shareholder-employee in consideration for services rendered are treated as being similar to guaranteed payments. The S corporation can deduct the contributions and they are includible in the shareholder-employee's gross income. In addition, if the requirements for the exclusion under Code Section 3121(a)(2)(B) are satisfied, the S corporation's contributions to an HSA of a 2% shareholder-employee are not wages subject to FICA tax, even though the amounts must be included in wages for income tax withholding purposes. An eligible 2% shareholder-employee can deduct the contributions as an adjustment to gross income on his or her federal income tax return. [Notice 2005-8, 2005-4 IRB 368]

Disability Insurance. A business can typically deduct short-term or long-term disability insurance paid as an ordinary and necessary business expense. [Reg §1.162-10] The cost of the premium is excluded from the employee's gross income. However, a 2% S corporation shareholder is treated as a partner in a partnership (not an employee) and cannot exclude from gross income disability insurance premiums paid by the S corporation. Thus, a partner or 2% shareholder must include the cost of disability insurance premiums in his or her income.

Group-Term Life Insurance. Code Section 79 provides an exclusion from income for premiums paid on group-term life insurance for coverage of no more than $50,000 per employee. The employer must report as compensation the amount of the premium for insurance that exceeds $50,000, according to a factor based on the age of the employee. [Reg. §1.79-3(d)] A partner and a 2% S corporation shareholder are not employees for purposes of the group-term life insurance rules. Therefore, a partner and a 2% shareholder cannot claim any exclusion for group-term life insurance.

Educational Assistance. An employer may establish a qualified educational assistance program. The employer's contributions are fully deductible, and the distributions may be tax-free to the employee who receives the benefit, up to $5,250 per year. [Code Sec. 127(a)(2)] The program must not discriminate in favor of highly-compensated employees. An individual who is self-employed is treated as an employee for this purpose, and distributions are excluded from his or her income. [Reg. §1.127-2(h)(1)(iii)]

Dependent Care Assistance. Self-employed individuals, including partners and S corporation 2% shareholders, can exclude dependent care assistance from their gross income. [Code Sec. 129(e)(3)] However, the

¶9.02

amount of benefits provided to principal shareholders or owners (those who own more than 5% of the stock or capital or profits interests) cannot exceed 25% of the total paid by the employer to all employees for the year. [Code Sec. 129(d)(4)]

Transportation Benefits. The Tax Cuts and Jobs Act of 2017 eliminates business deductions for most qualified transportation fringe benefits paid or incurred after 2017. However, certain transportation, transit passes, qualified parking, and qualified bicycle commuting reimbursements may be excluded from an employee's income. [Code Sec. 132(f)]

An employer may provide qualified transportation fringe benefits only to individuals who are currently employees of the employer at the time the qualified transportation benefit is provided. An employee includes only common-law employees and other statutory employees, such as officers of corporations. A self-employed person is not an employee for the purpose of excluding qualified transportation benefits from income. However, the *de minimis* fringe benefits rules may apply to exclude transit passes or parking provided to partners, 2% shareholders, and independent contractors.

Commuter Highway Vehicle Transportation. The 2018 exclusion for an employer-provided ride in a commuter highway vehicle between the employee's home and workplace is limited to $260 per month less the value of any transit passes provided. A commuter highway vehicle must seat at least six adults plus the driver. At least 80% of its mileage must be for transporting employees between their homes and the workplace, and the number of employees transported must be at least one-half of the adult seating capacity of the vehicle (not including the driver's seat). For tax years after 2017, the TCJA eliminates the employer's deduction for commuter highway vehicle transportation, except if the transportation is necessary to ensure the safety of the employee. The exclusion does not apply to non-employees.

Transit Passes. The 2018 exclusion for transit passes provided by an employer is limited to $260 per month less the value of any commuter highway vehicle expenses that the employer provides. Transit passes include any pass, token, farecard, voucher, or similar item that entitles a person to ride (free of charge or at a reduced rate) on mass transit or in a vehicle that seats at least six adults (not including the driver). The vehicle must be operated by a person in the business of transporting persons. Mass transit may be publicly or privately operated, and includes bus, rail, or ferry services.

For tax years after 2017, the TCJA eliminates the employer's deduction for transit passes, except as is necessary to ensure the safety of the employee. The exclusion does not apply to non-employees, but a recipient of a transit pass may be able to exclude the value of the pass if it has so little value that accounting for it would be unreasonable or administratively impracticable (a *de minimis* fringe benefit). Thus, for example, a 2% S corporation shareholder-employee may be able to exclude from income the value of local transportation fare that the corporation occasionally provides because the employee is working overtime.

Qualified Parking. The 2018 exclusion for qualified parking provided by an employer is limited to $260 per month. Parking is provided by an employer if: the parking is on property that the employer owns or leases, the employer pays for the parking, or the employer reimburses the employee for parking expenses. [Reg. §1.132-9]

Qualified parking must be located on or near the business premises, or on or near the location from which the business's employees commute using mass transit, commuter highway vehicles, or carpools. Parking on or near the employer's business premises includes parking on or near a work location at which the employee provides services for the employer. Parking on or near property used by the employee for residential purposes is not qualified parking.

For tax years after 2017, the TCJA eliminates the employer's deduction for parking, except as is necessary for the safety of the employee. Parking provided to a non-employee is not excludable from gross income, but it may be excludable under Code Section 132(a)(3) as a working condition fringe benefit if it is provided so that the partner, 2% shareholder, or independent contractor can do his or her job. It also may be excludable as a *de minimis* fringe benefit.

Qualified Bicycle Commuting Expenses. The exclusion for qualified bicycle commuting expenses provided by an employer (when allowed) is limited to $20 per month. Qualified bicycle commuting reimbursements can cover the purchase of a bicycle, bicycle improvements, repairs, and storage of a bicycle. The bicycle must be regularly used for commuting between the employee's residence and place of employment. A bicycle commuting fringe benefit is not excludable if the employee received any other qualified transportation fringe benefit for that month.

An employer can deduct amounts paid for qualified bicycle commuting expenses in tax years 2018 through 2025. Amounts paid on or after January 1, 2026, are not deductible. The Tax Cuts and Jobs Act of 2017 suspends the Section 132 qualified bicycle commuting reimbursement exclusion for tax years beginning after December 31, 2017 and before January 1, 2026. When available, the exclusion is only for employees, and partners and 2% S corporation shareholders cannot claim the exclusion.

¶9.02

Employee Meals and Lodging. Meals and lodging furnished on the employer's premises (the employee's place of work) and for the convenience of the employer are excluded from an employee's income. [Code Sec. 119] The employee cannot have an option to receive additional pay instead of meals or lodging. *De minimis* meal expenses are also excluded from a recipient's income. [Code Sec. 132(e)]

Meals are furnished for the employer's convenience in the following situations:

1. The meals are furnished during working hours so that the employees will be available for emergency calls during the meal period. The employer must be able to show that emergency calls have occurred or can reasonably be expected to occur.
2. The meals are furnished during working hours because the type of business restricts an employee to a short meal period (such as 30 or 45 minutes) and the employee cannot be expected to eat elsewhere in such a short time.
3. The meals are furnished during working hours if the employee cannot eat proper meals within a reasonable time because there are insufficient eating facilities near the place of employment.
4. The meals are provided to restaurant employees during (or immediately before or after) the employee's working hours.

If more than one-half of the employees who are furnished meals on the business premises are furnished meals for the employer's convenience, the employer can treat all meals furnished to employees on the business premises as furnished for the employer's convenience.

The value of lodging furnished to an employee by the employer is excluded from the employee's gross income if the following three tests are met:

1. The lodging is furnished on the business premises of the employer.
2. The lodging is furnished for the convenience of the employer.
3. The employee is required to accept such lodging as a condition of his employment.

The Tax Cuts and Jobs Act of 2017 reduces the business deduction for employer-provided meals from 100% to 50% after 2017, and it eliminates the deduction after 2025. The exclusion of the value of employer-provided meals and lodging from income is limited to employees. Partners and 2% shareholder-employees of S corporations cannot exclude the value of meals and lodging from their income.

¶9.02

Comment. After December 31, 2017, no deduction is allowed for expenses paid or incurred for an activity generally considered to be entertainment, amusement, or recreation, membership dues for a club organized for business, pleasure, recreation, or other social purposes, or a facility used in connection with these activities or clubs. The elimination of the deduction for entertainment expenses does not apply to the expenses authorized by Code Section 274(e) such as expenses for recreational, social, or similar activities (including facilities) primarily for the benefit of employees (other than employees who are highly-compensated employees), expenses directly related to business meetings of the taxpayer's employees, stockholders, agents, or directors, and expenses to attend a business league meeting or trade convention.

Code Section 132(e) allows the exclusion of *de minimis* meal expenses from a recipient's wages. Examples of *de minimis* fringe benefits include coffee, snacks, or soft drinks in the employee breakroom, and occasional parties or picnics for workers and their guests. The *de minimis* meals exclusion also applies to meals provided at an employer-operated eating facility for employees if the annual revenue from the facility equals or exceeds the direct operating costs of the facility. The eating facility must be available on substantially the same terms to members of a group of employees and cannot discriminate in favor of highly-compensated employees.

From 2018 through 2025, employers can deduct 50% of the cost of these meal expenses. After 2025, these costs are not deductible. The exclusion from income for *de minimis* meal expenses applies to any recipient, including partners and 2% S corporation shareholders.

¶9.02

Chapter 10

Conclusion: Tax Rates, Distributions and Entity Choice

¶10.01 In General

This Guide has discussed several important factors for the selection of a business entity. The general conclusion has been that, unless the owners are holding the business for growth and do not plan to withdraw substantial funds from the enterprise, the pass-through entity is preferred. However, the C corporation retains its viability as an enterprise in a few situations. One is where it is a profitable enterprise in which the investors' primary objective is to hold stock for growth. This is especially important if the stock qualifies in whole or in part for Code Section 1202 treatment. Another is where fringe benefits or expected nondeductible expenses are principal objectives. An example might be a professional service business, where the income is too high to qualify for the Section 199A deduction, the shareholders want to exclude medical insurance, and the business incurs significant entertainment expenses.

If there are to be significant distributions to owners, the pass-through entity generally provides an advantage over the C corporation. If the income is subject to self-employment tax, the S corporation may provide an advantage over the unincorporated entity (proprietorship or partnership). The advantage is greatest when the total income of the business is less than the FICA ceiling of approximately $130,000. Certain payments by an S corporation, such as medical insurance premiums and contributions to qualified retirement plans, are deductible by the corporation but are not subject to FICA. Moreover, at any level of business income, if the reasonable compensation of the owners is less than the net profit of the business, the owner may be able to mix compensation, which is subject to FICA, and distributions, which are not subject to FICA. However, setting compensation of shareholder-employees at an unreasonably low level can lead to penalties and interest. Most taxpayers who have attempted to fight the IRS on the imposition of such penalties have been unsuccessful.

The situation reverses when the income from the business is not subject to self-employment tax. Examples of such income include rents, royalties, interest and dividends. If these are the sources of income for an S corporation and if a shareholder provides any services for the business, he or she must take some salary from the corporation. This converts some or all of the income which would not be subject to self-employment tax in the unincorporated entity to FICA wages.

The analysis in this chapter compares the C corporation, the S corporation and the unincorporated entity over various income levels and varying levels of distributions. There are essentially four classifications of income:

1. Not eligible for the Section 199A deduction and subject to self-employment tax.
2. Eligible for the Section 199A deduction and subject to self-employment tax.
3. Not eligible for the Section 199A deduction and not subject to self-employment tax.
4. Eligible for the Section 199A deduction and not subject to self-employment tax.

In each of the Figures below, the horizontal axis represents the pre-tax income of the business and the vertical axis shows the after-tax income. The analyses assume that the owner has no other income or deductions other than the standard deduction. The after-tax income is net of the corporate income tax, the owner's income tax, the self-employment tax (if unincorporated), employer and employee FICA on the salary paid and the NII tax on dividends, when applicable. The analyses are all based on single filing status. Pre-tax income ranges from $50,000 to a top of $600,000, which covers the entire income tax rate schedule, as well as the varying rates of self-employment tax, FICA and NIIT.

Among other limitations, these analyses consider only a single year. The complexity of a multi-year analysis, with varying incomes, distributions and other aspects such as sources of income and deductions would be appropriate and necessary for an intelligent evaluation of an actual business. The conclusions presented in this material are appropriate guides for an initial evaluation of business structures.

Comment. From an early 2019 vantage point, it appears likely that there will be significant changes in federal tax policies in the future. One of the possibilities is an increase in the corporate income tax rate to 25%. The final portion of this chapter adapts the earlier analysis of a business that does not qualify for the Section 199A deduction, is subject to self-employment tax as an unincorporated entity, and distributes none of its income.

¶10.02 Not Eligible for Section 199A Deduction and Subject to Self-Employment Tax

When the entity is a C or S corporation, this model compensates the shareholder with 2/7 of the income. This keeps the analysis consistent with the relationships used in analyzing income streams that are eligible for the Section 199A deduction. This percentage may be below the level of compensation that is considered reasonable for an S corporation and its shareholder-employee for purposes of FICA.

Figure 1. Not Qualified Business; Subject to FICA/SET, Percent Distributed 0%, Wage to Owner 28.57% of Income

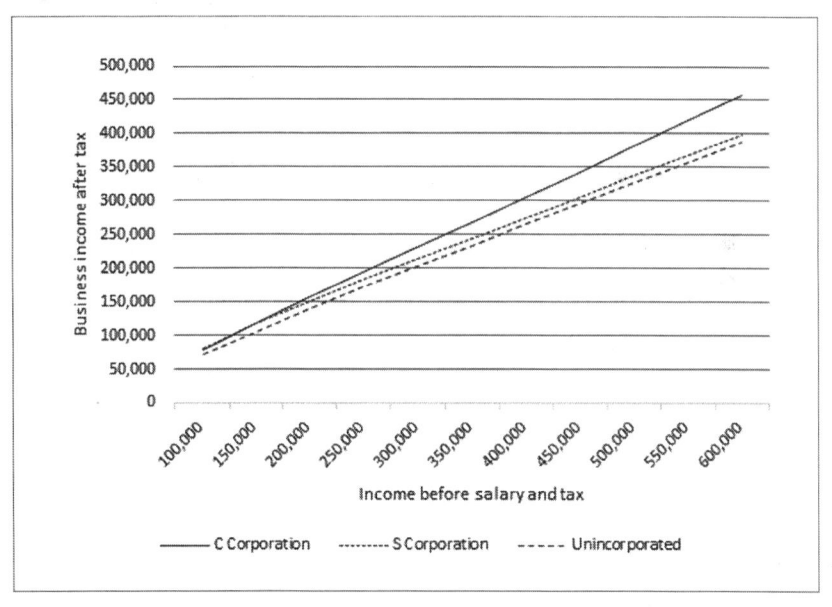

As Figure 1 indicates, results of the three entities are close until pretax income exceeds $300,000. At that level, the C corporation gains the upper hand. The S corporation is slightly better than the unincorporated entity at all ranges, due to the difference between the self-employment tax and FICA bases. The exact point at which the C corporation shows the slight advantage is at $126,411 of pretax income. At the top of the range the corporation results in $58,871 greater accumulation than the S corporation, or slightly less than 10% of the pretax income. However, this analysis provides for no distributions to the owner, other than salary.

The next part of the analysis shows the results with distributions of 50% of the pretax income, but the distributions include the corporate income tax. Accordingly, the C corporation pays 21% of its pretax income in tax and then distributes 29% as dividends. The amount of the distribution does not affect the tax on the owner of either pass-through entity.

Figure 2. Not Qualified Business; Subject to FICA/SET, Percent Distributed 50%, Wage to Owner 28.57% of Income

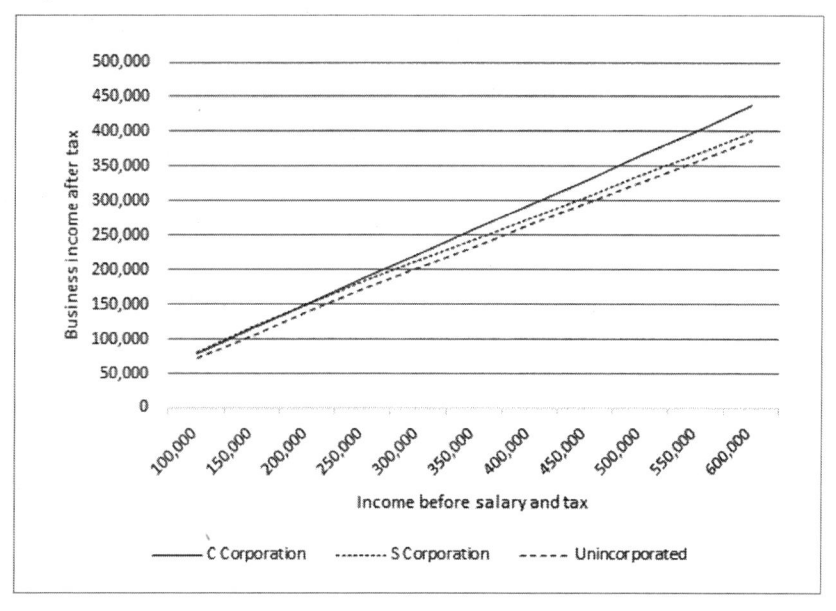

As Figure 2 shows, the C corporation again has an advantage at higher levels of income. However, the breakeven point moves to $202,610. The saving at the top of the range is $38,143 or about 6% of pretax income.

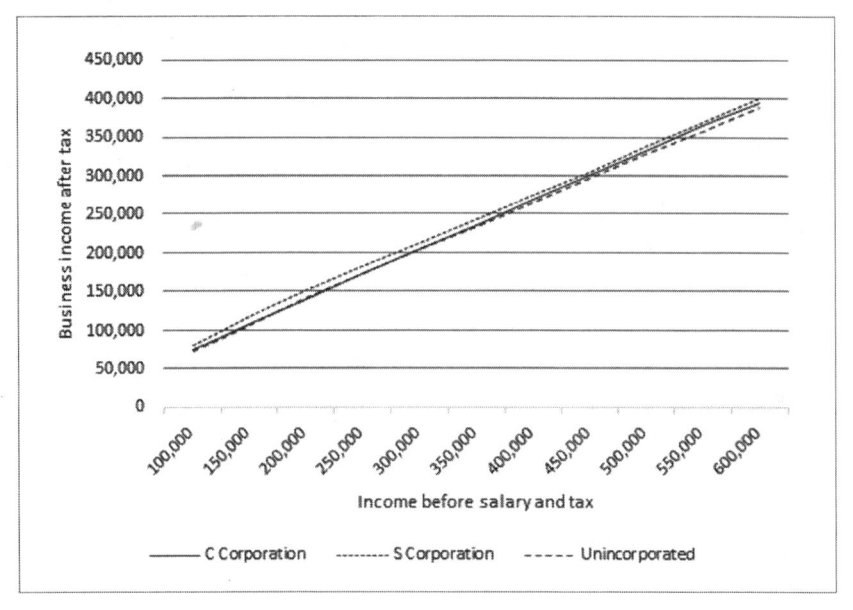

Figure 3. Not Qualified Business; Subject to FICA/SET, Percent Distributed 100%, Wage to Owner 28.57% of Income

Moving to 100% distribution, the results, as expected, are that the pass-through entity has the advantage at all income levels. This situation could reflect a professional service firm, where the income is high enough that it does not qualify for the Section 199A deduction, and the shareholders or partners distribute substantially all of the cash flow.

This scenario represents the most favorable circumstances for the C corporation. All of the income was subject to self-employment tax if the business was unincorporated. None of the income qualified for the Section 199A deduction.

¶10.03 Eligible for Section 199A Deduction and Subject to Self-Employment Tax

In this case, the pass-through entity gains an advantage, since the QBI deduction effectively reduces the tax rate on the owner of the pass-through entity by 20%. It has no effect on the C corporation. The analyses use the same assumptions as those in ¶10.02.

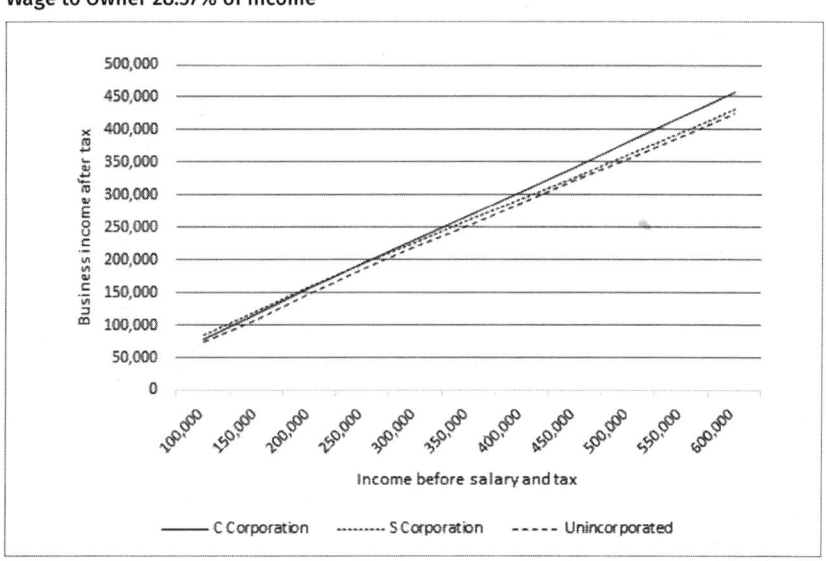

Figure 4. Qualified Business, Subject to FICA/SET, Percent Distributed 0%, Wage to Owner 28.57% of Income

The patterns are similar to those in the preceding section. The S corporation has the advantage at lower income levels. However, the breakeven point, with zero distributions, is now $254,751. The C corporation savings at $600,000 of pretax income are $28,052, less than 5% of the pretax income.

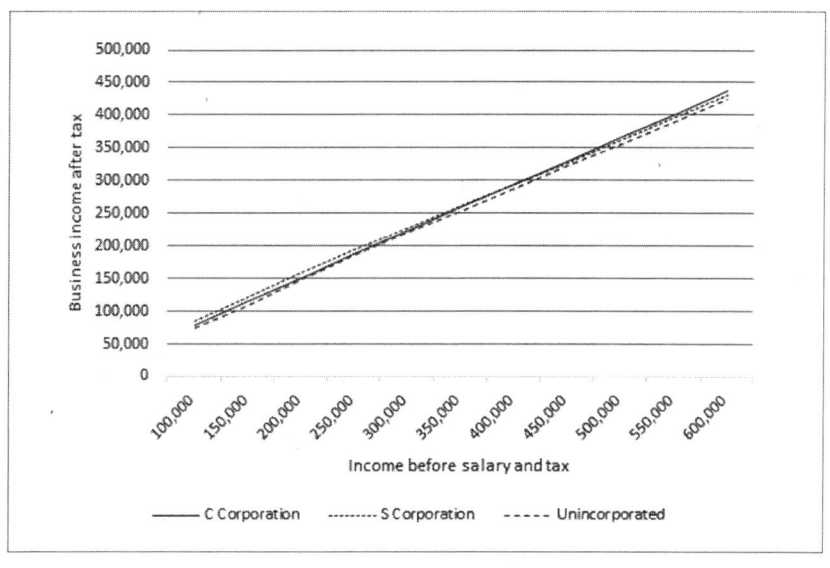

Figure 5. Qualified Business, Subject to FICA/SET, Percent Distributed 50%, Wage to Owner 28.57% of Income

¶10.03

Moving to a 50% distribution, the C corporation loses almost all advantage. The crossover point from S corporation to C corporation becomes $387,419. At $600,000 of pretax income, the C corporation's advantage is $7,323, slightly over 1% of pretax income.

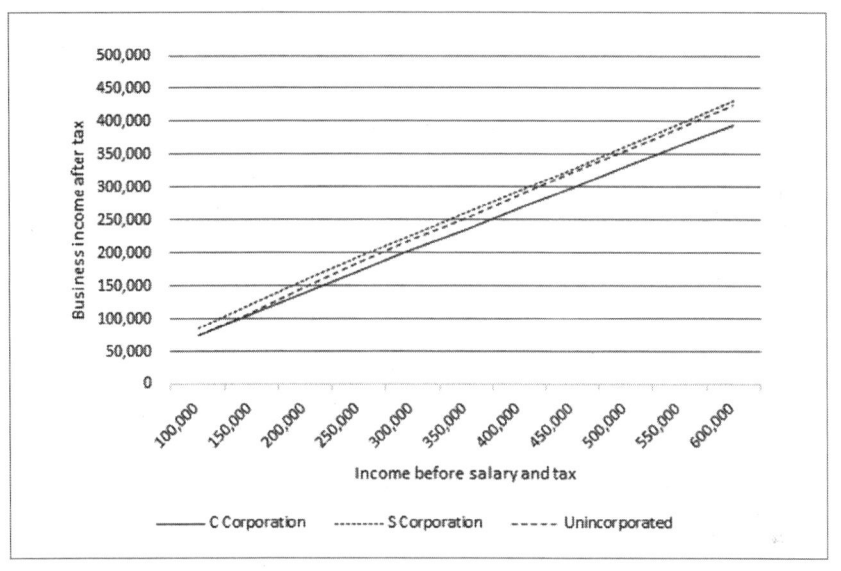

Figure 6. Qualified Business, Subject to FICA/SET, Percent Distributed 100%, Wage to Owner 28.57% of Income

At 100% distribution, the C corporation provides the worst tax results at all income levels. At $600,000 of pretax income, the cash flow from C corporation status is $36,160 less than it is with the S corporation, a loss of approximately 6% of pretax income.

¶10.04 Not Eligible for Section 199A Deduction and Not Subject to Self-Employment Tax

The principal difference of removing self-employment tax from the analysis is that the unincorporated entity shows better results than the S corporation. Again, the situation where the C corporation is most favorable is where the business does not qualify for the Section 199A deduction.

With zero distributions, the C corporation advantage is similar to what it was in Figure 1 where the business did not qualify under Section 199A.

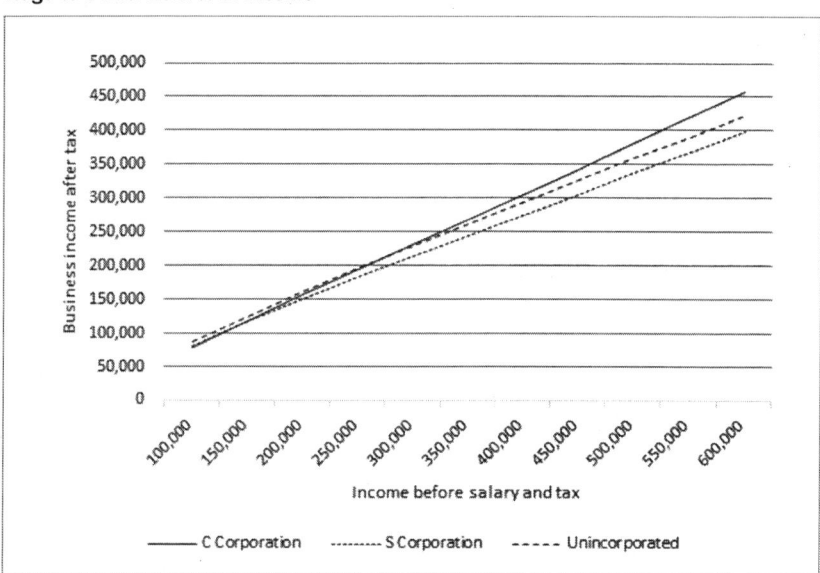

Figure 7. Not Qualified Business, Not Subject to FICA/SET, Percent Distributed 0%, Wage to Owner 28.57% of Income

The patterns are similar to those in the preceding section. The unincorporated entity has the advantage at lower income levels. The breakeven point, with zero distributions, is $126,411. The C corporation savings at $600,000 of pretax income are $35,925, less than 6% of the pretax income. The difference between the unincorporated entity and the S corporation is due to the FICA taxes imposed on the corporation and the shareholder-employee with the S corporation option.

¶10.04

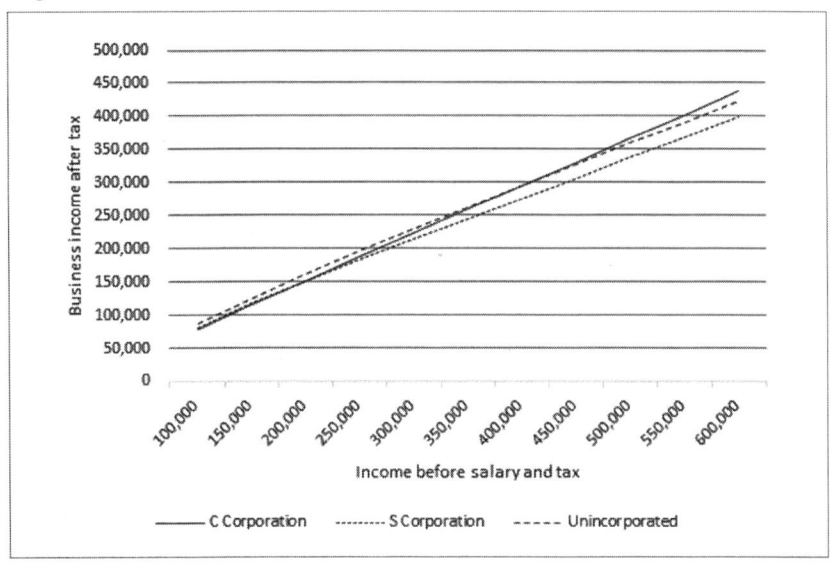

Figure 8. Not Qualified Business, Not Subject to FICA/SET, Percent Distributed 50%, Wage to Owner 28.57% of Income

Moving to a 50% distribution, the C corporation loses almost all advantage. The crossover point from unincorporated entity to C corporation becomes $202,600. At $600,000 of pretax income, the C corporation's advantage is $15,197, slightly over 2.5% of pretax income.

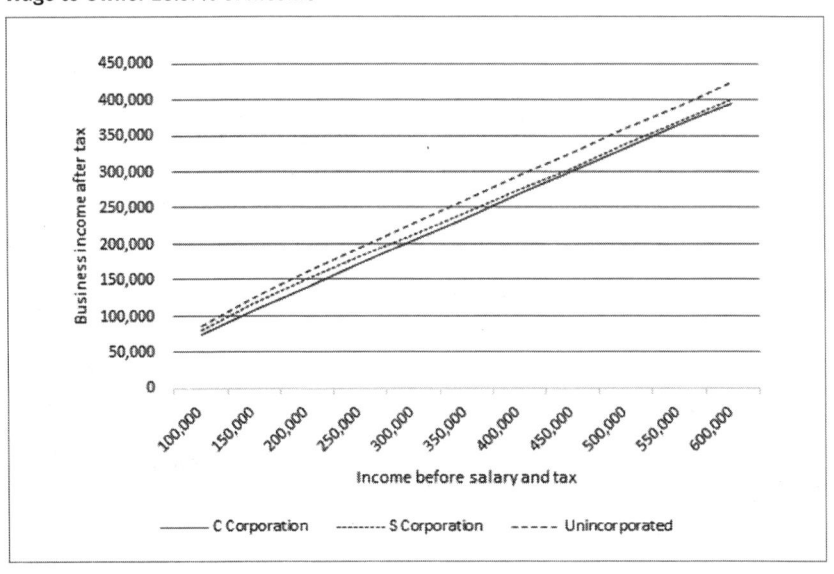

Figure 9. Not Qualified Business, Not Subject to FICA/SET, Percent Distributed 100%, Wage to Owner 28.57% of Income

¶10.04

At 100% distribution, the C corporation provides the worst tax results at all income levels. At $600,000 of pretax income, the cash flow from C corporation status is $28,286 less than it is with the unincorporated entity, a loss of approximately 4.7% of pretax income.

¶10.05 Eligible for Section 199A Deduction and Not Subject to Self-Employment Tax

Our final section of the analysis using existing tax laws (as of early 2019) is the situation where the unincorporated entity has the inherent advantage. The business qualifies for the Section 199A deduction and the income is not subject to self-employment tax when the entity is unincorporated.

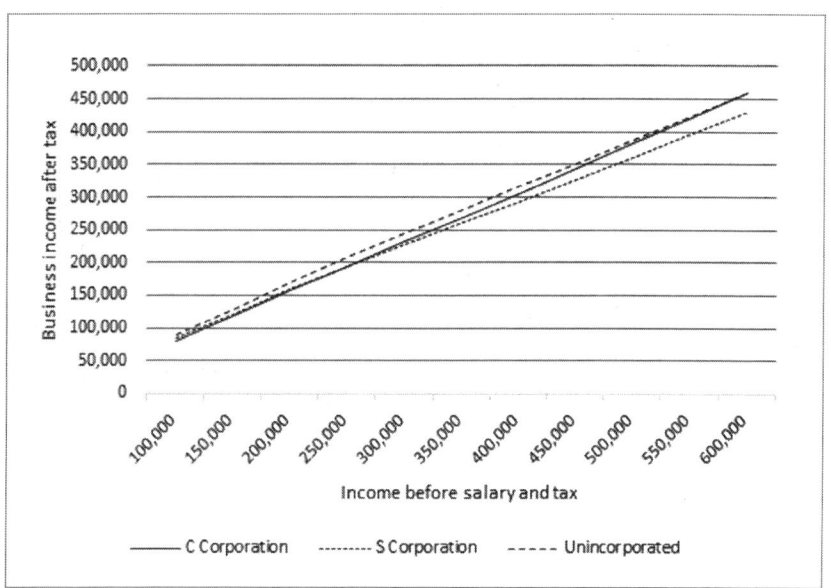

Figure 10. Qualified Business, Not Subject to FICA/SET, Percent Distributed 0%, Wage to Owner 28.57% of Income

At all levels of income, the unincorporated entity dominates. The S corporation is in second place until income reaches $254,751, at which point the C corporation gains the advantage. At $600,000 of income, the C corporation provides $28,052, or approximately 4.7% more cash flow than the S corporation.

Since the unincorporated entity dominates at every level of income, it may seem pointless to continue the analysis. However, if the business is already incorporated, it may be prohibitively expensive to liquidate. Therefore, the only realistic options may be C corporation or S corporation status. Accordingly, this scenario continues with entity comparisons at the 50% and 100% levels.

Figure 11. Qualified Business, Not Subject to FICA/SET, Percent Distributed 50%, Wage to Owner 28.57% of Income

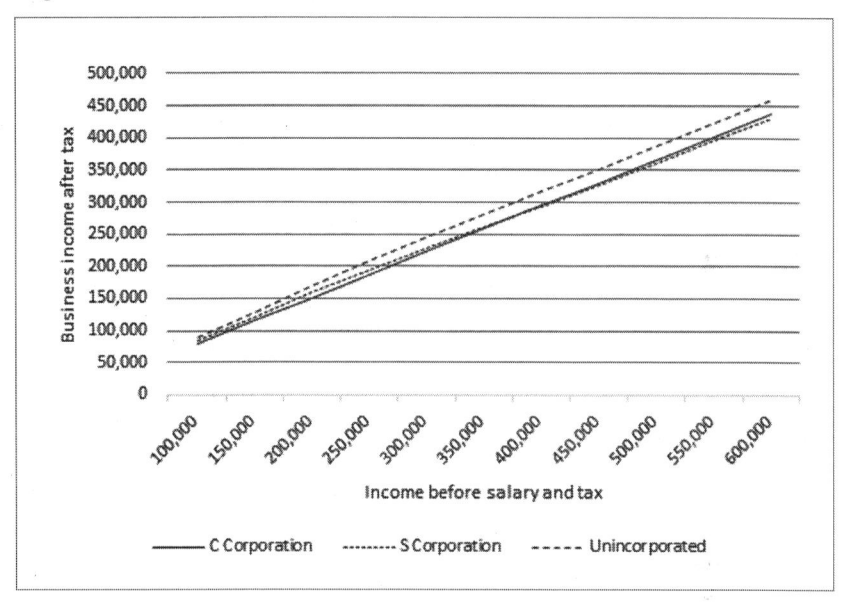

The breakeven between C and S corporation status occurs when the pretax income is $387,419. At $600,000 of pretax income, the C corporation savings compared to S corporation savings are $7,323, slightly more than 1% of the income. At $600,000 of pretax income the unincorporated entity produces $21,805 more cash flow than the C corporation.

¶10.05

Figure 12. Qualified Business, Not Subject to FICA/SET, Percent Distributed 100%, Wage to Owner 28.57% of Income

With 100% distributions, the S corporation produces better results than the C corporation at all levels. The unincorporated entity, as expected, dominates both corporate forms. At $600,000 of income The S corporation produces $36,160, or 6%, more cash flow than the C corporation. The unincorporated entity holds an advantage of $29,128 over the S corporation, approximately 5% of the pretax income.

In conclusion, each of the three business forms has advantages in certain situations. In order of importance, the factors to be taken into account are:

1. Percent of income to be distributed to the owners.
2. Eligibly of the income for the QBI deduction.
3. Classification of the income for self-employment tax purposes.

In view of the other aspects of owning, operating and selling a business entity discussed in this Guide, it would be foolish to assume that any one entity selection dominates. Since the savings resulting from the differences in business form are usually minor, the owners and tax advisors should proceed with caution before changing business forms. The cost of converting to corporate status may be low, although there are traps, especially when there are liabilities. Perhaps the more important aspect of changing to corporate status is that, for practical purposes, it may be irreversible without an onerous cost, which would have been unnecessary.

¶10.05

Appendix

Selected Code Sections Affected by the Tax Cuts and Jobs Act

[Sec. 168]
SEC. 168. ACCELERATED COST RECOVERY SYSTEM.
[Sec. 168(a)]
(a) GENERAL RULE.—Except as otherwise provided in this section, the depreciation deduction provided by section 167(a) for any tangible property shall be determined by using—
 (1) the applicable depreciation method,
 (2) the applicable recovery period, and
 (3) the applicable convention.

[Sec. 168(b)]
(b) APPLICABLE DEPRECIATION METHOD.—For purposes of this section—
 (1) IN GENERAL.—Except as provided in paragraphs (2) and (3), the applicable depreciation method is—
  (A) the 200 percent declining balance method,
  (B) switching to the straight line method for the 1st taxable year for which using the straight line method with respect to the adjusted basis as of the beginning of such year will yield a larger allowance.
 (2) 150 PERCENT DECLINING BALANCE METHOD IN CERTAIN CASES.—Paragraph (1) shall be applied by substituting "150 percent" for "200 percent" in the case of—
  (A) any 15-year or 20-year property not referred to in paragraph (3),
  (B) any property (other than property described in paragraph (3)) which is a qualified smart electric meter or qualified smart electric grid system, or
  (C) any property (other than property described in paragraph (3)) with respect to which the taxpayer elects under paragraph (5) to have the provisions of this paragraph apply.
 (3) PROPERTY TO WHICH STRAIGHT LINE METHOD APPLIES.—The applicable depreciation method shall be the straight line method in the case of the following property:
  (A) Nonresidential real property.
  (B) Residential rental property.
  (C) Any railroad grading or tunnel bore.
  (D) Property with respect to which the taxpayer elects under paragraph (5) to have the provisions of this paragraph apply.
  (E) Property described in subsection (e)(3)(D)(ii).
  (F) Water utility property described in subsection (e)(5).
  (G) Qualified improvement property described in subsection (e)(6).
 (4) SALVAGE VALUE TREATED AS ZERO.—Salvage value shall be treated as zero.
 (5) ELECTION.—An election under paragraph (2)(D) or (3)(D) may be made with respect to 1 or more classes of property for any taxable year and once made with respect to any class shall apply to all property in such class placed in service during such taxable year. Such an election, once made, shall be irrevocable.

Amendments

• **2017, Tax Cuts and Jobs Act (P.L. 115-97)**

P.L. 115-97, § 13203(b):

Amended Code Sec. 168(b)(2) by striking subparagraph (B) and by redesignating subparagraphs (C) and (D) as subparagraphs (B) and (C), respectively. **Effective** for property placed in service after 12-31-2017, in tax years ending after such date. Prior to being stricken, Code Sec. 168(b)(2)(B) read as follows:

(B) any property used in a farming business (within the meaning of section 263A(e)(4)),

P.L. 115-97, § 13204(a)(2)(A)-(B):

Amended Code Sec. 168(b)(3) by striking subparagraphs (G), (H), and (I), and by inserting after subparagraph (F) a new subparagraph (G). **Effective** for property placed in service after 12-31-2017. Prior to being stricken, Code Sec. 168(b)(3)(G)-(I) read as follows:

(G) Qualified leasehold improvement property described in subsection (e)(6).

(H) Qualified restaurant property described in subsection (e)(7).

(I) Qualified retail improvement property described in subsection (e)(8).

• **2014, Tax Technical Corrections Act of 2014 (P.L. 113-295)**

P.L. 113-295, § 210(g)(2)(A), Division A:

Amended Code Sec. 168(b)(5) by striking "(2)(C)" and inserting "(2)(D)". **Effective** as if included in the provision of the Energy Improvement and Extension Act of 2008 (P.L. 110-343) to which it relates [**effective** for property placed in service after 10-3-2008.—CCH].

• **2008, Tax Extenders and Alternative Minimum Tax Relief Act of 2008 (P.L. 110-343)**

P.L. 110-343, Division C, § 305(c)(3):

Amended Code Sec. 168(b)(3) by adding at the end a new subparagraph (I). **Effective** for property placed in service after 12-31-2008.

P.L. 110-343, Division B, § 306(c):

Amended Code Sec. 168(b)(2) by striking "or" at the end of subparagraph (B), redesignating subparagraph (C) as subparagraph (D), and by inserting after subparagraph (B) a new subparagraph (C). **Effective** for property placed in service after 10-3-2008.

• **2004, American Jobs Creation Act of 2004 (P.L. 108-357)**

P.L. 108-357, § 211(d)(1):

Amended Code Sec. 168(b)(3) by adding at the end new subparagraphs (G) and (H). **Effective** for property placed in service after 10-22-2004.

P.L. 108-357, § 211(d)(2):

Amended Code Sec. 168(b)(2)(A) by inserting before the comma "not referred to in paragraph (3)". **Effective** for property placed in service after 10-22-2004.

• **1998, Tax and Trade Relief Extension Act of 1998 (P.L. 105-277)**

P.L. 105-277, § 2022, provides:

SEC. 2022. DEPRECIATION STUDY.

The Secretary of the Treasury (or the Secretary's delegate)—

(1) shall conduct a comprehensive study of the recovery periods and depreciation methods under section 168 of the Internal Revenue Code of 1986, and

(2) not later than March 31, 2000, shall submit the results of such study, together with recommendations for determining such periods and methods in a more rational manner, to the Committee on Ways and Means of the House of Representatives and the Committee on Finance of the Senate.

- **1996, Small Business Job Protection Act of 1996 (P.L. 104-188)**

P.L. 104-188, §1613(b)(1):

Amended Code Sec. 168(b)(3) by adding at the end a new subparagraph (F). **Effective** for property placed in service after 6-12-96, other than property placed in service pursuant to a binding contract in effect before 6-10-96, and at all times thereafter before the property is placed in service.

- **1989, Omnibus Budget Reconciliation Act of 1989 (P.L. 101-239)**

P.L. 101-239, §7816(e)(1):

Amended Code Sec. 168(b)(5) by striking "paragraph (2)(B)" and inserting "paragraph (2)(C)". **Effective** as if included in the provision of P.L. 100-647 to which it relates.

P.L. 101-239, §7816(f):

Amended Code Sec. 168(b)(3) by redesignating subparagraph (D) as subparagraph (E). **Effective** as if included in the provision of P.L. 100-647 to which it relates.

- **1988, Technical and Miscellaneous Revenue Act of 1988 (P.L. 100-647)**

P.L. 100-647, §1002(a)(11)(A):

Amended Code Sec. 168(b)(2). **Effective** as if included in the provision of P.L. 99-514 to which it relates. Prior to amendment, Code Sec. 168(b)(2) read as follows:

(2) 15-YEAR AND 20-YEAR PROPERTY.—In the case of 15-year and 20-year property, paragraph (1) shall be applied by substituting "150 percent" for "200 percent".

P.L. 100-647, §1002(a)(11)(B):

Amended Code Sec. 168(b)(5) by striking out "under paragraph (3)(C)" and inserting in lieu thereof "under paragraph (2)(B) or (3)(C)". **Effective** as if included in the provision of P.L. 99-514 to which it relates.

P.L. 100-647, §1002(i)(2)(B)(i):

Amended Code Sec. 168(b)(3) by redesignating subparagraph (C) as subparagraph (D) and by inserting after subparagraph (B) a new subparagraph (C). **Effective** as if included in the provision of P.L. 99-514 to which it relates.

P.L. 100-647, §1002(i)(2)(B)(ii):

Amended Code Sec. 168(b)(5) by striking out "(3)(C)" and inserting in lieu thereof "(3)(D)". **Effective** as if included in the provision of P.L. 99-514 to which it relates.

P.L. 100-647, §6028(a):

Amended Code Sec. 168(b)(2) by striking out "or" at the end of subparagraph (A), by redesignating subparagraph (B) as subparagraph (C), and by inserting after subparagraph (A) a new subparagraph (B). **Effective**, generally, for property placed in service after 12-31-88. However, for an exception, see Act Sec. 6028(b)(2) below.

P.L. 100-647, §6028(b)(2), provides:

(b)(2) EXCEPTION.—The amendments made by this section shall not apply to any property if such property is placed in service before July 1, 1989, and if such property—

(A) is constructed, reconstructed, or acquired by the taxpayer pursuant to a written contract which was binding on July 14, 1988, or

(B) is constructed or reconstructed by the taxpayer and such construction or reconstruction began by July 14, 1988.

P.L. 100-647, §6029(b):

Amended Code Sec. 168(b)(3) by adding at the end thereof a new subparagraph (D)[(E)]. **Effective** for property placed in service after 12-31-88.

[Sec. 168(c)]

(c) APPLICABLE RECOVERY PERIOD.—For purposes of this section, the applicable recovery period shall be determined in accordance with the following table:

In the case of:	The applicable recovery period is:
3-year property	3 years
5-year property	5 years
7-year property	7 years
10-year property	10 years
15-year property	15 years
20-year property	20 years
Water utility property	25 years
Residential rental property	27.5 years
Nonresidential real property	39 years
Any railroad grading or tunnel bore	50 years

Amendments

- **1998, IRS Restructuring and Reform Act of 1998 (P.L. 105-206)**

P.L. 105-206, §6006(b)(1):

Amended Code Sec. 168(c) by striking paragraph (2). **Effective** as if included in the provision of P.L. 105-34 to which it relates [**effective** 8-5-97.—CCH]. Prior to being stricken, Code Sec. 168(c)(2) read as follows:

(2) PROPERTY FOR WHICH 150 PERCENT METHOD ELECTED.—In the case of property to which an election under subsection (b)(2)(C) applies, the applicable recovery period shall be determined under the table contained in subsection (g)(2)(C).

P.L. 105-206, §6006(b)(2):

Amended Code Sec. 168(c) by striking the portion of such subsection preceding the table in paragraph (1) and inserting new material. **Effective** as if included in the provision of P.L. 105-34 to which it relates [**effective** 8-5-97.—CCH]. Prior to amendment, the portion of Code Sec. 168(c) preceding the table read as follows:

(c) APPLICABLE RECOVERY PERIOD.—For purposes of this section—

(1) IN GENERAL.—Except as provided in paragraph (2), the applicable recovery period shall be determined in accordance with the following table:

- **1996, Small Business Job Protection Act of 1996 (P.L. 104-188)**

P.L. 104-188, §1613(b)(2):

Amended Code Sec. 168(c)(1) by inserting a new item in the table after the item relating to 20-year property. **Effective** for property placed in service after 6-12-96, other than property placed in service pursuant to a binding contract in effect before 6-10-96, and at all times thereafter before the property is placed in service.

- **1993, Omnibus Budget Reconciliation Act of 1993 (P.L. 103-66)**

P.L. 103-66, §13151(a):

Amended Code Sec. 168(c)(1) by striking the item relating to nonresidential real property and inserting a new item relating to nonresidential real property. **Effective**, generally, for property placed in service by the taxpayer on or after 5-13-93. For an exception, see Act Sec. 13151(b)(2) below.

Code Sec. 168

Prior to amendment, the item relating to nonresidential real property read as follows:
Nonresidential real property . . . . 31.5 years
P.L. 103-66, § 13151(b)(2), provides:
(2) EXCEPTION.—The amendments made by this section shall not apply to property placed in service by the taxpayer before January 1, 1994, if—
(A) the taxpayer or a qualified person entered into a binding written contract to purchase or construct such property before May 13, 1993, or
(B) the construction of such property was commenced by or for the taxpayer or a qualified person before May 13, 1993.
For purposes of this paragraph, the term "qualified person" means any person who transfers his rights in such a contract or such property to the taxpayer but only if the property is not placed in service by such person before such rights are transferred to the taxpayer.

- **1989, Omnibus Budget Reconciliation Act of 1989 (P.L. 101-239)**

P.L. 101-239, § 7816(e)(2):
Amended Code Sec. 168(c)(2) by striking "subsection (b)(2)(B)" and inserting "subsection (b)(2)(C)". **Effective** as if included in the provision of P.L. 100-647 to which it relates.

- **1988, Technical and Miscellaneous Revenue Act of 1988 (P.L. 100-647)**

P.L. 100-647, § 1002(a)(11)(C):
Amended Code Sec. 168(c). **Effective** as if included in the provision of P.L. 99-514 to which it relates. Prior to amendment, Code Sec. 168(c) read as follows:

(c) APPLICABLE RECOVERY PERIOD.—For purposes of this section, the applicable recovery period shall be determined in accordance with the following table:

In the case of:	The applicable recovery period is:
3-year property	3 years
5-year property	5 years
7-year property	7 years
10-year property	10 years
15-year property	15 years
20-year property	20 years
Residential rental property	27.5 years
Nonresidential real property	31.5 years

P.L. 100-647, § 1002(i)(2)(A):
Amended Code Sec. 168(c)(1) by adding at the end thereof a new item to the table. **Effective** as if included in the provision of P.L. 99-514 to which it relates.

[Sec. 168(d)]

(d) APPLICABLE CONVENTION.—For purposes of this section—

(1) IN GENERAL.—Except as otherwise provided in this subsection, the applicable convention is the half-year convention.

(2) REAL PROPERTY.—In the case of—
(A) nonresidential real property,
(B) residential rental property, and
(C) any railroad grading or tunnel bore,
the applicable convention is the mid-month convention.

(3) SPECIAL RULE WHERE SUBSTANTIAL PROPERTY PLACED IN SERVICE DURING LAST 3 MONTHS OF TAXABLE YEAR.—

(A) IN GENERAL.—Except as provided in regulations, if during any taxable year—
(i) the aggregate bases of property to which this section applies placed in service during the last 3 months of the taxable year, exceed
(ii) 40 percent of the aggregate bases of property to which this section applies placed in service during such taxable year,
the applicable convention for all property to which this section applies placed in service during such taxable year shall be the mid-quarter convention.

(B) CERTAIN PROPERTY NOT TAKEN INTO ACCOUNT.—For purposes of subparagraph (A), there shall not be taken into account—
(i) any nonresidential real property, and residential rental property and railroad grading or tunnel bore, and
(ii) any other property placed in service and disposed of during the same taxable year.

(4) DEFINITIONS.—
(A) HALF-YEAR CONVENTION.—The half-year convention is a convention which treats all property placed in service during any taxable year (or disposed of during any taxable year) as placed in service (or disposed of) on the mid-point of such taxable year.
(B) MID-MONTH CONVENTION.—The mid-month convention is a convention which treats all property placed in service during any month (or disposed of during any month) as placed in service (or disposed of) on the mid-point of such month.
(C) MID-QUARTER CONVENTION.—The mid-quarter convention is a convention which treats all property placed in service during any quarter of a taxable year (or disposed of during any quarter of a taxable year) as placed in service (or disposed of) on the mid-point of such quarter.

Amendments

- **2018, Tax Technical Corrections Act of 2018 (P.L. 115-141)**

P.L. 115-141, § 401(a)(49), Div. U:
Amended Code Sec. 168(d)(3)(B)(i) by inserting a comma after "real property". **Effective** 3-23-2018.

- **1988, Technical and Miscellaneous Revenue Act of 1988 (P.L. 100-647)**

P.L. 100-647, § 1002(a)(5):
Amended Code Sec. 168(d)(3)(A)(i) by striking out "and which are" after "applies". **Effective** as if included in the

APPENDIX: Selected Code Sections Affected by the Tax Cuts and Jobs Act

provision of P.L. 99-514 to which it relates. Prior to amendment, Code Sec. 168(d)(3)(A)(i) read as follows:

(i) the aggregate bases of property to which this section applies and which are placed in service during the last 3 months of the taxable year, exceed

P.L. 100-647, §1002(a)(23)(A):

Amended Code Sec. 168(d)(3)(B). **Effective**, generally, as if included in the provision of P.L. 99-514 to which it relates. However, for a special **effective** date, see Act Sec. 1002(a)(23)(B), below. Prior to amendment, Code Sec. 168(d)(3)(B) read as follows:

(B) CERTAIN REAL PROPERTY NOT TAKEN INTO ACCOUNT.—For purposes of subparagraph (A), nonresidential real property and residential rental property shall not be taken into account.

P.L. 100-647, §1002(a)(23)(B), provides:

(B) Clause (ii) of section 168(d)(3)(B) of the 1986 Code (as added by subparagraph (A)) shall apply to taxable years beginning after March 31, 1988, unless the taxpayer elects, at such time and in such manner as the Secretary of the Treasury or his delegate may prescribe, to have such clause apply to taxable years beginning on or before such date.

P.L. 100-647, §1002(i)(2)(D):

Amended Code Sec. 168(d)(2) by striking out "and" at the end of subparagraph (A), by inserting "and" at the end of subparagraph (B), and by inserting after subparagraph (B) a new subparagraph (C). **Effective** as if included in the provision of P.L. 99-514 to which it relates.

P.L. 100-647, §1002(i)(2)(E):

Amended Code Sec. 168(d)(3)(B)(i) by striking out "residential rental property" and inserting in lieu thereof "residential rental property and railroad grading or tunnel bore". **Effective** as if included in the provision of P.L. 99-514 to which it relates.

[Sec. 168(e)]

(e) CLASSIFICATION OF PROPERTY.—For purposes of this section—

(1) IN GENERAL.—Except as otherwise provided in this subsection, property shall be classified under the following table:

Property shall be treated as:	If such property has a class life (in years) of:
3-year property	4 or less
5-year property	More than 4 but less than 10
7-year property	10 or more but less than 16
10-year property	16 or more but less than 20
15-year property	20 or more but less than 25
20-year property	25 or more.

(2) RESIDENTIAL RENTAL OR NONRESIDENTIAL REAL PROPERTY.—

(A) RESIDENTIAL RENTAL PROPERTY.—

(i) RESIDENTIAL RENTAL PROPERTY.—The term "residential rental property" means any building or structure if 80 percent or more of the gross rental income from such building or structure for the taxable year is rental income from dwelling units.

(ii) DEFINITIONS.—For purposes of clause (i)—

(I) the term "dwelling unit" means a house or apartment used to provide living accommodations in a building or structure, but does not include a unit in a hotel, motel, or other establishment more than one-half of the units in which are used on a transient basis, and

(II) if any portion of the building or structure is occupied by the taxpayer, the gross rental income from such building or structure shall include the rental value of the portion so occupied.

(B) NONRESIDENTIAL REAL PROPERTY.—The term "nonresidential real property" means section 1250 property which is not—

(i) residential rental property, or

(ii) property with a class life of less than 27.5 years.

(3) CLASSIFICATION OF CERTAIN PROPERTY.—

(A) 3-YEAR PROPERTY.—The term "3-year property" includes—

(i) any race horse—

(I) which is placed in service before January 1, 2018, and

(II) which is placed in service after December 31, 2017, and which is more than 2 years old at the time such horse is placed in service by such purchaser,

(ii) any horse other than a race horse which is more than 12 years old at the time it is placed in service, and

(iii) any qualified rent-to-own property.

(B) 5-YEAR PROPERTY.—The term "5-year property" includes—

(i) any automobile or light general purpose truck,

(ii) any semi-conductor manufacturing equipment,

(iii) any computer-based telephone central office switching equipment,

(iv) any qualified technological equipment,

(v) any section 1245 property used in connection with research and experimentation,

(vi) any property which—

(I) is described in subparagraph (A) of section 48(a)(3) (or would be so described if "solar or wind energy" were substituted for "solar energy" in clause (i) thereof and the last sentence of such section did not apply to such subparagraph),

Code Sec. 168

(II) is described in paragraph (15) of section 48(l) (as in effect on the day before the date of the enactment of the Revenue Reconciliation Act of 1990) and has a power production capacity of not greater than 80 megawatts, or

(III) is described in section 48(l)(3)(A)(ix) (as in effect on the day before the date of the enactment of the Revenue Reconciliation Act of 1990), and

(vii) any machinery or equipment (other than any grain bin, cotton ginning asset, fence, or other land improvement) which is used in a farming business (as defined in section 263A(e)(4)), the original use of which commences with the taxpayer after December 31, 2017.

Nothing in any provision of law shall be construed to treat property as not being described in subclause (I) or (II) of clause (vi) by reason of being public utility property.

(C) 7-YEAR PROPERTY.—The term "7-year property" includes—
(i) any railroad track,
(ii) any motorsports entertainment complex,
(iii) any Alaska natural gas pipeline,
(iv) any natural gas gathering line the original use of which commences with the taxpayer after April 11, 2005, and
(v) any property which—
(I) does not have a class life, and
(II) is not otherwise classified under paragraph (2) or this paragraph.

(D) 10-YEAR PROPERTY.—The term "10-year property" includes—
(i) any single purpose agricultural or horticultural structure (within the meaning of subsection (i)(13)),
(ii) any tree or vine bearing fruit or nuts,
(iii) any qualified smart electric meter, and
(iv) any qualified smart electric grid system.

(E) 15-YEAR PROPERTY.—The term "15-year property" includes—
(i) any municipal wastewater treatment plant,
(ii) any telephone distribution plant and comparable equipment used for 2-way exchange of voice and data communications,
(iii) any section 1250 property which is a retail motor fuels outlet (whether or not food or other convenience items are sold at the outlet),
(iv) initial clearing and grading land improvements with respect to gas utility property,
(v) any section 1245 property (as defined in section 1245(a)(3)) used in the transmission at 69 or more kilovolts of electricity for sale and the original use of which commences with the taxpayer after April 11, 2005, and
(vi) any natural gas distribution line the original use of which commences with the taxpayer after April 11, 2005, and which is placed in service before January 1, 2011.

(F) 20-YEAR PROPERTY.—The term "20-year property" means initial clearing and grading land improvements with respect to any electric utility transmission and distribution plant.

(4) RAILROAD GRADING OR TUNNEL BORE.—The term "railroad grading or tunnel bore" means all improvements resulting from excavations (including tunneling), construction of embankments, clearings, diversions of roads and streams, sodding of slopes, and from similar work necessary to provide, construct, reconstruct, alter, protect, improve, replace, or restore a roadbed or right-of-way for railroad track.

(5) WATER UTILITY PROPERTY.—The term "water utility property" means property—
(A) which is an integral part of the gathering, treatment, or commercial distribution of water, and which, without regard to this paragraph, would be 20-year property, and
(B) any municipal sewer.

(6) QUALIFIED IMPROVEMENT PROPERTY.—
(A) IN GENERAL.—The term "qualified improvement property" means any improvement to an interior portion of a building which is nonresidential real property if such improvement is placed in service after the date such building was first placed in service.
(B) CERTAIN IMPROVEMENTS NOT INCLUDED.—Such term shall not include any improvement for which the expenditure is attributable to—
(i) the enlargement of the building,
(ii) any elevator or escalator, or
(iii) the internal structural framework of the building.

Amendments

- **2018, Tax Technical Corrections Act of 2018 (P.L. 115-141)**

P.L. 115-141, §302(a)(1), Div. U:

Amended Code Sec. 168(e)(3)(B)(vi)(II) by striking "is a qualifying small power production facility" and all that follows and inserting "has a power production capacity of not greater than 80 megawatts, or". **Effective** for property placed in service after 3-23-2018. Prior to amendment, Code Sec. 168(e)(3)(B)(vi)(II) read as follows:

(II) is described in paragraph (15) of section 48(l) (as in effect on the day before the date of the enactment of the Revenue Reconciliation Act of 1990) and is a qualifying small power production facility within the meaning of section 3(17)(C) of the Federal Power Act (16 U.S.C. 796(17)(C)), as in effect on September 1, 1986, or

APPENDIX: Selected Code Sections Affected by the Tax Cuts and Jobs Act

P.L. 115-141, §302(a)(2), Div. U:
Amended the last sentence of Code Sec. 168(e)(3)(B) by striking "clause (vi)(I)" and all that follows and inserting "subclause (I) or (II) of clause (vi) by reason of being public utility property". **Effective** for property placed in service after 3-23-2018. Prior to amendment, the last sentence of Code Sec. 168(e)(3)(B) read as follows:
Nothing in any provision of law shall be construed to treat property as not being described in clause (vi)(I) (or the corresponding provisions of prior law) by reason of being public utility property (within the meaning of section 48(a)(3)).

P.L. 115-141, §401(a)(50), Div. U:
Amended Code Sec. 168(e)(3)(C)(i) by striking "and". Effective 3-23-2018.

- **2018, Bipartisan Budget Act of 2018 (P.L. 115-123)**

P.L. 115-123, §40304(a)(1)-(2), Div. D:
Amended Code Sec. 168(e)(3)(A)(i) by striking "January 1, 2017" in subclause (I) and inserting "January 1, 2018", and by striking "December 31, 2016" in subclause (II) and inserting "December 31, 2017". **Effective** for property placed in service after 12-31-2016.

- **2017, Tax Cuts and Jobs Act (P.L. 115-97)**

P.L. 115-97, §13203(a):
Amended Code Sec. 168(e)(3)(B)(vii) by striking "after December 31, 2008, and which is placed in service before January 1, 2010" and inserting "after December 31, 2017". **Effective** for property placed in service after 12-31-2017, in tax years ending after such date.

P.L. 115-97, §13204(a)(1)(A)(i)-(iv):
Amended Code Sec. 168(e)(3)(E) by striking clauses (iv), (v), and (ix), by inserting "and" at the end of clause (vii), by striking ", and" in clause (viii) and inserting a period, and by redesignating clauses (vi), (vii), and (viii), as so amended, as clauses (iv), (v), and (vi), respectively. **Effective** for property placed in service after 12-31-2017. Prior to being stricken, Code Sec. 168(e)(3)(E)(iv), (v), and (ix) read as follows:
(iv) any qualified leasehold improvement property,
(v) any qualified restaurant property,

* * *

(ix) any qualified retail improvement property.

P.L. 115-97, §13204(a)(1)(B):
Amended Code Sec. 168(e) by striking paragraphs (6), (7), and (8). **Effective** for property placed in service after 12-31-2017. Prior to being stricken, Code Sec. 168(e)(6)-(8) read as follows:
(6) QUALIFIED LEASEHOLD IMPROVEMENT PROPERTY.—For purposes of this subsection—
(A) IN GENERAL.—The term "qualified leasehold improvement property" means any improvement to an interior portion of a building which is nonresidential real property if—
(i) such improvement is made under or pursuant to a lease (as defined in subsection (h)(7))—
(I) by the lessee (or any sublessee) of such portion, or
(II) by the lessor of such portion,
(ii) such portion is to be occupied exclusively by the lessee (or any sublessee) of such portion, and
(iii) such improvement is placed in service more than 3 years after the date the building was first placed in service.
(B) CERTAIN IMPROVEMENTS NOT INCLUDED.—Such term shall not include any improvement for which the expenditure is attributable to—
(i) the enlargement of the building,
(ii) any elevator or escalator,
(iii) any structural component benefitting a common area, or
(iv) the internal structural framework of the building.
(C) DEFINITIONS AND SPECIAL RULES.—For purposes of this paragraph—
(i) COMMITMENT TO LEASE TREATED AS LEASE.—A commitment to enter into a lease shall be treated as a lease, and the parties to such commitment shall be treated as lessor and lessee, respectively.
(ii) RELATED PERSONS.—A lease between related persons shall not be considered a lease. For purposes of the preceding sentence, the term "related persons" means—
(I) members of an affiliated group (as defined in section 1504), and
(II) persons having a relationship described in subsection (b) of section 267; except that, for purposes of this clause, the phrase "80 percent or more" shall be substituted for the phrase "more than 50 percent" each place it appears in such subsection.
(D) IMPROVEMENTS MADE BY LESSOR.—In the case of an improvement made by the person who was the lessor of such improvement when such improvement was placed in service, such improvement shall be qualified leasehold improvement property (if at all) only so long as such improvement is held by such person.
(E) EXCEPTION FOR CHANGES IN FORM OF BUSINESS.—Property shall not cease to be qualified leasehold improvement property under subparagraph (D) by reason of—
(i) death,
(ii) a transaction to which section 381(a) applies,
(iii) a mere change in the form of conducting the trade or business so long as the property is retained in such trade or business as qualified leasehold improvement property and the taxpayer retains a substantial interest in such trade or business,
(iv) the acquisition of such property in an exchange described in section 1031, 1033, or 1038 to the extent that the basis of such property includes an amount representing the adjusted basis of other property owned by the taxpayer or a related person, or
(v) the acquisition of such property by the taxpayer in a transaction described in section 332, 351, 361, 721, or 731 (or the acquisition of such property by the transferee from the transferee or acquiring corporation in a transaction described in such section), to the extent that the basis of the property in the hands of the taxpayer is determined by reference to its basis in the hands of the transferor or distributor.
(7) QUALIFIED RESTAURANT PROPERTY.—
(A) IN GENERAL.—The term "qualified restaurant property" means any section 1250 property which is—
(i) a building, or
(ii) an improvement to a building,
if more than 50 percent of the building's square footage is devoted to preparation of, and seating for on-premises consumption of, prepared meals.
(B) EXCLUSION FROM BONUS DEPRECIATION.—Property described in this paragraph which is not qualified improvement property shall not be considered qualified property for purposes of subsection (k).
(8) QUALIFIED RETAIL IMPROVEMENT PROPERTY.—
(A) IN GENERAL.—The term "qualified retail improvement property" means any improvement to an interior portion of a building which is nonresidential real property if—
(i) such portion is open to the general public and is used in the retail trade or business of selling tangible personal property to the general public, and
(ii) such improvement is placed in service more than 3 years after the date the building was first placed in service.
(B) IMPROVEMENTS MADE BY OWNER.—In the case of an improvement made by the owner of such improvement, such improvement shall be qualified retail improvement property (if at all) only so long as such improvement is held by such owner. Rules similar to the rules under paragraph (6)(B) shall apply for purposes of the preceding sentence.
(C) CERTAIN IMPROVEMENTS NOT INCLUDED.—Such term shall not include any improvement for which the expenditure is attributable to—
(i) the enlargement of the building,
(ii) any elevator or escalator,
(iii) any structural component benefitting a common area, or
(iv) the internal structural framework of the building.

P.L. 115-97, §13204(a)(4)(B)(i):
Amended Code Sec. 168(e), as amended by Act Sec. 13204(a)(1)(B), by adding at the end a new paragraph (6). **Effective** for property placed in service after 12-31-2017.

- **2015, Protecting Americans from Tax Hikes Act of 2015 (P.L. 114-113)**

P.L. 114-113, §123(a), Div. Q:
Amended Code Sec. 168(e)(3)(E)(iv)-(v) by striking "placed in service before January 1, 2015" each place it appears after "property". **Effective** for property placed in service after 12-31-2014.

P.L. 114-113, §123(b), Div. Q:
Amended Code Sec. 168(e)(3)(E)(ix) by striking "placed in service after December 31, 2008, and before January 1, 2015" before the period at the end. **Effective** for property placed in service after 12-31-2014.

P.L. 114-113, §143(b)(6)(A)(i)-(ii), Div. Q:

Amended Code Sec. 168(e)(6) by redesignating subparagraphs (A)-(B) as subparagraphs (D)-(E), respectively, by striking all that precedes subparagraph (D) (as so redesignated) and inserting:

"(6) QUALIFIED LEASEHOLD IMPROVEMENT PROPERTY.—For purposes of this subsection—"

and new subparagraphs (A)-(C), and by striking "subparagraph (A)" in subparagraph (E) (as so redesignated) and inserting "subparagraph (D)". **Effective** for property placed in service after 12-31-2015, in tax years ending after such date. Prior to being stricken, all that preceded subparagraph (D) (as so redesignated) in Code Sec. 168(e)(6) read as follows:

(6) QUALIFIED LEASEHOLD IMPROVEMENT PROPERTY.—The term "qualified leasehold improvement property" has the meaning given such term in section 168(k)(3) except that the following special rules shall apply:

P.L. 114-113, §143(b)(6)(B), Div. Q:

Amended Code Sec. 168(e)(7)(B) by striking "qualified leasehold improvement property" and inserting "qualified improvement property". **Effective** for property placed in service after 12-31-2015, in tax years ending after such date.

P.L. 114-113, §143(b)(6)(C), Div. Q:

Amended Code Sec. 168(e)(8) by striking subparagraph (D). **Effective** for property placed in service after 12-31-2015, in tax years ending after such date. Prior to being stricken, Code Sec. 168(e)(8)(D) read as follows:

(D) EXCLUSION FROM BONUS DEPRECIATION.—Property described in this paragraph which is not qualified leasehold improvement property shall not be considered qualified property for purposes of subsection (k).

P.L. 114-113, §165(a)(1)-(2), Div. Q:

Amended Code Sec. 168(e)(3)(A)(i) by striking "January 1, 2015" in subclause (I) and inserting "January 1, 2017", and by striking "December 31, 2014" in subclause (II) and inserting "December 31, 2016". **Effective** for property placed in service after 12-31-2014.

• **2014, Tax Increase Prevention Act of 2014 (P.L. 113-295)**

P.L. 113-295, §121(a)(1)-(2), Division A:

Amended Code Sec. 168(e)(3)(A)(i) by striking "January 1, 2014" in subclause (I) and inserting "January 1, 2015", and by striking "December 31, 2013" in subclause (II) and inserting "December 31, 2014". **Effective** for property placed in service after 12-31-2013.

P.L. 113-295, §122(a), Division A:

Amended Code Sec. 168(e)(3)(E)(iv), (v), and (ix) by striking "January 1, 2014" and inserting "January 1, 2015". **Effective** for property placed in service after 12-31-2013.

• **2014, Tax Technical Corrections Act of 2014 (P.L. 113-295)**

P.L. 113-295, §211(b), Division A:

Amended Code Sec. 168(e)(7)(B) and (8)(D) by inserting "which is not qualified leasehold improvement property" after "Property described in this paragraph". **Effective** as if included in the provision of the Tax Extenders and Alternative Minimum Tax Relief Act of 2008 (P.L. 110-343) to which it relates [**effective** for property placed in service after 12-31-2008.—CCH].

• **2013, American Taxpayer Relief Act of 2012 (P.L. 112-240)**

P.L. 112-240, §311(a):

Amended Code Sec. 168(e)(3)(E)(iv), (v), and (ix) by striking "January 1, 2012" and inserting "January 1, 2014". **Effective** for property placed in service after 12-31-2011.

• **2010, Tax Relief, Unemployment Insurance Reauthorization, and Job Creation Act of 2010 (P.L. 111-312)**

P.L. 111-312, §737(a):

Amended Code Sec. 168(e)(3)(E)(iv), (v), and (ix) by striking "January 1, 2010" and inserting "January 1, 2012". **Effective** for property placed in service after 12-31-2009.

P.L. 111-312, §737(b)(1):

Amended Code Sec. 168(e)(7)(A)(i) by striking "if building is placed in service after December 31, 2008, and before January 1, 2010," after "a building,". **Effective** for property placed in service after 12-31-2009.

P.L. 111-312, §737(b)(2):

Amended Code Sec. 168(e)(8) by striking subparagraph (E). **Effective** for property placed in service after 12-31-2009. Prior to being stricken, Code Sec. 168(e)(8)(E) read as follows:

(E) TERMINATION.—Such term shall not include any improvement placed in service after December 31, 2009.

• **2008, Energy Improvement and Extension Act of 2008 (P.L. 110-343)**

P.L. 110-343, Division B, §306(a):

Amended Code Sec. 168(e)(3)(D) by striking "and" at the end of clause (i), by striking the period at the end of clause (ii) and inserting a comma, and by inserting after clause (ii) new clauses (iii)-(iv). **Effective** for property placed in service after 10-3-2008.

• **2008, Tax Extenders and Alternative Minimum Tax Relief Act of 2008 (P.L. 110-343)**

P.L. 110-343, Division C, §305(a)(1):

Amended Code Sec. 168(e)(3)(E)(iv) and (v) by striking "January 1, 2008" and inserting "January 1, 2010". **Effective** for property placed in service after 12-31-2007.

P.L. 110-343, Division C, §305(b)(1):

Amended Code Sec. 168(e)(7). **Effective** for property placed in service after 12-31-2008. Prior to amendment, Code Sec. 168(e)(7) read as follows:

(7) QUALIFIED RESTAURANT PROPERTY.—The term "qualified restaurant property" means any section 1250 property which is an improvement to a building if—

(A) such improvement is placed in service more than 3 years after the date such building was first placed in service, and

(B) more than 50 percent of the building's square footage is devoted to preparation of, and seating for on-premises consumption of, prepared meals.

P.L. 110-343, Division C, §305(c)(1):

Amended Code Sec. 168(e)(3)(E) by striking "and" at the end of clause (vii), by striking the period at the end of clause (viii) and inserting ", and", and by adding at the end a new clause (ix). **Effective** for property placed in service after 12-31-2008.

P.L. 110-343, Division C, §305(c)(2):

Amended Code Sec. 168(e) by adding at the end a new paragraph (8). **Effective** for property placed in service after 12-31-2008.

P.L. 110-343, Division C, §505(a):

Amended Code Sec. 168(e)(3)(B) by striking "and" at the end of clause (v), by striking the period at the end of clause (vi)(III) and inserting ", and", and by inserting after clause (vi) a new clause (vii). **Effective** for property placed in service after 12-31-2008.

• **2008, Heartland, Habitat, Harvest, and Horticulture Act of 2008 (P.L. 110-246)**

P.L. 110-246, §15344(a):

Amended Code Sec. 168(e)(3)(A)(i). **Effective** for property placed in service after 12-31-2008. Prior to amendment, Code Sec. 168(e)(3)(A)(i) read as follows:

(i) any race horse which is more than 2 years old at the time it is placed in service,

• **2006, Tax Relief and Health Care Act of 2006 (P.L. 109-432)**

P.L. 109-432, Division A, §113(a):

Amended Code Sec. 168(e)(3)(E)(iv)-(v) by striking "2006" and inserting "2008". **Effective** for property placed in service after 12-31-2005.

• **2005, Gulf Opportunity Zone Act of 2005 (P.L. 109-135)**

P.L. 109-135, §410(a):

Amended Code Sec. 168(e)(3)(B)(vi)(I) by striking "if 'solar and wind' were substituted for 'solar' in clause (i) thereof" and inserting "if 'solar or wind energy' were substituted for 'solar energy' in clause (i) thereof". **Effective** as if included in section 11813 of the Omnibus Budget Reconciliation Act of 1990 (P.L. 101-508) [**effective** generally for property placed in service after 12-31-1990.—CCH].

APPENDIX: Selected Code Sections Affected by the Tax Cuts and Jobs Act

- **2005, Energy Tax Incentives Act of 2005 (P.L. 109-58)**

P.L. 109-58, §1301(f)(5):
Amended Code Sec. 168(e)(3)(B)(vi)(I). **Effective** as if included in the amendments made by section 710 of P.L. 108-357 [effective generally for electricity produced and sold after 10-22-2004, in tax years ending after such date.—CCH]. Prior to amendment, Code Sec. 168(e)(3)(B)(vi)(I) read as follows:

(I) is described in subparagraph (A) of section 48(a)(3) (or would be so described if "solar and wind" were substituted for "solar" in clause (i) thereof,

P.L. 109-58, §1308(a):
Amended Code Sec. 168(e)(3)(E) by striking "and" at the end of clause (v), by striking the period at the end of clause (vi) and inserting ", and", and by adding at the end a new clause (vii). **Effective** generally for property placed in service after 4-11-2005. For an exception, see Act Sec. 1308(c)(2), below.

P.L. 109-58, §1308(c)(2), provides:
(2) EXCEPTION.—The amendments made by this section shall not apply to any property with respect to which the taxpayer or a related party has entered into a binding contract for the construction thereof on or before April 11, 2005, or, in the case of self-constructed property, has started construction on or before such date.

P.L. 109-58, §1325(a):
Amended Code Sec. 168(e)(3)(E), as amended by this Act, by striking "and" at the end of clause (vi), by striking the period at the end of clause (vii) and by inserting ", and", and by adding at the end a new clause (viii). **Effective** generally for property placed in service after 4-11-2005. For an exception, see Act Sec. 1325(c)(2), below.

P.L. 109-58, §1325(c)(2), provides:
(2) EXCEPTION.—The amendments made by this section shall not apply to any property with respect to which the taxpayer or a related party has entered into a binding contract for the construction thereof on or before April 11, 2005, or, in the case of self-constructed property, has started construction on or before such date.

P.L. 109-58, §1326(a):
Amended Code Sec. 168(e)(3)(C) by striking "and" at the end of clause (iii), by redesignating clause (iv) as clause (v), and by inserting after clause (iii) a new clause (iv). **Effective** generally for property placed in service after 4-11-2005. For an exception, see Act Sec. 1326(e)(2), below.

P.L. 109-58, §1326(e)(2), provides:
(2) EXCEPTION.—The amendments made by this section shall not apply to any property with respect to which the taxpayer or a related party has entered into a binding contract for the construction thereof on or before April 11, 2005, or, in the case of self-constructed property, has started construction on or before such date.

- **2004, American Jobs Creation Act of 2004 (P.L. 108-357)**

P.L. 108-357, §211(a):
Amended Code Sec. 168(e)(3)(E) by striking "and" at the end of clause (ii), by striking the period at the end of clause (iii) and inserting a comma, and by adding at the end new clauses (iv) and (v). **Effective** for property placed in service after 10-22-2004.

P.L. 108-357, §211(b):
Amended Code Sec. 168(e) by adding at the end a new paragraph (6). **Effective** for property placed in service after 10-22-2004.

P.L. 108-357, §211(c):
Amended Code Sec. 168(e), as amended by Act Sec. 211(b), by adding at the end a new paragraph (7). **Effective** for property placed in service after 10-22-2004.

P.L. 108-357, §704(a):
Amended Code Sec. 168(e)(3)(C) by redesignating clause (ii) as clause (iii) and by inserting after clause (i) a new clause (ii). **Effective** generally for property placed in service after 10-22-2004. For special rules, see Act Secs. 704(c)(2)-(3), below.

P.L. 108-357, §704(c)(2)-(3), provides:
(2) SPECIAL RULE FOR ASSET CLASS 80.0.—In the case of race track facilities placed in service after the date of the enactment of this Act [10-22-2004.—CCH], such facilities shall not be treated as theme and amusement facilities classified under asset class 80.0.

(3) NO INFERENCE.—Nothing in this section or the amendments made by this section shall be construed to affect the treatment of property placed in service on or before the date of the enactment of this Act [10-22-2004.—CCH].

P.L. 108-357, §706(a):
Amended Code Sec. 168(e)(3)(C), as amended by this Act, by striking "and" at the end of clause (ii), by redesignating clause (iii) as clause (iv), and by inserting after clause (ii) a new clause (iii). **Effective** for property placed in service after 12-31-2004.

P.L. 108-357, §901(a):
Amended Code Sec. 168(e)(3)(E), as amended by this Act, by striking "and" at the end of clause (iv), by striking the period at the end of clause (v) and inserting ", and", and by adding at the end a new clause (vi). **Effective** for property placed in service after 10-22-2004.

P.L. 108-357, §901(b):
Amended Code Sec. 168(e)(3) by adding at the end a new subparagraph (F). **Effective** for property placed in service after 10-22-2004.

- **1997, Taxpayer Relief Act of 1997 (P.L. 105-34)**

P.L. 105-34, §1086(b)(1):
Amended Code Sec. 168(e)(3)(A) by striking "and" at the end of clause (i), by striking the period at the end of clause (ii) and inserting ", and", and by adding at the end a new clause. **Effective** for property placed in service after 8-5-97.

- **1996, Small Business Job Protection Act of 1996 (P.L. 104-188)**

P.L. 104-188, §1120(a):
Amended Code Sec. 168(e)(3)(E) by striking "and" at the end of clause (i), by striking the period at the end of clause (ii) and inserting ", and", and by adding at the end a new clause (iii). For the **effective** date, see Act Sec. 1120(c), below.

P.L. 104-188, §1120(c), provides:
(c) EFFECTIVE DATE.—The amendments made by this section shall apply to property which is placed in service on or after the date of the enactment of this Act and to which section 168 of the Internal Revenue Code of 1986 applies after the amendment made by section 201 of the Tax Reform Act of 1986. A taxpayer may elect (in such form and manner as the Secretary of the Treasury may prescribe) to have such amendments apply with respect to any property placed in service before such date and to which such section so applies.

P.L. 104-188, §1613(b)(3)(A):
Amended Code Sec. 168(e) by adding at the end a new paragraph. **Effective** for property placed in service after 6-12-96, other than property placed in service pursuant to a binding contract in effect before 6-10-96, and at all times thereafter before the property is placed in service.

P.L. 104-188, §1613(b)(3)(B)(i):
Amended Code Sec. 168(e)(3) by striking subparagraph (F). **Effective** for property placed in service after 6-12-96, other than property placed in service pursuant to a binding contract in effect before 6-10-96, and at all times thereafter before the property is placed in service. Prior to being stricken, Code Sec. 168(e)(3)(F) read as follows:

(F) 20-YEAR PROPERTY.—The term "20-year property" includes any municipal sewers.

P.L. 104-188, §1702(h)(1)(A):
Amended Code Sec. 168(e)(3)(B)(vi) by striking "or" at the end of subclause (I), by striking the period at the end of subclause (II) and inserting ", or", and by adding at the end thereof a new subclause (III). **Effective** as if included in the provision of P.L. 101-508 to which it relates.

P.L. 104-188, §1702(h)(1)(B):
Amended Code Sec. 168(e)(3)(B) by adding at the end a new flush sentence. **Effective** as if included in the provision of P.L. 101-508 to which it relates.

- **1990, Omnibus Budget Reconciliation Act of 1990 (P.L. 101-508)**

P.L. 101-508, §11812(b)(2)(A):
Amended Code Sec. 168(e)(2)(A). **Effective**, generally, for property placed in service after 11-5-90. However, for exceptions see Act Sec. 11812(c)(2)-(3) below. Prior to amendment, Code Sec. 168(e)(2)(A) read as follows:

(A) RESIDENTIAL RENTAL PROPERTY.—The term "residential rental property" has the meaning given such term by section 167(j)(2)(B).

Code Sec. 168

P.L. 101-508, §11812(c)(2)-(3), provides:

(2) EXCEPTION.—The amendments made by this section shall not apply to any property to which section 168 of the Internal Revenue Code of 1986 does not apply by reason of subsection (f)(5) thereof.

(3) EXCEPTION FOR PREVIOUSLY GRANDFATHER EXPENDITURES.—The amendments made by this section shall not apply to rehabilitation expenditures described in section 252(f)(5) of the Tax Reform Act of 1986 (as added by section 1002(l)(31) of the Technical and Miscellaneous Revenue Act of 1988).

P.L. 101-508, §11813(b)(9)(A)(i)-(ii) (as amended by P.L. 104-188, §1704(t)(54)):

Amended Code Sec. 168(e)(3)(B)(vi) by striking "paragraph (3)(A)(viii), (3)(A)(ix), or (4) of section 48(l)" in subclause (I) and inserting "subparagraph (A) of section 48(a)(3) (or would be so described if 'solar and wind' were substituted for 'solar' in clause (i) thereof)", and by inserting "(as in effect on the day before the date of the enactment of the Revenue Reconciliation Act of 1990)" after "48(l)" in subclause (II). **Effective**, generally, for property placed in service after 12-31-90. However, for exceptions see Act Sec. 11813(c)(2) below.

P.L. 101-508, §11813(b)(9)(B)(i):

Amended Code Sec. 168(e)(3)(D)(i) by striking "section 48(p)" and inserting "subsection (i)(13)". **Effective**, generally, for property placed in service after 12-31-90. However, for exceptions see Act Sec. 11813(c)(2) below.

P.L. 101-508, §11813(c)(2), provides:

(2) EXCEPTIONS.—The amendments made by this section shall not apply to—

(A) any transition property (as defined in section 49(e) of the Internal Revenue Code of 1986 (as in effect on the day before the date of the enactment of this Act),

(B) any property with respect to which qualified progress expenditures were previously taken into account under section 46(d) of such Code (as so in effect), and

(C) any property described in section 46(b)(2)(C) of such Code (as so in effect).

• 1988, Technical and Miscellaneous Revenue Act of 1988 (P.L. 100-647)

P.L. 100-647, §1002(a)(21):

Amended Code Sec. 168(e)(3)(B)(v) by striking out "any property" and inserting in lieu thereof "any section 1245 property". **Effective** as if included in the provision of P.L. 99-514 to which it relates.

P.L. 100-647, §1002(i)(2)(C):

Amended Code Sec. 168(e) by adding at the end thereof a new paragraph (4). **Effective** as if included in the provision of P.L. 99-514 to which it relates.

P.L. 100-647, §6027(a):

Amended Code Sec. 168(e)(3) by redesignating subparagraphs (D) and (E) as subparagraphs (E) and (F), respectively, and by inserting after subparagraph (C) a new subparagraph (D). **Effective**, generally, for property placed in service after 12-31-88. However, see Act Sec. 6027(c)(2), below, for an exception.

P.L. 100-647, §6027(b)(1):

Amended Code Sec. 168(e)(3)(C) by adding "and" at the end of clause (i), by striking out clause (ii) and by redesignating clause (iii) as clause (ii). **Effective**, generally, for property placed in service after 12-31-88. However, see Act Sec. 6027(c)(2), below, for an exception. Prior to amendment, Code Sec. 168(e)(3)(C)(ii) read as follows:

(ii) any single-purpose agricultural or horticultural structure (within the meaning of section 48(p)), and

P.L. 100-647, §6027(c)(2), provides:

(c)(2) EXCEPTION.—The amendments made by this section shall not apply to any property if such property is placed in service before January 1, 1990, and if such property—

(A) is constructed, reconstructed, or acquired by the taxpayer pursuant to a written contract which was binding on July 14, 1988, or

(B) is constructed or reconstructed by the taxpayer and such construction or reconstruction began by July 14, 1988.

P.L. 100-647, §6029(a):

Amended Code Sec. 168(e)(3)(D). **Effective** for property placed in service after 12-31-88. Prior to amendment, Code Sec. 168(e)(3)(D) read as follows:

(D) 10-YEAR PROPERTY.—The term "10-year property" includes any single purpose agricultural or horticultural structure (within the meaning of section 48(p)).

[Sec. 168(f)]

(f) PROPERTY TO WHICH SECTION DOES NOT APPLY.—This section shall not apply to—

(1) CERTAIN METHODS OF DEPRECIATION.—Any property if—

(A) the taxpayer elects to exclude such property from the application of this section, and

(B) for the 1st taxable year for which a depreciation deduction would be allowable with respect to such property in the hands of the taxpayer, the property is properly depreciated under the unit-of-production method or any method of depreciation not expressed in a term of years (other than the retirement-replacement-betterment method or similar method).

(2) CERTAIN PUBLIC UTILITY PROPERTY.—Any public utility property (within the meaning of subsection (i)(10)) if the taxpayer does not use a normalization method of accounting.

(3) FILMS AND VIDEO TAPE.—Any motion picture film or video tape.

(4) SOUND RECORDINGS.—Any works which result from the fixation of a series of musical, spoken, or other sounds, regardless of the nature of the material (such as discs, tapes, or other phonorecordings) in which such sounds are embodied.

(5) CERTAIN PROPERTY PLACED IN SERVICE IN CHURNING TRANSACTIONS.—

(A) IN GENERAL.—Property—

(i) described in paragraph (4) of section 168(e) (as in effect before the amendments made by the Tax Reform Act of 1986), or

(ii) which would be described in such paragraph if such paragraph were applied by substituting "1987" for "1981" and "1986" for "1980" each place such terms appear.

(B) SUBPARAGRAPH (A)(ii) NOT TO APPLY.—Clause (ii) of subparagraph (A) shall not apply to—

(i) any residential rental property or nonresidential real property,

(ii) any property if, for the 1st taxable year in which such property is placed in service—

(I) the amount allowable as a deduction under this section (as in effect before the date of the enactment of this paragraph) with respect to such property is greater than,

(II) the amount allowable as a deduction under this section (as in effect on or after such date and using the half-year convention) for such taxable year, or

(iii) any property to which this section (as amended by the Tax Reform Act of 1986) applied in the hands of the transferor.

(C) SPECIAL RULE.—In the case of any property to which this section would apply but for this paragraph, the depreciation deduction under section 167 shall be determined under the provisions of this section as in effect before the amendments made by section 201 of the Tax Reform Act of 1986.

Amendments

- **1990, Omnibus Budget Reconciliation Act of 1990 (P.L. 101-508)**
P.L. 101-508, § 11812(b)(2)(C):
Amended Code Sec. 168(f)(2) by striking "section 167(l)(3)(A)" and inserting "subsection (i)(10)". **Effective**, generally, for property placed in service after 11-5-90. However, for exceptions see Act Sec. 11812(c)(2)-(3) in the amendment notes following Code Sec. 168(e).

- **1988, Technical and Miscellaneous Revenue Act of 1988 (P.L. 100-647)**
P.L. 100-647, § 1002(a)(6)(A)(i)-(ii):
Amended Code Sec. 168(f)(5)(B) by striking out "1st full taxable year" in clause (ii) and inserting in lieu thereof "1st taxable year", and by striking out "or" at the end of clause (i), by striking out the period at the end of clause (ii) and inserting in lieu thereof ", or", and by adding at the end thereof new clause (iii). **Effective** as if included in the provision of P.L. 99-514 to which it relates.

P.L. 100-647, § 1002(a)(6)(B):
Amended Code Sec. 168(f)(5) by adding at the end thereof new subparagraph (C). **Effective** as if included in the provision of P.L. 99-514 to which it relates.

P.L. 100-647, § 1002(a)(16)(B):
Amended Code Sec. 168(f)(4). **Effective** as if included in the provision of P.L. 99-514 to which it relates. Prior to amendment, Code Sec. 168(f)(4) read as follows:

(4) SOUND RECORDINGS.—Any sound recording described in section 48(r)(5).

[Sec. 168(g)]

(g) ALTERNATIVE DEPRECIATION SYSTEM FOR CERTAIN PROPERTY.—
(1) IN GENERAL.—In the case of—
(A) any tangible property which during the taxable year is used predominantly outside the United States,
(B) any tax-exempt use property,
(C) any tax-exempt bond financed property,
(D) any imported property covered by an Executive order under paragraph (6),
(E) any property to which an election under paragraph (7) applies,
(F) any property described in paragraph (8), and
(G) any property with a recovery period of 10 years or more which is held by an electing farming business (as defined in section 163(j)(7)(C)),

the depreciation deduction provided by section 167(a) shall be determined under the alternative depreciation system.

(2) ALTERNATIVE DEPRECIATION SYSTEM.—For purposes of paragraph (1), the alternative depreciation system is depreciation determined by using—
(A) the straight line method (without regard to salvage value),
(B) the applicable convention determined under subsection (d), and
(C) a recovery period determined under the following table:

In the case of:	The recovery period shall be:
(i) Property not described in clause (ii) or (iii)	The class life.
(ii) Personal property with no class life	12 years.
(iii) Residential rental property	30 years
(iv) Nonresidential real property	40 years
(v) Any railroad grading or tunnel bore or water utility property	50 years

(3) SPECIAL RULES FOR DETERMINING CLASS LIFE.—
(A) TAX-EXEMPT USE PROPERTY SUBJECT TO LEASE.—In the case of any tax-exempt use property subject to a lease, the recovery period used for purposes of paragraph (2) shall (notwithstanding any other subparagraph of this paragraph) in no event be less than 125 percent of the lease term.

(B) SPECIAL RULE FOR CERTAIN PROPERTY ASSIGNED TO CLASSES.—For purposes of paragraph (2), in the case of property described in any of the following subparagraphs of subsection (e)(3), the class life shall be determined as follows:

If property is described in subparagraph:	The class life is:
(A)(iii)	4
(B)(ii)	5
(B)(iii)	9.5
(B)(vii)	10
(C)(i)	10
(C)(iii)	22
(C)(iv)	14
(D)(i)	15
(D)(ii)	20

If property is described in subparagraph:	The class life is:
(D)(v)	20
(E)(i)	24
(E)(ii)	24
(E)(iii)	20
(E)(iv)	20
(E)(v)	30
(E)(vi)	35
(F)	25

(C) QUALIFIED TECHNOLOGICAL EQUIPMENT.—In the case of any qualified technological equipment, the recovery period used for purposes of paragraph (2) shall be 5 years.

(D) AUTOMOBILES, ETC.—In the case of any automobile or light general purpose truck, the recovery period used for purposes of paragraph (2) shall be 5 years.

(E) CERTAIN REAL PROPERTY.—In the case of any section 1245 property which is real property with no class life, the recovery period used for purposes of paragraph (2) shall be 40 years.

(4) EXCEPTION FOR CERTAIN PROPERTY USED OUTSIDE UNITED STATES.—Subparagraph (A) of paragraph (1) shall not apply to—

(A) any aircraft which is registered by the Administrator of the Federal Aviation Agency and which is operated to and from the United States or is operated under contract with the United States;

(B) rolling stock which is used within and without the United States and which is—

(i) of a rail carrier subject to part A of subtitle IV of title 49, or

(ii) of a United States person (other than a corporation described in clause (i)) but only if the rolling stock is not leased to one or more foreign persons for periods aggregating more than 12 months in any 24-month period;

(C) any vessel documented under the laws of the United States which is operated in the foreign or domestic commerce of the United States;

(D) any motor vehicle of a United States person (as defined in section 7701(a)(30)) which is operated to and from the United States;

(E) any container of a United States person which is used in the transportation of property to and from the United States;

(F) any property (other than a vessel or an aircraft) of a United States person which is used for the purpose of exploring for, developing, removing, or transporting resources from the outer Continental Shelf (within the meaning of section 2 of the Outer Continental Shelf Lands Act, as amended and supplemented; (43 U.S.C. 1331));

(G) any property which is owned by a domestic corporation or by a United States citizen (other than a citizen entitled to the benefits of section 931 or 933) and which is used predominantly in a possession of the United States by such a corporation or such a citizen, or by a corporation created or organized in, or under the law of, a possession of the United States;

(H) any communications satellite (as defined in section 103(3) of the Communications Satellite Act of 1962, 47 U.S.C. 702(3)), or any interest therein, of a United States person;

(I) any cable, or any interest therein, of a domestic corporation engaged in furnishing telephone service to which section 168(i)(10)(C) applies (or of a wholly owned domestic subsidiary of such a corporation), if such cable is part of a submarine cable system which constitutes part of a communication link exclusively between the United States and one or more foreign countries;

(J) any property (other than a vessel or an aircraft) of a United States person which is used in international or territorial waters within the northern portion of the Western Hemisphere for the purpose of exploring for, developing, removing, or transporting resources from ocean waters or deposits under such waters;

(K) any property described in section 48(l)(3)(A)(ix) (as in effect on the day before the date of the enactment of the Revenue Reconciliation Act of 1990) which is owned by a United States person and which is used in international or territorial waters to generate energy for use in the United States; and

(L) any satellite (not described in subparagraph (H)) or other spacecraft (or any interest therein) held by a United States person if such satellite or other spacecraft was launched from within the United States.

For purposes of subparagraph (J), the term "northern portion of the Western Hemisphere" means the area lying west of the 30th meridian west of Greenwich, east of the international dateline, and north of the Equator, but not including any foreign country which is a country of South America.

(5) TAX-EXEMPT BOND FINANCED PROPERTY.—For purposes of this subsection—

(A) IN GENERAL.—Except as otherwise provided in this paragraph, the term "tax-exempt bond financed property" means any property to the extent such property is financed (directly or indirectly) by an obligation the interest on which is exempt from tax under section 103(a).

(B) ALLOCATION OF BOND PROCEEDS.—For purposes of subparagraph (A), the proceeds of any obligation shall be treated as used to finance property acquired in connection with the issuance of such obligation in the order in which such property is placed in service.

(C) QUALIFIED RESIDENTIAL RENTAL PROJECTS.—The term "tax-exempt bond financed property" shall not include any qualified residential rental project (within the meaning of section 142(a)(7)).

(6) IMPORTED PROPERTY.—

(A) COUNTRIES MAINTAINING TRADE RESTRICTIONS OR ENGAGING IN DISCRIMINATORY ACTS.—If the President determines that a foreign country—

(i) maintains nontariff trade restrictions, including variable import fees, which substantially burden United States commerce in a manner inconsistent with provisions of trade agreements, or

(ii) engages in discriminatory or other acts (including tolerance of international cartels) or policies unjustifiably restricting United States commerce,

the President may by Executive order provide for the application of paragraph (1)(D) to any article or class of articles manufactured or produced in such foreign country for such period as may be provided by such Executive order. Any period specified in the preceding sentence shall not apply to any property ordered before (or the construction, reconstruction, or erection of which began before) the date of the Executive order unless the President determines an earlier date to be in the public interest and specifies such date in the Executive order.

(B) IMPORTED PROPERTY.—For purposes of this subsection, the term "imported property" means any property if—

(i) such property was completed outside the United States, or

(ii) less than 50 percent of the basis of such property is attributable to value added within the United States.

For purposes of this subparagraph, the term "United States" includes the Commonwealth of Puerto Rico and the possessions of the United States.

(7) ELECTION TO USE ALTERNATIVE DEPRECIATION SYSTEM.—

(A) IN GENERAL.—If the taxpayer makes an election under this paragraph with respect to any class of property for any taxable year, the alternative depreciation system under this subsection shall apply to all property in such class placed in service during such taxable year. Notwithstanding the preceding sentence, in the case of nonresidential real property or residential rental property, such election may be made separately with respect to each property.

(B) ELECTION IRREVOCABLE.—An election under subparagraph (A), once made, shall be irrevocable.

(8) ELECTING REAL PROPERTY TRADE OR BUSINESS.—The property described in this paragraph shall consist of any nonresidential real property, residential rental property, and qualified improvement property held by an electing real property trade or business (as defined in 163(j)(7)(B)).

Amendments

• **2018, Tax Technical Corrections Act of 2018 (P.L. 115-141)**

P.L. 115-141, §401(d)(1)(D)(iv), Div. U:
Amended Code Sec. 168(g)(4)(G) by striking "other than a corporation which has an election in effect under section 936)" following "owned by a domestic corporation". **Effective** 3-23-2018. For a special rule, see Act Sec. 401(e), Div. U, below.

P.L. 115-141, §401(e), Div. U, provides:
(e) GENERAL SAVINGS PROVISION WITH RESPECT TO DEADWOOD PROVISIONS.—If—
(1) any provision amended or repealed by the amendments made by subsection (b) or (d) applied to—
(A) any transaction occurring before the date of the enactment of this Act,
(B) any property acquired before such date of enactment, or
(C) any item of income, loss, deduction, or credit taken into account before such date of enactment, and
(2) the treatment of such transaction, property, or item under such provision would (without regard to the amendments or repeals made by such subsection) affect the liability for tax for periods ending after such date of enactment, nothing in the amendments or repeals made by this section shall be construed to affect the treatment of such transaction, property, or item for purposes of determining liability for tax for periods ending after such date of enactment.

• **2017, Tax Cuts and Jobs Act (P.L. 115-97)**

P.L. 115-97, §13204(a)(3)(A)(i)(I)-(III):
Amended Code Sec. 168(g) in paragraph (1) by striking "and" at the end of subparagraph (D), by inserting "and" at the end of subparagraph (E), and by inserting after subparagraph (E) a new subparagraph (F). **Effective** for tax years beginning after 12-31-2017.

P.L. 115-97, §13204(a)(3)(A)(ii):
Amended Code Sec. 168(g) by adding at the end a new paragraph (8). **Effective** for tax years beginning after 12-31-2017.

P.L. 115-97, §13204(a)(3)(B)(i)-(ii):
Amended the table contained in Code Sec. 168(g)(3)(B) by inserting after the item relating to subparagraph (D)(ii) a new item relating to subparagraph (D)(v), and by striking the item relating to subparagraph (E)(iv) and all that follows through the item relating to subparagraph (E)(ix) and inserting new items relating to subparagraphs (E)(iv)-(E)(vi). **Effective** for property placed in service after 12-31-2017. Prior to being stricken, the items relating to subparagraphs (E)(iv) through (E)(ix) in the table read as follows:

(E)(iv)	39
(E)(v)	39
(E)(vi)	20
(E)(vii)	30

(E)(viii) 35
(E)(ix) 39

P.L. 115-97, §13204(a)(3)(C):

Amended the table contained in Code Sec. 168(g)(2)(C) by striking clauses (iii) and (iv) and inserting clauses (iii)-(v). **Effective** for property placed in service after 12-31-2017. Prior to being stricken, clauses (iii)-(iv) in the table read as follows:

(iii) Nonresidential real and residential rental property . . . . 40 years.

(iv) Any railroad grading or tunnel bore or water utility property . . . . 50 years.

P.L. 115-97, §13205(a):

Amended Code Sec. 168(g)(1), as amended by Act Sec. 13204, by striking "and" at the end of subparagraph (E), by inserting "and" at the end of subparagraph (F), and by inserting after subparagraph (F) a new subparagraph (G). **Effective** for tax years beginning after 12-31-2017.

- **2008, Tax Extenders and Alternative Minimum Tax Relief Act of 2008 (P.L. 110-343)**

P.L. 110-343, Division C, §305(c)(4):

Amended the table contained in Code Sec. 168(g)(3)(B) by inserting after the item relating to subparagraph (E)(viii) a new item. **Effective** for property placed in service after 12-31-2008.

P.L. 110-343, Division C, §505(b):

Amended the table contained in Code Sec. 168(g)(3)(B) by inserting after the item relating to subparagraph (B)(iii) a new item. **Effective** for property placed in service after 12-31-2008.

- **2005, Energy Tax Incentives Act of 2005 (P.L. 109-58)**

P.L. 109-58, §1308(b):

Amended the table contained in Code Sec. 168(g)(3)(B) by inserting after the item relating to subparagraph (E)(vi) a new item relating to subparagraph (E)(vii). **Effective** generally for property placed in service after 4-11-2005. For an exception, see Act Sec. 1308(c)(2), below.

P.L. 109-58, §1308(c)(2), provides:

(2) EXCEPTION.—The amendments made by this section shall not apply to any property with respect to which the taxpayer or a related party has entered into a binding contract for the construction thereof on or before April 11, 2005, or, in the case of self-constructed property, has started construction on or before such date.

P.L. 109-58, §1325(b):

Amended the table contained in Code Sec. 168(g)(3)(B), as amended by this Act, by inserting after the item relating to subparagraph (E)(vii) a new item relating to subparagraph (E)(viii). **Effective** generally for property placed in service after 4-11-2005. For an exception, see Act Sec. 1325(c)(2), below.

P.L. 109-58, §1325(c)(2), provides:

(2) EXCEPTION.—The amendments made by this section shall not apply to any property with respect to which the taxpayer or a related party has entered into a binding contract for the construction thereof on or before April 11, 2005, or, in the case of self-constructed property, has started construction on or before such date.

P.L. 109-58, §1326(c):

Amended the table contained in Code Sec. 168(g)(3)(B), as amended by this Act, by inserting after the item relating to subparagraph (C)(iii) a new item relating to subparagraph (C)(iv). **Effective** generally for property placed in service after 4-11-2005. For an exception, see Act Sec. 1326(e)(2), below.

P.L. 109-58, §1326(e)(2), provides:

(2) EXCEPTION.—The amendments made by this section shall not apply to any property with respect to which the taxpayer or a related party has entered into a binding contract for the construction thereof on or before April 11, 2005, or, in the case of self-constructed property, has started construction on or before such date.

- **2004, American Jobs Creation Act of 2004 (P.L. 108-357)**

P.L. 108-357, §211(e):

Amended the table contained in Code Sec. 168(g)(3)(B) by adding at the end two new items. **Effective** for property placed in service after 10-22-2004.

P.L. 108-357, §706(c):

Amended the table contained in Code Sec. 168(g)(3)(B) by inserting after the item relating to subparagraph (C)(ii)[(i)] a new item. **Effective** for property placed in service after 12-31-2004.

P.L. 108-357, §847(a):

Amended Code Sec. 168(g)(3)(A) by inserting "(notwithstanding any other subparagraph of this paragraph)" after "shall". **Effective** generally for leases entered into after 3-12-2004, and in the case of property treated as tax-exempt use property other than by reason of a lease, to property acquired after 3-12-2004 [effective date amended by P.L. 109-135, §403(ff)]. For an exception, see Act Sec. 849(b)(1)-(2), below.

P.L. 108-357, §849(b)(1)-(2), provides:

(b) EXCEPTION.—

(1) IN GENERAL.—The amendments made by this part shall not apply to qualified transportation property.

(2) QUALIFIED TRANSPORTATION PROPERTY.—For purposes of paragraph (1), the term "qualified transportation property" means domestic property subject to a lease with respect to which a formal application—

(A) was submitted for approval to the Federal Transit Administration (an agency of the Department of Transportation) after June 30, 2003, and before March 13, 2004,

(B) is approved by the Federal Transit Administration before January 1, 2006, and

(C) includes a description of such property and the value of such property.

P.L. 108-357, §901(c):

Amended the table contained in Code Sec. 168(g)(3)(B), as amended by this Act, by inserting after the item relating to subparagraph (E)(v) two new items. **Effective** for property placed in service after 10-22-2004.

- **1997, Taxpayer Relief Act of 1997 (P.L. 105-34)**

P.L. 105-34, §1086(b)(2):

Amended the table contained in Code Sec. 168(g)(3)(B) by inserting before the first item a new item. **Effective** for property placed in service after 8-5-97.

- **1996, Small Business Job Protection Act of 1996 (P.L. 104-188)**

P.L. 104-188, §1120(b):

Amended Code Sec. 168(g)(3)(B) by inserting after the item relating to subparagraph (E)(ii) in the table contained therein a new item relating to subparagraph (E)(iii). For the **effective** date, see Act Sec. 1120(c), below.

P.L. 104-188, §1120(c), provides:

(c) EFFECTIVE DATE.—The amendments made by this section shall apply to property which is placed in service on or after the date of the enactment of this Act and to which section 168 of the Internal Revenue Code of 1986 applies after the amendment made by section 201 of the Tax Reform Act of 1986. A taxpayer may elect (in such form and manner as the Secretary of the Treasury may prescribe) to have such amendments apply with respect to any property placed in service before such date and to which such section so applies.

P.L. 104-188, §1613(b)(3)(B)(ii):

Amended Code Sec. 168(g)(3) by striking the item relating to subparagraph (F) in the table. **Effective** for property placed in service after 6-12-96, other than property placed in service pursuant to a binding contract in effect before 6-10-96, and at all times thereafter before the property is placed in service. Prior to amendment, the item relating to subparagraph (F) in the table read as follows:

(F) 50

P.L. 104-188, §1613(b)(4):

Amended Code Sec. 168(g)(2)(C)(iv) by inserting "or water utility property" after "tunnel bore". **Effective** for

Code Sec. 168

property placed in service after 6-12-96, other than property placed in service pursuant to a binding contract in effect before 6-10-96, and at all times thereafter before the property is placed in service.

P.L. 104-188, § 1702(h)(1)(C):
Amended Code Sec. 168(g)(4)(K) by striking "section 48(a)(3)(A)(iii)" and inserting "section 48(l)(3)(A)(ix) (as in effect on the day before the date of the enactment of the Revenue Reconciliation Act of 1990)". **Effective** as if included in the provision of P.L. 101-508 to which it relates.

P.L. 104-188, § 304(a):
Amended Code Sec. 168(g)(4)(B)(i) by striking "domestic railroad corporation providing transportation subject to subchapter I of chapter 105" and inserting in lieu thereof "rail carrier subject to part A of subtitle IV". **Effective** 1-1-96.

- **1990, Omnibus Budget Reconciliation Act of 1990 (P.L. 101-508)**

P.L. 101-508, § 11813(b)(9)(C):
Amended Code Sec. 168(g)(4). **Effective**, generally, for property placed in service after 12-31-90. However, for exceptions see Act Sec. 11813(c)(2) in the amendment notes following Code Sec. 168(e). Prior to amendment, Code Sec. 168(g)(4) read as follows:

(4) PROPERTY USED PREDOMINANTLY OUTSIDE THE UNITED STATES.—For purposes of this subsection, rules similar to the rules under section 48(a)(2) (including the exceptions contained in subparagraph (B) thereof) shall apply in determining whether property is used predominantly outside the United States. In addition to the exceptions contained in such subparagraph (B), there shall be excepted any satellite or other spacecraft (or any interest therein) held by a United States person if such satellite or spacecraft was launched from within the United States.

- **1988, Technical and Miscellaneous Revenue Act of 1988 (P.L. 100-647)**

P.L. 100-647, § 1002(i)(2)(F):
Amended Code Sec. 168(g)(2)(C) by adding at the end of the table contained therein a new item. **Effective** as if included in the provision of P.L. 99-514 to which it relates.

P.L. 100-647, § 6027(b)(2):
Amended the table contained in Code Sec. 168(g)(3)(B). **Effective**, generally, for property placed in service after 12-31-88. For an exception see Act Sec. 6027(c)(2) in the amendment notes following 168(e). Prior to amendment, the table contained in Code Sec. 168(g)(3)(B) read as follows:

If property is described in subparagraph:	The class life is:
(B)(ii)	5
(B)(iii)	9.5
(C)(i)	10
(C)(ii)	15
(D)(i)	24
(D)(ii)	24
(E)	50

P.L. 100-647, § 6029(c):
Amended the table contained in Code Sec. 168(g)(3)(B), as amended by section 6027. **Effective** for property placed in service after 12-31-88. Prior to amendment, the table contained in Code Sec. 168(g)(3)(B) read as follows:

If property is described in subparagraph:	The class life is:
(B)(ii)	5
(B)(iii)	9.5
(C)(i)	10
(D)	15
(E)(i)	24
(E)(ii)	24
(F)	50

[Sec. 168(h)]

(h) TAX-EXEMPT USE PROPERTY.—

(1) IN GENERAL.—For purposes of this section—

(A) PROPERTY OTHER THAN NONRESIDENTIAL REAL PROPERTY.—Except as otherwise provided in this subsection, the term "tax-exempt use property" means that portion of any tangible property (other than nonresidential real property) leased to a tax-exempt entity.

(B) NONRESIDENTIAL REAL PROPERTY.—

(i) IN GENERAL.—In the case of nonresidential real property, the term "tax-exempt use property" means that portion of the property leased to a tax-exempt entity in a disqualified lease.

(ii) DISQUALIFIED LEASE.—For purposes of this subparagraph, the term "disqualified lease" means any lease of the property to a tax-exempt entity, but only if—

(I) part or all of the property was financed (directly or indirectly) by an obligation the interest on which is exempt from tax under section 103(a) and such entity (or a related entity) participated in such financing,

(II) under such lease there is a fixed or determinable price purchase or sale option which involves such entity (or a related entity) or there is the equivalent of such an option,

(III) such lease has a lease term in excess of 20 years, or

(IV) such lease occurs after a sale (or other transfer) of the property by, or lease of the property from, such entity (or a related entity) and such property has been used by such entity (or a related entity) before such sale (or other transfer) or lease.

(iii) 35-PERCENT THRESHOLD TEST.—Clause (i) shall apply to any property only if the portion of such property leased to tax-exempt entities in disqualified leases is more than 35 percent of the property.

(iv) TREATMENT OF IMPROVEMENTS.—For purposes of this subparagraph, improvements to a property (other than land) shall not be treated as a separate property.

(v) LEASEBACKS DURING 1ST 3 MONTHS OF USE NOT TAKEN INTO ACCOUNT.—Subclause (IV) of clause (ii) shall not apply to any property which is leased within 3 months after the date such property is first used by the tax-exempt entity (or a related entity).

(C) EXCEPTION FOR SHORT-TERM LEASES.—

(i) IN GENERAL.—Property shall not be treated as tax-exempt use property merely by reason of a short-term lease.

(ii) SHORT-TERM LEASE.—For purposes of clause (i), the term "short-term lease" means any lease the term of which is—
    (I) less than 3 years, and
    (II) less than the greater of 1 year or 30 percent of the property's present class life.

In the case of nonresidential real property and property with no present class life, subclause (II) shall not apply.

    (D) EXCEPTION WHERE PROPERTY USED IN UNRELATED TRADE OR BUSINESS.—The term "tax-exempt use property" shall not include any portion of a property if such portion is predominantly used by the tax-exempt entity (directly or through a partnership of which such entity is a partner) in an unrelated trade or business the income of which is subject to tax under section 511. For purposes of subparagraph (B)(iii), any portion of a property so used shall not be treated as leased to a tax-exempt entity in a disqualified lease.

    (E) NONRESIDENTIAL REAL PROPERTY DEFINED.—For purposes of this paragraph, the term "nonresidential real property" includes residential rental property.

(2) TAX-EXEMPT ENTITY.—

    (A) IN GENERAL.—For purposes of this subsection, the term "tax-exempt entity" means—
        (i) the United States, any State or political subdivision thereof, any possession of the United States, or any agency or instrumentality of any of the foregoing,
        (ii) an organization (other than a cooperative described in section 521) which is exempt from tax imposed by this chapter,
        (iii) any foreign person or entity, and
        (iv) any Indian tribal government described in section 7701(a)(40).

For purposes of applying this subsection, any Indian tribal government referred to in clause (iv) shall be treated in the same manner as a State.

    (B) EXCEPTION FOR CERTAIN PROPERTY SUBJECT TO UNITED STATES TAX AND USED BY FOREIGN PERSON OR ENTITY.—Clause (iii) of subparagraph (A) shall not apply with respect to any property if more than 50 percent of the gross income for the taxable year derived by the foreign person or entity from the use of such property is—
        (i) subject to tax under this chapter, or
        (ii) included under section 951 in the gross income of a United States shareholder for the taxable year with or within which ends the taxable year of the controlled foreign corporation in which such income was derived.

For purposes of the preceding sentence, any exclusion or exemption shall not apply for purposes of determining the amount of the gross income so derived, but shall apply for purposes of determining the portion of such gross income subject to tax under this chapter.

    (C) FOREIGN PERSON OR ENTITY.—For purposes of this paragraph, the term "foreign person or entity" means—
        (i) any foreign government, any international organization, or any agency or instrumentality of any of the foregoing, and
        (ii) any person who is not a United States person.

Such term does not include any foreign partnership or other foreign pass-thru entity.

    (D) TREATMENT OF CERTAIN TAXABLE INSTRUMENTALITIES.—For purposes of this subsection, a corporation shall not be treated as an instrumentality of the United States or of any State or political subdivision thereof if—
        (i) all of the activities of such corporation are subject to tax under this chapter, and
        (ii) a majority of the board of directors of such corporation is not selected by the United States or any State or political subdivision thereof.

    (E) CERTAIN PREVIOUSLY TAX-EXEMPT ORGANIZATIONS.—
        (i) IN GENERAL.—For purposes of this subsection, an organization shall be treated as an organization described in subparagraph (A)(ii) with respect to any property (other than property held by such organization) if such organization was an organization (other than a cooperative described in section 521) exempt from tax imposed by this chapter at any time during the 5-year period ending on the date such property was first used by such organization. The preceding sentence and subparagraph (D)(ii) shall not apply to the Federal Home Loan Mortgage Corporation.
        (ii) ELECTION NOT TO HAVE CLAUSE (I) [sic] APPLY.—
            (I) IN GENERAL.—In the case of an organization formerly exempt from tax under section 501(a) as an organization described in section 501(c)(12), clause (i) shall not apply to such organization with respect to any property if such organization elects not to be exempt from tax under section 501(a) during the tax-exempt use period with respect to such property.
            (II) TAX-EXEMPT USE PERIOD.—For purposes of subclause (I), the term "tax-exempt use period" means the period beginning with the taxable year in which the property described in subclause (I) is first used by the organization and ending with the close of the 15th taxable year following the last taxable year of the applicable recovery period of such property.

(III) ELECTION.—Any election under subclause (I), once made, shall be irrevocable.

(iii) TREATMENT OF SUCCESSOR ORGANIZATIONS.—Any organization which is engaged in activities substantially similar to those engaged in by a predecessor organization shall succeed to the treatment under this subparagraph of such predecessor organization.

(iv) FIRST USED.—For purposes of this subparagraph, property shall be treated as first used by the organization—

(I) when the property is first placed in service under a lease to such organization, or

(II) in the case of property leased to (or held by) a partnership (or other pass-thru entity) in which the organization is a member, the later of when such property is first used by such partnership or pass-thru entity or when such organization is first a member of such partnership or pass-thru entity.

(3) SPECIAL RULES FOR CERTAIN HIGH TECHNOLOGY EQUIPMENT.—

(A) EXEMPTION WHERE LEASE TERM IS 5 YEARS OR LESS.—For purposes of this section, the term "tax-exempt use property" shall not include any qualified technological equipment if the lease to the tax-exempt entity has a lease term of 5 years or less. Notwithstanding subsection (i)(3)(A)(i), in determining a lease term for purposes of the preceding sentence, there shall not be taken into account any option of the lessee to renew at the fair market value rent determined at the time of renewal; except that the aggregate period not taken into account by reason of this sentence shall not exceed 24 months.

(B) EXCEPTION FOR CERTAIN PROPERTY.—

(i) IN GENERAL.—For purposes of subparagraph (A), the term "qualified technological equipment" shall not include any property leased to a tax-exempt entity if—

(I) part or all of the property was financed (directly or indirectly) by an obligation the interest on which is exempt from tax under section 103(a),

(II) such lease occurs after a sale (or other transfer) of the property by, or lease of such property from, such entity (or related entity) and such property has been used by such entity (or a related entity) before such sale (or other transfer) or lease, or

(III) such tax-exempt entity is the United States or any agency or instrumentality of the United States.

(ii) LEASEBACKS DURING 1ST 3 MONTHS OF USE NOT TAKEN INTO ACCOUNT.—Subclause (II) of clause (i) shall not apply to any property which is leased within 3 months after the date such property is first used by the tax-exempt entity (or a related entity).

(4) RELATED ENTITIES.—For purposes of this subsection—

(A)(i) Each governmental unit and each agency or instrumentality of a governmental unit is related to each other such unit, agency, or instrumentality which directly or indirectly derives its powers, rights, and duties in whole or in part from the same sovereign authority.

(ii) For purposes of clause (i), the United States, each State, and each possession of the United States shall be treated as a separate sovereign authority.

(B) Any entity not described in subparagraph (A)(i) is related to any other entity if the 2 entities have—

(i) significant common purposes and substantial common membership, or

(ii) directly or indirectly substantial common direction or control.

(C)(i) An entity is related to another entity if either entity owns (directly or through 1 or more entities) a 50 percent or greater interest in the capital or profits of the other entity.

(ii) For purposes of clause (i), entities treated as related under subparagraph (A) or (B) shall be treated as 1 entity.

(D) An entity is related to another entity with respect to a transaction if such transaction is part of an attempt by such entities to avoid the application of this subsection.

(5) TAX-EXEMPT USE OF PROPERTY LEASED TO PARTNERSHIPS, ETC., DETERMINED AT PARTNER LEVEL.—For purposes of this subsection—

(A) IN GENERAL.—In the case of any property which is leased to a partnership, the determination of whether any portion of such property is tax-exempt use property shall be made by treating each tax-exempt entity partner's proportionate share (determined under paragraph (6)(C)) of such property as being leased to such partner.

(B) OTHER PASS-THRU ENTITIES; TIERED ENTITIES.—Rules similar to the rules of subparagraph (A) shall also apply in the case of any pass-thru entity other than a partnership and in the case of tiered partnerships and other entities.

(C) PRESUMPTION WITH RESPECT TO FOREIGN ENTITIES.—Unless it is otherwise established to the satisfaction of the Secretary, it shall be presumed that the partners of a foreign partnership (and the beneficiaries of any other foreign pass-thru entity) are persons who are not United States persons.

(6) TREATMENT OF PROPERTY OWNED BY PARTNERSHIPS, ETC.—

(A) IN GENERAL.—For purposes of this subsection, if—

(i) any property which (but for this subparagraph) is not tax-exempt use property is owned by a partnership which has both a tax-exempt entity and a person who is not a tax-exempt entity as partners, and

(ii) any allocation to the tax-exempt entity of partnership items is not a qualified allocation,

an amount equal to such tax-exempt entity's proportionate share of such property shall (except as provided in paragraph (1)(D)) be treated as tax-exempt use property.

(B) QUALIFIED ALLOCATION.—For purposes of subparagraph (A), the term "qualified allocation" means any allocation to a tax-exempt entity which—

(i) is consistent with such entity's being allocated the same distributive share of each item of income, gain, loss, deduction, credit, and basis and such share remains the same during the entire period the entity is a partner in the partnership, and

(ii) has substantial economic effect within the meaning of section 704(b)(2).

For purposes of this subparagraph, items allocated under section 704(c) shall not be taken into account.

(C) DETERMINATION OF PROPORTIONATE SHARE.—

(i) IN GENERAL.—For purposes of subparagraph (A), a tax-exempt entity's proportionate share of any property owned by a partnership shall be determined on the basis of such entity's share of partnership items of income or gain (excluding gain allocated under section 704(c)), whichever results in the largest proportionate share.

(ii) DETERMINATION WHERE ALLOCATIONS VARY.—For purposes of clause (i), if a tax-exempt entity's share of partnership items of income or gain (excluding gain allocated under section 704(c)) may vary during the period such entity is a partner in the partnership, such share shall be the highest share such entity may receive.

(D) DETERMINATION OF WHETHER PROPERTY USED IN UNRELATED TRADE OR BUSINESS.—For purposes of this subsection, in the case of any property which is owned by a partnership which has both a tax-exempt entity and a person who is not a tax-exempt entity as partners, the determination of whether such property is used in an unrelated trade or business of such an entity shall be made without regard to section 514.

(E) OTHER PASS-THRU ENTITIES; TIERED ENTITIES.—Rules similar to the rules of subparagraphs (A), (B), (C), and (D) shall also apply in the case of any pass-thru entity other than a partnership and in the case of tiered partnerships and other entities.

(F) TREATMENT OF CERTAIN TAXABLE ENTITIES.—

(i) IN GENERAL.—For purposes of this paragraph and paragraph (5), except as otherwise provided in this subparagraph, any tax-exempt controlled entity shall be treated as a tax-exempt entity.

(ii) ELECTION.—If a tax-exempt controlled entity makes an election under this clause—

(I) such entity shall not be treated as a tax-exempt entity for purposes of this paragraph and paragraph (5), and

(II) any gain recognized by a tax-exempt entity on any disposition of an interest in such entity (and any dividend or interest received or accrued by a tax-exempt entity from such tax-exempt controlled entity) shall be treated as unrelated business taxable income for purposes of section 511.

Any such election shall be irrevocable and shall bind all tax-exempt entities holding interests in such tax-exempt controlled entity. For purposes of subclause (II), there shall only be taken into account dividends which are properly allocable to income of the tax-exempt controlled entity which was not subject to tax under this chapter.

(iii) TAX-EXEMPT CONTROLLED ENTITY.—

(I) IN GENERAL.—The term "tax-exempt controlled entity" means any corporation (which is not a tax-exempt entity determined without regard to this subparagraph and paragraph (2)(E)) if 50 percent or more (in value) of the stock in such corporation is held by 1 or more tax-exempt entities (other than a foreign person or entity).

(II) ONLY 5-PERCENT SHAREHOLDERS TAKEN INTO ACCOUNT IN CASE OF PUBLICLY TRADED STOCK.—For purposes of subclause (I), in the case of a corporation the stock of which is publicly traded on an established securities market, stock held by a tax-exempt entity shall not be taken into account unless such entity holds at least 5 percent (in value) of the stock in such corporation. For purposes of this subclause, related entities (within the meaning of paragraph (4)) shall be treated as 1 entity.

(III) SECTION 318 TO APPLY.—For purposes of this clause, a tax-exempt entity shall be treated as holding stock which it holds through application of section 318 (determined without regard to the 50-percent limitation contained in subsection (a)(2)(C) thereof).

(G) REGULATIONS.—For purposes of determining whether there is a qualified allocation under subparagraph (B), the regulations prescribed under paragraph (8) for purposes of this paragraph—

(i) shall set forth the proper treatment for partnership guaranteed payments, and

(ii) may provide for the exclusion or segregation of items.

(7) LEASE.—For purposes of this subsection, the term "lease" includes any grant of a right to use property.

(8) REGULATIONS.—The Secretary shall prescribe such regulations as may be necessary or appropriate to carry out the purposes of this subsection.

Amendments

• **2004, American Jobs Creation Act of 2004 (P.L. 108-357)**

P.L. 108-357, § 847(d):
Amended Code Sec. 168(h)(3)(A) by adding at the end a new sentence. **Effective** generally for leases entered into after 3-12-2004, and in the case of property treated as tax-exempt use property other than by reason of a lease, to property acquired after 3-12-2004 [effective date amended by P.L. 109-135, § 403(ff)]. For an exception, see Act Sec. 849(b)(1)-(2), below.

P.L. 108-357, § 847(e):
Amended Code Sec. 168(h)(2)(A) by striking "and" at the end of clause (ii), by striking the period at the end of clause (iii) and inserting ", and" and by inserting at the end a new clause (iv) and a flush sentence that follows clause (iv). **Effective** for leases entered into after 10-3-2004. For an exception, see Act Sec. 849(b)(1)-(2), below.

P.L. 108-357, § 849(b)(1)-(2), provides:
(b) EXCEPTION.—
(1) IN GENERAL.—The amendments made by this part shall not apply to qualified transportation property.
(2) QUALIFIED TRANSPORTATION PROPERTY.—For purposes of paragraph (1), the term "qualified transportation property" means domestic property subject to a lease with respect to which a formal application—
(A) was submitted for approval to the Federal Transit Administration (an agency of the Department of Transportation) after June 30, 2003, and before March 13, 2004,
(B) is approved by the Federal Transit Administration before January 1, 2006, and

(C) includes a description of such property and the value of such property.

• **1988, Technical and Miscellaneous Revenue Act of 1988 (P.L. 100-647)**

P.L. 100-647, § 1002(a)(8):
Amended Code Sec. 168(h)(2)(B). **Effective** as if included in the provision of P.L. 99-514 to which it relates. Prior to amendment, Code Sec. 168(h)(2)(B) read as follows:
(B) EXCEPTIONS FOR CERTAIN PROPERTY SUBJECT TO UNITED STATES TAX AND USED BY FOREIGN PERSON OR ENTITY.—
(i) INCOME FROM PROPERTY SUBJECT TO UNITED STATES TAX.—Clause (iii) of subparagraph (A) shall not apply with respect to any property if more than 50 percent of the gross income for the taxable year derived by the foreign person or entity from the use of such property is—
(I) subject to tax under this chapter, or
(II) included under section 951 in the gross income of a United States shareholder for the taxable year with or within which ends the taxable year of the controlled foreign corporation in which such income was derived.
For purposes of the preceding sentence, any exclusion or exemption shall not apply for purposes of determining the amount of the gross income so derived, but shall apply for purposes of determining the portion of such gross income subject to tax under this chapter.
(ii) MOVIES AND SOUND RECORDINGS.—Clause (iii) of subparagraph (A) shall not apply with respect to any qualified film (as defined in section 48(k)(1)(B)) or any sound recording (as defined in section 48(r)(5)).

[Sec. 168(i)]

(i) DEFINITIONS AND SPECIAL RULES.—For purposes of this section—

(1) CLASS LIFE.—Except as provided in this section, the term "class life" means the class life (if any) which would be applicable with respect to any property as of January 1, 1986, under subsection (m) of section 167 (determined without regard to paragraph (4) and as if the taxpayer had made an election under such subsection). The Secretary, through an office established in the Treasury, shall monitor and analyze actual experience with respect to all depreciable assets. The reference in this paragraph to subsection (m) of section 167 shall be treated as a reference to such subsection as in effect on the day before the date of the enactment of the Revenue Reconciliation Act of 1990.

(2) QUALIFIED TECHNOLOGICAL EQUIPMENT.—

(A) IN GENERAL.—The term "qualified technological equipment" means—
(i) any computer or peripheral equipment,
(ii) any high technology telephone station equipment installed on the customer's premises, and
(iii) any high technology medical equipment.

(B) COMPUTER OR PERIPHERAL EQUIPMENT DEFINED.—For purposes of this paragraph—
(i) IN GENERAL.—The term "computer or peripheral equipment" means—
(I) any computer, and
(II) any related peripheral equipment.
(ii) COMPUTER.—The term "computer" means a programmable electronically activated device which—
(I) is capable of accepting information, applying prescribed processes to the information, and supplying the results of these processes with or without human intervention, and
(II) consists of a central processing unit containing extensive storage, logic, arithmetic, and control capabilities.
(iii) RELATED PERIPHERAL EQUIPMENT.—The term "related peripheral equipment" means any auxiliary machine (whether on-line or off-line) which is designed to be placed under the control of the central processing unit of a computer.
(iv) EXCEPTIONS.—The term "computer or peripheral equipment" shall not include—
(I) any equipment which is an integral part of other property which is not a computer,
(II) typewriters, calculators, adding and accounting machines, copiers, duplicating equipment, and similar equipment, and
(III) equipment of a kind used primarily for amusement or entertainment of the user.

(C) HIGH TECHNOLOGY MEDICAL EQUIPMENT.—For purposes of this paragraph, the term "high technology medical equipment" means any electronic, electromechanical, or computer-based high technology equipment used in the screening, monitoring, observation, diagnosis, or treatment of patients in a laboratory, medical, or hospital environment.

(3) Lease term.—

(A) In general.—In determining a lease term—

(i) there shall be taken into account options to renew,

(ii) the term of a lease shall include the term of any service contract or similar arrangement (whether or not treated as a lease under section 7701(e))—

(I) which is part of the same transaction (or series of related transactions) which includes the lease, and

(II) which is with respect to the property subject to the lease or substantially similar property,

(iii) 2 or more successive leases which are part of the same transaction (or a series of related transactions) with respect to the same or substantially similar property shall be treated as 1 lease.

(B) Special rule for fair rental options on nonresidential real property or residential rental property.—For purposes of clause (i) of subparagraph (A), in the case of nonresidential real property or residential rental property, there shall not be taken into account any option to renew at fair market value, determined at the time of renewal.

(4) General asset accounts.—Under regulations, a taxpayer may maintain 1 or more general asset accounts for any property to which this section applies. Except as provided in regulations, all proceeds realized on any disposition of property in a general asset account shall be included in income as ordinary income.

(5) Changes in use.—The Secretary shall, by regulations, provide for the method of determining the deduction allowable under section 167(a) with respect to any tangible property for any taxable year (and the succeeding taxable years) during which such property changes status under this section but continues to be held by the same person.

(6) Treatments of additions or improvements to property.—In the case of any addition to (or improvement of) any property—

(A) any deduction under subsection (a) for such addition or improvement shall be computed in the same manner as the deduction of such property would be computed if such property had been placed in service at the same time as such addition or improvement, and

(B) the applicable recovery period for such addition or improvement shall begin on the later of—

(i) the date on which such addition (or improvement) is placed in service, or

(ii) the date on which the property with respect to which such addition (or improvement) was made is placed in service.

(7) Treatment of certain transferees.—

(A) In general.—In the case of any property transferred in a transaction described in subparagraph (B), the transferee shall be treated as the transferor for purposes of computing the depreciation deduction determined under this section with respect to so much of the basis in the hands of the transferee as does not exceed the adjusted basis in the hands of the transferor. In any case where this section as in effect before the amendments made by section 201 of the Tax Reform Act of 1986 applied to the property in the hands of the transferor, the reference in the preceding sentence to this section shall be treated as a reference to this section as so in effect.

(B) Transactions covered.—The transactions described in this subparagraph are—

(i) any transaction described in section 332, 351, 361, 721, or 731, and

(ii) any transaction between members of the same affiliated group during any taxable year for which a consolidated return is made by such group.

(C) Property reacquired by the taxpayer.—Under regulations, property which is disposed of and then reacquired by the taxpayer shall be treated for purposes of computing the deduction allowable under subsection (a) as if such property had not been disposed of.

(D) [Repealed.]

(8) Treatment of leasehold improvements.—

(A) In general.—In the case of any building erected (or improvements made) on leased property, if such building or improvement is property to which this section applies, the depreciation deduction shall be determined under the provisions of this section.

(B) Treatment of lessor improvements which are abandoned at termination of lease.— An improvement—

(i) which is made by the lessor of leased property for the lessee of such property, and

(ii) which is irrevocably disposed of or abandoned by the lessor at the termination of the lease by such lessee, shall be treated for purposes of determining gain or loss under this title as disposed of by the lessor when so disposed of or abandoned.

(C) CROSS REFERENCE.—

For treatment of qualified long-term real property constructed or improved in connection with cash or rent reduction from lessor to lessee, see section 110(b).

(9) NORMALIZATION RULES.—

(A) IN GENERAL.—In order to use a normalization method of accounting with respect to any public utility property for purposes of subsection (f)(2)—

(i) the taxpayer must, in computing its tax expense for purposes of establishing its cost of service for ratemaking purposes and reflecting operating results in its regulated books of account, use a method of depreciation with respect to such property that is the same as, and a depreciation period for such property that is no shorter than, the method and period used to compute its depreciation expense for such purposes; and

(ii) if the amount allowable as a deduction under this section with respect to such property (respecting all elections made by the taxpayer under this section) differs from the amount that would be allowable as a deduction under section 167 using the method (including the period, first and last year convention, and salvage value) used to compute regulated tax expense under clause (i), the taxpayer must make adjustments to a reserve to reflect the deferral of taxes resulting from such difference.

(B) USE OF INCONSISTENT ESTIMATES AND PROJECTIONS, ETC.—

(i) IN GENERAL.—One way in which the requirements of subparagraph (A) are not met is if the taxpayer, for ratemaking purposes, uses a procedure or adjustment which is inconsistent with the requirements of subparagraph (A).

(ii) USE OF INCONSISTENT ESTIMATES AND PROJECTIONS.—The procedures and adjustments which are to be treated as inconsistent for purposes of clause (i) shall include any procedure or adjustment for ratemaking purposes which uses an estimate or projection of the taxpayer's tax expense, depreciation expense, or reserve for deferred taxes under subparagraph (A)(ii) unless such estimate or projection is also used, for ratemaking purposes, with respect to the other 2 such items and with respect to the rate base.

(iii) REGULATORY AUTHORITY.—The Secretary may by regulations prescribe procedures and adjustments (in addition to those specified in clause (ii)) which are to be treated as inconsistent for purposes of clause (i).

(C) PUBLIC UTILITY PROPERTY WHICH DOES NOT MEET NORMALIZATION RULES.—In the case of any public utility property to which this section does not apply by reason of subsection (f)(2), the allowance for depreciation under section 167(a) shall be an amount computed using the method and period referred to in subparagraph (A)(i).

(10) PUBLIC UTILITY PROPERTY.—The term "public utility property" means property used predominantly in the trade or business of the furnishing or sale of—

(A) electrical energy, water, or sewage disposal services,

(B) gas or steam through a local distribution system,

(C) telephone services, or other communication services if furnished or sold by the Communications Satellite Corporation for purposes authorized by the Communications Satellite Act of 1962 (47 U.S.C. 701), or

(D) transportation of gas or steam by pipeline,

if the rates for such furnishing or sale, as the case may be, have been established or approved by a State or political subdivision thereof, by any agency or instrumentality of the United States, or by a public service or public utility commission or other similar body of any State or political subdivision thereof.

(11) RESEARCH AND EXPERIMENTATION.—The term "research and experimentation" has the same meaning as the term research and experimental has under section 174.

(12) SECTION 1245 AND 1250 PROPERTY.—The terms "section 1245 property" and "section 1250 property" have the meanings given such terms by sections 1245(a)(3) and 1250(c), respectively.

(13) SINGLE PURPOSE AGRICULTURAL OR HORTICULTURAL STRUCTURE.—

(A) IN GENERAL.—The term "single purpose agricultural or horticultural structure" means—

(i) a single purpose livestock structure, and

(ii) a single purpose horticultural structure.

(B) DEFINITIONS.—For purposes of this paragraph—

(i) SINGLE PURPOSE LIVESTOCK STRUCTURE.—The term "single purpose livestock structure" means any enclosure or structure specifically designed, constructed, and used—

(I) for housing, raising, and feeding a particular type of livestock and their produce, and

(II) for housing the equipment (including any replacements) necessary for the housing, raising, and feeding referred to in subclause (I).

(ii) SINGLE PURPOSE HORTICULTURAL STRUCTURE.—The term "single purpose horticultural structure" means—

(I) a greenhouse specifically designed, constructed, and used for the commercial production of plants, and

Code Sec. 168

(II) a structure specifically designed, constructed, and used for the commercial production of mushrooms.

(iii) S‌TRUCTURES WHICH INCLUDE WORK SPACE.—An enclosure or structure which provides work space shall be treated as a single purpose agricultural or horticultural structure only if such work space is solely for—

(I) the stocking, caring for, or collecting of livestock or plants (as the case may be) or their produce,

(II) the maintenance of the enclosure or structure, and

(III) the maintenance or replacement of the equipment or stock enclosed or housed therein.

(iv) L‌IVESTOCK.—The term "livestock" includes poultry.

(14) Q‌UALIFIED RENT-TO-OWN PROPERTY.—

(A) I‌N GENERAL.—The term "qualified rent-to-own property" means property held by a rent-to-own dealer for purposes of being subject to a rent-to-own contract.

(B) R‌ENT-TO-OWN DEALER.—The term "rent-to-own dealer" means a person that, in the ordinary course of business, regularly enters into rent-to-own contracts with customers for the use of consumer property, if a substantial portion of those contracts terminate and the property is returned to such person before the receipt of all payments required to transfer ownership of the property from such person to the customer.

(C) C‌ONSUMER PROPERTY.—The term "consumer property" means tangible personal property of a type generally used within the home for personal use.

(D) R‌ENT-TO-OWN CONTRACT.—The term "rent-to-own contract" means any lease for the use of consumer property between a rent-to-own dealer and a customer who is an individual which—

(i) is titled "Rent-to-Own Agreement" or "Lease Agreement with Ownership Option," or uses other similar language,

(ii) provides for level (or decreasing where no payment is less than 40 percent of the largest payment), regular periodic payments (for a payment period which is a week or month),

(iii) provides that legal title to such property remains with the rent-to-own dealer until the customer makes all the payments described in clause (ii) or early purchase payments required under the contract to acquire legal title to the item of property,

(iv) provides a beginning date and a maximum period of time for which the contract may be in effect that does not exceed 156 weeks or 36 months from such beginning date (including renewals or options to extend),

(v) provides for payments within the 156-week or 36-month period that, in the aggregate, generally exceed the normal retail price of the consumer property plus interest,

(vi) provides for payments under the contract that, in the aggregate, do not exceed $10,000 per item of consumer property,

(vii) provides that the customer does not have any legal obligation to make all the payments referred to in clause (ii) set forth under the contract, and that at the end of each payment period the customer may either continue to use the consumer property by making the payment for the next payment period or return such property to the rent-to-own dealer in good working order, in which case the customer does not incur any further obligations under the contract and is not entitled to a return of any payments previously made under the contract, and

(viii) provides that the customer has no right to sell, sublease, mortgage, pawn, pledge, encumber, or otherwise dispose of the consumer property until all the payments stated in the contract have been made.

(15) M‌OTORSPORTS ENTERTAINMENT COMPLEX.—

(A) I‌N GENERAL.—The term "motorsports entertainment complex" means a racing track facility which—

(i) is permanently situated on land, and

(ii) during the 36-month period following the first day of the month in which the asset is placed in service, hosts 1 or more racing events for automobiles (of any type), trucks, or motorcycles which are open to the public for the price of admission.

(B) A‌NCILLARY AND SUPPORT FACILITIES.—Such term shall include, if owned by the taxpayer who owns the complex and provided for the benefit of patrons of the complex—

(i) ancillary facilities and land improvements in support of the complex's activities (including parking lots, sidewalks, waterways, bridges, fences, and landscaping),

(ii) support facilities (including food and beverage retailing, souvenir vending, and other nonlodging accommodations), and

(iii) appurtenances associated with such facilities and related attractions and amusements (including ticket booths, race track surfaces, suites and hospitality facilities, grandstands and viewing structures, props, walls, facilities that support the delivery of entertainment services, other special purpose structures, facades, shop interiors, and buildings).

Code Sec. 168

(C) EXCEPTION.—Such term shall not include any transportation equipment, administrative services assets, warehouses, administrative buildings, hotels, or motels.

(D) TERMINATION.—Such term shall not include any property placed in service after December 31, 2017.

(16) ALASKA NATURAL GAS PIPELINE.—The term "Alaska natural gas pipeline" means the natural gas pipeline system located in the State of Alaska which—

(A) has a capacity of more than 500,000,000,000 Btu of natural gas per day, and

(B) is—

(i) placed in service after December 31, 2013, or

(ii) treated as placed in service on January 1, 2014, if the taxpayer who places such system in service before January 1, 2014, elects such treatment.

Such term includes the pipe, trunk lines, related equipment, and appurtenances used to carry natural gas, but does not include any gas processing plant.

(17) NATURAL GAS GATHERING LINE.—The term "natural gas gathering line" means—

(A) the pipe, equipment, and appurtenances determined to be a gathering line by the Federal Energy Regulatory Commission, and

(B) the pipe, equipment, and appurtenances used to deliver natural gas from the wellhead or a commonpoint to the point at which such gas first reaches—

(i) a gas processing plant,

(ii) an interconnection with a transmission pipeline for which a certificate as an interstate transmission pipeline has been issued by the Federal Energy Regulatory Commission,

(iii) an interconnection with an intrastate transmission pipeline, or

(iv) a direct interconnection with a local distribution company, a gas storage facility, or an industrial consumer.

(18) QUALIFIED SMART ELECTRIC METERS.—

(A) IN GENERAL.—The term "qualified smart electric meter" means any smart electric meter which—

(i) is placed in service by a taxpayer who is a supplier of electric energy or a provider of electric energy services, and

(ii) does not have a class life (determined without regard to subsection (e)) of less than 16 years.

(B) SMART ELECTRIC METER.—For purposes of subparagraph (A), the term "smart electric meter" means any time-based meter and related communication equipment which is capable of being used by the taxpayer as part of a system that—

(i) measures and records electricity usage data on a time-differentiated basis in at least 24 separate time segments per day,

(ii) provides for the exchange of information between supplier or provider and the customer's electric meter in support of time-based rates or other forms of demand response,

(iii) provides data to such supplier or provider so that the supplier or provider can provide energy usage information to customers electronically, and

(iv) provides net metering.

(19) QUALIFIED SMART ELECTRIC GRID SYSTEMS.—

(A) IN GENERAL.—The term "qualified smart electric grid system" means any smart grid property which—

(i) is used as part of a system for electric distribution grid communications, monitoring, and management placed in service by a taxpayer who is a supplier of electric energy or a provider of electric energy services, and

(ii) does not have a class life (determined without regard to subsection (e)) of less than 16 years.

(B) SMART GRID PROPERTY.—For the purposes of subparagraph (A), the term "smart grid property" means electronics and related equipment that is capable of—

(i) sensing, collecting, and monitoring data of or from all portions of a utility's electric distribution grid,

(ii) providing real-time, two-way communications to monitor or manage such grid, and

(iii) providing real time analysis of and event prediction based upon collected data that can be used to improve electric distribution system reliability, quality, and performance.

Amendments

- **2018, Bipartisan Budget Act of 2018 (P.L. 115-123)**
P.L. 115-123, §40305(a), Div. D:
Amended Code Sec. 168(i)(15)(D) by striking "December 31, 2016" and inserting "December 31, 2017". Effective for property placed in service after 12-31-2016.

- **2017, Tax Cuts and Jobs Act (P.L. 115-97)**
P.L. 115-97, §13001(d), provides:
(d) NORMALIZATION REQUIREMENTS.—
(1) IN GENERAL.—A normalization method of accounting shall not be treated as being used with respect to any public utility property for purposes of section 167 or 168 of the

Internal Revenue Code of 1986 if the taxpayer, in computing its cost of service for ratemaking purposes and reflecting operating results in its regulated books of account, reduces the excess tax reserve more rapidly or to a greater extent than such reserve would be reduced under the average rate assumption method.

(2) ALTERNATIVE METHOD FOR CERTAIN TAX-PAYERS.—If, as of the first day of the taxable year that includes the date of enactment of this Act—

(A) the taxpayer was required by a regulatory agency to compute depreciation for public utility property on the basis of an average life or composite rate method, and

(B) the taxpayer's books and underlying records did not contain the vintage account data necessary to apply the average rate assumption method,

the taxpayer will be treated as using a normalization method of accounting if, with respect to such jurisdiction, the taxpayer uses the alternative method for public utility property that is subject to the regulatory authority of that jurisdiction.

(3) DEFINITIONS.—For purposes of this subsection—

(A) EXCESS TAX RESERVE.—The term "excess tax reserve" means the excess of—

(i) the reserve for deferred taxes (as described in section 168(i)(9)(A)(ii) of the Internal Revenue Code of 1986) as of the day before the corporate rate reductions provided in the amendments made by this section take effect, over

(ii) the amount which would be the balance in such reserve if the amount of such reserve were determined by assuming that the corporate rate reductions provided in this Act were in effect for all prior periods.

(B) AVERAGE RATE ASSUMPTION METHOD.—The average rate assumption method is the method under which the excess in the reserve for deferred taxes is reduced over the remaining lives of the property as used in its regulated books of account which gave rise to the reserve for deferred taxes. Under such method, during the time period in which the timing differences for the property reverse, the amount of the adjustment to the reserve for the deferred taxes is calculated by multiplying—

(i) the ratio of the aggregate deferred taxes for the property to the aggregate timing differences for the property as of the beginning of the period in question, by

(ii) the amount of the timing differences which reverse during such period.

(C) ALTERNATIVE METHOD.—The "alternative method" is the method in which the taxpayer—

(i) computes the excess tax reserve on all public utility property included in the plant account on the basis of the weighted average life or composite rate used to compute depreciation for regulatory purposes, and

(ii) reduces the excess tax reserve ratably over the remaining regulatory life of the property.

(4) TAX INCREASED FOR NORMALIZATION VIOLATION.—If, for any taxable year ending after the date of the enactment of this Act, the taxpayer does not use a normalization method of accounting for the corporate rate reductions provided in the amendments made by this section—

(A) the taxpayer's tax for the taxable year shall be increased by the amount by which it reduces its excess tax reserve more rapidly than permitted under a normalization method of accounting, and

(B) such taxpayer shall not be treated as using a normalization method of accounting for purposes of subsections (f)(2) and (i)(9)(C) of section 168 of the Internal Revenue Code of 1986.

P.L. 115-97, §13504(b)(1):

Amended Code Sec. 168(i)(7)(B) by striking the second sentence [the last sentence of Code Sec. 168(i)(7)]. **Effective** for partnership tax years beginning after 12-31-2017. Prior to being stricken, the second sentence of Code Sec. 168(i)(7)(B) [the last sentence of Code Sec. 168(i)(7)] read as follows:

Subparagraph (A) shall not apply in the case of a termination of a partnership under section 708(b)(1)(B).

• **2015, Protecting Americans from Tax Hikes Act of 2015 (P.L. 114-113)**

P.L. 114-113, §166(a), Div. Q:

Amended Code Sec. 168(i)(15)(D) by striking "December 31, 2014" and inserting "December 31, 2016". **Effective** for property placed in service after 12-31-2014.

• **2014, Tax Increase Prevention Act of 2014 (P.L. 113-295)**

P.L. 113-295, §123(a), Division A:

Amended Code Sec. 168(i)(15)(D) by striking "December 31, 2013" and inserting "December 31, 2014". **Effective** for property placed in service after 12-31-2013.

• **2014, Tax Technical Corrections Act of 2014 (P.L. 113-295)**

P.L. 113-295, §210(c)(1), Division A:

Amended Code Sec. 168(i)(18)(A)(ii) by striking "10 years" and inserting "16 years". **Effective** as if included in the provision of the Energy Improvement and Extension Act of 2008 (P.L. 110-343) to which it relates [**effective** for property placed in service after 10-3-2008.—CCH].

P.L. 113-295, §210(c)(2), Division A:

Amended Code Sec. 168(i)(19)(A)(ii) by striking "10 years" and inserting "16 years". **Effective** as if included in the provision of the Energy Improvement and Extension Act of 2008 (P.L. 110-343) to which it relates [**effective** for property placed in service after 10-3-2008.—CCH].

• **2013, American Taxpayer Relief Act of 2012 (P.L. 112-240)**

P.L. 112-240, §312(a):

Amended Code Sec. 168(i)(15)(D) by striking "December 31, 2011" and inserting "December 31, 2013". **Effective** for property placed in service after 12-31-2011.

P.L. 112-240, §331(d):

Amended Code Sec. 168(i)(9)(A)(ii) by inserting "(respecting all elections made by the taxpayer under this section)" after "such property". **Effective** for property placed in service after 12-31-2012, in tax years ending after such date.

• **2010, Tax Relief, Unemployment Insurance Reauthorization, and Job Creation Act of 2010 (P.L. 111-312)**

P.L. 111-312, §738(a):

Amended Code Sec. 168(i)(15)(D) by striking "December 31, 2009" and inserting "December 31, 2011". **Effective** for property placed in service after 12-31-2009.

• **2008, Energy Improvement and Extension Act of 2008 (P.L. 110-343)**

P.L. 110-343, Division B, §306(b):

Amended Code Sec. 168(i) by inserting at the end new paragraph[s] (18)-(19). **Effective** for property placed in service after 10-3-2008.

• **2008, Tax Extenders and Alternative Minimum Tax Relief Act of 2008 (P.L. 110-343)**

P.L. 110-343, Division C, §317(a):

Amended Code Sec. 168(i)(15)(D) by striking "December 31, 2007" and inserting "December 31, 2009". **Effective** for property placed in service after 12-31-2007.

• **2005, Gulf Opportunity Zone Act of 2005 (P.L. 109-135)**

P.L. 109-135, §412(s):

Amended Code Sec. 168(i)(15)(D) by striking "This paragraph shall not apply to" and inserting "Such term shall not include". **Effective** 12-21-2005.

• **2005, Energy Tax Incentives Act of 2005 (P.L. 109-58)**

P.L. 109-58, §1326(b):

Amended Code Sec. 168(i) by inserting after paragraph (16) a new paragraph (17). **Effective** generally for property placed in service after 4-11-2005. For an exception, see Act Sec. 1326(e)(2), below.

P.L. 109-58, §1326(e)(2), provides:

(2) EXCEPTION.—The amendments made by this section shall not apply to any property with respect to which the taxpayer or a related party has entered into a binding contract for the construction thereof on or before April 11, 2005, or, in the case of self-constructed property, has started construction on or before such date.

- **2004, American Jobs Creation Act of 2004 (P.L. 108-357)**

P.L. 108-357, § 704(b):
Amended Code Sec. 168(i) by adding at the end a new paragraph (15). **Effective** generally for any property placed in service after 10-22-2004. For special rules, see Act Secs. 704(c)(2)-(3), below.

P.L. 108-357, § 704(c)(2)-(3), provides:
(2) SPECIAL RULE FOR ASSET CLASS 80.0.—In the case of race track facilities placed in service after the date of the enactment of this Act [10-22-2004.—CCH], such facilities shall not be treated as theme and amusement facilities classified under asset class 80.0.

(3) NO INFERENCE.—Nothing in this section or the amendments made by this section shall be construed to affect the treatment of property placed in service on or before the date of the enactment of this Act [10-22-2004.—CCH].

P.L. 108-357, § 706(b):
Amended Code Sec. 168(i), as amended by this Act, by inserting after paragraph (15) a new paragraph (16). **Effective** for property placed in service after 12-31-2004.

P.L. 108-357, § 847(c):
Amended Code Sec. 168(i)(3)(A) by striking "and" at the end of clause (i), by redesignating clause (ii) as clause (iii) and by inserting after clause (i) a new clause (ii). **Effective** generally for leases entered into after 3-12-2004, and in the case of property treated as tax-exempt use property other than by reason of a lease, to property acquired after 3-12-2004 [effective date amended by P.L. 109-135, § 403(ff)]. For an exception, see Act Sec. 849(b)(1)-(2), below.

P.L. 108-357, § 849(b)(1)-(2), provides:
(b) EXCEPTION.—
(1) IN GENERAL.—The amendments made by this part shall not apply to qualified transportation property.
(2) QUALIFIED TRANSPORTATION PROPERTY.—For purposes of paragraph (1), the term "qualified transportation property" means domestic property subject to a lease with respect to which a formal application—
(A) was submitted for approval to the Federal Transit Administration (an agency of the Department of Transportation) after June 30, 2003, and before March 13, 2004,
(B) is approved by the Federal Transit Administration before January 1, 2006, and
(C) includes a description of such property and the value of such property.

- **1997, Taxpayer Relief Act of 1997 (P.L. 105-34)**

P.L. 105-34, § 1086(b)(3):
Amended Code Sec. 168(i) by adding at the end a new paragraph (14). **Effective** for property placed in service after 8-5-97.

P.L. 105-34, § 1213(c):
Amended Code Sec. 168(i)(8) by adding at the end a new subparagraph (C). **Effective** for leases entered into after 8-5-97.

- **1996, Small Business Job Protection Act of 1996 (P.L. 104-188)**

P.L. 104-188, § 1121(a):
Amended Code Sec. 168(i)(8). **Effective** for improvements disposed of or abandoned after 6-12-96. Prior to amendment, Code Sec. 168(i)(8) read as follows:
(8) TREATMENT OF LEASEHOLD IMPROVEMENTS.—In the case of any building erected (or improvements made) on leased property, if such building or improvement is property to which this section applies, the depreciation deduction shall be determined under the provisions of this section.

- **1990, Omnibus Budget Reconciliation Act of 1990 (P.L. 101-508)**

P.L. 101-508, § 11801(c)(8)(B):
Amended Code Sec. 168(i)(7)(B) by striking "371(a), 374(a)," after "361". **Effective** 11-5-90.

P.L. 101-508, § 11821(b), provides:
(b) SAVINGS PROVISION.—If—
(1) any provision amended or repealed by this part applied to—
(A) any transaction occurring before the date of the enactment of this Act,
(B) any property acquired before such date of enactment, or
(C) any item of income, loss, deduction, or credit taken into account before such date of enactment, and

(2) the treatment of such transaction, property, or item under such provision would (without regard to the amendments made by this part) affect liability for tax for periods ending after such date of enactment,
nothing in the amendments made by this part shall be construed to affect the treatment of such transaction, property, or item for purposes of determining liability for tax for periods ending after such date of enactment.

P.L. 101-508, § 11812(b)(2)(B):
Amended Code Sec. 168(i)(10). **Effective**, generally, for property placed in service after 11-5-90. However, for exceptions see Act Sec. 11812(c)(2)-(3) below. Prior to amendment, Code Sec. 168(i)(10) read as follows:
(10) PUBLIC UTILITY PROPERTY.—The term "public utility property" has the meaning given such term by section 167(l)(3)(A).

P.L. 101-508, § 11812(b)(2)(D):
Amended Code Sec. 168(i)(1) by adding a new sentence at the end thereof. **Effective**, generally, for property placed in service after 11-5-90. However, for exceptions see Act Sec. 11812(c)(2)-(3) below.

P.L. 101-508, § 11812(b)(2)(E):
Amended Code Sec. 168(i)(9)(A)(ii) by striking "(determined without regard to section 167(l))" after "section 167". **Effective**, generally, for property placed in service after 11-5-90. However, for exceptions see Act Sec. 11812(c)(2)-(3) below.

P.L. 101-508, § 11812(c)(2)-(3), provides:
(2) EXCEPTION.—The amendments made by this section shall not apply to any property to which section 168 of the Internal Revenue Code of 1986 does not apply by reason of subsection (f)(5) thereof.

(3) EXCEPTION FOR PREVIOUSLY GRANDFATHER EXPENDITURES.—The amendments made by this section shall not apply to rehabilitation expenditures described in section 252(f)(5) of the Tax Reform Act of 1986 (as added by section 1002(l)(31) of the Technical and Miscellaneous Revenue Act of 1988).

P.L. 101-508, § 11813(b)(9)(B)(ii):
Amended Code Sec. 168(i) by adding at the end thereof new paragraph (13). **Effective**, generally, for property placed in service after 12-31-90. However, for exceptions see Act Sec. 11813(c)(2) below.

P.L. 101-508, § 11813(c)(2), provides:
(2) EXCEPTIONS.—The amendments made by this section shall not apply to—
(A) any transition property (as defined in section 49(e) of the Internal Revenue Code of 1986 (as in effect on the day before the date of the enactment of this Act),
(B) any property with respect to which qualified progress expenditures were previously taken into account under section 46(d) of such Code (as so in effect), and
(C) any property described in section 46(b)(2)(C) of such Code (as so in effect).

- **1988, Technical and Miscellaneous Revenue Act of 1988 (P.L. 100-647)**

P.L. 100-647, § 1002(a)(7)(A):
Amended Code Sec. 168(i)(7)(A) by adding at the end thereof a new sentence. **Effective** as if included in the provision of P.L. 99-514 to which it relates.

P.L. 100-647, § 1002(a)(7)(B):
Amended Code Sec. 168(i)(7)(B). **Effective** as if included in the provision of P.L. 99-514 to which it relates. Prior to amendment, Code Sec. 168(i)(7)(B) read as follows:
(B) TRANSACTIONS COVERED.—The transactions described in this subparagraph are any transaction described in section 332, 351, 361, 371(a), 374(a), 721, or 731. Subparagraph (A) shall not apply in the case of a termination of a partnership under section 708(b)(1)(B).

P.L. 100-647, § 1002(a)(7)(C):
Repealed Code Sec. 168(i)(7)(D). **Effective** as if included in the provision of P.L. 99-514 to which it relates. Prior to repeal, Code Sec. 168(i)(7)(D) read as follows:
(D) EXCEPTION.—This paragraph shall not apply to any transaction to which subsection (f)(5) applies (relating to churning transactions).

P.L. 100-647, § 1002(i)(2)(G):
Amended the Code Sec. 168(i)(1)(E) by adding at the end thereof a new clause (iii). **Effective** as if included in the provision of P.L. 99-514 to which it relates.

P.L. 100-647, § 6253:
Amended Code Sec. 168(i)(1). **Effective** 11-10-88. Prior to amendment, Code Sec. 168(i)(1) read as follows:

(1) CLASS LIFE.—

(A) IN GENERAL.—Except as provided in this section, the term "class life" means the class life (if any) which would be applicable with respect to any property as of January 1, 1986, under subsection (m) of section 167 (determined without regard to paragraph (4) thereof and as if the taxpayer had made an election under such subsection).

(B) SECRETARIAL AUTHORITY.—The Secretary, through an office established in the Treasury—

(i) shall monitor and analyze actual experience with respect to all depreciable assets, and

(ii) except in the case of residential rental property or nonresidential real property—

(I) may prescribe a new class life for any property,

(II) in the case of assigned property, may modify any assigned item, or

(III) may prescribe a class life for any property which does not have a class life within the meaning of subparagraph (A).

Any class life or assigned item prescribed or modified under the preceding sentence shall reasonably reflect the anticipated useful life, and the anticipated decline in value over time, of the property to the industry or other group.

(C) EFFECT OF MODIFICATION.—Any class life or assigned item with respect to any property prescribed or modified under subparagraph (B) shall be used in classifying such property under subsection (e) and in applying subsection (g).

(D) NO MODIFICATION OF ASSIGNED PROPERTY BEFORE JANUARY 1, 1992.—

(i) IN GENERAL.—Except as otherwise provided in this subparagraph, the Secretary may not modify an assigned item under subparagraph (B)(ii)(II) with respect to any assigned property which is placed in service before January 1, 1992.

(ii) EXCEPTION FOR SHORTER CLASS LIFE.—In the case of assigned property which is placed in service before January 1, 1992, and for which the assigned item reflects a class life which is shorter than the class life under subparagraph (A), the Secretary may modify such assigned item under subparagraph (B)(ii)(II) if such modification results in an item which reflects a shorter class life than such assigned item.

(E) ASSIGNED PROPERTY AND ITEM.—For purposes of this paragraph—

(i) ASSIGNED PROPERTY.—The term "assigned property" means property for which a class life, classification, or recovery period is assigned under subsection (e)(3) or subparagraph (B), (C), or (D) of subsection (g)(3).

(ii) ASSIGNED ITEMS.—The term "assigned item" means the class life, classification, or recovery period assigned under subsection (e)(3) or subparagraph (B), (C), or (D) of subsection (g)(3).

(iii) SPECIAL RULE FOR RAILROAD GRADING OR TUNNEL BORES.—In the case of any property which is a railroad grading or tunnel bore—

(I) such property shall be treated as an assigned property,

(II) the recovery period applicable to such property shall be treated as an assigned item, and

(III) clause (ii) of subparagraph (D) shall not apply.

- **1986, Tax Reform Act of 1986 (P.L. 99-514)**

P.L. 99-514, § 201(a):

Amended Code Sec. 168. For **effective** dates and transitional rules, see Act Secs. 203, 204 and 251(d)(2)-7, below. Prior to amendment, Code Sec. 168 read as follows:

SEC. 168. ACCELERATED COST RECOVERY SYSTEM.

[Sec. 168(a)]

(a) ALLOWANCE OF DEDUCTION.—There shall be allowed as a deduction for any taxable year the amount determined under this section with respect to recovery property.

Amendments

- **1981, Economic Recovery Tax Act of 1981 (P.L. 97-34)**

P.L. 97-34, § 201(a):

Added Code Sec. 168(a). **Effective** for property placed in service after 12-31-80, in tax years ending after such date.

[Sec. 168(b)]

(b) AMOUNT OF DEDUCTION.—

(1) IN GENERAL.—Except as otherwise provided in this section, the amount of the deduction allowable by subsection (a) for any taxable year shall be the aggregate amount determined by applying to the unadjusted basis of recovery property the applicable percentage determined in accordance with the following table:

	The applicable percentage of the class of property is:			
If the recovery year is:	3-year	5-year	10-year	15-year public utility
1	25	15	8	5
2	38	22	14	10
3	37	21	12	9
4		21	10	8
5		21	10	7
6			10	7
7			9	6
8			9	6
9			9	6
10			9	6
11				6
12				6
13				6
14				6
15				6

(2) 19-YEAR REAL PROPERTY.—

(A) IN GENERAL.—In the case of 19-year real property, the applicable percentage shall be determined in accordance with a table prescribed by the Secretary. In prescribing such table, the Secretary shall—

(i) assign to the property a 19-year recovery period, and

(ii) assign percentages generally determined in accordance with use of the 175 percent declining balance method, switching to the method described in section 167(b)(1) at a time to maximize the deduction allowable under subsection (a).

(B) MID-MONTH CONVENTION FOR 19-YEAR REAL PROPERTY.—In the case of 19-year real property, the amount of the deduction determined under any provision of this section (or for purposes of section 57(a)(12)(B) or 312(k)) for any taxable year shall be determined on the basis of the number of months (using a mid-month convention) in which the property is in service.

(3) ELECTION OF DIFFERENT RECOVERY PERCENTAGE.—

(A) IN GENERAL.—Except as provided in subsection (f)(2), in lieu of any applicable percentage under paragraph (1), (2), or (4), the taxpayer may elect, with respect to one or more classes of recovery property placed in service during the taxable year, the applicable percentage determined by use of the straight line method over the recovery period elected by the taxpayer in accordance with the following table:

In the case of:	The taxpayer may elect a recovery period of:
3-year property	3, 5, or 12 years.
5-year property	5, 12, or 25 years.
10-year property	10, 25, or 35 years.
15-year public utility property	15, 35, or 45 years.
19-year real property	19, 35, or 45 years.
Low-income housing	15, 35, or 45 years.

(B) OPERATING RULES.—

(i) IN GENERAL.—Except as provided in clause (ii), the taxpayer may elect under subparagraph (A) only a single percentage for property in any class of recovery property placed in service during the taxable year. The percentage so elected shall apply to all property in such class placed in service during such taxable year and shall apply throughout the recovery period elected for such property.

(ii) REAL PROPERTY.—In the case of 19-year real property or low-income housing the taxpayer shall make the election under subparagraph (A) on a property-by-property basis.

(iii) CONVENTION.—Under regulations prescribed by the Secretary, the half-year convention shall apply to any election with respect to any recovery property (other than 19-year real property or low-income housing) with respect to which an election is made under this paragraph.

(4) LOW-INCOME HOUSING.—

(A) IN GENERAL.—In the case of low-income housing, the applicable percentage shall be determined in accordance with the table prescribed in paragraph (2) (without regard to the mid-month convention), except that in prescribing such table, the Secretary shall—

(i) assign to the property a 15-year recovery period, and

(ii) assign percentages generally determined in accordance with use of the 200 percent declining balance method, switching to the method described in section 167(b)(1) at a time to maximize the deduction allowable under subsection (a).

(B) MONTHLY CONVENTION.—In the case of low-income housing, the amount of the deduction determined under any provision of this section (or for purposes of section 57(a)(12)(B) or 312(k)) for any taxable year shall be determined on the basis of the number of months (treating all property placed in service or disposed of during any month as placed in service or disposed of on the first day of such month) in which the property is in service.

Amendments

• **1985 (P.L. 99-121)**
P.L. 99-121, §103(a):
Amended Code Sec. 168(b)(2)(A)(i) by striking out "18-year recovery period" and inserting in lieu thereof "19-year recovery period". **Effective** with respect to property placed in service by the taxpayer after 5-8-85. However, for an exception and special rule, see Act Sec. 105(b)(2) and (3), below.

P.L. 99-121, §103(b)(2):
Amended Code Sec. 168(b)(3) by striking out "18, 35, or 45" in the table contained in subparagraph (A) and inserting in lieu thereof "19, 35, or 45 years". **Effective** with respect to property placed in service by the taxpayer after 5-8-85. However, for an exception and special rule, see Act Sec. 105(b)(2) and (3), below.

P.L. 99-121, §105(b)(2) and (3), provides:
(2) EXCEPTION.—The amendments made by section 103 shall not apply to property placed in service by the taxpayer before January 1, 1987, if—
(A) the taxpayer or a qualified person entered into a binding contract to purchase or construct such property before May 9, 1985, or
(B) construction of such property was commenced by or for the taxpayer or a qualified person before May 9, 1985.
For purposes of this paragraph, the term "qualified person" means any person whose rights in such a contract or such property are transferred to the taxpayer, but only if such property is not placed in service before such rights are transferred to the taxpayer.

(3) SPECIAL RULE FOR COMPONENTS.—For purposes of applying section 168(f)(1)(B) of the Internal Revenue Code of 1954 (as amended by section 103) to components placed in service after December 31, 1986, property to which paragraph (2) of this subsection applies shall be treated as placed in service by the taxpayer before May 9, 1985.

• **1984, Deficit Reduction Act of 1984 (P.L. 98-369)**
P.L. 98-369, §111(a):
Amended Code Sec. 168(b)(2) by striking out "15-year real property" each place it appears in the text and heading thereof and inserting in lieu thereof "18-year real property", by striking out "15-year recovery period" in subparagraph (A)(i) and inserting in lieu thereof "18-year recovery period", and by striking out "(200 percent declining balance method in the case of low-income housing)". For the **effective** date as well as special rules, see Act Sec. 111(g)[f], below.

P.L. 98-369, §111(b)(1):
Amended Code Sec. 168(b) by adding at the end thereof new paragraph (4). For the **effective** date as well as special rules, see Act Sec. 111(g)[f], below.

P.L. 98-369, §111(b)(3)(A):
Amended Code Sec. 168(b)(2)(A) by striking out the last sentence thereof. For the **effective** date as well as special rules, see Act Sec. 111(g)[f], below. Prior to amendment, the last sentence read as follows:
For purposes of this subparagraph, the term "low-income housing" means property described in clause (i), (ii), (iii), or (iv) of section 1250(a)(1)(B).

P.L. 98-369, §111(d):
Amended Code Sec. 168(b)(2)(A) and (B) by inserting "(using a midmonth convention)" after "months". For the **effective** date as well as special rules, see Act Sec. 111(g)[f], below.

P.L. 98-369, §111(e)(1):
Amended Code Sec. 168(b)(3)(B)(iii) by striking out "15-year real property" each place it appears and inserting in lieu thereof "18-year real property or low-income housing". For the **effective** date as well as special rules, see Act Sec. 111(g)[f], below.

P.L. 98-369, §111(e)(2):
Amended Code Sec. 168(b)(3)(B)(ii) by striking out "15-year real property" and inserting in lieu thereof "18-year real property or low-income housing". For the **effective** date as well as special rules, see Act Sec. 111(g)[f], below.

P.L. 98-369, §111(e)(9):
Amended Code Sec. 168(b)(3)(A) by striking out "under paragraphs (1) and (2)" and inserting in lieu thereof "under paragraph (1), (2), or (4)", and by striking out the item in the table relating to 15-year real property and inserting in lieu thereof: "18-year real property and low-income housing. . . . 18, 35, or 45 [years]." For the **effective** date as well as special rules, see Act Sec. 111(g)[f], below.

P.L. 98-369, §111(g)[f] provides:
[f] Effective Date.—
(1) In General.—Except as otherwise provided in this subsection, the amendments made by this section shall apply with respect to property placed in service by the taxpayer after March 15, 1984.
(2) Exception.—The amendments made by this section shall not apply to property placed in service by the taxpayer before January 1, 1987, if—
(A) the taxpayer or a qualified person entered into a binding contract to purchase or construct such property before March 16, 1984, or
(B) construction of such property was commenced by or for the taxpayer or a qualified person before March 16, 1984.
For purposes of this paragraph the term "qualified person" means any person who transfers his rights in such a contract or such property to the taxpayer, but only if the property is not placed in service by such person before such rights are transferred to the taxpayer.
(3) Special Rules for Application of Paragraph (2).—
(A) Certain Inventory.—In the case of any property which—
(i) is held by a person as property described in section 1221(1), and
(ii) is disposed of by such person before January 1, 1985,
such person shall not, for purposes of paragraph (2), be treated as having placed such property in service before such property is disposed of merely because such person

rented such property or held such property for rental. No deduction for depreciation or amortization shall be allowed to such person with respect to such property,

(B) Certain Property Financed By Bonds.—In the case of any property with respect to which—,

(i) bonds were issued to finance such property before 1984, and

(ii) an architectural contract was entered into before March 16, 1984,

paragraph (2) shall be applied by substituting "May 2" for "March 16".

(4) SPECIAL RULE FOR COMPONENTS.—For purposes of applying section 168(f)(1)(B) of the Internal Revenue Code of 1954 (as amended by this section) to components placed in service after December 31, 1986, property to which paragraph (2) applies shall be treated as placed in service by the taxpayer before March 16, 1984.

(5) SPECIAL RULE FOR MID-MONTH CONVENTION.—In the case of the amendment made by subsection (d)—

(A) paragraph (1) shall be applied by substituting "June 22, 1984" for "March 15, 1984", and

(B) paragraph (2) shall be applied by substituting "June 23, 1984" for "March 15, 1984" each place it appears.

- **1983, Technical Corrections Act of 1982 (P.L. 97-448)**

P.L. 97-448, § 102(a)(5):

Amended the third sentence of Code Sec. 168(b)(2)(A) by striking out "For purposes of this subparagraph" and inserting in lieu thereof "In the case of 15-year real property". **Effective** as if it had been included in the provision of P.L. 97-34 to which it relates.

- **1982, Tax Equity and Fiscal Responsibility Act of 1982 (P.L. 97-248)**

P.L. 97-248, § 206(a)(1)(3):

Amended Code Sec. 168(b)(1) by striking out "tables" and inserting in lieu thereof "table", by striking out "(A) FOR PROPERTY PLACED IN SERVICE AFTER DECEMBER 31, 1980, AND BEFORE JANUARY 1, 1985.—", and by striking out subparagraphs (B) and (C). **Effective** as of 9-3-82. Prior to amendment, subparagraphs (B) and (C) read as follows:

"(B) For property placed in service in 1985.—

	The applicable percentage for the class of property is:			
If the recovery year is:	3-year	5-year	10-year	15-year public utility
1	29	18	9	6
2	47	33	19	12
3	24	25	16	12
4		16	14	11
5		8	12	10
6			10	9
7			8	8
8			6	7
9			4	6
10			2	5
11				4
12				4
13				3
14				2
15				1

(C) For property placed in service after December 31, 1985.—

	The applicable percentage for the class of property is:			
If the recovery year is:	3-year	5-year	10-year	15-year public utility
1	33	20	10	7
2	45	32	18	12
3	23	24	16	12
4		16	14	11
5		8	12	10
6			10	9
7			8	8
8			6	7

Code Sec. 168

9	4	6
10	2	5
11		4
12		3
13		3
14		2
15		1 ."

- **1981, Economic Recovery Tax Act of 1981 (P.L. 97-34)**

P.L. 97-34, §201(a):

Added Code Sec. 168(b). **Effective** for property placed in service after 12-31-80, in tax years ending after such date.

[Sec. 168(c)]

(c) RECOVERY PROPERTY.—For purposes of this title—

(1) RECOVERY PROPERTY DEFINED.—Except as provided in subsection (e), the term "recovery property" means tangible property of a character subject to the allowance for depreciation—

(A) used in a trade or business, or

(B) held for the production of income.

(2) CLASSES OF RECOVERY PROPERTY.—Each item of recovery property shall be assigned to one of the following classes of property:

(A) 3-YEAR PROPERTY.—The term "3-year property" means section 1245 class property—

(i) with a present class life of 4 years or less; or

(ii) used in connection with research and experimentation.

(B) 5-YEAR PROPERTY.—The term "5-year property" means recovery property which is section 1245 class property and which is not 3-year property, 10-year property, or 15-year public utility property.

(C) 10-YEAR PROPERTY.—The term "10-year property" means—

(i) public utility property (other than section 1250 class property or 3-year property) with a present class life of more than 18 years but not more than 25 years; and

(ii) section 1250 class property with a present class life of 12.5 years or less.

(D) 19-YEAR REAL PROPERTY.—The term "19-year real property" means section 1250 class property which—

(i) does not have a present class life of 12.5 years or less, and

(ii) is not low-income housing.

(E) 15-YEAR PUBLIC UTILITY PROPERTY.—The term "15-year public utility property" means public utility property (other than section 1250 class property or 3-year property) with a present class life of more than 25 years.

(F) LOW-INCOME HOUSING.—The term "low-income housing" means property described in clause (i), (ii), (iii), or (iv) of section 1250(a)(1)(B).

(G) SPECIAL RULE FOR THEME PARKS, ETC.—For purposes of subparagraphs (C) and (D), a building (and its structural components) shall not be treated as having a present class life of 12.5 years or less by reason of any use other than the use for which such building was originally placed in service.

Amendments

- **1984, Deficit Reduction Act of 1984 (P.L. 98-369)**

P.L. 98-369, §111(b)(2):

Amended Code Sec. 168(c)(2) by redesignating subparagraph (F) as subparagraph (G) and by inserting after subparagraph (E) new subparagraph (F). **Effective** with respect to property placed in service by the taxpayer after 3-15-84. Special rules appear in Act Sec. 111(g)[f]following former Code Sec. 168(f).

P.L. 98-369, §111(b)(3)(B):

Amended Code Sec. 168(c)(2)(D). Prior to amendment, it read as follows:

(D) 15-year Real Property.—The term "15-year real property" means section 1250 class property which does not have a present class life of 12.5 years or less. **Effective** with respect to property placed in service by the taxpayer after 3-15-84. Special rules appear in Act Sec. 111(g)[f] following former Code Sec. 168(f).

- **1983, Technical Corrections Act of 1982 (P.L. 97-448)**

P.L. 97-448, §102(a)(8):

Amended Code Sec. 168(c)(2) by adding at the end thereof new subparagraph (F). **Effective** as if it had been included in the provision of P.L. 97-34 to which it relates.

- **1981, Economic Recovery Tax Act of 1981 (P.L. 97-34)**

P.L. 97-34, §201(a):

Added Code Sec. 168(c). **Effective** for property placed in service after 12-31-80, in tax years ending after such date.

[Sec. 168(d)]

(d) UNADJUSTED BASIS; ADJUSTMENTS.—

(1) UNADJUSTED BASIS DEFINED.—

(A) IN GENERAL.—For purposes of this section, the term "unadjusted basis" means the excess of—

(i) the basis of the property determined under part II of subchapter O of chapter 1 for purposes of determining gain (determined without regard to the adjustments described in paragraph (2) or (3) of section 1016(a)), over

(ii) the sum of—

(I) that portion of the basis for which the taxpayer properly elects amortization (including the deduction allowed under section 167(k)) in lieu of depreciation, and

(II) that portion of the basis which the taxpayer properly elects to treat as an expense under section 179.

(B) TIME FOR TAKING BASIS INTO ACCOUNT.—

(i) IN GENERAL.—The unadjusted basis of property shall be first taken into account under subsection (b) for the taxable year in which the property is placed in service.

(ii) REDETERMINATIONS.—The Secretary shall by regulation provide for the method of determining the deduction allowable under subsection (a) for any taxable year (and succeeding taxable years) in which the basis is redetermined (including any reduction under section 1017).

(2) DISPOSITIONS.—

(A) MASS ASSET ACCOUNTS.—In lieu of recognizing gain or loss under this chapter, a taxpayer who maintains one or more mass asset accounts of recovery property may, under regulations prescribed by the Secretary, elect to include in income all proceeds realized on the disposition of such property.

(B) ADJUSTMENT TO BASIS.—Except as provided under regulations prescribed by the Secretary under paragraph (7) or (10) of subsection (f), if any recovery property (other than 19-year real property or low-income housing or property with respect to which an election under subparagraph (A) is made) is disposed of, the unadjusted basis of such property shall cease to be taken into account in determining any recovery deduction allowable under subsection (a) as of the beginning of the taxable year in which such disposition occurs.

(C) DISPOSITION INCLUDES RETIREMENT.—For purposes of this subparagraph, the term "disposition" includes retirement.

Amendments

- **1984, Deficit Reduction Act of 1984 (P.L. 98-369)**

P.L. 98-369, §111(e)(3):

Amended Code Sec. 168(d)(2)(B) by striking out "15-year real property" and inserting in lieu thereof "18-year real property or low-income housing". For the **effective** date, as well as special rules, see Act Sec. 111(g)[f] following former Code Sec. 168(f).

Code Sec. 168

- **1983, Technical Corrections Act of 1982 (P.L. 97-448)**

P.L. 97-448, §102(a)(2):
Amended Code Sec. 168(d)(2)(B) by striking out "subsection (f)(7)" and inserting in lieu thereof "paragraph (7) or (10) of subsection (f)". **Effective** as if it had been included in the provision of P.L. 97-34 to which it relates.

- **1981, Economic Recovery Tax Act of 1981 (P.L. 97-34)**

P.L. 97-34, §201(a):
Added Code Sec. 168(d). **Effective** for property placed in service after 12-31-80, in tax years ending after such date.

[Sec. 168(e)]

(e) PROPERTY EXCLUDED FROM APPLICATION OF SECTION.—For purposes of this title—

(1) PROPERTY PLACED IN SERVICE BEFORE JANUARY 1, 1981.—The term "recovery property" does not include property placed in service by the taxpayer before January 1, 1981.

(2) CERTAIN METHODS OF DEPRECIATION.—The term "recovery property" does not include property if—

(A) the taxpayer elects to exclude such property from the application of this section, and

(B) for the first taxable year for which a deduction would (but for this election) be allowable under this section with respect to such property in the hands of the taxpayer, the property is properly depreciated under the unit-of-production method or any method of depreciation not expressed in a term of years (other than the retirement-replacement-betterment method).

(3) SPECIAL RULE FOR CERTAIN PUBLIC UTILITY PROPERTY.—

(A) IN GENERAL.—The term "recovery property" does not include public utility property (within the meaning of section 167(l)(3)(A)) if the taxpayer does not use a normalization method of accounting.

(B) USE OF NORMALIZATION METHOD DEFINED.—For purposes of subparagraph (A), in order to use a normalization method of accounting with respect to any public utility property—

(i) the taxpayer must, in computing its tax expense for purposes of establishing its cost of service for ratemaking purposes and reflecting operating results in its regulated books of account, use a method of depreciation with respect to such property that is the same as, and a depreciation period for such property that is no shorter than, the method and period used to compute its depreciation expense for such purposes; and

(ii) if the amount allowable as a deduction under this section with respect to such property differs from the amount that would be allowable as a deduction under section 167 (determined without regard to section 167(l)) using the method (including the period, first and last year convention, and salvage value) used to compute regulated tax expense under subparagraph (B)(i), the taxpayer must make adjustments to a reserve to reflect the deferral of taxes resulting from such difference.

(C) USE OF INCONSISTENT ESTIMATES AND PROJECTIONS, ETC.—

(i) IN GENERAL.—One way in which the requirements of subparagraph (B) are not met is if the taxpayer, for ratemaking purposes, uses a procedure or adjustment which is inconsistent with the requirements of subparagraph (B).

(ii) USE OF INCONSISTENT ESTIMATES AND PROJECTIONS.—The procedures and adjustments which are to be treated as inconsistent for purposes of clause (i) shall include any procedure or adjustment for ratemaking purposes which uses an estimate or projection of the taxpayer's tax expense, depreciation expense, or reserve for deferred taxes under subparagraph (B)(ii) unless such estimate or projection is also used, for ratemaking purposes, with respect to the other 2 such items and with respect to the rate base.

(iii) REGULATORY AUTHORITY.—The Secretary may by regulations prescribe procedures and adjustments (in addition to those specified in clause (ii)) which are to be treated as inconsistent for purposes of clause (i).

(D) PUBLIC UTILITY PROPERTY WHICH IS NOT RECOVERY PROPERTY.—In the case of public utility property which, by reason of this paragraph, is not treated as recovery property, the allowance for depreciation under section 167(a) shall be an amount computed using the method and period referred to in subparagraph (B)(i).

(4) CERTAIN TRANSACTIONS IN PROPERTY PLACED IN SERVICE BEFORE 1980.—

(A) SECTION 1245 CLASS PROPERTY.—The term "recovery property" does not include section 1245 class property acquired by the taxpayer after December 31, 1980, if—

(i) the property was owned or used at any time during 1980 by the taxpayer or a related person,

(ii) the property is acquired from a person who owned such property at any time during 1980, and, as part of the transaction, the user of such property does not change,

(iii) the taxpayer leases such property to a person (or a person related to such person) who owned or used such property at any time during 1980, or

(iv) the property is acquired in a transaction as part of which the user of such property does not change and the property is not recovery property in the hands of the person from which the property is so acquired by reason of clause (ii) or (iii).

For purposes of this subparagraph and subparagraph (B), property shall not be treated as owned before it is placed in service. For purposes of this subparagraph, whether the user of property changes as part of a transaction shall be determined in accordance with regulations prescribed by the Secretary.

(B) SECTION 1250 CLASS PROPERTY.—The term "recovery property" does not include section 1250 class property acquired by the taxpayer after December 31, 1980, if—

(i) such property was owned by the taxpayer or by a related person at any time during 1980;

(ii) the taxpayer leases such property to a person (or a person related to such person) who owned such property at any time during 1980; or

(iii) such property is acquired in an exchange described in section 1031, 1033, 1038, or 1039 to the extent that the basis of such property includes an amount representing the adjusted basis of other property owned by the taxpayer or a related person during 1980.

(C) CERTAIN NONRECOGNITION TRANSACTIONS.—The term "recovery property" does not include property placed in service by the transferor or distributor before January 1, 1981, which is acquired by the taxpayer after December 31, 1980, in a transaction described in section 332, 351, 361, 371(a), 374(a), 721, or 731 (or such property acquired from the transferee or acquiring corporation in a transaction described in such section), to the extent that the basis of the property is determined by reference to the basis of the property in the hands of the transferor or distributor. In the case of property to which this subparagraph applies, rules similar to the rules described in section 381(c)(6) shall apply.

(D) RELATED PERSON DEFINED.—Except as provided in subparagraph (E), for purposes of this paragraph a person (hereinafter referred to as the related person) is related to any person if—

(i) the related person bears a relationship to such person specified in section 267(b) or section 707(b)(1), or

(ii) the related person and such person are engaged in trades or businesses under common control (within the meaning of subsections (a) and (b) of section 52).

For purposes of clause (i), in applying section 267(b) and section 707(b)(1) "10 percent" shall be substituted for "50 percent". The determination of whether a person is related to another person shall be made as of the time the taxpayer acquires the property involved. In the case of the acquisition of property by any partnership which results from the termination of another partnership under section 708(b)(1)(B), the determination of whether the acquiring partnership is related to the other partnership shall be made immediately before the event resulting in such termination occurs.

(E) LIQUIDATION OF SUBSIDIARY, ETC.—For purposes of this paragraph, a corporation is not a related person to the taxpayer—

(i) if such corporation is a distributing corporation in a transaction to which section 334(b)(2)(B) applies and the stock of such corporation referred to in such subparagraph (B) was acquired by the taxpayer by purchase after December 31, 1980, or

(ii) if such corporation is liquidated in a liquidation to which section 331(a) applies and the taxpayer (or a related person) by himself or together with 1 or more other persons acquires the stock of the liquidated corporation by purchase (meeting the requirements of section 334(b)(2)(B)) after December 31, 1980.

A similar rule shall apply in the case of a deemed liquidation under section 338.

(F) ANTIAVOIDANCE RULE.—The term "recovery property" does not include property acquired by the taxpayer after December 31, 1980, which, under regulations prescribed by the Secretary, is acquired in a transaction one of the principal purposes of which is to avoid the principles of paragraph (1) and this paragraph.

APPENDIX: Selected Code Sections Affected by the Tax Cuts and Jobs Act

(G) REDUCTION IN UNADJUSTED BASIS.—In the case of an acquisition of property described in subparagraph (B) or (C), the unadjusted basis of the property under subsection (d) shall be reduced to the extent that such property acquired is not recovery property.

(H) ACQUISITIONS BY REASON OF DEATH.—Subparagraphs (A) and (B) shall not apply to the acquisition of any property by the taxpayer if the basis of the property in the hands of the taxpayer is determined under section 1014(a).

(I) SECTION 1245 CLASS PROPERTY ACQUIRED INCIDENTAL TO ACQUISITION OF SECTION 1250 CLASS PROPERTY.—Under regulations prescribed by the Secretary, subparagraph (B) shall apply (and subparagraph (A) shall not apply) to section 1245 class property which is acquired incidental to the acquisition of section 1250 class property.

(5) FILMS AND VIDEO TAPES NOT RECOVERY PROPERTY.—The term "recovery property" shall not include any motion picture film or video tape.

Amendments

- **1984, Deficit Reduction Act of 1984 (P.L. 98-369)**

P.L. 98-369, § 113(b)(1):

Amended Code Sec. 168(e) by adding at the end thereof new paragraph (5). **Effective** for any motion picture film or video tape placed in service before, on, or after 7-18-84, except that such amendment shall not apply to—

(i) any qualified film placed in service by the taxpayer before March 15, 1984, if the taxpayer treated such film as recovery property for purposes of section 168 of the Internal Revenue Code of 1954 on a return of tax under chapter 1 of such Code filed before March 16, 1984, or

(ii) any qualified film placed in service by the taxpayer before January 1, 1985, if—

(I) 20 percent or more of the production costs of such film were incurred before March 16, 1984, and

(II) the taxpayer treats such film as recovery property for purposes of section 168 of such Code.

No credit shall be allowable under section 38 of such Code with respect to any qualified film described in clause (ii), except to the extent provided in section 48(k) of such Code.

For purposes of this paragraph, the terms "qualified film" and "production costs" have the same respective meanings as when used in section 48(k) of Internal Revenue Code of 1954.

P.L. 98-369, § 113(b)(2)(A):

Amended Code Sec. 168(e) by striking out "section" and inserting in lieu thereof "title" in the matter preceding paragraph (1). **Effective** as if included in the amendments made by P.L. 97-34.

- **1983, Technical Corrections Act of 1982 (P.L. 97-448)**

P.L. 97-448, § 102(a)(9):

Amended Code Sec. 168(e)(4) by adding the sentence at the end of subparagraph (D), and by adding at the end thereof new subparagraphs (H) and (I). **Effective** as if it had been included in the provision of P.L. 97-34 to which it relates.

- **1982, Surface Transportation Act of 1982 (P.L. 97-424)**

P.L. 97-424, § 541(a)(1):

Amended Code Sec. 168(e)(3) by redesignating subparagraph (C) as subparagraph (D) and by adding a new subparagraph (C). **Effective** for tax years beginning after 12-31-79. See, however, the amendment note for Act Sec. 541(c)(2)-(5) following Code Sec. 46(f), as amended by P.L. 97-448, for special rules.

- **1982, Tax Equity and Fiscal Responsibility Act of 1982 (P.L. 97-248)**

P.L. 97-248, § 206(b)(1)(2):

Amended Code Sec. 168(e)(4) by striking out paragraph (H) and by striking out "1986" in the heading thereof and inserting in lieu thereof "1981". **Effective** 9-3-82. Prior to amendment, paragraph (H) read as follows:

"(H) Special rules for property placed in service before certain percentages take effect.—Under regulations prescribed by the Secretary—

(i) rules similar to the rules of this paragraph shall be applied in determining whether the tables contained in subparagraph (B) or (C) of subsection (b)(1) apply with respect to recovery property, and

(ii) if the tables contained in subparagraph (B) or (C) of subsection (b)(1) do not apply to such property by reason of clause (i), the deduction allowable under subsection (a) shall be computed—

(I) in the case of a transaction described in subparagraph (C), under rules similar to the rules described in section 381(c)(6); and

(II) in the case of a transaction otherwise described in this paragraph, under the recovery period and method (including rates prescribed under subsection (b)(1)) used by the person from whom the taxpayer acquired such property (or, where such person had no recovery method and period for such property, under the recovery period and method (including rates prescribed under subsection (b)(1)) used by the person which transferred such property to such person)."

P.L. 97-248, § 224(c)(1):

Amended Code Sec. 168 by amending subparagraph (E) of section 168(e)(4) by adding at the end thereof the following new sentence: "A similar rule shall apply in the case of a deemed liquidation under section 338." **Effective** for any target corporation (within the meaning of Code Sec. 338) for which the acquisition date (within the meaning of such section) occurs after 8-31-82. For a special rule, see amendment notes under Code Sec. 338, as added by P.L. 97-248 Act Sec. 224.

- **1981, Economic Recovery Tax Act of 1981 (P.L. 97-34)**

P.L. 97-34, § 201(a):

Added Code Sec. 168(e). **Effective** for property placed in sevice after 12-31-80, in tax years ending after such date.

P.L. 97-34, § 209(d)(1) and (2), provides the following transitional rules applicable to public utilities:

(d) SPECIAL RULE FOR PUBLIC UTILITIES.—

(1) TRANSITIONAL RULE FOR NORMALIZATION REQUIREMENTS.—If, by the terms of the applicable rate order last entered before the date of the enactment of this Act by a regulatory commission having appropriate jurisdiction, a regulated public utility would (but for this provision) fail to meet the requirements of section 168(e)(3) of the Internal Revenue Code of 1954 with respect to property because, for an accounting period ending after December 31, 1980, such public utility used a method of accounting other than a normalization method of accounting, such regulated public utility shall not fail to meet such requirements if, by the terms of its first rate order determining cost of service with respect to such property which becomes effective after the date of the enactment of this Act and on or before January 1, 1983, such regulated public utility uses a normalization method of accounting. This provision shall not apply to any rate order which, under the rules in effect before the date of the enactment of this Act, required a regulated public utility to use a method of accounting with respect to the deduction allowable by section 167 which, under section 167(l), it was not permitted to use.

(2) TRANSITIONAL RULE FOR REQUIREMENTS OF SECTION 46(f).—If, by the terms of the applicable rate order last entered before the date of the enactment of this Act by a regulatory commission having appropriate jurisdiction, a regulated public utility would (but for this provision) fail to meet the requirements of paragraph (1) or (2) of section 46(f) of the Internal Revenue Code of 1954 with respect to property for an accounting period ending after December 31, 1980, such regulated public utility shall not fail to meet such requirements if, by the terms of its first rate order determining cost of service with respect to such property which becomes effective after the date of the enactment of this Act and on or before January 1, 1983, such regulated public utility meets such requirements. This provision shall not apply to any rate order which, under the rules in effect before the date of the enactment of this Act, was inconsistent with the requirements of paragraph (1) or (2) of section 46(f) of such Code (whichever would have been applicable).

P.L. 97-34, § 209(d)(4), provides:

(4) AUTHORITY TO PRESCRIBE INTERIM REGULATIONS WITH RESPECT TO NORMALIZATION.—Until Congress acts further, the Secretary of the Treasury or his delegate may prescribe such interim regulations as may be necessary or appropriate to determine whether the requirements of section 168(e)(3)(B) of the Internal Revenue Code of 1954 have been met with respect to property placed in service after December 31, 1980.

[Sec. 168(f)]

(f) SPECIAL RULES FOR APPLICATION OF THIS SECTION.—For purposes of this section—

(1) COMPONENTS OF SECTION 1250 CLASS PROPERTY.—

(A) IN GENERAL.—Except as otherwise provided in this paragraph—

(i) the deduction allowable under subsection (a) with respect to any component (which is section 1250 class property) of a building shall be computed in the same manner as the deduction allowable with respect to such building, and

(ii) the recovery period for such component shall begin on the later of—

(I) the date such component is placed in service, or

(II) the date on which the building is placed in service.

(B) TRANSITIONAL RULES.—

(i) BUILDINGS PLACED IN SERVICE BEFORE 1981.—In the case of any building placed in service by the taxpayer before January 1, 1981, for purposes of applying subparagraph (A) to components of such buildings placed in service after December 31, 1980, and before March 16, 1984, the deduction allowable under subsection (a) with respect to such components shall be computed in the same manner as the deduction allowable with respect to the first such component placed in service after December 31, 1980.

(ii) BUILDINGS PLACED IN SERVICE BEFORE MARCH 16, 1984.—In the case of any building placed in service by the taxpayer before March 16, 1984, for purposes of applying subparagraph (A) to components of such buildings placed in service after March 15, 1984, and before May 9, 1985, the deduction allowable under subsection (a) with respect to such components shall be computed in the same manner as the deduction allowable with respect to the first such component placed in service after March 15, 1984.

(iii) BUILDINGS PLACED IN SERVICE BEFORE MAY 9, 1985.—In the case of any building placed in service by the taxpayer before May 9, 1985, for purposes of applying subparagraph (A) to components of such buildings placed in service after May 8, 1985, the deduction allowable under subsection (a) with respect to such components shall be computed in the same manner as the deduction allowable with respect to the first component placed in service after May 8, 1985.

(iv) FIRST COMPONENT TREATED AS SEPARATE BUILDING.—For purposes of clause (i), (ii), or (iii), the method of computing the deduction allowable with respect to the first component described in such clause shall be determined as if it were a separate building.

(C) EXCEPTION FOR SUBSTANTIAL IMPROVEMENTS.—

(i) IN GENERAL.—For purposes of this paragraph, a substantial improvement shall be treated as a separate building.

(ii) SUBSTANTIAL IMPROVEMENT.—For purposes of clause (i), the term "substantial improvement" means the improvements added to capital account with respect to any building during any 24-month period, but only if the sum of the amounts added to such account during such period equals or exceeds 25 percent of the adjusted basis of the building (determined without regard to the adjustments provided in paragraphs (2) and (3) of section 1016(a)) as of the first day of such period.

(iii) IMPROVEMENTS MUST BE MADE AFTER BUILDING IN SERVICE FOR 3 YEARS.—For purposes of this paragraph, the term "substantial improvement" shall not include any improvement made before the date 3 years after the building was placed in service.

(2) RECOVERY PROPERTY USED PREDOMINANTLY OUTSIDE THE UNITED STATES.—

(A) IN GENERAL.—Except as provided in subparagraphs (B) and (C), in the case of recovery property which, during the taxable year, is used predominantly outside the United States, the recovery deduction for the taxable year shall be, in lieu of the amount determined under subsection (b), the amount determined by applying to the unadjusted basis of such property the applicable percentage determined under tables prescribed by the Secretary. For purposes of the preceding sentence, in prescribing such tables, the Secretary shall—

(i) assign the property described in this subparagraph to classes in accordance with the present class life (or 12 years in the case of personal property with no present class life) of such property;

(ii) assign percentages (taking into account the half-year convention) determined in accordance with use of the method of depreciation described in section 167(b)(2), switching to the method described in section 167(b)(1) at a time to maximize the deduction allowable under subsection (a).

(B) REAL PROPERTY.—Except as provided in subparagraph (C), in the case of 19-year real property or low-income housing which, during the taxable year, is predominantly used outside the United States, the recovery deduction for the taxable year shall be, in lieu of the amount determined under subsection (b), the amount determined by applying to the unadjusted basis of such property the applicable percentage determined under tables prescribed by the Secretary. For purposes of the preceding sentence, in prescribing such tables, the Secretary shall—

(i) assign to the property described in this subparagraph a 35-year recovery period, and

(ii) assign percentages determined in accordance with the use of the method of depreciation described in section 167(j)(1)(B), switching to the method described in section 167(b)(1) at a time to maximize the deduction allowable under subsection (a).

(C) ELECTION OF DIFFERENT RECOVERY PERCENTAGE.—

(i) GENERAL RULE.—The taxpayer may elect, with respect to one or more classes of recovery property described in this paragraph, to determine the applicable percentage under this paragraph by use of the straight-line method over the recovery period determined in accordance with the following table:

In the case of:	The taxpayer may elect a recovery period of:
3-year property	The present class life, 5 or 12 years.
5-year property	The present class life, 12 or 25 years.
10-year property	The present class life, 25 or 35 years.
15-year public utility property	The present class life, 35 or 45 years.
19-year real property or low-income housing	35 or 45 years.

(ii) OPERATING RULES.—

(I) PERIOD ELECTED BY TAXPAYER.—Except as provided in subclause (II), the taxpayer may elect under clause (i) for any taxable year only a single recovery period for recovery property described in this paragraph which is placed in service during such taxable year, which has the same present class life, and which is in the same class under subsection (c)(2). The period so elected shall not be shorter than such present class life.

(II) REAL PROPERTY.—In the case of 19-year real property or low-income housing, the election under clause (i) shall be made on a property-by-property basis.

(D) DETERMINATION OF PROPERTY USED PREDOMINANTLY OUTSIDE THE UNITED STATES.—For purposes of this paragraph, under regulations prescribed by the Secretary, rules similar to the rules under section 48(a)(2) (including the exceptions under subparagraph (B)) shall be applied in determining whether property is used predominantly outside the United States.

(E) CONVENTION.—Under regulations prescribed by the Secretary, the half year convention shall apply for purposes of any determination under subparagraph (C) (other than any determination with respect to 19-year real property or low-income housing).

(3) RRB REPLACEMENT PROPERTY.—

(A) IN GENERAL.—In the case of RRB replacement property placed in service before January 1, 1985, the recovery deduction for the taxable year shall be, in lieu of the amount determined under subsection (b), the amount determined by applying to the unadjusted basis of such property the applicable percentage determined under tables prescribed by the Secretary. For purposes of the preceding sentence, in prescribing such tables, the Secretary shall—

(i) use the recovery period determined in accordance with the following table:

Code Sec. 168

If the year property is placed in service is:	The recovery period is:
1981	1
1982	2
1983	3
1984	4

and

(ii) assign percentages determined in accordance with use of the method of depreciation described in section 167(b)(2), switching to the method described in section 167(b)(3) at a time to maximize the deduction allowable under subsection (a) (taking into account the half-year convention).

(B) RRB REPLACEMENT PROPERTY DEFINED.—For purposes of this section, the term "RRB replacement property" means replacement track material (including rail, ties, other track material, and ballast) installed by a railroad (including a railroad switching terminal company) if—

(i) the replacement is made pursuant to a scheduled program for replacement,

(ii) the replacement is made pursuant to observations by maintenance-of-way personnel of specific track material needing replacement,

(iii) the replacement is made pursuant to the detection by a rail-test car of specific track material needing replacement, or

(iv) the replacement is made as a result of a casualty.

Replacements made as a result of a casualty shall be RRB replacement property only to the extent that, in the case of each casualty, the replacement cost with respect to the replacement track material exceeds $50,000.

(4) MANNER AND TIME FOR MAKING ELECTIONS.—

(A) IN GENERAL.—Any election under this section shall be made for the taxable year in which the property is placed in service.

(B) ELECTION MADE ON RETURN.—

(i) IN GENERAL.—Except as provided in clause (ii), any election under this section shall be made on the taxpayer's return of the tax imposed by this chapter for the taxable year concerned.

(ii) SPECIAL RULE FOR QUALIFIED REHABILITATED BUILDINGS.—In the case of any qualified rehabilitated building (as defined in section 48(g)(1)), an election under subsection (b)(3) may be made at any time before the date 3 years after the building was placed in service.

(C) REVOCATION ONLY WITH CONSENT.—Any election under this section, once made, may be revoked only with the consent of the Secretary.

(5) SHORT TAXABLE YEARS.—In the case of a taxable year that is less than 12 months, the amount of the deduction under this section shall be an amount which bears the same relationship to the amount of the deduction, determined without regard to this paragraph, as the number of months in the short taxable year bears to 12. In such case, the amount of the deduction for subsequent taxable years shall be appropriately adjusted in accordance with regulations prescribed by the Secretary. The determination of when a taxable year begins shall be made in accordance with regulations prescribed by the Secretary. This paragraph shall not apply to any deduction with respect to any property for the first taxable year of the lessor for which an election under paragraph (8) is in effect with respect to such property. In the case of 19-year real property or low-income housing, the first sentence of this paragraph shall not apply to the taxable year in which the property is placed in service or disposed of.

(6) LEASEHOLD IMPROVEMENTS.—For purposes of determining whether a leasehold improvement which is recovery property shall be amortized over the term of the lease, the recovery period (taking into account any election under paragraph (2)(C) of this subsection or under subsection (b)(3) with respect to such property) of such property shall be taken into account in lieu of its useful life.

(7) SPECIAL RULE FOR ACQUISITIONS AND DISPOSITIONS IN NON-RECOGNITION TRANSACTIONS.—Notwithstanding any other provision of this section, the deduction allowed under this section in the taxable year in which recovery property is acquired or is disposed of in a transaction in which gain or loss is not recognized in whole or in part shall be determined in accordance with regulations prescribed by the Secretary.

[Caution: Code Sec. 168(f)(8), below, as amended by P.L. 97-248 and P.L. 98-369, is generally effective with respect to agreements entered into after July 1, 1982, or to property placed in service after July 1, 1982, and before 1984. But see amendment notes below for special rules.—CCH.]

(8) SPECIAL RULE FOR LEASES.—

(A) IN GENERAL.—In the case of an agreement with respect to qualified leased property, if all of the parties to the agreement characterize such agreement as a lease and elect to have the provisions of this paragraph apply with respect to such agreement, and if the requirements of subparagraph (B) are met, then, except as provided in subsection (i), for purposes of this subtitle—

(i) such agreement shall be treated as a lease entered into by the parties (and any party which is a corporation described in subparagraph (B)(i)(I) shall be deemed to have entered into the lease in the course of carrying on a trade or business), and

(ii) the lessor shall be treated as the owner of the property and the lessee shall be treated as the lessee of the property.

(B) CERTAIN REQUIREMENTS MUST BE MET.—The requirements of this subparagraph are met if—

(i) the lessor is—

(I) a corporation (other than an S corporation or a personal holding company (within the meaning of section 542(a))) which is not a related person with respect to the lessee,

(II) a partnership all of the partners of which are corporations described in subclause (I), or

(III) a grantor trust with respect to which the grantor and all beneficiaries of the trust are described in subclause (I) or (II),

(ii) the minimum investment of the lessor—

(I) at the time the property is first placed in service under the lease, and

(II) at all times during the term of the lease,

is not less than 10 percent of the adjusted basis of such property, and

(iii) the term of the lease (including any extensions) does not exceed the greater of—

(I) 120 percent of the present class life of the property, or

(II) the period equal to the recovery period determined with respect to such property under subsection (i)(2).

(C) NO OTHER FACTORS TAKEN INTO ACCOUNT.—If the requirements of subparagraphs (A) and (B) are met with respect to any transaction described in subparagraph (A), no other factors shall be taken into account in making a determination as to whether subparagraph (A)(i) or (ii) applies with respect to such transaction.

(D) QUALIFIED LEASED PROPERTY DEFINED.—For purposes of this section—

(i) IN GENERAL.—The term "qualified leased property" means recovery property—

(I) which is new section 38 property of the lessor, which is leased within 3 months after such property was placed in service, and which, if acquired by the lessee, would have been new section 38 property of the lessee, or

(II) which was new section 38 property of the lessee, which is leased within 3 months after such property is placed in service by the lessee, and with respect to which the adjusted basis of the lessor does not exceed the adjusted basis of the lessee at the time of the lease.

(ii) ONLY 45 PERCENT OF THE LESSEE'S PROPERTY MAY BE TREATED AS QUALIFIED.—The cost basis of all safe harbor lease property (determined without regard to this clause)—

(I) which is placed in service during any calendar year, and

(II) with respect to which the taxpayer is a lessee,

shall not exceed an amount equal to the 45 percent of the cost basis of the taxpayer's qualified base property placed in service during such calendar year.

(iii) ALLOCATION OF DISQUALIFIED BASIS.—The cost basis not treated as qualified leased property under clause (ii) shall be allocated to safe harbor lease property for such calendar year (determined without regard to clause (ii)) in reverse order to when the agreement described in subparagraph (A) with respect to such property was entered into.

(iv) CERTAIN PROPERTY MAY NOT BE TREATED AS QUALIFIED LEASED PROPERTY.—The term "qualified leased property" shall not include recovery property—

(I) which is a qualified rehabilitated building (within the meaning of section 48(g)(1)),

(II) which is public utility property (within the meaning of section 167(l)(3)(A)),

(III) which is property with respect to which a deduction is allowable by reason of section 291(b),

(IV) with respect to which the lessee of the property (other than property described in clause (v)) under the agreement described in subparagraph (A) is a nonqualified tax-exempt organization, or

(V) property with respect to which the user of such property is a person (other than a United States person) not subject to United States tax on income derived from the use of such property.

(v) QUALIFIED MASS COMMUTING VEHICLES INCLUDED.—The term "qualified leased property" includes recovery property which is a qualified mass commuting vehicle (as defined in section 103(b)(9)) which is financed in whole or in part by obligations the interest on which is excludable under section 103(a).

(vi) QUALIFIED BASE PROPERTY.—For purposes of this subparagraph, the term "qualified base property" means property placed in service during any calendar year which—

(I) is new section 38 property of the taxpayer,

(II) is safe harbor lease property (not described in subclause (I)) with respect to which the taxpayer is the lessee, or

(III) is designated leased property (other than property described in subclause (I) or (II)) with respect [to] which the taxpayer is the lessee.

Any designated leased property taken into account by any lessee under the preceding sentence shall not be taken into account by the lessor in determining the lessor's qualified base property. The lessor shall provide the lessee with such information with respect to the cost basis of such property as is necessary to carry out the purposes of this clause.

(vii) DEFINITION OF DESIGNATED LEASED PROPERTY.—For purposes of this subparagraph, the term "designated leased property" means property—

(I) which is new section 38 property,

(II) which is subject to a lease with respect to which the lessor of the property is treated (without regard to this paragraph) as the owner of the property for Federal tax purposes,

(III) with respect to which the term of the lease to which such property is subject is more than 50 percent of the present class life (or, if no present class life, the recovery period used in subsection (i)(2)) of such property, and

(IV) which the lessee designates on his return as designated leased property.

(viii) DEFINITION; SPECIAL RULE.—For purposes of this subparagraph—

(I) NEW SECTION 38 PROPERTY.—The term "new section 38 property" has the meaning given such term by section 48(b).

(II) PROPERTY PLACED IN SERVICE.—For purposes of this title (other than clause (i)), any property described in clause (i) to which subparagraph (A) applies shall be deemed originally placed in service not earlier than the date such property is used under the lease.

(E) MINIMUM INVESTMENT.—

(i) IN GENERAL.—For purposes of subparagraph (A), the term "minimum investment" means the amount the lessor has at risk with respect to the property (other than financing from the lessee or a related party of the lessee).

(ii) SPECIAL RULE FOR PURCHASE REQUIREMENT.—For purposes of clause (i), an agreement between the lessor and lessee requiring either or both parties to purchase or sell the qualified leased property at some price (whether or not fixed in the agreement) at the end of the lease term shall not affect the amount the lessor is treated as having at risk with respect to the property.

(F) CHARACTERIZATION BY PARTIES.—For purposes of this paragraph, any determination as to whether a person is a lessor or lessee or property is leased shall be made on the basis of the characterization of such person or property under the agreement described in subparagraph (A).

(G) REGULATIONS.—The Secretary shall prescribe such regulations as may be necessary to carry out the purposes of this paragraph, including (but not limited to) regulations consistent with such purposes which limit the aggregate amount of (and timing of) deductions and credits in respect of qualified leased property to the aggregate amount (and the timing) allowable without regard to this paragraph.

(H) DEFINITIONS.—For purposes of this paragraph—

(i) RELATED PERSON.—A person is related to another person if both persons are members of the same affiliated group (within the meaning of subsection (a) of section 1504 determined without regard to subsection (b) of section 1504).

(ii) NONQUALIFIED TAX-EXEMPT ORGANIZATION.—

(I) IN GENERAL.—The term "nonqualified tax-exempt organization" means, with respect to any agreement to which subparagraph (A) applies, any organization (or predecessor organization which was engaged in substantially similar activities) which was exempt from taxation under this title at any time during the 5-year period ending on the date such agreement was entered into.

(II) SPECIAL RULE FOR FARMERS' COOPERATIVES.—The term "nonqualified tax-exempt organization" shall not include any farmers' cooperative organization described in section 521 whether or not exempt from taxation under section 521.

(III) SPECIAL RULE FOR PROPERTY USED IN UNRELATED TRADE OR BUSINESS.—An organization shall not be treated as a nonqualified tax-exempt organization with respect to any property if such property is used in an unrelated trade or business (within the meaning of section 513) of such organization which is subject to tax under section 511.

(I) TRANSITIONAL RULES FOR CERTAIN TRANSACTIONS.—

(i) IN GENERAL.—Except as provided in clause (ii), clause (ii) of subparagraph (D) shall not apply to any transitional safe harbor lease property (within the meaning of section 208(d)(3) of the Tax Equity and Fiscal Responsibility Act of 1982).

(ii) SPECIAL RULES.—For purposes of subparagraph (D)(ii)—

(I) DETERMINATION OF QUALIFIED BASE PROPERTY.—The cost basis of property described in clause (i) (and other property placed in service during 1982 to which subparagraph (D)(ii) does not apply) shall be taken into account in determining the qualified base property of the taxpayer for the taxable year in which such property was placed in service.

(II) REDUCTION IN QUALIFIED LEASED PROPERTY.—The cost basis of property which may be treated as qualified leased property under subparagraph (D)(ii) for the taxable year in which such property was placed in service (determined without regard to this subparagraph) shall be reduced by the cost basis of the property taken into account under subclause (I).

(J) COORDINATION WITH AT RISK RULES.—

(i) IN GENERAL.—For purposes of section 465, in the case of property placed in service after the date of the enactment of this subparagraph, if—

(I) an activity involves the leasing of section 1245 property which is safe harbor lease property, and

(II) the lessee of such property (as determined under this paragraph) would, but for this paragraph, be treated as the owner of such property for purposes of this title,

then the lessor (as so determined) shall be considered to be at risk with respect to such property in an amount equal to the amount the lessee is considered at risk with respect to such property (determined under section 465 without regard to this paragraph).

(ii) SUBPARAGRAPH NOT TO APPLY TO CERTAIN SERVICE CORPORATIONS.—Clause (i) shall not apply to any lessor which is a corporation the principal function of which is the performance of services in the field of health, law, engineering, architecture, accounting, actuarial science, performing arts, athletics, or consulting.

(iii) SPECIAL RULE FOR PROPERTY PLACED IN SERVICE BEFORE DATE OF ENACTMENT OF THIS SUBPARAGRAPH.—This subparagraph shall apply to property placed in service before the date of enactment of this subparagraph if the provisions of section 465 did not apply to the lessor before such date but become applicable to such lessor after such date.

(K) CROSS REFERENCE.—

For special recapture in cases where lessee acquires qualified leased property, see section 1245.

[*Caution: Code Sec. 168(f)(8), below, as added by P.L. 97-248 and amended by P.L. 97-354 and P.L. 98-369, applies, generally, to agreements entered into after December 31, 1987. But see amendment notes below for special rules.—CCH.*]

(8) SPECIAL RULES FOR FINANCE LEASES.—

(A) IN GENERAL.—For purposes of this title, except as provided in subsection (i), in the case of any agreement with respect to any finance lease property, the fact that—

(i) a lessee has the right to purchase the property at a fixed price which is not less than 10 percent of the original cost of the property to the lessor, or

(ii) the property is of a type not readily usable by any person other than the lessee, shall not be taken into account in determining whether such agreement is a lease.

(B) FINANCE LEASE PROPERTY DEFINED.—For purposes of this section—

(i) IN GENERAL.—The term "finance lease property" means recovery property which is subject to an agreement which meets the requirements of subparagraph (C) and—

(I) which is new section 38 property of the lessor, which is leased within 3 months after such property was placed in service, and which, if acquired by the lessee, would have been new section 38 property of the lessee, or

(II) which was new section 38 property of the lessee, which is leased within 3 months after such property is placed in service by the lessee, and with respect to which the adjusted basis of the lessor does not exceed the adjusted basis of the lessee at the time of the lease.

(ii) ONLY 40 PERCENT OF THE LESSEE'S PROPERTY MAY BE TREATED AS QUALIFIED.—The cost basis of all finance lease property (determined without regard to this clause)—

(I) which is placed in service during any calendar year beginning before January 1, 1990, and

(II) with respect to which the taxpayer is a lessee,

shall not exceed an amount equal to 40 percent of the cost basis of the taxpayer's qualified base property placed in service during such calendar year.

(iii) ALLOCATION OF DISQUALIFIED BASIS.—The cost basis not treated as finance lease property under clause (ii) shall be allocated to finance lease property for such calendar year (determined without regard to clause (ii)) in reverse order to when the agreement described in subparagraph (A) with respect to such property was entered into.

(iv) CERTAIN PROPERTY MAY NOT BE TREATED AS FINANCE LEASE PROPERTY.—The term "finance lease proeprty" shall not include recovery property—

(I) which is a qualified rehabilitation building (within the meaning of section 48(g)(1)),

(II) which is public utility property (within the meaning of section 167(l)(3)(A)),

(III) which is property with respect to which a deduction is allowable by reason of section 291(b),

(IV) with respect to which the lessee of the property under the agreement described in subparagraph (A) is a nonqualified tax-exempt organization, or

(V) property with respect to which the user of such property is a person (other than a United States person) not subject to United States tax on income derived from the use of such property.

(v) QUALIFIED BASE PROPERTY.—For purposes of this subparagraph, the term "qualified base property" means property placed in service during any calendar year which—

(I) is new section 38 property of the taxpayer,

(II) is finance lease property (not described in subclause (I)) with respect to which the taxpayer is the lessee, or

(III) is designated leased property (other than property described in subclause (I) or (II)) with respect to which the taxpayer is the lessee.

Any designated leased property taken into account by any lessee under the preceding sentence shall not be taken into account by the lessor in determining the lessor's qualified base property. The lessor shall provide the lessee with such information with respect to the cost basis of such property as is necessary to carry out the purposes of this clause.

(vi) DEFINITION OF DESIGNATED LEASED PROPERTY.—For purposes of this subparagraph, the term "designated leased property" means property—

(I) which is new section 38 property,

(II) which is subject to a lease with respect to which the lessor of the property is treated (without regard to this paragraph) as the owner of the property for Federal tax purposes,

(III) with respect to which the term of the lease to which such property is subject is more than 50 percent of the present class life (or, if no present class life, the recovery period under subsection (a)) of such property, and

(IV) which the lessee designates on his return as designated leased property.

(vii) DEFINITION; SPECIAL RULES.—For purposes of this subparagraph—

(I) NEW SECTION 38 PROPERTY DEFINED.—The term "new section 38 property" has the meaning given such term by section 48(b).

(II) LESSEE LIMITATION NOT TO APPLY TO CERTAIN FARM PROPERTY.—Clause (ii) shall not apply to any property which is used for farming purposes (within the meaning of section 2032A(e)(5)) and which is placed in service during the calendar year but only if the cost basis of such property, when added to the cost basis of other finance lease property used for such purpose does not exceed $150,000 (determined under rules similar to the rules of section 209(d)(1)(B) of the Tax Equity and Fiscal Responsibility Act of 1982).

(III) PROPERTY PLACED IN SERVICE.—For purposes of this title (other than clause (i)), any finance lease property shall be deemed originally placed in service not earlier than the date such property is used under the lease.

(C) AGREEMENTS MUST MEET CERTAIN REQUIREMENTS.—The requirements of this subparagraph are met with respect to any agreement if—

(i) LESSOR REQUIREMENT.—Any lessor under the agreement must be—

(I) a corporation (other than an S corporation or a personal holding company within the meaning of section 542(a)),

(II) a partnership all of the partners of which are corporations described in subclause (I), or

(III) a grantor trust with respect to which the grantor and all the beneficiaries of the trust are described in subclause (I) or (II).

(ii) CHARACTERIZATION OF AGREEMENT.—The parties to the agreement characterize such agreement as a lease.

(iii) AGREEMENT CONTAINS CERTAIN PROVISIONS.—The agreement contains the provision described in clause (i) or (ii) of subparagraph (A), or both.

(iv) AGREEMENT OTHERWISE LEASE, ETC.—For purposes of this title (determined without regard to the provisions described in clause (iii)), the agreement would be treated as a lease and the lessor under the agreement would be treated as the owner of the property.

(D) PARAGRAPH NOT TO APPLY TO AGREEMENTS BETWEEN RELATED PERSONS.—This paragraph shall not apply to any agreement if the lessor and lessee are both persons who are members of the same affiliated group (within the meaning of subsection (a) of section 1504 and determined without regard to subsection (b) of section 1504).

(E) NONQUALIFIED TAX-EXEMPT ORGANIZATION.—

(i) IN GENERAL.—The term "nonqualified tax-exempt organization" means, with respect to any agreement to which subparagraph (A) applies, any organization (or predecessor organization which was engaged in substantially similar activities) which was exempt from taxation under this title at any time during the 5-year period ending on the date such agreement was entered into.

(ii) SPECIAL RULE FOR FARMERS' COOPERATIVES.—The term "nonqualified tax-exempt organization" shall not include any farmers' cooperative organization which is described in section 521 whether or not exempt from taxation under section 521.

(iii) SPECIAL RULE FOR PROPERTY USED IN UNRELATED TRADE OR BUSINESS.—An organization shall not be treated as a nonqualified tax-exempt organization with respect to any property if such property is used in an unrelated trade or business (within the meaning of section 513) of such organization which is subject to taxation under section 511.

(F) CROSS REFERENCE.—

For special recapture in case where lessee acquires financed recovery property, see section 1245.

(9) SALVAGE VALUE.—No salvage value shall be taken into account in determining the deduction allowable under subsection (a).

(10) TRANSFEREE BOUND BY TRANSFEROR'S PERIOD AND METHOD IN CERTAIN CASES.—

(A) IN GENERAL.—In the case of recovery property transferred in a transaction described in subparagraph (B), for purposes of computing the deduction allowable under subsection (a) with respect to so much of the basis in the hands of the transferee as does not exceed the adjusted basis in the hands of the transferor—

(i) if the transaction is described in subparagraph (B)(i), the transferee shall be treated in the same manner as the transferor, or

(ii) if the transaction is described in clause (ii) or (iii) of subparagraph (B) and the transferor made an election with respect to such property under subsection (b)(3) or (f)(2)(C), the transferee shall be treated as having made the same election (or its equivalent).

(B) TRANSFERS COVERED.—The transactions described in this subparagraph are—

(i) a transaction described in section 332, 351, 361, 371(a), 374(a), 721, or 731;

(ii) an acquisition (other than described in clause (i)) from a related person (as defined in subparagraph (D) of subsection (e)(4)); and

(iii) an acquisition followed by a leaseback to the person from whom the property is acquired.

Clause (i) shall not apply in the case of the termination of a partnership under section 708(b)(1)(B).

(C) PROPERTY REACQUIRED BY THE TAXPAYER.—Under regulations prescribed by the Secretary, recovery property which is disposed of and then reacquired by the taxpayer shall be treated for purposes of computing the deduction allowable under subsection (a) as if such property had not been disposed of.

(D) EXCEPTION.—This paragraph shall not apply to any transaction to which subsection (e)(4) applies.

(11) SPECIAL RULES FOR COOPERATIVES.—In the case of a cooperative organization described in section 1381(a), the Secretary may by regulations provide—

(A) for allowing allocation units to make separate elections under this section with respect to recovery property, and

(B) for the allocation of the deduction allowable under subsection (a) among allocation units.

(12) LIMITATIONS ON PROPERTY FINANCED WITH TAX-EXEMPT BONDS.—

(A) IN GENERAL.—Notwithstanding any other provision of this section, to the extent that any property is financed by the proceeds of an industrial development bond (within the meaning of section 103(b)(2)) the interest of which is exempt from taxation under section 103(a), the deduction allowed under subsection (a) (and any deduction allowable in lieu of the deduction allowable under subsection (a)) for any taxable year with respect to such property shall be determined under subparagraph (B).

(B) RECOVERY METHOD.—

(i) IN GENERAL.—Except as provided in clause (ii), the amount of the deduction allowed with respect to property described in subparagraph (A) shall be determined by using the straight-line method (with a half-year convention and without regard to salvage value) and a recovery period determined in accordance with the following table:

In the case of:	The recovery period is:
3-year property	3 years.
5-year property	5 years.
10-year property	10 years.
15-year public utility property	15 years.

(ii) 19-YEAR REAL PROPERTY.—In the case of 19-year real property, the amount of the deduction allowed shall be determined by using the straight-line method (without regard to salvage value) and a recovery period of 19 years.

(C) EXCEPTION FOR LOW- AND MODERATE-INCOME HOUSING.—Subparagraph (A) shall not apply to—

(i) any low-income housing, and

(ii) any other recovery property which is placed in service in connection with projects for residential rental property financed by the proceeds of obligations described in section 103(b)(4)(A).

(D) EXCEPTION WHERE LONGER RECOVERY PERIOD APPLICABLE.—Subparagraph (A) shall not apply to any recovery property if the recovery period which would be applicable to such property by reason of an election under subsection (b)(3) exceeds the recovery period for such property determined under subparagraph (B).

(13) CHANGES IN USE.—The Secretary shall, by regulation, provide for the method of determining the deduction allowable under subsection (a) with respect to any property for any taxable year (and for succeeding taxable years) during which such property changes status under this section but continues to be held by the same person.

(14) MOTOR VEHICLE OPERATING LEASES.—

(A) IN GENERAL.—For purposes of this title, in the case of a qualified motor vehicle operating agreement which contains a terminal rental adjustment clause—

(i) such agreement shall be treated as a lease if (but for such terminal rental adjustment clause) such agreement would be treated as a lease under this title, and

(ii) the lessee shall not be treated as the owner of the property subject to an agreement during any period such agreement is in effect.

(B) QUALIFIED MOTOR VEHICLE OPERATING AGREEMENT DEFINED.—For purposes of this paragraph—

(i) IN GENERAL.—The term "qualified motor vehicle operating agreement" means any agreement with respect to a motor vehicle (including a trailer) which meets the requirements of clauses (ii), (iii), and (iv) of this subparagraph.

(ii) MINIMUM LIABILITY OF LESSOR.—An agreement meets the requirements of this clause if under such agreement the sum of—

(I) the amount the lessor is personally liable to repay, and

(II) the net fair market value of the lessor's interest in any property pledged as security for property subject to the agreement,

equals or exceeds all amounts borrowed to finance the acquisition of property subject to the agreement. There shall not be taken into account under subclause (II) any property pledged which is property subject to the agreement or property directly or indirectly financed by indebtedness secured by property subject to the agreement.

(iii) CERTIFICATION BY LESSEE; NOTICE OF TAX OWNERSHIP.—An agreement meets the requirements of this clause if such agreement contains a separate written statement separately signed by the lessee—

(I) under which the lessee certifies, under penalty of perjury, that it intends that more than 50 percent of the use of the property subject to such agreement is to be in a trade or business of the lessee, and

(II) which clearly and legibly states that the lessee has been advised that it will not be treated as the owner of the property subject to the agreement for Federal income tax purposes.

(iv) LESSOR MUST HAVE NO KNOWLEDGE THAT CERTIFICATION IS FALSE.—An agreement meets the requirements of this clause if the lessor does not know that the certification described in clause (iii)(I) is false.

(C) TERMINAL RENTAL ADJUSTMENT CLAUSE DEFINED.—

(i) IN GENERAL.—For purposes of this paragraph, the term "terminal rental adjustment clause" means a provision of an agreement which permits or requires the rental price to be adjusted upward or downward by reference to the amount realized by the lessor under the agreement upon sale or other disposition of such property.

(ii) SPECIAL RULE FOR LESSEE DEALERS.—The term "terminal rental adjustment clause" also includes a provision of an agreement which requires a lessee who is a dealer in motor vehicles to purchase the motor vehicle for a predetermined price and then resell such vehicle where such provision achieves substantially the same results as a provision described in clause (i).

(15) SPECIAL RULES FOR SOUND RECORDINGS.—In the case of a sound recording (within the meaning of section 48(r)), the unadjusted basis of such property shall be equal to the production costs (within the meaning of section 48(r)(6)).

Amendments

• 1985 (P.L. 99-121)

P.L. 99-121, §103(b)(3)(A):

Amended Code Sec. 168(f)(1)(B) by redesignating clause (iii) as clause (iv) and by inserting after clause (ii) new clause (iii). **Effective** with respect to property placed in service by the taxpayer after 5-8-85. However, for an exception and special rule, see Act Sec. 105(b)(2) and (3), below.

P.L. 99-121, §103(b)(3)(B):

Amended Code Sec. 168(f)(1)(B)(ii) by striking out "March 15, 1984, the" and inserting in lieu thereof "March 15, 1984, and before May 9, 1985, the". **Effective** with respect to property placed in service by the taxpayer after 5-8-85. However, for an exception and special rule, see Act Sec. 105(b)(2) and (3), below.

P.L. 99-121, §103(b)(3)(C):

Amended Code Sec. 168(f)(1)(B)(iv), as redesignated by Act Sec. 103(b)(3)(A), by striking out "or (ii)" and inserting in lieu thereof ", (ii), or (iii)". **Effective** with respect to property placed in service by the taxpayer after 5-8-85. However, for an exception and special rule, see Act Sec. 105(b)(2) and (3), below.

P.L. 99-121, §103(b)(4)(A) and (B):

Amended Code Sec. 168(f)(12)(B)(ii) by striking out "15-year real property" each place it appears in the heading and the text and inserting in lieu thereof "19-year real property", and by striking out "15 years" and inserting in lieu thereof "19 years." **Effective** with respect to property placed in service by the taxpayer after 5-8-85. However, for an exception and special rule, see Act Sec. 105(b)(2) and (3), below.

P.L. 99-121, § 105(b)(2) and (3), provides:

(2) EXCEPTION.—The amendments made by section 103 shall not apply to property placed in service by the taxpayer before January 1, 1987, if—

(A) the taxpayer or a qualified person entered into a binding contract to purchase or construct such property before May 9, 1985, or

(B) construction of such property was commenced by or for the taxpayer or a qualified person before May 9, 1985.

For purposes of this paragraph, the term "qualified person" means any person whose rights in such a contract or such property are transferred to the taxpayer, but only if such property is not placed in service before such rights are transferred to the taxpayer.

(3) SPECIAL RULE FOR COMPONENTS.—For purposes of applying section 168(f)(1)(B) of the Internal Revenue Code of 1954 (as amended by section 103) to components placed in service after December 31, 1986, property to which paragraph (2) of this subsection applies shall be treated as placed in service by the taxpayer before May 9, 1985.

- **1984, Deficit Reduction Act of 1984 (P.L. 98-369)**

P.L. 98-369, § 12(a)(3):

Amended Code Sec. 168(f)(8)(B)(ii)(I) by striking out "1986" and inserting in lieu thereof "1990". **Effective**, generally, for tax years beginning after 12-31-83. See, however, Act Sec. 12(b)-(c), below.

P.L. 98-369, § 12(b)-(c), as amended by P.L. 99-514, § 1801(a)(1) and P.L. 100-647, § 1002(d)(7)(B), provides:

(b) Termination of Safe Harbor Leasing Rules.—Paragraph (8) of section 168(f) of the Internal Revenue Code of 1954 (relating to special rules for leasing), as in effect after the amendments made by section 208 of the Tax Equity and Fiscal Responsibility Act of 1982 but before the amendments made by section 209 of such Act, shall not apply to agreements entered into after December 31, 1983. The preceding sentence shall not apply to property described in paragraph (3)(G) or (5) of section 208(d) of such Act.

(c) Transitional Rules.—

(1) In General.—The amendments made by subsection (a) shall not apply with respect to any property if—

(A) A binding contract to acquire or to construct such property was entered into by or for the lessee before March 7, 1984, or

(B) such property was acquired by the lessee, or the construction of such property was begun, by or for the lessee, before March 7, 1984.

The preceding sentence shall not apply to any property with respect to which an election is made under this sentence at such time after the date of the enactment of the Tax Reform Act of 1986 as the Secretary of the Treasury or his delegate may prescribe.

(2) Special rule for certain automotive property.—

(A) In General.—The amendments made by subsection (a) shall not apply to property—

(i) which is automotive manufacturing property, and

(ii) with respect to which the lessee is a qualified lessee (within the meaning of section 208(d)(6) of the Tax Equity and Fiscal Responsibility Act of 1982).

(B) $150,000,000 limitation.—The provisions of subparagraph (A) shall not apply to any agreement if the sum of—

(i) the cost basis of the property subject to the agreement, plus

(ii) the cost basis of any property subject to an agreement to which subparagraph (A) previously applied and with respect to which the lessee was the lessee under the agreement described in clause (i) (or any related person within the meaning of section 168(e)(4)(D) of the Internal Revenue Code of 1954),

exceeds $150,000,000.

(C) Automotive Manufacturing Property.—For purposes of this paragraph, the term "automotive manufacturing property" means—

(i) property used principally by the taxpayer directly in connection with the trade or business of the taxpayer of the manufacturing of automobiles or trucks (other than truck tractors) with a gross vehicle weight of 13,000 pounds or less,

(ii) machinery, equipment, and special tools of the type included in former depreciation range guideline classes 37.11 and 37.12, and

(iii) any special tools owned by the taxpayer which are used by a vendor solely for the production of component parts for sale to the taxpayer.

(3) Special rule for certain cogeneration facilities.—The amendments made by subsection (a) shall not apply with respect to any property which is part of a coal-fired cogeneration facility—

(A) for which an application for a certification was filed with the Federal Energy Regulatory Commission on December 30, 1983,

(B) for which an application for a construction permit was filed with a State environmental protection agency on February 20, 1984, and

(C) which is placed in service before January 1, 1988.

P.L. 98-369, § 32(a):

Amended Code Sec. 168(f) by adding at the end thereof new paragraph (13)[14]. **Effective** for agreements described in Code Sec. 168(f)(14) (as added by Act Sec. 32(a)) entered into more than 90 days after 7-18-84.

P.L. 98-369, § 111(c):

Amended Code Sec. 168(f)(1)(B). For the **effective** date as well as special rules, see Act Sec. 111(g)[(f)], below. Prior to amendment, it read as follows:

(B) Transitional Rule.—In the case of any building placed in service by the taxpayer before January 1, 1981, for purposes of applying subparagraph (A) to components of such buildings placed in service after December 31, 1980, the deduction allowable under subsection (a) with respect to such components shall be computed in the same manner as the deduction allowable with respect to the first such component placed in service after December 31, 1980. For purposes of the preceding sentence, the method of computing the deduction allowable with respect to such first component shall be determined as if it were a separate building.

P.L. 98-369, § 111(e)(1):

Amended Code Sec. 168(b)(3)(B)(iii), (f)(2)(B), (f)(2)(C)(ii)(II), (f)(2)(E), and (f)(5) by striking out "15-year real property" each place it appears and inserting in lieu thereof "18-year real property or low-income housing". For the **effective** date as well as special rules, see Act Sec. 111(g)[(f)] below.

P.L. 98-369, § 111(e)(4):

Amended Code Sec. 168(f)(2)(C)(i) by striking out the item relating to 15-year real property in the table and inserting in lieu thereof: "18-year real property or low-income housing: 35 or 45 years.". For the **effective** date as well as special rules, see Act Sec. 111(g)[(f)], below.

P.L. 98-369, § 111(g)[(f)], provides:

[(f)] Effective Date.—

(1) In General.—Except as otherwise provided in this subsection, the amendments made by this section shall apply with respect to property placed in service by the taxpayer after March 15, 1984.

(2) Exception.—The amendments made by this section shall not apply to property placed in service by the taxpayer before January 1, 1987, if—

(A) the taxpayer or a qualified person entered into a binding contract to purchase or construct such property before March 16, 1984, or

(B) construction of such property was commenced by or for the taxpayer or a qualified person before March 16, 1984.

For purposes of this paragraph the term "qualified person" means any person who transfers his rights in such a contract or such property to the taxpayer, but only if the property is not placed in service by such person before such rights are transferred to the taxpayer.

(3) Special Rules for Application of Paragraph (2).—

(A) Certain Inventory.—In the case of any property which—

(i) is held by a person as property described in section 1221(1), and

(ii) is disposed of by such person before January 1, 1985, such person shall not, for purposes of paragraph (2), be treated as having placed such property in service before such property is disposed of merely because such person rented such property or held such property for rental.

No deduction for depreciation or amortization shall be allowed to such person with respect to such property,

(B) Certain Property Financed By Bonds.—In the case of any property with respect to which—

(i) bonds were issued to finance such property before 1984, and

(ii) an architectural contract was entered into before March 16, 1984,

paragraph (2) shall be applied by substituting "May 2" for "March 16".

(4) Special Rule for Components.—For purposes of applying section 168(f)(1)(B) of the Internal Revenue Code of 1954 (as amended by this section) to components placed in service after December 31, 1986, property to which paragraph (2) applies shall be treated as placed in service by the taxpayer before March 16, 1984.

(5) Special rule for mid-month convention.—In the case of the amendment made by subsection (d)—

(A) paragraph (1) shall be applied by substituting "June 22, 1984" for "March 15, 1984", and

(B) paragraph (2) shall be applied by substituting "June 23, 1984" for "March 15, 1984" each place it appears.

P.L. 98-369, §113(a)(2):

Amended Code Sec. 168(f) (as amended by this Act) by adding at the end thereof new paragraph (14)[15]. **Effective** for property placed in service after 3-15-84, in tax years ending after such date.

P.L. 98-369, §628(b)(1):

Amended Code Sec. 168(f)(12)(C). **Effective** for property placed in service after 12-31-83, to the extent such property is financed by the proceeds of an obligation (including a refunding obligation) issued after 10-18-83. However, see the exceptions provided by Act Sec. 631(b)(2), below. Prior to amendment, it read as follows:

(C) Exceptions.—Subparagraph (A) shall not apply to any recovery property which is placed in service—

(i) in connection with projects for residential rental property financed by the proceeds of obligations described in section 103(b)(4)(A),

(ii) in connection with a sewage or solid waste disposal facility—

(I) which provides sewage of solid waste disposal services for the residents of part or all of 1 or more governmental units, and

(II) with respect to which substantially all of the sewage or solid waste processed is collected from the general public,

(iii) as an air or water pollution control facility which is—

(I) installed in connection with an existing facility, or

(II) installed in connection with the conversion of an existing facility which uses oil or natural gas (or any product of oil or natural gas) as a primary fuel to a facility which uses coal as a primary fuel, or

(iv) in connection with a facility with respect to which an urban development action grant has been made under section 119 of the Housing and Community Development Act of 1974.

P.L. 98-369, §628(b)(2):

Amended Code Sec. 168(f)(12) by striking out subparagraph (D) and by redesignating subparagraph (E) as subparagraph (D). **Effective** for property placed in service after 12-31-83, to the extent such property is financed by the proceeds of an obligation (including a refunding obligation) issued after 10-18-83. However, see the exceptions provided by Act Sec. 631(b)(2), below. Prior to amendment Code Sec. 168(f)(12)(D) read as follows:

(D) Existing Facility.—For purposes of this paragraph, the term "existing facility" means a plant or property in operation before July 1, 1982.

P.L. 98-369, §631(b)(2), provides:

(b) Property Financed With Tax-Exempt Bonds Required To Be Depreciated on Straight-Line Basis.—

* * *

(2) Exceptions.—

(A) Construction or binding agreement.—The amendments made by section 628(b) shall not apply with respect to facilities—

(i) the original use of which commences with the taxpayer and the construction, reconstruction, or rehabilitation of which began before October 19, 1983, or

(ii) with respect to which a binding contract to incur significant expenditures was entered into before October 19, 1983.

(B) Refunding.—

(i) In General.—Except as provided in clause (ii), in the case of property placed in service after December 31, 1983, which is financed by the proceeds of an obligation which is issued solely to refund another obligation which was issued before October 19, 1983, the amendments made by section 628(b) shall apply only with respect to an amount equal to the basis in such property which has not been recovered before the date such refunded obligation is issued.

(ii) Significant expenditures.—In the case of facilities the original use of which commences with the taxpayer and with respect to which significant expenditures are made before January 1, 1984, the amendments made by section 628(b) shall not apply with respect to such facilities to the extent such facilities are financed by the proceeds of an obligation issued solely to refund another obligation which was issued before October 19, 1983.

(C) Facilities.—In the case of an inducement resolution or other comparable preliminary approval adopted by an issuing authority before October 19, 1983, for purposes of applying subparagraphs (A)(i) and (B)(ii) with respect to obligations described in such resolution, the term "facilities" means the facilities described in such resolution.

• **1983, Technical Corrections Act of 1982 (P.L. 97-448)**

P.L. 97-448, §102(a)(1):

Amended Code Sec. 168(f)(5) by adding the last sentence. **Effective** as if such it had been included in the provision of P.L. 97-34 to which it relates.

P.L. 97-448, §102(a)(3):

Amended Code Sec. 168(f) by adding at the end thereof new paragraph (13). **Effective** as if it had been included in the provision of P.L. 97-34 to which it relates.

P.L. 97-448, §102(a)(10)(A):

Amended Code Sec. 168(f)(8)(D), as in effect before the amendments made by P.L. 97-248, by adding the last sentence below. **Effective** with respect to property to which the provisions of Code Sec. 168(f)(8) (as in effect before the amendments made by P.L. 97-248) apply.

P.L. 97-448, §102(f)(4):

Amended Code Sec. 168(f)(4)(B). **Effective** as if it had been included in the provision of P.L. 97-34 to which it relates. Prior to amendment, Code Sec. 168(f)(4)(B) read as follows:

"(B) Made on return.—Any election under this section shall be made on the taxpayer's return of the tax imposed by this chapter for the taxable year concerned."

• **1982, Subchapter S Revision Act of 1982 (P.L. 97-354)**

P.L. 97-354, §5(a)(19):

Amended Code Sec. 168(f)(8)(B)(i)(I), as in effect before the enactment of P.L. 97-248 by striking out "an electing small business corporation (within the meaning of section 1371(b))" and inserting in lieu thereof "an S corporation". **Effective** for tax years beginning after 1982.

P.L. 97-354, §5(a)(20):

Amended Code Sec. 168(f)(8)(C)(i)(I) (as added by subsection (a) of section 209 of the Tax Equity and Fiscal Responsibility Act of 1982) by striking out "an electing small business corporation (within the meaning of section 1371(b))" and inserting in lieu thereof "an S corporation". **Effective** for tax years beginning after 1982 with respect to agreements entered into after 1983.

• **1982, Tax Equity and Fiscal Responsibility Act of 1982 (P.L. 97-248)**

P.L. 97-248, §208(a)(2)(A):

Amended Code Sec. 168(f)(8)(A) by inserting "except as provided in subsection (i)," before "for purposes of this subtitle". **Effective** for agreements entered into after 7-1-82, or to property placed in service after 7-1-82. For transitional rules, see amendment notes for P.L. 97-248, Act Sec. 208(d)(2)-(6)[7], following former Code Sec. 168(i).

P.L. 97-248, §208(b)(1):

Amended Code Sec. 168(f)(8)(B)(i)(I) by inserting "which is not a related person with respect to the lessee" before the comma at the end thereof. **Effective** for agreements entered into after 7-1-82, or to property placed in service after 7-1-82. For transitional rules, see amendment notes for P.L. 97-248, Act Sec. 208(d)(2)-(6)[7], following former Code Sec. 168(i).

P.L. 97-248, §208(b)(2):

Amended Code Sec. 168(f)(8)(B)(iii). **Effective** for agreements entered into after 7-1-82, or to property placed in service after 7-1-82. For transitional rules, see amendment notes for P.L. 97-248, Act Sec. 208(d)(2)-(6)[7], following former Code Sec. 168(i). Prior to amendment, it read as follows:

"(iii) the term of the lease (including any extensions) does not exceed the greater of—

Code Sec. 168

(I) 90 percent of the useful life of such property for purposes of section 167, or

(II) 150 percent of the present class life of such property."

P.L. 97-248, §208(b)(3), as amended by P.L. 97-448, §102(a)(10)(A):

Amended Code Sec. 168(f)(8)(D). **Effective** for property placed in service after 12-31-80, in tax years ending after such date. For transitional rules, see amendment notes for P.L. 97-248, Act Sec. 208(d)(2)-(6)[7], following former Code Sec. 168(i). Prior to amendment by P.L. 97-248, but after amendment by P.L. 97-448, it read as follows:

"(D) Qualified leased property defined.—For purposes of subparagraph (A), the term 'qualified leased property' means recovery property (other than a qualified rehabilitated building within the meaning of section 48(g)(1)) which is—

(i) new section 38 property (as defined in section 48(b)) of the lessor which is leased within 3 months after such property was placed in service and which, if acquired by the lessee, would have been new section 38 property of the lessee,

(ii) property—

(I) which was new section 38 property of the lessee,

(II) which was leased within 3 months after such property was placed in service by the lessee, and

(III) with respect to which the adjusted basis of the lessor does not exceed the adjusted basis of the lessee at the time of the lease, or

(iii) property which is a qualified mass commuting vehicle (as defined in section 103(b)(9)) and which is financed in whole or in part by obligations the interest on which is excludable from income under section 103(a).

For purposes of this title (other than this subparagraph), any property described in clause (i) or (ii) to which subparagraph (A) applies shall be deemed originally placed in service not earlier than the date such property is used under the lease. In the case of property placed in service after December 31, 1980, and before the date of the enactment of this subparagraph, this subparagraph shall be applied by submitting [substituting] 'the date of the enactment of this subparagraph' for 'such property was placed in service'. Under regulations prescribed by the Secretary, public utility property shall not be treated as qualified leased property unless the requirements of rules similar to the rules of subsection (e)(3) of this section and section 46(f) are met with respect to such property."

P.L. 97-248, §208(b)(4):

Amended Code Sec. 168(f)(8) by redesignating subparagraph (H) as subparagraph (K) and by inserting after subparagraph (G) new subparagraphs (H), (I) and (J). **Effective** for agreements entered into after 7-1-82, or to property placed in service after 7-1-82. For transitional rules, see amendment notes for P.L. 97-248, Act Sec. 208(d)(2)-(6)[7], following Code Sec. 168(i).

P.L. 97-248, §208(c), provides:

(c) Certain Leases Before October 20, 1981, Treated as Qualified Leases.—Nothing in paragraph (8) of section 168(f) of the Internal Revenue Code of 1954, or in any regulations prescribed thereunder, shall be treated as making such paragraph inapplicable to any agreement entered into before October 20, 1981, solely because under such agreement 1 party to such agreement is entitled to the credit allowable under section 38 of such Code with respect to property and another party to such agreement is entitled to the deduction allowable under section 168 of such Code with respect to such property. Section 168(f)(8)(B)(ii) of such Code shall not apply to the party entitled to such credit.

P.L. 97-248, §209(a):

Amended Code Sec. 168(f)(8). **Effective** for agreements entered into after 12-31-87. However, see Act Sec. 209(d)(1)(B), below. Prior to amendment by P.L. 97-248 but after the amendment made by P.L. 97-354, §5(a)(19), it read as follows:

"(8) Special rule for leases.—

(A) In general.—In the case of an agreement with respect to qualified leased property, if all of the parties to the agreement characterize such agreement as a lease and elect to have the provisions of this paragraph apply with respect to such agreement, and if the requirements of subparagraph (B) are met, then, for purposes of this subtitle—

(i) such agreement shall be treated as a lease entered into by the parties (and any party which is a corporation described in subparagraph (B)(i)(I) shall be deemed to have entered into the lease in the course of carrying on a trade or business), and

(ii) the lessor shall be treated as the owner of the property and the lessee shall be treated as the lessee of the property.

(B) Certain requirements must be met.—The requirements of this subparagraph are met if—

(i) the lessor is—

(I) a corporation (other than an S corporation or a personal holding company (within the meaning of section 542(a))),

(II) a partnership all of the partners of which are corporations described in subclause (I), or

(III) a grantor trust with respect to which the grantor and all beneficiaries of the trust are described in subclause (I) or (II),

(ii) the minimum investment of the lessor—

(I) at the time the property is first placed in service under the lease, and

(II) at all times during the term of the lease, is not less than 10 percent of the adjusted basis of such property, and

(iii) the term of the lease (including any extensions) does not exceed the greater of—

(I) 90 percent of the useful life of such property for purposes of section 167, or

(II) 150 percent of the present class life of such property.

(C) No other factors taken into account.—If the requirements of subparagraphs (A) and (B) are met with respect to any transaction described in subparagraph (A), no other factors shall be taken into account in making a determination as to whether subparagraph (A)(i) or (ii) applies with respect to such transaction.

(D) Qualified leased property defined.—For purposes of subparagraph (A), the term "qualified leased property" means recovery property (other than a qualified rehabilitated building within the meaning of section 48(g)(1)) which is—

(i) new section 38 property (as defined in section 48(b)) of the lessor which is leased within 3 months after such property was placed in service and which, if acquired by the lessee, would have been new section 38 property of the lessee,

(ii) property—

(I) which was new section 38 property of the lessee,

(II) which was leased within 3 months after such property was placed in service by the lessee, and

(III) with respect to which the adjusted basis of the lessor does not exceed the adjusted basis of the lessee at the time of the lease, or

(iii) property which is a qualified mass commuting vehicle (as defined in section 103(b)(9)) and which is financed in whole or in part by obligations the interest on which is excludable from income under section 103(a).

For purposes of this title (other than this subparagraph), any property described in clause (i) or (ii) to which subparagraph (A) applies shall be deemed originally placed in service not earlier than the date such property is used under the lease. In the case of property placed in service after December 31, 1980, and before the date of the enactment of this subparagraph, this subparagraph shall be applied by submitting "the date of the enactment of this subparagraph" for "such property was placed in service".

(E) Minimum investment.—

(i) In general.—For purposes of subparagraph (A), the term "minimum investment" means the amount the lessor has at risk with respect to the property (other than financing from the lessee or a related party of the lessee).

(ii) Special rule for purchase requirement.—For purposes of clause (i), an agreement between the lessor and lessee requiring either or both parties to purchase or sell the qualified leased property at some price (whether or not fixed in the agreement) at the end of the lease term shall not affect the amount the lessor is treated as having at risk with respect to the property.

(F) Characterization by parties.—For purposes of this paragraph, any determination as to whether a person is a lessor or lessee or property is leased shall be made on the basis of the characterization of such person or property under the agreement described in subparagraph (A).

(G) Regulations.—The Secretary shall prescribe such regulations as may be necessary to carry out the purposes of this paragraph, including (but not limited to) regulations consistent with such purposes which limit the aggregate amount of (and timing of) deductions and credits in respect of qualified leased property to the aggregate amount (and the timing) allowable without regard to this paragraph.

(H) Cross reference.—"

P.L. 97-248, §209(d)(1)(B), as amended by P.L. 98-369, §12(a), provides:

(B) Special rule for farm property aggregating $150,000 or less.—

(i) In general.—The amendments made by subsection (a) shall also apply to any agreement entered into after July 1, 1982, and before January 1, 1988, if the property subject to such agreement is section 38 property which is used for farming purposes (within the meaning of section 2032A(e)(5)).

(ii) $150,000 limitation.—The provisions of clause (i) shall not apply to any agreement if the sum of—

(I) the cost basis of the property subject to the agreement, plus

(II) the cost basis of any property subject to an agreement to which this subparagraph previously applied, which was entered into during the same calendar year, and with respect to which the lessee was the lessee of the agreement described in subclause (I) (or any related person within the meaning of section 168(e)(4)(D)), exceeds $150,000. For purposes of subclause (II), in the case of an individual, there shall not be taken into account any agreement of any individual who is a related person involving property which is used in a trade or business of farming of such related person which is separate from the trade or business of farming of the lessee described in subclause (II).

P.L. 97-248, §210, as amended by P.L. 98-369, §§32(b) and 712(d)(1), (2), provides:

SEC. 210 MOTOR VEHICLE OPERATING LEASES.

(a) In General.—In the case of any qualified motor vehicle agreement entered into on or before the 90th day after the date of the enactment of the Tax Reform Act of 1984, the fact that such agreement contains a terminal rental adjustment clause shall not be taken into account in determining whether such agreement is a lease.

(b) Definitions.—For purposes of this section—

(1) Qualified motor vehicle agreement.—The term "qualified motor vehicle agreement" means any agreement with respect to a motor vehicle (including a trailer)—

(A) which was entered into before—

(i) the enactment of any law, or

(ii) the publication by the Secretary of the Treasury or his delegate of any regulation, which provides that any agreement with a terminal rental adjustment clause is not a lease,

(B) with respect to which the lessor under the agreement—

(i) is personally liable for the repayment of, or

(ii) has pledged property (but only to the extent of the net fair market value of the lessor's interest in such property), other than property subject to the agreement or property directly or indirectly financed by indebtedness secured by property subject to the agreement, as security for,

all amounts borrowed to finance the acquisition of property subject to the agreement, and

(C) with respect to which the lessee under the agreement uses the property subject to the agreement in a trade or business or for the production of income.

(2) Terminal rental adjustment clause.—The term "terminal rental adjustment clause" means a provision of an agreement which permits or requires the rental price to be adjusted upward or downward by reference to the amount realized by the lessor under the agreement upon sale or other disposition of such property. Such term also includes a provision of an agreement which requires a lessee who is a dealer in motor vehicles to purchase the motor vehicle for a predetermined price and then resell such vehicle where such provision achieves substantially the same results as a provision described in the preceding sentence.

(c) Exception Where Lessee Took Position on Return.—Subsection (a) shall not apply to any deduction for interest paid or accrued claimed by a lessee with respect to a qualified motor vehicle agreement on a return of tax imposed by chapter 1 of the Internal Revenue Code of 1954 which was filed before the date of the enactment of this Act or to deny a credit for investment in depreciable property claimed by the lessee on such a return pursuant to an agreement with the lessor that the lessor would not claim the credit.

P.L. 97-248, §216(a):

Amended Code Sec. 168(f) by adding new paragraph (12). **Effective** with respect to property placed in service after 12-31-82, to the extent such property is financed by the proceeds of an obligation issued after 6-30-82. However, Act Sec. 216(b)(2) provides as follows:

(2) Exceptions.—

(A) Construction or binding agreement.—The amendments made by this section shall not apply with respect to facilities the original use of which commences with the taxpayer and—

(i) the construction, reconstruction, or rehabilitation of which began before July 1, 1982, or

(ii) with respect to which a binding agreement to incur significant expenditures was entered into before July 1, 1982.

(B) Refunding.—

(i) In general.—Except as provided in clause (ii), in the case of property placed in service after December 31, 1982 which is financed by the proceeds of an obligation which is issued solely to refund another obligation which was issued before July 1, 1982, the amendments made by this section shall apply only with respect to the basis in such property which has not been recovered before the date such refunding obligation is issued.

(ii) Significant expenditures.—In the case of facilities the original use of which commences with the taxpayer and with respect to which significant expenditures are made before January 1, 1983, the amendments made by this section shall not apply with respect to such facilities to the extent such facilities are financed by the proceeds of an obligation issued solely to refund another obligation which was issued before July 1, 1982.

In the case of an inducement resolution adopted by an issuing authority before July 1, 1982, for purposes of applying subparagraphs (A)(i) and (B)(ii) with respect to obligations described in such resolution, the term "facilities" means the facilities described in such resolution.

P.L. 97-248, §216(b)(3), provides:

(3) Certain projects for residential real property.—For purposes of clause (i) of section 168(f)(12)(C) of the Internal Revenue Code of 1954 (as added by this section), any obligation issued to finance a project described in the table contained in paragraph (1) of section 1104(n) of the Mortgage Subsidy Bond Tax Act of 1980 shall be treated as an obligation described in section 103(b)(4)(A) of the Internal Revenue Code of 1954.

P.L. 97-248, §224(c)(2):

Amended Code Sec. 168(f)(10)(B)(i) by striking out "(other than a transaction with respect to which the basis is determined under section 334(b)(2))." **Effective** for any target corporation (within the meaning of Code Sec. 338) with respect to which the acquisition date (within the meaning of such section) occurs after 8-31-82. For a special rule, see amendment notes under Code Sec. 338, as added by P.L. 97-248, Act Sec. 224.

• **1981, Black Lung Benefits Revenue Act of 1981 (P.L. 97-119)**

P.L. 97-119, §112, provides:

SEC. 112. INFORMATION RETURNS WITH RESPECT TO SAFE HARBOR LEASES.

(a) REQUIREMENT OF RETURN.—

(1) IN GENERAL.—Except as provided in paragraph (2), paragraph (8) of section 168(f) of the Internal Revenue Code of 1954 (relating to special rule for leases) shall not apply with respect to an agreement unless a return, signed by the lessor and lessee and containing the information required to be included in the return pursuant to subsection (b), has been filed with the Internal Revenue Service not later than the 30th day after the date on which the agreement is executed.

(2) SPECIAL RULES FOR AGREEMENTS EXECUTED BEFORE JANUARY 1, 1982.—

(A) IN GENERAL.—In the case of an agreement executed before January 1, 1982, such agreement shall cease on February 1, 1982, to be treated as a lease under section 168(f)(8) unless a return, signed by the lessor and containing the information required to be included in subsection (b), has been filed with the Internal Revenue Service not later than January 31, 1982.

(B) FILING BY LESSEE.—If the lessor does not file a return under subparagraph (A), the return requirement under subparagraph (A) shall be satisfied if such return is filed by the Lessee before January 31, 1982.

(3) CERTAIN FAILURE TO FILE.—If—

(A) a lessor or lessee fails to file any return within the time prescribed by this subsection, and

(B) such failure is shown to be due to reasonable cause and not due to willful neglect,

the lessor or lessee shall be treated as having filed a timely return if a return is filed within a reasonable time after the failure is ascertained.

(b) INFORMATION REQUIRED.—The information required to be included in the return pursuant to this subsection is as follows:

(1) The name, address, and taxpayer identifying number of the lessor and the lessee (and parent company if a consolidated return is filed);

(2) The district director's office with which the income tax returns of the lessor and lessee are filed;

(3) A description of each individual property with respect to which the election is made;

(4) The date on which the lessee places the property in service, the date on which the lease begins and the term of the lease;

(5) The recovery property class and the ADR midpoint life of the leased property;

(6) The payment terms between the parties to the lease transaction;

(7) Whether the ACRS deductions and the investment tax credit are allowable to the same taxpayer;

(8) The aggregate amount paid to outside parties to arrange or carry out the transaction;

(9) For the lessor only: the unadjusted basis of the property as defined in section 168(d)(1);

(10) For the lessor only: if the lessor is a partnership or a grantor trust, the name, address, and taxpayer identifying number of the partners or the beneficiaries, and the district director's office with which the income tax return of each partner or beneficiary is filed; and

(11) Such other information as may be required by the return or its instructions.

Paragraph (8) shall not apply with respect to any person for any calendar year if it is reasonable to estimate that the aggregate adjusted basis of the property of such person which will be subject to subsection (a) for such year is $1,000,000 or less.

(c) COORDINATION WITH OTHER INFORMATION REQUIREMENTS.—In the case of agreements executed after December 31, 1982, to the extent provided in regulations prescribed by the Secretary of the Treasury or his delegate, the provisions of this section shall be modified to coordinate such provisions with other information requirements of the Internal Revenue Code of 1954.

- **1981, Economic Recovery Tax Act of 1981 (P.L. 97-34)**

P.L. 97-34, § 201(a):

Added Code Sec. 168(f). **Effective** for property placed in service after 12-31-80, in tax years ending after such date.

[Sec. 168(g)]

(g) DEFINITIONS.—For purposes of this section—

(1) PUBLIC UTILITY PROPERTY.—The term "public utility property" means property described in section 167(l)(3)(A).

(2) PRESENT CLASS LIFE.—The term "present class life" means the class life (if any) which would be applicable with respect to any property as of January 1, 1981, under subsection (m) of section 167 (determined without regard to paragraph (4) thereof and as if the taxpayer had made an election under such subsection). If any property (other than section 1250 class property) does not have a present class life within the meaning of the preceding sentence, the Secretary may prescribe a present class life for such property which reasonably reflects the anticipated useful life of such property to the industry or other group.

(3) SECTION 1250 CLASS PROPERTY.—The term "section 1245 class property" means tangible property described in section 1245(a)(3) other than subparagraphs (C) and (D).

(4) SECTION 1250 CLASS PROPERTY.—The term "section 1250 class property" means property described in section 1250(c) and property described in section 1245(a)(3)(C).

(5) RESEARCH AND EXPERIMENTATION.—The term "research and experimentation" has the same meaning as the term research or experimental has under section 174.

(6) RRB PROPERTY DEFINED.—For purposes of this section, the term "RRB property" means property which under the taxpayer's method of depreciation before January 1, 1981, would have been depreciated using the retirement-replacement-betterment method.

(7) MANUFACTURED HOMES.—The term "manufactured home" has the same meaning as in section 603(6) of the Housing and Community Development Act of 1974, which is 1250 class property used as a dwelling unit.

(8) QUALIFIED COAL UTILIZATION PROPERTY.—

(A) QUALIFIED COAL UTILIZATION PROPERTY.—The term "qualified coal utilization property" means that portion of the unadjusted basis of coal utilization property which bears the same ratio (but not greater than 1) to such unadjusted basis as—

(i) the Btu's of energy produced by the powerplant or major fuel-burning installation before the conversion or replacement involving coal utilization property, bears to

(ii) the Btu's of energy produced by such powerplant or installation after such conversion or replacement.

(B) COAL UTILIZATION PROPERTY.—The term "coal utilization property" means—

(i) a boiler or burner—

(I) the primary fuel for which is coal (including lignite), and

(II) which replaces an existing boiler or burner which is part of a powerplant or major fuel-burning installation and the primary fuel for which is oil or natural gas or any product thereof, and

(ii) equipment for converting an existing boiler or burner described in clause (i)(II) to a boiler or burner the primary fuel for which will be coal.

(C) POWERPLANT AND MAJOR FUEL-BURNING INSTALLATION.—The terms "powerplant" and "major fuel-burning installation" have the meanings given such terms by paragraphs (7) and (10) of section 103(a) of the Powerplant and Industrial Fuel Use Act of 1978, respectively.

(D) EXISTING BOILER OR BURNER.—The term "existing boiler or burner" means a boiler or burner which was placed in service before January 1, 1981.

(E) REPLACEMENT OF EXISTING BOILER OR BURNER.—A boiler or burner shall be treated as replacing a boiler or burner if the taxpayer certifies that the boiler or burner which is to be replaced—

(i) was used during calendar year 1980 for more than 2,000 hours of full load peak use (or equivalent thereof), and

(ii) will not be used for more than 2,000 hours of such use during any 12-month period after the boiler or burner which is to replace such boiler or burner is placed in service.

Amendments

- **1984, Deficit Reduction Act of 1984 (P.L. 98-369)**

P.L. 98-369, § 31(d):

Added the sentence at the end of Code Sec. 168(g)(2). For the **effective** date as well as special rules, see Act Sec. 31(g) following former Code Sec. 168(j).

- **1983, Technical Corrections Act of 1982 (P.L. 97-448)**

P.L. 97-448, § 102(a)(4)(B):

Amended the heading of Code Sec. 168(g)(8)(A). **Effective** as if it had been included in the provision of P.L. 97-34 to which it relates. Prior to amendment, the heading read as follows:

"(A) In general.—"

P.L. 97-448, § 102(a)(4)(C):

Amended the heading of Code Sec. 168(g)(8)(B). **Effective** as if it had been included in the provision of P.L. 97-34 to which it relates. Prior to amendment, the heading read as follows:

(B) IN GENERAL.—

P.L. 97-34, § 201(a):

Added Code Sec. 168(g). **Effective** for property placed in service after 12-31-80, in tax years ending after such date.

[Sec. 168(h)]

(h) SPECIAL RULES FOR RECOVERY PROPERTY CLASSES.—For purposes of this section—

(1) CERTAIN HORSES.—The term "3-year property" includes—

(A) any race horse which is more than 2 years old at the time such horse is placed in service; or

(B) any other horse which is more than 12 years old at such time.

(2) RAILROAD TANK CARS.—The term "10-year property" includes railroad tank cars.

(3) MANUFACTURED HOMES.—The term "10-year property" includes manufactured homes.

(4) QUALIFIED COAL UTILIZATION PROPERTY.—The term "10-year property" includes qualified coal utilization property which would otherwise be 15-year public utility property.

(5) APPLICATION WITH OTHER CLASSES.—Any property which is treated as included in a class or property by reason of this subsection shall not be treated as included in any other class.

Amendments

- **1983, Technical Corrections Act of 1982 (P.L. 97-448)**

P.L. 97-448, §102(a)(4)(A):

Amended Code Sec. 168(h)(4). **Effective** as if it had been included in the provision of P.L. 97-34 to which it relates. Prior to amendment, Code Sec. 168(h)(4) read as follows:

"(4) Qualified coal utilization property.—The term '10-year property' includes qualified coal utilization property which is not 3-year property, 5-year property, or 10-year property (determined without regard to this paragraph)."

- **1981, Economic Recovery Tax Act of 1981 (P.L. 97-34)**

P.L. 97-34, §201(a):

Added Code Sec. 168(h). **Effective** for property placed in service after 12-31-80, in tax years ending after such date.

[*Caution: Code Sec. 168(i), below, as added by P.L. 97-248 and amended by P.L. 98-369, applies, generally, to agreements entered into after July 1, 1982, or to property placed in service after July 1, 1982. But see the amendment notes below for special rules.—CCH.*]

[Sec. 168(i)]

(i) LIMITATIONS RELATING TO LEASES OF QUALIFIED LEASED PROPERTY.—For purposes of this subtitle, in the case of safe harbor lease property, the following limitations shall apply:

(1) LESSOR MAY NOT REDUCE TAX LIABILITY BY MORE THAN 50 PERCENT.—

(A) IN GENERAL.—The aggregate amount allowable as deductions or credits for any taxable year which are allocable to all safe harbor lease property with respect to which the taxpayer is the lessor may not reduce the liability for tax of the taxpayer for such taxable year (determined without regard to safe harbor lease items) by more than 50 percent of such liability.

(B) CARRYOVER OF AMOUNTS NOT ALLOWABLE AS DEDUCTIONS OR CREDITS.—Any amount not allowable as a deduction or credit under subparagraph (A)—

(i) may be carried over to any subsequent taxable year, and

(ii) shall be treated as a deduction or credit allocable to safe harbor lease property in such subsequent taxable year.

(C) ALLOCATION AMONG DEDUCTIONS AND CREDITS.—The Secretary shall prescribe regulations for determining the amount—

(i) of any deduction or credit allocable to safe harbor lease property for any taxable year to which subparagraph (A) applies, and

(ii) of any carryover of any such deduction or credit under subparagraph (B) to any subsequent taxable year.

(D) LIABILITY FOR TAX AND SAFE HARBOR LEASE ITEMS DEFINED.—For purposes of this paragraph—

(i) LIABILITY FOR TAX DEFINED.—Except as provided in this subparagraph, the term "liability for tax" means the tax imposed by this chapter, reduced by the sum of the credits allowable under subparts A, B, and D of part IV of subchapter A of this chapter.

(ii) SAFE HARBOR LEASE ITEMS DEFINED.—The term "safe harbor lease items" means any of the following items which are properly allocable to safe harbor lease property with respect to which the taxpayer is the lessor:

(I) Any deduction or credit allowable under this chapter (other than any deduction for interest).

(II) Any rental income received by the taxpayer from any lessee of such property.

(III) Any interest allowable as a deduction under this chapter on indebtedness of the taxpayer (or any related person within the meaning of subsection (e)(4)(D)) which is paid or incurred to the lessee of such property (or any person so related to the lessee).

(iii) CERTAIN TAXES NOT INCLUDED.—The term "tax imposed by this chapter" shall not include any tax treated as not imposed by this chapter under section 26(b)(2) (other than the tax imposed by section 56).

(2) METHOD OF COST RECOVERY.—The deduction allowable under subsection (a) with respect to any safe harbor lease property shall be determined by using the 150 percent declining balance method, switching to the straight-line method at a time to maximize the deduction (with a half-year convention in the first recovery year and without regard to salvage value) and a recovery period determined in accordance with the following table:

In the case of:	The recovery period is:
3-year property	5 years.
5-year property	8 years.
10-year property	15 years.

(3) INVESTMENT CREDIT ALLOWED ONLY OVER 5-YEAR PERIOD.—In the case of any credit which would otherwise be allowable under section 38 with respect to any safe harbor lease property for any taxable year (determined without regard to this paragraph), only 20 percent of the amount of such credit shall be allowable in such taxable year and 20 percent of such amount shall be allowable in each of the succeeding 4 taxable years.

(4) NO CARRYBACKS OF CREDIT OR NET OPERATING LOSS ALLOCABLE TO ELECTED QUALIFIED LEASED PROPERTY.—

(A) CREDIT CARRYBACKS.—In determining the amount of any credit allowable under section 38 which may be carried back to any preceding taxable year—

(i) the liability for tax for the taxable year from which any such credit is to be carried shall be reduced first by any credit not properly allocable to safe harbor lease property, and

(ii) no credit which is properly allocable to safe harbor lease property shall be taken into account in determining the amount of any credit which may be carried back.

(B) NET OPERATING LOSS CARRYBACKS.—The net operating loss carryback provided in section 172(b) for any taxable year shall be reduced by that portion of the amount of such carryback which is properly allocable to the items described in paragraph (1)(D)(ii) with respect to all safe harbor lease property with respect to which the taxpayer is the lessor.

(5) LIMITATION ON DEDUCTION FOR INTEREST PAID BY THE LESSOR TO THE LESSEE.—In the case of interest described in paragraph (1)(D)(ii)(III), the amount allowable as a deduction for any taxable year with respect to such interest shall not exceed the amount which would have been computed if the rate of interest under the agreement were equal to the rate of interest in effect under section 6621 at the time the agreement was entered into.

(6) COMPUTATION OF TAXABLE INCOME OF LESSEE FOR PURPOSES OF PERCENTAGE DEPLETION.—

(A) IN GENERAL.—For purposes of section 613 or 613A, the taxable income of any taxpayer who is a lessee of any safe harbor lease property shall be computed as if the taxpayer was the owner of such property, except that the amount of the deduction under subsection (a) of this section shall be determined after application of paragraph (2) of this subsection.

(B) COORDINATION WITH CRUDE OIL WINDFALL PROFIT TAX.—Section 4988(b)(3)(A) shall be applied without regard to subparagraph (A).

(7) TRANSITIONAL RULE FOR APPLICATION OF PARAGRAPH (1) TO CERTAIN TRANSACTIONS.—In the case of any deduction or credit with respect to—

(A) any transitional safe harbor lease property (within the meaning of section 208(d)(3) of the Tax Equity and Fiscal Responsibility Act of 1982), or

(B) any other safe harbor lease property placed in service during 1982 and to which paragraph (1) does not apply,

paragraph (1) shall not operate to disallow any such deduction or credit for the taxable year for which such deduction or credit would otherwise be allowable but deductions and credits with respect to such property shall be taken into account first in determining whether any deduction or credit is allowable under paragraph (1) with respect to any other safe harbor lease property.

(8) SAFE HARBOR LEASE PROPERTY.—For purposes of this section, the term "safe harbor lease property" means qualified leased property with respect to which an election under section 168(f)(8) is in effect.

[*Caution: Code Sec. 168(i), below, as added by P.L. 97-248 and amended by P.L. 98-369, applies, generally, to agreements entered into after December 31, 1987. But see the amendment notes below for special rules.—CCH.*]

[Sec. 168(i)]

(i) LIMITATIONS RELATING TO LEASES OF FINANCE LEASE PROPERTY.—For purposes of this subtitle, in the case of finance lease property, the following limitations shall apply:

(1) LESSOR MAY NOT REDUCE TAX LIABILITY BY MORE THAN 50 PERCENT.—

(A) IN GENERAL.—The aggregate amount allowable as deductions or credits for any taxable year which are allocable to all finance lease property with respect to which the taxpayer is the lessor may not reduce the liability for tax of the taxpayer for such taxable year (determined without regard to finance lease items) by more than 50 percent of such liability.

(B) CARRYOVER OF AMOUNTS NOT ALLOWABLE AS DEDUCTIONS OR CREDITS.—Any amount not allowable as a deduction or credit under subparagraph (A)—

(i) may be carried over to any subsequent taxable year, and

(ii) shall be treated as a deduction or credit allocable to finance lease property in such subsequent taxable year.

(C) ALLOCATION AMONG DEDUCTIONS AND CREDITS.—The Secretary shall prescribe regulations for determining the amount—

(i) of any deduction or credit allocable to finance lease property for any taxable year to which subparagraph (A) applies, and

(ii) of any carryover of any such deduction or credit under subparagraph (B) to any subsequent taxable year.

(D) LIABILITY FOR TAX AND FINANCE LEASE ITEMS DEFINED.—For purposes of this paragraph—

(i) LIABILITY FOR TAX DEFINED.—Except as provided in this subparagraph, the term "liability for tax" means the tax imposed by this chapter, reduced by the sum of the credits allowable under subparts A, B, and D of part IV of subchapter A of this chapter.

(ii) FINANCE LEASE ITEMS DEFINED.—The term "finance lease items" means any of the following items which are properly allocable to finance lease property with respect to which the taxpayer is the lessor:

(I) Any deduction or credit allowable under this chapter.

(II) Any rental income received by the taxpayer from any lessee of such property.

(iii) CERTAIN TAXES NOT INCLUDED.—The term "tax imposed by this chapter" shall not include any tax treated as not imposed by this chapter under section 26(b)(2) (other than the tax imposed by section 56).

(E) CERTAIN SAFE HARBOR LEASE PROPERTY TAKEN INTO ACCOUNT.—Under regulations prescribed by the Secretary, deductions and credits and safe harbor lease items which are allocable to safe harbor lease property to which this paragraph (as in effect for taxable years beginning in 1983) applies shall be taken into account for purposes of applying this paragraph.

(2) INVESTMENT CREDIT ALLOWED ONLY OVER 5-YEAR PERIOD.—In the case of any credit which would otherwise be allowable under section 38 with respect to any finance lease property for any taxable year (determined without regard to this paragraph), only 20 percent of the amount of such credit shall be allowable in such taxable year and 20 percent of such amount shall be allowable in each of the succeeding 4 taxable years.

(3) COMPUTATION OF TAXABLE INCOME OF LESSEE FOR PURPOSES OF PERCENTAGE DEPLETION.—

(A) IN GENERAL.—For purposes of section 613 or 613A, the taxable income of any taxpayer who is a lessee of any financed recovery property shall be computed as if the taxpayer was the owner of such property, except that the amount of the deduction under subsection (a) of this section shall be determined after application of paragraph (2) of this subsection.

(B) COORDINATION WITH CRUDE OIL WINDFALL PROFIT TAX.—Section 4988(b)(3)(A) shall be applied without regard to subparagraph (A).

(4) LIMITATIONS.—

(A) TERMINATION OF CERTAIN PROVISIONS.—

(i) PARAGRAPH (1).—Paragraph (1) shall not apply to property placed in service after September 30, 1989, in taxable years beginning after such date.

(ii) PARAGRAPH (2).—Paragraph (2) shall not apply to property placed in service after September 30, 1989.

(B) CERTAIN FARM PROPERTY.—This subsection shall not apply to property which is used for farming purposes (within the meaning of section 2032A(e)(5)) and which is placed in service during the taxable year but only if the cost basis of such property, when added to the cost basis of other finance lease property used for such purpose, does not exceed $150,000 (determined under rules similar to the rules of section 209(d)(1)(B) of the Tax Equity and Fiscal Responsibility Act of 1982).

Amendments

• **1984, Deficit Reduction Act of 1984 (P.L. 98-369)**

P.L. 98-369, §12(a)(3):

Amended Code Sec. 168(i)(4) by striking out "1985" each place it appeared and inserting in lieu thereof "1989". **Effective**, generally, for tax years beginning after 12-31-83. See, however, the special rules provided in Act Sec. 12(b)-(c) following former Code Sec. 168(f).

P.L. 98-369, §474(r)(7)(A):

Amended Code Sec. 168(i)(1)(D)(i) by striking out "subpart A of part IV" and inserting in lieu thereof "subparts A, B, and D of part IV". **Effective** for tax years beginning after 12-31-83, and to carrybacks from such years.

P.L. 98-369, §474(r)(7)(B):

Amended Code Sec. 168(i)(1)(D)(iii) by striking out "under the last sentence of section 53(a)" and inserting in lieu thereof "under section 25(b)(2)". **Effective** for tax years beginning after 12-31-83, and to carrybacks from such years.

P.L. 98-369, §474(r)(7)(C):

Amended Code Sec. 168(i)(4)(A) by striking out "subpart A of part IV of subchapter A of this chapter" and inserting in lieu thereof "section 38". **Effective** for tax years beginning after 12-31-83, and to carrybacks from such years.

P.L. 98-369, §474(r)(7)(D):

Amended Code Sec. 168(i)(1)(D)(i) by striking out "subpart A of part IV" and inserting in lieu thereof "subparts A, B, and D of part IV". **Effective** for tax years beginning after 12-31-83, and to carrybacks from such years.

P.L. 98-369, §474(r)(7)(E):

Amended Code Sec. 168(i)(1)(D)(iii) by striking out "under the last sentence of section 53(a)" and inserting in lieu thereof "under section 25(b)(2)". **Effective** for tax years beginning after 12-31-83, and to carrybacks from such years.

P.L. 98-369, §612(e)(4):

Amended Code Sec. 168(i)(1)(D)(iii) as amended by Act Sec. 485(r)(7)(B), by striking out "section 25(b)(2)" and inserting in lieu thereof "section 26(b)(2)". **Effective** for interest paid or accrued after 12-31-84, on indebtedness incurred after 12-31-84.

P.L. 98-369, §612(e)(5):

Amended Code Sec. 168(i)(1)(D)(iii) as amended by Act Sec. 474(r)(7)(E) by striking out "section 25(b)(2)" and inserting in lieu thereof "section 26(b)(2)". **Effective** for interest paid or accrued after 12-31-84, on indebtedness incurred after 12-31-84.

• **1982, Tax Equity and Fiscal Responsibility Act of 1982 (P.L. 97-248)**

P.L. 97-248, §208(a)(1):

Amended Code Sec. 168 by redesignating subsection (i) as subsection (j) and by inserting after subsection (h) new subsection (i). **Effective** for agreements entered into after 7-1-82, or to property placed in service after 7-1-82.

P.L. 97-248, §208(d)(2)-(8), as amended by P.L. 97-448, §306(a)(4)(A)-(C) and P.L. 98-369, §1067(a), provides:

(2) Transitional rule for certain safe harbor lease property.—

(A) In general.—The amendments made by subsections (a) and (b) shall not apply to transitional safe harbor lease property.

(B) Special rule for certain provisions.—Subparagraph (A) shall not apply with respect to the provisions of paragraph (6) of section 168(i) of the Internal Revenue Code of 1954 (as added by subsection (a)(1)), to the provisions of section 168(f)(8)(J) of such Code (as added by subsection (b)(4)), or to the amendment made by subsection (b)(1).

(3) Transitional safe harbor lease property.—For purposes of this subsection, the term "transitional safe harbor lease property" means property described in any of the following subparagraphs:

(A) In general.—Property is described in this subparagraph if such property is placed in service before January 1, 1983, if—

(i) with respect to such property a binding contract to acquire or to construct such property was entered into by the lessee after December 31, 1980, and before July 2, 1982, or

(ii) such property was acquired by the lessee, or construction of such property was commenced by or for the lessee, after December 31, 1980, and before July 2, 1982.

(B) Certain qualified lessees.—Property is described in this subparagraph if such property is placed in service before July 1, 1982, and with respect to which—

(i) an agreement to which section 168(f)(8)(A) of the Internal Revenue Code of 1954 applies was entered into before August 15, 1982, and

(ii) the lessee under such agreement is a qualified lessee (within the meaning of paragraph (6)).

(C) Automotive Manufacturing Property.—

(i) In General.—Property is described in this subparagraph if—

(I) such property is used principally by the taxpayer directly in connection with the trade or business of the taxpayer of the manufacture of automobiles or light-duty trucks,

(II) such property is automotive manufacturing property, and

(III) such property would be described in subparagraph (A) if "October 1" were substituted for "January 1".

(ii) Light-Duty Truck.—For purposes of this subparagraph, the term "light-duty truck" means any truck with a gross vehicle weight of 13,000 pounds or less. Such term shall not include any truck tractor.

(iii) Automotive Manufacturing Property.—For purposes of this subparagraph, the term "automotive manufacturing property" means machinery, equipment, and special tools of the type included in the former asset depreciation range guideline classes 37.11 and 37.12.

(iv) Special Tools Used By Certain Vendors.—For purposes of this subparagraph, any special tools owned by a taxpayer described in subclause (I) of clause (i) which are used by a vendor solely for the production of component parts for sale to the taxpayer shall be treated as automotive manufacturing property used directly by such taxpayer.

(D) Certain aircraft.—Property is described in this subparagraph if such property—

(i) is a commercial passenger aircraft (other than a helicopter), and

(ii) would be described in subparagraph (A) if "January 1, 1984" were substituted for "January 1, 1983".

For purposes of determining whether property described in this subparagraph in described in subparagraph (A), subparagraph (A)(ii) shall be applied by substituting "June 25, 1981" for "December 31, 1980" and by substituting "February 20, 1982" for "July 2, 1982" and construction of the aircraft shall be treated as having been begun during the period referred to in subparagraph (A)(ii) if during such period construction or reconstruction of a subassembly was commenced, or the stub wing join occurred.

(E) Turbines and boilers.—Property is described in this subparagraph if such property—

(i) is a turbine or boiler of a cooperative organization engaged in the furnishing of electric energy to persons in rural areas, and

(ii) would be property described in subparagraph (A) if "July 1" were substituted for "January 1".

For purposes of determining whether property described in this subparagraph is described in subparagraph (A), such property shall be treated as having been acquired during the period referred to in subparagraph (A)(ii) if at least 20 percent of the cost of such property is paid during such period.

(F) Property used in the production of steel.—Property is described in this subparagraph if such property—

(i) is used by the taxpayer directly in connection with the trade or business of the taxpayer of the manufacture or production of steel, and

(ii) would be described in subparagraph (A) if "January 1, 1984" were substituted for "January 1, 1983".

(4) Special rule for antiavoidance provisions.—The provisions of paragraph (6) of section 168(i) of such Code (as added by subsection (a)(1)), and the amendment made by subsection (b)(1), shall apply to leases entered into after February 19, 1982, in taxable years ending after such date.

(5) Special rule for mass commuting vehicles.—The amendments made by this section (other than section 168(i)(1) and (7) of such Code, as added by subsection

(a)(1)), or section 168(f)(8)(J) of such Code, as added by subsection (b)(4), and section 209 shall not apply to qualified leased property described in section 168(f)(8)(D)(v) of such Code (as in effect after the amendments made by this section) which—

(A) is placed in service before January 1, 1988, or

(B) is placed in service after such date—

(i) pursuant to a binding contract or commitment entered into before April 1, 1983, and

(ii) solely because of conditions which, as determined by the Secretary of the Treasury or his delegate, are not within the control of the lessor or lessee.

(6) Qualified lessee defined.—

(A) In general.—The term "qualified lessee" means a taxpayer which is a lessee of an agreement to which section 168(f)(8)(A) of such Code applies and which—

(i) had net operating losses in each of the three most recent taxable years ending before July 1, 1982, and had an aggregate net operating loss for the five most recent taxable years ending before July 1, 1982, and

(ii) which uses the property subject to the agreement to manufacture and produce within the United States a class of products in an industry with respect to which—

(I) the taxpayer produced less than 5 percent of the total number of units (or value) of such products during the period covering the three most recent taxable years of the taxpayer ending before July 1, 1982, and

(II) four or fewer United States persons (including as one person an affiliated group as defined in section 1504(a)) other than the taxpayer manufactured 85 percent or more of the total number of all units (or value) within such class of products manufactured and produced in the United States during such period.

(B) Class of products.—For purposes of subparagraph (A)—

(i) the term "class of products" means any of the categories designated and numbered as a "class of products" in the 1977 Census of Manufacturers compiled and published by the Secretary of Commerce under title 13 of the United States Code, and

(ii) information—

(I) compiled or published by the Secretary of Commerce, as part of or in connection with the Statistical Abstract of the United States or the Census of Manufacturers, regarding the number of units (or value) of a class of products manufactured and produced in the United States during any period, or

(II) if information under subclause (I) is not available, so compiled or published with respect to the number of such units shipped or sold by such manufacturers during any period,

shall constitute prima facie evidence of the total number of all units of such class of products manufactured and produced in the United States in such period.

(6)[7] Underpayments of tax for 1982.—No addition to the tax shall be made under section 6655 of the Internal Revenue Code of 1954 (relating to failure by corporation to pay estimated income tax) or any period before October 15, 1982, with respect to any underpayment of estimated tax by a taxpayer with respect to any tax imposed by chapter 1 of such Code, to the extent that such underpayment was created or increased by any provision of this section.

(7)[8]Coordination with at risk rules.—Subparagraph (J) of section 168(f)(8) of the Internal Revenue Code of 1954 (as added by subsection (b)(4)) shall take effect as provided in such subparagraph (J).

(G) COAL GASIFICATION FACILITIES.—

(i) IN GENERAL.—Property is described in this subparagraph if such property—

(I) is used directly in connection with the manufacture or production of low sulfur gaseous fuel from coal, and

(II) would be described in subparagraph (A) if "July 1, 1984" were substituted for "January 1, 1983."

(ii) SPECIAL RULE.—For purposes of determining whether property described in this subparagraph is described in subparagraph (A), such property shall be treated as having been acquired during the period referred to in subparagraph (A)(ii) if at least 20 percent of the cost of such property is paid during such period.

(iii) LIMITATION ON AMOUNT.—Clause (i) shall only apply to the lease of an undivided interest in the property in an amount which does not exceed the lesser of—

(I) 50 percent of the cost basis of such property, or

Code Sec. 168

(II) $67,500,000.

(iv) PLACED IN SERVICE.—In the case of property to which this subparagraph applies—

(I) such property shall be treated as placed in service when the taxpayer receives an operating permit with respect to such property from a State environmental protection agency, and

(II) the term of the lease with respect to such property shall be treated as being 5 years.

P.L. 97-248, § 209(b):

Amended Code Sec. 168(i). **Effective** for agreements entered into after 12-31-87 (P.L. 98-369, § 12(a)(1) changed the effective date.). See also the amendment notes for P.L. 97-248, Act Sec. 209(c), following former Code Sec. 168(f) for special rules.

[Sec. 168(j)]

(j) PROPERTY LEASED TO GOVERNMENTS AND OTHER TAX-EXEMPT ENTITIES.—

(1) IN GENERAL.—Notwithstanding any other provision of this section, the deduction allowed under subsection (a) (and any other deduction allowable for depreciation or amortization) for any taxable year with respect to tax-exempt use property shall be determined—

(A) by using the straight-line method (without regard to salvage value), and

(B) by using a recovery period determined under the following table:

In the case of:	The recovery period shall be:
(I) Property not described in subclause (II) or subclause (III)	The present class life.
(II) Personal property with no present class life	12 years.
(III) 19-year real property	40 years.

(2) OPERATING RULES.—

(A) RECOVERY PERIOD MUST AT LEAST EQUAL 125 PERCENT OF LEASE TERM.—In the case of any tax-exempt use property, the recovery period used for purposes of paragraph (1) shall not be less than 125 percent of the lease term.

(B) CONVENTIONS.—

(i) PROPERTY OTHER THAN 19-YEAR REAL PROPERTY.—In the case of property other than 19-year real property, the half-year convention shall apply for purposes of paragraph (1).

(ii) CROSS REFERENCE.—

For other applicable conventions, see paragraphs (2)(B) and (4)(B) of subsection (b).

(C) EXCEPTION WHERE LONGER RECOVERY PERIOD APPLIES.—Paragraph (1) shall not apply to any recovery property if the recovery period which applies to such property (without regard to this subsection) exceeds the recovery period for such property determined under this subsection.

(D) DETERMINATION OF CLASS FOR REAL PROPERTY WHICH IS NOT RECOVERY PROPERTY.—In the case of any real property which is not recovery property, for purposes of this subsection, the determination of whether such property is 19-year real property shall be made as if such property were recovery property.

(E) COORDINATION WITH SUBSECTION (f)(12).—Paragraph (12) of subsection (f) shall not apply to any tax-exempt use property to which this subsection applies.

(F) 19-YEAR REAL PROPERTY.—For purposes of this subsection, the term "19-year real property" includes—

(i) low-income housing, and

(ii) any property which was treated as 15-year real property under this section (as in effect before the amendments made by the Tax Reform Act of 1984).

(3) TAX-EXEMPT USE PROPERTY.—For purposes of this subsection—

(A) PROPERTY OTHER THAN 19-YEAR REAL PROPERTY.—Except as otherwise provided in this subsection, the term "tax-exempt use property" means that portion of any tangible property (other than 19-year real property) leased to a tax-exempt entity.

(B) 19-YEAR REAL PROPERTY.—

(i) IN GENERAL.—In the case of 19-year real property, the term "tax-exempt use property" means that portion of the property leased to a tax-exempt entity in a disqualified lease.

(ii) DISQUALIFIED LEASE.—For purposes of this subparagraph, the term "disqualified lease" means any lease of the property to a tax-exempt entity, but only if—

(I) part or all of the property was financed (directly or indirectly) by an obligation the interest on which is exempt from tax under section 103 and such entity (or a related entity) participated in such financing,

(II) under such lease there is a fixed or determinable price purchase or sale option which involves such entity (or a related entity) or there is the equivalent of such an option,

(III) such lease has a lease term in excess of 20 years, or

(IV) such lease occurs after a sale (or other transfer) of the property by, or lease of the property from, such entity (or a related entity) and such property has been used by such entity (or a related entity) before such sale (or other transfer) or lease.

(iii) 35-PERCENT THRESHOLD TEST.—Clause (i) shall apply to any property only if the portion of such property leased to tax-exempt entities in disqualified leases is more than 35 percent of the property.

(iv) TREATMENT OF IMPROVEMENTS.—For purposes of this subparagraph, improvements to a property (other than land) shall not be treated as a separate property.

(v) LEASEBACKS DURING 1ST 3 MONTHS OF USE NOT TAKEN INTO ACCOUNT.—Subclause (IV) of clause (ii) shall not apply to any property which is leased within 3 months after the date such property is first used by the tax-exempt entity (or a related entity).

(C) EXCEPTION FOR SHORT-TERM LEASES.—

(i) IN GENERAL.—Property shall not be treated as tax-exempt use property merely by reason of a short-term lease.

(ii) SHORT-TERM LEASE.—For purposes of clause (i), the term "short-term lease" means any lease the term of which is—

(I) less than 3 years, and

(II) less than the greater of 1 year or 30 percent of the property's present class life.

In the case of 19-year real property and property with no present class life, subclause (II) shall not apply.

(D) EXCEPTION WHERE PROPERTY USED IN UNRELATED TRADE OR BUSINESS.—The term "tax-exempt use property" shall not include any portion of a property if such portion is predominantly used by the tax-exempt entity (directly or through a partnership of which such entity is a partner) in an unrelated trade or business the income of which is subject to tax under section 511. For purposes of subparagraph (B)(iii), any portion of a property so used shall not be treated as leased to a tax-exempt entity in a disqualified lease.

(4) TAX-EXEMPT ENTITY.—

(A) IN GENERAL.—For purposes of this subsection, the term "tax-exempt entity" means–

(i) the United States, any State or political subdivision thereof, any possession of the United States, or any agency or instrumentality of any of the foregoing,

(ii) an organization (other than a cooperative described in section 521) which is exempt from tax imposed by this chapter, and

(iii) any foreign person or entity.

(B) EXCEPTIONS FOR CERTAIN PROPERTY USED BY FOREIGN PERSON OR ENTITY.—

(i) INCOME FROM PROPERTY SUBJECT TO UNITED STATES TAX.—Clause (iii) of subparagraph (A) shall not apply with respect to any property if more than 50 percent of the gross income for the taxable year derived by the foreign person or entity from the use of such property is—

(I) subject to tax under this chapter, or

(II) included under section 951 in the gross income of a United States shareholder for the taxable year with or within which ends the taxable year of the controlled foreign corporation in which such income was derived.

For purposes of the preceding sentence, any exclusion or exemption shall not apply for purposes of determining the amount of the gross income so derived, but shall apply for purposes of determining the portion of such gross income subject to tax under this chapter.

(ii) MOVIES AND SOUND RECORDINGS.—Clause (iii) of subparagraph (A) shall not apply with respect to any qualified film (as defined in section 48(k)(1)(B)) or any sound recording (as defined in section 48(r)).

(C) FOREIGN PERSON OR ENTITY.—For purposes of this paragraph, the term "foreign person or entity" means—

(i) any foreign government, any international organization, or any agency or instrumentality of any of the foregoing, and

(ii) any person who is not a United States person.

Such term does not include any foreign partnership or other foreign pass-thru entity.

(D) TREATMENT OF CERTAIN TAXABLE INSTRUMENTALITIES.—For purposes of this subsection and paragraph (5) of section 48(a), a corporation shall not be treated as an instrumentality of the United States or of any State or political subdivision thereof if—

(i) all of the activities of such corporation are subject to tax under this chapter, and

(ii) a majority of the board of directors of such corporation is not selected by the United States or any State or political subdivision thereof.

(E) CERTAIN PREVIOUSLY TAX-EXEMPT ORGANIZATIONS.—

(i) IN GENERAL.—For purposes of this subsection and paragraph (4) of section 48(a), an organization shall be treated as an organization described in subparagraph (A)(ii) with respect to any property, (other than property held by such organization) if such organization was an organization (other than a cooperative described in section 521) exempt from tax imposed by this chapter at any time during the 5-year period ending on the date such property was first used by such organization. The preceding sentence and subparagraph (d)(ii) shall not apply to the Federal Home Loan Mortgage Corporation.

(ii) ELECTION NOT TO HAVE CLAUSE (i) APPLY.—

(I) IN GENERAL.—In the case of an organization formerly exempt from tax under section 501(a) as an organization described in section 501(c)(12), clause (i) shall not apply to such organization with respect to any property if such organization elects not to be exempt from tax under section 501(a) during the tax-exempt use period with respect to such property.

(II) TAX-EXEMPT USE PERIOD.—For purposes of subclause (I), the term "tax-exempt use period" means the period beginning with the taxable year in which the property described in subclause (I) is first used by the organization and ending with the close of the 15th taxable year following the last taxable year of the recovery period of such property.

(III) ELECTION.—Any election under subclause (I), once made, shall be irrevocable.

(iii) TREATMENT OF SUCCESSOR ORGANIZATIONS.—Any organization which is engaged in activities substantially similar to those engaged in by a predecessor organization shall succeed to the treatment under this subparagraph of such predecessor organization.

(iv) FIRST USED.—For purposes of this subparagraph, property shall be treated as first used by the organization—

(I) when the property is first placed in service under a lease to such organization, or

(II) in the case of property leased to (or held by) a partnership (or other pass-thru entity) in which the organization is a member, the later of when such property is first used by such partnership or pass-thru entity or when such organization is first a member of such partnership of pass-thru entity.

(5) SPECIAL RULES FOR CERTAIN HIGH TECHNOLOGY EQUIPMENT.—

(A) EXEMPTION WHERE LEASE TERM IS 5 YEARS OR LESS.—For purposes of this subsection, the term "tax-exempt use property" shall not include any qualified technological equipment if the lease to the tax-exempt entity has a lease term of 5 years or less.

(B) RECOVERY PERIOD WHERE LEASE TERM IS GREATER THAN 5 YEARS.—In the case of any qualified technological equipment not described in subparagraph (A) and which is not property to which subsection (f)(2) applies, the recovery period used for purposes of paragraph (1) shall be 5 years.

(C) QUALIFIED TECHNOLOGICAL EQUIPMENT.—For purposes of this paragraph—

(i) IN GENERAL.—Except as otherwise provided in this subparagraph, the term "qualified technological equipment" means—

(I) any computer or peripheral equipment,

(II) any high technology telephone station equipment installed on the customer's premises, and

(III) any high technology medical equipment,

(ii) EXCEPTION FOR CERTAIN PROPERTY.—The term "qualified technological equipment" shall not include any property leased to a tax-exempt entity if—

(I) part or all of the property was financed (directly or indirectly) by an obligation the interest on which is exempt from tax under section 103,

(II) such lease occurs after a sale (or other transfer) of the property by, or lease of such property from, such entity (or related entity) and such property has been used by such entity (or a related entity) before such sale (or other transfer) or lease, or

(III) such tax-exempt entity is the United States or any agency or instrumentality of the United States.

(iii) LEASEBACKS DURING 1ST 3 MONTHS OF USE NOT TAKEN INTO ACCOUNT.—Subclause (II) of clause (ii) shall not apply to any property which is leased within 3 months after the date such property is first used by the tax-exempt entity (or a related entity).

(D) COMPUTER OR PERIPHERAL EQUIPMENT DEFINED.—For purposes of this paragraph—

(i) IN GENERAL.—The term "computer or peripheral equipment" means—

(I) any computer, and

(II) any related peripheral equipment.

(ii) COMPUTER.—The term "computer" means a programmable electronically activated device which—

(I) is capable of accepting information, applying prescribed processes to the information, and supplying the results of these processes with or without human intervention, and

(II) consists of a central processing unit containing extensive storage, logic, arithmetic, and control capabilities.

(iii) RELATED PERIPHERAL EQUIPMENT.—The term "related peripheral equipment" means any auxiliary machine (whether on-line or off-line) which is designed to be placed under the control of the central processing unit of a computer.

(iv) EXCEPTIONS.—The term "computer or peripheral equipment" shall not include—

(I) any equipment which is an integral part of other property which is not a computer,

(II) typewriters, calculators, adding and accounting machines, copiers, duplicating equipment, and similar equipment, and

(III) equipment of a kind used primarily for amusement or entertainment of the user.

(E) HIGH TECHNOLOGY MEDICAL EQUIPMENT.—For purposes of this paragraph, the term "high technology medical equipment" means any electronic, eletromechanical, or computerbased high technology equipment used in the screening, monitoring, observation, diagnosis, or treatment of patients in a laboratory, medical, or hospital environment.

(6) OTHER SPECIAL RULES.—For purposes of this subsection—

(A) LEASE.—The term "lease" includes any grant of a right to use property.

(B) LEASE TERM.—In determining a lease term—

(i) there shall be taken into account options to renew, and

(ii) 2 or more successive leases which are part of the same transaction (or a series of related transactions) with respect to the same or substantially similar property shall be treated as 1 lease.

(C) SPECIAL RULE FOR FAIR RENTAL OPTIONS ON 19-YEAR REAL PROPERTY.—For purposes of clause (i) of subparagraph (B), in the case of 19-year real property, there shall not be taken into account any option to renew at fair market value, determined at the time of renewal.

(7) RELATED ENTITIES.—For purposes of this subsection—

(A)(i) Each governmental unit and each agency or instrumentality of a governmental unit is related to each other such unit, agency, or instrumentality which directly or indirectly derives its powers, rights, and duties in whole or in part from the same sovereign authority.

(ii) For purposes of clause (i), the United States, each State, and each possession of the United States shall be treated as a separate sovereign authority.

(B) Any entity not described in subparagraph (A)(i) is related to any other entity if the 2 entities have—

(i) significant common purposes and substantial common membership, or

(ii) directly or indirectly substantial common direction or control.

Code Sec. 168

(C)(i) An entity is related to another entity if either entity owns (directly or through 1 or more entities) a 50 percent or greater interest in the capital or profits of the other entity.

(ii) For purposes of clause (i), entities treated as related under subparagraph (A) or (B) shall be treated as 1 entity.

(D) An entity is related to another entity with respect to a transaction if such transaction is part of an attempt by such entities to avoid the application of this subsection, section 46(e), paragraph (4) or (5) of section 48(a), or clause (vi) of section 48(g)(2)(B).

(8) TAX-EXEMPT USE OF PROPERTY LEASED TO PARTNERSHIPS, ETC., DETERMINED AT PARTNER LEVEL.—For purposes of this subsection—

(A) IN GENERAL.—In the case of any property which is leased to a partnership, the determination of whether any portion of such property is tax-exempt use property shall be made by treating each tax-exempt entity partner's proportionate share (determined under paragraph (9)(C)) of such property as being leased to such partner.

(B) OTHER PASS-THRU ENTITIES; TIERED ENTITIES.—Rules similar to the rules of subparagraph (A) shall also apply in the case of any pass-thru entity other than a partnership and in the case of tiered partnerships and other entities.

(C) PRESUMPTION WITH RESPECT TO FOREIGN ENTITIES.—Unless it is otherwise established to the satisfaction of the Secretary, it shall be presumed that the partners of a foreign partnership (and the beneficiaries of any other foreign pass-thru entity) are persons who are not United States persons.

(9) TREATMENT OF PROPERTY OWNED BY PARTNERSHIPS, ETC.—

(A) IN GENERAL.—For purposes of this subsection, if

(i) any property which (but for this subparagraph) is not tax-exempt use property is owned by a partnership which has both tax-exempt entity and a person who is not a tax-exempt entity as partners and

(ii) any allocation to the tax-exempt entity of partnership items is not a qualified allocation,

an amount equal to such tax-exempt entity's proportionate share of such property shall (except as provided in paragraph (3)(D)) be treated as tax-exempt use property.

(B) QUALIFIED ALLOCATION.—For purposes of subparagraph (A), the term "qualified allocation" means any allocation to a tax-exempt entity which—

(i) is consistent with such entity's being allocated the same distributive share item of income, gain, loss, deduction, credit, and basis and such share remains the same during the entire period the entity is a partner in the partnership, and

(ii) has substantial economic effect within the meaning of section 704(b)(2).

For purposes of this subparagraph, items allocated under section 704(c) shall not be taken into account.

(C) DETERMINATION OF PROPORTION SHARE.—

(i) IN GENERAL.—For purposes of subparagraph (A), a tax-exempt entity's proportionate share of any property owned by a partnership shall be determined on the basis of such entity's share of partnership items of income or gain (excluding gain allocated under section 704(c)), whichever results in the largest proportionate share.

(ii) DETERMINATION WHERE ALLOCATIONS VARY.—For purposes of clause (i), if a tax-exempt entity's share of partnership items of income or gain (excluding gain allocated under section 704(c)) may vary during the period such entity is a partner in the partnership, such share shall be the highest share such entity may receive.

(D) DETERMINATION OF WHETHER PROPERTY USED IN UNRELATED TRADE OR BUSINESS.—For purposes of this subsection, in the case of any property which is owned by a partnership which has both a tax-exempt entity and a person who is not a tax-exempt entity as partners, the determination of whether such property is used in an unrelated trade or business of such an entity shall be made without regard to section 514.

(E) OTHER PASS-THRU ENTITIES; TIERED ENTITIES.—Rules similar to the rules of subparagraphs (A), (B), (C), and (D) shall also apply in the case of any pass-thru entity other than a partnership and in the case of tiered partnership and other entities.

(F) TREATMENT OF CERTAIN TAXABLE ENTITIES.—

(i) IN GENERAL.—For purposes of this paragraph and paragraph (8), except as otherwise provided in this subparagraph, any tax-exempt controlled entity shall be treated as a tax-exempt entity.

(ii) ELECTION.—If a tax-exempt controlled entity makes an election under this clause—

(I) such entity shall not be treated as a tax-exempt entity for purposes of this paragraph and paragraph (8),

(II) any gain recognized by a tax-exempt entity on any disposition of an interest in such entity (and any dividend or interest received or accrued by a tax-exempt entity from such tax-exempt controlled entity) shall be treated as unrelated business taxable income for purposes of section 511.

Any such election shall be irrevocable and shall bind all tax-exempt entities holding interests in such tax-exempt controlled entity. For purposes of subclause (II), there shall only be taken into account dividends which are properly allocable to income of the tax-exempt controlled entity which was not subject to tax under this chapter.

(iii) TAX-EXEMPT CONTROLLED ENTITY.—

(I) IN GENERAL.—The term "tax-exempt controlled entity" means any corporation (which is not a tax-exempt entity determined without regard to this subparagraph and paragraph (4)(E)) if 50 percent or more (in value) of the stock in such corporation is held by 1 or more tax-exempt entities (other than a foreign person or entity).

(II) ONLY 5-PERCENT SHAREHOLDERS TAKEN INTO ACCOUNT IN CASE OF PUBLICLY TRADED STOCK.—For purposes of subclause (I), in the case of a corporation the stock of which is publicly traded on an established securities market, stock held by a tax-exempt entity shall not be taken into account unless such entity holds at least 5 percent (in value) of the stock in such corporation. For purposes of this subclause, related entities (within the meaning of paragraph (7)) shall be treated as 1 entity.

(III) SECTION 318 TO APPLY.—For purposes of this clause, a tax-exempt entity shall be treated as holding stock which it holds through application of section 318 (determined without regard to the 50-percent limitation contained in subsection (a)(2)(C) thereof).

(G) REGULATIONS.—For purposes of determining whether there is a qualified allocation under subparagraph (B), the regulations prescribed under paragraph (10) for purposes of this paragraph—

(i) shall set forth the proper treatment for partnership guaranteed payments, and

(ii) may provide for the exclusion or segregation of items.

(10) REGULATIONS.—The Secretary shall prescribe such regulations as may be necessary or appropriate to carry out the purposes of this section.

Amendments

- **1988, Technical and Miscellaneous Revenue Act of 1988 (P.L. 100-647)**

P.L. 100-647, §1018(b)(2)(A)-(B):

Amended Code Sec. 168(j)(9)(E) (as amended by P.L. 99-514, §1802(a)(2) and as in effect before the amendments made by P.L. 99-514, §201) by striking out "this paragraph" in clauses (i) and (ii)(I) and inserting in lieu thereof "this paragraph and paragraph (8)", and by striking out clause (iii) and inserting in lieu thereof new clause (iii). **Effective** as if included in the provision of P.L. 99-514 to which it relates. Prior to amendment, Code Sec. 168(j)(9)(E)(iii) read as follows:

(iii) TAX-EXEMPT CONTROLLED ENTITY.—The term "tax-exempt controlled entity" means any corporation (which is not a tax-exempt entity determined without regard to this subparagraph and paragraph (4)(E)) if 50 percent or more (by value) of the stock in such corporation is held (directly or through the application of section 318 determined without regard to the 50-percent limitation contained in subsection (a)(2)(C) thereof) by 1 or more tax-exempt entities.

- **1984, Deficit Reduction Act of 1984 (P.L. 98-369)**

P.L. 98-369, §31(a):

Amended Code Sec. 168 by redesignating subsection (j) as subsection (k) and by inserting after subsection (i) new subsection (j). For the **effective** date as well as special rules, see Act Sec. 31(g), below.

P.L. 98-369, §31(g), as amended by P.L. 99-514 and P.L. 100-647, §1018(b)(1), provides:

(g) Effective Dates.—

(1) In General.—Except as otherwise provided in this subsection, the amendments made by this section shall apply—

(A) to property placed in service by the taxpayer after May 23, 1983, in taxable years ending after such date, and

(B) to property placed in service by the taxpayer on or before May 23, 1983, if the lease to the tax-exempt entity is entered into after May 23, 1983.

(2) Leases Entered into on or Before May 23, 1983.—The amendments made by this section shall not apply with

respect to any property leased to a tax-exempt entity if the property is leased pursuant to—

(A) a lease entered into on or before May 23, 1983 (or a sublease under such a lease), or

(B) any renewal or extension of a lease entered into on or before May 23, 1983, if such renewal or extension is pursuant to an option exercisable by the tax-exempt entity which was held by the tax-exempt entity on May 23, 1983.

(3) Binding Contracts, Etc.—

(A) The amendments made by this section shall not apply with respect to any property leased to a tax-exempt entity if such lease is pursuant to 1 or more written binding contracts which, on May 23, 1983, and at all times thereafter, required—

(i) the taxpayer (or his predecessor in interest under the contract) to acquire, construct, reconstruct, or rehabilitate such property, and

(ii) the tax-exempt entity (or a tax-exempt predecessor thereof) to be the lessee of such property.

(B) Paragraph (9) of section 168(j) of the Internal Revenue Code of 1954 (as added by this section) shall not apply with respect to any property owned by a partnership if—

(i) such property was acquired by such partnership on or before October 21, 1983, or

(ii) such partnership entered into a written binding contract which, on October 21, 1983, and at all times thereafter, required the partnership to acquire or construct such property.

(C) The amendments made by this section shall not apply with respect to any property leased to a tax-exempt entity (other than any foreign person or entity)—

(i) if—

(I) on or before May 23, 1983, the taxpayer (or his predecessor in interest under the contract) or the tax-exempt entity entered into a written binding contract to acquire, construct, reconstruct, or rehabilitate such property and such property had not previously been used by the tax-exempt entity, or

(II) the taxpayer or the tax-exempt entity acquired the property after June 30, 1982 and on or before May 23, 1983, or completed the construction, reconstruction, or rehabilitation of the property after December 31, 1982, and on or before May 23, 1983, and

(ii) if such lease is pursuant to a written binding contract entered into before January 1, 1985, which requires the tax-exempt entity to be the lessee of such property.

(4) Official Governmental Action on or Before November 1, 1983.—

(A) In General.—The amendments made by this section shall not apply with respect to any property leased to a tax-exempt entity (other than the United States, any agency or instrumentality thereof, or any foreign person or entity) if—

(i) on or before November 1, 1983—there was significant official governmental action with respect to the project or its design, and

(ii) the lease to the tax-exempt entity is pursuant to a written binding contract entered into before January 1, 1985, which requires the tax-exempt entity to be the lessee of the property.

(B) Significant Official Governmental Action.—For purposes of subparagraph (A), the term "significant official governmental action" does not include granting of permits, zoning changes, environmental impact statements, or similar governmental actions.

(C) Special Rule for Credit Unions.—In the case of any property leased to a credit union pursuant to a written binding contract with an expiration date of December 31, 1984, which was entered into by such organization on August 23, 1984—

(i) such credit union shall not be treated as an agency or instrumentality of the United States; and

(ii) clause (ii) of subparagraph (A) shall be applied by substituting "January 1, 1987" for "January 1, 1985".

(D) Special Rule for Greenville Auditorium Board.—For purposes of this paragraph, significant official governmental action taken by the Greenville County Auditorium Board of Greenville, South Carolina, before May 23, 1983, shall be treated as significant official governmental action with respect to the coliseum facility subject to a binding contract to lease which was in effect on January 1, 1985.

(E) Treatment of Certain Historic Structures.—If—

(i) On June 16, 1982, the legislative body of the local governmental unit adopted a bond ordinance to provide funds to renovate elevators in a deteriorating building owned by the local governmental unit and listed in the National Register, and

(ii) the chief executive officer of the local governmental unit, in connection with the renovation of such building, made an application on June 1, 1983, to a State agency for a Federal historic preservation grant and made an application on June 17, 1983, to the Economic Development Administration of the United States Department of Commerce for a grant,

the requirements of clauses (i) and (ii) of subparagraph (A) shall be treated as met.

(5) Mass Commuting Vehicles.—The amendments made by this section shall not apply to any qualified mass commuting vehicle (as defined in section 103(b)(9) of the Internal Revenue Code of 1954) which is financed in whole or in part by obligations the interest on which is excludable from gross income under section 103(a) of such Code if—

(A) such vehicle is placed in service before January 1, 1988, or

(B) such vehicle is placed in service on or after such date—

(i) pursuant to a binding contract or commitment entered into before April 1, 1983, and

(ii) solely because of conditions which, as determined by the Secretary of the Treasury or his delegate, are not within the control of the lessor or lessee.

(6) Certain Turbines and Boilers.—The amendments made by this section shall not apply to any property described in section 208(d)(3)(E) of the Tax Equity and Fiscal Responsibility Act of 1982.

(7) Certain Facilities for Which Ruling Requests Filed on or Before May 23, 1983.—The amendments made by this section shall not apply with respect to any facilities described in clause (ii) of section 168(f)(12)(C) of the Internal Revenue Code of 1954 (relating to certain sewage or solid waste disposal facilities), as in effect on the day before the date of the enactment of this Act, if a ruling request with respect to the lease of such facility to the tax-exempt entity was filed with the Internal Revenue Service on or before May 23, 1983.

(8) Recovery Period for Certain Qualified Sewage Facilities.—

(A) In General.—In the case of any property (other than 15-year real property) which is part of a qualified sewage facility, the recovery period used for purposes of paragraph (1) of section 168(j) of the Internal Revenue Code of 1954 (as added by this section) shall be 12 years. For purposes of the preceding sentence, the term "15-year real property" includes 18-year real property.

(B) Qualified Sewage Facility.—For purposes of subparagraph (A), the term "qualified sewage facility" means any facility which is part of the sewer system of a city, if—

(i) on June 15, 1983, the City Council approved a resolution under which the city authorized the procurement of equity investments for such facility, and

(ii) on July 12, 1983, the Industrial Development Board of the city approved a resolution to issue a $100,000,000 industrial development bond issue to provide funds to purchase such facility.

(9) Property Used by the Postal Service.—In the case of property used by the United States Postal Service, paragraphs (1) and (2) shall be applied by substituting "October 31" for "May 23".

(10) Existing Appropriations.—The amendments made by this section shall not apply to personal property leased to or used by the United States if—

(A) an express appropriation has been made for rentals under such lease for the fiscal year 1983 before May 23, 1983, and

(B) the United States or an agency or instrumentality thereof has not provided an indemnification against the loss of all or a portion of the tax benefits claimed under the lease or service contract.

(11) Special Rule for Certain Partnerships.—

(A) Partnerships for Which Qualifying Action Existed Before October 21, 1983.—Paragraph (9) of section 168(j) of the Internal Revenue Code of 1954 (as added by this section) shall not apply to any property acquired, directly or indirectly, before January 1, 1985, by any partnership described in subparagraph (B).

(B) Application Filed Before October 21, 1983.—A partnership is described in this subparagraph if—

(i) before October 21, 1983, the partnership was organized, a request for exemption with respect to such partnership was filed with the Department of Labor, and a private placement memorandum stating the maximum number of units in the partnership that would be offered had been circulated.

(ii) the interest in the property to be acquired, directly or indirectly (including through acquiring an interest in another partnership) by such partnership was described in such private placement memorandum, and

(iii) the marketing of partnership units in such partnership is completed not later than two years after the later of the date of the enactment of this Act or the date of publication in the Federal Register of such exemption by the Department of Labor and the aggregate number of units in such partnership sold does not exceed the amount described in clause (i).

(C) Partnerships For Which Qualifying Action Existed Before March 6, 1984.—Paragraph (9) of section 168(j) of the Internal Revenue Code of 1954 (as added by this section) shall not apply to any property acquired directly or indirectly, before January 1, 1986, by any partnership described in subparagraph (D). For purposes of this subparagraph, property shall be deemed to have been acquired prior to January 1, 1986, if the partnership had entered into a written binding contract to acquire such property prior to January 1, 1986 and the closing of such contract takes place within 6 months of the date of such contract (24 months in the case of new construction).

(D) Partnership Organized Before March 6, 1984.—A partnership is described in this subparagraph if—

(i) before March 6, 1984, the partnership was organized and publicly announced the maximum amount (as shown in the registration statement, prospectus or partnership agreement, whichever is greater) of interests which would be sold in the partnership, and

(ii) the marketing or partnership interests in such partnership was [sic] completed not later than the 90th day after the date of the enactment of this Act and the aggregate amount of interest in such partnership sold does not exceed the maximum amount described in clause (i).

(12) Special Rule for Amendment Made by Subsection (c)(2).—The amendment made by subsection (c)(2) to the extent it relates to subsection (f)(12) of section 168 of the Internal Revenue Code of 1954 shall take effect as if it had been included in the amendments made by section 216(a) of the Tax Equity and Fiscal Responsibility Act of 1982.

(13) Special Rule for Service Contracts Not Involving Tax-Exempt Entities.—In the case of a service contract or other arrangement described in section 7701(e) of the Internal Revenue Code of 1954 (as added by this section) with respect to which no party is a tax-exempt entity, such section 7701(e) shall not apply to—

(A) such contract or other arrangement if such contract or other arrangement was entered into before November 5, 1983, or

(B) any renewal or other extension of such contract or other arrangement pursuant to an option contained in such contract or other arrangement on November 5, 1983.

(14) Property Leased to Section 593 Organizations.—For purposes of the amendment made by subsection (f), paragraphs (1), (2), and (4) shall be applied by substituting—

(A) "November 5, 1983" for "May 23, 1983" and "November 1, 1983", as the case may be, and

(B) "organization described in section 593 of the Internal Revenue Code of 1954" for "tax-exempt entity".

(15) Special Rules Relating to Foreign Persons or Entities—

(A) In General.—In the case of tax-exempt use property which is used by a foreign person or entity, the amendments made by this section shall not apply to any property which—

(i) is placed in service by the taxpayer before January 1, 1984, and

(ii) is used by such foreign person or entity pursuant to a lease entered into before January 1, 1984.

(B) Special Rule for Subleases.—If tax-exempt use property is being used by a foreign person or entity pursuant to a sublease under a lease described in subparagraph (A)(ii), subparagraph (A) shall apply to such property only if such property was used before January 1, 1984, by any foreign person or entity pursuant to such lease.

(C) Binding Contracts, etc.—The amendments made by this section shall not apply with respect to any property (other than aircraft described in subparagraph (D)) to a foreign person or entity—

(i) if—

(I) on or before May 23, 1983, the taxpayer (or a predecessor in interest under the contract) or the foreign person or entity entered into a written binding conntract to acquire, construct, or rehabilitate such property and such property had not previously been used by the foreign person or entity, or

(II) the taxpayer or the foreign person or entity acquired the property or completed the construction, reconstruction, or rehabilitation of the property after December 31, 1982 and on or before May 23, 1983, and

(ii) if such lease is pursuant to a written binding contract entered into before January 1, 1984, which requires the foreign person or entity to be the lessee of such property.

(D) Certain Aircraft.—The amendments made by this section shall not apply with respect to any wide-body, fourengine, commercial aircraft used by a foreign person or entity if—

(i) on or before November 1, 1983, the foreign person or entity entered into a written binding contract to acquire such aircraft, and

(ii) such aircraft is originally placed in service by such foreign person or entity (or its successor in interest under the contract) after May 23, 1983, and before January 1, 1986.

(E) Use After 1983.—Qualified container equipment placed in service before January 1, 1984, which is used before such date by a foreign person shall not, for purposes of section 47 of the Internal Revenue Code of 1954, be treated as ceasing to be section 38 property by reason of the use of such equipment before January 1, 1985, by a foreign person or entity. For purposes of this subparagraph, the term "qualified container equipment" means any container, container chassis, or container trailer of United States person with a present class life of not more than 6 years.

(16) Organizations Electing Exemption From Rules Relating to Previously Tax-exempt Organizations Must Elect Taxation of Exempt Arbitrage Profits.—

(A) In General.—An organization may make the election under section 168(j)(4)(E)(ii) of the Internal Revenue Code of 1954 (relating to election not to have rules relating to previously tax-exempt organizations apply) only if such organization elects the tax treatment of exempt arbitrage profits described in subparagraph (B).

(B) Taxation of Exempt Arbitrage Profits.—

(i) In General.—In the case of an organization which elects the application of this subparagraph, there is hereby imposed a tax on the exempt arbitrage profits of such organization.

(ii) Rate of Tax, Etc.—The tax imposed by clause (i)—

(I) shall be the amount of tax which would be imposed by section 11 of such Code if the exempt arbitrage profits were taxable income (and there were no oher taxable income), and

(II) shall be imposed for the first taxable year of the taxexempt use period (as defined in section 168(j)(4)(E)(ii) of such Code).

(C) Exempt Arbitrage Profits.—

(i) In General.—For purposes of this paragraph, the term exempt arbitrage profits means the aggregate amount described in clauses (i) and (ii) of subparagraph (D) of section 103(c)(6) of such Code for all taxable years for which the organization was exempt from tax under section 501(a) of such Code with respect to obligations—

(I) associated with property described in section 168(j)(4)(E)(i), and

(II) issued before January 1, 1985.

(ii) Application of Section 103(b)(6).—For purposes of this paragraph, section 103(b)(6) of such Code shall apply to obligations issued before January 1, 1985, but the amount described in clauses (i) and (ii) of subparagraph (D) thereof shall be determined without regard to clauses (i)(II) and (ii) of subparagraph (F) thereof.

(D) Other Laws Applicable.—

(i) In General.—Except as provided in clause (ii), all provisions of law, including penalties applicable with respect to the tax imposed by section 11 of such Code shall apply with respect to the tax imposed by this paragraph.

(ii) No Credits Against Tax, Etc.—The tax imposed by this paragraph shall not be treated as imposed by section 11 of such Code for purposes of—

(I) part VI of subchapter A of chapter 1 of such Code (relating to minimum tax for tax preferences), and

(II) determining the amount of any credit allowable under subpart A of part IV of such subchapter.

(E) Election.—Any election under subparagraph (A)—
(i) shall be made at such time and in such manner as the Secretary may prescribe,
(ii) shall apply to any successor organization which is engaged in substantially similar activities, and
(iii) once made, shall be irrevocable.
(17) Certain Transitional Leased Property.—The amendments made by this section shall not apply to property described in section 168(c)(2)(D) of the Internal Revenue Code of 1954, as in effect on the day before the date of the enactment of this Act, and which is described in any of the following subparagraphs:
(A) Property is described in this subparagraph if such property is leased to a university, and—
(i) on June 16, 1983, the Board of Administrators of the university adopted a resolution approving the rehabilitation of the property in connection with an overall campus development program; and
(ii) the property houses a basketball arena and university offices.
(B) Property is described in this subparagraph if such property is leased to a charitable organization, and—
(i) on August 21, 1981, the charitable organization acquired the property, with a view towards rehabilitating the property; and
(ii) on June 12, 1982, an arson fire caused substantial damage to the property, delaying the planned rehabilitation.
(C) Property is described in this subparagraph if such property is leased to a corporation that is described in section 501(c)(3) of the Internal Revenue Code of 1954 (relating to organizations exempt from tax) pursuant to a contract—
(i) which was entered into on August 3, 1983; and
(ii) under which the corporation first occupied the property on December 22, 1983.
(D) Property is described in this subparagraph if such property is leased to an educational institution for use as an Arts and Humanities Center and with respect to which—
(i) in November 1982, an architect was engaged to design a planned renovation;
(ii) in January 1983, the architectural plans were completed;
(iii) in December 1983, a demolition contract was entered into; and
(iv) in March 1984, a renovation contract was entered into.
(E) Property is described in this subparagraph if such property is used by a college as a dormitory, and—
(i) in October 1981, the college purchased the property with a view towards renovating the property;
(ii) renovation plans were delayed because of a zoning dispute; and
(iii) in May 1983, the court of highest jurisdiction in the State in which the college is located resolved the zoning dispute in favor of the college.
(F) Property is described in this subparagraph if such property is a fraternity house related to a university with respect to which—
(i) in August 1982, the university retained attorneys to advise the university regarding the rehabilitation of the property;
(ii) on January 21, 1983, the governing body of the university established a committee to develop rehabilitation plans;
(iii) on January 10, 1984, the governor of the state in which the university is located approved historic district designation for an area that includes the property; and
(iv) on February 2, 1984, historic preservation certification applications for the property were filed with a historic landmarks commission.
(G) Property is described in this subparagraph if such property is leased to a retirement community with respect to which—
(i) on January 5, 1977, a certificate of incorporation was filed with the appropriate authority of the State in which the retirement community is located; and
(ii) on November 22, 1983, the Board of Trustees adopted a resolution evidencing the intention to begin immediate construction of the property.
(H) Property is described in this subparagraph if such property is used by a university, and—
(i) in July 1982, the Board of Trustees of the university adopted a master plan for the financing of the property; and
(ii) as of August 1, 1983, at least $60,000 in private expenditures had been expended in connection with the property.

In the case of Clemson University, the preceding sentence applies only to the Continuing Education Center and the component housing project.
(I) Property is described in this subparagraph if such property is used by a university as a fine arts center and the Board of Trustees of such university authorized the sale-leaseback agreement with respect to such property on March 7, 1984.
(J) Property is described in this subparagraph if such property is used by a tax-exempt entity as an international trade center, and
(i) prior to 1982, an environmental impact study for such property was completed;
(ii) on June 24, 1981, a developer made a written commitment to provide one-third of the financing for the development of such property; and
(iii) on October 20, 1983, such developer was approved by the Board of Directors of the tax-exempt entity.
(K) Property is described in this subparagraph if such property is used by [a] university of osteopathic medicine and health sciences, and on or before December 31, 1983, the Board of Trustees of such university approved the construction of such property.
(L) Property is described in this subparagraph if such property is used by a tax-exempt entity, and—
(i) such use is pursuant to a lease with a taxpayer which placed substantial improvements in service;
(ii) on May 23, 1983, there existed architectural plans and specifications (within the meaning of sec. 48(g)(1)(C)(ii) of the Internal Revenue Code of 1954); and
(iii) prior to May 23, 1983, at least 10 percent of the total cost of such improvements was actually paid or incurred.
Property is described in this subparagraph if such property was leased to a tax-exempt entity pursuant to a lease recorded in the Register of Deeds of Essex County, New Jersey, on May 7, 1984, and a deed of such property was recorded in the Register of Deeds of Essex County, New Jersey, on May 7, 1984.
(M) Property is described in this subparagraph if such property is used as a convention center, and on June 2, 1983, the City Council of the city in which the center is located provided for over $6 million for the project.
(18) Special Rule for Amendment Made by Subsection (c)(1).—
(A) In General.—The amendment made by subsection (c)(1) shall not apply to property—
(i) leased by the taxpayer on or before November 1, 1983, or
(ii) leased by the taxpayer after November 1, 1983, if on or before such date the taxpayer entered into a written binding contract requiring the taxpayer to lease such property.
(B) Limitation.—Subparagraph (A) shall apply to the amendment made by subsection (c)(1) only to the extent such amendment relates to property described in subclause (II), (III), or (IV) of section 168(j)(3)(B)(ii) of the Internal Revenue Code of 1954 (as added by this section).
(19) Special Rule for Certain Energy Management Contracts.—
(A) In General.—The amendments made by subsection (e) shall not apply to property used pursuant to a energy management contract that was entered into prior to May 1, 1984.
(B) Definition of energy management contract.—For purposes of subparagraph (A), the term "energy management contract" means a contract for the providing of energy conservation or energy management services.
(20) Definitions.—For purposes of this subsection—
(A) Tax-Exempt Entity.—The term "tax-exempt entity" has the same meaning as when used in section 168(j) of the Internal Revenue Code of 1954 (as added by this section), except that such term shall include any related entity (within the meaning of such section).
(B) Treatment of Improvements.—
(i) In General.—For purposes of this subsection, an improvement to property shall not be treated as a separate property unless such improvement is a substantial improvement with respect to such property.
(ii) Substantial Improvement.—For purposes of clause (i), the term "substantial improvement" has the meaning given such term by section 168(f)(1)(C) of such Code determined—
(I) by substituting "property" for "building" each place it appears therein,

(II) by substituting "20 percent" for "25 percent" in clause (ii) thereof, and

(III) without regard to clause (iii) thereof.

(C) Foreign Person or Entity.—The term "foreign person or entity" has the meaning given to such term by subparagraph (C) of section 168(j)(4) of such Code (as added by this section). For purposes of this subparagraph and subparagraph (A), such subparagraph (C) shall be applied without regard to the last sentence thereof.

(D) Leases and Subleases.—The determination of whether there is a lease or sublease to a tax-exempt entity shall take into account sections 168(j)(6)(A), 168(j)(8)(A) and 7701(e) of the Internal Revenue Code of 1954 (as added by this section).

[Sec. 168(k)]

(k) CROSS REFERENCE.—

For special rules with respect to certain gain derived from disposition of recovery property, see sections 1245 and 1250.

Amendments

- **1985 (P.L. 99-121)**

P.L. 99-121, § 103(b)(1)(A):

Amended Code Sec. 168 by striking out "18-year real property" each place it appeared in the text and headings thereof and inserting in lieu thereof "19-year real property". **Effective** with respect to property placed in service by the taxpayer after 5-8-85. However, for an exception and special rule, see Act Sec. 105(b)(2) and (3), below.

P.L. 99-121, § 105(b)(2) and (3), provides:

(2) EXCEPTION.—The amendments made by section 103 shall not apply to property placed in service by the taxpayer before January 1, 1987, if—

(A) the taxpayer or a qualified person entered into a binding contract to purchase or construct such property before May 9, 1985, or

(B) construction of such property was commenced by or for the taxpayer or a qualified person before May 9, 1985.

For purposes of this paragraph, the term "qualified person" means any person whose rights in such a contract or such property are transferred to the taxpayer, but only if such property is not placed in service before such rights are transferred to the taxpayer.

(3) SPECIAL RULE FOR COMPONENTS.—For purposes of applying section 168(f)(1)(B) of the Internal Revenue Code of 1954 (as amended by section 103) to components placed in service after December 31, 1986, property to which paragraph (2) of this subsection applies shall be treated as placed in service by the taxpayer before May 9, 1985.

- **1984, Deficit Reduction Act of 1984 (P.L. 98-369)**

P.L. 98-369, § 31(a):

Redesignated Code Sec. 168(j) as 168(k). **Effective** as noted in Act Sec. 31(g) following former Code Sec. 168(j).

- **1982, Tax Equity and Fiscal Responsibility Act of 1982 (P.L. 97-248)**

P.L. 97-248, § 208(a)(1):

Redesignated Code Sec. 168(i) as (j). **Effective** for agreements entered into after 7-1-82, or to property placed in service after 7-1-82.

- **1981, Economic Recovery Tax Act of 1981 (P.L. 97-34)**

P.L. 97-34, § 201(a):

Added Code Sec. 168(i). **Effective** for property placed in service after 12-31-80, in tax years ending after such date.

- **1976, Tax Reform Act of 1976 (P.L. 94-455)**

P.L. 94-455, § 1951(b)(4):

Repealed Code Sec. 168. **Effective** 1-1-77. Prior to repeal, Code Sec. 168 read as follows:

SEC. 168. AMORTIZATION OF EMERGENCY FACILITIES.

(a) General Rule.—Every person, at his election, shall be entitled to a deduction with respect to the amortization of the adjusted basis (for determining gain) of any emergency facility (as defined in subsection (d)), based on a period of 60 months. Such amortization deduction shall be an amount, with respect to each month of such period within the taxable year, equal to the adjusted basis of the facility at the end of such month divided by the number of months (including the month for which the deduction is computed) remaining in the period. Such adjusted basis at the end of the month shall be computed without regard to the amortization deduction for such month. The amortization deduction above provided with respect to any month shall, except to the extent provided in subsection (f), be in lieu of the depreciation deduction with respect to such facility for such month provided by section 167. The 60-month period shall begin as to any emergency facility, at the election of the taxpayer, with the month following the month in which the facility was completed or acquired, or with the succeeding taxable year.

(b) Election of Amortization.—The election of the taxpayer to take the amortization deduction and to begin the 60-month period with the month following the month in which the facility was completed or acquired, or with the taxable year succeeding the taxable year in which such facility was completed or acquired, shall be made by filing with the Secretary or his delegate, in such manner, in such form, and within such time, as the Secretary or his delegate may by regulations prescribe, a statement of such election.

(c) Termination of Amortization Deduction.—A taxpayer which has elected under subsection (b) to take the amortization deduction provided in subsection (a) may, at any time after making such election, discontinue the amortization deduction with respect to the remainder of the amortization period, such discontinuance to begin as of the beginning of any month specified by the taxpayer in a notice in writing filed with the Secretary or his delegate before the beginning of such month. The depreciation deduction provided under section 167 shall be allowed, beginning with the first month as to which the amortization deduction does not apply, and the taxpayer shall not be entitled to any further amortization deduction with respect to such emergency facility.

(d) Definitions.—

(1) Emergency facility.—For purposes of this section, the term "emergency facility" means any facility, land, building, machinery, or equipment, or any part thereof, the construction, reconstruction, erection, installation, or acquisition of which was completed after December 31, 1949, and with respect to which a certificate under subsection (e) has been made. In no event shall an amortization deduction be allowed in respect of any emergency facility for any taxable year unless a certificate in respect thereof under this paragraph shall have been made before the filing of the taxpayer's return for such taxable year.

(2) Emergency period.—For purposes of this section, the term "emergency period" means the period beginning January 1, 1950, and ending on the date on which the President proclaims that the utilization of a substantial portion of the emergency facilities with respect to which certifications under subsection (e) have been made is no longer required in the interest of national defense.

(e) Determination of Adjusted Basis of Emergency Facility.—In determining, for purposes of subsection (a) or (g), the adjusted basis of an emergency facility—

(1) Certifications on or before August 22, 1957.—In the case of a certificate made on or before August 22, 1957, there shall be included only so much of the amount of the adjusted basis of such facility (computed without regard to this section) as is properly attributable to such construction, reconstruction, erection, installation, or acquisition after December 31, 1949, as the certifying authority, designated by the President by Executive Order, has certified as necessary in the interest of national defense during the emergency period, and only such portion of such amount as such authority has certified as attributable to defense purposes. Such certification shall be under such regulations as may be prescribed from time to time by such certifying authority with the approval of the President. An application for a certificate must be filed at such time and in such manner as may be prescribed by such certifying authority under such regulations, but in no event shall such certificate have any effect unless an application therefor is filed before March 24, 1951, or before the expiration of 6 months after the beginning of such construction, reconstruction, erection, or installation or the date of such acquisition, whichever is later.

(2) Certifications after August 22, 1957.—In the case of a certificate made after August 22, 1957, there shall be included only so much of the amount of the adjusted basis of such facility (computed without regard to this section) as is properly attributable to such construction, reconstruction, erection, installation, or acquisition after December 31, 1949, as the certifying authority designated by the President by Executive Order, has certified is to be used—

(A) to produce new or specialized defense items or components of new or specialized defense items (as defined in paragraph (4)) during the emergency period,

(B) to provide research, developmental, or experimental services during the emergency period for the Department of Defense (or one of the component departments of such

Department), or for the Atomic Energy Commission as a part of the national defense program, or

(C) to provide primary processing for uranium ore or uranium concentrate under a program of the Atomic Energy Commission for the development of new sources of uranium ore or uranium concentrate,

and only such portion of such amount as such authority has certified is attributable to the national defense program. Such certification shall be under such regulations as may be prescribed from time to time by such certifying authority with the approval of the President. An application for a certificate must be filed at such time and in such manner as may be prescribed by such certifying authority under such regulations but in no event shall such certificate have any effect unless an application therefor is filed before the expiration of 6 months after the beginning of such construction, reconstruction, erection, or installation or the date of such acquisition. For purposes of the preceding sentence, an application which was timely filed under this subsection on or before August 22, 1957, and which was pending on such date, shall be considered to be an application timely filed under this paragraph.

(3) Separate facilities; special rule.—After the completion or acquisition of any emergency facility with respect to which a certificate under paragraph (1) or (2) has been made, any expenditure (attributable to such facility and to the period after such completion or acquisition) which does not represent construction, reconstruction, erection, installation, or acquisition included in such certificate, but with respect to which a separate certificate is made under paragraph (1) or (2), shall not be applied in adjustment of the basis of such facility, but a separate basis shall be computed therefor pursuant to paragraph (1) or (2), as the case may be, as if it were a new and separate emergency facility.

(4) Definitions.—For purposes of paragraph (2)—

(A) New or specialized defense item.—The term "new or specialized defense item" means only an item (excluding services)—

(i) which is produced, or will be produced, for sale to the Department of Defense (or one of the component departments of such Department), or to the Atomic Energy Commission, for use in the national defense program, and

(ii) for the production of which existing productive facilities are unsuitable because of its newness or of its specialized defense features.

(B) Component of new or specialized defense item.—The term "component of a new or specialized defense item" means only an item—

(i) which is, or will become, a physical part of a new or specialized defense item, and

(ii) for the production of which existing productive facilities are unsuitable because of its newness or of its specialized defense features.

(5) Limitation with respect to uranium ore or uranium concentrate processing facilities.—No certificate shall be made under paragraph (2)(C) with respect to any facility unless existing facilities for processing the uranium ore or uranium concentrate which will be processed by such facility are unsuitable because of their location.

(f) Depreciation Deduction.—If the adjusted basis of the emergency facility (computed without regard to this section) is in excess of the adjusted basis computed under subsection (e), the depreciation deduction provided by section 167 shall, despite the provisions of subsection (a) of this section, be allowed with respect to such emergency facility as if its adjusted basis for the purpose of such deduction were an amount equal to the amount of such excess.

(g) Payment by United States of Unamortized Cost of Facility.—If an amount is properly includible in the gross income of the taxpayer on account of a payment with respect to an emergency facility and such payment is certified as provided in paragraph (1), then, at the election of the taxpayer in its return for the taxable year in which such amount is so includible—

(1) The amortization deduction for the month in which such amount is so includible shall (in lieu of the amount of the deduction for such month computed under subsection (a)) be equal to the amount so includible but not in excess of the adjusted basis of the emergency facility as of the end of such month (computed without regard to any amortization deduction for such month). Payments referred to in this subsection shall be payments the amounts of which are certified, under such regulations as the President may prescribe, by the certifying authority designated by the President as compensation to the taxpayer for the unamortized cost of the emergency facility made because—

(A) a contract with the United States involving the use of the facility has been terminated by its terms or by cancellation, or

(B) the taxpayer had reasonable ground (either from provisions of a contract with the United States involving the use of the facility, or from written or oral representations made under authority of the United States) for anticipating future contracts involving the use of the facility, which future contracts have not been made.

(2) In case the taxpayer is not entitled to any amortization deduction with respect to the emergency facility, the depreciation deduction allowable under section 167 on account of the month in which such amount is so includible shall be increased by such amount, but such deduction on account of such month shall not be in excess of the adjusted basis of the emergency facility as of the end of such month (computed without regard to any amount allowable, on account of such month, under section 167 or this paragraph).

(h) Life Tenant and Remainderman.—In the case of property held by one person for life with remainder to another person, the deduction shall be computed as if the life tenant were the absolute owner of the property and shall be allowable to the life tenant.

(i) Termination.—No certificate under subsection (e) shall be made with respect to any emergency facility after December 31, 1959.

(j) Cross Reference.—

For special rule with respect to gain derived from the sale or exchange of property the adjusted basis of which is determined with regard to this section, see section 1238.

P.L. 94-455, § 1951(b)(4)(B), provides:

(B) SAVINGS PROVISION.—Notwithstanding the repeal made by subparagraph (A), if a certificate was issued before January 1, 1960, with respect to an emergency facility which is or has been placed in service before the date of the enactment of this Act, the provisions of section 168 shall not, with respect to such facility, be considered repealed. The benefit of deductions by reason of the preceding sentence shall be allowed to estates and trusts in the same manner as in the case of an individual. The allowable deduction shall be apportioned between the income beneficiaries and the fiduciary in accordance with regulations prescribed under section 642(f).

- **1986, Tax Reform Act of 1986 (P.L. 99-514)**
P.L. 99-514, §§ 203, 204 and 251(d)(2)-(7), as amended by P.L. 99-509 and P.L. 100-647, § 1002(c)-(d), provide:
SEC. 203. EFFECTIVE DATES; GENERAL TRANSITIONAL RULES.

(a) GENERAL EFFECTIVE DATES.—

(1) Section 201.—

(A) IN GENERAL.—Except as provided in this section, section 204, and section 251(d), the amendments made by section 201 shall apply to property placed in service after December 31, 1986, in taxable years ending after such date.

(B) ELECTION TO HAVE AMENDMENTS MADE BY SECTION 201 APPLY.—A taxpayer may elect (at such time and in such manner as the Secretary of the Treasury or his delegate may prescribe) to have the amendments made by section 201 apply to any property placed in service after July 31, 1986, and before January 1, 1987. No election may be made under this subparagraph with respect to property to which section 168 of the Internal Revenue Code of 1986 would not apply by reason of section 168(f)(5) of such Code if such property were placed in service after December 31, 1986.

(2) SECTION 202.—

(A) IN GENERAL.—The amendments made by section 202 shall apply to property placed in service after December 31, 1986, in taxable years ending after such date.

(B) SPECIAL RULE FOR FISCAL YEARS INCLUDING JANUARY 1, 1987.—In the case of any taxable year (other than a calendar year) which includes January 1, 1987, for purposes of applying the amendments made by section 202 to property placed in service during such taxable year and after December 31, 1986—

(i) the limitation of section 179(b)(1) of the Internal Revenue Code of 1986 (as amended by section 202) shall be reduced by the aggregate deduction under section 179 (as in effect on the day before the date of the enactment of the Tax Reform Act of 1986) for section 179 property placed in service during such taxable year and before January 1, 1987,

(ii) the limitation of section 179(b)(2) of such Code (as so amended) shall be applied by taking into account the cost of all section 179 property placed in service during such taxable year, and

(iii) the limitation of section 179(b)(3) of such Code shall be applied by taking into account the taxable income for the entire taxable year reduced by the amount of any deduction under section 179 of such Code for property placed in service during such taxable year and before January 1, 1987.

(b) GENERAL TRANSITIONAL RULE.—

(1) IN GENERAL.—The amendments made by section 201 shall not apply to—

(A) any property which is constructed, reconstructed, or acquired by the taxpayer pursuant to a written contract which was binding on March 1, 1986,

(B) property which is constructed or reconstructed by the taxpayer if—

(i) the lesser of (I) $1,000,000, or (II) 5 percent of the cost of such property has been incurred or committed by March 1, 1986, and

(ii) the construction or reconstruction of such property began by such date, or

(C) an equipped building or plant facility if construction has commenced as of March 1, 1986, pursuant to a written specific plan and more than one-half of the cost of such equipped building or facility has been incurred or committed by such date.

For purposes of this paragraph, all members of the same affiliated group of corporations (within the meaning of section 1504 of the Internal Revenue Code of 1986) filing a consolidated return shall be treated as one taxpayer.

(2) REQUIREMENT THAT CERTAIN PROPERTY BE PLACED IN SERVICE BEFORE CERTAIN DATE.—

(A) IN GENERAL.—Paragraph (1) and section 204(a) (other than paragraph (8) or (12) thereof) shall not apply to any property unless such property has a class life of at least 7 years and is placed in service before the applicable date determined under the following table:

In the case of property with a class life of:	The applicable date is:
At least 7 but less than 20 years	January 1, 1989
20 years or more	January 1, 1991

(B) RESIDENTIAL RENTAL AND NONRESIDENTIAL REAL PROPERTY.—In the case of residential rental property and nonresidential real property, the applicable date is January 1, 1991.

(C) CLASS LIVES.—For purposes of subparagraph (A)—

(i) the class life of property to which section 168(g)(3)(B) of the Internal Revenue Code of 1986 (as added by section 201) applies shall be the class life in effect on January 1, 1986, except that computer-based telephone central office switching equipment described in section 168(e)(3)(B)(iii) of such Code shall be treated as having a class life of 6 years,

(ii) property described in section 204(a) shall be treated as having a class life of 20 years, and

(iii) property with no class life shall be treated as having a class life of 12 years.

(D) SUBSTITUTION OF APPLICABLE DATES.—If any provision of this Act substitutes a date for an applicable date, this paragraph shall be applied by using such date.

(3) PROPERTY QUALIFIES IF SOLD AND LEASED BACK IN 3 MONTHS.—Property shall be treated as meeting the requirements of paragraphs (1) and (2) or section 204(a) with respect to any taxpayer if such property is acquired by the taxpayer from a person—

(A) in whose hands such property met the requirements of paragraphs (1) and (2) or section 204(a) (or would have met such requirements if placed in service by such person), or

(B) who placed the property in service before January 1, 1987,

and such property is leased back by the taxpayer to such person, or is leased to such person, not later than the earlier of the applicable date under paragraph (2) or the day which is 3 months after such property was placed in service.

(4) PLANT FACILITY.—For purposes of paragraph (1), the term "plant facility" means a facility which does not include any building (or with respect to which buildings constitute an insignificant portion) and which is—

(A) a self-contained single operating unit or processing operation,

(B) located on a single site, and

(C) identified as a single unitary project as of March 1, 1986.

(c) PROPERTY FINANCED WITH TAX-EXEMPT BONDS.—

(1) IN GENERAL.—Except as otherwise provided in this subsection or section 204, subparagraph (C) of section 168(g)(1) of the Internal Revenue Code of 1986 (as added by this Act) shall apply to property placed in service after December 31, 1986, in taxable years ending after such date, to the extent such property is financed by the proceeds of an obligation (including a refunding obligation) issued after March 1, 1986.

(2) EXCEPTIONS.—

(A) CONSTRUCTION OR BINDING AGREEMENTS.—Subparagraph (C) of section 168(g)(1) of such Code (as so added) shall not apply to obligations with respect to a facility—

(i)(I) the original use of which commences with the taxpayer, and the construction, reconstruction, or rehabilitation of which began before March 2, 1986, and was completed on or after such date,

(II) with respect to which a binding contract to incur significant expenditures for construction, reconstruction, or rehabilitation was entered into before March 2, 1986, and some of such expenditures are incurred on or after such date, or

(III) acquired on or after March 2, 1986, pursuant to a binding contract entered into before such date, and

(ii) described in an inducement resolution or other comparable preliminary approval adopted by the issuing authority (or by a voter referendum) before March 2, 1986.

(B) REFUNDING.—

(i) IN GENERAL.—Except as provided in clause (ii), in the case of property placed in service after December 31, 1986, which is financed by the proceeds of an obligation which is issued solely to refund another obligation which was issued before March 2, 1986, subparagraph (C) of section 168(g)(1) of such Code (as so added) shall apply only with respect to an amount equal to the basis in such property which has not been recovered before the date such refunded obligation is issued.

(ii) SIGNIFICANT EXPENDITURES.—In the case of facilities the original use of which commences with the taxpayer and with respect to which significant expenditures are made before January 1, 1987, subparagraph (C) of section 168(g)(1) of such Code (as so added) shall not apply with respect to such facilities to the extent such facilities are financed by the proceeds of an obligation issued solely to refund another obligation which was issued before March 2, 1986.

(C) FACILITIES.—In the case of an inducement resolution or other comparable preliminary approval adopted by an issuing authority before March 2, 1986, for purposes of subparagraphs (A) and (B)(ii) with respect to obligations described in such resolution, the term "facilities" means the facilities described in such resolution.

(D) SIGNIFICANT EXPENDITURES.—For purposes of this paragraph, the term "significant expenditures" means expenditures greater than 10 percent of the reasonably anticipated cost of the construction, reconstruction, or rehabilitation of the facility involved.

(d) MID-QUARTER CONVENTION.—In the case of any taxable year beginning before October 1, 1987 in which property to which the amendments made by section 201 do not apply is placed in service, such property shall be taken into account in determining whether section 168(d)(3) of the Internal Revenue Code of 1986 (as added by section 201) applies for such taxable year to property to which such amendments apply. The preceding sentence shall only apply to property which would be taken into account if such amendments did apply.

(e) NORMALIZATION REQUIREMENTS.—

(1) IN GENERAL.—A normalization method of accounting shall not be treated as being used with respect to any public utility property for purposes of section 167 or 168 of the Internal Revenue Code of 1986 if the taxpayer, in computing its cost of service for ratemaking purposes and reflecting operating results in its regulated books of account, reduces the excess tax reserve more rapidly or to a greater extent than such reserve would be reduced under the average rate assumption method.

Code Sec. 168

(2) DEFINITIONS.—For purpose of this subsection—
(A) EXCESS TAX RESERVE.—The term "excess tax reserve" means the excess of—
(i) the reserve for deferred taxes (as described in section 167(l)(3)(G)(ii) or 168(e)(3)(B)(ii) of the Internal Revenue Code of 1954 as in effect on the day before the date of the enactment of this Act), over
(ii) the amount which would be the balance in such reserve if the amount of such reserve were determined by assuming that the corporate rate reductions provided in this Act were in effect for all prior periods.
(B) AVERAGE RATE ASSUMPTION METHOD.—The average rate assumption method is the method under which the excess in the reserve for deferred taxes is reduced over the remaining lives of the property as used in its regulated books of account which gave rise to the reserve for deferred taxes. Under such method, if timing differences for the property reverse, the amount of the adjustment to the reserve for the deferred taxes is calculated by multiplying—
(i) the ratio of the aggregate deferred taxes for the property to the aggregate timing differences for the property as of the beginning of the period in question, by
(ii) the amount of the timing differences which reverse during such period.

SEC. 204. ADDITIONAL TRANSITIONAL RULES.
(a) OTHER TRANSITIONAL RULES.
(1) URBAN RENOVATION PROJECTS.—
(A) IN GENERAL.—The amendments made by section 201 shall not apply to any property which is an integral part of any qualified urban renovation project.
(B) QUALIFIED URBAN RENOVATION PROJECT.—For purposes of subparagraph (A), the term "qualified urban renovation project" means any project—
(i) described in subparagraph (C), (D), (E), or (G) which before March 1, 1986, was publicly announced by a political subdivision of a State for a renovation of an urban area within its jurisdiction,
(ii) described in subparagraph (C), (D) or (G) which before March 1, 1986, was identified as a single unitary project in the internal financing plans of the primary developer of the project,
(iii) described in subparagraph (C) or (D), which is not substantially modified on or after March 1, 1986, and
(iv) described in subparagraph (F) or (H).
(C) PROJECT WHERE AGREEMENT ON DECEMBER 19, 1984.—A project is described in this subparagraph if—
(i) a political subdivision granted on July 11, 1985, development rights to the primary developer-purchaser of such project, and
(ii) such project was the subject of a development agreement between a political subdivision and a bridge authority on December 19, 1984.
For purposes of this subparagraph, section 203(b)(2) shall be applied by substituting "January 1, 1994" for "January 1, 1991" each place it appears.
(D) CERTAIN ADDITIONAL PROJECTS.—A project is described in this subparagraph if it is described in any of the following clauses of this subparagraph and the primary developer of all such projects is the same person:
(i) A project is described in this clause if the development agreement with respect thereto was entered into during April 1984 and the estimated cost of the project is approximately $194,000,000.
(ii) A project is described in this clause if the development agreement with respect thereto was entered into during May 1984 and the estimated cost of the project is approximately $190,000,000.
(iii) A project is described in this clause if the project has an estimated cost of approximately $92,000,000 and at least $7,000,000 was spent before September 26, 1985, with respect to such project.
(iv) A project is described in this clause if the estimated project cost is approximately $39,000,000 and at least $2,000,000 of construction cost for such project were incurred before September 26, 1985.
(v) A project is described in this clause if the development agreement with respect thereto was entered into before September 26, 1985, and the estimated cost of the project is approximately $150,000,000.
(vi) A project is described in this clause if the board of directors of the primary developer approved such project in December 1982, and the estimated cost of such project is approximately $107,000,000.

(vii) A project is described in this clause if the board of directors of the primary developer approved such project in December 1982, and the estimated cost of such project is approximately $59,000,000.
(viii) A project is described in this clause if the Board of Directors of the primary developer approved such project in December 1983, following selection of the developer by a city council on September 26, 1983, and the estimated cost of such project is approximately $107,000,000.
(E) PROJECT WHERE PLAN CONFIRMED ON OCTOBER 4, 1984.—A project is described in this subparagraph if—
(i) a State or an agency, instrumentality, or political subdivision thereof approved the filing of a general project plan on June 18, 1981, and on October 4, 1984, a State or an agency, instrumentality, or political subdivision thereof confirmed such plan,
(ii) the project plan as confirmed on October 4, 1984, included construction or renovation of office buildings, a hotel, a trade mart, theaters, and a subway complex, and
(iii) significant segments of such project were the subject of one or more conditional designations granted by a State or an agency, instrumentality, or political subdivision thereof to one or more developers before January 1, 1985.
The preceding sentence shall apply with respect to a property only to the extent that a building on such property site was identified as part of the project plan before September 26, 1985, and only to the extent that the size of the building on such property site was not substantially increased by reason of a modification to the project plan with respect to such property on or after such date. For purposes of this subparagraph, section 203(b)(2) shall be applied by substituting "January 1, 1988" for "January 1, 1991" each place it appears.
(F) A project is described in this subparagraph if it is a sports and entertainment facility which—
(i) is to be used by both a National Hockey League team and a National Basketball Association team;
(ii) is to be constructed on a platform utilizing air rights over land acquired by a State authority and identified as site B in a report dated May 30, 1984, prepared for a State urban development corporation; and
(iii) is eligible for real property tax, and power and energy benefits pursuant to the provisions of State legislation approved and effective July 7, 1982.
A project is also described in this subparagraph if it is a mixed-use development which is—
(I) to be constructed above a public railroad station utilized by the national railroad passenger corporation and commuter railroads serving two States; and
(II) will include the reconstruction of such station so as to make it a more efficient transportation center and to better integrate the station with the development above, such reconstruction plans to be prepared in cooperation with a State transportation authority.
For purposes of this subparagraph, section 203(b)(2) shall be applied by substituting "January 1, 1998" for the applicable date that would otherwise apply.
(G) A project is described in this subparagraph if—
(i) an inducement resolution was passed on March 9, 1984, for the issuance of obligations with respect to such project,
(ii) such resolution was extended by resolutions passed on August 14, 1984, April 2, 1985, August 13, 1985, and July 8, 1986,
(iii) an application was submitted on January 31, 1984, for an Urban Development Action Grant with respect to such project, and
(iv) an Urban Development Action Grant was preliminarily approved for all or part of such project on July 3, 1986.
(H) A project is described in this subparagraph if it is a redevelopment project, with respect to which $10,000,000 in industrial revenue bonds were approved by a State Development Finance Authority on January 15, 1986, a village transferred approximately $4,000,000 of bond volume authority to the State in June 1986, and a binding Redevelopment Agreement was executed between a city and the development team on June 30, 1986.
(2) CERTAIN PROJECTS GRANTED FERC LICENSES, ETC.—The amendments made by section 201 shall not apply to any property which is part of a project—
(A) which is certified by the Federal Energy Regulatory Commission before March 2, 1986, as a qualifying facility for

purposes of the Public Utility Regulatory Policies Act of 1978,

(B) which was granted before March 2, 1986, a hydroelectric license for such project by the Federal Energy Regulatory Commission, or

(C) which is a hydroelectric project of less than 80 megawatts that filed an application for a permit, exemption, or license with the Federal Energy Regulatory Commission before March 2, 1986.

(3) SUPPLY OR SERVICE CONTRACTS.—The amendments made by section 201 shall not apply to any property which is readily identifiable with and necessary to carry out a written supply or service contract, or agreement to lease, which was binding on March 1, 1986.

(4) PROPERTY TREATED UNDER PRIOR TAX ACTS.—The amendments made by section 201 shall not apply—

(A) to property described in section 12(c)(2) (as amended by the Technical and Miscellaneous Revenue Act of 1988), 31(g)(5), or 31(g)(17)(J) of the Tax Reform Act of 1984,

(B) to property described in section 209(d)(1)(B) of the Tax Equity and Fiscal Responsibility Act of 1982, as amended by the Tax Reform Act of 1984, and

(C) to property described in section 216(b)(3) of the Tax Equity and Fiscal Responsibility Act of 1982.

(5) SPECIAL RULES FOR PROPERTY INCLUDED IN MASTER PLANS OF INTEGRATED PROJECTS.—The amendments made by section 201 shall not apply to any property placed in service pursuant to a master plan which is clearly identifiable as of March 1, 1986, for any project described in any of the following subparagraphs of this paragraph:

(A) A project is described in this subparagraph if—

(i) the project involves production platforms for off-shore drilling, oil and gas pipeline to shore, process and storage facilities, and a marine terminal, and

(ii) at least $900,000,000 of the costs of such project were incurred before September 26, 1985.

(B) A project is described in this subparagraph if—

(i) such project involves a fiber optic network of at least 20,000 miles, and

(ii) before September 26, 1985, construction commenced pursuant to the master plan and at least $85,000,000 was spent on construction.

(C) A project is described in this subparagraph if—

(i) such project passes through at least 10 States and involves intercity communication link[s] (including one or more repeater sites, terminals and junction stations for microwave transmissions, regenerators or fiber optics and other related equipment),

(ii) the lesser of $150,000,000 or 5 percent of the total project cost has been expended, incurred, or committed before March 2, 1986, by one or more taxpayers each of which is a member of the same affiliated group (as defined in section 1504(a)), and

(iii) such project consists of a comprehensive plan for meeting network capacity requirements as encompassed within either:

(I) a November 5, 1985, presentation made to and accepted by the Chairman of the Board and the president of the taxpayer, or

(II) the approvals by the Board of Directors of the parent company of the taxpayer on May 3, 1985, and September 22, 1985, and of the executive committee of said board on December 23, 1985.

(D) A project is described in this subparagraph if—

(i) such project is part of a flat rolled product modernization plan which was initially presented to the Board of Directors of the taxpayer on July 8, 1983,

(ii) such program will be carried out at 3 locations, and

(iii) such project will involve a total estimated minimum capital cost of at least $250,000,000.

(E) A project is described in this subparagraph if the project is being carried out by a corporation engaged in the production of paint, chemicals, fiberglass, and glass, and if—

(i) the project includes a production line which applied a thin coating to glass in the manufacture of energy efficient residential products, if approved by the management committee of the corporation on January 29, 1986,

(ii) the project is a turbogenerator which was approved by the president of such corporation and at least $1,000,000 of the cost of which was incurred or committed before such date,

(iii) the project is a waste-to-energy disposal system which was initially approved by the management commit-

tee of the corporation on March 29, 1982, and at least $5,000,000 of the cost of which was incurred before September 26, 1985,

(iv) the project, which involves the expansion of an existing service facility and the addition of new lab facilities needed to accommodate topcoat and undercoat production needs of a nearby automotive assembly plant, was approved by the corporation's management committee on March 5, 1986, or

(v) the project is part of a facility to consolidate and modernize the silica production of such corporation and the project was provided by the president of such corporation on August 19, 1985.

(F) A project is described in this subparagraph if—

(i) such project involves a port terminal and oil pipeline extending generally from the area of Los Angeles, California, to the area of Midland, Texas, and

(ii) before September 26, 1985, there is a binding contract for dredging and channeling with respect thereto and a management contract with a construction manager for such project.

(G) A project is described in this subparagraph if—

(i) the project is a newspaper printing and distribution plant project with respect to which a contract for the purchase of 8 printing press units and related equipment to be installed in a single press line was entered into on January 8, 1985, and

(ii) the contract price for such units and equipment represents at least 50 percent of the total cost of such project.

(H) A project is described in this subparagraph if it is the second phase of a project involving direct current transmission lines spanning approximately 190 miles from the United States-Canadian border to Ayer, Massachusetts, alternating current transmission lines in Massachusetts from Ayer to Milbury to West Medway, DC-AC converted terminals to Monroe, New Hampshire, and Ayer, Massachusetts, and other related equipment and facilities.

(I) A project is described in this subparagraph if it involves not more than two natural gas-fired combined cycle electric generating units each having a net electrical capability of approximately 233 megawatts, and a sale contract for approximately one-half of the output of the 1st unit was entered into in December 1985.

(J) A project is described in this subparagraph if—

(i) the project involves an automobile manufacturing facility (including equipment and incidental appurtenances) to be located in the United States, and

(ii) either—

(I) the project was the subject of a memorandum of understanding between 2 automobile manufacturers that was signed before September 25, 1985, the automobile manufacturing facility (including equipment and incidental appurtenances) will involve a total estimated cost of approximately $750,000,000, and will have an annual production capacity of approximately 240,000 vehicles or

(II) The Board of Directors of an automobile manufacturer approved a written plan for the conversion of existing facilities to produce new models of a vehicle not currently produced in the United States, such facilities will be placed in service by July 1, 1987, and such Board action occurred in July 1985 with respect to a $602,000,000 expenditure, a $438,000,000 expenditure, and a $321,000,000 expenditure.

(K) A project is described in this subparagraph if—

(i) the project involves a joint venture between a utility company and a paper company for a supercalendared paper mill, and at least $50,000,000 was incurred or committed with respect to such project before March 1, 1986, or

(ii) the project involves a paper mill for the manufacture of newsprint (including a cogeneration facility) is generally based on a written design and feasibility study that was completed on December 15, 1981, and will be placed in service before January 1, 1991, or

(iii) the project is undertaken by a Maine corporation and involves the modernization of pulp and paper mills in Millinocket and/or East Millinocket, Maine, or

(iv) the project involves the installation of a paper machine for production of coated publication papers, the modernization of a pulp mill, and the installation of machinery and equipment with respect to related processes, as of December 31, 1985, in excess of $50,000,000 was incurred for the project, as of July 1986, in excess of $150,000,000 was incurred for the project, and the project is located in Pine Bluff, Arkansas, or

Code Sec. 168

(v) the project involves property of a type described in ADR classes 26.1, 26.2, 25, 00.3 and 00.4 included in a paper plant which will manufacture and distribute tissue, towel or napkin products; is located in Effingham County, Georgia; and is generally based upon a written General Description which was submitted to the Georgia Department of Revenue on or about June 13, 1985.

(L) A project is described in this subparagraph if—

(i) a letter of intent with respect to such project was executed on June 4, 1985, and

(ii) a 5-percent downpayment was made in connection with such project for 2 10-unit press lines and related equipment.

(M) A project is described in this subparagraph if—

(i) the project involves the retrofit of ammonia plants,

(ii) as of March 1, 1986, more than $390,000 had been expended for engineering and equipment, and

(iii) more than $170,000 was expensed in 1985 as a portion of preliminary engineering expense.

(N) A project is described in this subparagraph if the project involves bulkhead intermodal flat cars which are placed in service before January 1, 1987, and either—

(i) more than $2,290,000 of expenditures were made before March 1, 1986, with respect to a project involving up to 300 platforms, or

(ii) more than $95,000 of expenditures were made before March 1, 1986, with respect to a project involving up to 850 platforms.

(O) A project is described in this subparagraph if—

(i) the project involves the production and transportation of oil and gas from a well located north of the Arctic Circle, and

(ii) more than $200,000,000 of cost had been incurred or committed before September 26, 1985.

(P) A project is described in this subparagraph if—

(i) a commitment letter was entered into with a financial institution on January 23, 1986, for the financing of the project,

(ii) the project involves intercity communication links (including microwave and fiber optics communications systems and related property),

(iii) the project consists of communications links between—

(I) Omaha, Nebraska, and Council Bluffs, Iowa,

(II) Waterloo, Iowa and Sioux City, Iowa,

(III) Davenport, Iowa and Springfield, Illinois, and

(iv) the estimated cost of such project is approximately $13,000,000.

(Q) A project is described in this subparagraph if—

(i) such project is a mining modernization project involving mining, transport, and milling operatons,

(ii) before September 26, 1985, at least $20,000,000 was expended for engineering studies which were approved by the Board of Directors of the taxpayer on January 27, 1983, and

(iii) such project will involve a total estimated minimum cost of $350,000,000.

(R) A project is described in this subparagraph if—

(i) such project is a dragline acquired in connection with a 3-stage program which began in 1980 to increase production from a coal mine,

(ii) at least $35,000,000 was spent before September 26, 1985, on the 1st 2 stages of the program, and

(iii) at least $4,000,000 was spent to prepare the mine site for the dragline.

(S) A project is described in this subparagraph if it is a project consisting of a mineral processing facility using a heap leaching system (including waste dumps, low-grade dumps, a leaching area, and mine roads) and if—

(i) convertible subordinated debentures were issued in August 1985, to finance the project,

(ii) construction of the project was authorized by the Board of Directors of the taxpayer on or before December 31, 1985,

(iii) at least $750,000 was paid or incurred with respect to the project on or before December 31, 1985, and

(iv) the project is placed in service on or before December 31, 1986.

(T) A project is described in this subparagraph if it is a plant facility on Alaska's North Slope which is placed in service before January 1, 1988, and—

(i) the approximate cost of which is $675,000,000, of which approximately $400,000,000 was spent on off-site construction,

(ii) the approximate cost of which is $445,000,000, of which approximately $400,000,000 was spent on off-site construction and more than 50 percent of the project cost was spent prior to December 31, 1985, or

(iii) the approximate cost of which is $375,000,000, of which approximately $260,000,000 was spent on off-site construction.

(U) A project is described in this subparagraph if it involves the connecting of existing retail stores in the downtown area of a city to a new covered area, the total project will be 250,000 square feet, a formal Memorandum of Understanding relating to development of the project was executed with the city on July 2, 1986, and the estimated cost of the project is $18,186,424.

(V) A project is described in this subparagraph if it includes a 200,000 square foot office tower, a 200-room hotel, a 300,000 square foot retail center, an 800-space parking facility, the total cost is projected to be $60,000,000, and $1,250,000 was expended with respect to the site before August 25, 1986.

(W) A project is described in this subparagraph if it is a joint use and development project including an integrated hotel, convention center, office, related retail facilities and public mass transportation terminal, and vehicle parking facilities which satisfies the following conditions:

(i) is developed within certain air space rights and upon real property exchanged for such joint use and development project which is owned or acquired by a state department of transportation, a regional mass transit district in a county with a population of at least 5,000,000 and a community redevelopment agency;

(ii) such project affects an existing, approximately forty (40) acre public mass transportation bus-way terminal facility located adjacent to an interstate highway;

(iii) a memorandum of understanding with respect to such joint use and development project is executed by a state department of transportation, such a county regional mass transit district and a community redevelopment agency on or before December 31, 1986, and

(iv) a major portion of such joint use and development project is placed in service by December 31, 1990.

(X) A project is described in this subparagraph if—

(i) it is an $8,000,000 project to provide advanced control technology for adipic acid at a plant, which was authorized by the company's Board of Directors in October 1985, at December 31, 1985, $1,400,000 was committed and $400,000 expended with respect to such project, or

(ii) it is an $8,300,000 project to achieve compliance with State and Federal regulations for particulates emissions, which was authorized by the company's Board of Directors in December 1985, by March 31, 1986, $250,000 was committed and $250,000 was expended with respect to such project, or

(iii) it is a $22,000,000 project for the retrofit of a plant that makes a raw material for aspartame, which was approved in the company's December 1985 capital budget, if approximately $3,000,000 of the $22,000,000 was spent before August 1, 1986.

(Y) A project is described in this subparagraph if such project passes through at least 9 states and involves an intercity communication link (including multiple repeater sites and junction stations for microwave transmissions and amplifiers for fiber optics); the link from Buffalo to New York/Elizabeth was completed in 1984; the link from Buffalo to Chicago was completed in 1985; and the link from New York to Washington is completed in 1986.

(Z) A project is described in this subparagraph if—

(i) such project involves a fiber optic network of at least 475 miles, passing through Minnesota and Wisconsin; and

(ii) before January 1, 1986, at least $15,000,000 was expended or committed for electronic equipment or fiber optic cable to be used in constructing the network.

(6) NATURAL GAS PIPELINE.—The amendments made by section 201 shall not apply to any interstate natural gas pipeline (and related equipment) if—

(A) 3 applications for the construction of such pipeline were filed with the Federal Energy Regulatory Commission before November 22, 1985 (and 2 of which were filed before September 26, 1985), and

(B) such pipeline has 1 of its terminal points near Bakersfield, California.

(7) CERTAIN LEASEHOLD IMPROVEMENTS.—The amendments made by section 201 shall not apply to any reasonable leasehold improvements, equipment and furnishings placed in service by a lessee or its affiliates if—

(A) the lessee or an affiliate is the original lessee of each building in which such property is to be used,

(B) such lessee is obligated to lease the building under an agreement to lease entered into before September 26, 1985, and such property is provided for such building, and

(C) such buildings are to serve as world headquarters of the lessee and its affiliates.

For purposes of this paragraph, a corporation is an affiliate of another corporation if both corporations are members of a controlled group of corporations within the meaning of section 1563(a) of the Internal Revenue Code of 1954 without regard to section 1563(b)(2) of such Code. Such lessee shall include a securities firm that meets the requirements of subparagraph (A), except the lessee is obligated to lease the building under a lessee entered into on June 18, 1986.

(8) SOLID WASTE DISPOSAL FACILITIES.—The amendments made by section 201 shall not apply to the taxpayer who originally places in service any qualified solid waste disposal facility (as defined in section 7701(e)(3)(B) of the Internal Revenue Code of 1986) if before March 2, 1986—

(A) there is a binding written contract between a service recipient and a service provider with respect to the operation of such facility to pay for the services to be provided by such facility,

(B) a service recipient or governmental unit (or any entity related to such recipient or unit) made a financial commitment of at least $200,000 for the financing or construction of such facility,

(C) such facility is the Tri-Cities Solid Waste Recovery Project involving Fremont, Newark, and Union City, California, and has received an authority to construct from the Environmental Protection Agency or from a State or local agency authorized by the Environmental Protection Agency to issue air quality permits under the Clean Air Act,

(D) a bond volume carryforward election was made for the facility and the facility is for Chattanooga, Knoxville, or Kingsport, Tennessee, or

(E) such facility is to serve Haverhill, Massachusetts.

(9) CERTAIN SUBMERSIBLE DRILLING UNITS.—In the case of a binding contract entered into on October 30, 1984, for the purchase of 6 semi-submersible drilling units at a cost of $425,000,000, such units shall be treated as having an applicable date under subsection 203(b)(2) of January 1, 1991.

(10) WASTEWATER OR SEWAGE TREATMENT FACILITY.—The amendments made by section 201 shall not apply to any property which is part of a wastewater or sewage treatment facility if—

(A) site preparation for such facility commenced before September 1985, and a parish council approved a service agreement with respect to such facility on December 4, 1985;

(B) a city-parish advertised in September 1985, for bids for construction of secondary treatment improvements for such facility, in May 1985, the city-parish received statements from 16 firms interested in privatizing the wastewater treatment facilities, and metropolitan council selected a privatizer at its meeting on November 20, 1985, and adopted a resolution authorizing the Mayor to enter into contractual negotiation with the selected privatizer;

(C) the property is part of a wastewater treatment facility serving Greenville, South Carolina with respect to which a binding service agreement between a privatizer and the Western Carolina Regional Sewer Authority with respect to such facility was signed before January 1, 1986; or

(D) such property is part of a wastewater treatment facility (located in Cameron County, Texas, within one mile of the City of Harlingen), an application for a wastewater discharge permit was filed with respect to such facility on December 4, 1985, and a City Commission approved a letter of intent relating to a service agreement with respect to such facility on August 7, 1986; or a wastewater facility (located in Harlingen, Texas) which is a subject of such letter of intent and service agreement of this paragraph and the design of which was contracted for in a letter of intent dated January 23, 1986.

(11) CERTAIN AIRCRAFT.—The amendments made by section 201 shall not apply to any new aircraft with 19 or fewer passenger seats if—

(A) The aircraft is manufactured in the United States. For purposes of this subparagraph, an aircraft is "manufactured" at the point of its final assembly,

(B) The aircraft was in inventory or in the planned production schedule of final assembly manufacturer, with orders placed for the engine(s) on or before August 16, 1986, and

(C) The aircraft is purchased or subject to a binding contract on or before December 31, 1986, and is delivered and placed in service by the purchaser, before July 1, 1987.

(12) CERTAIN SATELLITES.—The amendments made by section 201 shall not apply to any satellite with respect to which—

(A) on or before January 28, 1986, there was a binding contract to construct or acquire a satellite, and

(i) an agreement to launch was in existence on that date, or

(ii) on or before August 5, 1983, the Federal Communications Commission had authorized the construction and for which the authorized party has a specific although undesignated agreement to launch in existence on January 28, 1986;

(B) by order adopted on July 25, 1985, the Federal Communications Commission granted the taxpayer an orbital slot and authorized the taxpayer to launch and operate 2 satellites with a cost of approximately $300,000,000; or

(C) the International Telecommunications Satellite o rganization or the International Maritime Satellite Organization entered into written binding contracts before May 1, 1985.

(13) CERTAIN NONWIRE LINE CELLULAR TELEPHONE SYSTEMS.—The amendments made by section 201 shall not apply to property that is part of a nonwire line system in the Domestic Public Cellular Radio Telecommunications Service for which the Federal Communications Commission has issued a construction permit before September 26, 1985, but only if such property is placed in service before January 1, 1987.

(14) CERTAIN COGENERATION FACILITIES.—The amendments made by section 201 shall not apply to projects consisting of 1 or more facilities for the cogeneration and distribution of electricity and steam or other forms of thermal energy if—

(A) at least $100,000 was paid or incurred with respect to the project before March 1, 1986, a memorandum of understanding was executed on September 13, 1985, and the project is placed in service before January 1, 1989,

(B) at least $500,000 was paid or incurred with respect to the projects before May 6, 1986, the projects involve a 22-megawatt combined cycle gas turbine plant and a 45-megawatt coal waste plant, and applications for qualifying facility status were filed with the Federal Energy Regulatory Commission on March 5, 1986,

(C) the project cost approximates $125,000,000 to $140,000,000 and an application was made to the Federal Energy Regulatory Commission in July 1985,

(D) an inducement resolution for such facility was adopted on September 10, 1985, a development authority was given an inducement date of September 10, 1985, for a loan not to exceed $80,000,000 with respect to such facility, and such facility is expected to have a capacity of approximately 30 megawatts of electric power and 70,000 pounds of steam per hour,

(E) at least $1,000,000 was incurred with respect to the project before May 6, 1986, the project involves a 52-megawatt combined cycle gas turbine plant and a petition was filed with the Connecticut Department of Public Utility Control to approve a power sales agreement with respect to the project on March 27, 1986,

(F) the project has a planned scheduled capacity of approximately 38,000 kilowatts, the project property is placed in service before January 1, 1991, and the project is operated, established, or constructed pursuant to certain agreements, the negotiation of which began before 1986, with public or municipal utilities conducting business in Massachusetts, or

(G) the Board of Regents of Oklahoma State University took official action on July 25, 1986, with respect to the project.

In the case of the project described in subparagraph (F), section 203(b)(2)(A) shall be applied by substituting "January 1, 1991" for "January 1, 1989."

(15) CERTAIN ELECTRIC GENERATING STATIONS.—The amendments made by section 201 shall not apply to a project located in New Mexico consisting of a coal-fired electric

generating station (including multiple generating units, coal mine equipment, and transmission facilities) if—

(A) a tax-exempt entity will own an equity interest in all property included in the project (except the coal mine equipment), and

(B) at least $72,000,000 was expended in the acquisition of coal leases, land and water rights, engineering studies, and other development costs before May 6, 1986.

For purposes of this paragraph, section 203(b)(2) shall be applied by substituting "January 1, 1996" for "January 1, 1991" each place it appears.

(16) SPORTS ARENAS.—

(A) INDOOR SPORTS FACILITY.—The amendments made by section 201 shall not apply to up to $20,000,000 of improvements made by a lessee of any indoor sports facility pursuant to a lease from a State commission granting the right to make limited and specified improvements (including planned seat explanations), if architectural renderings of the project were commissioned and received before December 22, 1985.

(B) METROPOLITAN SPORTS ARENA.—The amendments made by section 201 shall not apply to any property which is part of an arena constructed for professional sports activities in a metropolitan area, provided that such arena is capable of seating no less than 18,000 spectators and a binding contract to incur significant expenditures for its construction was entered into before June 1, 1986.

(17) CERTAIN WASTE-TO-ENERGY FACILITIES.—The amendments made by section 201 shall not apply to 2 agricultural waste-to-energy powerplants (and required transmission facilities), in connection with which a contract to sell 100 megawatts of electricity to a city was executed in October 1984.

(18) CERTAIN COAL-FIRED PLANTS.—The amendments made by section 201 shall not apply to one of three 540 megawatt coal-fired plants that are placed in service after a sale leaseback occurring after January 1, 1986, if—

(A) the Board of Directors of an electric power cooperation authorized the investigation of a sale leaseback of a nuclear generation facility by resolution dated January 22, 1985, and

(B) a loan was extended by the Rural Electrification Administration on February 20, 1986, which contained a covenant with respect to used property leasing from unit II.

(19) CERTAIN RAIL SYSTEMS.—

(A) The amendments made by section 201 shall not apply to a light rail transit system, the approximate cost of which is $235,000,000, if, with respect to which, the board of directors of a corporation (formed in September 1984 for the purpose of developing, financing, and operating the system) authorized a $300,000 expenditure for a feasibility study in April 1985.

(B) The amendments made by section 201 shall not apply to any project for rehabilitation of regional railroad rights of way and properties including grade crossings which was authorized by the Board of Directors of such company prior to October 1985; and/or was modified, altered or enlarged as a result of termination of company contracts, but approved by said Board of Directors no later than January 30, 1986, and which is in the public interest, and which is subject to binding contracts or substantive commitments by December 31, 1987.

(20) CERTAIN DETERGENT MANUFACTURING FACILITY.—The amendments made by section 201 shall not apply to a laundry detergent manufacturing facility, the approximate cost of which is $13,200,000, with respect to which a project agreement was fully executed on March 17, 1986.

(21) CERTAIN RESOURCE RECOVERY FACILITY.—The amendments made by section 201 shall not apply to any of 3 resource recovery plants, the aggregate cost of which approximates $300,000,000, if an industrial development authority adopted a bond resolution with respect to such facilities on December 17, 1984, and the projects were approved by the department of commerce of a Commonwealth on December 27, 1984.

(22) The amendments made by section 201 shall not apply to a computer and office support center building in Minneapolis, with respect to which the first contract, with an architecture firm, was signed on April 30, 1985, and a construction contract was signed on March 12, 1986.

(23) CERTAIN DISTRICT HEATING AND COOLING FACILITIES.—The amendments made by section 201 shall not apply to pipes, mains, and related equipment included in district heating and cooling facilities, with respect to which the development authority of a State approved the project through an inducement resolution adopted on October 8, 1985, and in connection with which approximately $11,000,000 of tax-exempt bonds are to be issued.

(24) CERTAIN VESSELS.—

(A) CERTAIN OFFSHORE VESSELS.—The amendments made by section 201 shall not apply to any offshore vessel the construction contract for which was signed on February 28, 1986, and the approximate cost of which is $9,000,000.

(B) CERTAIN INLAND RIVER VESSEL.—The amendments made by section 201 shall not apply to a project involving the reconstruction of an inland river vessel docked on the Mississippi River at St. Louis, Missouri, on July 14, 1986, and with respect to which:

(i) the estimated cost of reconstruction is approximately $39,000,000;

(ii) reconstruction was commenced prior to December 1, 1985;

(iii) at least $17,000,000 was expended before December 31, 1985; and

(C) SPECIAL AUTOMOBILE CARRIER VESSELS.—The amendments made by section 201 shall not apply to two new automobile carrier vessels which will cost approximately $47,000,000 and will be constructed by a United States-flag carrier to operate, under the United States-flag with an American crew, to transport foreign automobiles to the United States, in a case where negotiations for such transportation arrangements commenced in April 1985, formal contract bids were submitted prior to the end of 1985, and definitive transportation contracts were awarded in May 1986.

(D) The amendments made by section 201 shall not apply to a 562-foot passenger cruise ship, which was purchased in 1980 for the purpose of returning the vessel to United States service, the approximate cost of refurbishment of which is approximately $47,000,000.

(E) The amendments made by section 201 shall not apply to the Muskegon, Michigan, Cross-Lake Ferry project having a projected cost of approximately $7,200,000.

(F) The amendments made by section 201 shall not apply to a new automobile carrier vessel, the contract price for which is no greater than $28,000,000, and which will be constructed for and placed in service by OSG Car Carriers, Inc., to transport, under the United States flag and with an American crew, foreign automobiles to North America in a case where negotiations for such transportation arrangements commenced in 1985, and definitive transportation contracts were awarded before June 1986.

(25) CERTAIN WOOD ENERGY PROJECTS.—The amendments made by section 201 shall not apply to two wood energy projects for which applications with the Federal Energy Regulatory Commission were filed before January 1, 1986, which are described as follows:

(A) a 26.5 megawatt plant in Fresno, California, and

(B) a 26.5 megawatt plant in Rocklin, California.

(26) The amendments made by section 201 shall not apply to property which is a geothermal project of less than 20 megawatts that was certified by the Federal Energy Regulatory Commission on July 14, 1986, as a qualifying small power production facility for purposes of the Public Utility Regulatory Policies Act of 1978 pursuant to an application filed with the Federal Energy Regulatory Commission on April 17, 1986.

(27) CERTAIN ECONOMIC DEVELOPMENT PROJECTS.—The amendments made by section 201 shall not apply to any of the following projects:

(A) A mixed use development on the East River the total cost of which is approximately $400,000,000, with respect to which a letter of intent was executed on January 24, 1984, and with respect to which approximately $2.5 million had been spent by March 1, 1986.

(B) A 356-room hotel, banquet, and conference facility (including 545,000 square feet of office space) the approximate cost of which is $158,000,000, with respect to which a letter of intent was executed on June 1, 1984 and with respect to which an inducement resolution and bond resolution was adopted on August 20, 1985.

(C) Phase 1 of a 4-phase project involving the construction of laboratory space and ground-floor retail space the estimated cost of which is $22,000,000 and with respect to which a memorandum of understanding was made on August 29, 1983.

(D) A project involving the development of a 490,000 square foot mixed-use building at 152 W. 57th Street, New York, New York, the estimated cost of which is $100,000,000, and with respect to which a building permit application was filed in May 1986.

(E) A mixed-use project containing a 300 unit, 12-story hotel, garage, two multi-rise office buildings, and also included a park, renovated riverboat, and barge with festival marketplace, the capital outlays for which approximate $68,000,000.

(F) The construction of a three-story office building that will serve as the home office for an insurance group and its affiliated companies, with respect to which a city agreed to transfer its ownership of the land for the project in a Redevelopment Agreement executed on September 18, 1985, once certain conditions are met.

(G) A commercial bank formed under the laws of the State of New York which entered into an agreement on September 5, 1985, to construct its headquarters at 60 Wall Street, New York, New York, with respect to such headquarters.

(H) Any property which is part of a commercial and residential project, the first phase of which is currently under construction, to be developed on land which is the subject of an ordinance passed on July 20, 1981, by the city council of the city in which such land is located, designating such land and the improvements to be placed thereon as a residential- business planned development, which development is being financed in part by the proceeds of industrial development bonds in the amount of $62,600,000 issued on December 4, 1985.

(I) A 600,000 square foot mixed use building known as Flushing Center with respect to which a letter of intent was executed on March 26, 1986.

In the case of the building described in subparagraph (I), section 203(b)(2)(A) shall be applied by substituting "January 1, 1993" for the applicable date which would otherwise apply.

(28) The amendments made by section 201 shall not apply to an $80 million capital project steel seamless tubular casings minimill and melting facility located in Youngstown, Ohio, which was purchased by the taxpayer in April 1985, and—

(A) the purchase and renovation of which was approved by a committee of the Board of Directors on February 22, 1985, and

(B) as of December 31, 1985, more than $20,000,000 was incurred or committed with respect to the renovation.

(29) The amendments made by section 201 shall not apply to any project for residential rental property if—

(A) an inducement resolution with respect to such project was adopted by the State housing development authority on January 25, 1985, and

(B) such project was the subject of a lawsuit filed on October 25, 1985.

(30) The amendments made by section 201 shall not apply to a 30 megawatt electric generating facility fueled by geothermal and wood waste, the approximate cost of which is $55,000,000, and with respect to which a 30-year power sales contract was executed on March 22, 1985.

(31) The amendments made by section 201 shall not apply to railroad maintenance-of-way equipment, with respect to which a Boston bank entered into a firm binding contract with a major northeastern railroad before March 2, 1986, to finance $10,500,000 of such equipment, if all of the equipment was placed in service before August 1, 1986.

(32) The amendment made by section 201 shall not apply to—

(A) a facility constructed on approximately seven acres of land located on Ogle's Poso Creek Oil field, the primary fuel of which will be bituminous coal from Utah or Wyoming, with respect to which an application for an authority to construct was filed on December 26, 1985, an authority to construct was issued on July 2, 1986, and a prevention of significant deterioration permit application was submitted in May 1985,

(B) a facility constructed on approximately seven acres of land located on Teorco's Jasmin oil field, the primary fuel of which will be bituminous coal from Utah or Wyoming, with respect to which an authority to construct was filed on December 26, 1985, an authority to construct was issued on July 2, 1986, and a prevention of significant deterioration permit application was submitted in July 1985,

(C) the Mountain View Apartments, in Hadley, Massachusetts,

(D) a facility expected to have a capacity of not less than 65 megawatts of electricity, the steam from which is to be sold to a pulp and paper mill, with respect to which application was made to the Federal Regulatory Commission for certification as a qualified facility on November 1, 1985, and received such certification on January 24, 1986,

(E) $5,000,000 of equipment ordered in 1986, in connection with a 60,000 square foot plant in Masontown, Pennsylvania, that was completed in 1983,

(F) a magnetic resonance imaging machine, with respect to which a binding contract to purchase was entered into in April 1986, in connection with the construction of a magnetic resonance imaging clinic with respect to which a Determination of Need certification was obtained from a State Department of Public Health on October 22, 1985, if such property is placed in service before December 31, 1986,

(G) a company, located in Salina, Kansas, which has been engaged in the construction of highways and city streets since 1946, but only to the extent of $1,410,000 of investment in new section 38 property,

(H) a $300,000 project undertaken by a small metal finishing company located in Minneapolis, Minnesota, the first parts of which were received and paid for in January 1986, with respect to which the company received Board approval to purchase the largest piece of machinery it has ever ordered in 1985,

(I) a $1.2 million finishing machine that was purchased on April 2, 1986 and placed into service in September 1986 by a company located in Davenport, Iowa,

(J) a 25 megawatt small power production facility, with respect to which Qualifying Facility status no. QF86-593-000 was granted on March 5, 1986,

(K) a 250 megawatt coal-fired electric plant in northeastern Nevada estimated to cost $600,000,000 and known as the Thousand Springs project, on which the Sierra Pacific Power Company, a subsidiary of Sierra Pacific Resources, began in 1980 work to design, finance, construct, and operate (and section 203(b)(2) shall be applied with respect to such plant by substituting "January 1, 1995" for "January 1, 1991"),

(L) 128 units of rental housing in connection with the Point Gloria Limited Partnership,

(M) property which is part of the Kenosha Downtown Redevelopment Project and which is financed with the proceeds of bonds issued pursuant to section 1317(6)(W),

(N) Lakeland Park Phase II, in Baton Rouge, Louisiana,

(O) the Santa Rosa Hotel, in Pensacola, Florida,

(P) the Sheraton Baton Rouge, in Baton Rouge, Louisiana,

(Q) $300,000 of equipment placed in service in 1986, in connection with the renovation of the Best Western Townhouse Convention Center in Cedar Rapids, Iowa,

(R) the segment of a nationwide fiber optics telecommunications network placed in service by SouthernNet, the total estimated cost of which is $37,000,000,

(S) two cogeneration facilities, to be placed in service by the Reading Anthracite Coal Company (or any subsidiary thereof), costing approximately $110,000,000 each, with respect to which filings were made with the Federal Energy Regulatory Commission by December 31, 1985, and which are located in Pennsylvania,

(T) a portion of a fiber optics network placed in service by LDX NET after December 31, 1988, but only to the extent the cost of such portion does not exceed $25,000,000,

(U) 3 newly constructed fishing vessels, and one vessel that is overhauled, constructed by Mid Coast Marine, but only to the extent of $6,700,000 of investment,

(V) $350,000 of equipment acquired in connection with the reopening of a plant in Bristol, Rhode Island, which plant was purchased by Buttonwoods, Ltd., Associates on February 7, 1986,

(W) $4,046,000 of equipment placed in service by Brendle's Incorporated, acquired in connection with a Distribution Center,

(X) a multi-family mixed-use housing project located in a home rule city, the zoning for which was changed to residential business planned development on November 26, 1985, and with respect to which both the home rule city on December 4, 1985, and the State housing finance agency on December 20, 1985, adopted inducement resolutions,

(Y) the Myrtle Beach Convention Center, in South Carolina, to the extent of $25,000,000 of investment, and

(Z) railroad cars placed in service by the Pullman Leasing Company, pursuant to an April 3, 1986 purchase order, costing approximately $10,000,000.

(33) The amendments made by section 201 shall not apply to—

(A) $400,000 of equipment placed in service by Super Key Market, if such equipment is placed in service before January 1, 1987,

(B) the Trolley Square project, the total project cost of which is $24,500,000, and the amount of depreciable real property of which is $14,700,000.

(C)(i) a waste-to-energy project in Derry, New Hampshire, costing approximately $60,000,000, and

(ii) a waste-to-energy project in Manchester, New Hampshire, costing approximately $60,000,000,

(D) the City of Los Angeles Co-composting project, the estimated cost of which is $62,000,000, with respect to which, on July 17, 1985, the California Pollution Control Financing Authority issued an initial resolution in the maximum amount of $75,000,000 to finance this project,

(E) the St. Charles, Missouri Mixed-Use Center,

(F) Oxford Place in Tulsa, Oklahoma,

(G) an amount of investment generating $20,000,000 of investment tax credits attributable to property used on the Illinois Diversatech Campus,

(H) $25,000,000 of equipment used in the Melrose Park Engine Plant that is sold and leased back by Navistar,

(I) 80,000 vending machines, for a cost approximating $3,400,000 placed into service by Folz Vending Co.,

(J) a 25.85 megawatt alternative energy facility located in Deblois, Maine, with respect to which certification by the Federal Energy Regulatory Commission was made on April 3, 1986,

(K) Burbank Manors, in Illinois, and

(L) a cogeneration facility to be built at a paper company in Turners Falls, Massachusetts, with respect to which a letter of intent was executed on behalf of the paper company on September 26, 1985.

(34) The amendments made by section 201 shall not apply to an approximately 240,000 square foot beverage container manufacturing plant located in Batesville, Mississippi, or plant equipment used exclusively on the plant premises if—

(A) a 2-year supply contract was signed by the taxpayer and a customer on November 1, 1985,

(B) such contract further obligated the customer to purchase beverage containers for an additional 5-year period if physical signs of construction of the plant are present before September 1986,

(C) ground clearing for such plant began before August 1986, and

(D) construction is completed, the equipment is installed, and operations are commenced before July 1, 1987.

(35) The amendments made by section 201 shall not apply to any property which is part of the multifamily housing at the Columbia Point Project in Boston, Massachusetts. A project shall be treated as not described in the preceding sentence and as not described in section 252(f)(1)(D) unless such project includes at substantially all times throughout the compliance period (within the meaning of section 42(i)(1) of the Internal Revenue Code of 1986), a facility which provides health services to the residents of such project for fees commensurate with the ability of such individuals to pay for such services.

(36) The amendments made by section 201 shall not apply to any ethanol facility located in Blair, Nebraska, if—

(A) in July of 1984 an initial binding construction contract was entered into for such facility,

(B) in June of 1986, certain Department of Energy recommended contract changes required a change of contractor, and

(C) in September of 1986, a new contract to construct such facility, consistent with such recommended changes, was entered into.

(37) The amendments made by section 201 shall not apply to any property which is part of a sewage treatment facility if, prior to January 1, 1986, the City of Conyers, Georgia, selected a privatizer to construct such facility, received a guaranteed maximum price bid for the construction of such facility, signed a letter of intent and began substantial negotiations of a service agreement with respect to such facility.

(38) The amendments made by section 201 shall not apply to—

(A) a $28,000,000 wood resource complex for which construction was authorized by the Board of Directors on August 9, 1985,

(B) an electrical cogeneration plant in Bethel, Maine which is to generate 2 megawatts of electricity from the burning of wood residues, with respect to which a contract was entered into on July 10, 1984, and with respect to which $200,000 of the expected $2,000,000 cost had been committed before June 15, 1986,

(C) a mixed income housing project in Portland, Maine which is known as the Back Bay Tower and which is expected to cost $17,300,000,

(D) the Eastman Place project and office building in Rochester, New York, which is projected to cost $20,000,000, with respect to which an inducement resolution was adopted in December 1986, and for which a binding contract of $500,000 was entered into on April 30, 1986,

(E) the Marquis Two project in Atlanta, Georgia which has a total budget of $72,000,000 and the construction phase of which began under a contract entered into on March 26, 1986,

(F) a 166-unit continuing care retirement center in New Orleans, Louisiana, the construction contract for which was signed on February 12, 1986, and is for a maximum amount not to exceed $8,500,000,

(G) the expansion of the capacity of an oil refining facility in Rosemont, Minnesota from 137,000 to 207,000 barrels per day which is expected to be completed by December 31, 1990, and

(H) a project in Ransom, Pennsylvania which will burn coal waste (known as 'culm') with an approximate cost of $64,000,000 and for which a certification from the Federal Energy Regulatory Commission was received on March 11, 1986.

(39) The amendments made by section 201 shall not apply to any facility for the manufacture of an improved particle board if a binding contract to purchase such equipment was executed March 3, 1986, such equipment will be placed in service by January 1, 1988, and such facility is located in or near Moncure, North Carolina.

(40) CERTAIN TRUCKS. ETC.—The amendments made by section 201 shall not apply to trucks, tractor units, and trailers which a privately held truck leasing company headquartered in Des Moines, Iowa, contracted to purchase in September 1985 but only to the extent the aggregate reduction in Federal tax liability by reason of the application of this paragraph does not exceed $8,500,000.

(b) SPECIAL RULE FOR CERTAIN PROPERTY.—The provisions of section 168(f)(8) of the Internal Revenue Code of 1954 (as amended by section 209 of the Tax Equity and Fiscal Responsibility Act of 1982) shall continue to apply to any transaction permitted by reason of section 12(c)(2) of the Tax Reform Act of 1984 or section 209(d)(1)(B) of the Tax Equity and Fiscal Responsibility Act of 1982 (as amended by the Tax Reform Act of 1984).

(c) APPLICABLE DATE IN CERTAIN CASES.—

(1) Section 203(b)(2) shall be applied by substituting "January 1, 1992" for "January 1, 1991" in the following cases:

(A) in the case of a 2-unit nuclear powered electric generating plant (and equipment and incidental appurtenances), located in Pennsylvania and constructed pursuant to contracts entered into by the owner operator of the facility before December 31, 1975, including contracts with the engineer/constructor and the nuclear steam system supplier, such contracts shall be treated as contracts described in section (b)(1)(A),

(B) a cogeneration facility with respect to which an application with the Federal Energy Regulatory Commission was filed on August 2, 1985, and approved October 15, 1985, and

(C) in the case of a 1,300 megawatt coal-fired steam powered electric generating plant (and related equipment and incidental appurtenances), which the three owners determined in 1984 to convert from nuclear power to coal power and for which more than $600,000,000 had been incurred or committed for construction before September 25, 1985, except that no investment tax credit will be allowable under section 49(d)(3) added by section 211(a) of this Act for any qualified progress expenditures made after December 31, 1990.

(2) Section 203(b)(2) shall be applied by substituting "April 1, 1992" for the applicable date that would otherwise apply, in the case of the second unit of a twin steam electric generating facility and related equipment which was granted a certificate of public convenience and necessity by a public service commission prior to January 1, 1982, if the first unit of the facility was placed in service prior to January 1, 1985, and before September 26, 1985, more than $100,000,000 had been expended toward the construction of the second unit.

(3) Section 203(b)(2) shall be applied by substituting "January 1, 1990," (or, in the case of a project described in

subparagraph (B), by substituting "April 1, 1992") for the applicable date that would otherwise apply in the case of—

(A) new commercial passenger aircraft used by a domestic airline, if a binding contract with respect to such aircraft was entered into on or before April 1, 1986, and such aircraft has a present class life of 12 years,

(B) a pumped storage hydroelectric project with respect to which an application was made to the Federal Energy Regulatory Commission for a license on February 4, 1974, and license was issued August 1, 1977, the project number of which is 2740, and

(C) a newsprint mill in Pend Oreille county, Washington, costing about $290,000,000.

In the case of an aircraft described in subparagraph (A), section 203(b)(1)(A) shall be applied by substituting "April 1, 1986" for "March 1, 1986" and section 49(e)(1)(B) of the Internal Revenue Code of 1986 shall not apply.

(4) The amendments made by section 201 shall not apply to a limited amount of the following property or a limited amount of property set forth in a submission before September 16, 1986, by the following taxpayers:

(A) Arena project, Michigan, but only with respect to $78,000,000 of investments.

(B) Campbell Soup Company, Pennsylvania, California, North Carolina, Ohio, Maryland, Florida, Nebraska, Michigan, South Carolina, Texas, New Jersey, and Delaware, but only with respect to $9,329,000 of regular investment tax credits.

(C) The Southeast Overtown/Park West development, Florida, but only with respect to $200,000,000 of investments.

(D) Equipment placed in service and operated by Leggett and Platt before July 1, 1987, but only with respect to $2,000,000 of regular investment tax credits, and subsections (c) and (d) of section 49 of the Internal Revenue Code of 1986 shall not apply to such equipment.

(E) East Bank Housing Project.

(F) $1,561,215 of investments by Standard Telephone Company.

(G) Five aircraft placed in service before January 1, 1987, by Presidential Air.

(H) A rehabilitation project by Ann Arbor Railroad, but only with respect to $2,900,000 of investments.

(I) Property that is part of a cogeneration project located in Ada, Michigan, but only with respect to $30,000,000 of investments.

(J) Anchor Store Project, Michigan, but only with respect to $21,000,000 of investments.

(K) A waste-fired electrical generating facility of Biogen Power, but only with respect to $34,000,000 of investments.

(L) $14,000,000 of television transmitting towers placed in service by Media General, Inc., which were subject to binding contracts as of January 21, 1986, and will be placed in service before January 1, 1988,

(M) Interests of Samuel A. Hardage (whether owned individually or in partnership form).

(N) Two aircraft of Mesa Airlines with an aggregate cost of $5,723,484.

(O) Yarn-spinning equipment used at Spray Cotton Mills, but only with respect to $3,000,000 of investments.

(P) 328 units of low-income housing at Angelus Plaza, but only with respect to $20,500,000 of investments.

(Q) One aircraft of Continental Aviation Services with a cost of approximately $15,000,000 that was purchased pursuant to a contract entered into during March of 1983 and that is placed in service by December 31, 1988.

(d) RAILROAD GRADING AND TUNNEL BORES.—

(1) IN GENERAL.—In the case of expenditures of railroad grading and tunnel bores which were incurred by a common carrier by railroad to replace property destroyed in a disaster occurring on or about April 17, 1983, near Thistle, Utah, such expenditures, to the extent not in excess of $15,000,000, shall be treated as recovery property which is 5-year property under section 168 of the Internal Revenue Code of 1954 (as in effect before the amendments made by this Act) and which is placed in service at the time such expenditures were incurred.

(2) BUSINESS INTERRUPTION PROCEEDS.—Business interruption proceeds received for loss of use, revenues, or profits in connection with the disaster described in paragraph (1) and devoted by the taxpayer described in paragraph (1) to the construction of replacement track and related grading and tunnel bore expenditures shall be treated as constituting an amount received from the involuntary conversion of property under section 1033(a)(2) of such Code.

(3) EFFECTIVE DATE.—This subsection shall apply to taxable years ending after April 17, 1983.

(e) TREATMENT OF CERTAIN DISASTER LOSSES.—

(1) IN GENERAL.—In a case of a disaster described in paragraph (2), at the election of the taxpayer, the amendments made by section 201 of this Act—

(A) shall not apply to any property placed in service during 1987 and 1988, or

(B) shall not apply to any property placed in service during 1985 and 1986,

which is property to replace property lost, damaged, or destroyed in such disaster.

(2) DISASTER TO WHICH SECTION APPLIES.—This section shall apply to a flood which occurred on November 3 through 7, 1985, and which was declared a natural disaster area by the President of the United States.

SEC. 251. MODIFICATION OF INVESTMENT TAX CREDIT FOR REHABILITATION EXPENDITURES.

* * *

(d) EFFECTIVE DATE.—

* * *

(2) GENERAL TRANSITIONAL RULE.—The amendments made by this section and section 201 shall not apply to any property placed in service before January 1, 1994, if such property is placed in service as part of—

(A) a rehabilitation which was completed pursuant to a written contract which was binding on March 1, 1986, or

(B) a rehabilitation incurred in connection with property (including any leasehold interest) acquired before March 2, 1986, or acquired on or after such date pursuant to a written contract that was binding on March 1, 1986, if—

(i) parts 1 and 2 of the Historic Preservation Certification Application were filed with the department of the Interior (or its designee) before March 2, 1986, or

(ii) the lesser of $1,000,000 or 5 percent of the cost of the rehabilitation is incurred before March 2, 1986, or is required to be incurred pursuant to a written contract which was binding on March 1, 1986.

(3) CERTAIN ADDITIONAL REHABILITATIONS.—The amendments made by this section and section 201 shall not apply to—

(A) the rehabilitation of 8 bathhouses within the Hot Springs National Park or of buildings in the Central Avenue Historic District at such Park,

(B) the rehabilitation of the Upper Pontalba Building in New Orleans, Louisiana,

(C) the rehabilitation of at least 60 buildings listed on the National Register at the Frankford Arsenal,

(D) the rehabilitation of De Baliveriere Arcade, St. Louis Centre, and Drake Apartments in Missouri,

(E) the rehabilitation of The Tides in Bristol, Rhode Island,

(F) the rehabilitation and renovation of the Outlet Company building and garage in Providence, Rhode Island,

(G) the rehabilitation of 10 structures in Harrisburg, Pennsylvania, with respect to which the Harristown Development Corporation was designated redeveloper and received an option to acquire title to the entire project site for $1 on June 27, 1984,

(H) the rehabilitation of a project involving the renovation of 3 historic structures on the Minneapolis riverfront, with respect to which the developer of the project entered into a redevelopment agreement with a municipality dated January 4, 1985, and industrial development bonds were sold in 3 separate issues in May, July, and October 1985,

(I) the rehabilitation of a bank's main office facilities of approximately 120,000 square feet, in connection with which the bank's board of directors authorized a $3,300,000 expenditure for the renovation and retrofit on March 20, 1984,

(J) the rehabilitation of 10 warehouse buildings built between 1906 and 1910 and purchased under a contract dated February 17, 1986,

(K) the rehabilitation of a facility which is customarily used for conventions and sporting events if an analysis of operations and recommendations of utilization of such facility was prepared by a certified public accounting firm pursuant to an engagement authorized on March 6, 1984, and presented on June 11, 1984, to officials of the city in which such facility is located,

(L) Mount Vernon Mills in Columbia, South Carolina,

(M) the Barbara Jordan II Apartments,

(N) the rehabilitation of the Federal Building and Post Office, 120 Hanover Street, Manchester, New Hampshire,
(O) the rehabilitation of the Charleston Waterfront project in South Carolina,
(P) the Hayes Mansion in San Jose, California,
(Q) the renovation of a facility owned by the National Railroad Passenger Corporation ("Amtrak") for which project Amtrak engaged a development team by letter agreement dated August 23, 1985, as modified by letter agreement dated September 9, 1985,
(R) the rehabilitation of a structure or its components which is listed in the National Register of Historic Places, is located in Allegheny County, Pennsylvania, will be substantially rehabilitated (as defined in section 48(g)(1)(C) prior to amendment by this Act), prior to December 31, 1989; and was previously utilized as a market and an auto dealership,
(S) The Bellevue Stratford Hotel in Philadelphia, Pennsylvania,
(T) the Dixon Mill Housing project in Jersey City, New Jersey,
(U) Motor Square Garden,
(V) the Blackstone Apartments, and the Shriver-Johnson building, in Sioux Falls, South Dakota,
(W) the Holy Name Academy in Spokane, Washington,
(X) the Nike/Clemson Mill in Exeter, New Hampshire,
(Y) the Central Bank Building in Grand Rapids, Michigan, and
(Z) the Heritage Hotel, in the City of Marquette, Michigan.
(4) ADDITIONAL REHABILITATIONS.—The amendments made by this section and section 201 shall not apply to—
(A) the Fort Worth Town Square Project in Texas,
(B) the American Youth Hostel in New York, New York,
(C) The Riverwest Loft Development (including all three phases, two of which do not involve rehabilitations),
(D) the Galsamp Quarter Historic District in California,
(E) the Eberhardt & Ober Brewery, in Pennsylvania,
(F) the Captain's Walk Limited Partnership-Harris Place Development, in Connecticut,
(G) the Velvet Mills in Connecticut,
(H) the Roycroft Inn, in New York,
(I) Old Main Village, in Mankato, Minnesota,
(J) the Washburn-Crosby A Mill, in Minneapolis, Minnesota,
(K) the Marble Arcade office building in Lakeland, Florida,
(L) the Willard Hotel, in Washington, D.C.,
(M) the H.P. Lau Building in Lincoln, Nebraska,
(N) the Starks Building, in Louisville, Kentucky,
(O) the Bellevue High School, in Bellevue, Kentucky,
(P) the Major Hampden Smith House, in Owensboro, Kentucky,
(Q) the Doe Run Inn, in Brandenburg, Kentucky,
(R) the State National Bank, in Frankfort, Kentucky,
(S) the Captain Jack House, in Fleming, Kentucky,
(T) the Elizabeth Arlinghaus House, in Covington, Kentucky,
(U) Limerick Shamrock, in Louisville, Kentucky,
(V) the Robert Mills Project, in South Carolina,
(W) the 620 Project, consisting of 3 buildings, in Kentucky,
(X) the Warrior Hotel, Ltd., the first two floors of the Martin Hotel, and the 105,000 square foot warehouse constructed in 1910, all in Sioux City, Iowa,
(Y) the waterpark condominium residential project, to the extent of $2 million of expenditures,
(Z) the Bigelow-Hartford Carpet Mill in Enfield, Connecticut,
(AA) properties abutting 125th Street in New York County from 7th Avenue west to Morningside and the pier area on the Hudson River at the end of such 125th Street,
(BB) the City of Los Angeles Central Library project pursuant to an agreement dated December 28, 1983,
(CC) the Warehouse Row project in Chattanooga, Tennessee,
(DD) any project described in section 204(a)(1)(F) of this Act,
(EE) the Wood Street Commons project in Pittsburgh, Pennsylvania,
(FF) any project described in section 803(d)(6) of this Act,
(GG) Union Station, Indianapolis, Indiana,
(HH) the Mattress Factory project in Pittsburgh, Pennsylvania,
(II) Union Station in Providence, Rhode Island,
(JJ) South Pack Plaza, Asheville, North Carolina,
(KK) Old Louisville Trust Project, Louisville, Kentucky,
(LL) Stewarts Rehabilitation Project, Louisville, Kentucky,
(MM) Bernheim Officenter, Louisville, Kentucky,
(NN) Springville Mill Project, Rockville, Connecticut, and
(OO) the D.J. Stewart Company Building, State and Main Streets, Rockford, Illinois.
(5) REDUCTION IN CREDIT FOR PROPERTY UNDER TRANSITIONAL RULES.—In the case of property placed in service after December 31, 1986, and to which the amendments made by this section do not apply, subparagraph (A) of section 46(b)(4) of the Internal Revenue Code of 1954 (as in effect before the enactment of this Act) shall be applied—
(A) by substituting "10 percent" for "15 percent", and
(B) by substituting "13 percent" for "20 percent".
(6) EXPENSING OF REHABILITATION EXPENSES FOR THE FRANKFORD ARSENAL.—In the case of any expenditures paid or incurred in connection with improvements (including repairs and maintenance) of the Frankford Arsenal pursuant to a contract and partnership agreement during the 8-year period specified in the contract or agreement, all such expenditures to be made during the period 1986 through and including 1993 shall—
(A) be treated as made (and allowable as a deduction) during 1986,
(B) be treated as qualified rehabilitation expenditures made during 1986, and
(C) be allocated in accordance with the partnership agreement regardless of when the interest in the partnership was acquired, except that—
(i) if the taxpayer is not the original holder of such interest, no person (other than the taxpayer) had claimed any benefits by reason of this paragraph,
(ii) no interest under section 6611 of the 1986 Code on any refund of income taxes which is solely attributable to this paragraph shall be paid for the period—
(I) beginning on the date which is 45 days after the later of April 15, 1987, or the date on which the return for such taxes was filed, and
(II) ending on the date the taxpayer acquired the interest in the partnership, and
(iii) if the expenditures to be made under this provision are not paid or incurred before January 1, 1994, then the tax imposed by chapter 1 of such Code for the taxpayer's last taxable year beginning in 1993 shall be increased by the amount of the tax benefits by reason of this paragraph which are attributable to the expenditures not so paid or incurred.
(7) SPECIAL RULE.—In the case of the rehabilitation of the Willard Hotel in Washington, D.C., section 205(c)(1)(B)(ii) of the Tax Equity and Fiscal Responsibility Act of 1982 shall be applied by substituting "1987" for "1986".

P.L. 99-514, §1801(a)(2), as amended by P.L. 100-647 §1018(c)(1), provides:
(2) TREATMENT OF CERTAIN FARM FINANCE LEASES.—
(A) IN GENERAL.—If—
(i) any partnership or grantor trust is the lessor under a specified agreement,
(ii) such partnership or grantor trust met the requirements of section 168(f)(8)(C)(i) of the Internal Revenue Code of 1954 (relating to special rules for finance leases) when the agreement was entered into, and
(iii) a person became a partner in such partnership (or a beneficiary in such trust) after its formation but before September 26, 1985,
then, for purposes of applying the revenue laws of the United States in respect to such agreement, the portion of the property allocable to partners (or beneficiaries) not described in clause (iii) shall be treated as if it were subject to a separate agreement and the portion of such property allocable to the partner or beneficiary described in clause (iii) shall be treated as if it were subject to a separate agreement.
(B) SPECIFIED AGREEMENT.—For purposes of subparagraph (A), the term "specified agreement" means an agreement to which subparagraph (B) of section 209(d) of the Tax Equity and Fiscal Responsibility Act of 1982 applies which is—
(i) an agreement dated as of December 20, 1982, as amended and restated as of February 1, 1983, involving approximately $8,734,000 of property at December 31, 1983,
(ii) an agreement dated as of December 15, 1983, as amended and restated as of January 3, 1984, involving approximately $13,199,000 of property at December 31, 1984, or

APPENDIX: Selected Code Sections Affected by the Tax Cuts and Jobs Act   155

(iii) an agreement dated as of October 25, 1984, as amended and restated as of December 1, 1984, involving approximately $966,000 of property at December 31, 1984.

P.L. 99-514, § 1802(a)(1):
Amended Code Sec. 168(j)(3)(D) by adding at the end thereof a new sentence. **Effective** as if included in the provision of P.L. 98-369 to which it relates.

P.L. 99-514, § 1802(a)(2)(A)(i) and (ii):
Amended Code Sec. 168(j)(4)(E)(i) by striking out "any property of which such organization is the lessee" and inserting in lieu thereof "any property (other than property held by such organization)", and by striking out "first leased to" and inserting in lieu thereof "first used by". **Effective** as if included in the provision of P.L. 98-369 to which it relates.

P.L. 99-514, § 1802(a)(2)(B):
Amended Code Sec. 168(j)(4)(E)(ii)(I) by striking out "of which such organization is the lessee". **Effective** as if included in the provision of P.L. 98-369 to which it relates. Prior to amendment, Code Sec. 168(j)(4)(E)(ii)(I) read as follows:

(I) IN GENERAL.—In the case of an organization formerly exempt from tax under section 501(a) as an organization described in section 501(c)(12), clause (i) shall not apply to such organization with respect to any property of which such organization is the lessee if such organization elects not to be exempt from tax under section 501(a) during the tax-exempt use period with respect to such property.

P.L. 99-514, § 1802(a)(2)(C):
Amended Code Sec. 168(j)(4)(E)(ii)(II) by striking out "is placed in service under the lease" and inserting in lieu thereof "is first used by the organization". **Effective** as if included in the provision of P.L. 98-369 to which it relates.

P.L. 99-514, § 1802(a)(2)(D):
Amended Code Sec. 168(j)(4)(E) by adding at the end thereof new clause (iv). **Effective** as if included in the provision of P.L. 98-369 to which it relates.

P.L. 99-514, § 1802(a)(2)(E)(i):
Amended Code Sec. 168(j)(9) by redesignating subparagraph (E) as subparagraph (F) and by inserting after subparagraph (D) new subparagraph (E). For the **effective** date, see Act Sec. 1802(a)(E)(ii), below.

P.L. 99-514, § 1802(a)(2)(E)(ii), provides:
(ii)(I) Except as otherwise provided in this clause, the amendment made by clause (i) shall apply to property placed in service after September 27, 1985; except that such amendment shall not apply to any property acquired pursuant to a binding written contract in effect on such date (and at all times thereafter).

(II) If an election under this subclause is made with respect to any property, the amendment made by clause (i) shall apply to such property whether or not placed in service on or before September 27, 1985.

P.L. 99-514, § 1802(a)(2)(G):
Amended Code Sec. 168(j)(4)(E)(i) by striking out "preceding sentence" and inserting in lieu thereof "preceding sentence and subparagraph (d)(ii)". **Effective** as if included in the provision of P.L. 98-369 to which it relates.

P.L. 99-514, § 1802(a)(3):
Repealed Code Sec. 168(j)(5)(C)(iv). **Effective** as if included in the provision of P.L. 98-369 to which it relates. Prior to repeal, Code Sec. 168(j)(5)(C)(iv) read as follows:

(iv) PROPERTY NOT SUBJECT TO RAPID OBSOLESCENCE MAY BE EXCLUDED.—The term "qualified technological equipment" shall not include any equipment described in subclause (II) or (III) of clause (i)—
(I) which the Secretary determines by regulations is not subject to rapid obsolescence, and
(II) which is placed in service after the date on which final regulations implementing such determination are published in the Federal Register.

P.L. 99-514, § 1802(a)(4)(A):
Amended Code Sec. 168(j)(8) by striking out "and paragraphs (4) and (5) of section 48(a)" in the matter preceding subparagraph (A). **Effective** as if included in the provision of P.L. 98-369 to which it relates. Prior to amendment, the matter preceding subparagraph (A) read as follows:

(8) TAX-EXEMPT USE OF PROPERTY LEASED TO PARTNERSHIPS, ETC., DETERMINED AT PARTNER LEVEL.—For purposes of this subsection and paragraphs (4) and (5) of section 48(a)—

P.L. 99-514, § 1802(a)(4)(B)(i) and (ii):
Amended Code Sec. 168(j)(9) by striking out "and paragraphs (4) and (5) of section 48(a)" in subparagraph (A), and by striking out "loss deduction" in subparagraph (B)(i) and inserting in lieu thereof "loss, deduction". **Effective** as if included in the provision of P.L. 98-369 to which it relates. Prior to amendment, Code Sec. 168(j)(9)(A) read as follows:

(A) IN GENERAL.—For purposes of this subsection and paragraphs (4) and (5) of section 48(a), if—
(i) any property which (but for this subparagraph) is not tax-exempt use property is owned by a partnership which has both tax-exempt entity and a person who is not a tax-exempt entity as partners and
(ii) any allocation to the tax-exempt entity of partnership items is not a qualified allocation,
an amount equal to such tax-exempt entity's proportionate share of such property shall (except as provided in paragraph (3)(D)) be treated as tax-exempt use property.

P.L. 99-514, § 1802(a)(7)(A):
Amended Code Sec. 168(j)(9) by redesignating subparagraphs (D), (E), and (F) as subparagraphs (E), (F), and (G), respectively, and by inserting after subparagraph (C) new subparagraph (D). **Effective** as if included in the provision of P.L. 98-369 to which it relates.

P.L. 99-514, § 1802(a)(7)(B):
Amended Code Sec. 168(j)(9)(E) (as redesignated by Act Sec. 1802(a)(7)(A)) by striking out "and (C)" and inserting in lieu thereof "(C), and (D)". **Effective** as if included in the provision of P.L. 98-369 to which it relates.

P.L. 99-514, § 1802(b)(1)(A) and (B):
Amended Code Sec. 168(f) by redesignating paragraph (13) as paragraph (14), and by redesignating paragraph (14) as paragraph (15). **Effective** as if included in the provision of P.L. 98-369 to which it relates.

P.L. 99-514, § 1809(a)(1)(A) and (B):
Amended Code Sec. 168(b)(3)(A) by striking out "and low-income housing" in the last item, and by adding at the end thereof a new item. **Effective** as if included in the provision of P.L. 98-369 to which it relates. Prior to amendment, Code Sec. 168(b)(3)(A) read as follows:

(A) IN GENERAL.—Except as provided in subsection (f)(2), in lieu of any applicable percentage under paragraph (1), (2), or (4), the taxpayer may elect, with respect to one or more classes of recovery property placed in service during the taxable year, the applicable percentage determined by use of the straight line method over the recovery period elected by the taxpayer in accordance with the following table:

In the case of:	The taxpayer may elect a recovery period of:
3-year property	3, 5, or 12 years.
5-year property	5, 12, or 25 years.
10-year property	10, 25, or 35 years.
15-year property	15, 35, or 45 years.
19-year property	19, 35, or 45 years.

P.L. 99-514, § 1809(a)(2)(A)(i)(I) and (II):
Amended Code Sec. 168(b)(2) by striking out the last sentence of subparagraph (A), and by amending subparagraph (B). **Effective** as if included in the provision of P.L. 98-369 to which it relates. Prior to amendment, the last sentence of subparagraph (A) and subparagraph (B) read as follows:

In the case of 19-year real property, the applicable percentage in the taxable year in which the property is placed in service shall be determined on the basis of the number of months (using a mid-month convention) in such year during which the property was in service.

(B) SPECIAL RULE FOR YEAR OF DISPOSITION.—In the case of a disposition of 19-year real property, the deduction allowable under subsection (a) for the taxable year in which the disposition occurs shall reflect only the months (using a mid-month convention) during such year the property was in service.

P.L. 99-514, § 1809(a)(2)(A)(ii):
Amended Code Sec. 168(f)(2)(B). **Effective** as if included in the provision of P.L. 98-369 to which it relates. Prior to amendment, Code Sec. 168(f)(2)(B) read as follows:

(B) REAL PROPERTY.—

Code Sec. 168

(i) IN GENERAL.—Except as provided in subparagraph (C), in the case of 19-year real property or low-income housing which, during the taxable year, is predominantly used outside the United States, the recovery deduction for the taxable year shall be, in lieu of the amount determined under subsection (b), the amount determined by applying to the unadjusted basis of such property the applicable percentage determined under tables prescribed by the Secretary. For purposes of the preceding sentence in prescribing such tables, the Secretary shall—

(I) assign to the property described in this subparagraph a 35-year recovery period, and

(II) assign percentages (taking into account the next to the last sentence of subsection (b)(2)(A)) determined in accordance with use of the method of depreciation described in section 167(j)(1)(B), switching to the method described in section 167(b)(1) at a time to maximize the deduction allowable under subsection (a).

(ii) SPECIAL RULE FOR DISPOSITION.—In the case of a disposition of 19-year real property or low-income housing described in clause (i), subsection (b)(2)(B) shall apply.

P.L. 99-514, §1809(a)(2)(B):

Amended Code Sec. 168(b)(4)(B). **Effective** as if included in the provision of P.L. 98-369 to which it relates. Prior to amendment, Code Sec. 168(b)(4)(B) read as follows:

(B) SPECIAL RULE FOR YEAR OF DISPOSITION.—In the case of a disposition of low-income housing, the deduction allowable under subsection (a) for the taxable year in which the disposition occurs shall reflect only the months during such year the property was placed in service.

P.L. 99-514, §1809(a)(2)(C)(i):

Amended Code Sec. 168(j)(2)(B)(ii). **Effective** on and after 10-22-86. Prior to amendment, Code Sec. 168(j)(2)(B)(ii) read as follows:

(ii) 19-YEAR REAL PROPERTY.—In the case of 19-year real property, the amount determined under paragraph (1) shall be determined on the basis of the number of months (using a mid-month convention) in the year in which the property is in service.

P.L. 99-514, §1809(a)(4)(A):

Amended Code Sec. 168(f)(12)(B)(ii). **Effective** as if included in the provision of P.L. 98-369 to which it relates. Prior to amendment, Code Sec. 168(f)(12)(B)(ii) read as follows:

(ii) 19-YEAR REAL PROPERTY.—In the case of 19-year real property, the amount of the deduction allowed shall be determined by using the straight-line method (determined on the basis of the number of months in the year in which such property was in service and without regard to salvage value) and a recovery period of 19 years.

P.L. 99-514, §1809(a)(4)(B):

Amended Code Sec. 168(f)(12)(C). **Effective** as if included in the provision of P.L. 98-369 to which it relates. Prior to amendment, Code Sec. 168(f)(12)(C) read as follows:

(C) EXCEPTION FOR PROJECTS FOR RESIDENTIAL RENTAL PROPERTY.—Subparagraph (A) shall not apply to any recovery property which is placed in service in connection with projects for residential rental property financed by the proceeds of obligations described in section 103(b)(4)(A).

P.L. 99-514, §1809(a)(4)(C), provides:

(C) Any property described in paragraph (3) of section 631(d) of the Tax Reform Act of 1984 shall be treated as property described in clause (ii) of section 168(f)(12)(C) of the Internal Revenue Code of 1954 as amended by subparagraph (B).

P.L. 99-514, §1809(a)(5), provides:

(5) COORDINATION WITH IMPUTED INTEREST CHANGES.—In the case of any property placed in service before May 9, 1985 (or treated as placed in service before such date by section 105(b)(3) of Public Law 99-121)—

(A) any reference in any amendment made by this subsection to 19-year real property shall be treated as a reference to 18-year real property, and

(B) section 168(f)(12)(B)(ii) of the Internal Revenue Code of 1954 (as amended by paragraph (4)(A)) shall be applied by substituting "18 years" for "19 years".

P.L. 99-514, §1809(b)(1):

Amended Code Sec. 168(f)(10)(A). **Effective** for property placed in service by the transferee after 12-31-85, in tax years ending after such date. Prior to amendment, Code Sec. 168(f)(10)(A) read as follows:

(A) IN GENERAL.—In the case of recovery property transferred in a transaction described in subparagraph (B), the transferee shall be treated as the transferor for purposes of computing the deduction allowable under subsection (a) with respect to so much of the basis in the hands of the transferee as does not exceed the adjusted basis in the hands of the transferor.

P.L. 99-514, §1809(b)(2):

Amended Code Sec. 168(f)(10)(B) by adding at the end thereof a new sentence. **Effective** for property placed in service by the transferee after 12-31-85, in tax years ending after such date.

[Sec. 168(j)]

(j) PROPERTY ON INDIAN RESERVATIONS.—

(1) IN GENERAL.—For purposes of subsection (a), the applicable recovery period for qualified Indian reservation property shall be determined in accordance with the table contained in paragraph (2) in lieu of the table contained in subsection (c).

(2) APPLICABLE RECOVERY PERIOD FOR INDIAN RESERVATION PROPERTY.—For purposes of paragraph (1)—

In the case of:	The applicable recovery period is:
3-year property	2 years
5-year property	3 years
7-year property	4 years
10-year property	6 years
15-year property	9 years
20-year property	12 years
Nonresidential real property	22 years

(3) DEDUCTION ALLOWED IN COMPUTING MINIMUM TAX.—For purposes of determining alternative minimum taxable income under section 55, the deduction under subsection (a) for qualified Indian reservation property shall be determined under this section without regard to any adjustment under section 56.

(4) QUALIFIED INDIAN RESERVATION PROPERTY DEFINED.—For purposes of this subsection—

(A) IN GENERAL.—The term "qualified Indian reservation property" means property which is property described in the table in paragraph (2) and which is—

(i) used by the taxpayer predominantly in the active conduct of a trade or business within an Indian reservation,

(ii) not used or located outside the Indian reservation on a regular basis,

(iii) not acquired (directly or indirectly) by the taxpayer from a person who is related to the taxpayer (within the meaning of section 465(b)(3)(C)), and

(iv) not property (or any portion thereof) placed in service for purposes of conducting or housing class I, II, or III gaming (as defined in section 4 of the Indian Regulatory Act (25 U.S.C. 2703)).

(B) EXCEPTION FOR ALTERNATIVE DEPRECIATION PROPERTY.—The term "qualified Indian reservation property" does not include any property to which the alternative depreciation system under subsection (g) applies, determined—

(i) without regard to subsection (g)(7) (relating to election to use alternative depreciation system), and

(ii) after the application of section 280F(b) (relating to listed property with limited business use).

(C) SPECIAL RULE FOR RESERVATION INFRASTRUCTURE INVESTMENT.—

(i) IN GENERAL.—Subparagraph (A)(ii) shall not apply to qualified infrastructure property located outside of the Indian reservation if the purpose of such property is to connect with qualified infrastructure property located within the Indian reservation.

(ii) QUALIFIED INFRASTRUCTURE PROPERTY.—For purposes of this subparagraph, the term "qualified infrastructure property" means qualified Indian reservation property (determined without regard to subparagraph (A)(ii)) which—

(I) benefits the tribal infrastructure,

(II) is available to the general public, and

(III) is placed in service in connection with the taxpayer's active conduct of a trade or business within an Indian reservation.

Such term includes, but is not limited to, roads, power lines, water systems, railroad spurs, and communications facilities.

(5) REAL ESTATE RENTALS.—For purposes of this subsection, the rental to others of real property located within an Indian reservation shall be treated as the active conduct of a trade or business within an Indian reservation.

(6) INDIAN RESERVATION DEFINED.—For purposes of this subsection, the term "Indian reservation" means a reservation, as defined in—

(A) section 3(d) of the Indian Financing Act of 1974 (25 U.S.C. 1452(d)), or

(B) section 4(10) of the Indian Child Welfare Act of 1978 (25 U.S.C. 1903(10)).

For purposes of the preceding sentence, such section 3(d) shall be applied by treating the term "former Indian reservations in Oklahoma" as including only lands which are within the jurisdictional area of an Oklahoma Indian tribe (as determined by the Secretary of the Interior) and are recognized by such Secretary as eligible for trust land status under 25 CFR Part 151 (as in effect on the date of the enactment of this sentence).

(7) COORDINATION WITH NONREVENUE LAWS.—Any reference in this subsection to a provision not contained in this title shall be treated for purposes of this subsection as a reference to such provision as in effect on the date of the enactment of this paragraph.

(8) ELECTION OUT.—If a taxpayer makes an election under this paragraph with respect to any class of property for any taxable year, paragraph (1) shall not apply to all property in such class placed in service during such taxable year. Such election, once made, shall be irrevocable.

(9) TERMINATION.—This subsection shall not apply to property placed in service after December 31, 2017.

Amendments

• **2018, Tax Technical Corrections Act of 2018 (P.L. 115-141)**

P.L. 115-141, § 101(e)(1), Div. U:

Amended Code Sec. 168(j)(3) by striking "property to which paragraph (1) applies" and inserting "qualified Indian reservation property". **Effective** as if included in the provision of the Protecting Americans from Tax Hikes Act of 2015 to which it relates [effective for tax years beginning after 12-31-2015.—CCH].

P.L. 115-141, § 101(e)(2), Div. U:

Amended Code Sec. 168(j)(8) by striking "this subsection" and inserting "paragraph (1)". **Effective** as if included in the provision of the Protecting Americans from Tax Hikes Act of 2015 to which it relates [effective for tax years beginning after 12-31-2015.—CCH].

• **2018, Bipartisan Budget Act of 2018 (P.L. 115-123)**

P.L. 115-123, § 40306(a), Div. D:

Amended Code Sec. 168(j)(9) by striking "December 31, 2016" and inserting "December 31, 2017". **Effective** for property placed in service after 12-31-2016.

• **2015, Protecting Americans from Tax Hikes Act of 2015 (P.L. 114-113)**

P.L. 114-113, § 167(a), Div. Q:

Amended Code Sec. 168(j)(8) by striking "December 31, 2014" and inserting "December 31, 2016". **Effective** for property placed in service after 12-31-2014.

P.L. 114-113, § 167(b), Div. Q:

Amended Code Sec. 168(j) by redesignating paragraph (8), as amended by Act Sec. 167(a), as paragraph (9), and by inserting after paragraph (7) a new paragraph (8). **Effective** for tax years beginning after 12-31-2015.

• **2014, Tax Increase Prevention Act of 2014 (P.L. 113-295)**

P.L. 113-295, § 124(a), Division A:

Amended Code Sec. 168(j)(8) by striking "December 31, 2013" and inserting "December 31, 2014". **Effective** for property placed in service after 12-31-2013.

• **2013, American Taxpayer Relief Act of 2012 (P.L. 112-240)**

P.L. 112-240, § 313(a):

Amended Code Sec. 168(j)(8) by striking "December 31, 2011" and inserting "December 31, 2013". **Effective** for property placed in service after 12-31-2011.

• **2010, Tax Relief, Unemployment Insurance Reauthorization, and Job Creation Act of 2010 (P.L. 111-312)**

P.L. 111-312, § 739(a):

Amended Code Sec. 168(j)(8) by striking "December 31, 2009" and inserting "December 31, 2011". **Effective** for property placed in service after 12-31-2009.

- **2008, Tax Extenders and Alternative Minimum Tax Relief Act of 2008 (P.L. 110-343)**
P.L. 110-343, Division C, § 315(a):
Amended Code Sec. 168(j)(8) by striking "December 31, 2007" and inserting "December 31, 2009". **Effective** for property placed in service after 12-31-2007.
- **2006, Tax Relief and Health Care Act of 2006 (P.L. 109-432)**
P.L. 109-432, Division A, § 112(a):
Amended Code Sec. 168(j)(8) by striking "2005" and inserting "2007". **Effective** for property placed in service after 12-31-2005.
- **2004, Working Families Tax Relief Act of 2004 (P.L. 108-311)**
P.L. 108-311, § 316:
Amended Code Sec. 168(j)(8) by striking "December 31, 2004" and inserting "December 31, 2005". **Effective** 10-4-2004.
- **2002, Job Creation and Worker Assistance Act of 2002 (P.L. 107-147)**
P.L. 107-147, § 613(b):
Amended Code Sec. 168(j)(8) by striking "December 31, 2003" and inserting "December 31, 2004". **Effective** on 3-9-2002.
- **1997, Taxpayer Relief Act of 1997 (P.L. 105-34)**
P.L. 105-34, § 1604(c)(1):
Amended Code Sec. 168(j)(6) by adding at the end a new flush sentence. For the **effective** date, see Act Sec. 1604(c)(2)(A)-(B), below.

P.L. 105-34, § 1604(c)(2)(A)-(B), provides:

(2) The amendment made by paragraph (1) shall apply as if included in the amendments made by section 13321 of the Omnibus Budget Reconciliation Act of 1993, except that such amendment shall not apply—

(A) with respect to property (with an applicable recovery period under section 168(j) of the Internal Revenue Code of 1986 of 6 years or less) held by the taxpayer if the taxpayer claimed the benefits of section 168(j) of such Code with respect to such property on a return filed before March 18, 1997, but only if such return is the first return of tax filed for the taxable year in which such property was placed in service, or

(B) with respect to wages for which the taxpayer claimed the benefits of section 45A of such Code for a taxable year on a return filed before March 18, 1997, but only if such return was the first return of tax filed for such taxable year.

- **1993, Omnibus Budget Reconciliation Act of 1993 (P.L. 103-66)**

P.L. 103-66, § 13321(a):

Amended Code Sec. 168 by adding at the end a new subsection (j). **Effective** for property placed in service after 12-31-93.

[Sec. 168(k)]

(k) SPECIAL ALLOWANCE FOR CERTAIN PROPERTY.—

(1) ADDITIONAL ALLOWANCE.—In the case of any qualified property—

(A) the depreciation deduction provided by section 167(a) for the taxable year in which such property is placed in service shall include an allowance equal to the applicable percentage of the adjusted basis of the qualified property, and

(B) the adjusted basis of the qualified property shall be reduced by the amount of such deduction before computing the amount otherwise allowable as a depreciation deduction under this chapter for such taxable year and any subsequent taxable year.

(2) QUALIFIED PROPERTY.—For purposes of this subsection—

(A) IN GENERAL.—The term "qualified property" means property—

(i)(I) to which this section applies which has a recovery period of 20 years or less,

(II) which is computer software (as defined in section 167(f)(1)(B)) for which a deduction is allowable under section 167(a) without regard to this subsection,

(III) which is water utility property, or

(IV) which is a qualified film or television production (as defined in subsection (d) of section 181) for which a deduction would have been allowable under section 181 without regard to subsections (a)(2) and (g) of such section or this subsection, or

(V) which is a qualified live theatrical production (as defined in subsection (e) of section 181) for which a deduction would have been allowable under section 181 without regard to subsections (a)(2) and (g) of such section or this subsection,

(ii) the original use of which begins with the taxpayer or the acquisition of which by the taxpayer meets the requirements of clause (ii) of subparagraph (E), and

(iii) which is placed in service by the taxpayer before January 1, 2027.

(B) CERTAIN PROPERTY HAVING LONGER PRODUCTION PERIODS TREATED AS QUALIFIED PROPERTY.—

(i) IN GENERAL.—The term "qualified property" includes any property if such property—

(I) meets the requirements of clauses (i) and (ii) of subparagraph (A),

(II) is placed in service by the taxpayer before January 1, 2028,

(III) is acquired by the taxpayer (or acquired pursuant to a written binding contract entered into) before January 1, 2027,

(IV) has a recovery period of at least 10 years or is transportation property,

(V) is subject to section 263A, and

(VI) meets the requirements of clause (iii) of section 263A(f)(1)(B) (determined as if such clause also applies to property which has a long useful life (within the meaning of section 263A(f))).

(ii) ONLY PRE-JANUARY 1, 2027 BASIS ELIGIBLE FOR ADDITIONAL ALLOWANCE.—In the case of property which is qualified property solely by reason of clause (i), paragraph (1) shall apply only to the extent of the adjusted basis thereof attributable to manufacture, construction, or production before January 1, 2027.

(iii) TRANSPORTATION PROPERTY.—For purposes of this subparagraph, the term "transportation property" means tangible personal property used in the trade or business of transporting persons or property.

(iv) APPLICATION OF SUBPARAGRAPH.—This subparagraph shall not apply to any property which is described in subparagraph (C).

(C) CERTAIN AIRCRAFT.—The term "qualified property" includes property—

(i) which meets the requirements of subparagraph (A)(ii) and subclauses (II) and (III) of subparagraph (B)(i),

(ii) which is an aircraft which is not a transportation property (as defined in subparagraph (B)(iii)) other than for agricultural or firefighting purposes,

(iii) which is purchased and on which such purchaser, at the time of the contract for purchase, has made a nonrefundable deposit of the lesser of—

(I) 10 percent of the cost, or
(II) $100,000, and

(iv) which has—

(I) an estimated production period exceeding 4 months, and
(II) a cost exceeding $200,000.

(D) EXCEPTION FOR ALTERNATIVE DEPRECIATION PROPERTY.—The term "qualified property" shall not include any property to which the alternative depreciation system under subsection (g) applies, determined—

(i) without regard to paragraph (7) of subsection (g) (relating to election to have system apply), and

(ii) after application of section 280F(b) (relating to listed property with limited business use).

(E) SPECIAL RULES.—

(i) SELF-CONSTRUCTED PROPERTY.—In the case of a taxpayer manufacturing, constructing, or producing property for the taxpayer's own use, the requirements of subclause (III) of subparagraph (B)(i) shall be treated as met if the taxpayer begins manufacturing, constructing, or producing the property before January 1, 2027.

(ii) ACQUISITION REQUIREMENTS.—An acquisition of property meets the requirements of this clause if—

(I) such property was not used by the taxpayer at any time prior to such acquisition, and

(II) the acquisition of such property meets the requirements of paragraphs (2)(A), (2)(B), (2)(C), and (3) of section 179(d).

(iii) SYNDICATION.—For purposes of subparagraph (A)(ii), if—

(I) property is used by a lessor of such property and such use is the lessor's first use of such property,

(II) such property is sold by such lessor or any subsequent purchaser within 3 months after the date such property was originally placed in service (or, in the case of multiple units of property subject to the same lease, within 3 months after the date the final unit is placed in service, so long as the period between the time the first unit is placed in service and the time the last unit is placed in service does not exceed 12 months), and

(III) the user of such property after the last sale during such 3-month period remains the same as when such property was originally placed in service,

such property shall be treated as originally placed in service not earlier than the date of such last sale.

(F) COORDINATION WITH SECTION 280F.—For purposes of section 280F—

(i) AUTOMOBILES.—In the case of a passenger automobile (as defined in section 280F(d)(5)) which is qualified property, the Secretary shall increase the limitation under section 280F(a)(1)(A)(i) by $8,000.

(ii) LISTED PROPERTY.—The deduction allowable under paragraph (1) shall be taken into account in computing any recapture amount under section 280F(b)(2).

(iii) PHASE DOWN.—In the case of a passenger automobile acquired by the taxpayer before September 28, 2017, and placed in service by the taxpayer after September 27, 2017, clause (i) shall be applied by substituting for "$8,000"—

(I) in the case of an automobile placed in service during 2018, $6,400, and
(II) in the case of an automobile placed in service during 2019, $4,800.

(G) DEDUCTION ALLOWED IN COMPUTING MINIMUM TAX.—For purposes of determining alternative minimum taxable income under section 55, the deduction under section 167 for qualified property shall be determined without regard to any adjustment under section 56.

(H) PRODUCTION PLACED IN SERVICE.—For purposes of subparagraph (A)—

(i) a qualified film or television production shall be considered to be placed in service at the time of initial release or broadcast, and

(ii) a qualified live theatrical production shall be considered to be placed in service at the time of the initial live staged performance.

(3) [Stricken.]
(4) [Stricken.]
(5) SPECIAL RULES FOR CERTAIN PLANTS BEARING FRUITS AND NUTS.—
(A) IN GENERAL.—In the case of any specified plant which is planted before January 1, 2027, or is grafted before such date to a plant that has already been planted, by the taxpayer in the ordinary course of the taxpayer's farming business (as defined in section 263A(e)(4)) during a taxable year for which the taxpayer has elected the application of this paragraph—
(i) a depreciation deduction equal to the applicable percentage of the adjusted basis of such specified plant shall be allowed under section 167(a) for the taxable year in which such specified plant is so planted or grafted, and
(ii) the adjusted basis of such specified plant shall be reduced by the amount of such deduction.
(B) SPECIFIED PLANT.—For purposes of this paragraph, the term "specified plant" means—
(i) any tree or vine which bears fruits or nuts, and
(ii) any other plant which will have more than one crop or yield of fruits or nuts and which generally has a pre-productive period of more than 2 years from the time of planting or grafting to the time at which such plant begins bearing a marketable crop or yield of fruits or nuts.
Such term shall not include any property which is planted or grafted outside of the United States.
(C) ELECTION REVOCABLE ONLY WITH CONSENT.—An election under this paragraph may be revoked only with the consent of the Secretary.
(D) ADDITIONAL DEPRECIATION MAY BE CLAIMED ONLY ONCE.—If this paragraph applies to any specified plant, such specified plant shall not be treated as qualified property in the taxable year in which placed in service.
(E) DEDUCTION ALLOWED IN COMPUTING MINIMUM TAX.—Rules similar to the rules of paragraph (2)(G) shall apply for purposes of this paragraph.
(6) APPLICABLE PERCENTAGE.—For purposes of this subsection—
(A) IN GENERAL.—Except as otherwise provided in this paragraph, the term "applicable percentage" means—
(i) in the case of property placed in service after September 27, 2017, and before January 1, 2023, 100 percent,
(ii) in the case of property placed in service after December 31, 2022, and before January 1, 2024, 80 percent,
(iii) in the case of property placed in service after December 31, 2023, and before January 1, 2025, 60 percent,
(iv) in the case of property placed in service after December 31, 2024, and before January 1, 2026, 40 percent, and
(v) in the case of property placed in service after December 31, 2025, and before January 1, 2027, 20 percent.
(B) RULE FOR PROPERTY WITH LONGER PRODUCTION PERIODS.—In the case of property described in subparagraph (B) or (C) of paragraph (2), the term "applicable percentage" means—
(i) in the case of property placed in service after September 27, 2017, and before January 1, 2024, 100 percent,
(ii) in the case of property placed in service after December 31, 2023, and before January 1, 2025, 80 percent,
(iii) in the case of property placed in service after December 31, 2024, and before January 1, 2026, 60 percent,
(iv) in the case of property placed in service after December 31, 2025, and before January 1, 2027, 40 percent, and
(v) in the case of property placed in service after December 31, 2026, and before January 1, 2028, 20 percent.
(C) RULE FOR PLANTS BEARING FRUITS AND NUTS.—In the case of a specified plant described in paragraph (5), the term "applicable percentage" means—
(i) in the case of a plant which is planted or grafted after September 27, 2017, and before January 1, 2023, 100 percent,
(ii) in the case of a plant which is planted or grafted after December 31, 2022, and before January 1, 2024, 80 percent,
(iii) in the case of a plant which is planted or grafted after December 31, 2023, and before January 1, 2025, 60 percent,
(iv) in the case of a plant which is planted or grafted after December 31, 2024, and before January 1, 2026, 40 percent, and
(v) in the case of a plant which is planted or grafted after December 31, 2025, and before January 1, 2027, 20 percent.

(7) ELECTION OUT.—If a taxpayer makes an election under this paragraph with respect to any class of property for any taxable year, paragraphs (1) and (2)(F) shall not apply to any qualified property in such class placed in service during such taxable year. An election under this paragraph may be revoked only with the consent of the Secretary.

(8) PHASE DOWN.—In the case of qualified property acquired by the taxpayer before September 28, 2017, and placed in service by the taxpayer after September 27, 2017, paragraph (6) shall be applied by substituting for each percentage therein—

(A) "50 percent" in the case of—
(i) property placed in service before January 1, 2018, and
(ii) property described in subparagraph (B) or (C) of paragraph (2) which is placed in service in 2018,

(B) "40 percent" in the case of—
(i) property placed in service in 2018 (other than property described in subparagraph (B) or (C) of paragraph (2)), and
(ii) property described in subparagraph (B) or (C) of paragraph (2) which is placed in service in 2019,

(C) "30 percent" in the case of—
(i) property placed in service in 2019 (other than property described in subparagraph (B) or (C) of paragraph (2)), and
(ii) property described in subparagraph (B) or (C) of paragraph (2) which is placed in service in 2020, and

(D) "0 percent" in the case of—
(i) property placed in service after 2019 (other than property described in subparagraph (B) or (C) of paragraph (2)), and
(ii) property described in subparagraph (B) or (C) of paragraph (2) which is placed in service after 2020.

(9) EXCEPTION FOR CERTAIN PROPERTY.—The term "qualified property" shall not include—

(A) any property which is primarily used in a trade or business described in clause (iv) of section 163(j)(7)(A), or

(B) any property used in a trade or business that has had floor plan financing indebtedness (as defined in paragraph (9) of section 163(j)), if the floor plan financing interest related to such indebtedness was taken into account under paragraph (1)(C) of such section.

(10) SPECIAL RULE FOR PROPERTY PLACED IN SERVICE DURING CERTAIN PERIODS.—

(A) IN GENERAL.—In the case of qualified property placed in service by the taxpayer during the first taxable year ending after September 27, 2017, if the taxpayer elects to have this paragraph apply for such taxable year, paragraphs (1)(A) and (5)(A)(i) shall be applied by substituting "50 percent" for "the applicable percentage".

(B) FORM OF ELECTION.—Any election under this paragraph shall be made at such time and in such form and manner as the Secretary may prescribe.

Amendments

- **2018, Tax Technical Corrections Act of 2018 (P.L. 115-141)**

P.L. 115-141, § 101(d)(1), Div. U:
Amended Code Sec. 168(k)(2)(B)(i)(III) by inserting "binding" before "contract". **Effective** as if included in the provision of the Protecting Americans from Tax Hikes Act of 2015 to which it relates [**effective** for property placed in service after 12-31-2015, in tax years ending after such date.—CCH].

P.L. 115-141, § 101(d)(2)(A)-(B), Div. U:
Amended Code Sec. 168(k)(5)(B)(ii) by inserting "crop or" after "more than one", and by inserting "a marketable crop or yield of" after "begins bearing". **Effective** as if included in the provision of the Protecting Americans from Tax Hikes Act of 2015 to which it relates [**effective** for specified plants (as defined in Code Sec. 168(k)(5)(B)) planted or grafted after 12-31-2015.—CCH].

P.L. 115-141, § 101(d)(3)-(4), Div. U, provides:
(3) For purposes of applying section 168(k) of the Internal Revenue Code of 1986, as in effect on the day before the date of the enactment of Public Law 115-97, with respect to property acquired before September 28, 2017, paragraph (6) thereof shall be treated as reading as follows (and as having been included in section 143 of the Protecting Americans from Tax Hikes Act of 2015):

"(6) PHASE-DOWN.—In the case of qualified property placed in service by the taxpayer after December 31, 2017 (December 31, 2018, in the case of property described in subparagraph (B) or (C) of paragraph (2)), paragraph (1)(A) shall be applied by substituting for '50 percent'—

"(A) '40 percent' in the case of—

"(i) property placed in service in 2018 (other than property described in subparagraph (B) or (C) of paragraph (2)), and

"(ii) property described in subparagraph (B) or (C) of paragraph (2) which is placed in service in 2019, and

"(B) '30 percent' in the case of—

"(i) property placed in service in 2019 (other than property described in subparagraph (B) or (C) of paragraph (2)), and

"(ii) property described in subparagraph (B) or (C) of paragraph (2) which is placed in service in 2020.".

(4) Section 168(k)(7) of the Internal Revenue Code of 1986, as in effect on the day before the date of the enactment of Public Law 115-97, shall be applied—

(A) by substituting "paragraphs (1), (2)(F), and (4)" for "paragraphs (1) and (2)(F)", and

(B) as if the application of such substitution had been included in section 143 of the Protecting Americans from Tax Hikes Act of 2015.

- **2017, Tax Cuts and Jobs Act (P.L. 115-97)**

P.L. 115-97, § 12001(b)(13):
Amended Code Sec. 168(k) by striking paragraph (4). **Effective** for tax years beginning after 12-31-2017. Prior to being stricken, Code Sec. 168(k)(4) read as follows:

(4) ELECTION TO ACCELERATE AMT CREDITS IN LIEU OF BONUS DEPRECIATION.—

(A) IN GENERAL.—If a corporation elects to have this paragraph apply for any taxable year—

(i) paragraphs (1) and (2)(F) shall not apply to any qualified property placed in service during such taxable year,

(ii) the applicable depreciation method used under this section with respect to such property shall be the straight line method, and

(iii) the limitation imposed by section 53(c) for such taxable year shall be increased by the bonus depreciation amount which is determined for such taxable year under subparagraph (B).

(B) BONUS DEPRECIATION AMOUNT.—For purposes of this paragraph—

(i) IN GENERAL.—The bonus depreciation amount for any taxable year is an amount equal to 20 percent of the excess (if any) of—

(I) the aggregate amount of depreciation which would be allowed under this section for qualified property placed in service by the taxpayer during such taxable year if paragraph (1) applied to all such property (and, in the case of any such property which is a passenger automobile (as defined in section 280F(d)(5)), if paragraph (2)(F) applied to such automobile), over

(II) the aggregate amount of depreciation which would be allowed under this section for qualified property placed in service by the taxpayer during such taxable year if paragraphs (1) and (2)(F) did not apply to any such property.

The aggregate amounts determined under subclauses (I) and (II) shall be determined without regard to any election made under subparagraph (A) or subsection (b)(2)(D), (b)(3)(D), or (g)(7).

(ii) LIMITATION.—The bonus depreciation amount for any taxable year shall not exceed the lesser of—

(I) 50 percent of the minimum tax credit under section 53(b) for the first taxable year ending after December 31, 2015, or

(II) the minimum tax credit under section 53(b) for such taxable year determined by taking into account only the adjusted net minimum tax for taxable years ending before January 1, 2016 (determined by treating credits as allowed on a first-in, first-out basis).

(iii) AGGREGATION RULE.—All corporations which are treated as a single employer under section 52(a) shall be treated—

(I) as 1 taxpayer for purposes of this paragraph, and

(II) as having elected the application of this paragraph if any such corporation so elects.

(C) CREDIT REFUNDABLE.—For purposes of section 6401(b), the aggregate increase in the credits allowable under part IV of subchapter A for any taxable year resulting from the application of this paragraph shall be treated as allowed under subpart C of such part (and not any other subpart).

(D) OTHER RULES.—

(i) ELECTION.—Any election under this paragraph may be revoked only with the consent of the Secretary.

(ii) PARTNERSHIPS WITH ELECTING PARTNERS.—In the case of a corporation which is a partner in a partnership and which makes an election under subparagraph (A) for the taxable year, for purposes of determining such corporation's distributive share of partnership items under section 702 for such taxable year—

(I) paragraphs (1) and (2)(F) shall not apply to any qualified property placed in service during such taxable year, and

(II) the applicable depreciation method used under this section with respect to such property shall be the straight line method.

(iii) CERTAIN PARTNERSHIPS.—In the case of a partnership in which more than 50 percent of the capital and profits interests are owned (directly or indirectly) at all times during the taxable year by 1 corporation (or by corporations treated as 1 taxpayer under subparagraph (B)(iii)), each partner shall compute its bonus depreciation amount under clause (i) of subparagraph (B) by taking into account its distributive share of the amounts determined by the partnership under subclauses (I) and (II) of such clause for the taxable year of the partnership ending with or within the taxable year of the partner.

P.L. 115-97, § 13201(a)(1)(A)-(B):

Amended Code Sec. 168(k) by striking "50 percent" in paragraph (1)(A) and inserting "the applicable percentage", and by striking "50 percent" in paragraph (5)(A)(i) and inserting "the applicable percentage". For the **effective** date, see Act Sec. 13201(h)(1)-(2), below.

P.L. 115-97, § 13201(a)(2):

Amended Code Sec. 168(k)(6). For the **effective** date, see Act Sec. 13201(h)(1)-(2), below. Prior to amendment, Code Sec. 168(k)(6) read as follows:

(6) PHASE DOWN.—In the case of qualified property placed in service by the taxpayer after December 31, 2017, paragraph (1)(A) shall be applied by substituting for "50 percent"—

(A) in the case of property placed in service in 2018 (or in the case of property placed in service in 2019 and described in paragraph (2)(B) or (C) (determined by substituting "2019" for "2020" in paragraphs (2)(B)(i)(III) and (ii) and paragraph (2)(E)(i)), "40 percent",

(B) in the case of property placed in service in 2019 (or in the case of property placed in service in 2020 and described in paragraph (2)(B) or (C), "30 percent".

P.L. 115-97, § 13201(a)(3)(A):

Amended Code Sec. 168(k)(5) by striking subparagraph (F). For the **effective** date, see Act Sec. 13201(h)(1)-(2), below. Prior to being stricken, Code Sec. 168(k)(5)(F) read as follows:

(F) PHASE DOWN.—In the case of a specified plant which is planted after December 31, 2017 (or is grafted to a plant that has already been planted before such date), subparagraph (A)(i) shall be applied by substituting for "50 percent"—

(i) in the case of a plant which is planted (or so grafted) in 2018, "40 percent", and

(ii) in the case of a plant which is planted (or so grafted) during 2019, "30 percent".

P.L. 115-97, § 13201(a)(3)(B):

Amended Code Sec. 168(k) by adding at the end a new paragraph (8). For the **effective** date, see Act Sec. 13201(h)(1)-(2), below.

P.L. 115-97, § 13201(b)(1)(A)(i):

Amended Code Sec. 168(k)(2)(A)(iii), (B)(i)(III) and (ii), and (E)(i) by striking "January 1, 2020" each place it appears and inserting "January 1, 2027". For the **effective** date, see Act Sec. 13201(h)(1)-(2), below.

P.L. 115-97, § 13201(b)(1)(A)(ii)(I)-(II):

Amended Code Sec. 168(k)(2)(B) by striking "January 1, 2021" in clause (i)(II) and inserting "January 1, 2028", and by striking "PRE-JANUARY 1, 2020" in the heading of clause (ii) and inserting "PRE-JANUARY 1, 2027". For the **effective** date, see Act Sec. 13201(h)(1)-(2), below.

P.L. 115-97, § 13201(b)(1)(B):

Amended Code Sec. 168(k)(5)(A) by striking "January 1, 2020" and inserting "January 1, 2027". For the **effective** date, see Act Sec. 13201(h)(1)-(2), below.

P.L. 115-97, § 13201(b)(2)(B):

Amended the heading of Code Sec. 168(k) by striking "ACQUIRED AFTER DECEMBER 31, 2007, AND BEFORE JANUARY 1, 2020" following "CERTAIN PROPERTY". For the **effective** date, see Act Sec. 13201(h)(1)-(2), below.

P.L. 115-97, § 13201(c)(1):

Amended Code Sec. 168(k)(2)(A)(ii). For the **effective** date, see Act Sec. 13201(h)(1)-(2), below. Prior to amendment, Code Sec. 168(k)(2)(A)(ii) read as follows:

(ii) the original use of which commences with the taxpayer, and

P.L. 115-97, § 13201(c)(2):

Amended Code Sec. 168(k)(2)(E)(ii). For the **effective** date, see Act Sec. 13201(h)(1)-(2), below. Prior to amendment, Code Sec. 168(k)(2)(E)(ii) read as follows:

(ii) SALE-LEASEBACKS.—For purposes of clause (iii) and subparagraph (A)(ii), if property is—

(I) originally placed in service by a person, and

(II) sold and leased back by such person within 3 months after the date such property was originally placed in service, such property shall be treated as originally placed in service not earlier than the date on which such property is used under the leaseback referred to in subclause (II).

P.L. 115-97, § 13201(c)(3):

Amended Code Sec. 168(k)(2)(E)(iii)(I). For the **effective** date, see Act Sec. 13201(h)(1)-(2), below. Prior to amendment, Code Sec. 168(k)(2)(E)(iii)(I) read as follows:

(I) property is originally placed in service by the lessor of such property,

P.L. 115-97, § 13201(d):

Amended Code Sec. 168(k), as amended by Act Sec. 13201, by adding at the end a new paragraph (9). For the **effective** date, see Act Sec. 13201(h)(1)-(2), below.

P.L. 115-97, § 13201(e):

Amended Code Sec. 168(k), as amended by Act Sec. 13201, by adding at the end a new paragraph (10). For the **effective** date, see Act Sec. 13201(h)(1)-(2), below.

P.L. 115-97, § 13201(f):

Amended Code Sec. 168(k)(2)(F)(iii) by striking "placed in service by the taxpayer after December 31, 2017" and inserting "acquired by the taxpayer before September 28, 2017, and placed in service by the taxpayer after September 27, 2017*ᵇ*. For the **effective** date, see Act Sec. 13201(h)(1)-(2), below.

P.L. 115-97, § 13201(g)(1)(A)-(C):
Amended Code Sec. 168(k)(2)(A)(i), as amended by Act Sec. 13204, by striking "or" in subclause (II), by adding "or" after the comma in subclause (III), and by adding at the end new subclauses (IV) and (V). For the **effective** date, see Act Sec. 13201(h)(1)-(2), below.

P.L. 115-97, § 13201(g)(2):
Amended Code Sec. 168(k)(2) by adding at the end a new subparagraph (H). For the **effective** date, see Act Sec. 13201(h)(1)-(2), below.

P.L. 115-97, § 13201(h)(1)-(2), provides:
(h) EFFECTIVE DATE.—
(1) IN GENERAL.—Except as provided by paragraph (2), the amendments made by this section shall apply to property which—
(A) is acquired after September 27, 2017, and
(B) is placed in service after such date.
For purposes of the preceding sentence, property shall not be treated as acquired after the date on which a written binding contract is entered into for such acquisition.
(2) SPECIFIED PLANTS.—The amendments made by this section shall apply to specified plants planted or grafted after September 27, 2017.

P.L. 115-97, § 13204(a)(4)(A)(i)-(iii):
Amended Code Sec. 168(k)(2)(A)(i) by inserting "or" after the comma in subclause (II), by striking "or" at the end of subclause (III), and by striking subclause (IV). **Effective** for property placed in service after 12-31-2017. Prior to being stricken, Code Sec. 168(k)(2)(A)(i)(IV) read as follows:
(IV) which is qualified improvement property,

P.L. 115-97, § 13204(a)(4)(B)(ii):
Amended Code Sec. 168(k) by striking paragraph (3). **Effective** for property placed in service after 12-31-2017. Prior to being stricken, Code Sec. 168(k)(3) read as follows:
(3) QUALIFIED IMPROVEMENT PROPERTY.—For purposes of this subsection—
(A) IN GENERAL.—The term "qualified improvement property" means any improvement to an interior portion of a building which is nonresidential real property if such improvement is placed in service after the date such building was first placed in service.
(B) CERTAIN IMPROVEMENTS NOT INCLUDED.—Such term shall not include any improvement for which the expenditure is attributable to—
(i) the enlargement of the building,
(ii) any elevator or escalator, or
(iii) the internal structural framework of the building.

- **2015, Protecting Americans from Tax Hikes Act of 2015 (P.L. 114-113)**

P.L. 114-113, § 143(a)(1)(A)-(B), Div. Q:
Amended Code Sec. 168(k)(2) by striking "January 1, 2016" in subparagraph (A)(iv) and inserting "January 1, 2017", and by striking "January 1, 2015" each place it appears and inserting "January 1, 2016". **Effective** for property placed in service after 12-31-2014, in tax years ending after such date.

P.L. 114-113, § 143(a)(3)(A), Div. Q:
Amended Code Sec. 168(k)(4)(D)(iii)(II) by striking "January 1, 2015" and inserting "January 1, 2016". **Effective** for tax years ending after 12-31-2014.

P.L. 114-113, § 143(a)(3)(B), Div. Q:
Amended Code Sec. 168(k)(4) by adding at the end a new subparagraph (L). **Effective** for tax years ending after 12-31-2014.

P.L. 114-113, § 143(a)(4)(A), Div. Q:
Amended the heading for Code Sec. 168(k) by striking "JANUARY 1, 2015" and inserting "JANUARY 1, 2016". **Effective** for property placed in service after 12-31-2014, in tax years ending after such date.

P.L. 114-113, § 143(a)(4)(B), Div. Q:
Amended the heading for Code Sec. 168(k)(2)(B)(ii) by striking "PRE-JANUARY 1, 2015" and inserting "PRE-JANUARY 1, 2016". **Effective** for property placed in service after 12-31-2014, in tax years ending after such date.

P.L. 114-113, § 143(b)(1), Div. Q:
Amended Code Sec. 168(k)(2), as amended by Act Sec. 143(a). **Effective** for property placed in service after 12-31-2015, in tax years ending after such date. Prior to amendment, Code Sec. 168(k)(2) read as follows:
(2) QUALIFIED PROPERTY.—For purposes of this subsection—
(A) IN GENERAL.—The term "qualified property" means property—
(i)(I) to which this section applies which has a recovery period of 20 years or less,
(II) which is computer software (as defined in section 167(f)(1)(B)) for which a deduction is allowable under section 167(a) without regard to this subsection,
(III) which is water utility property, or
(IV) which is qualified leasehold improvement property,
(ii) the original use of which commences with the taxpayer after December 31, 2007,
(iii) which is—
(I) acquired by the taxpayer after December 31, 2007, and before January 1, 2016, but only if no written binding contract for the acquisition was in effect before January 1, 2008, or
(II) acquired by the taxpayer pursuant to a written binding contract which was entered into after December 31, 2007, and before January 1, 2016, and
(iv) which is placed in service by the taxpayer before January 1, 2016, or, in the case of property described in subparagraph (B) or (C), before January 1, 2017.
(B) CERTAIN PROPERTY HAVING LONGER PRODUCTION PERIODS TREATED AS QUALIFIED PROPERTY.—
(i) IN GENERAL.—The term "qualified property" includes any property if such property—
(I) meets the requirements of clauses (i), (ii), (iii), and (iv) of subparagraph (A),
(II) has a recovery period of at least 10 years or is transportation property,
(III) is subject to section 263A, and
(IV) meets the requirements of clause (iii) of section 263A(f)(1)(B) (determined as if such clause also applies to property which has a long useful life (within the meaning of section 263A(f))).
(ii) ONLY PRE-JANUARY 1, 2016, BASIS ELIGIBLE FOR ADDITIONAL ALLOWANCE.—In the case of property which is qualified property solely by reason of clause (i), paragraph (1) shall apply only to the extent of the adjusted basis thereof attributable to manufacture, construction, or production before January 1, 2016.
(iii) TRANSPORTATION PROPERTY.—For purposes of this subparagraph, the term "transportation property" means tangible personal property used in the trade or business of transporting persons or property.
(iv) APPLICATION OF SUBPARAGRAPH.—This subparagraph shall not apply to any property which is described in subparagraph (C).
(C) CERTAIN AIRCRAFT.—The term "qualified property" includes property—
(i) which meets the requirements of clauses (ii), (iii), and (iv) of subparagraph (A),
(ii) which is an aircraft which is not a transportation property (as defined in subparagraph (B)(iii)) other than for agricultural or firefighting purposes,
(iii) which is purchased and on which such purchaser, at the time of the contract for purchase, has made a nonrefundable deposit of the lesser of—
(I) 10 percent of the cost, or
(II) $100,000, and
(iv) which has—
(I) an estimated production period exceeding 4 months, and
(II) a cost exceeding $200,000.
(D) EXCEPTIONS.—
(i) ALTERNATIVE DEPRECIATION PROPERTY.—The term "qualified property" shall not include any property to which the alternative depreciation system under subsection (g) applies, determined—
(I) without regard to paragraph (7) of subsection (g) (relating to election to have system apply), and
(II) after application of section 280F(b) (relating to listed property with limited business use).
(ii) QUALIFIED NEW YORK LIBERTY ZONE LEASEHOLD IMPROVEMENT PROPERTY.—The term "qualified property" shall not include any qualified New York Liberty Zone leasehold improvement property (as defined in section 1400L(c)(2)).

(iii) Election out.—If a taxpayer makes an election under this clause with respect to any class of property for any taxable year, this subsection shall not apply to all property in such class placed in service during such taxable year.

(E) Special rules.—

(i) Self-constructed property.—In the case of a taxpayer manufacturing, constructing, or producing property for the taxpayer's own use, the requirements of clause (iii) of subparagraph (A) shall be treated as met if the taxpayer begins manufacturing, constructing, or producing the property after December 31, 2007, and before January 1, 2016.

(ii) Sale-leasebacks.—For purposes of clause (iii) and subparagraph (A)(ii), if property is—

(I) originally placed in service after December 31, 2007, by a person, and

(II) sold and leased back by such person within 3 months after the date such property was originally placed in service, such property shall be treated as originally placed in service not earlier than the date on which such property is used under the leaseback referred to in subclause (II).

(iii) Syndication.—For purposes of subparagraph (A)(ii), if—

(I) property is originally placed in service after December 31, 2007, by the lessor of such property,

(II) such property is sold by such lessor or any subsequent purchaser within 3 months after the date such property was originally placed in service (or, in the case of multiple units of property subject to the same lease, within 3 months after the date the final unit is placed in service, so long as the period between the time the first unit is placed in service and the time the last unit is placed in service does not exceed 12 months), and

(III) the user of such property after the last sale during such 3-month period remains the same as when such property was originally placed in service,

such property shall be treated as originally placed in service not earlier than the date of such last sale.

(iv) Limitations related to users and related parties.—The term "qualified property" shall not include any property if—

(I) the user of such property (as of the date on which such property is originally placed in service) or a person which is related (within the meaning of section 267(b) or 707(b)) to such user or to the taxpayer had a written binding contract in effect for the acquisition of such property at any time on or before December 31, 2007, or

(II) in the case of property manufactured, constructed, or produced for such user's or person's own use, the manufacture, construction, or production of such property began at any time on or before December 31, 2007.

(F) Coordination with Section 280F.—For purposes of section 280F—

(i) Automobiles.—In the case of a passenger automobile (as defined in section 280F(d)(5)) which is qualified property, the Secretary shall increase the limitation under section 280F(a)(1)(A)(i) by $8,000.

(ii) Listed property.—The deduction allowable under paragraph (1) shall be taken into account in computing any recapture amount under section 280F(b)(2).

(G) Deduction allowed in computing minimum tax.—For purposes of determining alternative minimum taxable income under section 55, the deduction under subsection (a) for qualified property shall be determined under this section without regard to any adjustment under section 56.

P.L. 114-113, §143(b)(2), Div. Q:

Amended Code Sec. 168(k)(3). **Effective** for property placed in service after 12-31-2015, in tax years ending after such date. Prior to amendment, Code Sec. 168(k)(3) read as follows:

(3) Qualified leasehold improvement property.—For purposes of this subsection—

(A) In general.—The term "qualified leasehold improvement property" means any improvement to an interior portion of a building which is nonresidential real property if—

(i) such improvement is made under or pursuant to a lease (as defined in subsection (h)(7))—

(I) by the lessee (or any sublessee) of such portion, or

(II) by the lessor of such portion,

(ii) such portion is to be occupied exclusively by the lessee (or any sublessee) of such portion, and

(iii) such improvement is placed in service more than 3 years after the date the building was first placed in service.

(B) Certain improvements not included.—Such term shall not include any improvement for which the expenditure is attributable to—

(i) the enlargement of the building,

(ii) any elevator or escalator,

(iii) any structural component benefiting a common area, and

(iv) the internal structural framework of the building.

(C) Definitions and special rules.—For purposes of this paragraph—

(i) Commitment to lease treated as lease.—A commitment to enter into a lease shall be treated as a lease, and the parties to such commitment shall be treated as lessor and lessee, respectively.

(ii) Related persons.—A lease between related persons shall not be considered a lease. For purposes of the preceding sentence, the term "related persons" means—

(I) members of an affiliated group (as defined in section 1504), and

(II) persons having a relationship described in subsection (b) of section 267; except that, for purposes of this clause, the phrase "80 percent or more" shall be substituted for the phrase "more than 50 percent" each place it appears in such subsection.

P.L. 114-113, §143(b)(3), Div. Q:

Amended Code Sec. 168(k)(4), as amended by Act Sec. 143(a). For the **effective** date, see Act Sec. 143(b)(7)(B), below. Prior to amendment, Code Sec. 168(k)(4) read as follows:

(4) Election to accelerate the AMT and research credits in lieu of bonus depreciation.—

(A) In general.—If a corporation elects to have this paragraph apply for the first taxable year of the taxpayer ending after March 31, 2008, in the case of such taxable year and each subsequent taxable year—

(i) paragraph (1) shall not apply to any eligible qualified property placed in service by the taxpayer,

(ii) the applicable depreciation method used under this section with respect to such property shall be the straight line method, and

(iii) each of the limitations described in subparagraph (B) for any such taxable year shall be increased by the bonus depreciation amount which is—

(I) determined for such taxable year under subparagraph (C), and

(II) allocated to such limitation under subparagraph (E).

(B) Limitations to be increased.—The limitations described in this subparagraph are—

(i) the limitation imposed by section 38(c), and

(ii) the limitation imposed by section 53(c).

(C) Bonus depreciation amount.—For purposes of this paragraph—

(i) In general.—The bonus depreciation amount for any taxable year is an amount equal to 20 percent of the excess (if any) of—

(I) the aggregate amount of depreciation which would be allowed under this section for eligible qualified property placed in service by the taxpayer during such taxable year if paragraph (1) applied to all such property, over

(II) the aggregate amount of depreciation which would be allowed under this section for eligible qualified property placed in service by the taxpayer during such taxable year if paragraph (1) did not apply to any such property.

The aggregate amounts determined under subclauses (I) and (II) shall be determined without regard to any election made under subsection (b)(2)(D), (b)(3)(D), or (g)(7) and without regard to subparagraph (A)(ii).

(ii) Maximum amount.—The bonus depreciation amount for any taxable year shall not exceed the maximum increase amount under clause (iii), reduced (but not below zero) by the sum of the bonus depreciation amounts for all preceding taxable years.

(iii) Maximum increase amount.—For purposes of clause (ii), the term "maximum increase amount" means, with respect to any corporation, the lesser of—

(I) $30,000,000, or

(II) 6 percent of the sum of the business credit increase amount, and the AMT credit increase amount, determined with respect to such corporation under subparagraph (E).

(iv) AGGREGATION RULE.—All corporations which are treated as a single employer under section 52(a) shall be treated—

(I) as 1 taxpayer for purposes of this paragraph, and

(II) as having elected the application of this paragraph if any such corporation so elects.

(D) ELIGIBLE QUALIFIED PROPERTY.—For purposes of this paragraph, the term "eligible qualified property" means qualified property under paragraph (2), except that in applying paragraph (2) for purposes of this paragraph—

(i) "March 31, 2008" shall be substituted for "December 31, 2007" each place it appears in subparagraph (A) and clauses (i) and (ii) of subparagraph (E) thereof,

(ii) "April 1, 2008" shall be substituted for "January 1, 2008" in subparagraph (A)(iii)(I) thereof, and

(iii) only adjusted basis attributable to manufacture, construction, or production—

(I) after March 31, 2008, and before January 1, 2010, and

(II) after December 31, 2010, and before January 1, 2016,

shall be taken into account under subparagraph (B)(ii) thereof.

(E) ALLOCATION OF BONUS DEPRECIATION AMOUNTS.—

(i) IN GENERAL.—Subject to clauses (ii) and (iii), the taxpayer shall, at such time and in such manner as the Secretary may prescribe, specify the portion (if any) of the bonus depreciation amount for the taxable year which is to be allocated to each of the limitations described in subparagraph (B) for such taxable year.

(ii) LIMITATION ON ALLOCATIONS.—The portion of the bonus depreciation amount which may be allocated under clause (i) to the limitations described in subparagraph (B) for any taxable year shall not exceed—

(I) in the case of the limitation described in subparagraph (B)(i), the excess of the business credit increase amount over the bonus depreciation amount allocated to such limitation for all preceding taxable years, and

(II) in the case of the limitation described in subparagraph (B)(ii), the excess of the AMT credit increase amount over the bonus depreciation amount allocated to such limitation for all preceding taxable years.

(iii) BUSINESS CREDIT INCREASE AMOUNT.—For purposes of this paragraph, the term "business credit increase amount" means the amount equal to the portion of the credit allowable under section 38 (determined without regard to subsection (c) thereof) for the first taxable year ending after March 31, 2008, which is allocable to business credit carryforwards to such taxable year which are—

(I) from taxable years beginning before January 1, 2006, and

(II) properly allocable (determined under the rules of section 38(d)) to the research credit determined under section 41(a).

(iv) AMT CREDIT INCREASE AMOUNT.—For purposes of this paragraph, the term "AMT credit increase amount" means the amount equal to the portion of the minimum tax credit under section 53(b) for the first taxable year ending after March 31, 2008, determined by taking into account only the adjusted net minimum tax for taxable years beginning before January 1, 2006. For purposes of the preceding sentence, credits shall be treated as allowed on a first-in, first-out basis.

(F) CREDIT REFUNDABLE.—For purposes of section 6401(b), the aggregate increase in the credits allowable under part IV of subchapter A for any taxable year resulting from the application of this paragraph shall be treated as allowed under subpart C of such part (and not any other subpart).

(G) OTHER RULES.—

(i) ELECTION.—Any election under this paragraph (including any allocation under subparagraph (E)) may be revoked only with the consent of the Secretary.

(ii) PARTNERSHIPS WITH ELECTING PARTNERS.—In the case of a corporation making an election under subparagraph (A) and which is a partner in a partnership, for purposes of determining such corporation's distributive share of partnership items under section 702—

(I) paragraph (1) shall not apply to any eligible qualified property, and

(II) the applicable depreciation method used under this section with respect to such property shall be the straight line method.

(iii) SPECIAL RULE FOR PASSENGER AIRCRAFT.—In the case of any passenger aircraft, the written binding contract limitation under paragraph (2)(A)(iii)(I) shall not apply for purposes of subparagraphs (C)(i)(I) and (D).

(H) SPECIAL RULES FOR EXTENSION PROPERTY.—

(i) TAXPAYERS PREVIOUSLY ELECTING ACCELERATION.—In the case of a taxpayer who made the election under subparagraph (A) for its first taxable year ending after March 31, 2008—

(I) the taxpayer may elect not to have this paragraph apply to extension property, but

(II) if the taxpayer does not make the election under subclause (I), in applying this paragraph to the taxpayer a separate bonus depreciation amount, maximum amount, and maximum increase amount shall be computed and applied to eligible qualified property which is extension property and to eligible qualified property which is not extension property.

(ii) TAXPAYERS NOT PREVIOUSLY ELECTING ACCELERATION.—In the case of a taxpayer who did not make the election under subparagraph (A) for its first taxable year ending after March 31, 2008—

(I) the taxpayer may elect to have this paragraph apply to its first taxable year ending after December 31, 2008, and each subsequent taxable year, and

(II) if the taxpayer makes the election under subclause (I), this paragraph shall only apply to eligible qualified property which is extension property.

(iii) EXTENSION PROPERTY.—For purposes of this subparagraph, the term "extension property" means property which is eligible qualified property solely by reason of the extension of the application of the special allowance under paragraph (1) pursuant to the amendments made by section 1201(a) of the American Recovery and Reinvestment Tax Act of 2009 (and the application of such extension to this paragraph pursuant to the amendment made by section 1201(b)(1) of such Act).

(I) SPECIAL RULES FOR ROUND 2 EXTENSION PROPERTY.—

(i) IN GENERAL.—In the case of round 2 extension property, this paragraph shall be applied without regard to—

(I) the limitation described in subparagraph (B)(i) thereof, and

(II) the business credit increase amount under subparagraph (E)(iii) thereof.

(ii) TAXPAYERS PREVIOUSLY ELECTING ACCELERATION.—In the case of a taxpayer who made the election under subparagraph (A) for its first taxable year ending after March 31, 2008, or a taxpayer who made the election under subparagraph (H)(ii) for its first taxable year ending after December 31, 2008—

(I) the taxpayer may elect not to have this paragraph apply to round 2 extension property, but

(II) if the taxpayer does not make the election under subclause (I), in applying this paragraph to the taxpayer the bonus depreciation amount, maximum amount, and maximum increase amount shall be computed and applied to eligible qualified property which is round 2 extension property.

The amounts described in subclause (II) shall be computed separately from any amounts computed with respect to eligible qualified property which is not round 2 extension property.

(iii) TAXPAYERS NOT PREVIOUSLY ELECTING ACCELERATION.—In the case of a taxpayer who neither made the election under subparagraph (A) for its first taxable year ending after March 31, 2008, nor made the election under subparagraph (H)(ii) for its first taxable year ending after December 31, 2008—

(I) the taxpayer may elect to have this paragraph apply to its first taxable year ending after December 31, 2010, and each subsequent taxable year, and

(II) if the taxpayer makes the election under subclause (I), this paragraph shall only apply to eligible qualified property which is round 2 extension property.

(iv) ROUND 2 EXTENSION PROPERTY.—For purposes of this subparagraph, the term "round 2 extension property" means property which is eligible qualified property solely by reason of the extension of the application of the special allowance under paragraph (1) pursuant to the amendments made by section 401(a) of the Tax Relief, Unemployment Insurance Reauthorization, and Job Creation Act of 2010 (and the application of such extension to this paragraph pursuant to the amendment made by section 401(c)(1) of such Act).

(J) SPECIAL RULES FOR ROUND 3 EXTENSION PROPERTY.—

(i) IN GENERAL.—In the case of round 3 extension property, this paragraph shall be applied without regard to—

(I) the limitation described in subparagraph (B)(i) thereof, and

(II) the business credit increase amount under subparagraph (E)(iii) thereof.

(ii) TAXPAYERS PREVIOUSLY ELECTING ACCELERATION.—In the case of a taxpayer who made the election under subparagraph (A) for its first taxable year ending after March 31, 2008, a taxpayer who made the election under subparagraph (H)(ii) for its first taxable year ending after December 31, 2008, or a taxpayer who made the election under subparagraph (I)(iii) for its first taxable year ending after December 31, 2010—

(I) the taxpayer may elect not to have this paragraph apply to round 3 extension property, but

(II) if the taxpayer does not make the election under subclause (I), in applying this paragraph to the taxpayer the bonus depreciation amount, maximum amount, and maximum increase amount shall be computed and applied to eligible qualified property which is round 3 extension property.

The amounts described in subclause (II) shall be computed separately from any amounts computed with respect to eligible qualified property which is not round 3 extension property.

(iii) TAXPAYERS NOT PREVIOUSLY ELECTING ACCELERATION.—In the case of a taxpayer who neither made the election under subparagraph (A) for its first taxable year ending after March 31, 2008, nor made the election under subparagraph (H)(ii) for its first taxable year ending after December 31, 2008, nor made the election under subparagraph (I)(iii) for its first taxable year ending after December 31, 2010—

(I) the taxpayer may elect to have this paragraph apply to its first taxable year ending after December 31, 2012, and each subsequent taxable year, and

(II) if the taxpayer makes the election under subclause (I), this paragraph shall only apply to eligible qualified property which is round 3 extension property.

(iv) ROUND 3 EXTENSION PROPERTY.—For purposes of this subparagraph, the term "round 3 extension property" means property which is eligible qualified property solely by reason of the extension of the application of the special allowance under paragraph (1) pursuant to the amendments made by section 331(a) of the American Taxpayer Relief Act of 2012 (and the application of such extension to this paragraph pursuant to the amendment made by section 331(c)(1) of such Act).

(K) SPECIAL RULES FOR ROUND 4 EXTENSION PROPERTY.—

(i) IN GENERAL.—In the case of round 4 extension property, in applying this paragraph to any taxpayer—

(I) the limitation described in subparagraph (B)(i) and the business credit increase amount under subparagraph (E)(iii) thereof shall not apply, and

(II) the bonus depreciation amount, maximum amount, and maximum increase amount shall be computed separately from amounts computed with respect to eligible qualified property which is not round 4 extension property.

(ii) ELECTION.—

(I) A taxpayer who has an election in effect under this paragraph for round 3 extension property shall be treated as having an election in effect for round 4 extension property unless the taxpayer elects to not have this paragraph apply to round 4 extension property.

(II) A taxpayer who does not have an election in effect under this paragraph for round 3 extension property may elect to have this paragraph apply to round 4 extension property.

(iii) ROUND 4 EXTENSION PROPERTY.—For purposes of this subparagraph, the term "round 4 extension property" means property which is eligible qualified property solely by reason of the extension of the application of the special allowance under paragraph (1) pursuant to the amendments made by section 125(a) of the Tax Increase Prevention Act of 2014 (and the application of such extension to this paragraph pursuant to the amendment made by section 125(c) of such Act).

(L) SPECIAL RULES FOR ROUND 5 EXTENSION PROPERTY.—

(i) IN GENERAL.—In the case of round 5 extension property, in applying this paragraph to any taxpayer—

(I) the limitation described in subparagraph (B)(i) and the business credit increase amount under subparagraph (E)(iii) thereof shall not apply, and

(II) the bonus depreciation amount, maximum amount, and maximum increase amount shall be computed separately from amounts computed with respect to eligible qualified property which is not round 5 extension property.

(ii) ELECTION.—

(I) A taxpayer who has an election in effect under this paragraph for round 4 extension property shall be treated as having an election in effect for round 5 extension property unless the taxpayer elects to not have this paragraph apply to round 5 extension property.

(II) A taxpayer who does not have an election in effect under this paragraph for round 4 extension property may elect to have this paragraph apply to round 5 extension property.

(iii) ROUND 5 EXTENSION PROPERTY.—For purposes of this subparagraph, the term "round 5 extension property" means property which is eligible qualified property solely by reason of the extension of the application of the special allowance under paragraph (1) pursuant to the amendments made by section 143(a)(1) of the Protecting Americans from Tax Hikes Act of 2015 (and the application of such extension to this paragraph pursuant to the amendment made by section 143(a)(3) of such Act).

P.L. 114-113, §143(b)(4)(A)-(B), Div. Q:

Amended Code Sec. 168(k) by striking paragraph (5), and by inserting after paragraph (4) a new paragraph (5). For the **effective** date, see Act Sec. 143(b)(7)(A) and (C), below. Prior to being stricken, Code Sec. 168(k)(5) read as follows:

(5) SPECIAL RULE FOR PROPERTY ACQUIRED DURING CERTAIN PRE-2012 PERIODS.—In the case of qualified property acquired by the taxpayer (under rules similar to the rules of clauses (ii) and (iii) of paragraph (2)(A)) after September 8, 2010, and before January 1, 2012, and which is placed in service by the taxpayer before January 1, 2012 (January 1, 2013, in the case of property described in subparagraph (2)(B) or (2)(C)), paragraph (1)(A) shall be applied by substituting "100 percent" for "50 percent".

P.L. 114-113, §143(b)(5), Div. Q:

Amended Code Sec. 168(k) by adding at the end a new paragraph (6). **Effective** for property placed in service after 12-31-2015, in tax years ending after such date.

P.L. 114-113, §143(b)(6)(D), Div. Q:

Amended Code Sec. 168(k), as amended by this Act Sec. 143, by adding at the end a new paragraph (7). **Effective** for property placed in service after 12-31-2015, in tax years ending after such date.

P.L. 114-113, §143(b)(6)(J), Div. Q:

Amended Code Sec. 168(k), as amended by Act Sec. 143(a), by striking "AND BEFORE JANUARY 1, 2016" in the heading thereof and inserting "AND BEFORE JANUARY 1, 2020". **Effective** for property placed in service after 12-31-2015, in tax years ending after such date.

P.L. 114-113, §143(b)(7)(A)-(C), Div. Q, provides:

(7) EFFECTIVE DATES.—

(A) IN GENERAL.—Except as otherwise provided in this paragraph, the amendments made by this subsection shall apply to property placed in service after December 31, 2015, in taxable years ending after such date.

(B) EXPANSION OF ELECTION TO ACCELERATE AMT CREDITS IN LIEU OF BONUS DEPRECIATION.—The amendments made by paragraph (3) shall apply to taxable years ending after December 31, 2015, except that in the case of any taxable year beginning before January 1, 2016, and ending after December 31, 2015, the limitation under section 168(k)(4)(B)(ii) of the Internal Revenue Code of 1986 (as amended by this section) shall be the sum of—

(i) the product of—

(I) the maximum increase amount (within the meaning of section 168(k)(4)(C)(iii) of such Code, as in effect before the amendments made by this subsection), multiplied by

(II) a fraction the numerator of which is the number of days in the taxable year before January 1, 2016, and the denominator of which is the number of days in the taxable year, plus

(ii) the product of—

(I) such limitation (determined without regard to this subparagraph), multiplied by

(II) a fraction the numerator of which is the number of days in the taxable year after December 31, 2015, and the denominator of which is the number of days in the taxable year.

(C) SPECIAL RULES FOR CERTAIN PLANTS BEARING FRUITS AND NUTS.—The amendments made by paragraph (4) (other than subparagraph (A) thereof [striking Code Sec. 168(k)(5)]) shall apply to specified plants (as defined in section 168(k)(5)(B) of the Internal Revenue Code of 1986, as amended by this subsection) planted or grafted after December 31, 2015.

APPENDIX: Selected Code Sections Affected by the Tax Cuts and Jobs Act   167

- **2014, Tax Increase Prevention Act of 2014 (P.L. 113-295)**

P.L. 113-295, §125(a)(1)-(2), Division A:
Amended Code Sec. 168(k)(2) by striking "January 1, 2015" in subparagraph (A)(iv) and inserting "January 1, 2016", and by striking "January 1, 2014" each place it appears and inserting "January 1, 2015". **Effective** for property placed in service after 12-31-2013, in tax years ending after such date.

P.L. 113-295, §125(c)(1), Division A:
Amended Code Sec. 168(k)(4)(D)(iii)(II) by striking "January 1, 2014" and inserting "January 1, 2015". **Effective** for property placed in service after 12-31-2013, in tax years ending after such date.

P.L. 113-295, §125(c)(2), Division A:
Amended Code Sec. 168(k)(4) by adding at the end a new subparagraph (K). **Effective** for property placed in service after 12-31-2013, in tax years ending after such date.

P.L. 113-295, §125(d)(1), Division A:
Amended the heading for Code Sec. 168(k) by striking "JANUARY 1, 2014" and inserting "JANUARY 1, 2015". **Effective** for property placed in service after 12-31-2013, in tax years ending after such date.

P.L. 113-295, §125(d)(2), Division A:
Amended the heading for Code Sec. 168(k)(2)(B)(ii) by striking "PRE-JANUARY 1, 2014" and inserting "PRE-JANUARY 1, 2015". **Effective** for property placed in service after 12-31-2013, in tax years ending after such date.

- **2014, Tax Technical Corrections Act of 2014 (P.L. 113-295)**

P.L. 113-295, §202(e), Division A:
Amended Code Sec. 168(k)(4)(J)(iii) by striking "any taxable year" and inserting "its first taxable year". **Effective** as if included in the provision of the American Taxpayer Relief Act of 2012 (P.L. 110-240) to which it relates [effective for property placed in service after 12-31-2012, in tax years ending after such date.—CCH].

P.L. 113-295, §210(g)(2)(B), Division A:
Amended the last sentence of Code Sec. 168(k)(4)(C)(i) by striking "(b)(2)(C)" and inserting "(b)(2)(D)". **Effective** as if included in the provision of the Energy Improvement and Extension Act of 2008 (P.L. 110-343) to which it relates [effective for property placed in service after 10-3-2008.—CCH].

P.L. 113-295, §212(b), Division A:
Amended Code Sec. 168(k)(4)(E)(iv) by striking "adjusted minimum tax" and inserting "adjusted net minimum tax". **Effective** as if included in the provision of the Housing Assistance Tax Act of 2008 (P.L. 110-289) to which it relates [effective for tax years ending after 3-31-2008.—CCH].

P.L. 113-295, §214(b), Division A:
Amended Code Sec. 168(k)(2)(B)(i)(IV) by striking "clauses also apply" and inserting "clause also applies". **Effective** as if included in the provision of the Economic Stimulus Act of 2008 (P.L. 110-185) to which it relates [effective for property placed in service after 12-31-2007, in tax years ending after such date.—CCH].

- **2013, American Taxpayer Relief Act of 2012 (P.L. 112-240)**

P.L. 112-240, §331(a)(1)-(2):
Amended Code Sec. 168(k)(2) by striking "January 1, 2014" in subparagraph (A)(iv) and inserting "January 1, 2015", and by striking "January 1, 2013" each place it appears and inserting "January 1, 2014". **Effective** for property placed in service after 12-31-2012, in tax years ending after such date.

P.L. 112-240, §331(c)(1):
Amended Code Sec. 168(k)(4)(D)(iii)(II) by striking "2013" and inserting "2014". **Effective** for property placed in service after 12-31-2012, in tax years ending after such date.

P.L. 112-240, §331(c)(2):
Amended Code Sec. 168(k)(4) by adding at the end a new subparagraph (J). **Effective** for property placed in service after 12-31-2012, in tax years ending after such date.

P.L. 112-240, §331(e)(1):
Amended the heading for Code Sec. 168(k) by striking "JANUARY 1, 2013" and inserting "JANUARY 1, 2014". **Effective** for property placed in service after 12-31-2012, in tax years ending after such date.

P.L. 112-240, §331(e)(2):
Amended the heading for Code Sec. 168(k)(2)(B)(ii) by striking "PRE-JANUARY 1, 2013" and inserting "PRE-JANUARY 1, 2014". **Effective** for property placed in service after 12-31-2012, in tax years ending after such date.

- **2010, Tax Relief, Unemployment Insurance Reauthorization, and Job Creation Act of 2010 (P.L. 111-312)**

P.L. 111-312, §401(a)(1)-(2):
Amended Code Sec. 168(k)(2) by striking "January 1, 2012" in subparagraph (A)(iv) and inserting "January 1, 2014", and by striking "January 1, 2011" each place it appears and inserting "January 1, 2013". **Effective** for property placed in service after 12-31-2010, in tax years ending after such date.

P.L. 111-312, §401(b):
Amended Code Sec. 168(k) by adding at the end a new paragraph (5). **Effective** for property placed in service after 9-8-2010, in tax years ending after such date.

P.L. 111-312, §401(c)(1):
Amended Code Sec. 168(k)(4)(D)(iii) by striking "or production" and all that follows and inserting "or production—", new subclauses (I) and (II), and new flush text. **Effective** for property placed in service after 12-31-2010, in tax years ending after such date. Prior to being stricken, all that followed "or production" in Code Sec. 168(k)(4)(D)(iii) read as follows:

or production after March 31, 2008, and before January 1, 2010, shall be taken into account under subparagraph (B)(ii) thereof,

P.L. 111-312, §401(c)(2):
Amended Code Sec. 168(k)(4) by adding at the end a new subparagraph (I). **Effective** for property placed in service after 12-31-2010, in tax years ending after such date.

P.L. 111-312, §401(d)(1):
Amended the heading for Code Sec. 168(k) by striking "JANUARY 1, 2011" and inserting "JANUARY 1, 2013". **Effective** for property placed in service after 12-31-2010, in tax years ending after such date.

P.L. 111-312, §401(d)(2):
Amended the heading of Code Sec. 168(k)(2)(B)(ii) by striking "PRE-JANUARY 1, 2011" and inserting "PRE-JANUARY 1, 2013". **Effective** for property placed in service after 12-31-2010, in tax years ending after such date.

P.L. 111-312, §401(d)(3)(A)-(C):
Amended Code Sec. 168(k)(4)(D) by striking clauses (iv) and (v), by inserting "and" at the end of clause (ii), and by striking the comma at the end of clause (iii) and inserting a period. **Effective** for property placed in service after 12-31-2010, in tax years ending after such date. Prior to being stricken, Code Sec. 168(k)(4)(D)(iv)-(v) read as follows:

(iv) "January 1, 2011" shall be substituted for "January 1, 2012" in subparagraph (A)(iv) thereof, and

(v) "January 1, 2010" shall be substituted for "January 1, 2011" each place it appears in subparagraph (A) thereof.

- **2010, Creating Small Business Jobs Act of 2010 (P.L. 111-240)**

P.L. 111-240, §2022(a)(1)-(2):
Amended Code Sec. 168(k)(2) by striking "January 1, 2011" in subparagraph (A)(iv) and inserting "January 1, 2012", and by striking "January 1, 2010" each place it appears and inserting "January 1, 2011". **Effective** for property placed in service after 12-31-2009, in tax years ending after such date.

P.L. 111-240, §2022(b)(1):
Amended the heading for Code Sec. 168(k) by striking "JANUARY 1, 2010" and inserting "JANUARY 1, 2011". **Effective** for property placed in service after 12-31-2009, in tax years ending after such date.

P.L. 111-240, §2022(b)(2):
Amended the heading for Code Sec. 168(k)(2)(B)(ii) by striking "PRE-JANUARY 1, 2010" and inserting "PRE-JANUARY 1, 2011". **Effective** for property placed in service after 12-31-2009, in tax years ending after such date.

P.L. 111-240, §2022(b)(3):
Amended Code Sec. 168(k)(4)(D) by striking "and" at the end of clause (ii), by striking the period at the end of clause (iii) and inserting a comma, and by adding at the end new

clauses (iv) and (v). **Effective** for property placed in service after 12-31-2009, in tax years ending after such date.

• **2009, American Recovery and Reinvestment Tax Act of 2009 (P.L. 111-5)**
P.L. 111-5, §1201(a)(1)(A)-(B):
Amended Code Sec. 168(k)(2) by striking "January 1, 2010" and inserting "January 1, 2011", and by striking "January 1, 2009" each place it appears and inserting "January 1, 2010". **Effective** for property placed in service after 12-31-2008, in tax years ending after such date.
P.L. 111-5, §1201(a)(2)(A):
Amended the heading for Code Sec. 168(k) by striking "JANUARY 1, 2009" and inserting "JANUARY 1, 2010". **Effective** for property placed in service after 12-31-2008, in tax years ending after such date.
P.L. 111-5, §1201(a)(2)(B):
Amended the heading for Code Sec. 168(k)(2)(B)(ii) by striking "PRE-JANUARY 1, 2009" and inserting "PRE-JANUARY 1, 2010". **Effective** for property placed in service after 12-31-2008, in tax years ending after such date.
P.L. 111-5, §1201(a)(3)(A)(i)-(iii):
Amended Code Sec. 168(k)(4)(D) by striking "and" at the end of clause (i), by redesignating clause (ii) as clause (iii), and by inserting after clause (i) a new clause (ii). **Effective** for tax years ending after 3-31-2008.
P.L. 111-5, §1201(b)(1)(A)-(B):
Amended Code Sec. 168(k)(4) by striking "2009" and inserting "2010" in subparagraph (D)(iii) (as redesignated by Act Sec. 1201(a)(3)), and by adding at the end a new subparagraph (H). **Effective** for property placed in service after 12-31-2008, in tax years ending after such date.

• **2008, Housing Assistance Tax Act of 2008 (P.L. 110-289)**
P.L. 110-289, §3081(a):
Amended Code Sec. 168(k) by adding at the end a new paragraph (4). **Effective** for tax years ending after 3-31-2008. For a special rule, see Act Sec. 3081(b), below.
P.L. 110-289, §3081(b), provides:
(b) APPLICATION TO CERTAIN AUTOMOTIVE PARTNERSHIPS.—
(1) IN GENERAL.—If an applicable partnership elects the application of this subsection—
(A) the partnership shall be treated as having made a payment against the tax imposed by chapter 1 of the Internal Revenue Code of 1986 for any applicable taxable year of the partnership in the amount determined under paragraph (3),
(B) in the case of any eligible qualified property placed in service by the partnership during any applicable taxable year—
(i) section 168(k) of such Code shall not apply in determining the amount of the deduction allowable with respect to such property under section 168 of such Code,
(ii) the applicable depreciation method used with respect to such property shall be the straight line method, and
(C) the amount of the credit determined under section 41 of such Code for any applicable taxable year with respect to the partnership shall be reduced by the amount of the deemed payment under subparagraph (A) for the taxable year.
(2) TREATMENT OF DEEMED PAYMENT.—
(A) IN GENERAL.—Notwithstanding any other provision of the Internal Revenue Code of 1986, the Secretary of the Treasury or his delegate shall not use the payment of tax described in paragraph (1) as an offset or credit against any tax liability of the applicable partnership or any partner but shall refund such payment to the applicable partnership.
(B) NO INTEREST.—The payment described in paragraph (1) shall not be taken into account in determining any amount of interest under such Code.
(3) AMOUNT OF DEEMED PAYMENT.—The amount determined under this paragraph for any applicable taxable year shall be the least of the following:
(A) The amount which would be determined for the taxable year under section 168(k)(4)(C)(i) of the Internal Revenue Code of 1986 (as added by the amendments made by this section) if an election under section 168(k)(4) of such Code were in effect with respect to the partnership.
(B) The amount of the credit determined under section 41 of such Code for the taxable year with respect to the partnership.
(C) $30,000,000, reduced by the amount of any payment under this subsection for any preceding taxable year.

(4) DEFINITIONS.—For purposes of this subsection—
(A) APPLICABLE PARTNERSHIP.—The term "applicable partnership" means a domestic partnership that—
(i) was formed effective on August 3, 2007, and
(ii) will produce in excess of 675,000 automobiles during the period beginning on January 1, 2008, and ending on June 30, 2008.
(B) APPLICABLE TAXABLE YEAR.—The term "applicable taxable year" means any taxable year during which eligible qualified property is placed in service.
(C) ELIGIBLE QUALIFIED PROPERTY.— The term "eligible qualified property" has the meaning given such term by section 168(k)(4)(D) of the Internal Revenue Code of 1986 (as added by the amendments made by this section).

• **2008, Economic Stimulus Act of 2008 (P.L. 110-185)**
P.L. 110-185, §103(a)(1)-(4):
Amended Code Sec. 168(k) by striking "September 10, 2001" each place it appears and inserting "December 31, 2007", by striking "September 11, 2001" each place it appears and inserting "January 1, 2008", by striking "January 1, 2005" each place it appears and inserting "January 1, 2009", and by striking "January 1, 2006" each place it appears and inserting "January 1, 2010". **Effective** for property placed in service after 12-31-2007, in tax years ending after such date.
P.L. 110-185, §103(b):
Amended Code Sec. 168(k)(1)(A) by striking "30 percent" and inserting "50 percent". **Effective** for property placed in service after 12-31-2007, in tax years ending after such date.
P.L. 110-185, §103(c)(1):
Amended Code Sec. 168(k)(2)(B)(i)(I) by striking "and (iii)" and inserting "(iii), and (iv)". **Effective** for property placed in service after 12-31-2007, in tax years ending after such date.
P.L. 110-185, §103(c)(2):
Amended Code Sec. 168(k)(2)(B)(i)(IV) by striking "clauses (ii) and [sic] (iii)" and inserting "clause (iii)". **Effective** for property placed in service after 12-31-2007, in tax years ending after such date.
P.L. 110-185, §103(c)(3):
Amended Code Sec. 168(k)(2)(C)(i) by striking "and (iii)" and inserting ", (iii), and (iv)". **Effective** for property placed in service after 12-31-2007, in tax years ending after such date.
P.L. 110-185, §103(c)(4):
Amended Code Sec. 168(k)(2)(F)(i) by striking "$4,600" and inserting "$8,000". **Effective** for property placed in service after 12-31-2007, in tax years ending after such date.
P.L. 110-185, §103(c)(5)(A):
Amended Code Sec. 168(k) by striking paragraph (4). **Effective** for property placed in service after 12-31-2007, in tax years ending after such date. Prior to being stricken, Code Sec. 168(k)(4) read as follows:
(4) 50-PERCENT BONUS DEPRECIATION FOR CERTAIN PROPERTY.—
(A) IN GENERAL.—In the case of 50-percent bonus depreciation property—
(i) paragraph (1)(A) shall be applied by substituting "50 percent" for "30 percent", and
(ii) except as provided in paragraph (2)(D), such property shall be treated as qualified property for purposes of this subsection.
(B) 50-PERCENT BONUS DEPRECIATION PROPERTY.—For purposes of this subsection, the term "50-percent bonus depreciation property" means property described in paragraph (2)(A)(i)—
(i) the original use of which commences with the taxpayer after May 5, 2003,
(ii) which is—
(I) acquired by the taxpayer after May 5, 2003, and before January 1, 2009, but only if no written binding contract for the acquisition was in effect before May 6, 2003, or
(II) acquired by the taxpayer pursuant to a written binding contract which was entered into after May 5, 2003, and before January 1, 2009, and
(iii) which is placed in service by the taxpayer before January 1, 2009, or, in the case of property described in paragraph (2)(B) (as modified by subparagraph (C) of this paragraph) or paragraph (2)(C) (as so modified), before January 1, 2010.
(C) SPECIAL RULES.—Rules similar to the rules of subparagraphs (B), (C), and (E) of paragraph (2) shall apply for

purposes of this paragraph; except that references to December 31, 2007, shall be treated as references to May 5, 2003.

(D) AUTOMOBILES.—Paragraph (2)(F) shall be applied by substituting "$7,650" for "$4,600" in the case of 50-percent bonus depreciation property.

(E) ELECTION OF 30-PERCENT BONUS.—If a taxpayer makes an election under this subparagraph with respect to any class of property for any taxable year, subparagraph (A)(i) shall not apply to all property in such class placed in service during such taxable year.

P.L. 110-185, § 103(c)(5)(B):

Amended Code Sec. 168(k)(2)(D)(iii) by striking the last sentence. **Effective** for property placed in service after 12-31-2007, in tax years ending after such date. Prior to being stricken, the last sentence of Code Sec. 168(k)(2)(D)(iii) read as follows:

The preceding sentence shall be applied separately with respect to property treated as qualified property by paragraph (4) and other qualified property.

P.L. 110-185, § 103(c)(11)(A)-(B):

Amended the heading for Code Sec. 168(k) by striking "SEPTEMBER 10, 2001" and inserting "DECEMBER 31, 2007", and by striking "JANUARY 1, 2005" and inserting "JANUARY 1, 2009". **Effective** for property placed in service after 12-31-2007, in tax years ending after such date.

P.L. 110-185, § 103(c)(12):

Amended the heading for Code Sec. 168(k)(2)(B)(ii) by striking "PRE-JANUARY 1, 2005" and inserting "PRE-JANUARY 1, 2009". **Effective** for property placed in service after 12-31-2007, in tax years ending after such date.

• **2005, Gulf Opportunity Zone Act of 2005 (P.L. 109-135)**

P.L. 109-135, § 105, provides:

SEC. 105. SPECIAL EXTENSION OF BONUS DEPRECIATION PLACED IN SERVICE DATE FOR TAXPAYERS AFFECTED BY HURRICANES KATRINA, RITA, AND WILMA.

In applying the rule under section 168(k)(2)(A)(iv) of the Internal Revenue Code of 1986 to any property described in subparagraph (B) or (C) of section 168(k)(2) of such Code—

(1) the placement in service of which—

(A) is to be located in the GO Zone (as defined in section 1400M(1) of such Code), the Rita GO Zone (as defined in section 1400M(3) of such Code), or the Wilma GO Zone (as defined in section 1400M(5) of such Code), and

(B) is to be made by any taxpayer affected by Hurricane Katrina, Rita, or Wilma, or

(2) which is manufactured in such Zone by any person affected by Hurricane Katrina, Rita, or Wilma,

the Secretary of the Treasury may, on a taxpayer by taxpayer basis, extend the required date of the placement in service of such property under such section by such period of time as is determined necessary by the Secretary but not to exceed 1 year. For purposes of the preceding sentence, the determination shall be made by only taking into account the effect of one or more hurricanes on the date of such placement by the taxpayer.

P.L. 109-135, § 403(j)(1):

Amended Code Sec. 168(k)(2)(A)(iv) by striking "subparagraphs (B) and (C)" and inserting "subparagraph (B) or (C)". **Effective** as if included in the provision of the American Jobs Creation Act of 2004 (P.L. 108-357) to which it relates [**effective** for property placed in service after September 10, 2001, in tax years ending after such date.—CCH].

P.L. 109-135, § 403(j)(2):

Amended Code Sec. 168(k)(4)(B)(iii) by striking "and paragraph (2)(C)" and inserting "or paragraph (2)(C) (as so modified)". **Effective** as if included in the provision of the American Jobs Creation Act of 2004 (P.L. 108-357) to which it relates [**effective** for property placed in service after September 10, 2001, in tax years ending after such date.—CCH].

P.L. 109-135, § 405(a)(1):

Amended Code Sec. 168(k)(4)(B)(ii). **Effective** as if included in section 201 of the Jobs and Growth Tax Relief Reconciliation Act of 2003 (P.L. 108-27) [**effective** for tax years ending after 5-5-2003.—CCH]. Prior to amendment Code Sec. 168(k)(4)(B)(ii) read as follows:

(ii) which is acquired by the taxpayer after May 5, 2003, and before January 1, 2005, but only if no written binding contract for the acquisition was in effect before May 6, 2003, and

• **2004, American Jobs Creation Act of 2004 (P.L. 108-357)**

P.L. 108-357, § 336(a)(1):

Amended Code Sec. 168(k)(2) by redesignating subparagraphs (C) through (F) as subparagraphs (D) through (G), respectively, and by inserting after subparagraph (B) a new subparagraph (C). **Effective** as if included in the amendments made by section 101 of the Job Creation and Worker Assistance Act of 2002 (P.L. 107-147) [**effective** for property placed in service after 9-10-2001, in tax years ending after such date.—CCH].

P.L. 108-357, § 336(a)(2):

Amended Code Sec. 168(k)(2)(A)(iv) by striking "subparagraph (B)" and inserting "subparagraphs (B) and (C)". **Effective** as if included in the amendments made by section 101 of the Job Creation and Worker Assistance Act of 2002 (P.L. 107-147) [**effective** for property placed in service after 9-10-2001, in tax years ending after such date.—CCH].

P.L. 108-357, § 336(b)(1):

Amended Code Sec. 168(k)(2)(B) by adding at the end a new clause (iv). **Effective** as if included in the amendments made by section 101 of the Job Creation and Worker Assistance Act of 2002 (P.L. 107-147) [**effective** for property placed in service after 9-10-2001, in tax years ending after such date.—CCH].

P.L. 108-357, § 336(b)(2):

Amended Code Sec. 168(k)(4)(A)(ii) by striking "paragraph (2)(C)" and inserting "paragraph (2)(D)". **Effective** as if included in the amendments made by section 101 of the Job Creation and Worker Assistance Act of 2002 (P.L. 107-147) [**effective** for property placed in service after 9-10-2001, in tax years ending after such date.—CCH].

P.L. 108-357, § 336(b)(3):

Amended Code Sec. 168(k)(4)(B)(iii) by inserting "and paragraph (2)(C)" after "of this paragraph)". **Effective** as if included in the amendments made by section 101 of the Job Creation and Worker Assistance Act of 2002 (P.L. 107-147) [**effective** for property placed in service after 9-10-2001, in tax years ending after such date.—CCH].

P.L. 108-357, § 336(b)(4):

Amended Code Sec. 168(k)(4)(C) by striking "subparagraphs (B) and (D)" and inserting "subparagraphs (B), (C), and (E)". **Effective** as if included in the amendments made by section 101 of the Job Creation and Worker Assistance Act of 2002 (P.L. 107-147) [**effective** for property placed in service after 9-10-2001, in tax years ending after such date.—CCH].

P.L. 108-357, § 336(b)(5):

Amended Code Sec. 168(k)(4)(D) by striking "Paragraph (2)(E)" and inserting "Paragraph (2)(F)". **Effective** as if included in the amendments made by section 101 of the Job Creation and Worker Assistance Act of 2002 (P.L. 107-147) [**effective** for property placed in service after 9-10-2001, in tax years ending after such date.—CCH].

P.L. 108-357, § 337(a):

Amended Code Sec. 168(k)(2)(E)(iii)(II), as amended by the Working Families Tax Relief Act of 2004 (P.L. 108-311) and as redesignated by this Act, by inserting before the comma at the end the following: "(or, in the case of multiple units of property subject to the same lease, within 3 months after the date the final unit is placed in service, so long as the period between the time the first unit is placed in service and the time the last unit is placed in service does not exceed 12 months)". **Effective** for property sold after 6-4-2004.

• **2004, Working Families Tax Relief Act of 2004 (P.L. 108-311)**

P.L. 108-311, § 403(a)(1):

Amended Code Sec. 168(k)(2)(B)(i). **Effective** as if included in the provision of the Job Creation and Worker Assistance Act of 2002 (P.L. 107-147) to which it relates [**effective** for property placed in service after 9-10-2001, in tax years ending after that date.—CCH]. Prior to amendment, Code Sec. 168(k)(2)(B)(i) read as follows:

(i) IN GENERAL.—The term "qualified property" includes property—

(I) which meets the requirements of clauses (i), (ii), and (iii) of subparagraph (A),

(II) which has a recovery period of at least 10 years or is transportation property, and

Code Sec. 168

(III) which is subject to section 263A by reason of clause (ii) or (iii) of subsection (f)(1)(B) thereof.

P.L. 108-311, § 403(a)(2)(A):
Amended Code Sec. 168(k)(2)(D) by adding at the end new clauses (iii) and (iv). **Effective** as if included in the provision of the Job Creation and Worker Assistance Act of 2002 (P.L. 107-147) to which it relates [**effective** for property placed in service after 9-10-2001, in tax years ending after that date.—CCH].

P.L. 108-311, § 403(a)(2)(B):
Amended Code Sec. 168(k)(2)(D)(ii) by inserting "clause (iii) and" before "subparagraph (A)(ii)". **Effective** as if included in the provision of the Job Creation and Worker Assistance Act of 2002 (P.L. 107-147) to which it relates [**effective** for property placed in service after 9-10-2001, in tax years ending after that date.—CCH].

P.L. 108-311, § 408(a)(6)(A)-(B):
Amended Code Sec. 168(k)(2)(D)(ii) by inserting "is" after "if property", and by striking "is" in subclause (I) before "originally placed in service". **Effective** 10-4-2004.

P.L. 108-311, § 408(a)(8):
Amended the heading for Code Sec. 168(k)(2)(F) by striking "MINIUMUM" and inserting "MINIMUM". **Effective** 10-4-2004.

• **2003, Jobs and Growth Tax Relief Reconciliation Act of 2003 (P.L. 108-27)**

P.L. 108-27, § 201(a):
Amended Code Sec. 168(k) by adding at the end a new paragraph (4). **Effective** for tax years ending after 5-5-2003.

P.L. 108-27, § 201(b)(1)(A):
Amended Code Sec. 168(k)(2)(B)(ii) and (D)(i) by striking "September 11, 2004" each place it appears in the text and inserting "January 1, 2005". **Effective** for tax years ending after 5-5-2003.

P.L. 108-27, § 201(b)(1)(B):
Amended Code Sec. 168(k)(2)(B)(ii) by striking "PRE-SEPTEMBER 11, 2004" in the heading and inserting "PRE-JANUARY 1, 2005". **Effective** for tax years ending after 5-5-2003.

P.L. 108-27, § 201(b)(2):
Amended Code Sec. 168(k)(2)(A)(iii) by striking "September 11, 2004" each place it appears and inserting "January 1, 2005". **Effective** for tax years ending after 5-5-2003.

P.L. 108-27, § 201(b)(3):
Amended Code Sec. 168(k)(2)(C)(iii) by adding at the end a new sentence. **Effective** for tax years ending after 5-5-2003.

P.L. 108-27, § 201(c)(1):
Amended the subsection heading for Code Sec. 168(k) by striking "SEPTEMBER 11, 2004" and inserting "JANUARY 1, 2005". **Effective** for tax years ending after 5-5-2003.

• **2002, Job Creation and Worker Assistance Act of 2002 (P.L. 107-147)**

P.L. 107-147, § 101(a):
Amended Code Sec. 168 by adding at the end a new subsection (k). **Effective** for property placed in service after 9-10-2001, in tax years ending after such date.

[Sec. 168(l)]

(l) Special Allowance for Second Generation Biofuel Plant Property.—

(1) Additional Allowance.—In the case of any qualified second generation biofuel plant property—

(A) the depreciation deduction provided by section 167(a) for the taxable year in which such property is placed in service shall include an allowance equal to 50 percent of the adjusted basis of such property, and

(B) the adjusted basis of such property shall be reduced by the amount of such deduction before computing the amount otherwise allowable as a depreciation deduction under this chapter for such taxable year and any subsequent taxable year.

(2) Qualified Second Generation Biofuel Plant Property.—The term "qualified second generation biofuel plant property" means property of a character subject to the allowance for depreciation—

(A) which is used in the United States solely to produce second generation biofuel (as defined in section 40(b)(6)(E)),

(B) the original use of which commences with the taxpayer after the date of the enactment of this subsection,

(C) which is acquired by the taxpayer by purchase (as defined in section 179(d)) after the date of the enactment of this subsection, but only if no written binding contract for the acquisition was in effect on or before the date of the enactment of this subsection, and

(D) which is placed in service by the taxpayer before January 1, 2018.

(3) Exceptions.—

(A) Bonus Depreciation Property Under Subsection (k).—Such term shall not include any property to which subsection (k) applies.

(B) Alternative Depreciation Property.—Such term shall not include any property described in subsection (k)(2)(D).

(C) Tax-Exempt Bond-Financed Property.—Such term shall not include any property any portion of which is financed with the proceeds of any obligation the interest on which is exempt from tax under section 103.

(D) Election Out.—If a taxpayer makes an election under this subparagraph with respect to any class of property for any taxable year, this subsection shall not apply to all property in such class placed in service during such taxable year.

(4) Special Rules.—For purposes of this subsection, rules similar to the rules of subsection (k)(2)(E) shall apply.

(5) Allowance Against Alternative Minimum Tax.—For purposes of this subsection, rules similar to the rules of subsection (k)(2)(G) shall apply.

(6) Recapture.—For purposes of this subsection, rules similar to the rules under section 179(d)(10) shall apply with respect to any qualified second generation biofuel plant property which ceases to be qualified second generation biofuel plant property.

(7) Denial of Double Benefit.—Paragraph (1) shall not apply to any qualified second generation biofuel plant property with respect to which an election has been made under section 179C (relating to election to expense certain refineries).

Amendments

- **2018, Bipartisan Budget Act of 2018 (P.L. 115-123)**

P.L. 115-123, § 40412(a), Div. D:

Amended Code Sec. 168(l)(2)(D) by striking "January 1, 2017" and inserting "January 1, 2018". **Effective** for property placed in service after 12-31-2016.

- **2015, Protecting Americans from Tax Hikes Act of 2015 (P.L. 114-113)**

P.L. 114-113, § 143(b)(6)(E)(i)-(ii), Div. Q:

Amended Code Sec. 168(l)(3) by striking "section 168(k)" in subparagraph (A) and inserting "subsection (k)", and by striking "section 168(k)(2)(D)(i)" in subparagraph (B) and inserting "subsection (k)(2)(D)". **Effective** for property placed in service after 12-31-2015, in tax years ending after such date.

P.L. 114-113, § 143(b)(6)(F), Div. Q:

Amended Code Sec. 168(l)(4) by striking "subparagraph (E) of section 168(k)(2)" and all that follows and inserting "subsection (k)(2)(E) shall apply.". **Effective** for property placed in service after 12-31-2015, in tax years ending after such date. Prior to amendment, Code Sec. 168(l)(4) read as follows:

(4) SPECIAL RULES.—For purposes of this subsection, rules similar to the rules of subparagraph (E) of section 168(k)(2) shall apply, except that such subparagraph shall be applied—

(A) by substituting "the date of the enactment of subsection (l)" for "December 31, 2007" each place it appears therein, and

(B) by substituting "qualified second generation biofuel plant property" for "qualified property" in clause (iv) thereof.

P.L. 114-113, § 143(b)(6)(G), Div. Q:

Amended Code Sec. 168(l)(5) by striking "section 168(k)(2)(G)" and inserting "subsection (k)(2)(G)". **Effective** for property placed in service after 12-31-2015, in tax years ending after such date.

P.L. 114-113, § 189(a), Div. Q:

Amended Code Sec. 168(l)(2)(D) by striking "January 1, 2015" and inserting "January 1, 2017". **Effective** for property placed in service after 12-31-2014.

- **2014, Tax Increase Prevention Act of 2014 (P.L. 113-295)**

P.L. 113-295, § 157(a), Division A:

Amended Code Sec. 168(l)(2)(D) by striking "January 1, 2014" and inserting "January 1, 2015". **Effective** for property placed in service after 12-31-2013.

- **2013, American Taxpayer Relief Act of 2012 (P.L. 112-240)**

P.L. 112-240, § 410(a)(1):

Amended Code Sec. 168(l)(2)(D) by striking "January 1, 2013" and inserting "January 1, 2014". **Effective** for property placed in service after 12-31-2012.

P.L. 112-240, § 410(b)(1):

Amended Code Sec. 168(l)(2)(A) by striking "solely to produce cellulosic biofuel" and inserting "solely to produce second generation biofuel (as defined in section 40(b)(6)(E))". **Effective** for property placed in service after 1-2-2013.

P.L. 112-240, § 410(b)(2)(A)-(D):

Amended Code Sec. 168(l), as amended by Act Sec. 410(a), by striking "cellulosic biofuel" each place it appears in the text thereof and inserting "second generation biofuel", by striking paragraph (3) and redesignating paragraphs (4) through (8) as paragraphs (3) through (7), respectively, by striking "CELLULOSIC" in the heading of such subsection and inserting "SECOND GENERATION", and by striking "CELLULOSIC" in the heading of paragraph (2) and inserting "SECOND GENERATION". **Effective** for property placed in service after 1-2-2013. Prior to being stricken, Code Sec. 168(l)(4) read as follows:

(3) CELLULOSIC BIOFUEL.—The term "cellulosic biofuel" means any liquid fuel which is produced from any lignocellulosic or hemicellulosic matter that is available on a renewable or recurring basis.

- **2010, Tax Relief, Unemployment Insurance Reauthorization, and Job Creation Act of 2010 (P.L. 111-312)**

P.L. 111-312, § 401(d)(4)(A)-(C):

Amended Code Sec. 168(l)(5) by inserting "and" at the end of subparagraph (A), by striking subparagraph (B), and by redesignating subparagraph (C) as subparagraph (B). **Effective** for property placed in service after 12-31-2010, in tax years ending after such date. Prior to being stricken, Code Sec. 168(l)(5)(B) read as follows:

(B) by substituting "January 1, 2013" for "January 1, 2011" in clause (i) thereof, and

- **2010, Creating Small Business Jobs Act of 2010 (P.L. 111-240)**

P.L. 111-240, § 2022(b)(4):

Amended Code Sec. 168(l)(5)(B) by striking "January 1, 2010" and inserting "January 1, 2011". **Effective** for property placed in service after 12-31-2009, in tax years ending after such date.

- **2009, American Recovery and Reinvestment Tax Act of 2009 (P.L. 111-5)**

P.L. 111-5, § 1201(a)(2)(C):

Amended Code Sec. 168(l)(5)(B) by striking "January 1, 2009" and inserting "January 1, 2010". **Effective** for property placed in service after 12-31-2008, in tax years ending after such date.

- **2008, Energy Improvement and Extension Act of 2008 (P.L. 110-343)**

P.L. 110-343, Division B, § 201(a):

Amended Code Sec. 168(l)(3). **Effective** for property placed in service after 10-3-2008, in tax years ending after such date. Prior to amendment, Code Sec. 168(l)(3) read as follows:

(3) CELLULOSIC BIOMASS ETHANOL.—For purposes of this subsection, the term "cellulosic biomass ethanol" means ethanol produced by hydrolysis of any lignocellulosic or hemicellulosic matter that is available on a renewable or recurring basis.

P.L. 110-343, Division B, § 201(b)(1)-(3):

Amended Code Sec. 168(l) by striking "cellulosic biomass ethanol" each place it appears and inserting "cellulosic biofuel", by striking "CELLULOSIC BIOMASS ETHANOL" in the heading of such subsection and inserting "CELLULOSIC BIOFUEL", and by striking "CELLULOSIC BIOMASS ETHANOL" in the heading of paragraph (2) thereof and inserting "CELLULOSIC BIOFUEL". **Effective** for property placed in service after 10-3-2008, in tax years ending after such date.

- **2008, Economic Stimulus Act of 2008 (P.L. 110-185)**

P.L. 110-185, § 103(c)(6):

Amended Code Sec. 168(l)(4) by redesignating subparagraphs (A), (B), and (C) as subparagraphs (B), (C), and (D) and inserting before subparagraph (B) (as so redesignated) a new subparagraph (A). **Effective** for property placed in service after 12-31-2007, in tax years ending after such date.

P.L. 110-185, § 103(c)(7)(A)-(B):

Amended Code Sec. 168(l)(5) by striking "September 10, 2001" in subparagraph (A) and inserting "December 31, 2007", and by striking "January 1, 2005" in subparagraph (B) and inserting "January 1, 2009". **Effective** for property placed in service after 12-31-2007, in tax years ending after such date.

- **2007, Tax Technical Corrections Act of 2007 (P.L. 110-172)**

P.L. 110-172, § 11(b)(1):

Amended Code Sec. 168(l)(3) by striking "enzymatic" before "hydrolysis". **Effective** as if included in the provision of the Tax Relief and Health Care Act of 2006 (P.L. 109-432) to which it relates [**effective** for property placed in service after 12-20-2006 in tax years after such date.—CCH].

- **2006, Tax Relief and Health Care Act of 2006 (P.L. 109-432)**

P.L. 109-432, Division A, § 209(a):

Amended Code Sec. 168 by adding at the end a new subsection (l). **Effective** for property placed in service after 12-20-2006 in tax years ending after such date.

[Sec. 168(m)]

(m) SPECIAL ALLOWANCE FOR CERTAIN REUSE AND RECYCLING PROPERTY.—

(1) IN GENERAL.—In the case of any qualified reuse and recycling property—

(A) the depreciation deduction provided by section 167(a) for the taxable year in which such property is placed in service shall include an allowance equal to 50 percent of the adjusted basis of the qualified reuse and recycling property, and

(B) the adjusted basis of the qualified reuse and recycling property shall be reduced by the amount of such deduction before computing the amount otherwise allowable as a depreciation deduction under this chapter for such taxable year and any subsequent taxable year.

(2) QUALIFIED REUSE AND RECYCLING PROPERTY.—For purposes of this subsection—

(A) IN GENERAL.—The term "qualified reuse and recycling property" means any reuse and recycling property—

(i) to which this section applies,

(ii) which has a useful life of at least 5 years,

(iii) the original use of which commences with the taxpayer after August 31, 2008, and

(iv) which is—

(I) acquired by purchase (as defined in section 179(d)(2)) by the taxpayer after August 31, 2008, but only if no written binding contract for the acquisition was in effect before September 1, 2008, or

(II) acquired by the taxpayer pursuant to a written binding contract which was entered into after August 31, 2008.

(B) EXCEPTIONS.—

(i) BONUS DEPRECIATION PROPERTY UNDER SUBSECTION (k).—The term "qualified reuse and recycling property" shall not include any property to which subsection (k) (determined without regard to paragraph (4) thereof) applies.

(ii) ALTERNATIVE DEPRECIATION PROPERTY.—The term "qualified reuse and recycling property" shall not include any property to which the alternative depreciation system under subsection (g) applies, determined without regard to paragraph (7) of subsection (g) (relating to election to have system apply).

(iii) ELECTION OUT.—If a taxpayer makes an election under this clause with respect to any class of property for any taxable year, this subsection shall not apply to all property in such class placed in service during such taxable year.

(C) SPECIAL RULE FOR SELF-CONSTRUCTED PROPERTY.—In the case of a taxpayer manufacturing, constructing, or producing property for the taxpayer's own use, the requirements of clause (iv) of subparagraph (A) shall be treated as met if the taxpayer begins manufacturing, constructing, or producing the property after August 31, 2008.

(D) DEDUCTION ALLOWED IN COMPUTING MINIMUM TAX.—For purposes of determining alternative minimum taxable income under section 55, the deduction under subsection (a) for qualified reuse and recycling property shall be determined under this section without regard to any adjustment under section 56.

(3) DEFINITIONS.—For purposes of this subsection—

(A) REUSE AND RECYCLING PROPERTY.—

(i) IN GENERAL.—The term "reuse and recycling property" means any machinery and equipment (not including buildings or real estate), along with all appurtenances thereto, including software necessary to operate such equipment, which is used exclusively to collect, distribute, or recycle qualified reuse and recyclable materials.

(ii) EXCLUSION.—Such term does not include rolling stock or other equipment used to transport reuse and recyclable materials.

(B) QUALIFIED REUSE AND RECYCLABLE MATERIALS.—

(i) IN GENERAL.—The term "qualified reuse and recyclable materials" means scrap plastic, scrap glass, scrap textiles, scrap rubber, scrap packaging, recovered fiber, scrap ferrous and nonferrous metals, or electronic scrap generated by an individual or business.

(ii) ELECTRONIC SCRAP.—For purposes of clause (i), the term "electronic scrap" means—

(I) any cathode ray tube, flat panel screen, or similar video display device with a screen size greater than 4 inches measured diagonally, or

(II) any central processing unit.

(C) RECYCLING OR RECYCLE.—The term "recycling" or "recycle" means that process (including sorting) by which worn or superfluous materials are manufactured or processed into specification grade commodities that are suitable for use as a replacement or substitute for virgin materials in manufacturing tangible consumer and commercial products, including packaging.

Amendments

• 2014, Tax Technical Corrections Act of 2014 (P.L. 113-295)

P.L. 113-295, § 210(d), Division A:
Amended Code Sec. 168(m)(2)(B)(i) by striking "section 168(k)" and inserting "subsection (k) (determined without regard to paragraph (4) thereof)". **Effective** as if included in the provision of the Energy Improvement and Extension Act of 2008 (P.L. 110-343) to which it relates [**effective** for property placed in service after 8-31-2008.—CCH].

• 2008, Energy Improvement and Extension Act of 2008 (P.L. 110-343)

P.L. 110-343, Division B, § 308(a):
Amended Code Sec. 168 by adding at the end a new subsection (m). **Effective** for property placed in service after 8-31-2008.

[Sec. 168(n)—Stricken]

Amendments

• 2018, Tax Technical Corrections Act of 2018 (P.L. 115-141)

P.L. 115-141, § 401(b)(13)(A), Div. U:
Amended Code Sec. 168 by striking subsection (n). **Effective** 3-23-2018, but not applicable to property placed in service before such. For a special rule, see Act Sec. 401(e), Div. U, below. Prior to being stricken, Code Sec. 168(n) read as follows:

(n) SPECIAL ALLOWANCE FOR QUALIFIED DISASTER ASSISTANCE PROPERTY.—

(1) IN GENERAL.—In the case of any qualified disaster assistance property—

(A) the depreciation deduction provided by section 167(a) for the taxable year in which such property is placed in service shall include an allowance equal to 50 percent of the adjusted basis of the qualified disaster assistance property, and

(B) the adjusted basis of the qualified disaster assistance property shall be reduced by the amount of such deduction before computing the amount otherwise allowable as a depreciation deduction under this chapter for such taxable year and any subsequent taxable year.

(2) QUALIFIED DISASTER ASSISTANCE PROPERTY.—For purposes of this subsection—

(A) IN GENERAL.—The term "qualified disaster assistance property" means any property—

(i)(I) which is described in subsection (k)(2)(A)(i), or

(II) which is nonresidential real property or residential rental property,

(ii) substantially all of the use of which is—

(I) in a disaster area with respect to a federally declared disaster occurring before January 1, 2010, and

(II) in the active conduct of a trade or business by the taxpayer in such disaster area,

(iii) which—

(I) rehabilitates property damaged, or replaces property destroyed or condemned, as a result of such federally declared disaster, except that, for purposes of this clause, property shall be treated as replacing property destroyed or condemned if, as part of an integrated plan, such property replaces property which is included in a continuous area which includes real property destroyed or condemned, and

(II) is similar in nature to, and located in the same county as, the property being rehabilitated or replaced,

(iv) the original use of which in such disaster area commences with an eligible taxpayer on or after the applicable disaster date,

(v) which is acquired by such eligible taxpayer by purchase (as defined in section 179(d)) on or after the applicable disaster date, but only if no written binding contract for the acquisition was in effect before such date, and

(vi) which is placed in service by such eligible taxpayer on or before the date which is the last day of the third calendar year following the applicable disaster date (the fourth calendar year in the case of nonresidential real property and residential rental property).

(B) EXCEPTIONS.—

(i) OTHER BONUS DEPRECIATION PROPERTY.—The term "qualified disaster assistance property" shall not include—

(I) any property to which subsection (k) (determined without regard to paragraph (4)), (l), or (m) applies,

(II) any property to which section 1400N(d) applies, and

(III) any property described in section 1400N(p)(3).

(ii) ALTERNATIVE DEPRECIATION PROPERTY.—The term "qualified disaster assistance property" shall not include any property to which the alternative depreciation system under subsection (g) applies, determined without regard to paragraph (7) of subsection (g) (relating to election to have system apply).

(iii) TAX-EXEMPT BOND FINANCED PROPERTY.—Such term shall not include any property any portion of which is financed with the proceeds of any obligation the interest on which is exempt from tax under section 103.

(iv) QUALIFIED REVITALIZATION BUILDINGS.—Such term shall not include any qualified revitalization building with respect to which the taxpayer has elected the application of paragraph (1) or (2) of section 1400I(a).

(v) ELECTION OUT.—If a taxpayer makes an election under this clause with respect to any class of property for any taxable year, this subsection shall not apply to all property in such class placed in service during such taxable year.

(C) SPECIAL RULES.—For purposes of this subsection, rules similar to the rules of subparagraph (E) of subsection (k)(2) shall apply, except that such subparagraph shall be applied—

(i) by substituting "the applicable disaster date" for "December 31, 2007" each place it appears therein,

(ii) without regard to "and before January 1, 2015" in clause (i) thereof, and

(iii) by substituting "qualified disaster assistance property" for "qualified property" in clause (iv) thereof.

(D) ALLOWANCE AGAINST ALTERNATIVE MINIMUM TAX.—For purposes of this subsection, rules similar to the rules of subsection (k)(2)(G) shall apply.

(3) OTHER DEFINITIONS.—For purposes of this subsection—

(A) APPLICABLE DISASTER DATE .—The term "applicable disaster date" means, with respect to any federally declared disaster, the date on which such federally declared disaster occurs.

(B) FEDERALLY DECLARED DISASTER.—The term "federally declared disaster" has the meaning given such term under section 165(h)(3)(C)(i).

(C) DISASTER AREA.—The term "disaster area" has the meaning given such term under section 165(h)(3)(C)(ii).

(D) ELIGIBLE TAXPAYER.—The term "eligible taxpayer" means a taxpayer who has suffered an economic loss attributable to a federally declared disaster.

(4) RECAPTURE.—For purposes of this subsection, rules similar to the rules under section 179(d)(10) shall apply with respect to any qualified disaster assistance property which ceases to be qualified disaster assistance property.

P.L. 115-141, § 401(e), Div. U, provides:

(e) GENERAL SAVINGS PROVISION WITH RESPECT TO DEADWOOD PROVISIONS.—If—

(1) any provision amended or repealed by the amendments made by subsection (b) or (d) applied to—

(A) any transaction occurring before the date of the enactment of this Act,

(B) any property acquired before such date of enactment, or

(C) any item of income, loss, deduction, or credit taken into account before such date of enactment, and

(2) the treatment of such transaction, property, or item under such provision would (without regard to the amendments or repeals made by such subsection) affect the liability for tax for periods ending after such date of enactment,

nothing in the amendments or repeals made by this section shall be construed to affect the treatment of such transaction, property, or item for purposes of determining liability for tax for periods ending after such date of enactment.

• 2014, Tax Increase Prevention Act of 2014 (P.L. 113-295)

P.L. 113-295, § 125(d)(3), Division A:
Amended Code Sec. 168(n)(2)(C) by striking "January 1, 2014" and inserting "January 1, 2015". **Effective** for property placed in service after 12-31-2013, in tax years ending after such date.

- **2013, American Taxpayer Relief Act of 2012 (P.L. 112-240)**

  P.L. 112-240, §331(e)(3):
  Amended Code Sec. 168(n)(2)(C)[(ii)] by striking "January 1, 2013" and inserting "January 1, 2014". **Effective** for property placed in service after 12-31-2012, in tax years ending after such date.

- **2010, Tax Relief, Unemployment Insurance Reauthorization, and Job Creation Act of 2010 (P.L. 111-312)**

  P.L. 111-312, §401(d)(5):
  Amended Code Sec. 168(n)(2)(C) by striking "January 1, 2011" and inserting "January 1, 2013". **Effective** for property placed in service after 12-31-2010, in tax years ending after such date.

- **2010, Creating Small Business Jobs Act of 2010 (P.L. 111-240)**

  P.L. 111-240, §2022(b)(5):
  Amended Code Sec. 168(n)(2)(C) by striking "January 1, 2010" and inserting "January 1, 2011". **Effective** for property placed in service after 12-31-2009, in tax years ending after such date.

- **2009, American Recovery and Reinvestment Tax Act of 2009 (P.L. 111-5)**

  P.L. 111-5, §1201(a)(2)(D):
  Amended Code Sec. 168(n)(2)(C) by striking "January 1, 2009" and inserting "January 1, 2010". **Effective** for property placed in service after 12-31-2008, in tax years ending after such date.

- **2008, Tax Extenders and Alternative Minimum Tax Relief Act of 2008 (P.L. 110-343)**

  P.L. 110-343, Division C, §710(a):
  Amended Code Sec. 168, as amended by this Act, by adding at the end a new subsection (n). **Effective** for property placed in service after 12-31-2007, with respect [to] disasters declared after such date.

[Sec. 197]
SEC. 197. AMORTIZATION OF GOODWILL AND CERTAIN OTHER INTANGIBLES.

[Sec. 197(a)]

(a) GENERAL RULE.—A taxpayer shall be entitled to an amortization deduction with respect to any amortizable section 197 intangible. The amount of such deduction shall be determined by amortizing the adjusted basis (for purposes of determining gain) of such intangible ratably over the 15-year period beginning with the month in which such intangible was acquired.

[Sec. 197(b)]

(b) NO OTHER DEPRECIATION OR AMORTIZATION DEDUCTION ALLOWABLE.—Except as provided in subsection (a), no depreciation or amortization deduction shall be allowable with respect to any amortizable section 197 intangible.

[Sec. 197(c)]

(c) AMORTIZABLE SECTION 197 INTANGIBLE.—For purposes of this section—

(1) IN GENERAL.—Except as otherwise provided in this section, the term "amortizable section 197 intangible" means any section 197 intangible—

(A) which is acquired by the taxpayer after the date of the enactment of this section, and

(B) which is held in connection with the conduct of a trade or business or an activity described in section 212.

(2) EXCLUSION OF SELF-CREATED INTANGIBLES, ETC.—The term "amortizable section 197 intangible" shall not include any section 197 intangible—

(A) which is not described in subparagraph (D), (E), or (F) of subsection (d)(1), and

(B) which is created by the taxpayer.

This paragraph shall not apply if the intangible is created in connection with a transaction (or series of related transactions) involving the acquisition of assets constituting a trade or business or substantial portion thereof.

(3) ANTI-CHURNING RULES.—

For exclusion of intangibles acquired in certain transactions, see subsection (f)(9).

[Sec. 197(d)]

(d) SECTION 197 INTANGIBLE.—For purposes of this section—

(1) IN GENERAL.—Except as otherwise provided in this section, the term "section 197 intangible" means—

(A) goodwill,

(B) going concern value,

(C) any of the following intangible items:

(i) workforce in place including its composition and terms and conditions (contractual or otherwise) of its employment,

(ii) business books and records, operating systems, or any other information base (including lists or other information with respect to current or prospective customers),

(iii) any patent, copyright, formula, process, design, pattern, knowhow, format, or other similar item,

(iv) any customer-based intangible,

(v) any supplier-based intangible, and

(vi) any other similar item,

(D) any license, permit, or other right granted by a governmental unit or an agency or instrumentality thereof,

(E) any covenant not to compete (or other arrangement to the extent such arrangement has substantially the same effect as a covenant not to compete) entered into in connection with an acquisition (directly or indirectly) of an interest in a trade or business or substantial portion thereof, and

(F) any franchise, trademark, or trade name.

(2) CUSTOMER-BASED INTANGIBLE.—

(A) IN GENERAL.—The term "customer-based intangible" means—

(i) composition of market,

(ii) market share, and

(iii) any other value resulting from future provision of goods or services pursuant to relationships (contractual or otherwise) in the ordinary course of business with customers.

(B) SPECIAL RULE FOR FINANCIAL INSTITUTIONS.—In the case of a financial institution, the term "customer-based intangible" includes deposit base and similar items.

(3) SUPPLIER-BASED INTANGIBLE.—The term "supplier-based intangible" means any value resulting from future acquisitions of goods or services pursuant to relationships (contractual or otherwise) in the ordinary course of business with suppliers of goods or services to be used or sold by the taxpayer.

[Sec. 197(e)]

(e) EXCEPTIONS.—For purposes of this section, the term "section 197 intangible" shall not include any of the following:

(1) FINANCIAL INTERESTS.—Any interest—

(A) in a corporation, partnership, trust, or estate, or

(B) under an existing futures contract, foreign currency contract, notional principal contract, or other similar financial contract.

(2) LAND.—Any interest in land.

(3) COMPUTER SOFTWARE.—

(A) IN GENERAL.—Any—

(i) computer software which is readily available for purchase by the general public, is subject to a nonexclusive license, and has not been substantially modified, and

(ii) other computer software which is not acquired in a transaction (or series of related transactions) involving the acquisition of assets constituting a trade or business or substantial portion thereof.

(B) COMPUTER SOFTWARE DEFINED.—For purposes of subparagraph (A), the term "computer software" means any program designed to cause a computer to perform a desired function. Such term shall not include any data base or similar item unless the data base or item is in the public domain and is incidental to the operation of otherwise qualifying computer software.

(4) CERTAIN INTERESTS OR RIGHTS ACQUIRED SEPARATELY.—Any of the following not acquired in a transaction (or series of related transactions) involving the acquisition of assets constituting a trade business or substantial portion thereof:

(A) Any interest in a film, sound recording, video tape, book, or similar property.

(B) Any right to receive tangible property or services under a contract or granted by a governmental unit or agency or instrumentality thereof.

(C) Any interest in a patent or copyright.

(D) To the extent provided in regulations, any right under a contract (or granted by a governmental unit or an agency or instrumentality thereof) if such right—

(i) has a fixed duration of less than 15 years, or

(ii) is fixed as to amount and, without regard to this section, would be recoverable under a method similar to the unit-of-production method.

(5) INTERESTS UNDER LEASES AND DEBT INSTRUMENTS.—Any interest under—

(A) an existing lease of tangible property, or

(B) except as provided in subsection (d)(2)(B), any existing indebtedness.

(6) MORTGAGE SERVICING.—Any right to service indebtedness which is secured by residential real property unless such right is acquired in a transaction (or series of related transactions) involving the acquisition of assests (other than rights described in this paragraph) constituting a trade or business or substantial portion thereof.

(7) CERTAIN TRANSACTION COSTS.—Any fees for professional services, and any transaction costs, incurred by parties to a transaction with respect to which any portion of the gain or loss is not recognized under part III of subchapter C.

Amendments

• 2004, American Jobs Creation Act of 2004 (P.L. 108-357)

P.L. 108-357, §886(a):

Amended Code Sec. 197(e) by striking paragraph (6) and by redesignating paragraphs (7) and (8) as paragraphs (6) and (7), respectively. **Effective** for property acquired after 10-22-2004. Prior to being stricken, Code Sec. 197(e)(6) read as follows:

(6) TREATMENT OF SPORTS FRANCHISES.—A franchise to engage in professional football, basketball, baseball, or other professional sport, and any item acquired in connection with such a franchise.

[Sec. 197(f)]

(f) SPECIAL RULES.—

(1) TREATMENT OF CERTAIN DISPOSITIONS, ETC.—

(A) IN GENERAL.—If there is a disposition of any amortizable section 197 intangible acquired in a transaction or series of related transactions (or any such intangible becomes worthless) and one or more other amortizable section 197 intangibles acquired in such transaction or series of related transactions are retained—

(i) no loss shall be recognized by reason of such disposition (or such worthlessness), and

(ii) appropriate adjustments to the adjusted bases of such retained intangibles shall be made for any loss not recognized under clause (i).

(B) SPECIAL RULE FOR COVENANTS NOT TO COMPETE.—In the case of any section 197 intangible which is a covenant not to compete (or other arrangement) described in subsection (d)(1)(E), in no event shall such covenant or other arrangement be treated as disposed of (or becoming worthless) before the disposition of the entire interest described in such subsection in connection with which such covenant (or other arrangement) was entered into.

(C) SPECIAL RULE.—All persons treated as a single taxpayer under section 41(f)(1) shall be so treated for purposes of this paragraph.

(2) Treatment of Certain Transfers.—

(A) In General.—In the case of any section 197 intangible transferred in a transaction described in subparagraph (B), the transferee shall be treated as the transferor for purposes of applying this section with respect to so much of the adjusted basis in the hands of the transferee as does not exceed the adjusted basis in the hands of the transferor.

(B) Transactions Covered.—The transactions described in this subparagraph are—

(i) any transaction described in section 332, 351, 361, 721, 731, 1031, or 1033, and

(ii) any transaction between members of the same affiliated group during any taxable year for which a consolidated return is made by such group.

(3) Treatment of Amounts Paid Pursuant to Covenants Not to Compete, etc.—Any amount paid or incurred pursuant to a covenant or arrangement referred to in subsection (d)(1)(E) shall be treated as an amount chargeable to capital account.

(4) Treatment of Franchises, etc.—

(A) Franchise.—The term "franchise" has the meaning given to such term by section 1253(b)(1).

(B) Treatment of Renewals.—Any renewal of a franchise, trademark, or trade name (or of a license, a permit, or other right referred to in subsection (d)(1)(D)) shall be treated as an acquisition. The preceding sentence shall only apply with respect to costs incurred in connection with such renewal.

(C) Certain Amounts Not Taken Into Account.—Any amount to which section 1253(d)(1) applies shall not be taken into account under this section.

(5) Treatment of Certain Reinsurance Transactions.—In the case of any amortizable section 197 intangible resulting from an assumption reinsurance transaction, the amount taken into account as the adjusted basis of such intangible under this section shall be the excess of—

(A) the amount paid or incurred by the acquirer under the assumption reinsurance transaction, over

(B) the amount required to be capitalized under section 848 in connection with such transaction.

Subsection (b) shall not apply to any amount required to be capitalized under section 848.

(6) Treatment of Certain Subleases.—For purposes of this section, a sublease shall be treated in the same manner as a lease of the underlying property involved.

(7) Treatment as Depreciable.—For purposes of this chapter, any amortizable section 197 intangible shall be treated as property which is of a character subject to the allowance for depreciation provided in section 167.

(8) Treatment of Certain Increments in Value.—This section shall not apply to any increment in value if, without regard to this section, such increment is properly taken into account in determining the cost of property which is not a section 197 intangible.

(9) Anti-Churning Rules.—For purposes of this section—

(A) In General.—The term "amortizable section 197 intangible" shall not include any section 197 intangible which is described in subparagraph (A) or (B) of subsection (d)(1) (or for which depreciation or amortization would not have been allowable but for this section) and which is acquired by the taxpayer after the date of the enactment of this section, if—

(i) the intangible was held or used at any time on or after July 25, 1991, and on or before such date of enactment by the taxpayer or a related person,

(ii) the intangible was acquired from a person who held such intangible at any time on or after July 25, 1991, and on or before such date of enactment, and, as part of the transaction, the user of such intangible does not change, or

(iii) the taxpayer grants the right to use such intangible to a person (or a person related to such person) who held or used such intangible at any time on or after July 25, 1991, and on or before such date of enactment.

For purposes of this subparagraph, the determination of whether the user of property changes as part of a transaction shall be determined in accordance with regulations prescribed by the Secretary. For purposes of this subparagraph, deductions allowable under section 1253(d) shall be treated as deductions allowable for amortization.

(B) Exception Where Gain Recognized.—If—

(i) subparagraph (A) would not apply to an intangible acquired by the taxpayer but for the last sentence of subparagraph (C)(i), and

(ii) the person from whom the taxpayer acquired the intangible elects, notwithstanding any other provision of this title—

(I) to recognize gain on the disposition of the intangible, and

(II) to pay a tax on such gain which, when added to any other income tax on such gain under this title, equals such gain multiplied by the highest rate of income tax applicable to such person under this title,

then subparagraph (A) shall apply to the intangible only to the extent that the taxpayer's adjusted basis in the intangible exceeds the gain recognized under clause (ii)(I).

(C) Related Person Defined.—For purposes of this paragraph—

(i) Related Person.—A person (hereinafter in this paragraph referred to as the "related person") is related to any person if—

(I) the related person bears a relationship to such person specified in section 267(b) or section 707(b)(1), or

(II) the related person and such person are engaged in trades or businesses under common control (within the meaning of subparagraphs (A) and (B) of section 41(f)(1)).

For purposes of subclause (I), in applying section 267(b) or 707(b)(1), "20 percent" shall be substituted for "50 percent".

(ii) TIME FOR MAKING DETERMINATION.—A person shall be treated as related to another person if such relationship exists immediately before or immediately after the acquisition of the intangible involved.

(D) ACQUISITIONS BY REASON OF DEATH.—Subparagraph (A) shall not apply to the acquisition of any property by the taxpayer if the basis of the property in the hands of the taxpayer is determined under section 1014(a).

(E) SPECIAL RULE FOR PARTNERSHIPS.—With respect to any increase in the basis of partnership property under section 732, 734, or 743, determinations under this paragraph shall be made at the partner level and each partner shall be treated as having owned and used such partner's proportionate share of the partnership assets.

(F) ANTI-ABUSE RULES.—The term "amortizable section 197 intangible" does not include any section 197 intangible acquired in a transaction, one of the principal purposes of which is to avoid the requirement of subsection (c)(1) that the intangible be acquired after the date of the enactment of this section or to avoid the provisions of subparagraph (A).

(10) TAX-EXEMPT USE PROPERTY SUBJECT TO LEASE.—In the case of any section 197 intangible which would be tax-exempt use property as defined in subsection (h) of section 168 if such section applied to such intangible, the amortization period under this section shall not be less than 125 percent of the lease term (within the meaning of section 168(i)(3)).

Amendments

- **2004, American Jobs Creation Act of 2004 (P.L. 108-357)**

P.L. 108-357, § 847(b)(3):

Amended Code Sec. 197(f) by adding at the end a new paragraph (10). **Effective** for leases entered into after 10-3-2004. For an exception, see Act Sec. 849(b)(1)-(2) below.

P.L. 108-357, § 849(b)(1)-(2), provides:

(b) EXCEPTION.—

(1) IN GENERAL.—The amendments made by this part shall not apply to qualified transportation property.

(2) QUALIFIED TRANSPORTATION PROPERTY.—For purposes of paragraph (1), the term "qualified transportation property" means domestic property subject to a lease with respect to which a formal application—

(A) was submitted for approval to the Federal Transit Administration (an agency of the Department of Transportation) after June 30, 2003, and before March 13, 2004,

(B) is approved by the Federal Transit Administration before January 1, 2006, and

(C) includes a description of such property and the value of such property.

[Sec. 197(g)]

(g) REGULATIONS.—The Secretary shall prescribe such regulations as may be appropriate to carry out the purposes of this section, including such regulations as may be appropriate to prevent avoidance of the purposes of this section through related persons or otherwise.

Amendments

- **1993, Omnibus Budget Reconciliation Act of 1993 (P.L. 103-66)**

P.L. 103-66, § 13261(a):

Amended part VI of subchapter B of chapter 1 by adding at the end thereof new Code Sec. 197. **Effective**, generally, for property acquired after 8-10-93. For special rules, see Act Sec. 13261(g)(2)-(3) below.

P.L. 103-66, § 13261(g)(2)-(3), as amended by P.L. 104-188, § 1703(l), provides:

(2) ELECTION TO HAVE AMENDMENTS APPLY TO PROPERTY ACQUIRED AFTER JULY 25, 1991.—

(A) IN GENERAL.—If an election under this paragraph applies to the taxpayer—

(i) the amendments made by this section shall apply to property acquired by the taxpayer after July 25, 1991,

(ii) subsection (c)(1)(A) of section 197 of the Internal Revenue Code of 1986 (as added by this section) (and so much of subsection (f)(9)(A) of such section 197 as precedes clause (i) thereof) shall be applied with respect to the taxpayer by treating July 25, 1991, as the date of the enactment of such section, and

(iii) in applying subsection (f)(9) of such section, with respect to any property acquired by the taxpayer or a related person on or before the date of the enactment of this Act, only holding or use on July 25, 1991, shall be taken into account.

(B) ELECTION.—An election under this paragrph shall be made at such time and in such manner as the Secretary of the Treasury or his delegate may prescribe. Such an election by any taxpayer, once made—

(i) may be revoked only with the consent of the Secretary, and

(ii) shall apply to the taxpayer making such election and any other taxpayer under common control with the taxpayer (within the meaning of subparagraphs (A) and (B) of section 41(f)(1) of such Code) at any time after August 2, 1993, and on or before the date on which such election is made.

(3) ELECTIVE BINDING CONTRACT EXCEPTION.—

(A) IN GENERAL.—The amendments made by this section shall not apply to any acquisition of property by the taxpayer if—

(i) such acquisition is pursuant to a written binding contract in effect on the date of the enactment of this Act and at all times thereafter before such acquisition,

(ii) an election under paragraph (2) does not apply to the taxpayer, and

(iii) the taxpayer makes an election under this paragraph with respect to such contract.

(B) ELECTION.—An election under this paragraph shall be made at such time and in such manner as the Secretary of the Treasury or his delegate shall prescribe. Such an election, once made—

(i) may be revoked only with the consent of the Secretary, and

(ii) shall apply to all property acquired pursuant to the contract with respect to which such election was made.

[Sec. 199A]
SEC. 199A. QUALIFIED BUSINESS INCOME.
[Sec. 199A(a)]
(a) ALLOWANCE OF DEDUCTION.—In the case of a taxpayer other than a corporation, there shall be allowed as a deduction for any taxable year an amount equal to the lesser of—
    (1) the combined qualified business income amount of the taxpayer, or
    (2) an amount equal to 20 percent of the excess (if any) of—
        (A) the taxable income of the taxpayer for the taxable year, over
        (B) the net capital gain (as defined in section 1(h)) of the taxpayer for such taxable year.

Amendments

- **2018, Consolidated Appropriations Act, 2018 (P.L. 115-141)**

P.L. 115-141, §101(b)(1), Div. T:

Amended Code Sec. 199A(a). **Effective** as if included in section 11011 of Public Law 115–97 [**effective** for tax years beginning after 12-31-2017.—CCH]. Prior to amendment, Code Sec. 199A(a) read as follows:

(a) IN GENERAL.—In the case of a taxpayer other than a corporation, there shall be allowed as a deduction for any taxable year an amount equal to the sum of—

(1) the lesser of—

(A) the combined qualified business income amount of the taxpayer, or

(B) an amount equal to 20 percent of the excess (if any) of—

(i) the taxable income of the taxpayer for the taxable year, over

(ii) the sum of any net capital gain (as defined in section 1(h)), plus the aggregate amount of the qualified cooperative dividends, of the taxpayer for the taxable year, plus

(2) the lesser of—

(A) 20 percent of the aggregate amount of the qualified cooperative dividends of the taxpayer for the taxable year, or

(B) taxable income (reduced by the net capital gain (as so defined)) of the taxpayer for the taxable year.

The amount determined under the preceding sentence shall not exceed the taxable income (reduced by the net capital gain (as so defined)) of the taxpayer for the taxable year.

[Sec. 199A(b)]

(b) COMBINED QUALIFIED BUSINESS INCOME AMOUNT.—For purposes of this section—

(1) IN GENERAL.—The term "combined qualified business income amount" means, with respect to any taxable year, an amount equal to—

(A) the sum of the amounts determined under paragraph (2) for each qualified trade or business carried on by the taxpayer, plus

(B) 20 percent of the aggregate amount of the qualified REIT dividends and qualified publicly traded partnership income of the taxpayer for the taxable year.

(2) DETERMINATION OF DEDUCTIBLE AMOUNT FOR EACH TRADE OR BUSINESS.—The amount determined under this paragraph with respect to any qualified trade or business is the lesser of—

(A) 20 percent of the taxpayer's qualified business income with respect to the qualified trade or business, or

(B) the greater of—

(i) 50 percent of the W–2 wages with respect to the qualified trade or business, or

(ii) the sum of 25 percent of the W–2 wages with respect to the qualified trade or business, plus 2.5 percent of the unadjusted basis immediately after acquisition of all qualified property.

(3) MODIFICATIONS TO LIMIT BASED ON TAXABLE INCOME.—

(A) EXCEPTION FROM LIMIT.—In the case of any taxpayer whose taxable income for the taxable year does not exceed the threshold amount, paragraph (2) shall be applied without regard to subparagraph (B).

(B) PHASE-IN OF LIMIT FOR CERTAIN TAXPAYERS.—

(i) IN GENERAL.—If—

(I) the taxable income of a taxpayer for any taxable year exceeds the threshold amount, but does not exceed the sum of the threshold amount plus $50,000 ($100,000 in the case of a joint return), and

(II) the amount determined under paragraph (2)(B) (determined without regard to this subparagraph) with respect to any qualified trade or business carried on by the taxpayer is less than the amount determined under paragraph (2)(A) with respect [to] such trade or business,

then paragraph (2) shall be applied with respect to such trade or business without regard to subparagraph (B) thereof and by reducing the amount determined under subparagraph (A) thereof by the amount determined under clause (ii).

(ii) AMOUNT OF REDUCTION.—The amount determined under this subparagraph is the amount which bears the same ratio to the excess amount as—

(I) the amount by which the taxpayer's taxable income for the taxable year exceeds the threshold amount, bears to

(II) $50,000 ($100,000 in the case of a joint return).

(iii) EXCESS AMOUNT.—For purposes of clause (ii), the excess amount is the excess of—

(I) the amount determined under paragraph (2)(A) (determined without regard to this paragraph), over

(II) the amount determined under paragraph (2)(B) (determined without regard to this paragraph).

(4) WAGES, ETC.—

(A) IN GENERAL.—The term "W–2 wages" means, with respect to any person for any taxable year of such person, the amounts described in paragraphs (3) and (8) of section 6051(a) paid by such person with respect to employment of employees by such person during the calendar year ending during such taxable year.

(B) LIMITATION TO WAGES ATTRIBUTABLE TO QUALIFIED BUSINESS INCOME.—Such term shall not include any amount which is not properly allocable to qualified business income for purposes of subsection (c)(1).

(C) RETURN REQUIREMENT.—Such term shall not include any amount which is not properly included in a return filed with the Social Security Administration on or before the 60th day after the due date (including extensions) for such return.

(5) ACQUISITIONS, DISPOSITIONS, AND SHORT TAXABLE YEARS.—The Secretary shall provide for the application of this subsection in cases of a short taxable year or where the taxpayer acquires, or disposes of, the major portion of a trade or business or the major portion of a separate unit of a trade or business during the taxable year.

(6) QUALIFIED PROPERTY.—For purposes of this section:

(A) IN GENERAL.—The term "qualified property" means, with respect to any qualified trade or business for a taxable year, tangible property of a character subject to the allowance for depreciation under section 167—

(i) which is held by, and available for use in, the qualified trade or business at the close of the taxable year,

(ii) which is used at any point during the taxable year in the production of qualified business income, and

(iii) the depreciable period for which has not ended before the close of the taxable year.

(B) DEPRECIABLE PERIOD.—The term "depreciable period" means, with respect to qualified property of a taxpayer, the period beginning on the date the property was first placed in service by the taxpayer and ending on the later of—

(i) the date that is 10 years after such date, or

(ii) the last day of the last full year in the applicable recovery period that would apply to the property under section 168 (determined without regard to subsection (g) thereof).

(7) SPECIAL RULE WITH RESPECT TO INCOME RECEIVED FROM COOPERATIVES.—In the case of any qualified trade or business of a patron of a specified agricultural or horticultural cooperative, the amount determined under paragraph (2) with respect to such trade or business shall be reduced by the lesser of—

(A) 9 percent of so much of the qualified business income with respect to such trade or business as is properly allocable to qualified payments received from such cooperative, or

(B) 50 percent of so much of the W-2 wages with respect to such trade or business as are so allocable.

Amendments
- **2018, Consolidated Appropriations Act, 2018 (P.L. 115-141)**
P.L. 115-141, § 101(b)(3), Div. T:
Amended Code Sec. 199A(b) by adding at the end a new paragraph (7). **Effective** as if included in section 11011 of Public Law 115-97 [**effective** for tax years beginning after 12-31-2017.—CCH].

[Sec. 199A(c)]

(c) QUALIFIED BUSINESS INCOME.—For purposes of this section—

(1) IN GENERAL.—The term "qualified business income" means, for any taxable year, the net amount of qualified items of income, gain, deduction, and loss with respect to any qualified trade or business of the taxpayer. Such term shall not include any qualified REIT dividends or qualified publicly traded partnership income.

(2) CARRYOVER OF LOSSES.—If the net amount of qualified income, gain, deduction, and loss with respect to qualified trades or businesses of the taxpayer for any taxable year is less than zero, such amount shall be treated as a loss from a qualified trade or business in the succeeding taxable year.

(3) QUALIFIED ITEMS OF INCOME, GAIN, DEDUCTION, AND LOSS.—For purposes of this subsection—

(A) IN GENERAL.—The term "qualified items of income, gain, deduction, and loss" means items of income, gain, deduction, and loss to the extent such items are—

(i) effectively connected with the conduct of a trade or business within the United States (within the meaning of section 864(c), determined by substituting "qualified trade or business (within the meaning of section 199A)" for "nonresident alien individual or a foreign corporation" or for "a foreign corporation" each place it appears), and

(ii) included or allowed in determining taxable income for the taxable year.

(B) EXCEPTIONS.—The following items shall not be taken into account as a qualified item of income, gain, deduction, or loss:

(i) Any item of short-term capital gain, short-term capital loss, long-term capital gain, or long-term capital loss.

(ii) Any dividend, income equivalent to a dividend, or payment in lieu of dividends described in section 954(c)(1)(G). Any amount described in section 1385(a)(1) shall not be treated as described in this clause.

(iii) Any interest income other than interest income which is properly allocable to a trade or business.

(iv) Any item of gain or loss described in subparagraph (C) or (D) of section 954(c)(1) (applied by substituting "qualified trade or business" for "controlled foreign corporation").

(v) Any item of income, gain, deduction, or loss taken into account under section 954(c)(1)(F) (determined without regard to clause (ii) thereof and other than items attributable to notional principal contracts entered into in transactions qualifying under section 1221(a)(7)).

(vi) Any amount received from an annuity which is not received in connection with the trade or business.

(vii) Any item of deduction or loss properly allocable to an amount described in any of the preceding clauses.

(4) TREATMENT OF REASONABLE COMPENSATION AND GUARANTEED PAYMENTS.—Qualified business income shall not include—

(A) reasonable compensation paid to the taxpayer by any qualified trade or business of the taxpayer for services rendered with respect to the trade or business,

(B) any guaranteed payment described in section 707(c) paid to a partner for services rendered with respect to the trade or business, and

(C) to the extent provided in regulations, any payment described in section 707(a) to a partner for services rendered with respect to the trade or business.

Amendments

- **2018, Consolidated Appropriations Act, 2018 (P.L. 115-141)**

P.L. 115-141, § 101(b)(2)(A), Div. T:
Amended Code Sec. 199A(c)(1) by striking ", qualified cooperative dividends," following "any qualified REIT dividends". **Effective** as if included in section 11011 of Public Law 115-97 [**effective** for tax years beginning after 12-31-2017.—CCH].

P.L. 115-141, § 101(b)(2)(B)(i)(I)-(II), Div. T:
Amended Code Sec. 199A(c)(3)(B) by striking "investment" in the matter preceding clause (i), and by adding at the end of clause (ii) "Any amount described in section 1385(a)(1) shall not be treated as described in this clause.". **Effective** as if included in section 11011 of Public Law 115-97 [**effective** for tax years beginning after 12-31-2017.—CCH].

[Sec. 199A(d)]

(d) QUALIFIED TRADE OR BUSINESS.—For purposes of this section—

(1) IN GENERAL.—The term "qualified trade or business" means any trade or business other than—

(A) a specified service trade or business, or

(B) the trade or business of performing services as an employee.

(2) SPECIFIED SERVICE TRADE OR BUSINESS.—The term "specified service trade or business" means any trade or business—

(A) which is described in section 1202(e)(3)(A) (applied without regard to the words "engineering, architecture,") or which would be so described if the term "employees or owners" were substituted for "employees" therein, or

(B) which involves the performance of services that consist of investing and investment management, trading, or dealing in securities (as defined in section 475(c)(2)), partnership interests, or commodities (as defined in section 475(e)(2)).

(3) EXCEPTION FOR SPECIFIED SERVICE BUSINESSES BASED ON TAXPAYER'S INCOME.—

(A) IN GENERAL.—If, for any taxable year, the taxable income of any taxpayer is less than the sum of the threshold amount plus $50,000 ($100,000 in the case of a joint return), then—

(i) any specified service trade or business of the taxpayer shall not fail to be treated as a qualified trade or business due to paragraph (1)(A), but

(ii) only the applicable percentage of qualified items of income, gain, deduction, or loss, and the W–2 wages and the unadjusted basis immediately after acquisition of qualified property, of the taxpayer allocable to such specified service trade or business shall be taken into account in computing the qualified business income, W–2 wages, and the unadjusted basis immediately after acquisition of qualified property of the taxpayer for the taxable year for purposes of applying this section.

(B) APPLICABLE PERCENTAGE.—For purposes of subparagraph (A), the term "applicable percentage" means, with respect to any taxable year, 100 percent reduced (not below zero) by the percentage equal to the ratio of—

(i) the taxable income of the taxpayer for the taxable year in excess of the threshold amount, bears to

(ii) $50,000 ($100,000 in the case of a joint return).

[Sec. 199A(e)]

(e) OTHER DEFINITIONS.—For purposes of this section—

(1) TAXABLE INCOME.—Except as otherwise provided in subsection (g)(2)(B), taxable income shall be computed without regard to any deduction allowable under this section.

(2) THRESHOLD AMOUNT.—

(A) IN GENERAL.—The term "threshold amount" means $157,500 (200 percent of such amount in the case of a joint return).

(B) INFLATION ADJUSTMENT.—In the case of any taxable year beginning after 2018, the dollar amount in subparagraph (A) shall be increased by an amount equal to—

(i) such dollar amount, multiplied by

(ii) the cost-of-living adjustment determined under section 1(f)(3) for the calendar year in which the taxable year begins, determined by substituting "calendar year 2017" for "calendar year 2016" in subparagraph (A)(ii) thereof.

The amount of any increase under the preceding sentence shall be rounded as provided in section 1(f)(7).

(3) QUALIFIED REIT DIVIDEND.—The term "qualified REIT dividend" means any dividend from a real estate investment trust received during the taxable year which—

(A) is not a capital gain dividend, as defined in section 857(b)(3), and

(B) is not qualified dividend income, as defined in section 1(h)(11).

(4) QUALIFIED PUBLICLY TRADED PARTNERSHIP INCOME.—The term "qualified publicly traded partnership income" means, with respect to any qualified trade or business of a taxpayer, the sum of—

(A) the net amount of such taxpayer's allocable share of each qualified item of income, gain, deduction, and loss (as defined in subsection (c)(3) and determined after the application of subsection (c)(4)) from a publicly traded partnership (as defined in section 7704(a)) which is not treated as a corporation under section 7704(c), plus

(B) any gain recognized by such taxpayer upon disposition of its interest in such partnership to the extent such gain is treated as an amount realized from the sale or exchange of property other than a capital asset under section 751(a).

Amendments

- **2018, Consolidated Appropriations Act, 2018 (P.L. 115-141)**

P.L. 115-141, §101(a)(2)(A), Div. T:
Amended Code Sec. 199A(e)(1) by striking "the deduction" and inserting "any deduction". **Effective** as if included in section 11011 of Public Law 115-97 [**effective** for tax years beginning after 12-31-2017.—CCH].

P.L. 115-141, §101(a)(2)(C), Div. T:
Amended Code Sec. 199A(e)(1) by striking "Taxable income" and inserting "Except as otherwise provided in subsection (g)(2)(B), taxable income". **Effective** as if included in section 11011 of Public Law 115-97 [**effective** for tax years beginning after 12-31-2017.—CCH].

P.L. 115-141, §101(b)(2)(B)(ii), Div. T:
Amended Code Sec. 199A(e) by striking paragraph (4) and by redesignating paragraph (5) as paragraph (4). **Effec-**

tive as if included in section 11011 of Public Law 115-97 [**effective** for tax years beginning after 12-31-2017.—CCH]. Prior to being stricken, Code Sec. 199A(e)(4) read as follows:

(4) QUALIFIED COOPERATIVE DIVIDEND.—The term "qualified cooperative dividend" means any patronage dividend (as defined in section 1388(a)), any per-unit retain allocation (as defined in section 1388(f)), and any qualified written notice of allocation (as defined in section 1388(c)), or any similar amount received from an organization described in subparagraph (B)(ii), which—

(A) is includible in gross income, and

(B) is received from—

(i) an organization or corporation described in section 501(c)(12) or 1381(a), or

(ii) an organization which is governed under this title by the rules applicable to cooperatives under this title before the enactment of subchapter T.

[Sec. 199A(f)]

(f) SPECIAL RULES.—

(1) APPLICATION TO PARTNERSHIPS AND S CORPORATIONS.—

(A) IN GENERAL.—In the case of a partnership or S corporation—

(i) this section shall be applied at the partner or shareholder level,

(ii) each partner or shareholder shall take into account such person's allocable share of each qualified item of income, gain, deduction, and loss, and

(iii) each partner or shareholder shall be treated for purposes of subsection (b) as having W–2 wages and unadjusted basis immediately after acquisition of qualified property for the taxable year in an amount equal to such person's allocable share of the W–2 wages and the unadjusted basis immediately after acquisition of qualified property of the partnership or S corporation for the taxable year (as determined under regulations prescribed by the Secretary).

For purposes of clause (iii), a partner's or shareholder's allocable share of W–2 wages shall be determined in the same manner as the partner's or shareholder's allocable share of wage expenses. For purposes of such clause, partner's or shareholder's allocable share of the unadjusted basis immediately after acquisition of qualified property shall be determined in the same manner as the partner's or shareholder's allocable share of depreciation. For purposes of this subparagraph, in the case of an S corporation, an allocable share shall be the shareholder's pro rata share of an item.

(B) APPLICATION TO TRUSTS AND ESTATES.—Rules similar to the rules under section 199(d)(1)(B)(i) (as in effect on December 1, 2017) for the apportionment of W–2 wages shall apply to the apportionment of W–2 wages and the apportionment of unadjusted basis immediately after acquisition of qualified property under this section.

(C) TREATMENT OF TRADES OR BUSINESS IN PUERTO RICO.—

(i) IN GENERAL.—In the case of any taxpayer with qualified business income from sources within the commonwealth of Puerto Rico, if all such income is taxable under section 1 for such taxable year, then for purposes of determining the qualified business income of such taxpayer for such taxable year, the term "United States" shall include the Commonwealth of Puerto Rico.

(ii) SPECIAL RULE FOR APPLYING LIMIT.—In the case of any taxpayer described in clause (i), the determination of W–2 wages of such taxpayer with respect to any qualified trade or business conducted in Puerto Rico shall be made without regard to any exclusion under section 3401(a)(8) for remuneration paid for services in Puerto Rico.

(2) Coordination with minimum tax.—For purposes of determining alternative minimum taxable income under section 55, qualified business income shall be determined without regard to any adjustments under sections 56 through 59.

(3) Deduction limited to income taxes.—The deduction under subsection (a) shall only be allowed for purposes of this chapter.

(4) Regulations.—The Secretary shall prescribe such regulations as are necessary to carry out the purposes of this section, including regulations—

(A) for requiring or restricting the allocation of items and wages under this section and such reporting requirements as the Secretary determines appropriate, and

(B) for the application of this section in the case of tiered entities.

[Sec. 199A(g)]

(g) Deduction for Income Attributable to Domestic Production Activities of Specified Agricultural or Horticultural Cooperatives.—

(1) Allowance of deduction.—

(A) In general.—In the case of a taxpayer which is a specified agricultural or horticultural cooperative, there shall be allowed as a deduction an amount equal to 9 percent of the lesser of—

(i) the qualified production activities income of the taxpayer for the taxable year, or

(ii) the taxable income of the taxpayer for the taxable year.

(B) Limitation.—

(i) In general.—The deduction allowable under subparagraph (A) for any taxable year shall not exceed 50 percent of the W-2 wages of the taxpayer for the taxable year.

(ii) W-2 wages.—For purposes of this subparagraph, the W-2 wages of the taxpayer shall be determined in the same manner as under subsection (b)(4) (without regard to subparagraph (B) thereof and after application of subsection (b)(5)), except that such wages shall not include any amount which is not properly allocable to domestic production gross receipts for purposes of paragraph (3)(A).

(C) Taxable income of cooperatives determined without regard to certain deductions.—For purposes of this subsection, the taxable income of a specified agricultural or horticultural cooperative shall be computed without regard to any deduction allowable under subsection (b) or (c) of section 1382 (relating to patronage dividends, per-unit retain allocations, and nonpatronage distributions).

(2) Deduction allowed to patrons.—

(A) In general.—In the case of any eligible taxpayer who receives a qualified payment from a specified agricultural or horticultural cooperative, there shall be allowed as a deduction for the taxable year in which such payment is received an amount equal to the portion of the deduction allowed under paragraph (1) to such cooperative which is—

(i) allowed with respect to the portion of the qualified production activities income to which such payment is attributable, and

(ii) identified by such cooperative in a written notice mailed to such taxpayer during the payment period described in section 1382(d).

(B) Limitation based on taxable income.—The deduction allowed to any taxpayer under this paragraph shall not exceed the taxable income of the taxpayer determined without regard to the deduction allowed under this paragraph and after taking into account any deduction allowed to the taxpayer under subsection (a) for the taxable year.

(C) Cooperative denied deduction for portion of qualified payments.—The taxable income of a specified agricultural or horticultural cooperative shall not be reduced under section 1382 by reason of that portion of any qualified payment as does not exceed the deduction allowable under subparagraph (A) with respect to such payment.

(D) Eligible taxpayer.—For purposes of this paragraph, the term "eligible taxpayer" means—

(i) a taxpayer other than a corporation, or

(ii) a specified agricultural or horticultural cooperative.

(E) Qualified payment.—For purposes of this section, the term "qualified payment" means, with respect to any eligible taxpayer, any amount which—

(i) is described in paragraph (1) or (3) of section 1385(a),

(ii) is received by such taxpayer from a specified agricultural or horticultural cooperative, and

(iii) is attributable to qualified production activities income with respect to which a deduction is allowed to such cooperative under paragraph (1).

(3) Qualified production activities income.—For purposes of this subsection—

(A) In general.—The term "qualified production activities income" for any taxable year means an amount equal to the excess (if any) of—

(i) the taxpayer's domestic production gross receipts for such taxable year, over

(ii) the sum of—

(I) the cost of goods sold that are allocable to such receipts, and

(II) other expenses, losses, or deductions (other than the deduction allowed under this subsection), which are properly allocable to such receipts.

(B) ALLOCATION METHOD.—The Secretary shall prescribe rules for the proper allocation of items described in subparagraph (A) for purposes of determining qualified production activities income. Such rules shall provide for the proper allocation of items whether or not such items are directly allocable to domestic production gross receipts.

(C) SPECIAL RULES FOR DETERMINING COSTS.—

(i) IN GENERAL.—For purposes of determining costs under subclause (I) of subparagraph (A)(ii), any item or service brought into the United States shall be treated as acquired by purchase, and its cost shall be treated as not less than its value immediately after it entered the United States. A similar rule shall apply in determining the adjusted basis of leased or rented property where the lease or rental gives rise to domestic production gross receipts.

(ii) EXPORTS FOR FURTHER MANUFACTURE.—In the case of any property described in clause (i) that had been exported by the taxpayer for further manufacture, the increase in cost or adjusted basis under clause (i) shall not exceed the difference between the value of the property when exported and the value of the property when brought back into the United States after the further manufacture.

(D) DOMESTIC PRODUCTION GROSS RECEIPTS.—

(i) IN GENERAL.—The term "domestic production gross receipts" means the gross receipts of the taxpayer which are derived from any lease, rental, license, sale, exchange, or other disposition of any agricultural or horticultural product which was manufactured, produced, grown, or extracted by the taxpayer (determined after the application of paragraph (4)(B)) in whole or significant part within the United States. Such term shall not include gross receipts of the taxpayer which are derived from the lease, rental, license, sale, exchange, or other disposition of land.

(ii) RELATED PERSONS.—

(I) IN GENERAL.—The term "domestic production gross receipts" shall not include any gross receipts of the taxpayer derived from property leased, licensed, or rented by the taxpayer for use by any related person.

(II) RELATED PERSON.—For purposes of subclause (I), a person shall be treated as related to another person if such persons are treated as a single employer under subsection (a) or (b) of section 52 or subsection (m) or (o) of section 414, except that determinations under subsections (a) and (b) of section 52 shall be made without regard to section 1563(b).

(4) SPECIFIED AGRICULTURAL OR HORTICULTURAL COOPERATIVE.—For purposes of this section—

(A) IN GENERAL.—The term "specified agricultural or horticultural cooperative" means an organization to which part I of subchapter T applies which is engaged—

(i) in the manufacturing, production, growth, or extraction in whole or significant part of any agricultural or horticultural product, or

(ii) in the marketing of agricultural or horticultural products.

(B) APPLICATION TO MARKETING COOPERATIVES.—A specified agricultural or horticultural cooperative described in subparagraph (A)(ii) shall be treated as having manufactured, produced, grown, or extracted in whole or significant part any agricultural or horticultural product marketed by the specified agricultural or horticultural cooperative which its patrons have so manufactured, produced, grown, or extracted.

(5) DEFINITIONS AND SPECIAL RULES.—

(A) SPECIAL RULE FOR AFFILIATED GROUPS.—

(i) IN GENERAL.—All members of an expanded affiliated group shall be treated as a single corporation for purposes of this subsection.

(ii) PARTNERSHIPS OWNED BY EXPANDED AFFILIATED GROUPS.—For purposes of paragraph (3)(D), if all of the interests in the capital and profits of a partnership are owned by members of a single expanded affiliated group at all times during the taxable year of such partnership, the partnership and all members of such group shall be treated as a single taxpayer during such period.

(iii) EXPANDED AFFILIATED GROUP.—For purposes of this subsection, the term "expanded affiliated group" means an affiliated group as defined in section 1504(a), determined—

(I) by substituting "more than 50 percent" for "at least 80 percent" each place it appears, and

(II) without regard to paragraphs (2) and (4) of section 1504(b).

(iv) ALLOCATION OF DEDUCTION.—Except as provided in regulations, the deduction under paragraph (1) shall be allocated among the members of the expanded affiliated group in proportion to each member's respective amount (if any) of qualified production activities income.

(B) SPECIAL RULE FOR COOPERATIVE PARTNERS.—In the case of a specified agricultural or horticultural cooperative which is a partner in a partnership, rules similar to the rules of subsection (f)(1) shall apply for purposes of this subsection.

(C) TRADE OR BUSINESS REQUIREMENT.—This subsection shall be applied by only taking into account items which are attributable to the actual conduct of a trade or business.

(D) UNRELATED BUSINESS TAXABLE INCOME.—For purposes of determining the tax imposed by section 511, this section shall be applied by substituting "unrelated business taxable income" for "taxable income" each place it appears in this section (other than this subparagraph).

(E) SPECIAL RULE FOR COOPERATIVE WITH OIL RELATED QUALIFIED PRODUCTION ACTIVITIES INCOME.—

(i) IN GENERAL.—If a specified agricultural or horticultural cooperative has oil related qualified production activities income for any taxable year, the amount otherwise allowable as a deduction under paragraph (1) shall be reduced by 3 percent of the least of—

(I) the oil related qualified production activities income of the cooperative for the taxable year,

(II) the qualified production activities income of the cooperative for the taxable year, or

(III) taxable income.

(ii) OIL RELATED QUALIFIED PRODUCTION ACTIVITIES INCOME.—For purposes of this subparagraph, the term "oil related qualified production activities income" means for any taxable year the qualified production activities income which is attributable to the production, refining, processing, transportation, or distribution of oil, gas, or any primary product thereof (within the meaning of section 927(a)(2)(C), as in effect before its repeal) during such taxable year.

(6) REGULATIONS.—The Secretary shall prescribe such regulations as are necessary to carry out the purposes of this subsection, including regulations which prevent more than 1 taxpayer from being allowed a deduction under this subsection with respect to any activity described in paragraph (3)(D)(i). Such regulations shall be based on the regulations applicable to cooperatives and their patrons under section 199 (as in effect before its repeal).

Amendments
- **2018, Consolidated Appropriations Act, 2018 (P.L. 115-141)**

P.L. 115-141, §101(a)(1), Div. T:

Amended Code Sec. 199A(g). **Effective** as if included in section 11011 of Public Law 115-97 [**effective** for tax years beginning after 12-31-2017.—CCH]. Prior to amendment, Code Sec. 199A(g) read as follows:

(g) DEDUCTION ALLOWED TO SPECIFIED AGRICULTURAL OR HORTICULTURAL COOPERATIVES.—

(1) IN GENERAL.—In the case of any taxable year of a specified agricultural or horticultural cooperative beginning after December 31, 2017, there shall be allowed a deduction in an amount equal to the lesser of—

(A) 20 percent of the excess (if any) of—

(i) the gross income of a specified agricultural or horticultural cooperative, over

(ii) the qualified cooperative dividends (as defined in subsection (e)(4)) paid during the taxable year for the taxable year, or

(B) the greater of—

(i) 50 percent of the W-2 wages of the cooperative with respect to its trade or business, or

(ii) the sum of 25 percent of the W-2 wages of the cooperative with respect to its trade or business, plus 2.5 percent of the unadjusted basis immediately after acquisition of all qualified property of the cooperative.

(2) LIMITATION.—The amount determined under paragraph (1) shall not exceed the taxable income of the specified agricultural or horticultural for the taxable year.

(3) SPECIFIED AGRICULTURAL OR HORTICULTURAL COOPERATIVE.—For purposes of this subsection, the term "specified agricultural or horticultural cooperative" means an organization to which part I of subchapter T applies which is engaged in—

(A) the manufacturing, production, growth, or extraction in whole or significant part of any agricultural or horticultural product,

(B) the marketing of agricultural or horticultural products which its patrons have so manufactured, produced, grown, or extracted, or

(C) the provision of supplies, equipment, or services to farmers or to organizations described in subparagraph (A) or (B).

[Sec. 199A(h)]

(h) ANTI-ABUSE RULES.—The Secretary shall—

(1) apply rules similar to the rules under section 179(d)(2) in order to prevent the manipulation of the depreciable period of qualified property using transactions between related parties, and

(2) prescribe rules for determining the unadjusted basis immediately after acquisition of qualified property acquired in like-kind exchanges or involuntary conversions.

[Sec. 199A(i)]

(i) TERMINATION.—This section shall not apply to taxable years beginning after December 31, 2025.

Amendments
- **2017, Tax Cuts and Jobs Act (P.L. 115-97)**

P.L. 115-97, §11011(a):

Amended part VI of subchapter B of chapter 1 by adding at the end a new Code Sec. 199A. **Effective** for tax years beginning after 12-31-2017.

APPENDIX: Selected Code Sections Affected by the Tax Cuts and Jobs Act

[Sec. 311]
SEC. 311. TAXABILITY OF CORPORATION ON DISTRIBUTION.

[Sec. 311(a)]
(a) GENERAL RULE.—Except as provided in subsection (b), no gain or loss shall be recognized to a corporation on the distribution (not in complete liquidation) with respect to its stock of—
 (1) its stock (or rights to acquire its stock), or
 (2) property.

Amendments

• **1988, Technical and Miscellaneous Revenue Act of 1988 (P.L. 100-647)**
P.L. 100-647, § 1018(d)(5)(E):
Amended Code Sec. 311(a) by striking out "distribution, with respect to its stock," and inserting in lieu thereof "distribution (not in complete liquidation) with respect to its stock". **Effective** as if included in the provision of P.L. 99-514 to which it relates.

[Sec. 311(b)]
(b) DISTRIBUTIONS OF APPRECIATED PROPERTY.—
 (1) IN GENERAL.—If—
  (A) a corporation distributes property (other than an obligation of such corporation) to a shareholder in a distribution to which subpart A applies, and
  (B) the fair market value of such property exceeds its adjusted basis (in the hands of the distributing corporation),
then gain shall be recognized to the distributing corporation as if such property were sold to the distributee at its fair market value.
 (2) TREATMENT OF LIABILITIES.—Rules similar to the rules of section 336(b) shall apply for purposes of this subsection.
 (3) SPECIAL RULE FOR CERTAIN DISTRIBUTIONS OF PARTNERSHIP OR TRUST INTERESTS.—If the property distributed consists of an interest in a partnership or trust, the Secretary may by regulations provide that the amount of the gain recognized under paragraph (1) shall be computed without regard to any loss attributable to property contributed to the partnership or trust for the principal purpose of recognizing such loss on the distribution.

Amendments

• **1988, Technical and Miscellaneous Revenue Act of 1988 (P.L. 100-647)**
P.L. 100-647, § 1006(e)(21)(B):
Amended Code Sec. 311(b)(2) by striking out "in Excess of Basis" after "Liabilities" in the heading. **Effective** as if included in the provision of P.L. 99-514 to which it relates.

P.L. 100-647, § 1006(e)(8)(B):
Amended Code Sec. 311(b) by adding at the end thereof new paragraph (3). **Effective** as if included in the provision of P.L. 99-514 to which it relates.

• **1986, Tax Reform Act of 1986 (P.L. 99-514)**
P.L. 99-514, § 631(c):
Amended Code Sec. 311. For the **effective** date, as well as special rules, see Act Sec. 633, below. Text of Code Sec. 311 before amendment is reproduced below.

P.L. 99-514, § 633, as amended by P.L. 100-647, § 1006(g), provides:
SEC. 633. EFFECTIVE DATES.
(a) GENERAL RULE.—Except as otherwise provided in this section, the amendments made by this subtitle shall apply to—
 (1) any distribution in complete liquidation, and any sale or exchange, made by a corporation after July 31, 1986, unless such corporation is completely liquidated before January 1, 1987,
 (2) any transaction described in section 338 of the Internal Revenue Code of 1986 for which the acquisition date occurs after December 31, 1986, and
 (3) any distribution (not in complete liquidation) made after December 31, 1986.
(b) BUILT-IN GAINS OF S CORPORATIONS.—
 (1) IN GENERAL.—The amendments made by section 632 (other than subsection (b) thereof) shall apply to taxable years beginning after December 31, 1986, but only in cases where the return for the taxable year is filed pursuant to an S election made after December 31, 1986.
 (2) APPLICATION OF PRIOR LAW.—In the case of any taxable year of an S corporation which begins after December 31, 1986, and to which the amendments made by section 632 (other than subsection (b) thereof) do not apply, paragraph (1) of section 1374(b) of the Internal Revenue Code of 1954 (as in effect on the date before the date of the enactment of this Act) shall be applied as if it read as follows:

"(1) an amount equal to 34 percent of the amount by which the net capital gain of the corporation for the taxable year exceeds $25,000, or".

(c) EXCEPTION FOR CERTAIN PLANS OF LIQUIDATION AND BINDING CONTRACTS.—
 (1) IN GENERAL.—The amendments made by this subtitle shall not apply to—
  (A) any distribution or sale or exchange made pursuant to a plan of liquidation adopted before August 1, 1986, if the liquidating corporation is completely liquidated before January 1, 1988,
  (B) any distribution or sale or exchange made by any corporation if more than 50 percent of the voting stock by value of such corporation is acquired on or after August 1, 1986, pursuant to a written binding contract in effect before such date and if such corporation is completely liquidated before January 1, 1988,
  (C) any distribution or sale or exchange made by any corporation if substantially all of the assets of such corporation are sold on or after August 1, 1986, pursuant to 1 or more written binding contracts in effect before such date and if such corporation is completely liquidated before January 1, 1988, or
  (D) any transaction described in section 338 of the Internal Revenue Code of 1986 with respect to any target corporation if a qualified stock purchase of such target corporation is made on or after August 1, 1986, pursuant to a written binding contract in effect before such date and the acquisition date (within the meaning of such section 338) is before January 1, 1988.
 (2) SPECIAL RULE FOR CERTAIN ACTIONS TAKEN BEFORE NOVEMBER 20, 1985.—For purposes of paragraph (1), transactions shall be treated as pursuant to a plan of liquidation adopted before August 1, 1986, if—
  (A) before November 20, 1985—
   (i) the board of directors of the liquidating corporation adopted a resolution to solicit shareholder approval for a transaction of a kind described in section 336 or 337, or
   (ii) the shareholders or board of directors have approved such a transaction,
  (B) before November 20, 1985—
   (i) there has been an offer to purchase a majority of the voting stock of the liquidating corporation, or
   (ii) the board of directors of the liquidating corporation has adopted a resolution approving an acquisition or recom-

mending the approval of an acquisition to the shareholders, or

(C) before November 20, 1985, a ruling request was submitted to the Secretary of the Treasury or his delegate with respect to a transaction of a kind described in section 336 or 337 of the Internal Revenue Code of 1954 (as in effect before the amendments made by this subtitle).

For purposes of the preceding sentence, any action taken by the board of directors or shareholders of a corporation with respect to any subsidiary of such corporation shall be treated as taken by the board of directors or shareholders of such subsidiary.

(d) TRANSITIONAL RULE FOR CERTAIN SMALL CORPORATIONS.—

(1) IN GENERAL.—In the case of the complete liquidation before January 1, 1989, of a qualified corporation, the amendments made by this subtitle shall not apply to the applicable percentage of each gain or loss which (but for this paragraph) would be recognized by the liquidating corporation by reason of the amendments made by this subtitle. Section 333 of the Internal Revenue Code of 1954 (as in effect on the day before the date of the enactment of this Act) shall continue to apply to any complete liquidation described in the preceding sentence.

(2) PARAGRAPH (1) NOT TO APPLY TO CERTAIN ITEMS.—Paragraph (1) shall not apply to—

(A) any gain or loss which is an ordinary gain or loss (determined without regard to section 1239 of the Internal Revenue Code of 1986),

(B) any gain or loss on a capital asset held for not more than 6 months, and

(C) any gain on an asset acquired by the qualified corporation if—

(i) the basis of such asset in the hands of the qualified corporation is determined (in whole or in part) by reference to the basis of such asset in the hands of the person from whom acquired, and

(ii) a principal purpose for the transfer of such asset to the qualified corporation was to secure the benefits of this subsection.

(3) APPLICABLE PERCENTAGE.—For purposes of this subsection, the term "applicable percentage" means—

(A) 100 percent if the applicable value of the qualified corporation is less than $5,000,000, or

(B) 100 percent reduced by an amount which bears the same ratio to 100 percent as—

(i) the excess of the applicable value of the corporation over $5,000,000, bears to

(ii) $5,000,000.

(4) APPLICABLE VALUE.—For purposes of this subsection, the applicable value is the fair market value of all of the stock of the corporation on the date of the adoption of the plan of complete liquidation (or if greater, on August 1, 1986).

(5) QUALIFIED CORPORATION.—For purposes of this subsection, the term "qualified corporation" means any corporation if—

(A) on August 1, 1986, and at all times thereafter before the corporation is completely liquidated, more than 50 percent (by value) of the stock in such corporation is held by a qualified group, and

(B) the applicable value of such corporation does not exceed $10,000,000.

(6) DEFINITIONS AND SPECIAL RULES.—For purposes of this subsection—

(A) QUALIFIED GROUP.—

(i) IN GENERAL.—Except as provided in clause (ii), the term "qualified group" means any group of 10 or fewer qualified persons who at all times during the 5-year period ending on the date of the adoption of the plan of complete liquidation (or, if shorter, the period during which the corporation or any predecessor was in existence) owned (or was treated as owning under the rules of subparagraph (C)) more than 50 percent (by value) of the stock in such corporation.

(ii) 5-YEAR OWNERSHIP REQUIREMENT NOT TO APPLY IN CERTAIN CASES.—In the case of—

(I) any complete liquidation pursuant to a plan of liquidation adopted before March 31, 1988,

(II) any distribution not in liquidation made before March 31, 1988,

(III) an election to be an S corporation filed before March 31, 1988, or

(IV) a transaction described in section 338 of the Internal Revenue Code of 1986 where the acquisition date (within the meaning of such section 338) is before March 31, 1988,

the term "qualified group" means any group of 10 or fewer qualified persons.

(B) QUALIFIED PERSON.—The term "qualified person" means—

(i) an individual,

(ii) an estate, or

(iii) any trust described in clause (ii) or clause (iii) of section 1361(c)(2)(A) of the Internal Revenue Code of 1986.

(C) ATTRIBUTION RULES.—

(i) IN GENERAL.—Any stock owned by a corporation, trust (other than a trust referred to in subparagraph (B)(iii), or partnership shall be treated as owned proportionately by its shareholders, beneficiaries, or partners, and shall not be treated as owned by such corporation, trust, or partnership. Stock considered to be owned by a person by reason of the application of the preceding sentence shall, for purposes of applying such sentence, be treated as actually owned by such person.

(ii) FAMILY MEMBERS.—Stock owned (or treated as owned) by members of the same family (within the meaning of section 318(a)(1) of the Internal Revenue Code of 1986) shall be treated as owned by 1 person, and shall be treated as owned by such 1 person for any period during which it was owned (or treated as owned) by any such member.

(iii) TREATMENT OF CERTAIN TRUSTS.—Stock owned (or treated as owned) by the estate of any decedent or by any trust referred to in subparagraph (B)(iii) with respect to such decedent shall be treated as owned by 1 person and shall be treated as owned by such 1 person for the period during which it was owned (or treated as owned) by such estate or any such trust or by the decedent.

(D) SPECIAL HOLDING PERIOD RULES.—Any property acquired by reason of the death of an individual shall be treated as owned at all times during which such property was owned (or treated as owned) by the decedent.

(E) CONTROLLED GROUP OF CORPORATIONS.—All members of the same controlled group (as defined in section 267(f)(1) of such Code) shall be treated as 1 corporation for purposes of determining whether any of such corporations met the requirement of paragraph (5)(B) and for purposes of determining the applicable percentage with respect to any of such corporations. For purposes of the preceding sentence, an S corporation shall not be treated as a member of a controlled group unless such corporation was a C corporation for its taxable year which includes August 1, 1988, or it was not described for such taxable year in paragraph (1) or (2) of section 1374(c) of such Code (as in effect on the day before the date of the enactment of this Act).

(7) SECTION 338 TRANSACTIONS.—The provisions of this subsection shall also apply in the case of a transaction described in section 338 of the Internal Revenue Code of 1986 where the acquisition date (within the meaning of such section 338) is before January 1, 1989.

(8) APPLICATION OF SECTION 1374.—Rules similar to the rules of this subsection shall apply for purposes of applying section 1374 of the Internal Revenue Code of 1986 (as amended by section 632) in the case of a qualified corporation which makes an election to be an S corporation under section 1362 of such Code before January 1, 1989, without regard to whether such corporation is completely liquidated.

(9) APPLICATION TO NONLIQUIDATING DISTRIBUTIONS.—The provisions of this subsection shall also apply in the case of any distribution (not in complete liquidation) made by a qualified corporation before January 1, 1989, without regard to whether such corporation is completely liquidated.

(e) COMPLETE LIQUIDATION DEFINED.—For purposes of this section, a corporation shall be treated as completely liquidated if all of the assets of such corporation are distributed in complete liquidation, less assets retained to meet claims.

(f) OTHER TRANSITIONAL RULES.—

(1) The amendments made by this subtitle shall not apply to any liquidation of a corporation incorporated under the laws of Pennsylvania on August 3, 1970, if—

(A) the board of directors of such corporation approved a plan of liquidation before January 1, 1986,

(B) an agreement for the sale of a material portion of the assets of such corporation was signed on May 9, 1986 (whether or not the assets are sold in accordance with such agreement), and

(C) the corporation is completely liquidated on or before December 31, 1988.

(2) The amendments made by this subtitle shall not apply to any liquidation (or deemed liquidation under section 338

of the Internal Revenue Code of 1986) of a diversified financial services corporation incorporated under the laws of Delaware on May 9, 1929 (or any direct or indirect subsidiary of such corporation), pursuant to a binding written contract entered into on or before December 31, 1986; but only if the liquidation is completed (or in the case of a section 338 election, the acquisition date occurs) before January 1, 1988.

(3) The amendments made by this subtitle shall not apply to any distribution, or sale, or exchange—

(A) of the assets owned (directly or indirectly) by a testamentary trust established under the will of a decedent dying on June 15, 1956, to its beneficiaries,

(B) made pursuant to a court order in an action filed on January 18, 1984, if such order—

(i) is issued after July 31, 1986, and

(ii) directs the disposition of the assets of such trust and the division of the trust corpus into 3 separate subtrusts.

For purposes of the preceding sentence, an election under section 338(g) of the Internal Revenue Code of 1986 (or an election under section 338(h)(10) of such Code, qualifying as a section 337 liquidation pursuant to regulations prescribed by the Secretary under section 1.338(h)(10)-1T(j)) made in connection with a sale or exchange pursuant to a court order described in subparagraph (B) shall be treated as a sale of [or] exchange.

(4)(A) The amendments made by this subtitle shall not apply to any distribution, or sale, or exchange—

(i) if—

(I) an option agreement to sell substantially all of the assets of a selling corporation organized under the laws of Massachusetts on October 20, 1976, is executed before August 1, 1986, the corporation adopts (by approval of its shareholders) a conditional plan of liquidation before August 1, 1986 to become effective upon the exercise of such option agreement (or modification thereto), and the assets are sold pursuant to the exercise of the option (as originally executed or subsequently modified provided that the purchase price is not thereby increased), or

(II) in the event that the optionee does not acquire substantially all the assets of the coporation, the optionor corporation sells substantially all its assets to another purchaser at a purchase price not greater than that contemplated by such option agreement pursuant to an effective plan of liquidation, and

(ii) the complete liquidation of the corporation occurs within 12 months of the time the plan of liquidation becomes effective, but in no event later than December 31, 1989.

(B) For purposes of subparagraph (A), a distribution, or sale, or exchange, of a distributee corporation (within the meaning of section 337(c)(3) of the Internal Revenue Code of 1986) shall be treated as satisfying the requirements of subparagraph (A) if its subsidiary satisfies the requirements of subparagraph (A).

(C) For purposes of section 56 of the Internal Revenue Code of 1986 (as amended by this Act), any gain or loss not recognized by reason of this paragraph shall not be taken into account in determining the adjusted net book income of the corporation.

(5) In the case of a corporation incorporated under the laws of Wisconsin on April 3, 1948—

(A) a voting trust established not later than December 31, 1987, shall qualify as a trust permitted as a shareholder of an S corporation and shall be treated as only 1 shareholder if the holders of beneficial interests in such voting trust are—

(i) employees or retirees of such corporation, or

(ii) in the case of stock or voting trust certificates acquired from an employee or retiree of such corporation, the spouse, child, or estate of such employee or retiree or a

trust created by such employee or retiree which is described in section 1361(c)(2) of the Internal Revenue Code of 1986 (or treated as described in such section by reason of section 1361(d) of such Code), and

(B) the amendment made by section 632 (other than subsection (b) thereof) shall not apply to such corporation if it elects to be an S corporation before January 1, 1989.

(6) The amendments made by this subtitle shall not apply to the liquidation of a corporation incorporated on January 26, 1982, under the laws of the State of Alabama with a principal place of business in Colbert County, Alabama, but only if such corporation is completely liquidated on or before December 31, 1987.

(7) The amendments made by this subtitle shall not apply to the acquisition by a Delaware Bank holding company of all of the assets of an Iowa bank holding company pursuant to a written contract dated December 9, 1981.

(8) The amendments made by this subtitle shall not apply to the liquidation of a corporation incorporated under the laws of Delaware on January 20, 1984, if more than 40 percent of the stock of such corporation was acquired by purchase on June 11, 1986, and there was a tender offer with respect to all additional outstanding shares of such corporation on July 29, 1986, but only if the corporation is completely liquidated on or before December 31, 1987.

(g) TREATMENT OF CERTAIN DISTRIBUTIONS IN RESPONSE TO HOSTILE TENDER OFFER.—

(1) IN GENERAL.—No gain or loss shall be recognized under the Internal Revenue Code of 1986 to a corporation (hereinafter in this subsection referred to as "parent") on a qualified distribution.

(2) QUALIFIED DISTRIBUTION DEFINED.—For purposes of paragraph (1)—

(A) IN GENERAL.—The term "qualified distribution" means a distribution—

(i) by parent of all of the stock of a qualified subsidiary in exchange for stock of parent which was acquired for purposes of such exchange pursuant to a tender offer dated February 16, 1982, and

(ii) pursuant to a contract dated February 13, 1982, and

(iii) which was made not more than 60 days after the board of directors of parent recommended rejection of an unsolicited tender offer to obtain control of parent.

(B) QUALIFIED SUBSIDIARY.—The term "qualified subsidiary" means a corporation created or organized under the laws of Delaware on September 7, 1976, all of the stock of which was owned by parent immediately before the qualified distribution.

Reproduced immediately below is the text of Code Sec. 311 before the amendment made by P.L. 99-514.

SEC. 311. TAXABILITY OF CORPORATION ON DISTRIBUTION.

[Sec. 311(a)]

(a) GENERAL RULE.—Except as provided in subsections (b), (c), and (d) of this section and section 453B, no gain or loss shall be recognized to a corporation on the distribution, with respect to its stock, of—

(1) its stock (or rights to acquire its stock), or

(2) property.

Amendments

• **1980, Installment Sales Revision Act of 1980 (P.L. 96-471)**

P.L. 96-471, §2(b)(1):

Amended Code Sec. 311(a) by substituting "section 453B" for "section 453(d)".

• **1969, Tax Reform Act of 1969 (P.L. 91-172)**

P.L. 91-172, §905(b)(1):

Amended Code Sec. 311(a) by changing "subsections (b) and (c)" to "subsections (b), (c), and (d)". **Effective** 12-1-69.

[Sec. 311(b)]

(b) LIFO INVENTORY.—

(1) RECOGNITION OF GAIN.—If a corporation inventorying goods under the method provided in section 472 (relating to last-in, first-out inventories) distributes inventory assets (as defined in paragraph (2) (A)), then the amount (if any) by which—

(A) the inventory amount (as defined in paragraph (2) (B)) of such assets under a method authorized by section 471 (relating to general rule for inventories), exceeds

(B) the inventory amount of such assets under the method provided in section 472,

shall be treated as gain to the corporation recognized from the sale of such inventory assets.

(2) DEFINITIONS.—For purposes of paragraph (1)—

(A) INVENTORY ASSETS.—The term "inventory assets" means stock in trade of the corporation, or other property of a kind which would properly be included in the inventory of the corporation if on hand at the close of the taxable year.

(B) INVENTORY AMOUNT.—The term "inventory amount" means, in the case of inventory assets distributed during a taxable year, the amount of such inventory assets determined as if the taxable year closed at the time of such distribution.

(3) METHOD OF DETERMINING INVENTORY AMOUNT.—For purposes of this subsection, the inventory amount of assets under a method authorized by section 471 shall be determined—

(A) if the corporation uses the retail method of valuing inventories under section 472, by using such method, or

(B) if subparagraph (A) does not apply, by using cost or market, whichever is lower.

[Sec. 311(c)]

(c) LIABILITY IN EXCESS OF BASIS.—If—

(1) a corporation distributes property to a shareholder with respect to its stock,

(2) such property is subject to a liability, or the shareholder assumes a liability of the corporation in connection with the distribution, and

(3) the amount of such liability exceeds the adjusted basis (in the hands of the distributing corporation) of such property,

then gain shall be recognized to the distributing corporation in an amount equal to such excess as if the property distributed had been sold at the time of the distribution. In the case of a distribution of property subject to a liability which is not assumed by the shareholder, the amount of gain to be recognized under the preceding sentence shall not exceed the excess, if any, of the fair market value of such property over its adjusted basis.

[Sec. 311(d)]

(d) DISTRIBUTIONS OF APPRECIATED PROPERTY.—

(1) IN GENERAL.—If—

(A) a corporation distributes property (other than an obligation of such corporation) to a shareholder in a distribution to which subpart A applies, and

(B) the fair market value of such property exceeds its adjusted basis (in the hands of the distributing corporation), then a gain shall be recognized to the distributing corporation in an amount equal to such excess as if the property distributed had been sold at the time of the distribution. This subsection shall be applied after the application of subsections (b) and (c).

(2) EXCEPTIONS AND LIMITATIONS.—Paragraph (1) shall not apply to—

(A) a distribution which is made with respect to qualified stock if—

(i) section 302(b)(4) applies to such distribution, or

(ii) such distribution is a qualified dividend;

(B) a distribution of stock or an obligation of a corporation if the requirements of paragraph (2) of subsection (e) are met with respect to the distribution;

(C) a distribution to the extent that section 303(a) (relating to distributions in redemption of stock to pay death taxes) applies to such distribution;

(D) a distribution to a private foundation in redemption of stock which is described in section 537(b)(2)(A) and (B); and

(E) a distribution by a corporation to which part I of subchapter M (relating to regulated investment companies) applies, if such distribution is in redemption of its stock upon the demand of the shareholder.

Amendments

- **1984, Deficit Reduction Act of 1984 (P.L. 98-369)**

P.L. 98-369, § 54(a)(1):

Amended Code Sec. 311(d)(1). **Effective** for distributions declared on or after 6-14-84, in tax years ending after such date. For special rules and exceptions, see Act Sec. 54(d)(3)-(6), below. Prior to amendment, Code Sec. 311 (d)(1) read as follows:

(1) In General.—If—

(A) a corporation distributes property (other than an obligation of such corporation) to a shareholder in a redemption (to which subpart A applies) of part or all of his stock in such corporation, and

(B) the fair market value of such property exceeds its adjusted basis (in the hands of the distributing corporation), then a gain shall be recognized to the distributing corporation in an amount equal to such excess as if the property distributed had been sold at the time of the distribution. Subsections (b) and (c) shall not apply to any distribution to which this subsection applies.

P.L. 98-369, § 54(a)(2)(A):

Amended Code Sec. 311(d)(2) by striking out subparagraphs (A) and (B) and inserting in lieu thereof new subparagraph (A). **Effective** for distributions declared on or after 6-14-84, in tax years ending after such date. For special rules and exceptions, see Act Sec. 54(d)(3)-(6), below. Prior to amendment, Code Sec. 311(d)(2)(A) and (B) read as follows:

(A) a distribution to a corporate shareholder if the basis of the property distributed is determined under section 301(d)(2);

(B) a distribution to which section 302(b)(4) applies and which is made with respect to qualified stock;

P.L. 98-369, § 54(a)(2)(B):

Amended Code Sec. 311(d)(2) by redesignating subparagraphs (C), (D), (E), and (F) as (B), (C), (D), and (E), respectively. **Effective** for distributions declared on or after 6-14-84, in tax years ending after such date. For special rules and exceptions, see Act Sec. 54(d)(3)-(6), below.

P.L. 98-369, § 54(a)(3):

Amended the heading of Code Sec. 311(d). **Effective** for distributions declared on or after 6-14-84, in tax years ending after such date. For special rules and exceptions, see Act Sec. 54(d)(3)-(6), below. Prior to amendment, the heading for Code Sec. 311(d) read as follows:

(d) Appreciated Property Used to Redeem Stock.—

P.L. 98-369, § 54(d)(3)-(6), as amended by P.L. 99-514, § 1804(b)(3) and P.L. 100-647, § 1018(d)(2)-(3), provides:

(3) Exception for Distributions Before January 1, 1985, to 80-Percent Corporate Shareholders.—

(A) In General.—The amendments made by subsection (a) shall not apply to any distribution before January 1, 1985, to an 80-percent corporate shareholder if the basis of the property distributed is determined under section 301(d)(2) of the Internal Revenue Code of 1954.

(B) 80-Percent Corporate Shareholder.—The term "80-percent corporate shareholder" means, with respect to any distribution, any corporation which owns—

(i) stock in the corporation making the distribution possessing at least 80 percent of the total combined voting power of all classes of stock entitled to vote, and

(ii) at least 80 percent of the total number of shares of all other classes of stock of the distributing corporation (except nonvoting stock which is limited and preferred as to dividends).

(C) Special Rule for Affiliated Group Filing Consolidated Return.—For purposes of this paragraph and paragraph (4), all members of the same affiliated group (as defined in section 1504 of the Internal Revenue Code of 1954) which file a consolidated return for the taxable year which includes the date of the distribution shall be treated as 1 corporation.

(D) Special Rule for Certain Distributions Before January 1, 1988.—

(i) In General.—In the case of a transaction to which this subparagraph applies, subparagraph (A) shall be applied by substituting "1988" for "1985" and the amendments made by subtitle D of title VI of the Tax Reform Act of 1986 shall not apply.

(ii) Transaction to Which Subparagraph Applies.—This subparagraph applies to a transaction in which a Delaware corporation which was incorporated on May 31, 1927, and which was acquired by the transferee on December 10, 1968, transfers to the transferee stock in a corporation—

(I) with respect to which such Delaware corporation is a 100-percent corporate shareholder, and

(II) which is a Tennessee corporation which was incorporated on March 2, 1978, and which is a successor to an Indiana corporation which was incorporated on June 28, 1946, and acquired by the transferee on December 10, 1968.

(4) Exception for Certain Distributions Where Tender Offer Commenced on May 23, 1984.—

(A) In General.—The amendments made by subsection (a) shall not apply to any distribution made before September 1, 1986, if—

(i) such distribution consists of qualified stock held (directly or indirectly) on June 15, 1984, by the distributing corporation,

(ii) control of the distributing corporation (as defined in section 368(c) of the Internal Revenue Code of 1954) is acquired other than in a tax-free transaction after January 1, 1984, but before January 1, 1985,

(iii) a tender offer for the shares of the distributing corporation was commenced on May 23, 1984, and was amended on May 24, 1984, and

(iv) the distributing corporation and the distributee corporation are members of the same affiliated group (as defined in section 1504 of such Code) which filed a consolidated return for the taxable year which includes the date of the distribution.

If the common parent of any affiliated group filing a consolidated return meets the requirements of clauses (ii) and (iii), each other member of such group shall be treated as meeting such requirements.

(B) Qualified Stock.—For purposes of subparagraph (A), the term "qualified stock" means any stock in a corporation which on June 15, 1984, was a member of the same affiliated group as the distributing corporation and which filed a consolidated return with the distributing corporation for the taxable year which included June 15, 1984.

(5) Exception for Certain Distributions.—

(A) In General.—The amendments made by this section shall not apply to distributions before February 1, 1986, if—

(i) the distribution consists of property held on March 7, 1984 (or property acquired thereafter in the ordinary course of a trade or business) by—

(I) the controlled corporation, or

(II) any subsidiary controlled corporation,

(ii) a group of 1 or more shareholders (acting in concert)—

(I) acquired, during the 1-year period ending on February 1, 1984, at least 10 percent of the outstanding stock of the controlled corporation,

(II) held at least 10 percent of the outstanding stock of the common parent on February 1, 1984, and

(III) submitted a proposal for distributions of interests in a royalty trust from the common parent or the controlled corporation, and

(iii) the common parent acquired control of the controlled corporation during the 1-year period ending on February 1, 1984.

(B) Definitions.—For purposes of this paragraph—

(i) The term "common parent" has the meaning given such term by section 1504(a) of the Internal Revenue Code of 1954.

(ii) The term "controlled corporation" means a corporation with respect to which 50 percent or more of the outstanding stock of its common parent is tendered for pursuant to a tender offer outstanding on March 7, 1984.

(iii) The term "subsidiary controlled corporation" means any corporation with respect to which the controlled corporation has control (within the meaning of section 368(c) of such Code) on March 7, 1984.

(6) Exception for Certain Distribution of Partnership Interests.—The amendments made by this section shall not apply to any distribution before February 1 1986, of an interest in a partnership the interests of which were being traded on a national securities exchange on March 7, 1984, if—

(A) such interest was owned by the distributing corporation (or any member of an affiliated group within the meaning of section 1504(a) of such Code of which the distributing corporation was a member) on March 7, 1984,

(B) the distributing corporation (or any such affiliated member) owned more than 80 percent of the interests in such partnership on March 7, 1984, and

(C) more than 10 percent of the interests in such partnership was offered for sale to the public during the 1-year period ending on March 7, 1984.

• **1982, Tax Equity and Fiscal Responsibility Act of 1982 (P.L. 97-248)**

P.L. 97-248, §223(a)(1):

Amended Code Sec. 311(d)(2)(A)-(C). **Effective**, generally, for distributions after 8-31-82. But see amendment notes for P.L. 97-248, §223(b)(2)-(5), below, for special rules. Prior to amendment Code Sec. 311(d)(2)(A)-(C) read as follows:

(A) a distribution in complete redemption of all of the stock of a shareholder who, at all times within the 12-month period ending on the date of such distribution, owns at least 10 percent in value of the outstanding stock of the distributing corporation, but only if the redemption qualifies under section 302(b)(3) (determined without the application of section 302(c)(2)(A)(ii));

(B) a distribution of stock or an obligation of a corporation—

(i) which is engaged in at least one trade or business,

(ii) which has not received property constituting a substantial part of its assets from the distributing corporation, in a transaction to which section 351 applied or as a contribution to capital, within the 5-year period ending on the date of the distribution, and

(iii) at least 50 percent in value of the outstanding stock of which is owned by the distributing corporation at any time within the 9-year period ending one year before the date of the distribution;

(C) a distribution of stock or securities pursuant to the terms of a final judgment rendered by a court with respect to the distributing corporation in a court proceeding under the Sherman Act (15 U.S.C. 1-7) or the Clayton Act (15 U.S.C. 12-27), or both, to which the United States is a party, but only if the distribution of such stock or securities in redemption of the distributing corporation's stock is in furtherance of the purposes of the judgment;

P.L. 97-248, §223(a)(3)(A)-(C):

Amended Code Sec. 311(d)(2) by inserting "and" at the end of subparagraph (E); by striking out the semicolon and "and" at the end of subparagraph (F) and inserting in lieu thereof a period; and by striking out paragraph (G). **Effective** for distributions after 8-31-82. Prior to amendment, paragraph (G) read as follows:

"(G) a distribution of stock to a distributee which is not an organization exempt from tax under section 501(a), if with respect to such distributee, subsection (a)(1) or (b)(1) of section 1101 (relating to distributions pursuant to Bank Holding Company Act) applies to such distribution."

P.L. 97-248, §223(b)(2)-(5), as amended by P.L. 97-448, §306(a)(7), provides:

(2) Distributions pursuant to ruling requests before July 23, 1982.—In the case of a ruling request under section 311(d)(2)(A) of the Internal Revenue Code of 1954 (as in effect before the amendments made by this section) made before July 23, 1982, the amendments made by this section shall not apply to distributions made—

(A) pursuant to a ruling granted pursuant to such request, and

(B) either before October 21, 1982, or within 90 days after the date of such ruling.

(3) Distributions pursuant to final judgments of court.—In the case of a final judgment described in section 311(d)(2)(C) of such Code (as in effect before the amendments made by this section) rendered before July 23, 1982, the amendments made by this section shall not apply to distributions made before January 1, 1986, pursuant to such judgment.

(4) Certain distributions with respect to stock acquired before May 1982.—The amendments made by this section shall not apply to distributions—

(A) which meet the requirements of section 311(d)(2)(A) of such Code (as in effect on the day before the date of the enactment of this Act),

(B) which are made on or before August 31, 1983, and

(C) which are made with respect to stock acquired after 1980 and before May 1982.

(5) Distributions of timberland with respect to stock of forest products company.—If—

(A) a forest products company distributes timberland to a shareholder in redemption of the common and preferred stock in such corporation held by such shareholder,

(B) section 311(d)(2)(A) of the Internal Revenue Code of 1954 (as in effect before the amendments made by this section) would have applied to such distributions, and

(C) such distributions are made pursuant to 1 or 2 options contained in a contract between such company and such shareholder which is binding on August 31, 1982, and at all times thereafter,

then such distributions of timberland having an aggregate fair market value on August 31, 1982, not in excess of $10,000,000 shall be treated as distributions to which section 311(d)(2)(A) of such Code (as in effect before the date of the enactment of this Act) applies.

• **1978, Revenue Act of 1978 (P.L. 95-600)**

P.L. 95-600, §703(j)(2)(B), (C):

Redesignated Code Sec. 311(d)(2)(H) as subparagraph (G). **Effective** as if included in P.L. 94-452, §2(b).

• **1976, Tax Reform Act of 1976 (P.L. 94-455)**

P.L. 94-455, §1901(a)(42):

Amended Code Sec. 311(d) by (1) substituting "then a gain shall be recognized" for "then again shall be recognized" in paragraph (1); (2) striking paragraph (2)(C) and redesignating paragraphs (2)(D), (2)(E), (2)(F), and (2)(G) as paragraphs (2)(C), (2)(D), (2)(E), and (2)(F), respectively; (3) striking "26 Stat. 209;" before "15 U.S.C. 1-7" in redesignated Code Sec. 311(d)(2)(C); and (4) striking "38 Stat. 730;" before "15 U.S.C. 12-27" in redesignated Code Sec. 311(d)(2)(C). **Effective** for tax years beginning after 12-31-76, except that the amendment made at (2) above apply only with respect to distributions after 11-30-74. Prior to repeal, Code Sec. 311(d)(2)(C) read as follows:

(C) a distribution before December 1, 1974, of stock of a corporation substantially all of the assets of which the distributing corporation (or a corporation which is a member of the same affiliated group (as defined in section 1504(a)) as the distributing corporation) held on November 30, 1969, if such assets constitute a trade or business which has been actively conducted throughout the one-year period ending on the date of the distribution;

- **1976, Bank Holding Company Tax Act of 1976 (P.L. 94-452)**

P.L. 94-452, §2(b):

Amended Code Sec. 311(d)(2) by adding subparagraph (H) [(G)]. **Effective** 10-1-77 with respect to distributions after 12-31-75, in tax years ending after 12-31-75.

- **1969, Tax Reform Act of 1969 (P.L. 91-172)**

P.L. 91-172, §905(a):

Amended Code Sec. 311 by adding subsection (d). P.L. 91-675, §1, approved 1-12-71, amended P.L. 91-172, §905(c), which governs the **effective** date of the amendments made to Code Sec. 311 by P.L. 91-172. The **effective** date provision, as amended by P.L. 91-675, read as follows:

"(c) Effective Date.—

"(1) Except as provided in paragraphs (2), (3), (4), and (5), the amendments made by subsections (a) and (b) shall apply with respect to distributions after November 30, 1969.

"(2) The amendments made by subsections (a) and (b) shall not apply to a distribution before April 1, 1970, pursuant to the terms of—

"(A) a written contract which was binding on the distributing corporation on November 30, 1969, and at all times thereafter before the distribution,

"(B) an offer made by the distributing corporation before December 1, 1969,

"(C) an offer made in accordance with a request for a ruling filed by the distributing corporation with the Internal Revenue Service before December 1, 1969, or

"(D) an offer made in accordance with a registration statement filed with the Securities and Exchange Commission before December 1, 1969.

"For purposes of subparagraphs (B), (C), and (D), an offer shall be treated as an offer only if it was in writing and not revocable by its express terms.

"(3) The amendments made by subsections (a) and (b) shall not apply to a distribution by a corporation of specific property in redemption of stock outstanding on November 30, 1969, if—

"(A) every holder of such stock on such date had the right to demand redemption of his stock in such specific property, and

"(B) the corporation had such specific property on hand on such date in a quantity sufficient to redeem all of such stock.

"For purposes of the preceding sentence, stock shall be considered to have been outstanding on November 30, 1969, if it could have been acquired on such date through the exercise of an existing right of conversion contained in other stock held on such date.

"(4) The amendments made by subsections (a) and (b) shall not apply to a distribution by a corporation of property (held on December 1, 1969, by the distributing corporation or a corporation which was a wholly owned subsidiary of the distributing corporation on such date) in redemption of stock outstanding on November 30, 1969, which is redeemed and canceled before July 31, 1971, if—

"(A) such redemption is pursuant to a resolution adopted before November 1, 1969, by the Board of Directors authorizing the redemption of a specific amount of stock constituting more than 10 percent of the outstanding stock of the corporation at the time of the adoption of such resolution; and

"(B) more than 40 percent of the stock authorized to be redeemed pursuant to such resolution was redeemed before December 30, 1969, and more than one-half of the stock so redeemed was redeemed with property other than money.

"(5) The amendments made by subsections (a) and (b) shall not apply to a distribution of stock by a corporation organized prior to December 1, 1969, for the principal purpose of providing an equity participation plan for employees of the corporation whose stock is being distributed (hereinafter referred to as the 'employer corporation') if—

"(A) the stock being distributed was owned by the distributing corporation on November 30, 1969,

"(B) the stock being redeemed was acquired before January 1, 1973, pursuant to such equity participation plan by the shareholder presenting such stock for redemption (or by a predecessor of such shareholder),

"(C) the employment of the shareholder presenting the stock for redemption (or the predecessor of such shareholder) by the employer corporation commenced before January 1, 1971,

"(D) at least 90 percent in value of the assets of the distributing corporation on November 30, 1969, consisted of common stock of the employer corporation, and

"(E) at least 50 percent of the outstanding voting stock of the employer corporation is owned by the distributing corporation at any time within the nine-year period ending one year before the date of such distribution."

[Sec. 311(e)]

(e) DEFINITIONS AND SPECIAL RULES FOR SUBSECTION (d)(2).—For purposes of subsection (d)(2) and this subsection—

(1) QUALIFIED STOCK.—

(A) IN GENERAL.—The term "qualified stock" means stock held by a person (other than a corporation) who at all times during the lesser of—

(i) the 5-year period ending on the date of distribution, or

(ii) the period during which the distributing corporation (or a predecessor corporation) was in existence,

held at least 10 percent in value of the outstanding stock of the distributing corporation (or predecessor corporation).

(B) DETERMINATION OF STOCK HELD.—Section 318 shall apply in determining ownership of stock under subparagraph (A); except that, in applying section 318(a)(1), the term "family" includes any individual described in section 267(c)(4) and any spouse of any such individual.

(C) RULES FOR PASSTHRU ENTITIES.—In the case of an S corporation, partnership, trust, or estate—

(i) the determination of whether subparagraph (A) is satisfied shall be made at the shareholder, partner, or beneficiary level (rather than at the entity level), and

(ii) the distribution shall be treated as made directly to the shareholders, partners, or beneficiaries in proportion to their respective interests in the entity.

(2) DISTRIBUTIONS OF STOCK OR OBLIGATIONS OF CONTROLLED CORPORATIONS.—

(A) REQUIREMENTS.—A distribution of stock or an obligation of a corporation (hereinafter in this paragraph referred to as the "controlled corporation") meets the requirements of this paragraph if—

(i) such distribution is made with respect to qualified stock,

(ii) substantially all of the assets of the controlled corporation consists of the assets of 1 or more qualified businesses,

(iii) no substantial part of the controlled corporation's nonbusiness assets were acquired from the distributing corporation, in a transaction to which section 351 applied or as a contribution to capital, within the 5-year period ending on the date of the distribution, and

(iv) more than 50 percent in value of the outstanding stock of the controlled corporation is distributed by the distributing corporation with respect to qualified stock.

(B) DEFINITIONS.—For purposes of subparagraph (A)—

(i) QUALIFIED BUSINESS.—The term "qualified business" means any trade or business which—

(I) was actively conducted throughout the 5-year period ending on the date of the distribution, and

(II) was not acquired by any person within such period in a transaction in which gain or loss was recognized in whole or in part.

(ii) NONBUSINESS ASSET.—The term "nonbusiness asset" means any asset not used in the active conduct of a trade or business.

(3) QUALIFIED DIVIDEND.—The term "qualified dividend" means any distribution of property to a shareholder other than a corporation if—

(A) such distribution is a dividend,

(B) such property was used by the distributing corporation in the active conduct of a qualified business (as defined in paragraph (2)), and

(C) such property is not property described in paragraph (1) or (4) of section 1221.

Amendments

• **1984, Deficit Reduction Act of 1984 (P.L. 98-369)**
P.L. 98-369, §54(a)(2)(C):
Amended Code Sec. 311(e) by adding new paragraph (3). **Effective** for distributions declared on or after 6-14-84, in tax years ending after such date. Special rules and exceptions appear following former Code Sec. 311(d).

P.L. 98-369, §712(j):
Added subparagraph (C) to Code Sec. 311(e)(1). **Effective** as if included in the provision of P.L. 97-248 to which it relates.

• **1982, Tax Equity and Fiscal Responsibility Act of 1982 (P.L. 97-248)**
P.L. 97-248, §223(a)(2):
Amended Code Sec. 311 by adding at the end thereof new paragraph (e). **Effective**, generally, for distributions after 8-31-82. But see amendment notes for P.L. 97-248, Act Sec. 223(b)(2)-(5) following former Code Sec. 311(d) for special rules.

[Sec. 318]
SEC. 318. CONSTRUCTIVE OWNERSHIP OF STOCK.
[Sec. 318(a)]

(a) GENERAL RULE.—For purposes of those provisions of this subchapter to which the rules contained in this section are expressly made applicable—

(1) MEMBERS OF FAMILY.—

(A) IN GENERAL.—An individual shall be considered as owning the stock owned, directly or indirectly, by or for—

(i) his spouse (other than a spouse who is legally separated from the individual under a decree of divorce or separate maintenance), and

(ii) his children, grandchildren, and parents.

(B) EFFECT OF ADOPTION.—For purposes of subparagraph (A)(ii), a legally adopted child of an individual shall be treated as a child of such individual by blood.

(2) ATTRIBUTION FROM PARTNERSHIPS, ESTATES, TRUSTS, AND CORPORATIONS.—

(A) FROM PARTNERSHIPS AND ESTATES.—Stock owned, directly or indirectly, by or for a partnership or estate shall be considered as owned proportionately by its partners or beneficiaries.

(B) FROM TRUSTS.—

(i) Stock owned, directly or indirectly, by or for a trust (other than an employees' trust described in section 401(a) which is exempt from tax under section 501(a)) shall be considered as owned by its beneficiaries in proportion to the actuarial interest of such beneficiaries in such trust.

(ii) Stock owned, directly or indirectly, by or for any portion of a trust of which a person is considered the owner under subpart E of part I of subchapter J (relating to grantors and others treated as substantial owners) shall be considered as owned by such person.

(C) From corporations.—If 50 percent or more in value of the stock in a corporation is owned, directly or indirectly, by or for any person, such person shall be considered as owning the stock owned, directly or indirectly, by or for such corporation, in that proportion which the value of the stock which such person so owns bears to the value of all the stock in such corporation.

(3) Attribution to partnerships, estates, trusts, and corporations.—

(A) To partnerships and estates.—Stock owned, directly or indirectly, by or for a partner or a beneficiary of an estate shall be considered as owned by the partnership or estate.

(B) To trusts.—

(i) Stock owned, directly or indirectly, by or for a beneficiary of a trust (other than an employees' trust described in section 401(a) which is exempt from tax under section 501(a)) shall be considered as owned by the trust, unless such beneficiary's interest in the trust is a remote contingent interest. For purposes of this clause, a contingent interest of a beneficiary in a trust shall be considered remote if, under the maximum exercise of discretion by the trustee in favor of such beneficiary, the value of such interest, computed actuarially, is 5 percent or less of the value of the trust property.

(ii) Stock owned, directly or indirectly, by or for a person who is considered the owner of any portion of a trust under subpart E of part I of subchapter J (relating to grantors and others treated as substantial owners) shall be considered as owned by the trust.

(C) To corporations.—If 50 percent or more in value of the stock in a corporation is owned, directly or indirectly, by or for any person, such corporation shall be considered as owning the stock owned, directly or indirectly, by or for such person.

(4) Options.—If any person has an option to acquire stock, such stock shall be considered as owned by such person. For purposes of this paragraph, an option to acquire such an option, and each one of a series of such options, shall be considered as an option to acquire such stock.

(5) Operating rules.—

(A) In general.—Except as provided in subparagraphs (B) and (C), stock constructively owned by a person by reason of the application of paragraph (1), (2), (3), or (4), shall, for purposes of applying paragraphs (1), (2), (3), and (4), be considered as actually owned by such person.

(B) Members of family.—Stock constructively owned by an individual by reason of the application of paragraph (1) shall not be considered as owned by him for purposes of again applying paragraph (1) in order to make another the constructive owner of such stock.

(C) Partnerships, estates, trusts, and corporations.—Stock constructively owned by a partnership, estate, trust, or corporation by reason of the application of paragraph (3) shall not be considered as owned by it for purposes of applying paragraph (2) in order to make another the constructive owner of such stock.

(D) Option rule in lieu of family rule.—For purposes of this paragraph, if stock may be considered as owned by an individual under paragraph (1) or (4), it shall be considered as owned by him under paragraph (4).

(E) S corporation treated as partnership.—For purposes of this subsection—

(i) an S corporation shall be treated as a partnership, and

(ii) any shareholder of the S corporation shall be treated as a partner of such partnership.

The preceding sentence shall not apply for purposes of determining whether stock in the S corporation is constructively owned by any person.

Amendments

- **1984, Deficit Reduction Act of 1984 (P.L. 98-369)**

P.L. 98-369, §721(j):

Added Code Sec. 318(a)(5)(E). **Effective** as if included in the provision of P.L. 97-354 to which it relates.

- **1964 (P.L. 88-554)**

P.L. 88-554, §5(a):

Amended Code Sec. 318(a)(2), (3), and (4), and added Code Sec. 318(a)(5). **Effective** 8-31-64. Prior to amendment, subsections (a)(2), (3), and (4) read as follows:

(2) Partnerships, estates, trusts, and corporations.—

(A) Partnerships and estates.—Stock owned, directly or indirectly, by or for a partnership or estate shall be considered as being owned proportionately by its partners or beneficiaries. Stock owned, directly or indirectly, by or for a partner or a beneficiary of an estate shall be considered as being owned by the partnership or estate.

(B) Trusts.—Stock owned, directly or indirectly, by or for a trust shall be considered as being owned by its beneficiaries in proportion to the actuarial interest of such beneficiaries in such trust. Stock owned, directly or indirectly, by or for a beneficiary of a trust shall be considered as being owned by the trust, unless such beneficiary's interest in the trust is a remote contingent interest. For purposes of the preceding sentence, a contingent interest of a beneficiary in a trust shall be considered remote if, under the maximum exercise of discretion by the trustee in favor of such beneficiary, the value of such interest, computed actuarially, is 5 percent or less of the value of the trust property. Stock owned, directly or indirectly, by or for any portion of a trust of which a person is considered the owner under subpart E of part I of subchapter J (relating to grantors and others treated as substantial owners) shall be considered as being owned by such person; and such trust shall be treated as owning the stock owned, directly or indirectly, by or for such person. This subparagraph shall not apply with respect to any employees' trust described in section 401(a) which is exempt from tax under section 501(a).

(C) Corporations.—If 50 percent or more in value of the stock in a corporation is owned, directly or indirectly, by or for any person, then—

(i) such person shall be considered as owning the stock owned, directly or indirectly, by or for that corporation, in that proportion which the value of the stock which such person so owns bears to the value of all the stock in such corporation; and

(ii) such corporation shall be considered as owning the stock owned, directly or indirectly, by or for that person.

(3) Options.—If any person has an option to acquire stock, such stock shall be considered as owned by such person. For purposes of this paragraph, an option to acquire such an option, and each one of a series of such options, shall be considered as an option to acquire such stock.

(4) Constructive ownership as actual ownership.—

(A) In general.—Except as provided in subparagraph (B), stock constructively owned by a person by reason of the application of paragraph (1), (2), or (3) shall, for purposes of applying paragraph (1), (2), or (3), be treated as actually owned by such person.

(B) Members of family.—Stock constructively owned by an individual by reason of the application of paragraph (1) shall not be treated as owned by him for purposes of again applying paragraph (1) in order to make another the constructive owner of such stock.

(C) Option rule in lieu of family rule.—For purposes of this paragraph, if stock may be considered as owned by an individual under paragraph (1) or (3), it shall be considered as owned by him under paragraph (3).

[Sec. 318(b)]

(b) CROSS REFERENCES.—

For provisions to which the rules contained in subsection (a) apply, see—

(1) section 302 (relating to redemption of stock);

(2) section 304 (relating to redemption by related corporations);

(3) section 306(b)(1)(A) (relating to disposition of section 306 stock);

(4) section 338(h)(3) (defining purchase);

(5) section 382(l)(3) (relating to special limitations on net operating loss carryovers);

(6) section 856(d) (relating to definition of rents from real property in the case of real estate investment trusts);

(7) section 958(b) (relating to constructive ownership rules with respect to controlled foreign corporations); and

(8) section 6038(e)(2) (relating to information with respect to certain foreign corporations).

Amendments

• **2005, Gulf Opportunity Zone Act of 2005 (P.L. 109-135)**

P.L. 109-135, §412(u):

Amended Code Sec. 318(b)(8) by striking "section 6038(d)(2)" and inserting "section 6038(e)(2)". **Effective** 12-21-2005.

• **1997, Taxpayer Relief Act of 1997 (P.L. 105-34)**

P.L. 105-34, §1142(e)(3):

Amended Code Sec. 318(b)(8) by striking "6038(d)(1)" and inserting "6038(d)(2)". **Effective** for annual accounting periods beginning after 8-5-97.

• **1986, Tax Reform Act of 1986 (P.L. 99-514)**

P.L. 99-514, §621(c)(1):

Amended Code Sec. 318(b)(5) by striking out "section 382(a)(3)" and inserting in lieu thereof "section 382(l)(3)". For the **effective** date, see Act Sec. 621(f)(1), below. For special rules, see Act Sec. 621(f)(2)-(9) following Code Sec. 368.

P.L. 99-514, §621(f)(1), provides:

(1) IN GENERAL.—The amendments made by subsections (a), (b), and (c) shall apply to any ownership change following—

(A) an owner shift involving a 5-percent shareholder occurring after December 31, 1986, or

(B) an equity structure shift occurring pursuant to a plan of reorganization adopted after December 31, 1986.

• **1984, Deficit Reduction Act of 1984 (P.L. 98-369)**

P.L. 98-369, §712(k)(5)(E):

Amended Code Sec. 318(b)(4). **Effective** as if included in the provision of P.L. 97-248 to which it relates. Prior to amendment Code Sec. 318(b)(4) read as follows:

(4) section 338(h)(3)(B) (relating to purchase of stock from subsidiaries, etc.);

• **1982, Tax Equity and Fiscal Responsibility Act of 1982 (P.L. 97-248)**

P.L. 97-248, §224(c)(3):

Amended Code Sec. 318(b)(4). **Effective** for any target corporation (with the meaning of Code Sec. 338) with respect to which the acquisition date (within the meaning of such section) occurs after 8-31-82. See, however, P.L. 97-248, §224(a), which appears in the amendment notes for Code Sec. 338, for special rules. Prior to amendment, it read as follows:

(4) section 334(b)(3)(C) (relating to basis of property received in certain liquidations of subsidiaries);

• **1964 (P.L. 88-554)**

P.L. 88-554, §5(b)(2):

Amended Code Sec. 318(b) by striking out "and" at the end of paragraph (6), by renumbering paragraph (7) as paragraph (8), and by adding new paragraph (7). **Effective** 8-31-64.

• **1962, Revenue Act of 1962 (P.L. 87-834)**

P.L. 87-834, §20:

Amended Code Sec. 318(b) by striking out "and" at the end of paragraph (5), by substituting "; and" for the period at the end of paragraph (6), and by adding at the end thereof a new paragraph (7). **Effective** 10-17-62.

• **1960 (P.L. 86-779)**

P.L. 86-779, §10(h):

Amended Code Sec. 318(b) by striking out "and" at the end of paragraph (4), by striking out the period at the end of paragraph (5) and substituting "; and", and by adding a new paragraph (6). **Effective** 1-1-61.

[Sec. 338]
SEC. 338. CERTAIN STOCK PURCHASES TREATED AS ASSET ACQUISITIONS.
[Sec. 338(a)]

(a) GENERAL RULE.—For purposes of this subtitle, if a purchasing corporation makes an election under this section (or is treated under subsection (e) as having made such an election), then, in the case of any qualified stock purchase, the target corporation—

(1) shall be treated as having sold all of its assets at the close of the acquisition date at fair market value in a single transaction, and

(2) shall be treated as a new corporation which purchased all of the assets referred to in paragraph (1) as of the beginning of the day after the acquisition date.

Amendments

• **1986, Tax Reform Act of 1986 (P.L. 99-514)**

P.L. 99-514, §631(b)(1):

Amended Code Sec. 338(a) by striking out "to which section 337 applies" after "single transaction". **Effective**, generally, for:

(1) any distribution in complete liquidation, and any sale or exchange, made by a corporation after 7-31-86, unless such corporation is completely liquidated before 1-1-87,

(2) any transaction described in section 338 of the Internal Revenue Code of 1986 for which the acquisition date occurs after 12-31-86, and

(3) any distribution (not in complete liquidation) made after 12-31-86. However, for special rules and exceptions, see Act Sec. 633(b)-(f) in the Amendment Notes following Code Sec. 311.

• **1984, Deficit Reduction Act of 1984 (P.L. 98-369)**

P.L. 98-369, §712(k)(1)(A):

Amended Code Sec. 338(a)(1) by inserting "at fair market value" after "the acquisition date". **Effective** as if included in the provision of P.L. 97-248 to which it relates. Special rules appear in Act Sec. 712(k)(9) following Code Sec. 338(h).

[Sec. 338(b)]

(b) BASIS OF ASSETS AFTER DEEMED PURCHASE.—

(1) IN GENERAL.—For purposes of subsection (a), the assets of the target corporation shall be treated as purchased for an amount equal to the sum of—

(A) the grossed-up basis of the purchasing corporation's recently purchased stock, and

(B) the basis of the purchasing corporation's nonrecently purchased stock.

(2) ADJUSTMENT FOR LIABILITIES AND OTHER RELEVANT ITEMS.—The amount described in paragraph (1) shall be adjusted under regulations prescribed by the Secretary for liabilities of the target corporation and other relevant items.

(3) ELECTION TO STEP-UP THE BASIS OF CERTAIN TARGET STOCK.—

(A) IN GENERAL.—Under regulations prescribed by the Secretary, the basis of the purchasing corporation's nonrecently purchased stock shall be the basis amount determined under subparagraph (B) of this paragraph if the purchasing corporation makes an election to recognize gain as if such stock were sold on the acquisition date for an amount equal to the basis amount determined under subparagraph (B).

(B) DETERMINATION OF BASIS AMOUNT.—For purposes of subparagraph (A), the basis amount determined under this subparagraph shall be an amount equal to the grossed-up basis determined under subparagraph (A) of paragraph (1) multiplied by a fraction—

(i) the numerator of which is the percentage of stock (by value) in the target corporation attributable to the purchasing corporation's nonrecently purchased stock, and

(ii) the denominator of which is 100 percent minus the percentage referred to in clause (i).

(4) GROSSED-UP BASIS.—For purposes of paragraph (1), the grossed-up basis shall be an amount equal to the basis of the corporation's recently purchased stock, multiplied by a fraction—

(A) the numerator of which is 100 percent, minus the percentage of stock (by value) in the target corporation attributable to the purchasing corporation's nonrecently purchased stock, and

(B) the denominator of which is the percentage of stock (by value) in the target corporation attributable to the purchasing corporation's recently purchased stock.

(5) ALLOCATION AMONG ASSETS.—The amount determined under paragraphs (1) and (2) shall be allocated among the assets of the target corporation under regulations prescribed by the Secretary.

(6) DEFINITIONS OF RECENTLY PURCHASED STOCK AND NONRECENTLY PURCHASED STOCK.—For purposes of this subsection—

(A) RECENTLY PURCHASED STOCK.—The term "recently purchased stock" means any stock in the target corporation which is held by the purchasing corporation on the acquisition date and which was purchased by such corporation during the 12-month acquisition period.

(B) NONRECENTLY PURCHASED STOCK.—The term "nonrecently purchased stock" means any stock in the target corporation which is held by the purchasing corporation on the acquisition date and which is not recently purchased stock.

Amendments

• **1984, Deficit Reduction Act of 1984 (P.L. 98-369)**

P.L. 98-369, §712(k)(1)(B):

Amended Code Sec. 338(b). **Effective** as if included in the provision of P.L. 97-248 to which it relates. Special rules appear in Act Sec. 712(k)(9) following Code Sec. 338(h). Prior to amendment, Code Sec. 338(b) read as follows:

(b) PRICE AT WHICH DEEMED SALE MADE.—

(1) IN GENERAL.—For purposes of subsection (a), the assets of the target corporation shall be treated as sold (and purchased) at an amount equal to—

(A) the grossed-up basis of the purchasing corporation's stock in the target corporation on the acquisition date, and

(B) properly adjusted under regulations prescribed by the Secretary for liabilities of the target corporation and other relevant items.

(2) GROSSED-UP BASIS.—For purposes of paragraph (1), the grossed-up basis shall be an amount equal to the basis of the purchasing corporation's stock in the target corporation on the acquisition date multiplied by a fraction—

(A) the numerator of which is 100 percent, and

(B) the denominator of which is the percentage of stock (by value) of the target corporation held by the purchasing corporation on the acquisition date.

(3) ALLOCATION AMONG ASSETS.—The amount determined under paragraph (1) shall be allocated among the assets of the target corporation under regulations prescribed by the Secretary.

[Sec. 338(c)—Repealed]

Amendments

• **1986, Tax Reform Act of 1986 (P.L. 99-514)**

P.L. 99-514, §631(b)(2):

Repealed Code Sec. 338(c). **Effective**, generally, for:

(1) any distribution in complete liquidation, and any sale or exchange, made by a corporation after 7-31-86, unless such corporation is completely liquidated before 1-1-87,

(2) any transaction described in section 338 of the Internal Revenue Code of 1986 for which the acquisition date occurs after 12-31-86, and

(3) any distribution (not in complete liquidation) made after 12-31-86. However, for special rules and exceptions, see Act Sec. 633(b)-(f) in the Amendment Notes following Code Sec. 311. Prior to repeal, Code Sec. 338(c) read as follows:

(c) SPECIAL RULES.—

(1) COORDINATION WITH SECTION 337 WHERE PURCHASING CORPORATION HOLDS LESS THAN 100 PERCENT OF STOCK.—If during the 1-year period beginning on the acquisition date the maximum percentage (by value) of stock in the target corporation held by the purchasing corporation is less than 100 percent, then in applying section 337 for purposes of subsection (a)(1), the nonrecognition of gain or loss shall be limited to an amount determined by applying such maximum percentage to such gain or loss. The preceding sentence shall not apply if the target corporation is liquidated during such 1-year period and section 333 does not apply to such liquidation.

(2) CERTAIN REDEMPTIONS WHERE ELECTION MADE.—If, in connection with a qualified stock purchase with respect to which an election is made under this section, the target corporation makes a distribution in complete redemption of all of the stock of a shareholder which qualifies under section 302(b)(3) (determined without regard to the application of section 302(c)(2)(A)(ii)), section 336 shall apply to such distribution as if it were a distribution in complete liquidation.

• **1984, Deficit Reduction Act of 1984 (P.L. 98-369)**

P.L. 98-369, §712(k)(2):

Amended the last sentence of Code Sec. 338(c)(1) by striking out "such 1-year period" and inserting in lieu thereof "such 1-year period and section 333 does not apply to such liquidation". **Effective** as if included in the provision of P.L. 97-248 to which it relates. Special rules appear in Act Sec. 712(k)(9) following Code Sec. 338(h).

[Sec. 338(d)]

(d) PURCHASING CORPORATION; TARGET CORPORATION; QUALIFIED STOCK PURCHASE.—For purposes of this section—

    (1) PURCHASING CORPORATION.—The term "purchasing corporation" means any corporation which makes a qualified stock purchase of stock of another corporation.

    (2) TARGET CORPORATION.—The term "target corporation" means any corporation the stock of which is acquired by another corporation in a qualified stock purchase.

    (3) QUALIFIED STOCK PURCHASE.—The term "qualified stock purchase" means any transaction or series of transactions in which stock (meeting the requirements of section 1504(a)(2)) of 1 corporation is acquired by another corporation by purchase during the 12-month acquisition period.

Amendments

• **1986, Tax Reform Act of 1986 (P.L. 99-514)**
P.L. 99-514, §1804(e)(8)(A):
Amended Code Sec. 338(d)(3). **Effective** in cases where the 12-month acquisition period (as defined in section 338(h)(1) of the Internal Revenue Code of 1954) begins after 12-31-85. Prior to amendment, Code Sec. 338(d)(3) read as follows:

(3) QUALIFIED STOCK PURCHASE.—The term "qualified stock purchase" means any transaction or series of transactions in which stock of 1 corporation possessing—

(A) at least 80 percent of total combined voting power of all classes of stock entitled to vote, and

(B) at least 80 percent of the total number of shares of all other classes of stock (except nonvoting stock which is limited and preferred as to dividends),

is acquired by another corporation by purchase during the 12-month acquisition period.

[Sec. 338(e)]

(e) DEEMED ELECTION WHERE PURCHASING CORPORATION ACQUIRES ASSET OF TARGET CORPORATION.—

    (1) IN GENERAL.—A purchasing corporation shall be treated as having made an election under this section with respect to any target corporation if, at any time during the consistency period, it acquires any asset of the target corporation (or a target affiliate).

    (2) EXCEPTIONS.—Paragraph (1) shall not apply with respect to any acquisition by the purchasing corporation if—

        (A) such acquisition is pursuant to a sale by the target corporation (or the target affiliate) in the ordinary course of its trade or business,

        (B) the basis of the property acquired is determined (wholly) by reference to the adjusted basis of such property in the hands of the person from whom acquired,

        (C) such acquisition was before September 1, 1982, or

        (D) such acquisition is described in regulations prescribed by the Secretary and meets such conditions as such regulations may provide.

    (3) ANTI-AVOIDANCE RULE.—Whenever necessary to carry out the purpose of this subsection and subsection (f), the Secretary may treat stock acquisitions which are pursuant to a plan and which meet the requirements of section 1504(a)(2) as qualified stock purchases.

Amendments

• **1988, Technical and Miscellaneous Revenue Act of 1988 (P.L. 100-647)**
P.L. 100-647, §1018(d)(9):
Amended Code Sec. 338(e)(3) by striking out "which meet the 80 percent requirements of subparagraphs (A) and (B) of subsection (d)(3)" and inserting in lieu thereof "which meet the requirements of section 1504(a)(2)". **Effective** as if included in the provision of P.L. 99-514 to which it relates.

• **1984, Deficit Reduction Act of 1984 (P.L. 98-369)**
P.L. 98-369, §712(k)(3):
Amended Code Sec. 338(e)(2) by striking out "(in whole or in part)" in subparagraph (B) and inserting in lieu thereof

"(wholly)", by inserting "or" at the end of subparagraph (C) and by striking out subparagraphs (D) and (E) and inserting in lieu thereof subparagraph (D) above. **Effective** as if included in the provision of P.L. 97-248 to which it relates. Special rules appear in Act Sec. 712(k)(9) following Code Sec. 338(h). Prior to amendment, subparagraph (D) and (E) read as follows:

(D) to the extent provided in regulations, the property acquired is located outside the United States, or

(E) such acquisition is described in regulations prescribed by the Secretary.

[Sec. 338(f)]

(f) CONSISTENCY REQUIRED FOR ALL STOCK ACQUISITIONS FROM SAME AFFILIATED GROUP.—If a purchasing corporation makes qualified stock purchases with respect to the target corporation and 1 or more target affiliates during any consistency period, then (except as otherwise provided in subsection (e))—

    (1) any election under this section with respect to the first such purchase shall apply to each other such purchase, and

    (2) no election may be made under this section with respect to the second or subsequent such purchase if such an election was not made with respect to the first such purchase.

[Sec. 338(g)]

(g) ELECTION.—

    (1) WHEN MADE.—Except as otherwise provided in regulations, an election under this section shall be made not later than the 15th day of the 9th month, beginning after the month in which the acquisition date occurs.

    (2) MANNER.—An election by the purchasing corporation under this section shall be made in such manner as the Secretary shall by regulations prescribe.

    (3) ELECTION IRREVOCABLE.—An election by a purchasing corporation under this section, once made, shall be irrevocable.

Amendments

- **1984, Deficit Reduction Act of 1984 (P.L. 98-369)**

P.L. 98-369, §712(k)(4):

Amended Code Sec. 338(g)(1). **Effective** as if included in the provision of P.L. 97-248 to which it relates. Special rules appear in Act Sec. 712(k)(9) following Code Sec. 338(h). Prior to amendment, Code Sec. 338(g)(1) read as follows:

(1) When Made.—Except as otherwise provided in regulations, an election under this section shall be made not later than 75 days after the acquisition date.

[Sec. 338(h)]

(h) DEFINITIONS AND SPECIAL RULES.—For purposes of this section—

(1) 12-MONTH ACQUISITION PERIOD.—The term "12-month acquisition period" means the 12-month period beginning with the date of the first acquisition by purchase of stock included in a qualified stock purchase (or, if any of such stock was acquired in an acquisition which is a purchase by reason of subparagraph (C) of paragraph (3), the date on which the acquiring corporation is first considered under section 318(a) (other than paragraph (4) thereof) as owning stock owned by the corporation from which such acquisition was made).

(2) ACQUISITION DATE.—The term "acquisition date" means, with respect to any corporation, the first day on which there is a qualified stock purchase with respect to the stock of such corporation.

(3) PURCHASE.—

(A) IN GENERAL.—The term "purchase" means any acquisition of stock, but only if—

(i) the basis of the stock in the hands of the purchasing corporation is not determined (I) in whole or in part by reference to the adjusted basis of such stock in the hands of the person from whom acquired, or (II) under section 1014(a) (relating to property acquired from a decedent),

(ii) the stock is not acquired in an exchange to which section 351, 354, 355, or 356 applies and is not acquired in any other transaction described in regulations in which the transferor does not recognize the entire amount of the gain or loss realized on the transaction, and

(iii) the stock is not acquired from a person the ownership of whose stock would, under section 318(a) (other than paragraph (4) thereof), be attributed to the person acquiring such stock.

(B) DEEMED PURCHASE UNDER SUBSECTION (a).—The term "purchase" includes any deemed purchase under subsection (a)(2). The acquisition date for a corporation which is deemed purchased under subsection (a)(2) shall be determined under regulations prescribed by the Secretary.

(C) CERTAIN STOCK ACQUISITIONS FROM RELATED CORPORATIONS.—

(i) IN GENERAL.—Clause (iii) of subparagraph (A) shall not apply to an acquisition of stock from a related corporation if at least 50 percent in value of the stock of such related corporation was acquired by purchase (within the meaning of subparagraphs (A) and (B)).

(ii) CERTAIN DISTRIBUTIONS.—Clause (i) of subparagraph (A) shall not apply to an acquisition of stock described in clause (i) of this subparagraph if the corporation acquiring such stock—

(I) made a qualified stock purchase of stock of the related corporation, and

(II) made an election under this section (or is treated under subsection (e) as having made such an election) with respect to such qualified stock purchase.

(iii) RELATED CORPORATION DEFINED.—For purposes of this subparagraph, a corporation is a related corporation if stock owned by such corporation is treated (under section 318(a) other than paragraph (4) thereof) as owned by the corporation acquiring the stock.

(4) CONSISTENCY PERIOD.—

(A) IN GENERAL.—Except as provided in subparagraph (B), the term "consistency period" means the period consisting of—

(i) the 1-year period before the beginning of the 12-month acquisition period for the target corporation,

(ii) such acquisition period (up to and including the acquisition date), and

(iii) the 1-year period beginning on the day after the acquisition date.

(B) EXTENSION WHERE THERE IS PLAN.—The period referred to in subparagraph (A) shall also include any period during which the Secretary determines that there was in effect a plan to make a qualified stock purchase plus 1 or more other qualified stock purchases (or asset acquisitions described in subsection (e)) with respect to the target corporation or any target affiliate.

(5) AFFILIATED GROUP.—The term "affiliated group" has the meaning given to such term by section 1504(a) (determined without regard to the exceptions contained in section 1504(b)).

(6) TARGET AFFILIATE.—

(A) IN GENERAL.—A corporation shall be treated as a target affiliate of the target corporation if each of such corporations was, at any time during so much of the consistency period as ends on the acquisition date of the target corporation, a member of an affiliated group which had the same common parent.

(B) CERTAIN FOREIGN CORPORATIONS, ETC.—Except as otherwise provided in regulations (and subject to such conditions as may be provided in regulations)—

(i) the term "target affiliate" does not include a foreign corporation or a DISC, and

(ii) stock held by a target affiliate in a foreign corporation or a domestic corporation which is a DISC or described in section 1248(e) shall be excluded from the operation of this section.

(7) [Repealed.]

(8) ACQUISITIONS BY AFFILIATED GROUP TREATED AS MADE BY 1 CORPORATION.—Except as provided in regulations prescribed by the Secretary, stock and asset acquisitions made by members of the same affiliated group shall be treated as made by 1 corporation.

(9) TARGET NOT TREATED AS MEMBER OF AFFILIATED GROUP.—Except as otherwise provided in paragraph (10) or in regulations prescribed under this paragraph, the target corporation shall not be treated as a member of an affiliated group with respect to the sale described in subsection (a)(1).

(10) ELECTIVE RECOGNITION OF GAIN OR LOSS BY TARGET CORPORATION, TOGETHER WITH NONRECOGNITION OF GAIN OR LOSS ON STOCK SOLD BY SELLING CONSOLIDATED GROUP.—

(A) IN GENERAL.—Under regulations prescribed by the Secretary, an election may be made under which if—

(i) the target corporation was, before the transaction, a member of the selling consolidated group, and

(ii) the target corporation recognizes gain or loss with respect to the transaction as if it sold all of its assets in a single transaction,

then the target corporation shall be treated as a member of the selling consolidated group with respect to such sale, and (to the extent provided in regulations) no gain or loss will be recognized on stock sold or exchanged in the transaction by members of the selling consolidated group.

(B) SELLING CONSOLIDATED GROUP.—For purposes of subparagraph (A), the term "selling consolidated group" means any group of corporations which (for the taxable period which includes the transaction)—

(i) includes the target corporation, and

(ii) files a consolidated return.

To the extent provided in regulations, such term also includes any affiliated group of corporations which includes the target corporation (whether or not such group files a consolidated return).

(C) INFORMATION REQUIRED TO BE FURNISHED TO THE SECRETARY.—Under regulations, where an election is made under subparagraph (A), the purchasing corporation and the common parent of the selling consolidated group shall, at such times and in such manner as may be provided in regulations, furnish to the Secretary the following information:

(i) The amount allocated under subsection (b)(5) to goodwill or going concern value.

(ii) Any modification of the amount described in clause (i).

(iii) Any other information as the Secretary deems necessary to carry out the provisions of this paragraph.

(11) ELECTIVE FORMULA FOR DETERMINING FAIR MARKET VALUE.—For purposes of subsection (a)(1), fair market value may be determined on the basis of a formula provided in regulations prescribed by the Secretary which takes into account liabilities and other relevant items.

(12) [Repealed.]

(13) TAX ON DEEMED SALE NOT TAKEN INTO ACCOUNT FOR ESTIMATED TAX PURPOSES.—For purposes of section 6655, tax attributable to the sale described in subsection (a)(1) shall not be taken into account. The preceding sentence shall not apply with respect to a qualified stock purchase for which an election is made under paragraph (10).

(14) [Stricken.]

(15) COMBINED DEEMED SALE RETURN.—Under regulations prescribed by the Secretary, a combined deemed sale return may be filed by all target corporations acquired by a purchasing corporation on the same acquisition date if such target corporations were members of the same selling consolidated group (as defined in subparagraph (B) of paragraph (10)).

(16) COORDINATION WITH FOREIGN TAX CREDIT PROVISIONS.—Except as provided in regulations, this section shall not apply for purposes of determining the source or character of any item for purposes of subpart A of part III of subchapter N of this chapter (relating to foreign tax credit). The preceding sentence shall not apply to any gain to the extent such gain is includible in gross income as a dividend under section 1248 (determined without regard to any deemed sale under this section by a foreign corporation).

Amendments

- **2018, Tax Technical Corrections Act of 2018 (P.L. 115-141)**

P.L. 115-141, § 401(a)(64), Div. U:

Amended Code Sec. 338(h)(3)(A)(iii) by striking "paragraph" and inserting "paragraph". **Effective** 3-23-2018.

P.L. 115-141, § 401(d)(1)(D)(vii), Div. U:

Amended Code Sec. 338(h)(6)(B)(i) by striking ", a DISC, or a corporation to which an election under section 936 applies" and inserting "or a DISC". **Effective** 3-23-2018. For a special rule, see Act Sec. 401(e), Div. U, below.

P.L. 115-141, §401(e), Div. U, provides:
(e) GENERAL SAVINGS PROVISION WITH RESPECT TO DEADWOOD PROVISIONS.—If—
(1) any provision amended or repealed by the amendments made by subsection (b) or (d) applied to—
(A) any transaction occurring before the date of the enactment of this Act,
(B) any property acquired before such date of enactment, or
(C) any item of income, loss, deduction, or credit taken into account before such date of enactment, and
(2) the treatment of such transaction, property, or item under such provision would (without regard to the amendments or repeals made by such subsection) affect the liability for tax for periods ending after such date of enactment, nothing in the amendments or repeals made by this section shall be construed to affect the treatment of such transaction, property, or item for purposes of determining liability for tax for periods ending after such date of enactment.

- **2013, American Taxpayer Relief Act of 2012 (P.L. 112-240)**

P.L. 112-240, §102(a), provides:
SEC. 102. PERMANENT EXTENSION AND MODIFICATION OF 2003 TAX RELIEF.
(a) PERMANENT EXTENSION.—The Jobs and Growth Tax Relief Reconciliation Act of 2003 is amended by striking section 303.

- **2004, American Jobs Creation Act of 2004 (P.L. 108-357)**

P.L. 108-357, §839(a):
Amended Code Sec. 338(h)(13) by adding at the end a new sentence. **Effective** for transactions occurring after 10-22-2004.

- **2003, Jobs and Growth Tax Relief Reconciliation Act of 2003 (P.L. 108-27)**

P.L. 108-27, §302(e)(4)(B)(i):
Amended Code Sec. 338(h) by striking paragraph (14). For the **effective** date, see Act Sec. 302(f), as amended by P.L. 108-311, §402(a)(6), below. Prior to being stricken, Code Sec. 338(h)(14) read as follows:
(14) COORDINATION WITH SECTION 341.—For purposes of determining whether section 341 applies to a disposition within 1 year after the acquisition date of stock by a shareholder (other than the acquiring corporation) who held stock in the target corporation on the acquisition date, section 341 shall be applied without regard to this section.

P.L. 108-27, §302(f), as amended by P.L. 108-311, §402(a)(6), provides:
(f) EFFECTIVE DATE.—
(1) IN GENERAL.—Except as provided in paragraph (2), the amendments made by this section shall apply to taxable years beginning after December 31, 2002.
(2) PASS-THRU ENTITIES.—In the case of a pass-thru entity described in subparagraph (A), (B), (C), (D), (E), or (F) of section 1(h)(10) of the Internal Revenue Code of 1986, as amended by this Act, the amendments made by this section shall apply to taxable years ending after December 31, 2002; except that dividends received by such an entity on or before such date shall not be treated as qualified dividend income (as defined in section 1(h)(11)(B) of such Code, as added by this Act).

P.L. 108-27, §303, as amended by P.L. 109-222, §102, and P.L. 111-312, §102(a), provides [but see P.L. 112-240, §102(a), above]:
SEC. 303. SUNSET OF TITLE.
All provisions of, and amendments made by, this title shall not apply to taxable years beginning after December 31, 2012, and the Internal Revenue Code of 1986 shall be applied and administered to such years as if such provisions and amendments had never been enacted.

- **1990, Omnibus Budget Reconciliation Act of 1990 (P.L. 101-508)**

P.L. 101-508, §11323(c)(1):
Amended Code Sec. 338(h)(10) by adding at the end thereof a new subparagraph (C). **Effective**, generally, for acquisitions after 10-9-90. For an exception, see Act Sec. 11323(d)(2), below.

P.L. 101-508, §11323(d)(2), provides:
(2) BINDING CONTRACT EXCEPTION.—The amendments made by this section shall not apply to any acquisition pursuant to a written binding contract in effect on October 9, 1990, and at all times thereafter before such acquisition.

- **1988, Technical and Miscellaneous Revenue Act of 1988 (P.L. 100-647)**

P.L. 100-647, §1006(e)(20):
Repealed Code Sec. 338(h)(7). **Effective** as if included in the provision of P.L. 99-514 to which it relates. Prior to repeal, Code Sec. 338(h)(7) read as follows:
(7) ADDITIONAL PERCENTAGE MUST BE ATTRIBUTABLE TO PURCHASE, ETC.—For purposes of subsection (c)(1), any increase in the maximum percentage of stock taken into account over the percentage of stock (by value) of the target corporation held by the purchasing corporation on the acquisition date shall be taken into account only to the extent such increase is attributable to—
(A) purchase, or
(B) a redemption of stock of the target corporation—
(i) to which section 302(a) applies, or
(ii) in the case of a shareholder who is not a corporation, to which section 301 applies.

P.L. 100-647, §1012(bb)(5)(A):
Amended Code Sec. 338(h) by adding at the end thereof a new paragraph (16). **Effective** for qualified stock purchases (as defined in section 338(d)(3) of the 1986 Code) after 3-31-88, except that, in the case of an election under section 338(h)(10) of the 1986 Code, such amendment shall apply to qualified stock purchases (as so defined) after 6-10-87.

- **1986, Tax Reform Act of 1986 (P.L. 99-514)**

P.L. 99-514, §631(b)(3):
Amended Code Sec. 338(h)(10)(B) by adding to the end thereof a new sentence. **Effective**, generally, for:
(1) any distribution in complete liquidation, and any sale or exchange, made by a corporation after 7-31-86, unless such corporation is completely liquidated before 1-1-87,
(2) any transaction described in section 338 of the Internal Revenue Code of 1986 for which the acquisition date occurs after 12-31-86, and
(3) any distribution (not in complete liquidation) made after 12-31-86. However, for special rules and exceptions, see Act Sec. 633(b)-(f) in the Amendment Notes following Code Sec. 311.

P.L. 99-514, §631(e)(5):
Repealed Code Sec. 338(h)(12). **Effective**, generally, for:
(1) any distribution in complete liquidation, and any sale or exchange, made by a corporation after 7-31-86, unless such corporation is completely liquidated before 1-1-87,
(2) any transaction described in section 338 of the Internal Revenue Code of 1986 for which the acquisition date occurs after 12-31-86, and
(3) any distribution (not in complete liquidation) made after 12-31-86. However, for special rules and exceptions, see Act Sec. 633(b)-(f) in the Amendment Notes following Code Sec. 311. Prior to repeal, Code Sec. 338(h)(12) read as follows:
(12) SECTION 337 TO APPLY WHERE TARGET HAD ADOPTED PLAN FOR COMPLETE LIQUIDATION.—If—
(A) during the 12-month period ending on the acquisition date the target corporation adopted a plan of complete liquidation,
(B) such plan was not rescinded before the close of the acquisition date, and
(C) the purchasing corporation makes an election under this section (or is treated under subsection (e) as having made such an election) with respect to the target corporation, then, subject to rules similar to the rules of subsection (c)(1), for purposes of section 337 (and other provisions which relate to section 337), the target corporation shall be treated as having distributed all of its assets as of the close of the acquisition date.

P.L. 99-514, §1275(c)(6):
Amended Code Sec. 338(h)(6)(B)(i) by striking out "a corporation described in section 934(b)," after "a DISC". **Effective**, generally, for tax years beginning after 12-31-86. For special rules and exceptions see Act Sec. 1277(b)-(c) in the Amendment Notes following Code Sec. 48.

P.L. 99-514, §1899A(7):
Amended Code Sec. 338(h)(3)(C)(i) by striking out "subparagraph (A) and (B)" and inserting in lieu thereof "subparagraphs (A) and (B)". **Effective** 10-22-86.

- **1984, Deficit Reduction Act of 1984 (P.L. 98-369)**

P.L. 98-369, §712(k)(5)(A):
Amended Code Sec. 338(h)(3)(B). **Effective** as if included in the provision of P.L. 97-248 to which it relates. A special rule appears below. Prior to amendment, Code Sec. 338(h)(3)(B) read as follows:

(B) Deemed Purchase of Stock of Subsidiaries.—If stock in a corporation is acquired by purchase (within the meaning of subparagraph (A)) and, as a result of such acquisition, the corporation making such purchase is treated (by reason of section 318(a)) as owning stock in a 3rd corporation, the corporation making such purchase shall be treated as having purchased such stock in such 3rd corporation. The corporation making such purchase shall be treated as purchasing stock in the 3rd corporation by reason of the preceding sentence on the first day on which the purchasing corporation is considered under section 318(a) as owning such stock.

P.L. 98-369, §712(k)(5)(B):
Amended Code Sec. 338(h)(3)(C). **Effective** as if included in the provision of P.L. 97-248 to which it relates. A special rule appears below.

P.L. 98-369, §712(k)(5)(C):
Amended Code Sec. 338(h)(1) by inserting before the period at the end thereof the following: "(or, if any of such stock was acquired in an acquisition which is a purchase by reason of subparagraph (C) of paragraph (3), the date on which the acquiring corporation is first considered under section 318(a) (other than paragraph (4) thereof) as owning stock owned by the corporation from which such acquisition was made)". **Effective** as if included in the provision of P.L. 97-248 to which it relates. A special rule appears below.

P.L. 98-369, §712(k)(5)(D):
Amended Code Sec. 338(h)(3)(A)(ii). **Effective** as if included in the provision of P.L. 97-248 to which it relates. A special rule appears below. Prior to amendment, it read as follows:

(ii) the stock is not acquired in an exchange to which section 351 applies, and

P.L. 98-369, §712(k)(6)(A):
Amended Code Sec. 338(h) by striking out paragraph (7), by redesignating paragraphs (8) and (9) as paragraphs (9) and (10), respectively, and by inserting after paragraph (6) new paragraphs (7) and (8). **Effective** as if included in the provision of P.L. 97-248 to which it relates. A special rule appears below. Prior to its deletion, paragraph (7) read as follows:

(7) Acquisitions by Purchasing Corporation Include Acquisitions by Corporations Affiliated with Purchasing Corporation.—Except as otherwise provided in regulations, an acquisition of stock or assets by any member of an affiliated group which includes a purchasing corporation shall be treated as made by the purchasing corporation.

P.L. 98-369, §712(k)(6)(B):
Amended Code Sec. 338(h)(9), as redesignated by Act Sec. 712(k)(6)(A), by striking out "paragraph (9)" and inserting in lieu thereof "paragraph (10)". **Effective** as if included in the provision of P.L. 97-248 to which it relates. A special rule appears below.

P.L. 98-369, §712(k)(6)(C):
Added Code Secs. 338(h)(11)—(15). **Effective** as if included in the provision of P.L. 97-248 to which it relates. A special rule appears below.

P.L. 98-369, §712(k)(9)-(10), provides:
(9) Amendments Not to Apply to Acquisitions before September 1, 1982.—

(A) In General.—The amendments made by this subsection shall not apply to any qualified stock purchase (as defined in section 338(d)(3) of the Internal Revenue Code of 1954) where the acquisition date (as defined in section 338(h)(2) of such Code) is before September 1, 1982.

(B) Extension of Time for Making Election.—In the case of any qualified stock purchase described in subparagraph (A), the time for making an election under section 338 of such Code shall not expire before the close of the 60th day after the date of the enactment of this Act.

(10) Special Rules for Deemed Purchases Under Prior Law.—If, before October 20, 1984, a corporation was treated as making a qualified stock purchase (as defined in section 338(d)(3) of the Internal Revenue Code of 1954), but would not be so treated under the amendments made by paragraphs (5) and (6) of this subsection, the amendments made by such paragraphs shall not apply to such purchase unless such corporation elects (at such time and in such manner as the Secretary of the Treasury or his delegate may by regulations prescribe) to have the amendments made by such paragraphs apply.

- **1983, Technical Corrections Act of 1982 (P.L. 97-448)**

P.L. 97-448, §306(a)(8)(B)(i):
Added Code Sec. 338(h)(8) and (9). **Effective** as if included in the provision of P.L. 97-248 to which it relates.

P.L. 97-448, §306(a)(8)(A)(ii), as amended by P.L. 98-369, §722(a)(3), provides:
(ii) If—

(I) any portion of a qualified stock purchase is pursuant to a binding contract entered into on or after September 1, 1982, and on or before the date of the enactment of this Act, and

(II) the purchasing corporation establishes by clear and convincing evidence that such contract was negotiated on the contemplation that, with respect to the deemed sale under section 338 of the Internal Revenue Code of 1954, the target corporation would be treated as a member of the affiliated group which includes the selling corporation,

then the amendment made by clause (i) shall not apply to such qualified stock purchase.

- **1982, Tax Equity and Fiscal Responsibility Act of 1982 (P.L. 97-248)**

P.L. 97-248, §222(e)(4):
Repealed Code Sec. 338 as in effect on 9-2-82. Prior to amendment, this section read as follows:

SEC. 338. EFFECT ON EARNINGS AND PROFITS.
For special rule relating to the effect on earnings and profits of certain distributions in partial liquidation, see section 312(e).

Applicable to distributions after August 31, 1982. See exceptions under P.L. 97-248, Act Sec. 222(f), following Code Sec. 331(b) for special rules.

P.L. 97-248, §224(a):
Amended Subchapter [part] B of Part II of Subchapter C of Chapter I by adding Code Sec. 338. **Effective** for any target corporation with respect to which the acquisition date occurs after 8-31-82.

P.L. 97-248, §224(d), as amended by P.L. 97-448, §306(a)(8)(B)(i) and (ii), provides:
As to certain acquisitions before September 1, 1982, if

(1) an acquisition date (within the meaning of section 338 of such Code without regard to paragraph (5) of this subsection) occurred after August 31, 1980, and before September 1, 1982,

(2) the target corporation (within the meaning of section 338 of such Code) is not liquidated before September 1, 1982, and

(3) the purchasing corporation (within the meaning of Code Sec. 338) makes, not later than November 15, 1982, an election under Code Sec. 338,

then the amendments made by this section shall apply to the acquisition of such target corporation.

In any case in which—

(1) there is, on July 22, 1982, a binding contract to acquire control (within the meaning of Code Sec. 368(c)) of any financial institution,

(2) the approval of one or more regulatory authorities is required in order to complete such acquisition, and

(3) within 90 days after the date of the final approval of the last such regulatory authority granting final approval, a plan of complete liquidation of such financial institution is adopted,

then the purchasing corporation may elect not to have the amendments made by this section apply to the acquisition pursuant to such contract.

(4) Extension of time for making elections; revocation of elections.—

(A) Extension.—The time for making an election under section 338 of such Code shall not expire before the close of February 28, 1983.

(B) Revocation.—Any election made under section 338 of such Code may be revoked by the purchasing corporation if revoked before March 1, 1983.

(5) Rules for acquisitions described in paragraph (2).—

(A) In general.—For purposes of applying section 338 of such Code with respect to any acquisition described in paragraph (2)—

(i) the date selected under subparagraph (B) of this paragraph shall be treated as the acquisition date,

Code Sec. 338

(ii) a rule similar to the last sentence of section 334(b)(2) of such Code (as in effect on August 31, 1982) shall apply, and

(iii) subsections (e), (f), and (i) of such section 338, and paragraphs (4), (6), (8), and (9) of subsection (h) of such section 338, shall not apply.

(B) Selection of acquisition date by purchasing corporation.—The purchasing corporation may select any date for purposes of subparagraph (A)(i) if such date—

(i) is after the later of June 30, 1982, or the acquisition date (within the meaning of section 338 of such Code without regard to this paragraph), and

(ii) is on or before the date on which the election described in paragraph (2)(C) is made.

For additional rules, see amendment notes for P.L. 97-248, Act Sec. 222(f) under Code Sec. 331(b).

[Sec. 338(i)]

(i) REGULATIONS.—The Secretary shall prescribe such regulations as may be necessary or appropriate to carry out the purposes of this section, including—

(1) regulations to ensure that the purpose of this section to require consistency of treatment of stock and asset sales and purchases may not be circumvented through the use of any provision of law or regulations (including the consolidated return regulations) and

(2) regulations providing for the coordination of the provisions of this section with the provision of this title relating to foreign corporations and their shareholders.

Amendments

• 1984, Deficit Reduction Act of 1984 (P.L. 98-369)

P.L. 98-369, §712(k)(7):

Amended Code Sec. 338(i). **Effective** as if included in the provision of P.L. 97-248 to which it relates. Special rules appear in Act Sec. 712(k)(9) following Code Sec. 338(h). Prior to amendment, it read as follows:

(i) Regulations.—The Secretary shall precribe such regulations as may be necessary to ensure that the purposes of this section to require consistency of treatment of stock and asset purchases with respect to a target corporation and its target affiliates (whether by treating all of them as stock purchases or as asset purchases) may not be circumvented through the use of any provision of law or regulations (including the consolidated return regulations).

[Sec. 351]
SEC. 351. TRANSFER TO CORPORATION CONTROLLED BY TRANSFEROR.

[Sec. 351(a)]

(a) GENERAL RULE.—No gain or loss shall be recognized if property is transferred to a corporation by one or more persons solely in exchange for stock in such corporation and immediately after the exchange such person or persons are in control (as defined in section 368(c)) of the corporation.

Amendments

• 1989, Omnibus Budget Reconciliation Act of 1989 (P.L. 101-239)

P.L. 101-239, §7203(a):

Amended Code Sec. 351(a) by striking "or securities" after "for stock". **Effective**, generally, for transfers after 10-2-89, in tax years ending after such date. For exceptions, see Act Sec. 7203(c)(2)-(3), below.

P.L. 101-239, §7203(c)(2)-(3), provides:

(2) BINDING CONTRACT.—The amendments made by this section shall not apply to any transfer pursuant to a written

binding contract in effect on October 2, 1989, and at all times thereafter before such transfer.

(3) CORPORATE TRANSFERS.—In the case of property transferred (directly or indirectly through a partnership or otherwise) by a C corporation, paragraphs (1) and (2) shall be applied by substituting "July 11, 1989" for "October 2, 1989". The preceding sentence shall not apply where the corporation meets the requirements of section 1504(a)(2) of the Internal Revenue Code of 1986 with respect to the transferee corporation (and where the transfer is not part of a plan pursuant to which the transferor subsequently fails to meet such requirements).

- **1980, Bankruptcy Tax Act of 1980 (P.L. 96-589)**

P.L. 96-589, §5(e)(2).

Amended Code Sec. 351(a) by striking out the last sentence. For the **effective** date, see the historical comment for P.L. 96-589 under Code Sec. 370(a). Prior to amendment, the last sentence of Code Sec. 351(a) provided:

"For purposes of this section, stock or securities issued for services shall not be considered as issued in return for property."

- **1976, Tax Reform Act of 1976 (P.L. 94-455)**

P.L. 94-455, §1901(a)(48)(A):

Struck out "(including, in the case of transfers made on or before June 30, 1967, an investment company" after "transferred to a corporation" in Code Sec. 351(a). **Effective** for transfers of property occurring after 10-4-76.

- **1966, Foreign Investors Tax Act of 1966 (P.L. 89-809)**

P.L. 89-809, §203(a):

Amended the first sentence of Code Sec. 351(a) by inserting "(including, in the case of transfers made on or before June 30, 1967, an investment company)" immediately after "to a corporation". **Effective** with respect to transfers of property to investment companies, whether made before, on, or after 11-13-66, the date of enactment.

[Sec. 351(b)]

(b) RECEIPT OF PROPERTY.—If subsection (a) would apply to an exchange but for the fact that there is received, in addition to the stock permitted to be received under subsection (a), other property or money, then—

(1) gain (if any) to such recipient shall be recognized, but not in excess of—

(A) the amount of money received, plus

(B) the fair market value of such other property received; and

(2) no loss to such recipient shall be recognized.

Amendments

- **1989, Omnibus Budget Reconciliation Act of 1989 (P.L. 101-239)**

P.L. 101-239, §7203(b)(1):

Amended Code Sec. 351(b) by striking "or securities" after "stock". **Effective**, generally, for transfers after 10-2-89,

in tax years ending after such date. For exceptions, see Act Sec. 7203(c)(2)-(3) in the amendment notes following Code Sec. 351(a).

[Sec. 351(c)]

(c) SPECIAL RULES WHERE DISTRIBUTION TO SHAREHOLDERS.—

(1) IN GENERAL.—In determining control for purposes of this section, the fact that any corporate transferor distributes part or all of the stock in the corporation which it receives in the exchange to its shareholders shall not be taken into account.

(2) SPECIAL RULE FOR SECTION 355.—If the requirements of section 355 (or so much of section 356 as relates to section 355) are met with respect to a distribution described in paragraph (1), then, solely for purposes of determining the tax treatment of the transfers of property to the controlled corporation by the distributing corporation, the fact that the shareholders of the distributing corporation dispose of part or all of the distributed stock, or the fact that the corporation whose stock was distributed issues additional stock, shall not be taken into account in determining control for purposes of this section.

Amendments

- **1998, Tax and Trade Relief Extension Act of 1998 (P.L. 105-277)**

P.L. 105-277, §4003(f)(1):

Amended Code Sec. 351(c)(2) by inserting ", or the fact that the corporation whose stock was distributed issues additional stock," after "dispose of part or all of the distributed stock". **Effective** as if included in the provision of P.L. 105-34 to which it relates [generally **effective** for transfers after 8-5-97—CCH].

- **1998, IRS Restructuring and Reform Act of 1998 (P.L. 105-206)**

P.L. 105-206, §6010(c)(3)(A):

Amended Code Sec. 351(c). **Effective** as if included in the provision of P.L. 105-34 to which it relates [generally **effective** for transfers after 8-5-97.—CCH]. Prior to amendment, Code Sec. 351(c) read as follows:

(c) SPECIAL RULES WHERE DISTRIBUTION TO SHAREHOLDERS.—In determining control for purposes of this section—

(1) the fact that any corporate transferor distributes part or all of the stock in the corporation which it receives in the exchange to its shareholders shall not be taken into account, and

(2) if the requirements of section 355 are met with respect to such distribution, the shareholders shall be treated as in control of such corporation immediately after the exchange if the shareholders own (immediately after the distribution) stock possessing—

(A) more than 50 percent of the total combined voting power of all classes of stock of such corporation entitled to vote, and

(B) more than 50 percent of the total value of shares of all classes of stock of such corporation.

- **1997, Taxpayer Relief Act of 1997 (P.L. 105-34)**

P.L. 105-34, §1012(c)(1):

Amended Code Sec. 351(c). **Effective**, generally, for transfers after 8-5-97. For a transition rule, see Act Sec.1012(d)(3), below. Prior to amendment, Code Sec. 351(c) read as follows:

(c) SPECIAL RULE.—In determining control, for purposes of this section, the fact that any corporate transferor distributes part or all of the stock which it receives in the exchange to its shareholders shall not be taken into account.

P.L. 105-34, §1012(d)(3), provides:

(3) TRANSITION RULE.—The amendments made by this section shall not apply to any distribution pursuant to a plan (or series of related transactions) which involves an acquisition described in section 355(e)(2)(A)(ii) of the Internal Revenue Code of 1986 (or, in the case of the amendments made by subsection (c), any transfer) occurring after April 16, 1997, if such acquisition or transfer is—

(A) made pursuant to an agreement which was binding on such date and at all times thereafter,

(B) described in a ruling request submitted to the Internal Revenue Service on or before such date, or

(C) described on or before such date in a public announcement or in a filing with the Securities and Exchange Commission required solely by reason of the acquisition or transfer.

This paragraph shall not apply to any agreement, ruling request, or public announcement or filing unless it identifies the acquirer of the distributing corporation or any controlled corporation, or the transferee, whichever is applicable.

[Sec. 351(d)]

(d) SERVICES, CERTAIN INDEBTEDNESS, AND ACCRUED INTEREST NOT TREATED AS PROPERTY.—For purposes of this section, stock issued for—

(1) services,

(2) indebtedness of the transferee corporation which is not evidenced by a security, or

(3) interest on indebtedness of the transferee corporation which accrued on or after the beginning of the transferor's holding period for the debt,

shall not be considered as issued in return for property.

Amendments

• **1989, Omnibus Budget Reconciliation Act of 1989 (P.L. 101-239)**

P.L. 101-239, §7203(b)(1):

Amended Code Sec. 351(d) by striking "or securities" after "stock". **Effective**, generally, for transfers after 10-2-89, in tax years ending after such date. For exceptions, see Act Sec. 7203(c)(2)-(3) in the amendment notes following Code Sec. 351(a).

• **1980, Bankruptcy Tax Act of 1980 (P.L. 96-589)**

P.L. 96-589, §5(e)(1):

Amended Code Sec. 351 by striking out subsection (d) and inserting in lieu thereof a new subsection (d). For the **effective** date, see the historical comment for P.L. 96-589 under Code Sec. 370(a). Prior to amendment, Code Sec. 351(d) provided:

"(d) EXCEPTION.—This section shall not apply to a transfer of property to an investment company."

• **1976, Tax Reform Act of 1976 (P.L. 94-455)**

P.L. 94-455, §1901(a)(48)(B):

Amended Code Sec. 351(d). **Effective** for transfers of property occurring after 10-4-76. Prior to amendment, Code Sec. 351(d) read as follows:

(d) APPLICATION OF JUNE 30, 1967, DATE.—For purposes of this section, if, in connection with the transaction, a registration statement is required to be filed with the Securities and Exchange Commission, a transfer of property to an investment company shall be treated as made on or before June 30, 1967, only if—

(1) such transfer is made on or before such date,

(2) the registration statement was filed with the Securities and Exchange Commission before January 1, 1967, and the aggregate issue price of the stock and securities of the investment company which are issued in the transaction does not exceed the aggregate amount therefor specified in the registration statement as of the close of December 31, 1966, and

(3) the transfer of property to the investment company in the transaction includes only property deposited before May 1, 1967.

• **1966, Foreign Investors Tax Act of 1966 (P.L. 89-809)**

P.L. 89-809, §203(b):

Redesignated former Code Sec. 351(d) as Sec. 351(e) and added new Code Sec. 351(d). **Effective** for transfers of property to investment companies, whether made on, before, or after 11-13-66, the date of enactment.

[Sec. 351(e)]

(e) EXCEPTIONS.—This section shall not apply to—

(1) TRANSFER OF PROPERTY TO AN INVESTMENT COMPANY.—A transfer of property to an investment company. For purposes of the preceding sentence, the determination of whether a company is an investment company shall be made—

(A) by taking into account all stock and securities held by the company, and

(B) by treating as stock and securities—

(i) money,

(ii) stocks and other equity interests in a corporation, evidences of indebtedness, options, forward or futures contracts, notional principal contracts and derivatives,

(iii) any foreign currency,

(iv) any interest in a real estate investment trust, a common trust fund, a regulated investment company, a publicly-traded partnership (as defined in section 7704(b)) or any other equity interest (other than in a corporation) which pursuant to its terms or any other arrangement is readily convertible into, or exchangeable for, any asset described in any preceding clause, this clause or clause (v) or (viii),

(v) except to the extent provided in regulations prescribed by the Secretary, any interest in a precious metal, unless such metal is used or held in the active conduct of a trade or business after the contribution,

(vi) except as otherwise provided in regulations prescribed by the Secretary, interests in any entity if substantially all of the assets of such entity consist (directly or indirectly) of any assets described in any preceding clause or clause (viii),

(vii) to the extent provided in regulations prescribed by the Secretary, any interest in any entity not described in clause (vi), but only to the extent of the value of such interest that is attributable to assets listed in clauses (i) through (v) or clause (viii), or

(viii) any other asset specified in regulations prescribed by the Secretary.

The Secretary may prescribe regulations that, under appropriate circumstances, treat any asset described in clauses (i) through (v) as not so listed.

(2) TITLE 11 OR SIMILAR CASE.—A transfer of property of a debtor pursuant to a plan while the debtor is under the jurisdiction of a court in a title 11 or similar case (within the meaning of section 368(a)(3)(A)), to the extent that the stock received in the exchange is used to satisfy the indebtedness of such debtor.

Amendments

• **1997, Taxpayer Relief Act of 1997 (P.L. 105-34)**

P.L. 105-34, §1002(a):

Amended Code Sec. 351(e)(1) by adding at the end new material. **Effective**, generally, for transfers after 6-8-97, in tax years ending after such date. For a special rule, see Act Sec. 1002(b)(2), below. Prior to amendment, Code Sec. 351(e)(1) read as follows:

(1) TRANSFER OF PROPERTY TO AN INVESTMENT COMPANY.—A transfer of property to an investment company.

P.L. 105-34, §1002(b)(2), provides:

(2) BINDING CONTRACTS.—The amendment made by subsection (a) shall not apply to any transfer pursuant to a written binding contract in effect on June 8, 1997, and at all times thereafter before such transfer if such contract provides for the transfer of a fixed amount of property.

• **1990, Omnibus Budget Reconciliation Act of 1990 (P.L. 101-508)**

P.L. 101-508, §11704(a)(3):

Amended Code Sec. 351(e)(2) by striking "are used" and inserting "is used". **Effective** 11-5-90.

• **1989, Omnibus Budget Reconciliation Act of 1989 (P.L. 101-239)**

P.L. 101-239, §7203(b)(1):

Amended Code Sec. 351(e)(2) by striking "or securities" after "stock". **Effective**, generally, for transfers after 10-2-89, in tax years ending after such date. For exceptions, see Act Sec. 7203(c)(2)-(3) in the amendment notes following Code Sec. 351(a).

• **1980, Bankruptcy Tax Act of 1980 (P.L. 96-589)**

P.L. 96-589, §5(e)(1):

Redesignated former Code Sec. 351(e) as Code Sec. 351(f) and added a new Code Sec. 351(e). For the **effective** date, see the historical comment for P.L. 96-589 under Code Sec. 370(a).

[Sec. 351(f)]

(f) TREATMENT OF CONTROLLED CORPORATION.—If—

(1) property is transferred to a corporation (hereinafter in this subsection referred to as the "controlled corporation") in an exchange with respect to which gain or loss is not recognized (in whole or in part) to the transferor under this section, and

(2) such exchange is not in pursuance of a plan of reorganization,

section 311 shall apply to any transfer in such exchange by the controlled corporation in the same manner as if such transfer were a distribution to which subpart A of part I applies.

Amendments

• **1988, Technical and Miscellaneous Revenue Act of 1988 (P.L. 100-647)**

P.L. 100-647, §1018(d)(5)(G):

Amended Code Sec. 351 by redesignating subsection (f) as subsection (g) and inserting after subsection (e) new subsection (f). **Effective** with respect to transfers on or after 6-21-88.

[Sec. 351(g)]

(g) NONQUALIFIED PREFERRED STOCK NOT TREATED AS STOCK.—

(1) IN GENERAL.—In the case of a person who transfers property to a corporation and receives nonqualified preferred stock—

(A) subsection (a) shall not apply to such transferor, and

(B) if (and only if) the transferor receives stock other than nonqualified preferred stock—

(i) subsection (b) shall apply to such transferor; and

(ii) such nonqualified preferred stock shall be treated as other property for purposes of applying subsection (b).

(2) NONQUALIFIED PREFERRED STOCK.—For purposes of paragraph (1)—

(A) IN GENERAL.—The term "nonqualified preferred stock" means preferred stock if—

(i) the holder of such stock has the right to require the issuer or a related person to redeem or purchase the stock,

(ii) the issuer or a related person is required to redeem or purchase such stock,

(iii) the issuer or a related person has the right to redeem or purchase the stock and, as of the issue date, it is more likely than not that such right will be exercised, or

(iv) the dividend rate on such stock varies in whole or in part (directly or indirectly) with reference to interest rates, commodity prices, or other similar indices.

(B) LIMITATIONS.—Clauses (i), (ii), and (iii) of subparagraph (A) shall apply only if the right or obligation referred to therein may be exercised within the 20-year period beginning on the issue date of such stock and such right or obligation is not subject to a contingency which, as of the issue date, makes remote the likelihood of the redemption or purchase.

(C) EXCEPTIONS FOR CERTAIN RIGHTS OR OBLIGATIONS.—

(i) IN GENERAL.—A right or obligation shall not be treated as described in clause (i), (ii), or (iii) of subparagraph (A) if—

(I) it may be exercised only upon the death, disability, or mental incompetency of the holder, or

(II) in the case of a right or obligation to redeem or purchase stock transferred in connection with the performance of services for the issuer or a related person (and which represents reasonable compensation), it may be exercised only upon the holder's separation from service from the issuer or a related person.

(ii) EXCEPTION.—Clause (i)(I) shall not apply if the stock relinquished in the exchange, or the stock acquired in the exchange is in—

APPENDIX: Selected Code Sections Affected by the Tax Cuts and Jobs Act 207

(I) a corporation if any class of stock in such corporation or a related party is readily tradable on an established securities market or otherwise, or

(II) any other corporation if such exchange is part of a transaction or series of transactions in which such corporation is to become a corporation described in subclause (I).

(3) DEFINITIONS.—For purposes of this subsection—

(A) PREFERRED STOCK.—The term "preferred stock" means stock which is limited and preferred as to dividends and does not participate in corporate growth to any significant extent. Stock shall not be treated as participating in corporate growth to any significant extent unless there is a real and meaningful likelihood of the shareholder actually participating in the earnings and growth of the corporation. If there is not a real and meaningful likelihood that dividends beyond any limitation or preference will actually be paid, the possibility of such payments will be disregarded in determining whether stock is limited and preferred as to dividends.

(B) RELATED PERSON.—A person shall be treated as related to another person if they bear a relationship to such other person described in section 267(b) or 707(b).

(4) REGULATIONS.—The Secretary may prescribe such regulations as may be necessary or appropriate to carry out the purposes of this subsection and sections 354(a)(2)(C), 355(a)(3)(D), and 356(e). The Secretary may also prescribe regulations, consistent with the treatment under this subsection and such sections, for the treatment of nonqualified preferred stock under other provisions of this title.

Amendments

• **2005, Gulf Opportunity Zone Act of 2005 (P.L. 109-135)**

P.L. 109-135, §403(kk):
Amended Code Sec. 351(g)(3)(A) by adding at the end a new sentence. **Effective** as if included in the provision of the American Jobs Creation Act of 2004 (P.L. 108-357) to which it relates [**effective** for transactions after 5-14-2003.—CCH].

• **2004, American Jobs Creation Act of 2004 (P.L. 108-357)**

P.L. 108-357, §899(a):
Amended Code Sec. 351(g)(3)(A) by adding at the end a new sentence. **Effective** for transactions after 5-14-2003.

• **1998, IRS Restructuring and Reform Act of 1998 (P.L. 105-206)**

P.L. 105-206, §6010(e)(1):
Amended Code Sec. 351(g)(1) by adding "and" at the end of subparagraph (A) and by striking subparagraphs (B) and (C) and inserting a new subparagraph (B). **Effective** as if included in the provision of P.L. 105-34 to which it relates [generally **effective** for transactions after 6-8-97.—CCH]. Prior to being stricken, Code Sec. 351(g)(1)(B)-(C) read as follows:

(B) subsection (b) shall apply to such transferor, and

(C) such nonqualified preferred stock shall be treated as other property for purposes of applying subsection (b).

• **1997, Taxpayer Relief Act of 1997 (P.L. 105-34)**

P.L. 105-34, §1014(a):
Act Sec. 1014(a) amended Code Sec. 351 by redesignating subsection (g) as subsection (h), and by inserting after subsection (f) a new subsection (g). **Effective**, generally, for transactions after 6-8-97. For a transition rule, see Act Sec. 1014(f)(2), below.

P.L. 105-34, §1014(f)(2), provides:

(2) TRANSITION RULE.—The amendments made by this section shall not apply to any transaction after June 8, 1997, if such transaction is—

(A) made pursuant to a written agreement which was binding on such date and at all times thereafter,

(B) described in a ruling request submitted to the Internal Revenue Service on or before such date, or

(C) described on or before such date in a public announcement or in a filing with the Securities and Exchange Commission required solely by reason of the transaction.

[Sec. 351(h)]

(h) CROSS REFERENCES.—

(1) For special rule where another party to the exchange assumes a liability, see section 357.

(2) For the basis of stock or property received in an exchange to which this section applies, see sections 358 and 362.

(3) For special rule in the case of an exchange described in this section but which results in a gift, see section 2501 and following.

(4) For special rule in the case of an exchange described in this section but which has the effect of the payment of compensation by the corporation or by a transferor, see section 61(a)(1).

(5) For coordination of this section with section 304, see section 304(b)(3).

Amendments

• **2002, Job Creation and Worker Assistance Act of 2002 (P.L. 107-147)**

P.L. 107-147, §417(9):
Amended Code Sec. 351(h)(1) by inserting a comma after "liability". **Effective** 3-9-2002.

• **1999, Miscellaneous Trade and Technical Corrections Act of 1999 (P.L. 106-36)**

P.L. 106-36, §3001(d)(1):
Amended Code Sec. 351(h)(1) by striking ", or acquires property subject to a liability," following "liability". **Effective** for transfers after 10-18-98.

• **1997, Taxpayer Relief Act of 1997 (P.L. 105-34)**

P.L. 105-34, §1014(a):
Amended Code Sec. 351 by redesignating subsection (g) as subsection (h). **Effective**, generally, for transactions after 6-8-97. For a transitional rule, see Act Sec. 1014(f)(2) in the amendment notes following Code Sec. 351(g).

• **1989, Omnibus Budget Reconciliation Act of 1989 (P.L. 101-239)**

P.L. 101-239, §7203(b)(2):
Amended Code Sec. 351(g)(2) by striking "stock, securities, or property" and inserting "stock or property". **Effective**, generally, for transfers after 10-2-89, in tax years ending after such date. For exceptions, see Act Sec. 7203(c)(2)-(3) in the amendment notes following Code Sec. 351(a).

Code Sec. 351

- **1988, Technical and Miscellaneous Revenue Act of 1988 (P.L. 100-647)**

P.L. 100-647, § 1018(d)(5)(G):

Amended Code Sec. 351 by redesignating subsection (f) as subsection (g). **Effective** with respect to transfers on or after 6-21-88.

- **1982, Tax Equity and Fiscal Responsibility Act of 1982 (P.L. 97-248)**

P.L. 97-248, § 226(a)(1)(B):

Added Code Sec. 351(f)(5). **Effective** for transfers occurring after 8-31-82, in tax years ending after such date. See P.L. 97-248, Act Sec. 226(c)(2), in the amendment notes under Code Sec. 306(c) for an exception.

- **1980, Bankruptcy Tax Act of 1980 (P.L. 96-589)**

P.L. 96-589, § 5(e)(1):

Redesignated former Code Sec. 351(e) as Code Sec. 351(f). For the **effective** date, see the historical comment for P.L. 96-589 under Code Sec. 370(a).

- **1966, Foreign Investors Tax Act of 1966 (P.L. 89-809)**

P.L. 89-809, § 203(b):

Redesignated former Code Sec. 351(d) as Sec. 351(e). **Effective** for transfers of property to investment companies, whether made before, on, or after 11-13-66, the date of enactment.

Code Sec. 351

[Sec. 357]
SEC. 357. ASSUMPTION OF LIABILITY.

[Sec. 357(a)]
(a) GENERAL RULE.—Except as provided in subsections (b) and (c), if—
(1) the taxpayer receives property which would be permitted to be received under section 351 or 361 without the recognition of gain if it were the sole consideration, and
(2) as part of the consideration, another party to the exchange assumes a liability of the taxpayer,

then such assumption shall not be treated as money or other property, and shall not prevent the exchange from being within the provisions of section 351 or 361, as the case may be.

Amendments
- **1999, Miscellaneous Trade and Technical Corrections Act of 1999 (P.L. 106-36)**
P.L. 106-36, § 3001(a)(1):
Amended Code Sec. 357(a)(2) by striking ", or acquires from the taxpayer property subject to a liability" following "taxpayer". **Effective** for transfers after 10-18-98.

P.L. 106-36, § 3001(d)(2):
Amended Code Sec. 357(a) by striking " or acquisition" following "then such assumption". **Effective** for transfers after 10-18-98.

- **1990, Omnibus Budget Reconciliation Act of 1990 (P.L. 101-508)**
P.L. 101-508, § 11801(c)(8)(F)(i):
Amended Code Sec. 357 by striking "351, 361, 371, or 374" each place it appears and inserting "351 or 361". **Effective** 11-5-90.

P.L. 101-508, § 11821(b)(1)-(2), provides:
(b) SAVINGS PROVISION.—If—

(1) any provision amended or repealed by this part applied to—
(A) any transaction occurring before the date of the enactment of this Act,
(B) any property acquired before such date of enactment, or
(C) any item of income, loss, deduction, or credit taken into account before such date of enactment, and
(2) the treatment of such transaction, property, or item under such provision would (without regard to the amendments made by this part) affect liability for tax for periods ending after such date of enactment,

nothing in the amendments made by this part shall be construed to affect the treatment of such transaction, property, or item for purposes of determining liability for tax for periods ending after such date of enactment.

- **1956 (P.L. 628, 84th Cong.)**
P.L. 628, 84th Cong., § 2(1):
Amended subsection (a) by substituting wherever it appears therein "371, or 374" for "or 371".

[Sec. 357(b)]
(b) TAX AVOIDANCE PURPOSE.—
(1) IN GENERAL.—If, taking into consideration the nature of the liability and the circumstances in the light of which the arrangement for the assumption was made, it appears that the principal purpose of the taxpayer with respect to the assumption described in subsection (a)—
(A) was a purpose to avoid Federal income tax on the exchange, or
(B) if not such purpose, was not a bona fide business purpose,

then such assumption (in the total amount of the liability assumed pursuant to such exchange) shall, for purposes of section 351 or 361 (as the case may be), be considered as money received by the taxpayer on the exchange.
(2) BURDEN OF PROOF.—In any suit or proceeding where the burden is on the taxpayer to prove such assumption is not to be treated as money received by the taxpayer, such burden shall not be considered as sustained unless the taxpayer sustains such burden by the clear preponderance of the evidence.

Amendments
- **1999, Miscellaneous Trade and Technical Corrections Act of 1999 (P.L. 106-36)**
P.L. 106-36, § 3001(d)(2):
Act Sec. 3001(d)(2) amended Code Sec. 357(b) by striking "or acquisition" following "assumption" each place it appeared. **Effective** for transfers after 10-18-98.

P.L. 106-36, § 3001(d)(3):
Act Sec. 3001(d)(3) amended Code Sec. 357(b)(1) by striking "or acquired" following "assumed". **Effective** for transfers after 10-18-98.

- **1990, Omnibus Budget Reconciliation Act of 1990 (P.L. 101-508)**
P.L. 101-508, § 11801(c)(8)(F)(i):
Act Sec. 11801(c)(8)(F)(i) amended Code Sec. 357 by striking "351, 361, 371, or 374" each place it appears and inserting "351 or 361". **Effective** 11-5-90.

P.L. 101-508, § 11821(b)(1)-(2), provides:
(b) SAVINGS PROVISION.—If—

(1) any provision amended or repealed by this part applied to—
(A) any transaction occurring before the date of the enactment of this Act,
(B) any property acquired before such date of enactment, or
(C) any item of income, loss, deduction, or credit taken into account before such date of enactment, and
(2) the treatment of such transaction, property, or item under such provision would (without regard to the amendments made by this part) affect liability for tax for periods ending after such date of enactment,

nothing in the amendments made by this part shall be construed to affect the treatment of such transaction, property, or item for purposes of determining liability for tax for periods ending after such date of enactment.

P.L. 628, 84th Cong., 2d Sess., § 2(1):
Amended subsection (b) by substituting "371, or 374" for "or 371". **Effective** 6-29-56.

[Sec. 357(c)]
(c) LIABILITIES IN EXCESS OF BASIS.—
(1) IN GENERAL.—In the case of an exchange—
(A) to which section 351 applies, or
(B) to which section 361 applies by reason of a plan of reorganization within the meaning of section 368(a)(1)(D) with respect to which stock or securities of the corporation to which the assets are transferred are distributed in a transaction which qualifies under section 355,

if the sum of the amount of the liabilities assumed exceeds the total of the adjusted basis of the property transferred pursuant to such exchange, then such excess shall be considered as a gain from the sale or exchange of a capital asset or of property which is not a capital asset, as the case may be.

(2) EXCEPTIONS.—Paragraph (1) shall not apply to any exchange—

(A) to which subsection (b)(1) of this section applies, or

(B) which is pursuant to a plan of reorganization within the meaning of section 368(a)(1)(G) where no former shareholder of the transferor corporation receives any consideration for his stock.

(3) CERTAIN LIABILITIES EXCLUDED.—

(A) IN GENERAL.—If a taxpayer transfers, in an exchange to which section 351 applies, a liability the payment of which either—

(i) would give rise to a deduction, or

(ii) would be described in section 736(a),

then, for purposes of paragraph (1), the amount of such liability shall be excluded in determining the amount of liabilities assumed.

(B) EXCEPTION.—Subparagraph (A) shall not apply to any liability to the extent that the incurrence of the liability resulted in the creation of, or an increase in, the basis of any property.

Amendments

- **2004, American Jobs Creation Act of 2004 (P.L. 108-357)**

P.L. 108-357, §898(b):

Amended Code Sec. 357(c)(1)(B) by inserting "with respect to which stock or securities of the corporation to which the assets are transferred are distributed in a transaction which qualifies under section 355" after "section 368(a)(1)(D)". **Effective** for transfers of money or other property, or liabilities assumed, in connection with a reorganization occurring on or after 10-22-2004.

- **1999, Miscellaneous Trade and Technical Corrections Act of 1999 (P.L. 106-36)**

P.L. 106-36, §3001(d)(4):

Amended Code Sec. 357(c)(1) by striking ", plus the amount of the liabilities to which the property is subject," following "assumed". **Effective** for transfers after 10-18-98.

P.L. 106-36, §3001(d)(5):

Amended Code Sec. 357(c)(3) by striking "or to which the property transferred is subject" following "assumed". **Effective** for transfers after 10-18-98.

- **1990, Omnibus Budget Reconciliation Act of 1990 (P.L. 101-508)**

P.L. 101-508, §11801(c)(8)(F)(ii):

Amended Code Sec. 357(c)(2) by inserting "or" at the end of subparagraph (A), by striking subparagraph (B), and by redesignating subparagraph (C) as subparagraph (B). **Effective** 11-5-90. Prior to amendment, Code Sec. 357(c)(2)(B) read as follows:

(B) to which section 371 or 374 applies, or

P.L. 101-508, §11821(b)(1)-(2), provides:

(b) SAVINGS PROVISION.—If—

(1) any provision amended or repealed by this part applied to—

(A) any transaction occurring before the date of the enactment of this Act,

(B) any property acquired before such date of enactment, or

(C) any item of income, loss, deduction, or credit taken into account before such date of enactment, and

(2) the treatment of such transaction, property, or item under such provision would (without regard to the amendments made by this part) affect liability for tax for periods ending after such date of enactment,

nothing in the amendments made by this part shall be construed to affect the treatment of such transaction, property, or item for purposes of determining liability for tax for periods ending after such date of enactment.

- **1980, Bankruptcy Tax Act of 1980 (P.L. 96-589)**

P.L. 96-589, §4(h)(2):

Amended Code Sec. 357(c)(2). For the **effective** date, see the historical comment for P.L. 96-589 under Code Sec. 370(a). Prior to amendment, Code Sec. 357(c)(2) provided:

(2) EXCEPTIONS.—Paragraph (1) shall not apply to any exchange to which—

(A) subsection (b)(1) of this section applies, or

(B) section 371 or 374 applies.

- **1980, Technical Corrections Act of 1979 (P.L. 96-222)**

P.L. 96-222, §103(a)(12):

Amended Code Sec. 357(c)(3)(A). **Effective** for transfers made after 11-6-78. Prior to amendment, Code Sec. 357(c)(3)(A) read as follows:

(A) IN GENERAL.—If—

(i) the taxpayer's taxable income is computed under the cash receipts and disbursements method of accounting, and

(ii) such taxpayer transfers, in an exchange to which section 351 applies, a liability which is either—

(I) an account payable payment of which would give rise to a deduction, or

(II) an amount payable which is described in section 736(a),

then, for purposes of paragraph (1), the amount of such liability shall be excluded in determining the amount of liabilities assumed or to which the property transferred is subject.

- **1978, Revenue Act of 1978 (P.L. 95-600)**

P.L. 95-600, §365(a), (c):

Added Code Sec. 357(c)(3). **Effective** for transfers occurring on or after 11-6-78.

- **1956 (P.L. 628, 84th Cong.)**

P.L. 628, 84th Cong., §2(2):

Amended subsection (c)(2)(B) by substituting "371 or 374" for "371".

[Sec. 357(d)]

(d) DETERMINATION OF AMOUNT OF LIABILITY ASSUMED.—

(1) IN GENERAL.—For purposes of this section, section 358(d), section 358(h), section 361(b)(3), section 362(d), section 368(a)(1)(C), and section 368(a)(2)(B), except as provided in regulations—

(A) a recourse liability (or portion thereof) shall be treated as having been assumed if, as determined on the basis of all facts and circumstances, the transferee has agreed to, and is expected to, satisfy such liability (or portion), whether or not the transferor has been relieved of such liability; and

(B) except to the extent provided in paragraph (2), a nonrecourse liability shall be treated as having been assumed by the transferee of any asset subject to such liability.

(2) EXCEPTION FOR NONRECOURSE LIABILITY.—The amount of the nonrecourse liability treated as described in paragraph (1)(B) shall be reduced by the lesser of—

(A) the amount of such liability which an owner of other assets not transferred to the transferee and also subject to such liability has agreed with the transferee to, and is expected to, satisfy, or

(B) the fair market value of such other assets (determined without regard to section 7701(g)).

(3) REGULATIONS.—The Secretary shall prescribe such regulations as may be necessary to carry out the purposes of this subsection and section 362(d). The Secretary may also prescribe regulations which provide that the manner in which a liability is treated as assumed under this subsection is applied, where appropriate, elsewhere in this title.

Amendments

• **2005, Gulf Opportunity Zone Act of 2005 (P.L. 109-135)**

P.L. 109-135, §403(jj)(2):

Amended Code Sec. 357(d)(1) by inserting "section 361(b)(3)," after "section 358(h),". **Effective** as if included in the provision of the American Jobs Creation Act of 2004 (P.L. 108-357) to which it relates [**effective** for transfers of money or other property, or liabilities assumed, in connection with a reorganization occurring on or after 10-22-2004.—CCH].

• **2000, Community Renewal Tax Relief Act of 2000 (P.L. 106-554)**

P.L. 106-554, §309(b):

Amended Code Sec. 357(d)(1) by inserting "section 358(h)," after "section 358(d),". **Effective**, generally, for assumptions of liability after 10-18-99. For special rules, see Act Sec. 309(c)(1)-(2) and (d)(2), below.

Act Sec. 309(c)(1)-(2) and (d)(2) provide:

(c) APPLICATION OF COMPARABLE RULES TO PARTNERSHIPS AND S CORPORATIONS.—The Secretary of the Treasury or his delegate—

(1) shall prescribe rules which provide appropriate adjustments under subchapter K of chapter 1 of the Internal Revenue Code of 1986 to prevent the acceleration or duplication of losses through the assumption of (or transfer of assets subject to) liabilities described in section 358(h)(3) of such Code (as added by subsection (a)) in transactions involving partnerships, and

(2) may prescribe rules which provide appropriate adjustments under subchapter S of chapter 1 of such Code in transactions described in paragraph (1) involving S corporations rather than partnerships.

(d) EFFECTIVE DATES.—

* * *

(2) RULES.—The rules prescribed under subsection (c) shall apply to assumptions of liability after October 18, 1999, or such later date as may be prescribed in such rules.

• **1999, Miscellaneous Trade and Technical Corrections Act of 1999 (P.L. 106-36)**

P.L. 106-36, §3001(b)(1):

Amended Code Sec. 357 by adding at the end new subsection (d). **Effective** for transfers after 10-18-98.

[Sec. 531]
SEC. 531. IMPOSITION OF ACCUMULATED EARNINGS TAX.

In addition to other taxes imposed by this chapter, there is hereby imposed for each taxable year on the accumulated taxable income (as defined in section 535) of each corporation described in section 532, an accumulated earnings tax equal to 20 percent of the accumulated taxable income.

Amendments

• **2013, American Taxpayer Relief Act of 2012 (P.L. 112-240)**

P.L. 112-240, §102(a), provides:

SEC. 102. PERMANENT EXTENSION AND MODIFICATION OF 2003 TAX RELIEF.

(a) PERMANENT EXTENSION.—The Jobs and Growth Tax Relief Reconciliation Act of 2003 is amended by striking section 303.

P.L. 112-240, §102(c)(1)(A):

Amended Code Sec. 531 by striking "15 percent" and inserting "20 percent". **Effective** for tax years beginning after 12-31-2012.

• **2003, Jobs and Growth Tax Relief Reconciliation Act of 2003 (P.L. 108-27)**

P.L. 108-27, §302(e)(5):

Amended Code Sec. 531 by striking "equal to" and all that follows and inserting "equal to 15 percent of the accumulated taxable income.". For the **effective** date, see Act Sec. 302(f), as amended by P.L. 108-311, §402(a)(6), below. Prior to amendment, Code Sec. 531 read as follows:

SEC. 531. IMPOSITION OF ACCUMULATED EARNINGS TAX.

In addition to other taxes imposed by this chapter, there is hereby imposed for each taxable year on the accumulated taxable income (as defined in section 535) of each corporation described in section 532, an accumulated earnings tax equal to the product of the highest rate of tax under section 1(c) and the accumulated taxable income.

P.L. 108-27, §302(f), as amended by P.L. 108-311, §402(a)(6), provides:

(f) EFFECTIVE DATE.—

(1) IN GENERAL.—Except as provided in paragraph (2), the amendments made by this section shall apply to taxable years beginning after December 31, 2002.

(2) PASS-THRU ENTITIES.—In the case of a pass-thru entity described in subparagraph (A), (B), (C), (D), (E), or (F) of section 1(h)(10) of the Internal Revenue Code of 1986, as amended by this Act, the amendments made by this section shall apply to taxable years ending after December 31, 2002; except that dividends received by such an entity on or before such date shall not be treated as qualified dividend income (as defined in section 1(h)(11)(B) of such Code, as added by this Act).

P.L. 108-27, §303, as amended by P.L. 109-222, §102, and P.L. 111-312, §102(a), provides [but see P.L. 112-240, §102(a), above]:

SEC. 303. SUNSET OF TITLE.

All provisions of, and amendments made by, this title shall not apply to taxable years beginning after December 31, 2012, and the Internal Revenue Code of 1986 shall be applied and administered to such years as if such provisions and amendments had never been enacted.

• **2001, Economic Growth and Tax Relief Reconciliation Act of 2001 (P.L. 107-16)**

P.L. 107-16, §101(c)(4):

Amended Code Sec. 531 by striking "equal to" and all that follows and inserting "equal to the product of the highest rate of tax under section 1(c) and the accumulated taxable income.". **Effective** for tax years beginning after 12-31-2000. Prior to amendment, Code Sec. 531 read as follows:

SEC. 531. IMPOSITION OF ACCUMULATED EARNINGS TAX.

In addition to other taxes imposed by this chapter, there is hereby imposed for each taxable year on the accumulated taxable income (as defined in section 535) of each corporation described in section 532, an accumulated earnings tax equal to 39.6 percent of the accumulated taxable income.

P.L. 107-16, §901(a)-(b), as amended by P.L. 111-312, §101(a)(1), provides:

SEC. 901. SUNSET OF PROVISIONS OF ACT.

(a) IN GENERAL.—All provisions of, and amendments made by, this Act shall not apply—

(1) to taxable, plan, or limitation years beginning after December 31, 2012, or

(2) in the case of title V, to estates of decedents dying, gifts made, or generation skipping transfers, after December 31, 2012.

(b) APPLICATION OF CERTAIN LAWS.—The Internal Revenue Code of 1986 and the Employee Retirement Income Security Act of 1974 shall be applied and administered to years, estates, gifts, and transfers described in subsection (a) as if the provisions and amendments described in subsection (a) had never been enacted.

- **1993, Omnibus Budget Reconciliation Act of 1993 (P.L. 103-66)**

P.L. 103-66, §13201(b)(1):

Amended Code Sec. 531 by striking "28 percent" and inserting "36 percent". **Effective** for tax years beginning after 12-31-92.

P.L. 103-66, §13202(b):

Amended Code Sec. 531 (as amended by Act Sec. 13201) by striking "36 percent" and inserting "39.6 percent". **Effective** for tax years beginning after 12-31-92.

- **1988, Technical and Miscellaneous Revenue Act of 1988 (P.L. 100-647)**

P.L. 100-647, §1001(a)(2)(A):

Amended Code Sec. 531. **Effective** for tax years beginning after 12-31-87. It shall not be treated as a change in a rate of tax for purposes of section 15 of the 1986 Code. Prior to amendment, Code Sec. 531 read as follows:

SEC. 531. IMPOSITION OF ACCUMULATED EARNINGS TAX.

In addition to other taxes imposed by this chapter, there is hereby imposed for each taxable year on the accumulated taxable income (as defined in section 535) of every corporation described in section 532, an accumulated earnings tax equal to the sum of—

(1) $27\frac{1}{2}$ percent of the accumulated taxable income not in excess of $100,000, plus

(2) $38\frac{1}{2}$ percent of the accumulated taxable income in excess of $100,000.

[Sec. 541]
SEC. 541. IMPOSITION OF PERSONAL HOLDING COMPANY TAX.
In addition to other taxes imposed by this chapter, there is hereby imposed for each taxable year on the undistributed personal holding company income (as defined in section 545) of every personal holding company (as defined in section 542) a personal holding company tax equal to 20 percent of the undistributed personal holding company income.

Amendments
- **2013, American Taxpayer Relief Act of 2012 (P.L. 112-240)**

P.L. 112-240, §102(a), provides:
SEC. 102. PERMANENT EXTENSION AND MODIFICATION OF 2003 TAX RELIEF.
(a) PERMANENT EXTENSION.—The Jobs and Growth Tax Relief Reconciliation Act of 2003 is amended by striking section 303.

P.L. 112-240, §102(c)(1)(B):
Amended Code Sec. 541 by striking "15 percent" and inserting "20 percent". **Effective** for tax years beginning after 12-31-2012.

- **2003, Jobs and Growth Tax Relief Reconciliation Act of 2003 (P.L. 108-27)**

P.L. 108-27, §302(e)(6):
Amended Code Sec. 541 by striking "equal to" and all that follows and inserting "equal to 15 percent of the undistributed personal holding company income.". For the **effective** date, see Act Sec. 302(f), as amended by P.L. 108-311, §402(a)(6), below. Prior to amendment, Code Sec. 541 read as follows:
SEC. 541. IMPOSITION OF PERSONAL HOLDING COMPANY TAX.
In addition to other taxes imposed by this chapter, there is hereby imposed for each taxable year on the undistributed personal holding company income (as defined in section 545) of every personal holding company (as defined in section 542) a personal holding company tax equal to the product of the highest rate of tax under section 1(c) and the undistributed personal holding company income.

P.L. 108-27, §302(f), as amended by P.L. 108-311, §402(a)(6), provides:
(f) EFFECTIVE DATE.—
(1) IN GENERAL.—Except as provided in paragraph (2), the amendments made by this section shall apply to taxable years beginning after December 31, 2002.
(2) PASS-THRU ENTITIES.—In the case of a pass-thru entity described in subparagraph (A), (B), (C), (D), (E), or (F) of section 1(h)(10) of the Internal Revenue Code of 1986, as amended by this Act, the amendments made by this section shall apply to taxable years ending after December 31, 2002; except that dividends received by such an entity on or before such date shall not be treated as qualified dividend income (as defined in section 1(h)(11)(B) of such Code, as added by this Act).

P.L. 108-27, §303, as amended by P.L. 109-222, §102, and P.L. 111-312, §102(a), provides [but see P.L. 112-240, §102(a), above]:
SEC. 303. SUNSET OF TITLE.
All provisions of, and amendments made by, this title shall not apply to taxable years beginning after December 31, 2012, and the Internal Revenue Code of 1986 shall be applied and administered to such years as if such provisions and amendments had never been enacted.

- **2001, Economic Growth and Tax Relief Reconciliation Act of 2001 (P.L. 107-16)**

P.L. 107-16, §101(c)(5):
Amended Code Sec. 541 by striking "equal to" and all that follows and inserting "equal to the product of the highest rate of tax under section 1(c) and the undistributed personal holding company income." **Effective** for tax years beginning after 12-31-2000. Prior to amendment, Code Sec. 541 read as follows:
SEC. 541. IMPOSITION OF PERSONAL HOLDING COMPANY TAX.
In addition to other taxes imposed by this chapter, there is hereby imposed for each taxable year on the undistributed personal holding company income (as defined in section 545) of every personal holding company (as defined in section 542) a personal holding company tax equal to 39.6 percent of the undistributed personal holding company income.

P.L. 107-16, §901(a)-(b), as amended by P.L. 111-312, §101(a)(1), provides:
SEC. 901. SUNSET OF PROVISIONS OF ACT.
(a) IN GENERAL.—All provisions of, and amendments made by, this Act shall not apply—
(1) to taxable, plan, or limitation years beginning after December 31, 2012, or
(2) in the case of title V, to estates of decedents dying, gifts made, or generation skipping transfers, after December 31, 2012.
(b) APPLICATION OF CERTAIN LAWS.—The Internal Revenue Code of 1986 and the Employee Retirement Income Security Act of 1974 shall be applied and administered to years, estates, gifts, and transfers described in subsection (a) as if the provisions and amendments described in subsection (a) had never been enacted.

- **1993, Omnibus Budget Reconciliation Act of 1993 (P.L. 103-66)**

P.L. 103-66, §13201(b)(2):
Amended Code Sec. 541 by striking "28 percent" and inserting "36 percent". **Effective** for tax years beginning after 12-31-92.

P.L. 103-66, §13202(b):
Amended Code Sec. 541 (as amended by Act Sec. 13201) by striking "36 percent" and inserting "39.6 percent". **Effective** for tax years beginning after 12-31-92.

- **1990, Omnibus Budget Reconciliation Act of 1990 (P.L. 101-508)**

P.L. 101-508, §11802(f)(1):
Amended Code Sec. 541 by striking "(38.5 percent in the case of tax years beginning in 1987)" after "28 percent". **Effective** 11-5-90.

P.L. 101-508, §11821(b), provides:
(b) SAVINGS PROVISION.—If—
(1) any provision amended or repealed by this part applied to—
(A) any transaction occurring before the date of the enactment of this Act,
(B) any property acquired before such date of enactment, or
(C) any item of income, loss, deduction, or credit taken into account before such date of enactment, and
(2) the treatment of such transaction, property, or item under such provision would (without regard to the amendments made by this part) effect liability for tax for periods ending after such date of enactment,
nothing in the amendments made by this part shall be construed to affect the treatment of such transaction, property, or item for purposes of determining liability for tax for periods ending after such date of enactment.

- **1986, Tax Reform Act of 1986 (P.L. 99-514)**

P.L. 99-514, §104(b)(8):
Amended Code Sec. 541 by striking out "50 percent" and inserting in lieu thereof "28 percent (38.5 percent in the case of taxable years beginning in 1987". **Effective** for tax years beginning after 12-31-86.

- **1981, Economic Recovery Tax Act of 1981 (P.L. 97-34)**

P.L. 97-34, §101(d)(2):
Amended Code Sec. 541 by striking out "70 percent" and inserting in lieu thereof "50 percent". **Effective** for tax years beginning after 12-31-81.

- **1964, Revenue Act of 1964 (P.L. 88-272)**

P.L. 88-272, §225(a):
Amended Code Sec. 541. **Effective** with respect to tax years beginning after 12-31-63. Prior to amendment, Sec. 541 read as follows:
"In addition to other taxes imposed by this chapter, there is hereby imposed for each taxable year on the undistributed personal holding company income (as defined in section 545) of every personal holding company (as defined in

section 542) a personal holding company tax equal to the sum of—

(1) 75 percent of the undistributed personal holding company income not in excess of $2,000, plus

(2) 85 percent of the undistributed personal holding company income in excess of $2,000."

[Sec. 704]
SEC. 704. PARTNER'S DISTRIBUTIVE SHARE.

[Sec. 704(a)]

(a) EFFECT OF PARTNERSHIP AGREEMENT.—A partner's distributive share of income, gain, loss, deduction, or credit shall, except as otherwise provided in this chapter, be determined by the partnership agreement.

Amendments

• **1976, Tax Reform Act of 1976 (P.L. 94-455)**
P.L. 94-455, § 213(c)(2):
Substituted "except as otherwise provided in this chapter" for "except as otherwise provided in this section" in Code Sec. 704(a). **Effective** for partnership tax years beginning after 12-31-75.

[Sec. 704(b)]

(b) DETERMINATION OF DISTRIBUTIVE SHARE.—A partner's distributive share of income, gain, loss, deduction, or credit (or item thereof) shall be determined in accordance with the partner's interest in the partnership (determined by taking into account all facts and circumstances), if—

(1) the partnership agreement does not provide as to the partner's distributive share of income, gain, loss, deduction, or credit (or item thereof), or

(2) the allocation to a partner under the agreement of income, gain, loss, deduction, or credit (or item thereof) does not have substantial economic effect.

Amendments

• **1976, Tax Reform Act of 1976 (P.L. 94-455)**
P.L. 94-455, §213(d):
Amended Code Sec. 704(b). **Effective** in the case of partnership tax years beginning after 12-31-75. Prior to amendment, Code Sec. 704(b) read as follows:
(b) DISTRIBUTIVE SHARE DETERMINED BY INCOME OR LOSS RATIO.—A partner's distributive share of any item of income, gain, loss, deduction, or credit shall be determined in accordance with his distributive share of taxable income or loss of the partnership, as described in section 702(a)(9), for the taxable year, if—

(1) the partnership agreement does not provide as to the partner's distributive share of such item, or

(2) the principal purpose of any provision in the partnership agreement with respect to the partner's distributive share of such item is the avoidance or evasion of any tax imposed by this subtitle.

[Sec. 704(c)]

(c) CONTRIBUTED PROPERTY.—

(1) IN GENERAL.—Under regulations prescribed by the Secretary—

(A) income, gain, loss, and deduction with respect to property contributed to the partnership by a partner shall be shared among the partners so as to take account of the variation between the basis of the property to the partnership and its fair market value at the time of contribution,

(B) if any property so contributed is distributed (directly or indirectly) by the partnership (other than to the contributing partner) within 7 years of being contributed—

(i) the contributing partner shall be treated as recognizing gain or loss (as the case may be) from the sale of such property in an amount equal to the gain or loss which would have been allocated to such partner under subparagraph (A) by reason of the variation described in subparagraph (A) if the property had been sold at its fair market value at the time of the distribution,

(ii) the character of such gain or loss shall be determined by reference to the character of the gain or loss which would have resulted if such property had been sold by the partnership to the distributee, and

(iii) appropriate adjustments shall be made to the adjusted basis of the contributing partner's interest in the partnership and to the adjusted basis of the property distributed to reflect any gain or loss recognized under this subparagraph, and

(C) if any property so contributed has a built-in loss—

(i) such built-in loss shall be taken into account only in determining the amount of items allocated to the contributing partner, and

(ii) except as provided in regulations, in determining the amount of items allocated to other partners, the basis of the contributed property in the hands of the partnership shall be treated as being equal to its fair market value at the time of contribution.

For purposes of subparagraph (C), the term "built-in loss" means the excess of the adjusted basis of the property (determined without regard to subparagraph (C)(ii)) over its fair market value at the time of contribution.

(2) SPECIAL RULE FOR DISTRIBUTIONS WHERE GAIN OR LOSS WOULD NOT BE RECOGNIZED OUTSIDE PARTNERSHIPS.—Under regulations prescribed by the Secretary, if—

(A) property contributed by a partner (hereinafter referred to as the "contributing partner") is distributed by the partnership to another partner, and

(B) other property of a like kind (within the meaning of section 1031) is distributed by the partnership to the contributing partner not later than the earlier of—

(i) the 180th day after the date of the distribution described in subparagraph (A), or

(ii) the due date (determined with regard to extensions) for the contributing partner's return of the tax imposed by this chapter for the taxable year in which the distribution described in subparagraph (A) occurs,

then to the extent of the value of the property described in subparagraph (B), paragraph (1)(B) shall be applied as if the contributing partner had contributed to the partnership the property described in subparagraph (B).

(3) OTHER RULES.—Under regulations prescribed by the Secretary, rules similar to the rules of paragraph (1) shall apply to contributions by a partner (using the cash receipts and disbursements method of accounting) of accounts payable and other accrued but unpaid items. Any reference in paragraph (1) or (2) to the contributing partner shall be treated as including a reference to any successor of such partner.

Amendments

• **2004, American Jobs Creation Act of 2004 (P.L. 108-357)**

P.L. 108-357, §833(a):
Amended Code Sec. 704(c)(1) by striking "and" at the end of subparagraph (A), by striking the period at the end of subparagraph (B) and inserting ", and", and by adding at the end a new subparagraph (C). **Effective** for contributions made after 10-22-2004.

• **1997, Taxpayer Relief Act of 1997 (P.L. 105-34)**
P.L. 105-34, §1063(a):
Amended Code Sec. 704(c)(1)(B) by striking "5 years" and inserting "7 years". **Effective** for property contributed to a partnership after 6-8-97. For a special rule, see Act Sec. 1063(b)(2), below.

P.L. 105-34, §1063(b)(2), provides:

(2) BINDING CONTRACTS.—The amendment made by subsection (a) shall not apply to any property contributed pursuant to a written binding contract in effect on June 8, 1997, and at all times thereafter before such contribution if such contract provides for the contribution of a fixed amount of property.

- **1992, Energy Policy Act of 1992 (P.L. 102-486)**

P.L. 102-486, §1937(b)(1):

Amended Code Sec. 704(c)(1)(B) by striking out "is distributed" in the material preceding clause (i) and inserting "is distributed (directly or indirectly)". **Effective** for distributions on or after 6-25-92.

- **1989, Omnibus Budget Reconciliation Act of 1989 (P.L. 101-239)**

P.L. 101-239, §7642(a):

Amended Code Sec. 704(c). **Effective** in the case of property contributed to the partnership after 10-3-89, in tax years ending after such date. Prior to amendment, Code Sec. 704(c) read as follows:

(c) CONTRIBUTED PROPERTY.—Under regulations prescribed by the Secretary, income, gain, loss, and deduction with respect to property contributed to the partnership by a partner shall be shared among partners so as to take account of the variation between the basis of the property to the partnership and its fair market value at the time of contribution. Under regulations prescribed by the Secretary, rules similar to the rules of the preceding sentence shall apply to contributions by a partner (using the cash receipts and disbursements method of accounting) of accounts payable and other accrued but unpaid items.

- **1984, Deficit Reduction Act of 1984 (P.L. 98-369)**

P.L. 98-369, §71(a):

Amended Code Sec. 704(c). **Effective** with respect to property contributed to the partnership after 3-31-84, in tax years ending after such date. Prior to amendment, Code Sec. 704(c) read as follows:

(c) Contributed Property.—

(1) General Rule.—In determining a partner's distributive share of items described in section 702(a), depreciation, depletion, or gain or loss with respect to property contributed to the partnership by a partner shall, except to the extent otherwise provided in paragraph (2) or (3), be allocated among the partners in the same manner as if such property had been purchased by the partnership.

(2) Effect of Partnership Agreement.—If the partnership agreement so provides, depreciation, depletion, or gain or loss with respect to property contributed to the partnership by a partner shall, under regulations prescribed by the Secretary, be shared among the partners so as to take account of the variation between the basis of the property to the partnership and its fair market value at the time of contribution.

(3) Undivided Interests.—If the partnership agreement does not provide otherwise, depreciation, depletion, or gain or loss with respect to undivided interests in property contributed to a partnership shall be determined as though such undivided interests had not been contributed to the partnership. This paragraph shall apply only if all the partners had undivided interests in such property prior to contribution and their interests in the capital and profits of the partnership correspond with such undivided interests.

- **1976, Tax Reform Act of 1976 (P.L. 94-455)**

P.L. 94-455, §1906(b)(13)(A):

Amended 1954 Code by substituting "Secretary" for "Secretary or his delegate" each place it appeared. **Effective** 2-1-77.

[Sec. 704(d)]

(d) LIMITATION ON ALLOWANCE OF LOSSES.—

(1) IN GENERAL.—A partner's distributive share of partnership loss (including capital loss) shall be allowed only to the extent of the adjusted basis of such partner's interest in the partnership at the end of the partnership year in which such loss occurred.

(2) CARRYOVER.—Any excess of such loss over such basis shall be allowed as a deduction at the end of the partnership year in which such excess is repaid to the partnership.

(3) SPECIAL RULES.—

(A) IN GENERAL.—In determining the amount of any loss under paragraph (1), there shall be taken into account the partner's distributive share of amounts described in paragraphs (4) and (6) of section 702(a).

(B) EXCEPTION.—In the case of a charitable contribution of property whose fair market value exceeds its adjusted basis, subparagraph (A) shall not apply to the extent of the partner's distributive share of such excess.

Amendments

- **2017, Tax Cuts and Jobs Act (P.L. 115-97)**

P.L. 115-97, §13503(a)(1)-(3):

Amended Code Sec. 704(d) by striking "A partner's distributive share" and inserting

"(1) IN GENERAL.—A partner's distributive share",

by striking "Any excess of such loss" and inserting

"(2) CARRYOVER.—Any excess of such loss",

and by adding at the end a new paragraph (3). **Effective** for partnership tax years beginning after 12-31-2017.

- **1978, Revenue Act of 1978 (P.L. 95-600)**

P.L. 95-600, §§201(b)(1), 204(a):

Amended Code Sec. 704(d) by striking out the last two sentences. **Effective** for tax years beginning after 12-31-78. Prior to amendment, the last two sentences read as follows:

For purposes of this subsection, the adjusted basis of any partner's interest in the partnership shall not include any portion of any partnership liability with respect to which the partner has no personal liability. The preceding sentence shall not apply with respect to any activity to the extent that section 465 (relating to limiting deductions to amounts at risk in case of certain activities) applies, nor shall it apply to any partnership the principal activity of which is investing in real property (other than mineral property).

P.L. 95-600, §201(b)(2), provides:

(2) TRANSITIONAL RULE.—In the case of a loss which was not allowed for any taxable year by reason of the last 2 sentences of section 704(d) of the Internal Revenue Code of 1954 (as in effect before November 6, 1978), such loss shall be treated as a deduction (subject to section 465(a) of such Code) for the first taxable year beginning after December 31, 1978. Section 465(a) of such Code (as amended by this section) shall not apply with respect to partnership liabilities to which the last 2 sentences of section 704(d) of such Code (as in effect on November 5, 1978) did not apply because of the provisions of section 213(f)(2) of the Tax Reform Act of 1976.

- **1976, Tax Reform Act of 1976 (P.L. 94-455)**

P.L. 94-455, §213(e):

Added the last two sentences to Code Sec. 704(d). **Effective** for liabilities incurred after 12-31-76.

[Sec. 704(e)]

(e) PARTNERSHIP INTERESTS CREATED BY GIFT.—

(1) DISTRIBUTIVE SHARE OF DONEE INCLUDIBLE IN GROSS INCOME.—In the case of any partnership interest created by gift, the distributive share of the donee under the partnership agreement shall

be includible in his gross income, except to the extent that such share is determined without allowance of reasonable compensation for services rendered to the partnership by the donor, and except to the extent that the portion of such share attributable to donated capital is proportionately greater than the share of the donor attributable to the donor's capital. The distributive share of a partner in the earnings of the partnership shall not be diminished because of absence due to military service.

(2) PURCHASE OF INTEREST BY MEMBER OF FAMILY.—For purposes of this subsection, an interest purchased by one member of a family from another shall be considered to be created by gift from the seller, and the fair market value of the purchased interest shall be considered to be donated capital. The "family" of any individual shall include only his spouse, ancestors, and lineal descendants, and any trusts for the primary benefit of such persons.

Amendments

• **2015, Bipartisan Budget Act of 2015 (P.L. 114-74)**

P.L. 114-74, § 1102(b)(1)-(3):

Amended Code Sec. 704(e) by striking paragraph (1) and by redesignating paragraphs (2) and (3) as paragraphs (1) and (2), respectively, by striking "this section" in paragraph (2), as redesignated, and inserting "this subsection", and by striking "FAMILY PARTNERSHIPS" in the heading and inserting "PARTNERSHIP INTERESTS CREATED BY GIFT". **Effective** for partnership tax years beginning after 12-31-2015. Prior to being stricken, Code Sec. 704(e)(1) read as follows:

(1) RECOGNITION OF INTEREST CREATED BY PURCHASE OR GIFT.—A person shall be recognized as a partner for purposes of this subtitle if he owns a capital interest in a partnership in which capital is a material income-producing factor, whether or not such interest was derived by purchase or gift from any other person.

[Sec. 704(f)]

(f) CROSS REFERENCE.—

For rules in the case of the sale, exchange, liquidation, or reduction of a partner's interest, see section 706(c)(2).

Amendments

• **1976, Tax Reform Act of 1976 (P.L. 94-455)**

P.L. 94-455, § 213(c)(3)(A):

Added Code Sec. 704(f). **Effective** in the case of partnership tax years beginning after 12-31-75.

[Sec. 721]
SEC. 721. NONRECOGNITION OF GAIN OR LOSS ON CONTRIBUTION.
[Sec. 721(a)]
(a) GENERAL RULE.—No gain or loss shall be recognized to a partnership or to any of its partners in the case of a contribution of property to the partnership in exchange for an interest in the partnership.

Amendments
- **1976, Tax Reform Act of 1976 (P.L. 94-455)**

P.L. 94-455, §2131(b):
Inserted subsection designation "(a)" before the provisions of former Code Sec. 721. For the **effective** date, see Act Sec. 2131(f)(3)-(5), below.

P.L. 94-455, §2131(f)(3)-(5), provides:
(3) Except as provided in paragraph (4), the amendments made by subsections (b) and (c) shall apply to transfers made after February 17, 1976, in taxable years ending after such date.

(4) The amendments made by subsections (b) and (c) shall not apply to transfers to a partnership made on or before the 90th day after the date of the enactment of this Act if—

(A) either—

(i) a ruling request with respect to such transfers was filed with the Internal Revenue Service before March 27, 1976, or

(ii) a registration statement with respect to such transfers was filed with the Securities and Exchange Commission before March 27, 1976,

(B) the securities transferred were deposited on or before the 60th day after the date of the enactment of this Act, and

(C) either—

(i) the aggregate value (determined as of the close of the 60th day referred to in subparagraph (B), or, if earlier, the close of the deposit period) of the securities so transferred does not exceed $100,000,000, or

(ii) the securities transferred were all on deposit on February 29, 1976, pursuant to a registration statement referred to in subparagraph (A)(ii).

(5) If no registration statement was required to be filed with the Securities and Exchange Commission with respect to the transfer of securities to any partnership, then paragraph (4) shall be applied to such transfers—

(A) as if paragraph (4) did not contain subparagraph (A)(ii) thereof, and

(B) by substituting "$25,000,000" for "$100,000,000" in subparagraph (C)(i) thereof.

[Sec. 721(b)]
(b) SPECIAL RULE.—Subsection (a) shall not apply to gain realized on a transfer of property to a partnership which would be treated as an investment company (within the meaning of section 351) if the partnership were incorporated.

Amendments
- **1976, Tax Reform Act of 1976 (P.L. 94-455)**

P.L. 94-455, §2131(b):
Added Code Sec. 721(b). For **effective** date, see Act Sec. 2131(f)(3)-(5) under Code Sec. 721(a).

[Sec. 721(c)]
(c) REGULATIONS RELATING TO CERTAIN TRANSFERS TO PARTNERSHIPS.—The Secretary may provide by regulations that subsection (a) shall not apply to gain realized on the transfer of property to a partnership if such gain, when recognized, will be includible in the gross income of a person other than a United States person.

Amendments
- **1997, Taxpayer Relief Act of 1997 (P.L. 105-34)**

P.L. 105-34, §1131(b)[(c)](3):
Amended Code Sec. 721 by adding at the end a new subsection (c). **Effective** 8-5-97.

[Sec. 721(d)]
(d) TRANSFERS OF INTANGIBLES.—

For regulatory authority to treat intangibles transferred to a partnership as sold, see section 367(d)(3).

Amendments
- **1997, Taxpayer Relief Act of 1997 (P.L. 105-34)**

P.L. 105-34, §1131(b)[(c)](5)(B):
Amended Code Sec. 721 by adding at the end a new subsection (d). **Effective** 8-5-97.

[Sec. 731]
SEC. 731. EXTENT OF RECOGNITION OF GAIN OR LOSS ON DISTRIBUTION.
[Sec. 731(a)]

(a) PARTNERS.—In the case of a distribution by a partnership to a partner—

(1) gain shall not be recognized to such partner, except to the extent that any money distributed exceeds the adjusted basis of such partner's interest in the partnership immediately before the distribution, and

(2) loss shall not be recognized to such partner, except that upon a distribution in liquidation of a partner's interest in a partnership where no property other than that described in subparagraph (A) or (B) is distributed to such partner, loss shall be recognized to the extent of the excess of the adjusted basis of such partner's interest in the partnership over the sum of—

(A) any money distributed, and

(B) the basis to the distributee, as determined under section 732, of any unrealized receivables (as defined in section 751(c)) and inventory (as defined in section 751(d)).

Any gain or loss recognized under this subsection shall be considered as gain or loss from the sale or exchange of the partnership interest of the distributee partner.

Amendments

- **1997, Taxpayer Relief Act of 1997 (P.L. 105-34) P.L. 105-34, §1062(b)(3):**

Amended Code Sec. 731(a)(2)(B) by striking "section 751(d)(2)" and inserting "section 751(d)". **Effective** for sales, exchanges, and distributions after 8-5-97. For a special rule, see Act Sec. 1062(c)(2), below.

P.L. 105-34, §1062(c)(2), provides:

(2) BINDING CONTRACTS.—The amendments made by this section shall not apply to any sale or exchange pursuant to a written binding contract in effect on June 8, 1997, and at all times thereafter before such sale or exchange.

[Sec. 731(b)]

(b) PARTNERSHIPS.—No gain or loss shall be recognized to a partnership on a distribution to a partner of property, including money.

[Sec. 731(c)]

(c) Treatment of Marketable Securities.—

(1) In General.—For purposes of subsection (a)(1) and section 737—

(A) the term "money" includes marketable securities, and

(B) such securities shall be taken into account at their fair market value as of the date of the distribution.

(2) Marketable Securities.—For purposes of this subsection:

(A) In General.—The term "marketable securities" means financial instruments and foreign currencies which are, as of the date of the distribution, actively traded (within the meaning of section 1092(d)(1)).

(B) Other Property.—Such term includes—

(i) any interest in—

(I) a common trust fund, or

(II) a regulated investment company which is offering for sale or has outstanding any redeemable security (as defined in section 2(a)(32) of the Investment Company Act of 1940) of which it is the issuer,

(ii) any financial instrument which, pursuant to its terms or any other arrangement, is readily convertible into, or exchangeable for, money or marketable securities,

(iii) any financial instrument the value of which is determined substantially by reference to marketable securities,

(iv) except to the extent provided in regulations prescribed by the Secretary, any interest in a precious metal which, as of the date of the distribution, is actively traded (within the meaning of section 1092(d)(1)) unless such metal was produced, used, or held in the active conduct of a trade or business by the partnership,

(v) except as otherwise provided in regulations prescribed by the Secretary, interests in any entity if substantially all of the assets of such entity consist (directly or indirectly) of marketable securities, money, or both, and

(vi) to the extent provided in regulations prescribed by the Secretary, any interest in an entity not described in clause (v) but only to the extent of the value of such interest which is attributable to marketable securities, money, or both.

(C) Financial Instrument.—The term "financial instrument" includes stocks and other equity interests, evidences of indebtedness, options, forward or futures contracts, notional principal contracts, and derivatives.

(3) Exceptions.—

(A) In General.—Paragraph (1) shall not apply to the distribution from a partnership of a marketable security to a partner if—

(i) the security was contributed to the partnership by such partner, except to the extent that the value of the distributed security is attributable to marketable securities or money contributed (directly or indirectly) to the entity to which the distributed security relates,

(ii) to the extent provided in regulations prescribed by the Secretary, the property was not a marketable security when acquired by such partnership, or

(iii) such partnership is an investment partnership and such partner is an eligible partner thereof.

(B) Limitation on Gain Recognized.—In the case of a distribution of marketable securities to a partner, the amount taken into account under paragraph (1) shall be reduced (but not below zero) by the excess (if any) of—

(i) such partner's distributive share of the net gain which would be recognized if all of the marketable securities of the same class and issuer as the distributed securities held by the partnership were sold (immediately before the transaction to which the distribution relates) by the partnership for fair market value, over

(ii) such partner's distributive share of the net gain which is attributable to the marketable securities of the same class and issuer as the distributed securities held by the partnership immediately after the transaction, determined by using the same fair market value as used under clause (i).

Under regulations prescribed by the Secretary, all marketable securities held by the partnership may be treated as marketable securities of the same class and issuer as the distributed securities.

(C) Definitions Relating to Investment Partnerships.—For purposes of subparagraph (A)(iii):

(i) Investment Partnership.—The term "investment partnership" means any partnership which has never been engaged in a trade or business and substantially all of the assets (by value) of which have always consisted of—

(I) money,

(II) stock in a corporation,

(III) notes, bonds, debentures, or other evidences of indebtedness,

(IV) interest rate, currency, or equity notional principal contracts,

(V) foreign currencies,

(VI) interests in or derivative financial instruments (including options, forward or futures contracts, short positions, and similar financial instruments) in any asset described in any other subclause of this clause or in any commodity traded on or subject to the rules of a board of trade or commodity exchange,

(VII) other assets specified in regulations prescribed by the Secretary, or

(VIII) any combination of the foregoing.

(ii) EXCEPTION FOR CERTAIN ACTIVITIES.—A partnership shall not be treated as engaged in a trade or business by reason of—

(I) any activity undertaken as an investor, trader, or dealer in any asset described in clause (i), or

(II) any other activity specified in regulations prescribed by the Secretary.

(iii) ELIGIBLE PARTNER.—

(I) IN GENERAL.—The term "eligible partner" means any partner who, before the date of the distribution, did not contribute to the partnership any property other than assets described in clause (i).

(II) EXCEPTION FOR CERTAIN NONRECOGNITION TRANSACTIONS.—The term "eligible partner" shall not include the transferor or transferee in a nonrecognition transaction involving a transfer of any portion of an interest in a partnership with respect to which the transferor was not an eligible partner.

(iv) LOOK-THRU OF PARTNERSHIP TIERS.—Except as otherwise provided in regulations prescribed by the Secretary—

(I) a partnership shall be treated as engaged in any trade or business engaged in by, and as holding (instead of a partnership interest) a proportionate share of the assets of, any other partnership in which the partnership holds a partnership interest, and

(II) a partner who contributes to a partnership an interest in another partnership shall be treated as contributing a proportionate share of the assets of the other partnership.

If the preceding sentence does not apply under such regulations with respect to any interest held by a partnership in another partnership, the interest in such other partnership shall be treated as if it were specified in a subclause of clause (i).

(4) BASIS OF SECURITIES DISTRIBUTED.—

(A) IN GENERAL.—The basis of marketable securities with respect to which gain is recognized by reason of this subsection shall be—

(i) their basis determined under section 732, increased by

(ii) the amount of such gain.

(B) ALLOCATION OF BASIS INCREASE.—Any increase in basis attributable to the gain described in subparagraph (A)(ii) shall be allocated to marketable securities in proportion to their respective amounts of unrealized appreciation before such increase.

(5) SUBSECTION DISREGARDED IN DETERMINING BASIS OF PARTNER'S INTEREST IN PARTNERSHIP AND OF BASIS OF PARTNERSHIP PROPERTY.—Sections 733 and 734 shall be applied as if no gain were recognized, and no adjustment were made to the basis of property, under this subsection.

(6) CHARACTER OF GAIN RECOGNIZED.—In the case of a distribution of a marketable security which is an unrealized receivable (as defined in section 751(c)) or an inventory item (as defined in section 751(d)), any gain recognized under this subsection shall be treated as ordinary income to the extent of any increase in the basis of such security attributable to the gain described in paragraph (4)(A)(ii).

(7) REGULATIONS.—The Secretary shall prescribe such regulations as may be necessary or appropriate to carry out the purposes of this subsection, including regulations to prevent the avoidance of such purposes.

Amendments

- **1997, Taxpayer Relief Act of 1997 (P.L. 105-34)**

P.L. 105-34, § 1062(b)(3):

Amended Code Sec. 731(c)(6) by striking "section 751(d)(2)" and inserting "section 751(d)". **Effective** for sales, exchanges, and distributions after 8-5-97. For a special rule, see Act Sec. 1062(c)(2), below.

P.L. 105-34, § 1062(c)(2), provides:

(2) BINDING CONTRACTS.—The amendments made by this section shall not apply to any sale or exchange pursuant to a written binding contract in effect on June 8, 1997, and at all times thereafter before such sale or exchange.

- **1994, Uruguay Round Agreements Act (P.L. 103-465)**

P.L. 103-465, § 741(a):

Amended Code Sec. 731 by redesignating subsection (c) as subsection (d) and by inserting after subsection (b) a new subsection (c). **Effective** for distributions after 12-8-94. For special rules, see Act Sec. 741(c)(2)-(5), below.

P.L. 103-465, § 741(c)(2)-(5), provides:

(2) CERTAIN DISTRIBUTIONS BEFORE JANUARY 1, 1995.—The amendments made by this section shall not apply to any marketable security distributed before January 1, 1995, by the partnership which held such security on July 27, 1994.

(3) DISTRIBUTIONS IN LIQUIDATION OF PARTNER'S INTEREST.—The amendments made by this section shall not apply to the distribution of a marketable security in liquidation of a partner's interest in a partnership if—

(A) such liquidation is pursuant to a written contract which was binding on July 15, 1994, and at all times thereafter before the distribution, and

(B) such contract provides for the purchase of such interest not later than a date certain for—

(i) a fixed value of marketable securities that are specified in the contract, or

(ii) other property.

The preceding sentence shall not apply if the partner has the right to elect that such distribution be made other than in marketable securities.

(4) DISTRIBUTIONS IN COMPLETE LIQUIDATION OF PUBLICLY TRADED PARTNERSHIPS.—

(A) IN GENERAL.—The amendments made by this section shall not apply to the distribution of a marketable security in a qualified partnership liquidation if—

(i) the marketable securities were received by the partnership in a nonrecognition transaction in exchange for substantially all of the assets of the partnership,

(ii) the marketable securities are distributed by the partnership within 90 days after their receipt by the partnership, and

(iii) the partnership is liquidated before the beginning of the 1st taxable year of the partnership beginning after December 31, 1997.

(B) QUALIFIED PARTNERSHIP LIQUIDATION.—For purposes of subparagraph (A), the term "qualified partnership liquidation" means—

(i) a complete liquidation of a publicly traded partnership (as defined in section 7704(b) of the Internal Revenue Code of 1986) which is an existing partnership (as defined in section 10211(c)(2) of the Revenue Act of 1987), and

(ii) a complete liquidation of a partnership which is related to a partnership described in clause (i) if such liquidation is related to a complete liquidation of the partnership described in clause (i).

(5) MARKETABLE SECURITIES.—For purposes of this subsection, the term "marketable securities" has the meaning given such term by section 731(c) of the Internal Revenue Code of 1986, as added by this section.

[Sec. 731(d)]

(d) EXCEPTIONS.—This section shall not apply to the extent otherwise provided by section 736 (relating to payments to a retiring partner or a deceased partner's successor in interest), section 751 (relating to unrealized receivables and inventory items), and section 737 (relating to recognition of precontribution gain in case of certain distributions).

Amendments

• 1994, Uruguay Round Agreements Act (P.L. 103-465)

P.L. 103-465, §741(a):

Amended Code Sec. 731 by redesignating subsection (c) as subsection (d). **Effective** for distributions after 12-8-94. For special rules, see Act Sec. 741(c)(2)-(5) in the amendments following Code Sec. 731(c).

• 1992, Energy Policy Act of 1992 (P.L. 102-486)

P.L. 102-486, §1937(b)(2)(A)-(B):

Amended Code Sec. 731(c) by striking "and section 751" and inserting ", section 751", and by inserting ", and section 737 (relating to recognition of precontribution gain in case of certain distributions)" before the period at the end thereof. **Effective** for distributions on or after 6-25-92.

[Sec. 741]

SEC. 741. RECOGNITION AND CHARACTER OF GAIN OR LOSS ON SALE OR EXCHANGE.

In the case of a sale or exchange of an interest in a partnership, gain or loss shall be recognized to the transferor partner. Such gain or loss shall be considered as gain or loss from the sale or exchange of a capital asset, except as otherwise provided in section 751 (relating to unrealized receivables and inventory items).

Amendments

• 2002, Job Creation and Worker Assistance Act of 2002 (P.L. 107-147)

P.L. 107-147, §417(12):

Amended Code Sec. 741 by striking "which have appreciated substantially in value" following "inventory items". **Effective** 3-9-2002.

[Sec. 743]
SEC. 743. SPECIAL RULES WHERE SECTION 754 ELECTION OR SUBSTANTIAL BUILT-IN LOSS.

[Sec. 743(a)]

(a) GENERAL RULE.—The basis of partnership property shall not be adjusted as the result of a transfer of an interest in a partnership by sale or exchange or on the death of a partner unless the election provided by section 754 (relating to optional adjustment to basis of partnership property) is in effect with respect to such partnership or unless the partnership has a substantial built-in loss immediately after such transfer.

Amendments
- **2004, American Jobs Creation Act of 2004 (P.L. 108-357)**

P.L. 108-357, §833(b)(1):

Amended Code Sec. 743(a) by inserting before the period "or unless the partnership has a substantial built-in loss immediately after such transfer". **Effective** for transfers after 10-22-2004. For a transition rule, see Act Sec. 833(d)(2)(B), below.

P.L. 108-357, §833(b)(6)(A):

Amended the heading for Code Sec. 743. **Effective** for transfers after 10-22-2004. For a transition rule, see Act Sec. 833(d)(2)(B), below. Prior to amendment, the heading for Code Sec. 743 read as follows:

SEC. 743. OPTIONAL ADJUSTMENT TO BASIS OF PARTNERSHIP PROPERTY.

P.L. 108-357, §833(d)(2)(B), provides:

(B) TRANSITION RULE.—In the case of an electing investment partnership which is in existence on June 4, 2004, section 743(e)(6)(H) of the Internal Revenue Code of 1986, as added by this section, shall not apply to such partnership and section 743(e)(6)(I) of such Code, as so added, shall be applied by substituting "20 years" for "15 years".

[Sec. 743(b)]

(b) ADJUSTMENT TO BASIS OF PARTNERSHIP PROPERTY.—In the case of a transfer of an interest in a partnership by sale or exchange or upon the death of a partner, a partnership with respect to which the election provided in section 754 is in effect or which has a substantial built-in loss immediately after such transfer shall—

(1) increase the adjusted basis of the partnership property by the excess of the basis to the transferee partner of his interest in the partnership over his proportionate share of the adjusted basis of the partnership property, or

(2) decrease the adjusted basis of the partnership property by the excess of the transferee partner's proportionate share of the adjusted basis of the partnership property over the basis of his interest in the partnership.

Under regulations prescribed by the Secretary, such increase or decrease shall constitute an adjustment to the basis of partnership property with respect to the transferee partner only. A partner's proportionate share of the adjusted basis of partnership property shall be determined in accordance with his interest in partnership capital and, in the case of property contributed to the partnership by a partner, section 704(c) (relating to contributed property) shall apply in determining such share. In the case of an adjustment under this subsection to the basis of partnership property subject to depletion, any depletion allowable shall be determined separately for the transferee partner with respect to his interest in such property.

Amendments
- **2004, American Jobs Creation Act of 2004 (P.L. 108-357)**

P.L. 108-357, §833(b)(2):

Amended Code Sec. 743(b) by inserting "or which has a substantial built-in loss immediately after such transfer" after "section 754 is in effect". **Effective** for transfers after 10-22-2004. For a transition rule, see Act Sec. 833(d)(2)(B), below.

P.L. 108-357, §833(d)(2)(B), provides:

(B) TRANSITION RULE.—In the case of an electing investment partnership which is in existence on June 4, 2004, section 743(e)(6)(H) of the Internal Revenue Code of 1986, as added by this section, shall not apply to such partnership and section 743(e)(6)(I) of such Code, as so added, shall be applied by substituting "20 years" for "15 years".

- **1984, Deficit Reduction Act of 1984 (P.L. 98-369)**

P.L. 98-369, §71(b):

Amended the third sentence of Code Sec. 743(b) by striking out "an agreement described in section 704(c)(2) (relating to effect of partnership agreement on contributed property), such share shall be determined by taking such agreement into account" and inserting in lieu thereof "property contributed to the partnership by a partner, section 704(c) (relating to contributed property) shall apply in determining such share". **Effective** with respect to property contributed to the partnership after 3-31-84, in tax years ending after such date.

- **1976, Tax Reform Act of 1976 (P.L. 94-455)**

P.L. 94-455, §1906(b)(13)(A):

Amended 1954 Code by substituting "Secretary" for "Secretary or his delegate" each place it appeared. **Effective** 2-1-77.

[Sec. 743(c)]

(c) ALLOCATION OF BASIS.—The allocation of basis among partnership properties where subsection (b) is applicable shall be made in accordance with the rules provided in section 755.

[Sec. 743(d)]

(d) SUBSTANTIAL BUILT-IN LOSS.—

(1) IN GENERAL.—For purposes of this section, a partnership has a substantial built-in loss with respect to a transfer of an interest in the partnership if—

(A) the partnership's adjusted basis in the partnership property exceeds by more than $250,000 the fair market value of such property, or

(B) the transferee partner would be allocated a loss of more than $250,000 if the partnership assets were sold for cash equal to their fair market value immediately after such transfer.

(2) REGULATIONS.—The Secretary shall prescribe such regulations as may be appropriate to carry out the purposes of paragraph (1) and section 734(d), including regulations aggregating related partnerships and disregarding property acquired by the partnership in an attempt to avoid such purposes.

Amendments

• 2017, Tax Cuts and Jobs Act (P.L. 115-97)

P.L. 115-97, §13502(a):

Amended Code Sec. 743(d)(1). **Effective** for transfers of partnership interests after 12-31-2017. Prior to amendment, Code Sec. 743(d)(1) read as follows:

(1) IN GENERAL.—For purposes of this section, a partnership has a substantial built-in loss with respect to a transfer of an interest in a partnership if the partnership's adjusted basis in the partnership property exceeds by more than $250,000 the fair market value of such property.

• 2004, American Jobs Creation Act of 2004 (P.L. 108-357)

P.L. 108-357, §833(b)(3):

Amended Code Sec. 743 by adding at the end a new subsection (d). **Effective** for transfers after 10-22-2004. For a transition rule, see Act Sec. 833(d)(2)(B), below.

P.L. 108-357, §833(d)(2)(B), provides:

(B) TRANSITION RULE.—In the case of an electing investment partnership which is in existence on June 4, 2004, section 743(e)(6)(H) of the Internal Revenue Code of 1986, as added by this section, shall not apply to such partnership and section 743(e)(6)(I) of such Code, as so added, shall be applied by substituting "20 years" for "15 years".

[Sec. 743(e)]

(e) ALTERNATIVE RULES FOR ELECTING INVESTMENT PARTNERSHIPS.—

(1) NO ADJUSTMENT OF PARTNERSHIP BASIS.—For purposes of this section, an electing investment partnership shall not be treated as having a substantial built-in loss with respect to any transfer occurring while the election under paragraph (6)(A) is in effect.

(2) LOSS DEFERRAL FOR TRANSFEREE PARTNER.—In the case of a transfer of an interest in an electing investment partnership, the transferee partner's distributive share of losses (without regard to gains) from the sale or exchange of partnership property shall not be allowed except to the extent that it is established that such losses exceed the loss (if any) recognized by the transferor (or any prior transferor to the extent not fully offset by a prior disallowance under this paragraph) on the transfer of the partnership interest.

(3) NO REDUCTION IN PARTNERSHIP BASIS.—Losses disallowed under paragraph (2) shall not decrease the transferee partner's basis in the partnership interest.

(4) CERTAIN BASIS REDUCTIONS TREATED AS LOSSES.—In the case of a transferee partner whose basis in property distributed by the partnership is reduced under section 732(a)(2), the amount of the loss recognized by the transferor on the transfer of the partnership interest which is taken into account under paragraph (2) shall be reduced by the amount of such basis reduction.

(5) ELECTING INVESTMENT PARTNERSHIP.—For purposes of this subsection, the term "electing investment partnership" means any partnership if—

(A) the partnership makes an election to have this subsection apply,

(B) the partnership would be an investment company under section 3(a)(1)(A) of the Investment Company Act of 1940 but for an exemption under paragraph (1) or (7) of section 3(c) of such Act,

(C) such partnership has never been engaged in a trade or business,

(D) substantially all of the assets of such partnership are held for investment,

(E) at least 95 percent of the assets contributed to such partnership consist of money,

(F) no assets contributed to such partnership had an adjusted basis in excess of fair market value at the time of contribution,

(G) all partnership interests of such partnership are issued by such partnership pursuant to a private offering before the date which is 24 months after the date of the first capital contribution to such partnership,

(H) the partnership agreement of such partnership has substantive restrictions on each partner's ability to cause a redemption of the partner's interest, and

(I) the partnership agreement of such partnership provides for a term that is not in excess of 15 years.

The election described in subparagraph (A), once made, shall be irrevocable except with the consent of the Secretary.

(6) REGULATIONS.—The Secretary shall prescribe such regulations as may be appropriate to carry out the purposes of this subsection, including regulations for applying this subsection to tiered partnerships.

Amendments

- **2017, Tax Cuts and Jobs Act (P.L. 115-97)**

P.L. 115-97, §13504(b)(2):

Amended Code Sec. 743(e) by striking paragraph (4) and redesignating paragraphs (5), (6), and (7) as paragraphs (4), (5), and (6). **Effective** for partnership tax years beginning after 12-31-2017. Prior to being stricken, Code Sec. 743(e)(4) read as follows:

(4) EFFECT OF TERMINATION OF PARTNERSHIP.—This subsection shall be applied without regard to any termination of a partnership under section 708(b)(1)(B).

- **2004, American Jobs Creation Act of 2004 (P.L. 108-357)**

P.L. 108-357, §833(b)(4)(A):

Amended Code Sec. 743 by adding after subsection (d) a new subsection (e). **Effective** for transfers after 10-22-2004. For a transition rule, see Act Sec. 833(d)(2)(B), below.

P.L. 108-357, §833(d)(2)(B), provides:

(B) TRANSITION RULE.—In the case of an electing investment partnership which is in existence on June 4, 2004, section 743(e)(6)(H) of the Internal Revenue Code of 1986, as added by this section, shall not apply to such partnership and section 743(e)(6)(I) of such Code, as so added, shall be applied by substituting "20 years" for "15 years".

[Sec. 743(f)]

(f) EXCEPTION FOR SECURITIZATION PARTNERSHIPS.—

(1) NO ADJUSTMENT OF PARTNERSHIP BASIS.—For purposes of this section, a securitization partnership shall not be treated as having a substantial built-in loss with respect to any transfer.

(2) SECURITIZATION PARTNERSHIP.—For purposes of paragraph (1), the term "securitization partnership" means any partnership the sole business activity of which is to issue securities which provide for a fixed principal (or similar) amount and which are primarily serviced by the cash flows of a discrete pool (either fixed or revolving) of receivables or other financial assets that by their terms convert into cash in a finite period, but only if the sponsor of the pool reasonably believes that the receivables and other financial assets comprising the pool are not acquired so as to be disposed of.

Amendments

- **2004, American Jobs Creation Act of 2004 (P.L. 108-357)**

P.L. 108-357, §833(b)(5):

Amended Code Sec. 743 by adding after subsection (e) a new subsection (f). **Effective** for transfers after 10-22-2004. For a transition rule, see Act Sec. 833(d)(2)(B), below.

P.L. 108-357, §833(d)(2)(B), provides:

(B) TRANSITION RULE.—In the case of an electing investment partnership which is in existence on June 4, 2004, section 743(e)(6)(H) of the Internal Revenue Code of 1986, as added by this section, shall not apply to such partnership and section 743(e)(6)(I) of such Code, as so added, shall be applied by substituting "20 years" for "15 years".

[Sec. 751]
SEC. 751. UNREALIZED RECEIVABLES AND INVENTORY ITEMS.

[Sec. 751(a)]

(a) SALE OR EXCHANGE OF INTEREST IN PARTNERSHIP.—The amount of any money, or the fair market value of any property, received by a transferor partner in exchange for all or a part of his interest in the partnership attributable to—

(1) unrealized receivables of the partnership, or

(2) inventory items of the partnership,

shall be considered as an amount realized from the sale or exchange of property other than a capital asset.

Amendments

- **1997, Taxpayer Relief Act of 1997 (P.L. 105-34)**

P.L. 105-34, §1062(a):

Amended Code Sec. 751(a)(2). **Effective**, generally, for sales, exchanges, and distributions after 8-5-97. For a special rule, see Act Sec. 1062(c)(2), below. Prior to amendment, Code Sec. 751(a)(2) read as follows:

(2) inventory items of the partnership which have appreciated substantially in value,

P.L. 105-34, §1062(c)(2), provides:

(2) BINDING CONTRACTS.—The amendments made by this section shall not apply to any sale or exchange pursuant to a written binding contract in effect on June 8, 1997, and at all times thereafter before such sale or exchange.

[Sec. 751(b)]

(b) CERTAIN DISTRIBUTIONS TREATED AS SALES OR EXCHANGES.—

(1) GENERAL RULE.—To the extent a partner receives in a distribution—

(A) partnership property which is—

(i) unrealized receivables, or

(ii) inventory items which have appreciated substantially in value,

in exchange for all or a part of his interest in other partnership property (including money), or

(B) partnership property (including money) other than property described in subparagraph (A)(i) or (ii) in exchange for all or a part of his interest in partnership property described in subparagraph (A)(i) or (ii),

such transactions shall, under regulations prescribed by the Secretary, be considered as a sale or exchange of such property between the distributee and the partnership (as constituted after the distribution).

(2) EXCEPTIONS.—Paragraph (1) shall not apply to—

(A) a distribution of property which the distributee contributed to the partnership, or

(B) payments, described in section 736(a), to a retiring partner or successor in interest of a deceased partner.

(3) SUBSTANTIAL APPRECIATION.—For purposes of paragraph (1)—

(A) IN GENERAL.—Inventory items of the partnership shall be considered to have appreciated substantially in value if their fair market value exceeds 120 percent of the adjusted basis to the partnership of such property.

(B) CERTAIN PROPERTY EXCLUDED.—For purposes of subparagraph (A), there shall be excluded any inventory property if a principal purpose for acquiring such property was to avoid the provisions of this subsection relating to inventory items.

Amendments

• **1997, Taxpayer Relief Act of 1997 (P.L. 105-34)**

P.L. 105-34, §1062(b)(1)(A):

Amended Code Sec. 751(b)(1) by striking subparagraphs (A) and (B) and inserting new subparagraphs (A) and (B). **Effective**, generally, for sales, exchanges, and distributions after 8-5-97. For a special rule, see Act Sec. 1062(c)(2), below. Prior to being stricken, Code Sec. 751(b)(1)(A)-(B) read as follows:

(A) partnership property described in subsection (a)(1) or (2) in exchange for all or a part of his interest in other partnership property (including money), or

(B) partnership property (including money) other than property described in subsection (a) (1) or (2) in exchange for all or a part of his interest in partnership property described in subsection (a) (1) or (2),

P.L. 105-34, §1062(b)(1)(B):

Amended Code Sec. 751(b) by adding at the end a new paragraph (3). **Effective**, generally, for sales, exchanges, and distributions after 8-5-97. For a special rule, see Act Sec. 1062(c)(2), below.

P.L. 105-34, §1062(c)(2), provides:

(2) BINDING CONTRACTS.—The amendments made by this section shall not apply to any sale or exchange pursuant to a written binding contract in effect on June 8, 1997, and at all times thereafter before such sale or exchange.

• **1976, Tax Reform Act of 1976 (P.L. 94-455)**

P.L. 94-455, §1906(b)(13)(A):

Amended 1954 Code by substituting "Secretary" for "Secretary or his delegate" each place it appeared. **Effective** 2-1-77.

[Sec. 751(c)]

(c) UNREALIZED RECEIVABLES.—For purposes of this subchapter, the term "unrealized receivables" includes, to the extent not previously includible in income under the method of accounting used by the partnership, any rights (contractual or otherwise) to payment for—

(1) goods delivered, or to be delivered, to the extent the proceeds therefrom would be treated as amounts received from the sale or exchange of property other than a capital asset, or

(2) services rendered, or to be rendered.

For purposes of this section and sections 731, 732, and 741 (but not for purposes of section 736), such term also includes mining property (as defined in section 617(f)(2)), stock in a DISC (as described in section 992(a)), section 1245 property (as defined in section 1245(a)(3)), stock in certain foreign corporations (as described in section 1248), section 1250 property (as defined in section 1250(c)), farm land (as defined in section 1252(a)), franchises, trademarks, or trade names (referred to in section 1253(a)), and an oil, gas, or geothermal property (described in section 1254) but only to the extent of the amount which would be treated as gain to which section 617(d)(1), 995(c), 1245(a), 1248(a), 1250(a), 1252(a), 1253(a) or 1254(a) would apply if (at the time of the transaction described in this section or section 731, 732, or 741, as the case may be) such property had been sold by the partnership at its fair market value. For purposes of this section and sections 731, 732, and 741 (but not for purposes of section 736), such term also includes any market discount bond (as defined in section 1278) and any short-term obligation (as defined in section 1283) but only to the extent of the amount which would be treated as ordinary income if (at the time of the transaction described in this section or section 731, 732, or 741, as the case may be) such property had been sold by the partnership.

Amendments

• **2018, Tax Technical Corrections Act of 2018 (P.L. 115-141)**

P.L. 115-141, §401(a)(140), Div. U:

Amended Code Sec. 751(c) by striking "and, sections" both places it appears and inserting "and sections". **Effective** 3-23-2018.

• **1998, IRS Restructuring and Reform Act of 1998 (P.L. 105-206)**

P.L. 105-206, §6010(m):

Amended Code Sec. 751(c) by striking "731" each place it appears and inserting "731, 732,". **Effective** as if included in the provision of P.L. 105-34 to which it relates [**effective** for distributions after 8-5-97.—CCH].

• **1993, Omnibus Budget Reconciliation Act of 1993 (P.L. 103-66)**

P.L. 103-66, §13262(b)(1)(A)-(B):

Amended Code Sec. 751(c) by striking "sections 731, 736, and 741" each place they appear and inserting ", sections 731 and 741 (but not for purposes of section 736)", and by striking "section 731, 736, or 741" each place it appears and inserting "section 731 or 741". **Effective**, generally, in the case of partners retiring or dying on or after 1-5-93. However, for exceptions, see Act Sec. 13262(c)(2) below.

P.L. 103-66, §13262(c)(2), provides:

(2) BINDING CONTRACT EXCEPTION.—The amendments made by this section shall not apply to any partner retiring on or after January 5, 1993, if a written contract to purchase such

partner's interest in the partnership was binding on January 4, 1993, and at all times thereafter before such purchase.

- **1986, Tax Reform Act of 1986 (P.L. 99-514)**

P.L. 99-514, §201(d)(10):
Amended Code Sec. 751(c) by striking out "section 1245 recovery property (as defined in section 1245(a)(5))," after "section 1245(a)(3)),". **Effective**, generally, for property placed in service after 12-31-86, in tax years ending after such date. However, for transitional rules see Act Secs. 203, 204, and 251(d) following Code Sec. 168.

P.L. 99-514, §1899A(19):
Amended Code Sec. 751(c) by striking out "section 617(f)(2), stock" and inserting in lieu thereof "section 617(f)(2)), stock". **Effective** 10-22-86.

- **1984, Deficit Reduction Act of 1984 (P.L. 98-369)**

P.L. 98-369, §43(c):
Added the sentence at the end of Code Sec. 751(c). **Effective** for tax years ending after 7-18-84.

P.L. 98-369, §492(b)(4):
Amended the second sentence of Code Sec. 751(c) by striking out "farm recapture property (as defined in section 1251(e)(1)),", and by striking out "1251(c),". **Effective** for tax years beginning after 12-31-83.

- **1983, Technical Corrections Act of 1982 (P.L. 97-448)**

P.L. 97-448, §102(a)(6):
Amended the second sentence of Code Sec. 751(c) by inserting "section 1245 recovery property (as defined in section 1245(a)(5))," after "section 1245(a)(3)),". **Effective** as if included in the provision of P.L. 97-34 to which it relates.

- **1978, Energy Tax Act of 1978 (P.L. 95-618)**

P.L. 95-618, §402(c)(5):
Amended Code Sec. 751(c) by striking out "oil or gas property" and inserting in lieu thereof "oil, gas, or geothermal property". For **effective** date, see historical comment for P.L. 95-618, §402(e), under Code Sec. 263(c).

- **1976, Tax Reform Act of 1976 (P.L. 94-455)**

P.L. 94-455, §205(b):
Added "and an oil or gas property (described in section 1254)" and struck out "or 1252(a)" and inserted in its place "1252(a), or 1254(a)". **Effective** for tax years ending after 12-31-75.

P.L. 94-455, §1042(c):
Struck out "(as defined in section 1245(a)(3))," and inserted in its place "(as defined in section 1245(a)(3)), stock in certain foreign corporations (as described in section 1248)," and substituted "1245(a), 1248(a)" for "1245(a)". **Effective** for transfers beginning after 10-9-75, and to sales, exchanges, and distributions taking place after such date.

P.L. 94-455, §1101(d):
Substituted "(as defined in section 617(f)(2), stock in a DISC (as described in section 992(a))," for "(as defined in section 617(f)(2))," and struck out "617(d)(1), 1245(a)," and inserted in its place "617(d)(1), 995(c), 1245(a),". **Effective** for sales, exchanges, or other dispositions after 12-31-76 (as amended by P.L. 95-600, §701(u)(12)(A)), in tax years ending after such date.

P.L. 94-455, §1901(a)(93):
Substituted "1245(a), 1250(a)," for "1245(a), or 1250(a)". **Effective** for tax years beginning after 1976.

P.L. 94-455, §2110(a):
Added "franchises, trademarks, or trade names (referred to in section 1253(a))," and substituted "1252(a), 1253(a)" for "1252(a)". **Effective** for transactions described in section 731, 736, 741, or 751 of the Internal Revenue Code of 1954 which occur after 12-31-76, in tax years ending after that date.

- **1969, Tax Reform Act of 1969 (P.L. 91-172)**

P.L. 91-172, §211(b):
Amended Code Sec. 751(c) by striking out "and section 1250 property (as defined in section 1250(c))" and inserting in lieu thereof "section 1250 property (as defined in section 1250(c)), farm recapture property (as defined in section 1251(e)(1)), and farm land (as defined in section 1252(a))"; and by striking out "1250(a)" and inserting in lieu thereof "1250(a), 1251(c), or 1252(a)". **Effective** for tax years beginning after 12-31-69.

- **1966 (P.L. 89-570)**

P.L. 89-570, §[1(c)]:
Amended the last sentence of Code Sec. 751(c) by substituting "mining property (as defined in section 617(f)(2)), section 1245 property (as defined in section 1245(a)(3))," for "section 1245 property (as defined in section 1245(a)(3))" and by substituting "section 617(d)(1), 1245(a)," for "section 1245(a)". **Effective** for tax years ending after 9-12-66, the date of enactment, but only in respect of expenditures paid or incurred after that date.

- **1964, Revenue Act of 1964 (P.L. 88-272)**

P.L. 88-272, §231(b)(6):
Amended the last sentence of Code Sec. 751(c) by inserting "and section 1250 property (as defined in section 1250(c))" and by adding "or 1250(a)" following "1245(a)". **Effective** as to dispositions after 12-31-63, in tax years ending after such date.

- **1962, Revenue Act of 1962 (P.L. 87-834)**

P.L. 87-834, §13(f)(1):
Amended Code Sec. 751(c) by adding the last sentence. **Effective** for tax years beginning after 12-31-62.

[Sec. 751(d)]

(d) INVENTORY ITEMS.—For purposes of this subchapter, the term "inventory items" means—

(1) property of the partnership of the kind described in section 1221(a)(1),

(2) any other property of the partnership which, on sale or exchange by the partnership, would be considered property other than a capital asset and other than property described in section 1231, and

(3) any other property held by the partnership which, if held by the selling or distributee partner, would be considered property of the type described in paragraph (1) or (2).

Amendments

- **2004, American Jobs Creation Act of 2004 (P.L. 108-357)**

P.L. 108-357, §413(c)(11):
Amended Code Sec. 751(d) by adding "and" at the end of paragraph (2), by striking paragraph (3), by redesignating paragraph (4) as paragraph (3), and by striking "paragraph (1), (2), or (3)" in paragraph (3) (as so redesignated) and inserting "paragraph (1) or (2)". **Effective** for tax years of foreign corporations beginning after 12-31-2004, and for tax years of United States shareholders with or within which such tax years of foreign corporations end. Prior to being stricken, Code Sec. 751(d)(3) read as follows:

(3) any other property of the partnership which, if sold or exchanged by the partnership, would result in a gain taxable under subsection (a) of section 1246 (relating to gain on foreign investment company stock), and

- **1999, Tax Relief Extension Act of 1999 (P.L. 106-170)**

P.L. 106-170, §532(c)(2)(F):
Amended Code Sec. 751(d)(1) by striking "section 1221(1)" and inserting "section 1221(a)(1)". **Effective** for any instrument held, acquired, or entered into, any transaction entered into, and supplies held or acquired on or after 12-17-99.

- **1997, Taxpayer Relief Act of 1997 (P.L. 105-34)**

P.L. 105-34, §1062(b)(2):
Amended Code Sec. 751(d). **Effective**, generally, for sales, exchanges, and distributions after 8-5-97. For a special rule, see Act Sec. 1062(c)(2), below. Prior to amendment, Code Sec. 751(d) read as follows:

(d) INVENTORY ITEMS WHICH HAVE APPRECIATED SUBSTANTIALLY IN VALUE.—

(1) SUBSTANTIAL APPRECIATION.—
(A) IN GENERAL.—Inventory items of the partnership shall be considered to have appreciated substantially in value if their fair market value exceeds 120 percent of the adjusted basis to the partnership of such property.
(B) CERTAIN PROPERTY EXCLUDED.—For purposes of subparagraph (A), there shall be excluded any inventory property if a principal purpose for acquiring such property was to avoid the provisions of this section relating to inventory items.
(2) INVENTORY ITEMS.—For purposes of this subchapter the term "inventory items" means—
(A) property of the partnership of the kind described in section 1221(1),
(B) any other property of the partnership which, on sale or exchange by the partnership, would be considered property other than a capital asset and other than property described in section 1231,
(C) any other property of the partnership which, if sold or exchanged by the partnership, would result in a gain taxable under subsection (a) of section 1246 (relating to gain on foreign investment company stock), and
(D) any other property held by the partnership which, if held by the selling or distributee partner, would be considered property of the type described in subparagraph (A), (B), or (C).

P.L. 105-34, §1062(c)(2), provides:
(2) BINDING CONTRACTS.—The amendments made by this section shall not apply to any sale or exchange pursuant to a written binding contract in effect on June 8, 1997, and at all times thereafter before such sale or exchange.

• **1993, Omnibus Budget Reconciliation Act of 1993 (P.L. 103-66)**
P.L. 103-66, §13206(e)(1):
Amended Code Sec. 751(d)(1). **Effective** for sales, exchanges, and distributions after 4-30-93. Prior to amendment, Code Sec. 751(d)(1) read as follows:
(1) SUBSTANTIAL APPRECIATION.—Inventory items of the partnership shall be considered to have appreciated substantially in value if their fair market value exceeds—
(A) 120 percent of the adjusted basis to the partnership of such property, and
(B) 10 percent of the fair market value of all partnership property, other than money.

• **1962, Revenue Act of 1962 (P.L. 87-834)**
P.L. 87-834, §14(b)(2):
Amended Code Sec. 751(d)(2) by deleting "and" at the end of paragraph (B), and by amending paragraph (C) and adding paragraph (D). **Effective** for tax years beginning after 12-31-62. Prior to amendment, paragraph (C) read as follows:
"(C) any other property held by the partnership which, if held by the selling or distributee partner, would be considered property of the type described in subparagraph (A) or (B)."

[Sec. 751(e)]
(e) LIMITATION ON TAX ATTRIBUTABLE TO DEEMED SALES OF SECTION 1248 STOCK.—For purposes of applying this section and sections 731 and 741 to any amount resulting from the reference to section 1248(a) in the second sentence of subsection (c), in the case of an individual, the tax attributable to such amount shall be limited in the manner provided by subsection (b) of section 1248 (relating to gain from certain sales or exchanges of stock in certain foreign corporation).

Amendments
• **1993, Omnibus Budget Reconciliation Act of 1993 (P.L. 103-66)**
P.L. 103-66, §13262(b)(2)(A):
Amended Code Sec. 751(e) by striking "sections 731, 736, and 741" and by inserting "sections 731 and 741". **Effective**, generally, in the case of partners retiring or dying on or after 1-5-93. However, for exceptions, see Act Sec. 13262(c)(2) below.

P.L. 103-66, §13262(c)(2), provides:
(2) BINDING CONTRACT EXCEPTION.—The amendments made by this section shall not apply to any partner retiring on or after January 5, 1993, if a written contract to purchase such partner's interest in the partnership was binding on January 4, 1993, and at all times thereafter before such purchase.

• **1978, Energy Tax Act of 1978 (P.L. 95-618)**
P.L. 95-618, §701(u)(13)(A):
Added Code Sec. 751(e). **Effective** for transfers beginning after 10-9-75, and to sales, exchanges, and distributions taking place after such date.

[Sec. 751(f)]
(f) SPECIAL RULES IN THE CASE OF TIERED PARTNERSHIPS, ETC.—In determining whether property of a partnership is—
(1) an unrealized receivable, or
(2) an inventory item,
such partnership shall be treated as owning its proportionate share of the property of any other partnership in which it is a partner. Under regulations, rules similar to the rules of the preceding sentence shall also apply in the case of interests in trusts.

Amendments
• **1984, Deficit Reduction Act of 1984 (P.L. 98-369)**
P.L. 98-369, §76(a):
Added Code Sec. 751(f). **Effective** for distributions, sales, and exchanges made after 3-31-84, in tax years ending after such date.

[Sec. 754]
SEC. 754. MANNER OF ELECTING OPTIONAL ADJUSTMENT TO BASIS OF PARTNERSHIP PROPERTY.

If a partnership files an election, in accordance with regulations prescribed by the Secretary, the basis of partnership property shall be adjusted, in the case of a distribution of property, in the manner provided in section 734 and, in the case of a transfer of a partnership interest, in the manner provided in section 743. Such an election shall apply with respect to all distributions of property by the partnership and to all transfers of interests in the partnership during the taxable year with respect to which such election was filed and all subsequent taxable years. Such election may be revoked by the partnership, subject to such limitations as may be provided by regulations prescribed by the Secretary.

Amendments

- **1976, Tax Reform Act of 1976 (P.L. 94-455)**

P.L. 94-455, § 1906(b)(13)(A):

Amended 1954 Code by substituting "Secretary" for "Secretary or his delegate" each place it appeared. **Effective** 2-1-77.

[Sec. 1042]
SEC. 1042. SALES OF STOCK TO EMPLOYEE STOCK OWNERSHIP PLANS OR CERTAIN COOPERATIVES.

[Sec. 1042(a)]

(a) NONRECOGNITION OF GAIN.—If—

(1) the taxpayer or executor elects in such form as the Secretary may prescribe the application of this section with respect to any sale of qualified securities,

(2) the taxpayer purchases qualified replacement property within the replacement period, and

(3) the requirements of subsection (b) are met with respect to such sale,

then the gain (if any) on such sale which would be recognized as long-term capital gain shall be recognized only to the extent that the amount realized on such sale exceeds the cost to the taxpayer of such qualified replacement property.

Amendments

- **1986, Tax Reform Act of 1986 (P.L. 99-514)**

P.L. 99-514, § 1854(a)(1)(A) and (B):

Amended Code Sec. 1042(a) by striking out "gain (if any) on such sale" and inserting in lieu thereof "gain (if any) on such sale which would be recognized as long-term capital gain", and by striking out "the taxpayer elects" in paragraph (1) and inserting in lieu thereof "the taxpayer or executor elects in such form as the Secretary may prescribe". **Effective** as if included in the provision of P.L. 98-369 to which it relates.

[Sec. 1042(b)]

(b) REQUIREMENTS TO QUALIFY FOR NONRECOGNITION.—A sale of qualified securities meets the requirements of this subsection if—

(1) SALE TO EMPLOYEE ORGANIZATIONS.—The qualified securities are sold to—

(A) an employee stock ownership plan (as defined in section 4975(e)(7)), or

(B) an eligible worker-owned cooperative.

(2) PLAN MUST HOLD 30 PERCENT OF STOCK AFTER SALE.—The plan or cooperative referred to in paragraph (1) owns (after application of section 318(a)(4)), immediately after the sale, at least 30 percent of—

(A) each class of outstanding stock of the corporation (other than stock described in section 1504(a)(4)) which issued the qualified securities, or

(B) the total value of all outstanding stock of the corporation (other than stock described in section 1504(a)(4)).

(3) WRITTEN STATEMENT REQUIRED.—

(A) IN GENERAL.—The taxpayer files with the Secretary the written statement described in subparagraph (B).

(B) STATEMENT.—A statement is described in this subparagraph if it is a verified written statement of—

(i) the employer whose employees are covered by the plan described in paragraph (1), or

(ii) any authorized officer of the cooperative described in paragraph (1),

consenting to the application of sections 4978 and 4979A with respect to such employer or cooperative.

(4) 3-YEAR HOLDING PERIOD.—The taxpayer's holding period with respect to the qualified securities is at least 3 years (determined as of the time of the sale).

Amendments

• **1989, Omnibus Budget Reconciliation Act of 1989 (P.L. 101-239)**

P.L. 101-239, § 7303(a):

Amended Code Sec. 1042(b) by adding at the end thereof a new paragraph (4). **Effective** for sales after 7-10-89.

• **1986, Tax Reform Act of 1986 (P.L. 99-514)**

P.L. 99-514, § 1854(a)(2)(A):

Amended Code Sec. 1042(b)(2). For the **effective** date, see Act Sec. 1854(b)(2)(B)(i), below.

P.L. 99-514, § 1854(b)(2)(B)(i), provides:

(B)(i) The requirement that section 1042(b) of the Internal Revenue Code of 1954 shall be applied with regard to section 318(a)(4) of such Code shall apply to sales after May 6, 1986.

P.L. 99-514, § 1854(a)(2)(B)(ii):

Amended Code Sec. 1042(b)(2). **Effective** for sales after 7-18-84, and before 10-22-86. Prior to amendment by Act Sec. 1854(a)(2)(A) and (B)(ii), Code Sec. 1042(b)(2) read as follows:

(2) EMPLOYEES MUST OWN 30 PERCENT OF STOCK AFTER SALE.—The plan or cooperative referred to in paragraph (1) owns, immediately after the sale, at least 30 percent of the total value of the employer securities (within the meaning of section 409(l)) outstanding as of such time.

P.L. 99-514, § 1854(a)(3)(B), as amended by P.L. 100-647, § 1018(t)(4)(F)-(G):

Amended Code Sec. 1042(b) by striking out paragraph (3) and redesignating paragraph (4) as paragraph (3). **Effective**, generally, for sales of securities after 10-22-86. For a special rule, see Act Sec. 1854(a)(3)(C)(ii) below. Prior to amendment, Code Sec. 1042(b)(3) read as follows:

(3) PLAN MAINTAINED FOR BENEFIT OF EMPLOYEES.—No portion of the assets of the plan or cooperative attributable to employer securities (within the meaning of section 409(l)) acquired by the plan or cooperative described in paragraph (1) accrue under such plan, or are allocated by such cooperative, for the benefit of—

(A) the taxpayer,

(B) any person who is a member of the family of the taxpayer (within the meaning of section 267(c)(4)), or

(C) any other person who owns (after application of section 318(a)) more than 25 percent in value of any class of outstanding employer securities (within the meaning of section 409(l)).

P.L. 99-514, § 1854(a)(3)(C)(ii), provides:

(ii) A taxpayer or executor may elect to have section 1042(b)(3) of the Internal Revenue Code of 1954 (as in effect before the amendment made by subparagraph (B)) apply to sales before the date of the enactment of this Act as if such section included the last sentence of section 409(n)(1) of the Internal Revenue Code of 1986 (as added by subparagraph (A)).

P.L. 99-514, § 1854(a)(9)(B):

Amended Code Sec. 1042(b)(3)(B) by striking out "section 4978(a)" and inserting in lieu thereof "sections 4978 and 4979A". **Effective** for sales of securities after 10-22-86.

P.L. 99-514, § 1854(f)(3)(B):

Amended Code Sec. 1042(b)(3)(B) by inserting "and 4979A" after "section 4978(a)". **Effective** 10-22-86.

[Sec. 1042(c)]

(c) DEFINITIONS; SPECIAL RULES.—For purposes of this section—

(1) QUALIFIED SECURITIES.—The term "qualified securities" means employer securities (as defined in section 409(l)) which—

(A) are issued by a domestic C corporation that has no stock outstanding that are readily tradable on an established securities market, and

(B) were not received by the taxpayer in—

(i) a distribution from a plan described in section 401(a), or

(ii) a transfer pursuant to an option or other right to acquire stock to which section 83, 422, or 423 applied (or to which section 422 or 424 (as in effect on the day before the date of the enactment of the Revenue Reconciliation Act of 1990) applied).

(2) ELIGIBLE WORKER-OWNED COOPERATIVE.—The term "eligible worker-owned cooperative" means any organization—

(A) to which part I of subchapter T applies,

(B) a majority of the membership of which is composed of employees of such organization,

(C) a majority of the voting stock of which is owned by members,

(D) a majority of the board of directors of which is elected by the members on the basis of 1 person 1 vote, and

(E) a majority of the allocated earnings and losses of which are allocated to members on the basis of—

(i) patronage,

(ii) capital contributions, or

(iii) some combination of clauses (i) and (ii).

(3) REPLACEMENT PERIOD.—The term "replacement period" means the period which begins 3 months before the date on which the sale of qualified securities occurs and which ends 12 months after the date of such sale.

(4) QUALIFIED REPLACEMENT PROPERTY.—

(A) IN GENERAL.— The term "qualified replacement property" means any security issued by a domestic operating corporation which—

(i) did not, for the taxable year preceding the taxable year in which such security was purchased, have passive investment income (as defined in section 1362(d)(3)(C)) in excess of 25 percent of the gross receipts of such corporation for such preceding taxable year, and

(ii) is not the corporation which issued the qualified securities which such security is replacing or a member of the same controlled group of corporations (within the meaning of section 1563(a)(1)) as such corporation.

For purposes of clause (i), income which is described in section 954(c)(3) (as in effect immediately before the Tax Reform Act of 1986) shall not be treated as passive investment income.

(B) OPERATING CORPORATION.—For purposes of this paragraph—

(i) IN GENERAL.—The term "operating corporation" means a corporation more than 50 percent of the assets of which were, at the time the security was purchased or before the close of the replacement period, used in the active conduct of the trade or business.

(ii) FINANCIAL INSTITUTIONS AND INSURANCE COMPANIES.—The term "operating corporation" shall include—

(I) any financial institution described in section 581, and

(II) an insurance company subject to tax under subchapter L.

(C) CONTROLLING AND CONTROLLED CORPORATIONS TREATED AS 1 CORPORATION.—

(i) IN GENERAL.—For purposes of applying this paragraph, if—

(I) the corporation issuing the security owns stock representing control of 1 or more other corporations,

(II) 1 or more other corporations own stock representing control of the corporation issuing the security, or

(III) both,

then all such corporations shall be treated as 1 corporation.

(ii) CONTROL.—For purposes of clause (i), the term "control" has the meaning given such term by section 304(c). In determining control, there shall be disregarded any qualified replacement property of the taxpayer with respect to the section 1042 sale being tested.

(D) SECURITY DEFINED.—For purposes of this paragraph the term "security" has the meaning given such term by section 165(g)(2), except that such term shall not include any security issued by a government or political subdivision thereof.

(5) SECURITIES SOLD BY UNDERWRITER.—No sale of securities by an underwriter to an employee stock ownership plan or eligible worker-owned cooperative in the ordinary course of his trade or business as an underwriter, whether or not guaranteed, shall be treated as a sale for purposes of subsection (a).

(6) TIME FOR FILING ELECTION.—An election under subsection (a) shall be filed not later than the last day prescribed by law (including extensions thereof) for filing the return of tax imposed by this chapter for the taxable year in which the sale occurs.

(7) SECTION NOT TO APPLY TO GAIN OF C CORPORATION.—Subsection (a) shall not apply to any gain on the sale of any qualified securities which is includible in the gross income of any C corporation.

Amendments

• 1996, Small Business Job Protection Act of 1996 (P.L. 104-188)

P.L. 104-188, § 1311(b)(3):
Amended Code Sec. 1042(c)(4)(A)(i) by striking "section 1362(d)(3)(D)" and inserting "section 1362(d)(3)(C)". Effective, generally, for tax years beginning after 12-31-96.

P.L. 104-188, § 1316(d)(3):
Amended Code Sec. 1042(c)(1)(A) by striking "domestic corporation" and inserting "domestic C corporation". Effective for tax years beginning after 12-31-97.

P.L. 104-188, § 1616(b)(13):
Amended Code Sec. 1042(c)(4)(B)(ii)[I] by striking "or 593" after "581". Effective, generally, for tax years beginning after 12-31-95.

• 1990, Omnibus Budget Reconciliation Act of 1990 (P.L. 101-508)

P.L. 101-508, § 11801(c)(9)(H) (as amended by P.L. 104-188, § 1704(t)(50)):
Amended Code Sec. 1042(c)(1)(B)(ii) by striking "section 83, 422, 422A, 423, or 424 applies" and inserting "section 83, 422, or 423 applied (or to which section 422 or 424 (as in effect on the day before the date of the enactment of the Revenue Reconciliation Act of 1990) applied)". Effective 11-5-90.

P.L. 101-508, § 11821(b)(1)-(2), provides:

(b) SAVINGS PROVISION.—If—

(1) any provision amended or repealed by this part applied to—

Code Sec. 1042

(A) any transaction occurring before the date of the enactment of this Act,
(B) any property acquired before such date of enactment, or
(C) any item of income, loss, deduction, or credit taken into account before such date of enactment, and
(2) the treatment of such transaction, property, or item under such provision would (without regard to the amendments made by this part) affect liability for tax for periods ending after such date of enactment,
nothing in the amendments made by this part shall be construed to affect the treatment of such transaction, property, or item for purposes of determining liability for tax for periods ending after such date of enactment.

- **1988, Technical and Miscellaneous Revenue Act of 1988 (P.L. 100-647)**

P.L. 100-647, § 1018(t)(4)(D):
Amended Code Sec. 1042(c)(4)(A) by inserting "(as in effect immediately before the Tax Reform Act of 1986)" after "section 954(c)(3)". **Effective** as if included in the provision of P.L. 99-514 to which it relates.

P.L. 100-647, § 1018(t)(4)(E):
Amended Code Sec. 1042(c)(4)(B)(i) by striking out "placement period" and inserting in lieu thereof "replacement period". **Effective** as if included in the provision of P.L. 99-514 to which it relates.

- **1986, Tax Reform Act of 1986 (P.L. 99-514)**

P.L. 99-514, § 1854(a)(4)(A)-(C):
Amended Code Sec. 1042(c)(1) by striking out "securities outstanding that are" in subparagraph (A) and inserting in lieu thereof "stock outstanding that is", by inserting "and" at the end of subparagraph (A), and by striking out subparagraph (B) and redesignating subparagraph (C) as subparagraph (B). **Effective** as if included in the provision of P.L. 98-369 to which it relates. Prior to amendment, Code Sec. 1042(c)(1)(B) read as follows:
(B) at the time of the sale described in subsection (a)(1), have been held by the taxpayer for more than 1 year.

P.L. 99-514, § 1854(a)(5)(A):
Amended Code Sec. 1042(c)(4). **Effective** as if included in the provision of P.L. 98-369 to which it relates. Prior to amendment, Code Sec. 1042(c)(4) read as follows:
(4) QUALIFIED REPLACEMENT PROPERTY.—The term "qualified replacement property" means any securities (as defined in section 165(g)(2)) issued by a domestic corporation which does not, for the taxable year in which such stock is issued, have passive investment income (as defined in section 1362(d)(3)(D)) that exceeds 25 percent of the gross receipts of such corporation for such taxable year.

P.L. 99-514, § 1854(a)(5)(B), provides:
(B) If—
(i) before January 1, 1987, the taxpayer acquired any security (as defined in section 165(g)(2) of the Internal Revenue Code of 1954) issued by a domestic corporation or by any State or political subdivision thereof,
(ii) the taxpayer treated such security as qualified replacement property for purposes of section 1042 of such Code, and
(iii) such property does not meet the requirements of section 1042(c)(4) of such Code (as amended by subparagraph (A)),
then, with respect to so much of any gain which the taxpayer treated as not recognized under section 1042(a) by reason of the acquisition of such property, the replacement period for purposes of such section shall not expire before January 1, 1987.

P.L. 99-514, § 1854(a)(6)(A):
Amended Code Sec. 1042(c) by adding at the end thereof new paragraph (7). For the **effective** date, see Act Sec. 1854(a)(6)(B)-(D), below.

P.L. 99-514, § 1854(a)(6)(B)-(D), provides:
(B) The amendment made by subparagraph (A) shall apply to sales after March 28, 1985, except that such amendment shall not apply to sales made before July 1, 1985, if made pursuant to a binding contract in effect on March 28, 1985, and at all times thereafter.
(C) The amendment made by subparagraph (A) shall not apply to any sale occurring on December 20, 1985, with respect to which—
(i) a commitment letter was issued by a bank on October 31, 1984, and
(ii) a final purchase agreement was entered into on November 5, 1985.
(D) In the case of a sale on September 27, 1985, with respect to which a preliminary commitment letter was issued by a bank on April 10, 1985, and with respect to which a commitment letter was issued by a bank on June 28, 1985, the amendment made by subparagraph (A) shall apply but such sale shall be treated as having occurred on September 27, 1986.

P.L. 99-514, § 1854(a)(10)(A)-(C):
Amended Code Sec. 1042(c)(5) by striking out "acquisition" and inserting in lieu thereof "sale", by inserting "to an employee stock ownership plan or eligible worker-owned cooperative" before "in", and by striking out "ACQUIRED" in the heading thereof and inserting in lieu thereof "SOLD". **Effective** as if included in the provision of P.L. 98-369 to which it relates.

P.L. 99-514, § 1854(a)(11):
Amended Code Sec. 1042 by inserting "EMPLOYEE" before "STOCK" in the heading for such section. **Effective** as if included in the provision of P.L. 98-369 to which it relates.

P.L. 99-514, § 1899A(26):
Amended Code Sec. 1042(c) by striking out "this section.—" in the material preceding paragraph (1) and inserting in lieu thereof "this section—". **Effective** 10-22-86.

[Sec. 1042(d)]

(d) BASIS OF QUALIFIED REPLACEMENT PROPERTY.—The basis of the taxpayer in qualified replacement property purchased by the taxpayer during the replacement period shall be reduced by the amount of gain not recognized by reason of such purchase and the application of subsection (a). If more than one item of qualified replacement property is purchased, the basis of each of such items shall be reduced by an amount determined by multiplying the total gain not recognized by reason of such purchase and the application of subsection (a) by a fraction—

(1) the numerator of which is the cost of such item of property, and
(2) the denominator of which is the total cost of all such items of property.

Any reduction in basis under this subsection shall not be taken into account for purposes of section 1278(a)(2)(A)(ii) (relating to definition of market discount).

Amendments
- **1986, Tax Reform Act of 1986 (P.L. 99-514)**

P.L. 99-514, § 1854(a)(7):
Amended Code Sec. 1042(d) by adding at the end thereof a new flush sentence. **Effective** as if included in the provision of P.L. 98-369 to which it relates.

[Sec. 1042(e)]

(e) RECAPTURE OF GAIN ON DISPOSITION OF QUALIFIED REPLACEMENT PROPERTY.—

(1) IN GENERAL.—If a taxpayer disposes of any qualified replacement property, then, notwithstanding any other provision of this title, gain (if any) shall be recognized to the extent of the gain which was not recognized under subsection (a) by reason of the acquisition by such taxpayer of such qualified replacement property.

(2) SPECIAL RULE FOR CORPORATIONS CONTROLLED BY THE TAXPAYER.—If—

Code Sec. 1042

(A) a corporation issuing qualified replacement property disposes of a substantial portion of its assets other than in the ordinary course of its trade or business, and

(B) any taxpayer owning stock representing control (within the meaning of section 304(c)) of such corporation at the time of such disposition holds any qualified replacement property of such corporation at such time,

then the taxpayer shall be treated as having disposed of such qualified replacement property at such time.

(3) RECAPTURE NOT TO APPLY IN CERTAIN CASES.—Paragraph (1) shall not apply to any transfer of qualified replacement property—

(A) in any reorganization (within the meaning of section 368) unless the person making the election under subsection (a)(1) owns stock representing control in the acquiring or acquired corporation and such property is substituted basis property in the hands of the transferee,

(B) by reason of the death of the person making such election,

(C) by gift, or

(D) in any transaction to which section 1042(a) applies.

Amendments

• **1986, Tax Reform Act of 1986 (P.L. 99-514)**
P.L. 99-514, §1854(a)(8)(A):
Amended Code Sec. 1042 by redesignating subsection (e) as subsection (f) and by inserting after subsection (d) new subsection (e). **Effective** for dispositions after 10-22-86, in tax years ending after such date.

[Sec. 1042(f)]

(f) STATUTE OF LIMITATIONS.—If any gain is realized by the taxpayer on the sale or exchange of any qualified securities and there is in effect an election under subsection (a) with respect to such gain, then—

(1) the statutory period for the assessment of any deficiency with respect to such gain shall not expire before the expiration of 3 years from the date the Secretary is notified by the taxpayer (in such manner as the Secretary may by regulations prescribe) of—

(A) the taxpayer's cost of purchasing qualified replacement property which the taxpayer claims results in nonrecognition of any part of such gain,

(B) the taxpayer's intention not to purchase qualified replacement property within the replacement period, or

(C) a failure to make such purchase within the replacement period, and

(2) such deficiency may be assessed before the expiration of such 3-year period notwithstanding the provisions of any other law or rule of law which would otherwise prevent such assessment.

Amendments

• **1986, Tax Reform Act of 1986 (P.L. 99-514)**
P.L. 99-514, §1854(a)(8)(A):
Amended Code Sec. 1042 by redesignating subsection (e) as subsection (f) and by inserting after subsection (d) new subsection (e). **Effective** for dispositions after 10-22-86, in tax years ending after such date.

• **1984, Deficit Reduction Act of 1984 (P.L. 98-369)**
P.L. 98-369, §541(a):
Added Code Sec. 1042. **Effective** for sales of securities in tax years beginning after 7-18-84.

[Sec. 1042(g)]

(g) APPLICATION OF SECTION TO SALES OF STOCK IN AGRICULTURAL REFINERS AND PROCESSORS TO ELIGIBLE FARM COOPERATIVES.—

(1) IN GENERAL.—This section shall apply to the sale of stock of a qualified refiner or processor to an eligible farmers' cooperative.

(2) QUALIFIED REFINER OR PROCESSOR.—For purposes of this subsection, the term "qualified refiner or processor" means a domestic corporation—

(A) substantially all of the activities of which consist of the active conduct of the trade or business of refining or processing agricultural or horticultural products, and

(B) which, during the 1-year period ending on the date of the sale, purchases more than one-half of such products to be refined or processed from—

(i) farmers who make up the eligible farmers' cooperative which is purchasing stock in the corporation in a transaction to which this subsection is to apply, or

(ii) such cooperative.

(3) ELIGIBLE FARMERS' COOPERATIVE.—For purposes of this section, the term "eligible farmers' cooperative" means an organization to which part I of subchapter T applies and which is engaged in the marketing of agricultural or horticultural products.

(4) SPECIAL RULES.—In applying this section to a sale to which paragraph (1) applies—

(A) the eligible farmers' cooperative shall be treated in the same manner as a cooperative described in subsection (b)(1)(B),

(B) subsection (b)(2) shall be applied by substituting "100 percent" for "30 percent" each place it appears,

(C) the determination as to whether any stock in the domestic corporation is a qualified security shall be made without regard to whether the stock is an employer security or to subsection (c)(1)(A), and

(D) paragraphs (2)(D) and (7) of subsection (c) shall not apply.

Amendments

• **1997, Taxpayer Relief Act of 1997 (P.L. 105-34)**
P.L. 105-34, § 968(a):
Amended Code Sec. 1042 by adding at the end a new subsection (g). **Effective** for sales after 12-31-97.

[Sec. 1045]
SEC. 1045. ROLLOVER OF GAIN FROM QUALIFIED SMALL BUSINESS STOCK TO ANOTHER QUALIFIED SMALL BUSINESS STOCK.

[Sec. 1045(a)]

(a) NONRECOGNITION OF GAIN.—In the case of any sale of qualified small business stock held by a taxpayer other than a corporation for more than 6 months and with respect to which such taxpayer elects the application of this section, gain from such sale shall be recognized only to the extent that the amount realized on such sale exceeds—

(1) the cost of any qualified small business stock purchased by the taxpayer during the 60-day period beginning on the date of such sale, reduced by

(2) any portion of such cost previously taken into account under this section.

This section shall not apply to any gain which is treated as ordinary income for purposes of this title.

Amendments

• **1998, IRS Restructuring and Reform Act of 1998 (P.L. 105-206)**
P.L. 105-206, § 6005(f)(1)(A)-(B):
Amended Code Sec. 1045(a) by striking "an individual" and inserting "a taxpayer other than a corporation", and by striking "such individual" and inserting "such taxpayer". **Effective** as if included in the provision of P.L. 105-34 to which it relates [**effective** for sales after 8-5-97.—CCH].

[Sec. 1045(b)]

(b) DEFINITIONS AND SPECIAL RULES.—For purposes of this section—

(1) QUALIFIED SMALL BUSINESS STOCK.—The term "qualified small business stock" has the meaning given such term by section 1202(c).

(2) PURCHASE.—A taxpayer shall be treated as having purchased any property if, but for paragraph (3), the unadjusted basis of such property in the hands of the taxpayer would be its cost (within the meaning of section 1012).

(3) BASIS ADJUSTMENTS.—If gain from any sale is not recognized by reason of subsection (a), such gain shall be applied to reduce (in the order acquired) the basis for determining gain or loss of any qualified small business stock which is purchased by the taxpayer during the 60-day period described in subsection (a).

(4) HOLDING PERIOD.—For purposes of determining whether the nonrecognition of gain under subsection (a) applies to stock which is sold—

(A) the taxpayer's holding period for such stock and the stock referred to in subsection (a)(1) shall be determined without regard to section 1223, and

(B) only the first 6 months of the taxpayer's holding period for the stock referred to in subsection (a)(1) shall be taken into account for purposes of applying section 1202(c)(2).

(5) CERTAIN RULES TO APPLY.—Rules similar to the rules of subsections (f), (g), (h), (i), (j), and (k) of section 1202 shall apply.

Amendments

• **1998, IRS Restructuring and Reform Act of 1998 (P.L. 105-206)**
P.L. 105-206, § 6005(f)(2):
Amended Code Sec. 1045(b) by adding at the end a new paragraph (5). **Effective** as if included in the provision of P.L. 105-34 to which it relates [**effective** for sales after 8-5-97.—CCH].

• **1997, Taxpayer Relief Act of 1997 (P.L. 105-34)**
P.L. 105-34, § 313(a):
Amended part III of subchapter O of chapter 1 by adding at the end a new Code Sec. 1045. **Effective** for sales after 8-5-97.

SEC. 1060. SPECIAL ALLOCATION RULES FOR CERTAIN ASSET ACQUISITIONS.

[Sec. 1060(a)]

(a) GENERAL RULE.—In the case of any applicable asset acquisition, for purposes of determining both—

(1) the transferee's basis in such assets, and

(2) the gain or loss of the transferor with respect to such acquisition,

the consideration received for such assets shall be allocated among such assets acquired in such acquisition in the same manner as amounts are allocated to assets under section 338(b)(5). If in connection with an applicable asset acquisition, the transferee and transferor agree in writing as to the allocation of any consideration, or as to the fair market value of any of the assets, such agreement shall be binding on both the transferee and transferor unless the Secretary determines that such allocation (or fair market value) is not appropriate.

Amendments

• **1990, Omnibus Budget Reconciliation Act of 1990 (P.L. 101-508)**
P.L. 101-508, § 1132(a):
Amended Code Sec. 1060(a) by adding at the end thereof a new sentence. **Effective**, generally, for acquisitions after 10-9-90. For an exception, see 11323(d)(2), below.

P.L. 101-508, § 11323(d)(2), provides:
(2) BINDING CONTRACT EXCEPTION.—The amendments made by this section shall not apply to any acquisition pursuant to a written binding contract in effect on October 9, 1990, and at all times thereafter before such acquisition.

[Sec. 1060(b)]

(b) INFORMATION REQUIRED TO BE FURNISHED TO SECRETARY.—Under regulations, the transferor and transferee in an applicable asset acquisition shall, at such times and in such manner as may be provided in such regulations, furnish to the Secretary the following information:

(1) The amount of the consideration received for the assets which is allocated to Section 197 intangibles.

(2) Any modification of the amount described in paragraph (1).

(3) Any other information with respect to other assets transferred in such acquisition as the Secretary deems necessary to carry out the provisions of this section.

Amendments

• **1993, Omnibus Budget Reconciliation Act of 1993 (P.L. 103-66)**
P.L. 103-66, § 13261(e)(1):
Amended Code Sec. 1060(b)(1) by striking "goodwill or going concern value" and inserting "section 197 intangibles". **Effective**, generally, with respect to property acquired after 8-10-93. For special rules, see Act Sec. 13261(g)(2)-(3) in the amendment notes following Code Sec. 197.

• **1988, Technical and Miscellaneous Revenue Act of 1988 (P.L. 100-647)**
P.L. 100-647, § 1006(h)(1):
Amended Code Sec. 1060(b)(3) by striking out "the Secretary may find necessary" and inserting in lieu thereof "the Secretary deems necessary". **Effective** as if included in the provision of P.L. 99-514 to which it relates.

[Sec. 1060(c)]

(c) APPLICABLE ASSET ACQUISITION.—For purposes of this section, the term "applicable asset acquisition" means any transfer (whether directly or indirectly)—

(1) of assets which constitute a trade or business, and

(2) with respect to which the transferee's basis in such assets is determined wholly by reference to the consideration paid for such assets.

A transfer shall not be treated as failing to be an applicable asset acquisition merely because section 1031 applies to a portion of the assets transferred.

Amendments

• **1986, Tax Reform Act of 1986 (P.L. 99-514)**
P.L. 99-514, § 641(a):
Amended part IV of subchapter O of chapter 1 by redesignating section 1060 as section 1061 and by inserting after section 1059 new section 1060. **Effective** for any acquisition of assets after 5-6-86, unless such acquisition is pursuant to a binding contract which was in effect on 5-6-86, and at all times thereafter.

[Sec. 1060(d)]

(d) TREATMENT OF CERTAIN PARTNERSHIP TRANSACTIONS.—In the case of a distribution of partnership property or a transfer of an interest in a partnership—

(1) the rules of subsection (a) shall apply but only for purposes of determining the value of section 197 intangibles for purposes of applying section 755, and

(2) if section 755 applies, such distribution or transfer (as the case may be) shall be treated as an applicable asset acquisition for purposes of subsection (b).

Amendments

• **1993, Omnibus Budget Reconciliation Act of 1993 (P.L. 103-66)**
P.L. 103-66, § 13261(e)(2):
Amended Code Sec. 1060(d)(1) by striking "goodwill or going concern value (or similar items)" and inserting "sec-

tion 197 intangibles". **Effective**, generally, for property acquired after 8-10-93. For special rules, see Act Sec. 13261(g)(2)-(3) in the amendment notes following Code Sec. 197.

- 1988, Technical and Miscellaneous Revenue Act of 1988 (P.L. 100-647)
P.L. 100-647, § 1006(h)(2):
Amended Code Sec. 1060 by adding at the end thereof new subsection (d). **Effective** as if included in the provision of P.L. 99-514 to which it relates.

[Sec. 1060(e)]

(e) INFORMATION REQUIRED IN CASE OF CERTAIN TRANSFERS OF INTERESTS IN ENTITIES.—
   (1) IN GENERAL.—If—
      (A) a person who is a 10-percent owner with respect to any entity transfers an interest in such entity, and
      (B) in connection with such transfer, such owner (or a related person) enters into an employment contract, covenant not to compete, royalty or lease agreement, or other agreement with the transferee,
   such owner and the transferee shall, at such time and in such manner as the Secretary may prescribe, furnish such information as the Secretary may require.
   (2) 10-PERCENT OWNER.—For purposes of this subsection—
      (A) IN GENERAL.—The term "10-percent owner" means, with respect to any entity, any person who holds 10 percent or more (by value) of the interests in such entity immediately before the transfer.
      (B) CONSTRUCTIVE OWNERSHIP.—Section 318 shall apply in determining ownership of stock in a corporation. Similar principles shall apply in determining the ownership of interests in any other entity.
   (3) RELATED PERSON.—For purposes of this subsection, the term "related person" means any person who is related (within the meaning of section 267(b) or 707(b)(1)) to the 10-percent owner.

Amendments

- 1990, Omnibus Budget Reconciliation Act of 1990 (P.L. 101-508)
P.L. 101-508, § 11323(b)(1):
Amended Code Sec. 1060 by redesignating subsection (e) as subsection (f) and by inserting after subsection (d) a new subsection (e). **Effective**, generally, for acquisitions after 10-9-90. For an exception, see 11323(d)(2), below.

P.L. 101-508, § 11323(d)(2), provides:
(2) BINDING CONTRACT EXCEPTION.—The amendments made by this section shall not apply to any acquisition pursuant to a written binding contract in effect on October 9, 1990, and at all times thereafter before such acquisition.

[Sec. 1060(f)]

(f) CROSS REFERENCE.—
   For provisions relating to penalties for failure to file a return required by this section, see section 6721.

Amendments

- 1990, Omnibus Budget Reconciliation Act of 1990 (P.L. 101-508)
P.L. 101-508, § 11323(b)(1):
Amended Code Sec. 1060 by redesignating subsection (e) as subsection (f). **Effective**, generally, for acquisitions after 10-9-90. For an exception, see 11323(d)(2), below.
P.L. 101-508, § 11323(d)(2), provides:
(2) BINDING CONTRACT EXCEPTION.—The amendments made by this section shall not apply to any acquisition pursuant to a written binding contract in effect on October 9, 1990, and at all times thereafter before such acquisition.

- 1988, Technical and Miscellaneous Revenue Act of 1988 (P.L. 100-647)
P.L. 100-647, § 1006(h)(3)(B):
Amended Code Sec. 1060 by adding at the end thereof new subsection (e). **Effective** as if included in the provision of P.L. 99-514 to which it relates.

[Sec. 1202]

SEC. 1202. PARTIAL EXCLUSION FOR GAIN FROM CERTAIN SMALL BUSINESS STOCK.

[Sec. 1202(a)]

(a) EXCLUSION.—
   (1) IN GENERAL.—In the case of a taxpayer other than a corporation, gross income shall not include 50 percent of any gain from the sale or exchange of qualified small business stock held for more than 5 years.
   (2) EMPOWERMENT ZONE BUSINESSES.—
      (A) IN GENERAL.—In the case of qualified small business stock acquired after the date of the enactment of this paragraph in a corporation which is a qualified business entity (as defined in section 1397C(b)) during substantially all of the taxpayer's holding period for such stock, paragraph (1) shall be applied by substituting "60 percent" for "50 percent".
      (B) CERTAIN RULES TO APPLY.—Rules similar to the rules of paragraphs (5) and (7) of section 1400B(b) (as in effect before its repeal) shall apply for purposes of this paragraph.
      (C) GAIN AFTER 2018 NOT QUALIFIED.—Subparagraph (A) shall not apply to gain attributable to periods after December 31, 2018.
      (D) TREATMENT OF DC ZONE.—The District of Columbia Enterprise Zone shall not be treated as an empowerment zone for purposes of this paragraph.
   (3) SPECIAL RULES FOR 2009 AND CERTAIN PERIODS IN 2010.—In the case of qualified small business stock acquired after the date of the enactment of this paragraph and on or before the date of the enactment of the Creating Small Business Jobs Act of 2010—

(A) paragraph (1) shall be applied by substituting "75 percent" for "50 percent", and
(B) paragraph (2) shall not apply.

In the case of any stock which would be described in the preceding sentence (but for this sentence), the acquisition date for purposes of this subsection shall be the first day on which such stock was held by the taxpayer determined after the application of section 1223.

(4) 100 PERCENT EXCLUSION FOR STOCK ACQUIRED DURING CERTAIN PERIODS IN 2010 AND THEREAFTER.—In the case of qualified small business stock acquired after the date of the enactment of the Creating Small Business Jobs Act of 2010—
(A) paragraph (1) shall be applied by substituting "100 percent" for "50 percent",
(B) paragraph (2) shall not apply, and
(C) paragraph (7) of section 57(a) shall not apply.

In the case of any stock which would be described in the preceding sentence (but for this sentence), the acquisition date for purposes of this subsection shall be the first day on which such stock was held by the taxpayer determined after the application of section 1223.

Amendments

• **2018, Tax Technical Corrections Act of 2018 (P.L. 115-141)**

P.L. 115-141, §401(d)(4)(B)(v), Div. U:
Amended Code Sec. 1202(a)(2)(B) by inserting "(as in effect before its repeal)" after "1400B(b)". **Effective** 3-23-2018. For a special rule, see Act Sec. 401(e), Div. U, below.

P.L. 115-141, §401(e), Div. U, provides:
(e) GENERAL SAVINGS PROVISION WITH RESPECT TO DEADWOOD PROVISIONS.—If—
(1) any provision amended or repealed by the amendments made by subsection (b) or (d) applied to—
(A) any transaction occurring before the date of the enactment of this Act,
(B) any property acquired before such date of enactment, or
(C) any item of income, loss, deduction, or credit taken into account before such date of enactment, and
(2) the treatment of such transaction, property, or item under such provision would (without regard to the amendments or repeals made by such subsection) affect the liability for tax for periods ending after such date of enactment, nothing in the amendments or repeals made by this section shall be construed to affect the treatment of such transaction, property, or item for purposes of determining liability for tax for periods ending after such date of enactment.

• **2015, Protecting Americans from Tax Hikes Act of 2015 (P.L. 114-113)**

P.L. 114-113, §126(a)(1)-(2), Div. Q:
Amended Code Sec. 1202(a)(4) by striking "and before January 1, 2015" following "Creating Small Business Jobs Act of 2010", and by striking ", 2011, 2012, 2013, AND 2014" in the heading and inserting "AND THEREAFTER". **Effective** for stock acquired after 12-31-2014.

• **2014, Tax Increase Prevention Act of 2014 (P.L. 113-295)**

P.L. 113-295, §136(a)(1)-(2), Division A:
Amended Code Sec. 1202(a)(4) by striking "January 1, 2014" and inserting "January 1, 2015", and by striking "AND 2013" in the heading and inserting "2013, AND 2014". **Effective** for stock acquired after 12-31-2013.

• **2013, American Taxpayer Relief Act of 2012 (P.L. 112-240)**

P.L. 112-240, §324(a)(1)-(2):
Amended Code Sec. 1202(a)(4) by striking "January 1, 2012" and inserting "January 1, 2014", and by striking "AND 2011" and inserting ", 2011, 2012, AND 2013" in the heading thereof. **Effective** for stock acquired after 12-31-2011.

P.L. 112-240, §324(b)(1):
Amended Code Sec. 1202(a)(3) by adding at the end a new flush sentence. **Effective** as if included in section 1241(a) of division B of the American Recovery and Reinvestment Act of 2009 (P.L. 111-5) [effective for stock acquired after 2-17-2009.—CCH].

P.L. 112-240, §324(b)(2):
Amended Code Sec. 1202(a)(4) by adding at the end a new flush sentence. **Effective** as if included in section 2011(a) of the Creating Small Business Jobs Act of 2010 (P.L. 111-240) [effective for stock acquired after 9-27-2010.—CCH].

P.L. 112-240, §327(b)(1)-(2):
Amended Code Sec. 1202(a)(2)(C) by striking "December 31, 2016" and inserting "December 31, 2018"; and by striking "2016" in the heading and inserting "2018". **Effective** for periods after 12-31-2011.

• **2010, Tax Relief, Unemployment Insurance Reauthorization, and Job Creation Act of 2010 (P.L. 111-312)**

P.L. 111-312, §753(b)(1)-(2):
Amended Code Sec. 1202(a)(2)(C) by striking "December 31, 2014" and inserting "December 31, 2016"; and by striking "2014" in the heading and inserting "2016". **Effective** for periods after 12-31-2009.

P.L. 111-312, §760(a)(1)-(2):
Amended Code Sec. 1202(a)(4) by striking "January 1, 2011" and inserting "January 1, 2012", and by inserting "AND 2011" after "2010" in the heading thereof. **Effective** for stock acquired after 12-31-2010.

• **2010, Creating Small Business Jobs Act of 2010 (P.L. 111-240)**

P.L. 111-240, §2011(a):
Amended Code Sec. 1202(a) by adding at the end a new paragraph (4). **Effective** for stock acquired after 9-27-2010.

P.L. 111-240, §2011(b)(1)-(2):
Amended Code Sec. 1202(a)(3) by inserting "CERTAIN PERIODS IN" before "2010" in the heading, and by striking "before January 1, 2011" and inserting "on or before the date of the enactment of the Creating Small Business Jobs Act of 2010". **Effective** for stock acquired after 9-27-2010.

• **2009, American Recovery and Reinvestment Tax Act of 2009 (P.L. 111-5)**

P.L. 111-5, §1241(a):
Amended Code Sec. 1202(a) by adding at the end a new paragraph (3). **Effective** for stock acquired after 2-17-2009.

• **2000, Community Renewal Tax Relief Act of 2000 (P.L. 106-554)**

P.L. 106-554, §117(a):
Amended Code Sec. 1202(a). **Effective** for stock acquired after 12-21-2000. Prior to amendment, Code Sec. 1202(a) read as follows:
(a) 50-PERCENT EXCLUSION.—In the case of a taxpayer other than a corporation, gross income shall not include 50 percent of any gain from the sale or exchange of qualified small business stock held for more than 5 years.

P.L. 106-554, §117(b)(2):
Amended the section heading for Code Sec. 1202 by striking "50-PERCENT" and inserting "PARTIAL". **Effective** for stock acquired after 12-21-2000.

[Sec. 1202(b)]—

(b) PER-ISSUER LIMITATION ON TAXPAYER'S ELIGIBLE GAIN.—

(1) IN GENERAL.—If the taxpayer has eligible gain for the taxable year from 1 or more dispositions of stock issued by any corporation, the aggregate amount of such gain from dispositions of stock issued by such corporation which may be taken into account under subsection (a) for the taxable year shall not exceed the greater of—

(A) $10,000,000 reduced by the aggregate amount of eligible gain taken into account by the taxpayer under subsection (a) for prior taxable years attributable to dispositions of stock issued by such corporation, or

(B) 10 times the aggregate adjusted bases of qualified small business stock issued by such corporation and disposed of by the taxpayer during the taxable year.

For purposes of subparagraph (B), the adjusted basis of any stock shall be determined without regard to any addition to basis after the date on which such stock was originally issued.

(2) Eligible gain.—For purposes of this subsection, the term "eligible gain" means any gain from the sale or exchange of qualified small business stock held for more than 5 years.

(3) Treatment of married individuals.—

(A) Separate returns.—In the case of a separate return by a married individual, paragraph (1)(A) shall be applied by substituting "$5,000,000" for "$10,000,000".

(B) Allocation of exclusion.—In the case of any joint return, the amount of gain taken into account under subsection (a) shall be allocated equally between the spouses for purposes of applying this subsection to subsequent taxable years.

(C) Marital status.—For purposes of this subsection, marital status shall be determined under section 7703.

[Sec. 1202(c)]

(c) Qualified Small Business Stock.—For purposes of this section—

(1) In general.—Except as otherwise provided in this section, the term "qualified small business stock" means any stock in a C corporation which is originally issued after the date of the enactment of the Revenue Reconciliation Act of 1993, if—

(A) as of the date of issuance, such corporation is a qualified small business, and

(B) except as provided in subsections (f) and (h), such stock is acquired by the taxpayer at its original issue (directly or through an underwriter)—

(i) in exchange for money or other property (not including stock), or

(ii) as compensation for services provided to such corporation (other than services performed as an underwriter of such stock).

(2) Active business requirement; etc.—

(A) In general.—Stock in a corporation shall not be treated as qualified small business stock unless, during substantially all of the taxpayer's holding period for such stock, such corporation meets the active business requirements of subsection (e) and such corporation is a C corporation.

(B) Special rule for certain small business investment companies.—

(i) Waiver of active business requirement.—Notwithstanding any provision of subsection (e), a corporation shall be treated as meeting the active business requirements of such subsection for any period during which such corporation qualifies as a specialized small business investment company.

(ii) Specialized small business investment company.—For purposes of clause (i), the term "specialized small business investment company" means any eligible corporation (as defined in subsection (e)(4)) which is licensed to operate under section 301(d) of the Small Business Investment Act of 1958 (as in effect on May 13, 1993).

(3) Certain purchases by corporation of its own stock.—

(A) Redemptions from taxpayer or related person.—Stock acquired by the taxpayer shall not be treated as qualified small business stock if, at any time during the 4-year period beginning on the date 2 years before the issuance of such stock, the corporation issuing such stock purchased (directly or indirectly) any of its stock from the taxpayer or from a person related (within the meaning of section 267(b) or 707(b)) to the taxpayer.

(B) Significant redemptions.—Stock issued by a corporation shall not be treated as qualified business stock if, during the 2-year period beginning on the date 1 year before the issuance of such stock, such corporation made 1 or more purchases of its stock with an aggregate value (as of the time of the respective purchases) exceeding 5 percent of the aggregate value of all of its stock as of the beginning of such 2-year period.

(C) Treatment of certain transactions.—If any transaction is treated under section 304(a) as a distribution in redemption of the stock of any corporation, for purposes of subparagraphs (A) and (B), such corporation shall be treated as purchasing an amount of its stock equal to the amount treated as such a distribution under section 304(a).

[Sec. 1202(d)]

(d) Qualified Small Business.—For purposes of this section—

(1) In general.—The term "qualified small business" means any domestic corporation which is a C corporation if—

(A) the aggregate gross assets of such corporation (or any predecessor thereof) at all times on or after the date of the enactment of the Revenue Reconciliation Act of 1993 and before the issuance did not exceed $50,000,000,

(B) the aggregate gross assets of such corporation immediately after the issuance (determined by taking into account amounts received in the issuance) do not exceed $50,000,000, and

(C) such corporation agrees to submit such reports to the Secretary and to shareholders as the Secretary may require to carry out the purposes of this section.

(2) AGGREGATE GROSS ASSETS.—

(A) IN GENERAL.—For purposes of paragraph (1), the term "aggregate gross assets" means the amount of cash and the aggregate adjusted bases of other property held by the corporation.

(B) TREATMENT OF CONTRIBUTED PROPERTY.—For purposes of subparagraph (A), the adjusted basis of any property contributed to the corporation (or other property with a basis determined in whole or in part by reference to the adjusted basis of property so contributed) shall be determined as if the basis of the property contributed to the corporation (immediately after such contribution) were equal to its fair market value as of the time of such contribution.

(3) AGGREGATION RULES.—

(A) IN GENERAL.—All corporations which are members of the same parent-subsidiary controlled group shall be treated as 1 corporation for purposes of this subsection.

(B) PARENT-SUBSIDIARY CONTROLLED GROUP.—For purposes of subparagraph (A), the term "parent-subsidiary controlled group" means any controlled group of corporations as defined in section 1563(a)(1), except that—

(i) "more than 50 percent" shall be substituted for "at least 80 percent" each place it appears in section 1563(a)(1), and

(ii) section 1563(a)(4) shall not apply.

[Sec. 1202(e)]

(e) ACTIVE BUSINESS REQUIREMENT.—

(1) IN GENERAL.—For purposes of subsection (c)(2), the requirements of this subsection are met by a corporation for any period if during such period—

(A) at least 80 percent (by value) of the assets of such corporation are used by such corporation in the active conduct of 1 or more qualified trades or businesses, and

(B) such corporation is an eligible corporation.

(2) SPECIAL RULE FOR CERTAIN ACTIVITIES.—For purposes of paragraph (1), if, in connection with any future qualified trade or business, a corporation is engaged in—

(A) start-up activities described in section 195(c)(1)(A),

(B) activities resulting in the payment or incurring of expenditures which may be treated as research and experimental expenditures under section 174, or

(C) activities with respect to in-house research expenses described in section 41(b)(4),

assets used in such activities shall be treated as used in the active conduct of a qualified trade or business. Any determination under this paragraph shall be made without regard to whether a corporation has any gross income from such activities at the time of the determination.

(3) QUALIFIED TRADE OR BUSINESS.—For purposes of this subsection, the term "qualified trade or business" means any trade or business other than—

(A) any trade or business involving the performance of services in the fields of health, law, engineering, architecture, accounting, actuarial science, performing arts, consulting, athletics, financial services, brokerage services, or any trade or business where the principal asset of such trade or business is the reputation or skill of 1 or more of its employees,

(B) any banking, insurance, financing, leasing, investing, or similar business,

(C) any farming business (including the business of raising or harvesting trees),

(D) any business involving the production or extraction of products of a character with respect to which a deduction is allowable under section 613 or 613A, and

(E) any business of operating a hotel, motel, restaurant, or similar business.

(4) ELIGIBLE CORPORATION.—For purposes of this subsection, the term "eligible corporation" means any domestic corporation; except that such term shall not include—

(A) a DISC or former DISC,

(B) a regulated investment company, real estate investment trust, or REMIC, and

(C) a cooperative.

(5) STOCK IN OTHER CORPORATIONS.—

(A) LOOK-THRU IN CASE OF SUBSIDIARIES.—For purposes of this subsection, stock and debt in any subsidiary corporation shall be disregarded and the parent corporation shall be deemed to own its ratable share of the subsidiary's assets, and to conduct its ratable share of the subsidiary's activities.

(B) PORTFOLIO STOCK OR SECURITIES.—A corporation shall be treated as failing to meet the requirements of paragraph (1) for any period during which more than 10 percent of the value of its assets (in excess of liabilities) consists of stock or securities in other corporations which are not subsidiaries of such corporation (other than assets described in paragraph (6)).

(C) SUBSIDIARY.—For purposes of this paragraph, a corporation shall be considered a subsidiary if the parent owns more than 50 percent of the combined voting power of all classes of stock entitled to vote, or more than 50 percent in value of all outstanding stock, of such corporation.

(6) WORKING CAPITAL.—For purposes of paragraph (1)(A), any assets which—

(A) are held as a part of the reasonably required working capital needs of a qualified trade or business of the corporation, or

(B) are held for investment and are reasonably expected to be used within 2 years to finance research and experimentation in a qualified trade or business or increases in working capital needs of a qualified trade or business,

shall be treated as used in the active conduct of a qualified trade or business. For periods after the corporation has been in existence for at least 2 years, in no event may more than 50 percent of the assets of the corporation qualify as used in the active conduct of a qualified trade or business by reason of this paragraph.

(7) MAXIMUM REAL ESTATE HOLDINGS.—A corporation shall not be treated as meeting the requirements of paragraph (1) for any period during which more than 10 percent of the total value of its assets consists of real property which is not used in the active conduct of a qualified trade or business. For purposes of the preceding sentence, the ownership of, dealing in, or renting of real property shall not be treated as the active conduct of a qualified trade or business.

(8) COMPUTER SOFTWARE ROYALTIES.—For purposes of paragraph (1), rights to computer software which produces active business computer software royalties (within the meaning of section 543(d)(1)) shall be treated as an asset used in the active conduct of a trade or business.

Amendments

- **2018, Tax Technical Corrections Act of 2018 (P.L. 115-141)**

P.L. 115-141, §401(d)(1)(D)(xv), Div. U:
Amended Code Sec. 1202(e)(4) by striking subparagraph (B) and by redesignating subparagraphs (C) and (D) as subparagraphs (B) and (C), respectively. **Effective** 3-23-2018. For a special rule, see Act Sec. 401(e), Div. U, below. Prior to being stricken, Code Sec. 1202(e)(4)(B) read as follows:

(B) a corporation with respect to which an election under section 936 is in effect or which has a direct or indirect subsidiary with respect to which such an election is in effect,

P.L. 115-141, §401(e), Div. U, provides:
(e) GENERAL SAVINGS PROVISION WITH RESPECT TO DEADWOOD PROVISIONS.—If—
(1) any provision amended or repealed by the amendments made by subsection (b) or (d) applied to—
(A) any transaction occurring before the date of the enactment of this Act,
(B) any property acquired before such date of enactment, or
(C) any item of income, loss, deduction, or credit taken into account before such date of enactment, and
(2) the treatment of such transaction, property, or item under such provision would (without regard to the amendments or repeals made by such subsection) affect the liability for tax for periods ending after such date of enactment,

nothing in the amendments or repeals made by this section shall be construed to affect the treatment of such transaction, property, or item for purposes of determining liability for tax for periods ending after such date of enactment.

- **2004, American Jobs Creation Act of 2004 (P.L. 108-357)**

P.L. 108-357, §835(b)(9):
Amended Code Sec. 1202(e)(4)(C) by striking "REMIC, or FASIT" and inserting "or REMIC". For the **effective** date, see Act Sec. 835(c), below.

P.L. 108-357, §835(c), provides:
(c) EFFECTIVE DATE.—
(1) IN GENERAL.—Except as provided in paragraph (2), the amendments made by this section shall take effect on January 1, 2005.
(2) EXCEPTION FOR EXISTING FASITS.—Paragraph (1) shall not apply to any FASIT in existence on the date of the enactment of this Act [10-22-2004.—CCH] to the extent that regular interests issued by the FASIT before such date continue to remain outstanding in accordance with the original terms of issuance.

- **1996, Small Business Job Protection Act of 1996 (P.L. 104-188)**

P.L. 104-188, §1621(b)(7):
Amended Code Sec. 1202(e)(4)(C) by striking "or REMIC" and inserting "REMIC, or FASIT". **Effective** 9-1-97.

[Sec. 1202(f)]

(f) STOCK ACQUIRED ON CONVERSION OF OTHER STOCK.—If any stock in a corporation is acquired solely through the conversion of other stock in such corporation which is qualified small business stock in the hands of the taxpayer—

(1) the stock so acquired shall be treated as qualified small business stock in the hands of the taxpayer, and

(2) the stock so acquired shall be treated as having been held during the period during which the converted stock was held.

[Sec. 1202(g)]

(g) TREATMENT OF PASS-THRU ENTITIES.—

(1) IN GENERAL.—If any amount included in gross income by reason of holding an interest in a pass-thru entity meets the requirements of paragraph (2)—

(A) such amount shall be treated as gain described in subsection (a), and

(B) for purposes of applying subsection (b), such amount shall be treated as gain from a disposition of stock in the corporation issuing the stock disposed of by the pass-thru entity and the taxpayer's proportionate share of the adjusted basis of the pass-thru entity in such stock shall be taken into account.

(2) REQUIREMENTS.—An amount meets the requirements of this paragraph if—

(A) such amount is attributable to gain on the sale or exchange by the pass-thru entity of stock which is qualified small business stock in the hands of such entity (determined by treating such entity as an individual) and which was held by such entity for more than 5 years, and

(B) such amount is includible in the gross income of the taxpayer by reason of the holding of an interest in such entity which was held by the taxpayer on the date on which such pass-thru entity acquired such stock and at all times thereafter before the disposition of such stock by such pass-thru entity.

(3) LIMITATION BASED ON INTEREST ORIGINALLY HELD BY TAXPAYER.—Paragraph (1) shall not apply to any amount to the extent such amount exceeds the amount to which paragraph (1) would have applied if such amount were determined by reference to the interest the taxpayer held in the pass-thru entity on the date the qualified small business stock was acquired.

(4) PASS-THRU ENTITY.—For purposes of this subsection, the term "pass-thru entity" means—

(A) any partnership,
(B) any S corporation,
(C) any regulated investment company, and
(D) any common trust fund.

[Sec. 1202(h)]

(h) CERTAIN TAX-FREE AND OTHER TRANSFERS.—For purposes of this section—

(1) IN GENERAL.—In the case of a transfer described in paragraph (2), the transferee shall be treated as—

(A) having acquired such stock in the same manner as the transferor, and

(B) having held such stock during any continuous period immediately preceding the transfer during which it was held (or treated as held under this subsection) by the transferor.

(2) DESCRIPTION OF TRANSFERS.—A transfer is described in this subsection if such transfer is—

(A) by gift,

(B) at death, or

(C) from a partnership to a partner of stock with respect to which requirements similar to the requirements of subsection (g) are met at the time of the transfer (without regard to the 5-year holding period requirement).

(3) CERTAIN RULES MADE APPLICABLE.—Rules similar to the rules of section 1244(d)(2) shall apply for purposes of this section.

(4) INCORPORATIONS AND REORGANIZATIONS INVOLVING NONQUALIFIED STOCK.—

(A) IN GENERAL.—In the case of a transaction described in section 351 or a reorganization described in section 368, if qualified small business stock is exchanged for other stock which would not qualify as qualified small business stock but for this subparagraph, such other stock shall be treated as qualified small business stock acquired on the date on which the exchanged stock was acquired.

(B) LIMITATION.—This section shall apply to gain from the sale or exchange of stock treated as qualified small business stock by reason of subparagraph (A) only to the extent of the gain which would have been recognized at the time of the transfer described in subparagraph (A) if section 351 or 368 had not applied at such time. The preceding sentence shall not apply if the stock which is treated as qualified small business stock by reason of subparagraph (A) is issued by a corporation which (as of the time of the transfer described in subparagraph (A)) is a qualified small business.

(C) SUCCESSIVE APPLICATION.—For purposes of this paragraph, stock treated as qualified small business stock under subparagraph (A) shall be so treated for subsequent transactions or reorganizations, except that the limitation of subparagraph (B) shall be applied as of the time of the first transfer to which such limitation applied (determined after the application of the second sentence of subparagraph (B)).

(D) CONTROL TEST.—In the case of a transaction described in section 351, this paragraph shall apply only if, immediately after the transaction, the corporation issuing the stock owns directly or indirectly stock representing control (within the meaning of section 368(c)) of the corporation whose stock was exchanged.

[Sec. 1202(i)]

(i) BASIS RULES.—For purposes of this section—

(1) STOCK EXCHANGED FOR PROPERTY.—In the case where the taxpayer transfers property (other than money or stock) to a corporation in exchange for stock in such corporation—

(A) such stock shall be treated as having been acquired by the taxpayer on the date of such exchange, and

(B) the basis of such stock in the hands of the taxpayer shall in no event be less than the fair market value of the property exchanged.

(2) TREATMENT OF CONTRIBUTIONS TO CAPITAL.—If the adjusted basis of any qualified small business stock is adjusted by reason of any contribution to capital after the date on which such stock was originally issued, in determining the amount of the adjustment by reason of such contribution, the basis of the contributed property shall in no event be treated as less than its fair market value on the date of the contribution.

[Sec. 1202(j)]

(j) TREATMENT OF CERTAIN SHORT POSITIONS.—

(1) IN GENERAL.—If the taxpayer has an offsetting short position with respect to any qualified small business stock, subsection (a) shall not apply to any gain from the sale or exchange of such stock unless—

(A) such stock was held by the taxpayer for more than 5 years as of the first day on which there was such a short position, and

(B) the taxpayer elects to recognize gain as if such stock were sold on such first day for its fair market value.

(2) OFFSETTING SHORT POSITION.—For purposes of paragraph (1), the taxpayer shall be treated as having an offsetting short position with respect to any qualified small business stock if—

(A) the taxpayer has made a short sale of substantially identical property,

(B) the taxpayer has acquired an option to sell substantially identical property at a fixed price, or

(C) to the extent provided in regulations, the taxpayer has entered into any other transaction which substantially reduces the risk of loss from holding such qualified small business stock.

For purposes of the preceding sentence, any reference to the taxpayer shall be treated as including a reference to any person who is related (within the meaning of section 267(b) or 707(b)) to the taxpayer.

[Sec. 1202(k)]

(k) REGULATIONS.—The Secretary shall prescribe such regulations as may be appropriate to carry out the purposes of this section, including regulations to prevent the avoidance of the purposes of this section through split-ups, shell corporations, partnerships, or otherwise.

Amendments

• 1993, Omnibus Budget Reconciliation Act of 1993 (P.L. 103-66)

P.L. 103-66, § 13113(a):

Amended Part I of subchapter P of chapter 1 by adding at the end thereof a new section 1202. **Effective** for stock issued after 8-10-93.

[Sec. 1202—Repealed]

Amendments

• 1986, Tax Reform Act of 1986 (P.L. 99-514)

P.L. 99-514, § 301(a):

Repealed Code Sec. 1202. **Effective** for tax years beginning after 12-31-86. Prior to repeal, Code Sec. 1202 read a follows:

SEC. 1202. DEDUCTION FOR CAPITAL GAINS.

(a) IN GENERAL.—If for any taxable year a taxpayer other than a corporation has a net capital gain, 60 percent of the amount of the net capital gain shall be a deduction from gross income.

(b) ESTATES AND TRUSTS.—In the case of an estate or trust, the deduction shall be computed by excluding the portion (if any) of the gains for the taxable year from sales or exchanges of capital assets which, under sections 652 and 662 (relating to inclusions of amounts in gross income of beneficiaries of trusts), is includible by the income beneficiaries as gain derived from the sale or exchange of capital assets.

(c) TRANSITIONAL RULE.—If for any taxable year ending after October 31, 1978, and beginning before November 1, 1979, a taxpayer other than a corporation has a net capital gain, the deduction under subsection (a) shall be the sum of—

(1) 60 percent of the lesser of—

(A) the net capital gain for the taxable year, or

(B) the net capital gain taking into account only gain or loss properly taken into account for the portion of the taxable year after October 31, 1978, plus

(2) 50 percent of the excess of—

(A) the net capital gain for the taxable year, over

(B) the amount of net capital gain taken into account under paragraph (1).

• 1981, Economic Recovery Tax Act of 1981 (P.L. 97-34)

P.L. 97-34, § 102 provides:

SEC. 102. 20-PERCENT MAXIMUM RATE ON NET CAPITAL GAIN FOR PORTION OF 1981.

(a) IN GENERAL.—If for any taxable year ending after June 9, 1981, and beginning before January 1, 1982, a taxpayer other than a corporation has qualified net capital gain, then the tax imposed under section 1 of the Internal Revenue Code of 1954 for such taxable year shall be equal to the lesser of—

(1) the tax imposed under such section determined without regard to this subsection, or

(2) the sum of—

(A) the tax imposed under such section on the excess of—

(i) the taxable income of the taxpayer, over

(ii) 40 percent of the qualified net capital gain of the taxpayer, and

(B) 20 percent of the qualified net capital gain.

(b) APPLICATION WITH ALTERNATIVE MINIMUM TAX.—

(1) IN GENERAL.—If subsection (a) applies to any taxpayer for any taxable year, then the amount determined under section 55(a)(1) of the Internal Revenue Code of 1954 for such taxable year shall be equal to the lesser of—

(A) the amount determined under section 55(a)(1) determined without regard to this subsection, or

(B) the sum of—

(i) the amount which would be determined under such section 55(a)(1) if the alternative minimum taxable income was the excess of—

(I) the alternative minimum taxable income (within the meaning of section 55(b)(1) of such Code) of the taxpayer, over

(II) the qualified net capital gain of the taxpayer, and

(ii) 20 percent of the qualified net capital gain.

(2) NO CREDITS ALLOWABLE.—For purposes of section 55(c) of such Code, no credit allowable under subpart A of part IV of subchapter A of chapter 1 of such Code (other than section 33(a) of such Code) shall be allowable against the amount described in paragraph (1)(B)(ii).

(c) QUALIFIED NET CAPITAL GAIN.—

(1) IN GENERAL.—For purposes of this section, the term "qualified net capital gain" means the lesser of—

(A) the net capital gain for the taxable year, or

(B) the net capital gain for the taxable year taking into account only gain or loss from sales or exchanges occurring after June 9, 1981.

(2) NET CAPITAL GAIN.—For purposes of this subsection, the term "net capital gain" has the meaning given such term by section 1222(11) of the Internal Revenue Code of 1954.

(d) SPECIAL RULE FOR PASS-THRU ENTITIES.—

(1) IN GENERAL.—In applying subsections (a), (b), and (c) with respect to any pass-thru entity, the determination of when a sale or exchange has occurred shall be made at the entity level.

(2) PASS-THRU ENTITY DEFINED.—For purposes of paragraph (1), the term "pass-thru entity" means—

(A) a regulated investment company,

(B) a real estate investment trust,

(C) an electing small business corporation,

(D) a partnership,

(E) an estate or trust, and

(F) a common trust fund.

• 1980, Technical Corrections Act of 1979 (P.L. 96-222)

P.L. 96-222, § 104(a)(2)(A)(i):

Amended Code Sec. 1202(c) by changing "(c) TAXABLE YEARS WHICH INCLUDE NOVEMBER 1, 1978.—If for any taxable year beginning before November 1, 1978, and ending after October 31, 1978," to "(c) TRANSITIONAL RULE.—If for any taxable year ending after October 31, 1978, and beginning before November 1, 1979,". **Effective** for tax years ending after 10-31-78.

P.L. 96-222, § 104(a)(2)(A)(ii):

Amended Code Sec. 1202(c)(1)(B). **Effective** for tax years ending after 10-31-78. Prior to amendment, Code Sec. 1202(c)(1)(B) read as follows:

(B) the net capital gain taking into account only sales and exchanges after October 31, 1978, plus

For a special rule for pass-through entities, see P.L. 96-222, § 104(a)(3)(A)(ii), following Code Sec. 1201(c).

• 1978, Revenue Act of 1978 (P.L. 95-600)

P.L. 95-600, §§ 402(a), (c)(1):

Amended Code Sec. 1202. **Effective** for tax years ending after 10-31-78. Before amendment, such code section read: "SEC. 1202. DEDUCTION FOR CAPITAL GAINS.

If for any taxable year, a taxpayer other than a corporation has a net capital gain, 50 percent of the amount of the net capital gain shall be a deduction from gross income. In the case of an estate or trust, the deduction shall be computed by excluding the portion (if any), of the gains for the taxable year from sales or exchanges of capital assets, which, under sections 652 and 662 (relating to inclusions of amounts in gross income of beneficiaries of trusts), is includible by the income beneficiaries as gain derived from the sale or exchange of capital assets." ration has a net capital gain, 50 percent of the amount of the net capital gain shall be a deduction from gross income." rather than "In the case of a taxpayer other than a corporation, if for any taxable year the net long-term capital gain exceeds the net short-term capital loss, 50 percent of the amount of such excess shall be a deduction from gross income." **Effective** with respect to tax years beginning after 12-31-76.

- **1976, Tax Reform Act of 1976 (P.L. 94-455)**

P.L. 94-455, §1901(b)(33)(M):

Amended Code Sec. 1202 by having the first sentence read "If for any taxable year, a taxpayer other than a corpo-

[Sec. 1361]

SEC. 1361. S CORPORATION DEFINED.

[Sec. 1361(a)]

(a) S CORPORATION DEFINED.—

(1) IN GENERAL.—For purposes of this title, the term "S corporation" means, with respect to any taxable year, a small business corporation for which an election under section 1362(a) is in effect for such year.

(2) C CORPORATION.—For purposes of this title, the term "C corporation" means, with respect to any taxable year, a corporation which is not an S corporation for such year.

[Sec. 1361(b)]

(b) SMALL BUSINESS CORPORATION.—

(1) IN GENERAL.—For purposes of this subchapter, the term "small business corporation" means a domestic corporation which is not an ineligible corporation and which does not—

(A) have more than 100 shareholders,

(B) have as a shareholder a person (other than an estate, a trust described in subsection (c)(2), or an organization described in subsection (c)(6)) who is not an individual,

(C) have a nonresident alien as a shareholder, and

(D) have more than 1 class of stock.

(2) INELIGIBLE CORPORATION DEFINED.—For purposes of paragraph (1), the term "ineligible corporation" means any corporation which is—

(A) a financial institution which uses the reserve method of accounting for bad debts described in section 585,

(B) an insurance company subject to tax under subchapter L, or

(C) a DISC or former DISC.

(3) TREATMENT OF CERTAIN WHOLLY OWNED SUBSIDIARIES.—

(A) IN GENERAL.—Except as provided in regulations prescribed by the Secretary, for purposes of this title—

(i) a corporation which is a qualified subchapter S subsidiary shall not be treated as a separate corporation, and

(ii) all assets, liabilities, and items of income, deduction, and credit of a qualified subchapter S subsidiary shall be treated as assets, liabilities, and such items (as the case may be) of the S corporation.

(B) QUALIFIED SUBCHAPTER S SUBSIDIARY.—For purposes of this paragraph, the term "qualified subchapter S subsidiary" means any domestic corporation which is not an ineligible corporation (as defined in paragraph (2)), if—

(i) 100 percent of the stock of such corporation is held by the S corporation, and

(ii) the S corporation elects to treat such corporation as a qualified subchapter S subsidiary.

(C) TREATMENT OF TERMINATIONS OF QUALIFIED SUBCHAPTER S SUBSIDIARY STATUS.—

(i) IN GENERAL.—For purposes of this title, if any corporation which was a qualified subchapter S subsidiary ceases to meet the requirements of subparagraph (B), such corporation shall be treated as a new corporation acquiring all of its assets (and assuming all of its liabilities) immediately before such cessation from the S corporation in exchange for its stock.

(ii) TERMINATION BY REASON OF SALE OF STOCK.—If the failure to meet the requirements of subparagraph (B) is by reason of the sale of stock of a corporation which is a qualified subchapter S subsidiary, the sale of such stock shall be treated as if—

(I) the sale were a sale of an undivided interest in the assets of such corporation (based on the percentage of the corporation's stock sold), and

(II) the sale were followed by an acquisition by such corporation of all of its assets (and the assumption by such corporation of all of its liabilities) in a transaction to which section 351 applies.

(D) ELECTION AFTER TERMINATION.—If a corporation's status as a qualified subchapter S subsidiary terminates, such corporation (and any successor corporation) shall not be eligible to make—

(i) an election under subparagraph (B)(ii) to be treated as a qualified subchapter S subsidiary, or

(ii) an election under section 1362(a) to be treated as an S corporation,

before its 5th taxable year which begins after the 1st taxable year for which such termination was effective, unless the Secretary consents to such election.

(E) INFORMATION RETURNS.—Except to the extent provided by the Secretary, this paragraph shall not apply to part III of subchapter A of chapter 61 (relating to information returns).

Amendments

• **2018, Tax Technical Corrections Act of 2018 (P.L. 115-141)**

P.L. 115-141, §401(d)(1)(D)(xvi), Div. U:

Amended Code Sec. 1361(b)(2) by adding "or" at the end of subparagraph (B), by striking subparagraph (C), and by redesignating subparagraph (D) as subparagraph (C). **Effective** 3-23-2018. For a special rule, see Act Sec. 401(e), Div. U, below. Prior to being stricken, Code Sec. 1361(b)(2)(C) read as follows:

(C) a corporation to which an election under section 936 applies, or

P.L. 115-141, §401(e), Div. U, provides:

(e) GENERAL SAVINGS PROVISION WITH RESPECT TO DEADWOOD PROVISIONS.—If—

(1) any provision amended or repealed by the amendments made by subsection (b) or (d) applied to—

(A) any transaction occurring before the date of the enactment of this Act,

(B) any property acquired before such date of enactment, or

(C) any item of income, loss, deduction, or credit taken into account before such date of enactment, and

(2) the treatment of such transaction, property, or item under such provision would (without regard to the amendments or repeals made by such subsection) affect the liability for tax for periods ending after such date of enactment, nothing in the amendments or repeals made by this section shall be construed to affect the treatment of such transaction, property, or item for purposes of determining liability for tax for periods ending after such date of enactment.

• **2007, Small Business and Work Opportunity Tax Act of 2007 (P.L. 110-28)**

P.L. 110-28, §8234(a)(1)-(2):

Amended Code Sec. 1361(b)(3)(C) by striking "For purposes of this title" and inserting "(i) IN GENERAL.—For purposes of this title,", and by inserting at the end a new clause (ii). **Effective** for tax years beginning after 12-31-2006.

• **2005, Gulf Opportunity Zone Act of 2005 (P.L. 109-135)**

P.L. 109-135, §413(c)(1)-(2):

Amended Code Sec. 1361(b)(3) by striking "and in the case of information returns required under part III of subchapter A of chapter 61" after "Secretary" in subparagraph (A), and by adding at the end a new subparagraph (E). **Effective** as if included in the provision of the American Jobs Creation Act of 2004 (P.L. 108-357) to which it relates [**effective** for tax years beginning after 12-31-2004.—CCH].

• **2004, American Jobs Creation Act of 2004 (P.L. 108-357)**

P.L. 108-357, §232(a):

Amended Code Sec. 1361(b)(1)(A) by striking "75" and inserting "100". **Effective** for tax years beginning after 12-31-2004.

APPENDIX: Selected Code Sections Affected by the Tax Cuts and Jobs Act 245

P.L. 108-357, § 239(a):
Amended Code Sec. 1361(b)(3)(A) by inserting "and in the case of information returns required under part III of subchapter A of chapter 61" after "Secretary". **Effective** for tax years beginning after 12-31-2004.

- **1997, Taxpayer Relief Act of 1997 (P.L. 105-34)**

P.L. 105-34, § 1601(c)(3):
Amended Code Sec. 1361(b)(3)(A) by striking "For purposes of this title" and inserting "Except as provided in regulations prescribed by the Secretary, for purposes of this title". **Effective** as if included in the provision of P.L. 104-188 to which it relates [effective for tax years beginning after 12-31-96.—CCH].

P.L. 105-34, § 1601(c)(4)(C):
Amended Code Sec. 1361(b)(1)(B) by striking "subsection (c)(7)" and inserting "subsection (c)(6)". **Effective** as if included in the provision of P.L. 104-188 to which it relates [effective for tax years beginning after 12-31-96.—CCH].

- **1996, Small Business Job Protection Act of 1996 (P.L. 104-188)**

P.L. 104-188, § 1301:
Amended Code Sec. 1361(b)(1)(A) by striking "35 shareholders" and inserting "75 shareholders". **Effective** for tax years beginning after 12-31-96.

P.L. 104-188, § 1308(a):
Amended Code Sec. 1361(b)(2) by striking subparagraph (A) and by redesignating subparagraphs (B), (C), (D) and (E) as subparagraphs (A), (B), (C) and (D), respectively. **Effective** for tax years beginning after 12-31-96. Prior to amendment, Code Sec. 1361(b)(2)(A) read as follows:
(A) a member of an affiliated group (determined under section 1504 without regard to the exceptions contained in subsection (b) thereof),

P.L. 104-188, § 1308(b):
Amended Code Sec. 1361(b) by adding at the end a new paragraph (3). **Effective** for tax years beginning after 12-31-96.

P.L. 104-188, § 1315:
Amended Code Sec. 1361(b)(2)(A), as redesignated by Act Sec. 1308(a). **Effective** for tax years beginning after 12-31-96. Prior to amendment, Code Sec. 1361(b)(2)(A) read as follows:
(A) a financial institution to which section 585 applies (or would apply but for subsection (c) thereof),

P.L. 104-188, § 1316(a)(1):
Amended Code Sec. 1361(b)(1)(B). **Effective** for tax years beginning after 12-31-97. Prior to amendment, Code Sec. 1361(b)(1)(B) read as follows:
(B) have as a shareholder a person (other than an estate and other than a trust described in subsection (c)(2)) who is not an individual,

P.L. 104-188, § 1616(b)(15):
Amended Code Sec. 1361(b)(2)(B) by striking "or to which section 593 applies" before the comma at the end. **Effective** for tax years beginning after 12-31-95.

- **1989, Omnibus Budget Reconciliation Act of 1989 (P.L. 101-239)**

P.L. 101-239, § 7811(c)(6):
Amended Code Sec. 1361(b)(2)(B). **Effective** as if included in the provision of P.L. 100-647 to which it relates. Prior to amendment, Code Sec. 1361(b)(2)(B) read as follows:
(B) a financial institution which is a bank (as defined in section 585(a)(2)) or to which section 593 applies,

- **1986, Tax Reform Act of 1986 (P.L. 99-514)**

P.L. 99-514, § 901(d)(4)(G):
Amended Code Sec. 1361(b)(2)(B) by striking out "to which section 585 or 593 applies" and inserting in lieu thereof "which is a bank (as defined in section 585(a)(2)) or to which section 593 applies". **Effective** for tax years beginning after 12-31-86.

[Sec. 1361(c)]

(c) SPECIAL RULES FOR APPLYING SUBSECTION (b).—
(1) MEMBERS OF A FAMILY TREATED AS 1 SHAREHOLDER.—
(A) IN GENERAL.—For purposes of subsection (b)(1)(A), there shall be treated as one shareholder—
(i) a husband and wife (and their estates), and
(ii) all members of a family (and their estates).
(B) MEMBERS OF A FAMILY.—For purposes of this paragraph—
(i) IN GENERAL.—The term "members of a family" means a common ancestor, any lineal descendant of such common ancestor, and any spouse or former spouse of such common ancestor or any such lineal descendant.
(ii) COMMON ANCESTOR.—An individual shall not be considered to be a common ancestor if, on the applicable date, the individual is more than 6 generations removed from the youngest generation of shareholders who would (but for this subparagraph) be members of the family. For purposes of the preceding sentence, a spouse (or former spouse) shall be treated as being of the same generation as the individual to whom such spouse is (or was) married.
(iii) APPLICABLE DATE.—The term "applicable date" means the latest of—
(I) the date the election under section 1362(a) is made,
(II) the earliest date that an individual described in clause (i) holds stock in the S corporation, or
(III) October 22, 2004.
(C) EFFECT OF ADOPTION, ETC.—Any legally adopted child of an individual, any child who is lawfully placed with an individual for legal adoption by the individual, and any eligible foster child of an individual (within the meaning of section 152(f)(1)(C)), shall be treated as a child of such individual by blood.
(2) CERTAIN TRUSTS PERMITTED AS SHAREHOLDERS.—
(A) IN GENERAL.—For purposes of subsection (b)(1)(B), the following trusts may be shareholders:
(i) A trust all of which is treated (under subpart E of part I of subchapter J of this chapter) as owned by an individual who is a citizen or resident of the United States.
(ii) A trust which was described in clause (i) immediately before the death of the deemed owner and which continues in existence after such death, but only for the 2-year period beginning on the day of the deemed owner's death.
(iii) A trust with respect to stock transferred to it pursuant to the terms of a will, but only for the 2-year period beginning on the day on which such stock is transferred to it.
(iv) A trust created primarily to exercise the voting power of stock transferred to it.

Code Sec. 1361

(v) An electing small business trust.

(vi) In the case of a corporation which is a bank (as defined in section 581) or a depository institution holding company (as defined in section 3(w)(1) of the Federal Deposit Insurance Act (12 U.S.C. 1813(w)(1)), a trust which constitutes an individual retirement account under section 408(a), including one designated as a Roth IRA under section 408A, but only to the extent of the stock held by such trust in such bank or company as of the date of the enactment of this clause.

This subparagraph shall not apply to any foreign trust.

(B) TREATMENT AS SHAREHOLDERS.—For purposes of subsection (b)(1)—

(i) In the case of a trust described in clause (i) of subparagraph (A), the deemed owner shall be treated as the shareholder.

(ii) In the case of a trust described in clause (ii) of subparagraph (A), the estate of the deemed owner shall be treated as the shareholder.

(iii) In the case of a trust described in clause (iii) of subparagraph (A), the estate of the testator shall be treated as the shareholder.

(iv) In the case of a trust described in clause (iv) of subparagraph (A), each beneficiary of the trust shall be treated as a shareholder.

(v) In the case of a trust described in clause (v) of subparagraph (A), each potential current beneficiary of such trust shall be treated as a shareholder; except that, if for any period there is no potential current beneficiary of such trust, such trust shall be treated as the shareholder during such period. This clause shall not apply for purposes of subsection (b)(1)(C).

(vi) In the case of a trust described in clause (vi) of subparagraph (A), the individual for whose benefit the trust was created shall be treated as the shareholder.

(3) ESTATE OF INDIVIDUAL IN BANKRUPTCY MAY BE SHAREHOLDER.—For purposes of subsection (b)(1)(B), the term "estate" includes the estate of an individual in a case under title 11 of the United States Code.

(4) DIFFERENCES IN COMMON STOCK VOTING RIGHTS DISREGARDED.—For purposes of subsection (b)(1)(D), a corporation shall not be treated as having more than 1 class of stock solely because there are differences in voting rights among the shares of common stock.

(5) STRAIGHT DEBT SAFE HARBOR.—

(A) IN GENERAL.—For purposes of subsection (b)(1)(D), straight debt shall not be treated as a second class of stock.

(B) STRAIGHT DEBT DEFINED.—For purposes of this paragraph, the term "straight debt" means any written unconditional promise to pay on demand or on a specified date a sum certain in money if—

(i) the interest rate (and interest payment dates) are not contingent on profits, the borrower's discretion, or similar factors,

(ii) there is no convertibility (directly or indirectly) into stock, and

(iii) the creditor is an individual (other than a nonresident alien), an estate, a trust described in paragraph (2), or a person which is actively and regularly engaged in the business of lending money.

(C) REGULATIONS.—The Secretary shall prescribe such regulations as may be necessary or appropriate to provide for the proper treatment of straight debt under this subchapter and for the coordination of such treatment with other provisions of this title.

(6) CERTAIN EXEMPT ORGANIZATIONS PERMITTED AS SHAREHOLDERS.—For purposes of subsection (b)(1)(B), an organization which is—

(A) described in section 401(a) or 501(c)(3), and

(B) exempt from taxation under section 501(a),

may be a shareholder in an S corporation.

Amendments

• **2018, Tax Technical Corrections Act of 2018 (P.L. 115-141)**

P.L. 115-141, §109(a), Div. U:

Amended Code Sec. 1361(c)(2)(B)(vi) by striking "a shareholder" and inserting "the shareholder". **Effective** as if included in section 319 of the American Jobs Creation Act of 2004 [**effective** for tax years beginning after 10-22-2004.—CCH].

• **2017, Tax Cuts and Jobs Act (P.L. 115-97)**

P.L. 115-97, §13541(a):

Amended Code Sec. 1361(c)(2)(B)(v) by adding at the end a new sentence. **Effective** 1-1-2018.

• **2005, Gulf Opportunity Zone Act of 2005 (P.L. 109-135)**

P.L. 109-135, §403(b):

Amended Code Sec. 1361(c)(1). **Effective** as if included in the provision of the American Jobs Creation Act of 2004 (P.L. 108-357) to which it relates [**effective** for tax years beginning after 12-31-2004.—CCH]. Prior to amendment, Code Sec. 1361(c)(1) read as follows:

(1) MEMBERS OF FAMILY TREATED AS 1 SHAREHOLDER.—

(A) IN GENERAL.—For purpose of subsection (b)(1)(A)—

(i) except as provided in clause (ii), a husband and wife (and their estates) shall be treated as 1 shareholder, and

(ii) in the case of a family with respect to which an election is in effect under subparagraph (D), all members of the family shall be treated as 1 shareholder.

(B) MEMBERS OF THE FAMILY.—For purpose of subparagraph (A)(ii)—

(i) IN GENERAL.—The term "members of the family" means the common ancestor, lineal descendants of the common ancestor, and the spouses (or former spouses) of such lineal descendants or common ancestor.

(ii) COMMON ANCESTOR.—For purposes of this paragraph, an individual shall not be considered a common ancestor if, as of the later of the effective date of this paragraph or the time the election under section 1362(a) is made, the individual is more than 6 generations removed from the youngest generation of shareholders who would (but for this clause) be members of the family. For purposes of the preceding sentence, a spouse (or former spouse) shall be treated as being of the same generation as the individual to which such spouse is (or was) married.

(C) EFFECT OF ADOPTION, ETC.—In determining whether any relationship specified in subparagraph (B) exists, the rules of section 152(b)(2) shall apply.

(D) ELECTION.—An election under subparagraph (A)(ii)—

(i) may, except as otherwise provided in regulations prescribed by the Secretary, be made by any member of the family, and

(ii) shall remain in effect until terminated as provided in regulations prescribed by the Secretary.

P.L. 109-135, §413(a)(1)(A)-(B):

Amended Code Sec. 1361(c)(2)(A)(vi) by inserting "or a depository institution holding company (as defined in section 3(w)(1) of the Federal Deposit Insurance Act (12 U.S.C. 1813(w)(1))" after "a bank (as defined in section 581)", and by inserting "or company" after "such bank". **Effective** as if included in the provision of the American Jobs Creation Act of 2004 (P.L. 108-357) to which it relates [effective 10-22-2004.—CCH].

- **2004, American Jobs Creation Act of 2004 (P.L. 108-357)**

P.L. 108-357, §231(a):

Amended Code Sec. 1361(c)(1). **Effective** for tax years beginning after 12-31-2004. Prior to amendment, Code Sec. 1361(c)(1) read as follows:

(1) HUSBAND AND WIFE TREATED AS 1 SHAREHOLDER.—For purposes of subsection (b)(1)(A), a husband and wife (and their estates) shall be treated as 1 shareholder.

P.L. 108-357, §233(a):

Amended Code Sec. 1361(c)(2)(A) by inserting after clause (v) a new clause (vi). **Effective** 10-22-2004.

P.L. 108-357, §233(b):

Amended Code Sec. 1361(c)(2)(B) by adding at the end a new clause (vi). **Effective** 10-22-2004.

- **1997, Taxpayer Relief Act of 1997 (P.L. 105-34)**

P.L. 105-34, §1601(c)(4)(B):

Amended Code Sec. 1361(c) by redesignating paragraph (7) as paragraph (6). **Effective** as if included in the provision of P.L. 104-188 to which it relates [effective for tax years beginning after 12-31-97.—CCH].

- **1996, Small Business Job Protection Act of 1996 (P.L. 104-188)**

P.L. 104-188, §1302(a):

Amended Code Sec. 1361(c)(2)(A) by inserting after clause (iv) a new clause (v). **Effective** for tax years beginning after 12-31-96.

P.L. 104-188, §1302(b):

Amended Code Sec. 1361(c)(2)(B) by adding at the end a new clause (v). **Effective** for tax years beginning after 12-31-96.

P.L. 104-188, §1303(1)-(2):

Amended Code Sec. 1361(c)(2)(A) by striking "60-day period" each place it appears in clauses (ii) and (iii) and inserting "2-year period", and by striking the last sentence of clause (ii). **Effective** for tax years beginning after 12-31-96. Prior to amendment, the last sentence of Code Sec. 1361(c)(2)(A)(ii) read as follows:

If a trust is described in the preceding sentence and if the entire corpus of the trust is includible in the gross estate of the deemed owner, the preceding sentence shall be applied by substituting "2-year period" for "60-day period".

P.L. 104-188, §1304:

Amended Code Sec. 1361(c)(5)(B)(iii) by striking "or a trust described in paragraph (2)" and inserting "a trust described in paragraph (2), or a person which is actively and regularly engaged in the business of lending money". **Effective** for tax years beginning after 12-31-96.

P.L. 104-188, §1308(d)(1):

Amended Code Sec. 1361(c) by striking paragraph (6). **Effective** for tax years beginning after 12-31-96. Prior to amendment, Code Sec. 1361(c)(6) read as follows:

(6) OWNERSHIP OF STOCK IN CERTAIN INACTIVE CORPORATIONS.—For purposes of subsection (b)(2)(A), a corporation shall not be treated as a member of an affiliated group during any period within a taxable year by reason of the ownership of stock in another corporation if such other corporation—

(A) has not begun business at any time on or before the close of such period, and

(B) does not have gross income for such period.

P.L. 104-188, §1316(a)(2):

Amended Code Sec. 1361(c) by adding at the end a new paragraph (7)[6]. **Effective** for tax years beginning after 12-31-97.

- **1984, Deficit Reduction Act of 1984 (P.L. 98-369)**

P.L. 98-369, §721(c):

Amended Code Sec. 1361(c)(6). **Effective** as if included in P.L. 97-354. Prior to amendment, Code Sec. 1361(c)(6) read as follows:

(6) Ownership of Stock in Certain Inactive Corporations.—For purposes of subsection (b)(2)(A), a corporation shall not be treated as a member of an affiliated group at any time during any taxable year by reason of the ownership of stock in another corporation if such other corporation—

(A) has not begun business at any time on or after the date of its incorporation and before the close of such taxable year, and

(B) does not have taxable income for the period included within such taxable year.

[Sec. 1361(d)]

(d) SPECIAL RULE FOR QUALIFIED SUBCHAPTER S TRUST.—

(1) IN GENERAL.—In the case of a qualified subchapter S trust with respect to which a beneficiary makes an election under paragraph (2)—

(A) such trust shall be treated as a trust described in subsection (c)(2)(A)(i),

(B) for purposes of section 678(a), the beneficiary of such trust shall be treated as the owner of that portion of the trust which consists of stock in an S corporation with respect to which the election under paragraph (2) is made, and

(C) for purposes of applying sections 465 and 469 to the beneficiary of the trust, the disposition of the S corporation stock by the trust shall be treated as a disposition by such beneficiary.

(2) ELECTION.—

(A) IN GENERAL.—A beneficiary of a qualified subchapter S trust (or his legal representative) may elect to have this subsection apply.

(B) MANNER AND TIME OF ELECTION.—

(i) SEPARATE ELECTION WITH RESPECT TO EACH CORPORATION.—An election under this paragraph shall be made separately with respect to each corporation the stock of which is held by the trust.

(ii) ELECTIONS WITH RESPECT TO SUCCESSIVE INCOME BENEFICIARIES.—If there is an election under this paragraph with respect to any beneficiary, an election under this paragraph shall be treated as made by each successive beneficiary unless such beneficiary affirmatively refuses to consent to such election.

(iii) TIME, MANNER, AND FORM OF ELECTION.—Any election, or refusal, under this paragraph shall be made in such manner and form, and at such time, as the Secretary may prescribe.

(C) ELECTION IRREVOCABLE.—An election under this paragraph, once made, may be revoked only with the consent of the Secretary.

(D) GRACE PERIOD.—An election under this paragraph shall be effective up to 15 days and 2 months before the date of the election.

(3) QUALIFIED SUBCHAPTER S TRUST.—For purposes of this subsection, the term "qualified subchapter S trust" means a trust—

(A) the terms of which require that—

(i) during the life of the current income beneficiary, there shall be only 1 income beneficiary of the trust,

(ii) any corpus distributed during the life of the current income beneficiary may be distributed only to such beneficiary,

(iii) the income interest of the current income beneficiary in the trust shall terminate on the earlier of such beneficiary's death or the termination of the trust, and

(iv) upon the termination of the trust during the life of the current income beneficiary, the trust shall distribute all of its assets to such beneficiary, and

(B) all of the income (within the meaning of section 643(b)) of which is distributed (or required to be distributed) currently to 1 individual who is a citizen or resident of the United States.

A substantially separate and independent share of a trust within the meaning of 663(c) shall be treated as a separate trust for purposes of this subsection and subsection (c).

(4) TRUST CEASING TO BE QUALIFIED.—

(A) FAILURE TO MEET REQUIREMENTS OF PARAGRAPH (3)(A).—If a qualified subchapter S trust ceases to meet any requirement of paragraph (3)(A), the provisions of this subsection shall not apply to such trust as of the date it ceases to meet such requirement.

(B) FAILURE TO MEET REQUIREMENTS OF PARAGRAPH (3)(B).—If any qualified subchapter S trust ceases to meet any requirement of paragraph (3)(B) but continues to meet the requirements of paragraph (3)(A), the provisions of this subsection shall not apply to such trust as of the first day of the first taxable year beginning after the first taxable year for which it failed to meet the requirements of paragraph (3)(B).

Amendments

- **2004, American Jobs Creation Act of 2004 (P.L. 108-357)**

P.L. 108-357, § 236(a)(1)-(3):

Amended Code Sec. 1361(d)(1) by striking "and" at the end of subparagraph (A), by striking the period at the end of subparagraph (B) and inserting ", and", and by adding at the end a new subparagraph (C). **Effective** for transfers made after 12-31-2004.

- **1988, Technical and Miscellaneous Revenue Act of 1988 (P.L. 100-647)**

P.L. 100-647, § 1018(q)(2):

Amended Code Sec. 1361(d)(3) by striking out "treated as a separate trust under section 663(c)" in the last sentence and inserting in lieu thereof "within the meaning of section 663(c)". **Effective** as if included in the provision of P.L. 99-514 to which it relates.

- **1986, Tax Reform Act of 1986 (P.L. 99-514)**

P.L. 99-514, § 1879(m)(1)(A):

Amended Code Sec. 1361(d)(3) by adding to the end thereof the last sentence. **Effective** for tax years beginning after 12-31-82.

- **1984, Deficit Reduction Act of 1984 (P.L. 98-369)**

P.L. 98-369, § 721(f)(1):

Amended Code Sec. 1361(d)(2)(D) by striking out "60 days" and inserting in lieu thereof "15 days and 2 months". **Effective** as if included in P.L. 97-354.

P.L. 98-369, § 721(f)(2):

Amended Code Sec. 1361(d) by striking out paragraphs (3) and (4) and inserting in lieu thereof paragraphs (3) and (4). **Effective** as if included in P.L. 97-354. Prior to amendment, paragraphs (3) and (4) read as follows:

(3) QUALIFIED SUBCHAPTER S TRUST.—For purposes of this subsection, the term "qualified subchapter S trust" means a trust—

(A) which owns stock in 1 or more S corporations,

(B) all of the income (within the meaning of section 643(b)) of which is distributed (or required to be distributed) currently to 1 individual who is a citizen or resident of the United States, and

(C) the terms of which require that—

(i) during the life of the current income beneficiary there shall be only 1 income beneficiary of the trust,

(ii) any corpus distributed during the life of the current income beneficiary may be distributed only to such beneficiary,

(iii) the income interest of the current income beneficiary in the trust shall terminate on the earlier of such beneficiary's death or the termination of the trust, and

(iv) upon the termination of the trust during the life of the current income beneficiary, the trust shall distribute all of its assets to such beneficiary.

(4) TRUST CEASING TO BE QUALIFIED.—If a qualified subchapter S trust ceases to meet any requirement under paragraph (3), the provisions of this subsection shall not apply to such trust as of the date it ceases to meet such requirements.

P.L. 98-369, § 721(f)(3):

Amended Code Sec. 1361(d)(2)(B)(i) by striking out "S corporation" each place it appeared and inserting in lieu thereof "corporation". **Effective** as if included in P.L. 97-354.

- **1982, Subchapter S Revision Act of 1982 (P.L. 97-354)**

P.L. 97-354, § 2:

Added Code Sec. 1361. **Effective** for tax years beginning after 12-31-82. For special rules, see Act Sec. 6(c)(2)-(4), below. For a special rule for subsidiaries that are foreign corporations or DISCs, see P.L. 97-354, § 6(c)(1), below.

P.L. 97-354, § 6(c)(1), provides:

(c) GRANDFATHER RULES.—

(1) SUBSIDIARIES WHICH ARE FOREIGN CORPORATIONS OR DISC'S.—In the case of any corporation which on September 28, 1982, would have been a member of the same affiliated group as an electing small business corporation but for paragraph (3) or (7) of section 1504(b) of the Internal Revenue Code of 1954, subparagraph (A) of section 1361(b)(2) of such Code (as amended by section 2) shall be applied by substituting "without regard to the exceptions contained in paragraphs (1), (2), (3), (5), and (6) of subsection (b) thereof" for "without regard to the exceptions contained in subsection (b) thereof".

P.L. 97-354, § 6(c)(2)–(4), provides:

(2) CASUALTY INSURANCE COMPANIES.—

(A) IN GENERAL.—In the case of any qualified casualty insurance electing small business corporation—

(i) the amendments made by this Act shall not apply, and

(ii) subchapter S (as in effect on July 1, 1982) of chapter 1 of the Internal Revenue Code of 1954 and part III of subchapter L of chapter 1 of such Code shall apply.

(B) QUALIFIED CASUALTY INSURANCE ELECTING SMALL BUSINESS CORPORATION.—The term "qualified casualty insurance electing small business corporation" means any corporation described in section 831(a) of the Internal Revenue Code of 1954 if—

(i) as of July 12, 1982, such corporation was an electing small business corporation and was described in section 831(a) of such Code,

(ii) such corporation was formed before April 1, 1982, and proposed (through a written private offering first circulated to investors before such date) to elect to be taxed as a subchapter S corporation and to be operated on an established insurance exchange, or

(iii) such corporation is approved for membership on an established insurance exchange pursuant to a written agreement entered into before December 31, 1982, and such corporation is described in section 831(a) of such Code as of December 31, 1984.

A corporation shall not be treated as a qualified casualty insurance electing small business corporation unless an election under subchapter S of chapter 1 of such Code is in effect for its first taxable year beginning after December 31, 1984.

(3) CERTAIN CORPORATIONS WITH OIL AND GAS PRODUCTION.—

(A) IN GENERAL.—In the case of any qualified oil corporation—

(i) the amendments made by this Act shall not apply, and

(ii) subchapter S (as in effect on July 1, 1982) of chapter 1 of the Internal Revenue Code of 1954 shall apply.

(B) QUALIFIED OIL CORPORATION.—For purposes of this paragraph, the term "qualified oil corporation" means any corporation if—

(i) as of September 28, 1982, such corporation—

(I) was an electing small business corporation, or

(II) was a small business corporation which made an election under section 1372(a) after December 31, 1981, and before September 28, 1982,

(ii) for calendar year 1982, the combined average daily production of domestic crude oil or natural gas of such corporation and any one of its substantial shareholders exceeds 1,000 barrels, and

(iii) such corporation makes an election under this subparagraph at such time and in such manner as the Secretary of the Treasury or his delegate shall prescribe.

(C) AVERAGE DAILY PRODUCTION.—For purposes of subparagraph (B), the average daily production of domestic crude oil or domestic natural gas shall be determined under section 613A(c)(2) of such Code without regard to the last sentence thereof.

(D) SUBSTANTIAL SHAREHOLDER.—For purposes of subparagraph (B), the term "substantial shareholder" means any person who on July 1, 1982, owns more than 40 percent (in value) of the stock of the corporation.

(4) CONTINUITY REQUIRED.—

(A) IN GENERAL.—This subsection shall cease to apply with respect to any corporation after—

(i) any termination of the election of the corporation under subchapter S of chapter 1 of such Code, or

(ii) the first day on which more than 50 percent of the stock of the corporation is newly owned stock within the meaning of section 1378(c)(2) of such Code (as amended by this Act).

(B) SPECIAL RULES FOR PARAGRAPH (2).—

(i) Paragraph (2) shall also cease to apply with respect to any corporation after the corporation ceases to be described in section 831(a) of such Code.

(ii) For purposes of determining under subparagraph (A)(ii) whether paragraph (2) ceases to apply to any corporation, section 1378(c)(2) of such Code (as amended by this Act) shall be applied by substituting "December 31, 1984" for "December 31, 1982" each place it appears therein.

[Sec. 1361(e)]

(e) ELECTING SMALL BUSINESS TRUST DEFINED.—

(1) ELECTING SMALL BUSINESS TRUST.—For purposes of this section—

(A) IN GENERAL.—Except as provided in subparagraph (B), the term "electing small business trust" means any trust if—

(i) such trust does not have as a beneficiary any person other than (I) an individual, (II) an estate, (III) an organization described in paragraph (2), (3), (4), or (5) of section 170(c), or (IV) an organization described in section 170(c)(1) which holds a contingent interest in such trust and is not a potential current beneficiary,

(ii) no interest in such trust was acquired by purchase, and

(iii) an election under this subsection applies to such trust.

(B) CERTAIN TRUSTS NOT ELIGIBLE.—The term "electing small business trust" shall not include—

(i) any qualified subchapter S trust (as defined in subsection (d)(3)) if an election under subsection (d)(2) applies to any corporation the stock of which is held by such trust,

(ii) any trust exempt from tax under this subtitle, and

(iii) any charitable remainder annuity trust or charitable remainder unitrust (as defined in section 664(d)).

(C) PURCHASE.—For purposes of subparagraph (A), the term "purchase" means any acquisition if the basis of the property acquired is determined under section 1012.

(2) POTENTIAL CURRENT BENEFICIARY.—For purposes of this section, the term "potential current beneficiary" means, with respect to any period, any person who at any time during such period is entitled to, or at the discretion of any person may receive, a distribution from the principal or income of the trust (determined without regard to any power of appointment to the extent such power remains unexercised at the end of such period). If a trust disposes of all of the stock which it holds in an S corporation, then, with respect to such corporation, the term "potential current beneficiary" does not include any person who first met the requirements of the preceding sentence during the 1-year period ending on the date of such disposition.

(3) ELECTION.—An election under this subsection shall be made by the trustee. Any such election shall apply to the taxable year of the trust for which made and all subsequent taxable years of such trust unless revoked with the consent of the Secretary.

(4) CROSS REFERENCE.—

For special treatment of electing small business trusts, see section 641(c).

Amendments

• **2004, American Jobs Creation Act of 2004 (P.L. 108-357)**

P.L. 108-357, §234(a)(1)-(2):

Amended Code Sec. 1361(e)(2) by inserting "(determined without regard to any power of appointment to the extent such power remains unexercised at the end of such period)" after "of the trust" in the first sentence, and by striking "60-day" and inserting "1-year" in the second sentence. **Effective** for tax years beginning after 12-31-2004.

• **2000, Community Renewal Tax Relief Act of 2000 (P.L. 106-554)**

P.L. 106-554, §316(b):

Amended Code Sec. 1361(e)(1)(A)(i) by striking "or" before "(III)" and by adding at the end new text. **Effective** as if included in the provision of P.L. 104-188 to which it relates [effective for tax years beginning after 12-31-96.—CCH].

- **1998, IRS Restructuring and Reform Act of 1998 (P.L. 105-206)**

P.L. 105-206, §6007(f)(3):
Amended Code Sec. 1361(e)(4) by striking "section 641(d)" and inserting "section 641(c)". **Effective** as if included in the provision of P.L. 105-134 to which it relates [effective for sales or exchanges after 8-5-97.—CCH].

- **1997, Taxpayer Relief Act of 1997 (P.L. 105-34)**

P.L. 105-34, §1601(c)(1):
Amended Code Sec. 1361(e)(1)(B) by striking "and" at the end of clause (i), striking the period at the end of clause (ii) and inserting ", and", and adding at the end a new clause

(iii). **Effective** as if included in the provision of P.L. 104-188 to which it relates [effective for tax years beginning after 12-31-96.—CCH].

- **1996, Small Business Job Protection Act of 1996 (P.L. 104-188)**

P.L. 104-188, §1302(c):
Amended Code Sec. 1361 by adding at the end a new subsection (e). **Effective** for tax years beginning after 12-31-96.

P.L. 104-188, §1316(e):
Amended Code Sec. 1361(e)(1)(A)(i), as added by section 1302, by striking "which holds a contingent interest and is not a potential current beneficiary". **Effective** for tax years beginning after 12-31-97.

[Sec. 1361(f)]

(f) RESTRICTED BANK DIRECTOR STOCK.—
  (1) IN GENERAL.—Restricted bank director stock shall not be taken into account as outstanding stock of the S corporation in applying this subchapter (other than section 1368(f)).
  (2) RESTRICTED BANK DIRECTOR STOCK.—For purposes of this subsection, the term "restricted bank director stock" means stock in a bank (as defined in section 581) or a depository institution holding company (as defined in section 3(w)(1) of the Federal Deposit Insurance Act (12 U.S.C. 1813(w)(1))), if such stock—
    (A) is required to be held by an individual under applicable Federal or State law in order to permit such individual to serve as a director, and
    (B) is subject to an agreement with such bank or company (or a corporation which controls (within the meaning of section 368(c)) such bank or company) pursuant to which the holder is required to sell back such stock (at the same price as the individual acquired such stock) upon ceasing to hold the office of director.
  (3) CROSS REFERENCE.—
    For treatment of certain distributions with respect to restricted bank director stock, see section 1368(f).

Amendments

- **2018, Tax Technical Corrections Act of 2018 (P.L. 115-141)**

P.L. 115-141, §401(a)(190), Div. U:
Amended Code Sec. 1361(f)(2) by striking "1813(w)(1))," and inserting "1813(w)(1))),". **Effective** 3-23-2018.

- **2007, Small Business and Work Opportunity Tax Act of 2007 (P.L. 110-28)**

P.L. 110-28, §8232(a):
Amended Code Sec. 1361 by adding at the end a new subsection (f). **Effective** generally for tax years beginning after 12-31-2006. For a special rule, see Act Sec. 8232(c)(2), below.

P.L. 110-28, §8232(c)(2), provides:

(2) SPECIAL RULE FOR TREATMENT AS SECOND CLASS OF STOCK.—In the case of any taxable year beginning after December 31, 1996, restricted bank director stock (as defined in section 1361(f) of the Internal Revenue Code of 1986, as added by this section) shall not be taken into account in determining whether an S corporation has more than 1 class of stock.

[Sec. 1361(g)]

(g) SPECIAL RULE FOR BANK REQUIRED TO CHANGE FROM THE RESERVE METHOD OF ACCOUNTING ON BECOMING S CORPORATION.—In the case of a bank which changes from the reserve method of accounting for bad debts described in section 585 or 593 for its first taxable year for which an election under section 1362(a) is in effect, the bank may elect to take into account any adjustments under section 481 by reason of such change for the taxable year immediately preceding such first taxable year.

Amendments

- **2007, Small Business and Work Opportunity Tax Act of 2007 (P.L. 110-28)**

P.L. 110-28, §8233(a):
Amended Code Sec. 1361, as amended by this Act, by adding at the end a new subsection (g). **Effective** for tax years beginning after 12-31-2006.

[Sec. 1362]

SEC. 1362. ELECTION; REVOCATION; TERMINATION.

[Sec. 1362(a)]

(a) ELECTION.—
  (1) IN GENERAL.—Except as provided in subsection (g), a small business corporation may elect, in accordance with the provisions of this section, to be an S corporation.
  (2) ALL SHAREHOLDERS MUST CONSENT TO ELECTION.—An election under this subsection shall be valid only if all persons who are shareholders in such corporation on the day on which such election is made consent to such election.

[Sec. 1362(b)]

(b) WHEN MADE.—
  (1) IN GENERAL.—An election under subsection (a) may be made by a small business corporation for any taxable year—
    (A) at any time during the preceding taxable year, or

(B) at any time during the taxable year and on or before the 15th day of the 3d month of the taxable year.

(2) CERTAIN ELECTIONS MADE DURING 1ST 2½ MONTHS TREATED AS MADE FOR NEXT TAXABLE YEAR.—If—

(A) an election under subsection (a) is made for any taxable year during such year and on or before the 15th day of the 3d month of such year, but

(B) either—

(i) on 1 or more days in such taxable year before the day on which the election was made the corporation did not meet the requirements of subsection (b) of section 1361, or

(ii) 1 or more of the persons who held stock in the corporation during such taxable year and before the election was made did not consent to the election,

then such election shall be treated as made for the following taxable year.

(3) ELECTION MADE AFTER 1ST 2½ MONTHS TREATED AS MADE FOR FOLLOWING TAXABLE YEAR.—If—

(A) a small business corporation makes an election under subsection (a) for any taxable year, and

(B) such election is made after the 15th day of the 3d month of the taxable year and on or before the 15th day of the 3rd month of the following taxable year,

then such election shall be treated as made for the following taxable year.

(4) TAXABLE YEARS OF 2½ MONTHS OR LESS.—For purposes of this subsection, an election for a taxable year made not later than 2 months and 15 days after the first day of the taxable year shall be treated as timely made during such year.

(5) AUTHORITY TO TREAT LATE ELECTIONS, ETC., AS TIMELY.—If—

(A) an election under subsection (a) is made for any taxable year (determined without regard to paragraph (3)) after the date prescribed by this subsection for making such election for such taxable year or no such election is made for any taxable year, and

(B) the Secretary determines that there was reasonable cause for the failure to timely make such election,

the Secretary may treat such an election as timely made for such taxable year (and paragraph (3) shall not apply).

Amendments

- **1996, Small Business Job Protection Act of 1996 (P.L. 104-188)**

P.L. 104-188, §1305(b):

Amended Code Sec. 1362(b) by adding at the end a new paragraph (5). **Effective** with respect to elections for tax years beginning after 12-31-82.

- **1984, Deficit Reduction Act of 1984 (P.L. 98-369)**

P.L. 98-369, §721(l)(1):

Amended Code Sec. 1362(b) by adding paragraph (4). **Effective** for any election under section 1362 of the Internal Revenue Code of 1954 (or any corresponding provision of prior law) made after 10-19-82.

P.L. 98-369, §721(l)(2):

Amended Code Sec. 1362(b)(3) by striking out "on or before the last day of such taxable year" and inserting in lieu thereof "on or before the 15th day of the 3rd month of the following taxable year". **Effective** for any election under section 1362 of the Internal Revenue Code of 1954 (or any corresponding provision of prior law) made after 10-19-82.

[Sec. 1362(c)]

(c) YEARS FOR WHICH EFFECTIVE.—An election under subsection (a) shall be effective for the taxable year of the corporation for which it is made and for all succeeding taxable years of the corporation, until such election is terminated under subsection (d).

[Sec. 1362(d)]

(d) TERMINATION.—

(1) BY REVOCATION.—

(A) IN GENERAL.—An election under subsection (a) may be terminated by revocation.

(B) MORE THAN ONE-HALF OF SHARES MUST CONSENT TO REVOCATION.—An election may be revoked only if shareholders holding more than one-half of the shares of stock of the corporation on the day on which the revocation is made consent to the revocation.

(C) WHEN EFFECTIVE.—Except as provided in subparagraph (D)—

(i) a revocation made during the taxable year and on or before the 15th day of the 3d month thereof shall be effective on the 1st day of such taxable year, and

(ii) a revocation made during the taxable year but after such 15th day shall be effective on the 1st day of the following taxable year.

(D) REVOCATION MAY SPECIFY PROSPECTIVE DATE.—If the revocation specifies a date for revocation which is on or after the day on which the revocation is made, the revocation shall be effective on and after the date so specified.

(2) BY CORPORATION CEASING TO BE SMALL BUSINESS CORPORATION.—

(A) IN GENERAL.—An election under subsection (a) shall be terminated whenever (at any time on or after the 1st day of the 1st taxable year for which the corporation is an S corporation) such corporation ceases to be a small business corporation.

(B) WHEN EFFECTIVE.—Any termination under this paragraph shall be effective on and after the date of cessation.

(3) WHERE PASSIVE INVESTMENT INCOME EXCEEDS 25 PERCENT OF GROSS RECEIPTS FOR 3 CONSECUTIVE TAXABLE YEARS AND CORPORATION HAS ACCUMULATED EARNINGS AND PROFITS.—

(A) TERMINATION.—

(i) IN GENERAL.—An election under subsection (a) shall be terminated whenever the corporation—

(I) has accumulated earnings and profits at the close of each of 3 consecutive taxable years, and

(II) has gross receipts for each of such taxable years more than 25 percent of which are passive investment income.

(ii) WHEN EFFECTIVE.—Any termination under this paragraph shall be effective on and after the first day of the first taxable year beginning after the third consecutive taxable year referred to in clause (i).

(iii) YEARS TAKEN INTO ACCOUNT.—A prior taxable year shall not be taken into account under clause (i) unless the corporation was an S corporation for such taxable year.

(B) GROSS RECEIPTS FROM THE SALES OF CERTAIN ASSETS.—For purposes of this paragraph—

(i) in the case of dispositions of capital assets (other than stock and securities), gross receipts from such dispositions shall be taken into account only to the extent of the capital gain net income therefrom, and

(ii) in the case of sales or exchanges of stock or securities, gross receipts shall be taken into account only to the extent of the gains therefrom.

(C) PASSIVE INVESTMENT INCOME DEFINED.—

(i) IN GENERAL.—Except as otherwise provided in this subparagraph, the term "passive investment income" means gross receipts derived from royalties, rents, dividends, interest, and annuities.

(ii) EXCEPTION FOR INTEREST ON NOTES FROM SALES OF INVENTORY.—The term "passive investment income" shall not include interest on any obligation acquired in the ordinary course of the corporation's trade or business from its sale of property described in section 1221(a)(1).

(iii) TREATMENT OF CERTAIN LENDING OR FINANCE COMPANIES.—If the S corporation meets the requirements of section 542(c)(6) for the taxable year, the term "passive investment income" shall not include gross receipts for the taxable year which are derived directly from the active and regular conduct of a lending or finance business (as defined in section 542(d)(1)).

(iv) TREATMENT OF CERTAIN DIVIDENDS.—If an S corporation holds stock in a C corporation meeting the requirements of section 1504(a)(2), the term "passive investment income" shall not include dividends from such C corporation to the extent such dividends are attributable to the earnings and profits of such C corporation derived from the active conduct of a trade or business.

(v) EXCEPTION FOR BANKS, ETC.—In the case of a bank (as defined in section 581) or a depository institution holding company (as defined in section 3(w)(1) of the Federal Deposit Insurance Act (12 U.S.C. 1813(w)(1))), the term "passive investment income" shall not include—

(I) interest income earned by such bank or company, or

(II) dividends on assets required to be held by such bank or company, including stock in the Federal Reserve Bank, the Federal Home Loan Bank, or the Federal Agricultural Mortgage Bank or participation certificates issued by a Federal Intermediate Credit Bank.

Amendments

- **2018, Tax Technical Corrections Act of 2018 (P.L. 115-141)**

P.L. 115-141, §401(a)(190), Div. U:

Amended Code Sec. 1362(d)(3)(C)(v) by striking "1813(w)(1))," and inserting "1813(w)(1)))," . **Effective** 3-23-2018.

- **2014, Tax Technical Corrections Act of 2014 (P.L. 113-295)**

P.L. 113-295, §221(a)(88), Division A:

Amended Code Sec. 1362(d)(3)(A)(iii) by striking "unless" and all that follows and inserting "unless the corporation was an S corporation for such taxable year.". **Effective** generally 12-19-2014. For a special rule, see Act Sec. 221(b)(2), Division A, below. Prior to amendment, Code Sec. 1362(d)(3)(A)(iii) read as follows:

(iii) YEARS TAKEN INTO ACCOUNT.—A prior taxable year shall not be taken into account under clause (i) unless—

(I) such taxable year began after December 31, 1981, and

(II) the corporation was an S corporation for such taxable year.

P.L. 113-295, §221(b)(2), Division A, provides:

(2) SAVINGS PROVISION.—If—

(A) any provision amended or repealed by the amendments made by this section applied to—

(i) any transaction occurring before the date of the enactment of this Act,

(ii) any property acquired before such date of enactment, or

(iii) any item of income, loss, deduction, or credit taken into account before such date of enactment, and

(B) the treatment of such transaction, property, or item under such provision would (without regard to the amendments or repeals made by this section) affect the liability for tax for periods ending after date of enactment, nothing in the amendments or repeals made by this section shall be construed to affect the treatment of such transaction, property, or item for purposes of determining liability for tax for periods ending after such date of enactment.

- **2007, Small Business and Work Opportunity Tax Act of 2007 (P.L. 110-28)**

P.L. 110-28, §8231(a):

Amended Code Sec. 1362(d)(3) by striking subparagraphs (B)-(F) and inserting new subparagraphs (B) and (C). **Effective** for tax years beginning after 5-25-2007. Prior to being stricken, Code Sec. 1362(d)(3)(B)-(F) read as follows:

(B) GROSS RECEIPTS FROM SALES OF CAPITAL ASSETS (OTHER THAN STOCK AND SECURITIES).—For purposes of this paragraph, in the case of dispositions of capital assets (other than stock and securities), gross receipts from such dispositions shall be taken into account only to the extent of the capital gain net income therefrom.

(C) PASSIVE INVESTMENT INCOME DEFINED.—For purposes of this paragraph—

(i) IN GENERAL.—Except as otherwise provided in this subparagraph, the term "passive investment income" means gross receipts derived from royalties, rents, dividends, interest, annuities, and sales or exchanges of stock or securities (gross receipts from such sales or exchanges being taken into account for purposes of this paragraph only to the extent of gains therefrom).

(ii) EXCEPTION FOR INTEREST ON NOTES FROM SALES OF INVENTORY.—The term "passive investment income" shall not include interest on any obligation acquired in the ordinary course of the corporation's trade or business from its sale of property described in section 1221(a)(1).

(iii) TREATMENT OF CERTAIN LENDING OR FINANCE COMPANIES.—If the S corporation meets the requirements of section 542(c)(6) for the taxable year, the term "passive investment income" shall not include gross receipts for the taxable year which are derived directly from the active and regular conduct of a lending or finance business (as defined in section 542(d)(1)).

(iv) TREATMENT OF CERTAIN LIQUIDATIONS.—Gross receipts derived from sales or exchanges of stock or securities shall not include amounts received by an S corporation which are treated under section 331 (relating to corporate liquidations) as payments in exchange for stock where the S corporation owned more than 50 percent of each class of stock of the liquidating corporation.

(D) SPECIAL RULE FOR OPTIONS AND COMMODITY DEALINGS.—

(i) IN GENERAL.—In the case of any options dealer or commodities dealer, passive investment income shall be determined by not taking into account any gain or loss (in the normal course of the taxpayer's activity of dealing in or trading section 1256 contracts) from any section 1256 contract or property related to such a contract.

(ii) DEFINITIONS.—For purposes of this subparagraph—

(I) OPTIONS DEALER.—The term "options dealer" has the meaning given such term by section 1256(g)(8).

(II) COMMODITIES DEALER.—The term "commodities dealer" means a person who is actively engaged in trading section 1256 contracts and is registered with a domestic board of trade which is designated as a contract market by the Commodities Futures Trading Commission.

(III) SECTION 1256 CONTRACT.—The term "section 1256 contract" has the meaning given to such term by section 1256(b).

(E) TREATMENT OF CERTAIN DIVIDENDS.—If an S corporation holds stock in a C corporation meeting the requirements of section 1504(a)(2), the term "passive investment income" shall not include dividends from such C corporation to the extent such dividends are attributable to the earnings and profits of such C corporation derived from the active conduct of a trade or business.

(F) EXCEPTION FOR BANKS; ETC.—In the case of a bank (as defined in section 581), [or] a depository institution holding company (as defined in section 3(w)(1) of the Federal Deposit Insurance Act (12 U.S.C. 1813(w)(1)), the term "passive investment income" shall not include—

(i) interest income earned by such bank or company, or

(ii) dividends on assets required to be held by such bank or company, including stock in the Federal Reserve Bank, the Federal Home Loan Bank, or the Federal Agricultural Mortgage Bank or participation certificates issued by a Federal Intermediate Credit Bank.

• **2005, Gulf Opportunity Zone Act of 2005 (P.L. 109-135)**

P.L. 109-135, §413(b):

Amended Code Sec. 1362(d)(3)(F) by striking "a bank holding company" and all that follows through "section 2(p) of such Act)" and inserting "[or] a depository institution holding company (as defined in section 3(w)(1) of the Federal Deposit Insurance Act (12 U.S.C. 1813(w)(1))". **Effective** as if included in the provision of the American Jobs Creation Act of 2004 (P.L. 108-357) to which it relates **[effective** for tax years beginning after 12-31-2004.—CCH]. Prior to amendment, Code Sec. 1362(d)(3)(F) read as follows:

(F) EXCEPTION FOR BANKS; ETC.—In the case of a bank (as defined in section 581), a bank holding company (within the meaning of section 2(a) of the Bank Holding Company Act of 1956 (12 U.S.C. 1841(a))), or a financial holding company (within the meaning of section 2(p) of such Act), the term "passive investment income" shall not include—

(i) interest income earned by such bank or company, or

(ii) dividends on assets required to be held by such bank or company, including stock in the Federal Reserve Bank, the Federal Home Loan Bank, or the Federal Agricultural Mortgage Bank or participation certificates issued by a Federal Intermediate Credit Bank.

• **2004, American Jobs Creation Act of 2004 (P.L. 108-357)**

P.L. 108-357, §237(a):

Amended Code Sec. 1362(d)(3) by adding at the end a new subparagraph (F). **Effective** for tax years beginning after 12-31-2004.

• **1999, Tax Relief Extension Act of 1999 (P.L. 106-170)**

P.L. 106-170, §532(c)(2)(T):

Amended Code Sec. 1362(d)(3)(C)(ii) by striking "section 1221(1)" and inserting "section 1221(a)(1)". **Effective** for any instrument held, acquired, or entered into, any transaction entered into, and supplies held or acquired on or after 12-17-99.

• **1996, Small Business Job Protection Act of 1996 (P.L. 104-188)**

P.L. 104-188, §1308(c):

Amended Code Sec. 1362(d)(3) by adding at the end a new subparagraph (F). **Effective** for tax years beginning after 12-31-96.

P.L. 104-188, §1311(b)(1)(A)-(C):

Amended Code Sec. 1362(d)(3) by striking "SUBCHAPTER C" in the paragraph heading and inserting "ACCUMULATED", by striking "subchapter C" in subparagraph (A)(i)(I) and inserting "accumulated", and by striking subparagraph (B) and redesignating the following subparagraphs accordingly. **Effective** for tax years beginning after 12-31-96. Prior to amendment, Code Sec. 1362(d)(3)(B) read as follows:

(B) SUBCHAPTER C EARNINGS AND PROFITS.—For purposes of subparagraph (A), the term "subchapter C earnings and profits" means earnings and profits of any corporation for any taxable year with respect to which an election under section 1362(a) (or under section 1372 of prior law) was not in effect.

• **1988, Technical and Miscellaneous Revenue Act of 1988 (P.L. 100-647)**

P.L. 100-647, §1006(f)(6)(A)-(B):

Amended Code Sec. 1362(d)(3) by striking out clause (v) of subparagraph (D), and by adding at the end thereof new subparagraph (E). **Effective** as if included in the provision of P.L. 99-514 to which it relates. Prior to amendment, Code Sec. 1362(d)(3)(D)(v) read as follows:

(v) SPECIAL RULE FOR OPTIONS AND COMMODITIES DEALERS.—In the case of any options or commodities dealer, passive investment income shall be determined by not taking into account any gain or loss described in section 1374(c)(4)(A).

• **1984, Deficit Reduction Act of 1984 (P.L. 98-369)**

P.L. 98-369, §102(d)(2):

Amended Code Sec. 1362(d)(3)(D) by adding new clause (v). **Effective** for positions established after 7-18-84, in tax years ending after such date. For a special rule, see Act Sec. 102(d)(3), below.

P.L. 98-369, §102(d)(3), as amended by P.L. 99-514, §1808(a), provides:

(3) SUBCHAPTER S ELECTION.—If a commodities dealer or an options dealer—

(A) becomes a small business corporation (as defined in section 1361(b) of the Internal Revenue Code of 1954) at any time before the close of the 75th day after the date of the enactment of this Act, and

(B) makes the election under section 1362(a) of such Code before the close of such 75th day,

then such dealer shall be treated as having received approval for and adopted a taxable year beginning on the first day during 1984 on which it was a small business corporation (as so defined) or such other day as may be permitted under regulations and ending on the date determined under section 1378 of such Code and such election shall be effective for such taxable year.

Code Sec. 1362

[Sec. 1362(e)]

(e) TREATMENT OF S TERMINATION YEAR.—
(1) IN GENERAL.—In the case of an S termination year, for purposes of this title—
(A) S SHORT YEAR.—The portion of such year ending before the 1st day for which the termination is effective shall be treated as a short taxable year for which the corporation is an S corporation.
(B) C SHORT YEAR.—The portion of such year beginning on such 1st day shall be treated as a short taxable year for which the corporation is a C corporation.
(2) PRO RATA ALLOCATION.—Except as provided in paragraph (3) and subparagraphs (C) and (D) of paragraph (6), the determination of which items are to be taken into account for each of the short taxable years referred to in paragraph (1) shall be made—
(A) first by determining for the S termination year—
(i) the amount of each of the items of income, loss, deduction, or credit described in section 1366(a)(1)(A), and
(ii) the amount of the nonseparately computed income or loss, and
(B) then by assigning an equal portion of each amount determined under subparagraph (A) to each day of the S termination year.
(3) ELECTION TO HAVE ITEMS ASSIGNED TO EACH SHORT TAXABLE YEAR UNDER NORMAL TAX ACCOUNTING RULES.—
(A) IN GENERAL.—A corporation may elect to have paragraph (2) not apply.
(B) SHAREHOLDERS MUST CONSENT TO ELECTION.—An election under this subsection shall be valid only if all persons who are shareholders in the corporation at any time during the S short year and all persons who are shareholders in the corporation on the first day of the C short year consent to such election.
(4) S TERMINATION YEAR.—For purposes of this subsection, the term "S termination year" means any taxable year of a corporation (determined without regard to this subsection) in which a termination of an election made under subsection (a) takes effect (other than on the 1st day thereof).
(5) TAX FOR C SHORT YEAR DETERMINED ON ANNUALIZED BASIS.—
(A) IN GENERAL.—The taxable income for the short year described in subparagraph (B) of paragraph (1) shall be placed on an annual basis by multiplying the taxable income for such short year by the number of days in the S termination year and by dividing the result by the number of days in the short year. The tax shall be the same part of the tax computed on the annual basis as the number of days in such short year is of the number of days in the S termination year.
(B) SECTION 443(d)(2) TO APPLY.—Subsection (d) of section 443 shall apply to the short taxable year described in subparagraph (B) of paragraph (1).
(6) OTHER SPECIAL RULES.—For purposes of this title—
(A) SHORT YEARS TREATED AS 1 YEAR FOR CARRYOVER PURPOSES.—The short taxable year described in subparagraph (A) of paragraph (1) shall not be taken into account for purposes of determining the number of taxable years to which any item may be carried back or carried forward by the corporation.
(B) DUE DATE FOR S YEAR.—The due date for filing the return for the short taxable year described in subparagraph (A) of paragraph (1) shall be the same as the due date for filing the return for the short taxable year described in subparagraph (B) of paragraph (1) (including extensions thereof).
(C) PARAGRAPH (2) NOT TO APPLY TO ITEMS RESULTING FROM SECTION 338.—Paragraph (2) shall not apply with respect to any item resulting from the application of section 338.
(D) PRO RATA ALLOCATION FOR S TERMINATION YEAR NOT TO APPLY IF 50-PERCENT CHANGE IN OWNERSHIP.—Paragraph (2) shall not apply to an S termination year if there is a sale or exchange of 50 percent or more of the stock in such corporation during such year.

Amendments

- **1988, Technical and Miscellaneous Revenue Act of 1988 (P.L. 100-647)**

P.L. 100-647, §1007(g)(9):
Amended Code Sec. 1362(e)(5)(B) by striking out "Subsection (d)(2)" and inserting in lieu thereof "Subsection (d)". **Effective** as if included in the provision of P.L. 99-514 to which it relates.

- **1984, Deficit Reduction Act of 1984 (P.L. 98-369)**

P.L. 98-369, §721(g)(1):
Amended Code Sec. 1362(e)(6) by adding subparagraph (C). **Effective** as if included in P.L. 97-354, except as noted in Act Sec. 721(y)(3), below.

P.L. 98-369, §721(g)(2):
Amended Code Sec. 1362(e)(2) by striking out "as provided in paragraph (3)" and inserting in lieu thereof "as provided in paragraph (3) and subparagraphs (C) and (D) of paragraph (6)". **Effective** as if included in P.L. 97-354.

P.L. 98-369, §721(h):
Amended Code Sec. 1362(e)(3)(B). **Effective** as if included in P.L. 97-354. Prior to amendment, Code Sec. 1362(e)(3)(B) read as follows:
(B) ALL SHAREHOLDERS MUST CONSENT TO ELECTION.—An election under this paragraph shall be valid only if all persons who are shareholders in the corporation at any time during the S termination year consent to such election.

P.L. 98-369, §721(t):
Amended Code Sec. 1362(e)(6) by adding subparagraph (D). **Effective** as if included in P.L. 97-354, except as noted in Act Sec. 721(y)(5), below.

P.L. 98-369, §721(y)(3), provides:
(3) AMENDMENT MADE BY SUBSECTION (g)(1).—If—
(A) any portion of a qualified stock purchase is pursuant to a binding contract entered into on or after October 19, 1982, and before the date of the enactment of this Act, and
(B) the purchasing corporation establishes by clear and convincing evidence that such contract was negotiated on the contemplation that, with respect to the deemed sale under section 338 of the Internal Revenue Code of 1954, paragraph (2) of section 1362(e) of such Code would apply, then the amendment made by paragraph (1) of subsection (g) shall not apply to such qualified stock purchase.

P.L. 98-369, §721(y)(5), provides:
(5) AMENDMENT MADE BY SUBSECTION (t).—If—
(A) on or before the date of the enactment of this Act 50 percent or more of the stock of an S corporation has been sold or exchanged in 1 or more transactions, and

(B) the person (or persons) acquiring such stock establish by clear and convincing evidence that such acquisitions were negotiated on the contemplation that paragraph (2) of section 1362(e) of the Internal Revenue Code of 1954 would apply to the S termination year in which such sales or exchanges occur,

then the amendment made by subsection (t) shall not apply to such S termination year.

[Sec. 1362(f)]

(f) INADVERTENT INVALID ELECTIONS OR TERMINATIONS.—If—

(1) an election under subsection (a) or section 1361(b)(3)(B)(ii) by any corporation—

(A) was not effective for the taxable year for which made (determined without regard to subsection (b)(2)) by reason of a failure to meet the requirements of section 1361(b) or to obtain shareholder consents, or

(B) was terminated under paragraph (2) or (3) of subsection (d) or section 1361(b)(3)(C),

(2) the Secretary determines that the circumstances resulting in such ineffectiveness or termination were inadvertent,

(3) no later than a reasonable period of time after discovery of the circumstances resulting in such ineffectiveness or termination, steps were taken—

(A) so that the corporation for which the election was made or the termination occurred is a small business corporation or a qualified subchapter S subsidiary, as the case may be, or

(B) to acquire the required shareholder consents, and

(4) the corporation for which the election was made or the termination occurred, and each person who was a shareholder in such corporation at any time during the period specified pursuant to this subsection, agrees to make such adjustments (consistent with the treatment of such corporation as an S corporation or a qualified subchapter S subsidiary, as the case may be) as may be required by the Secretary with respect to such period,

then, notwithstanding the circumstances resulting in such ineffectiveness or termination, such corporation shall be treated as an S corporation or a qualified subchapter S subsidiary, as the case may be, during the period specified by the Secretary.

Amendments

• **2018, Tax Technical Corrections Act of 2018 (P.L. 115-141)**

P.L. 115-141, §401(a)(191), Div. U:

Amended Code Sec. 1362(f) by striking "may be during" and inserting "may be, during". **Effective** 3-23-2018.

• **2007, Tax Technical Corrections Act of 2007 (P.L. 110-172)**

P.L. 110-172, §11(a)(25)(A)-(B):

Amended Code Sec. 1362(f)(1) by striking ", section 1361(b)(3)(B)(ii), or section 1361(c)(1)(A)(ii)" and inserting "or section 1361(b)(3)(B)(ii)", and by striking ", section 1361(b)(3)(C), or section 1361(c)(1)(D)(iii)" in subparagraph (B) and inserting "or section 1361(b)(3)(C)". **Effective** 12-29-2007.

• **2004, American Jobs Creation Act of 2004 (P.L. 108-357)**

P.L. 108-357, §231(b)(1):

Amended Code Sec. 1362(f)(1), as amended by this Act, by inserting "or section 1361(c)(1)(A)(ii)" after "section 1361(b)(3)(B)(ii),". **Effective** for elections made and terminations made after 12-31-2004.

P.L. 108-357, §231(b)(2):

Amended Code Sec. 1362(f)(1)(B), as amended by this Act, by inserting "or section 1361(c)(1)(D)(iii)" after "section 1361(b)(3)(C),". **Effective** for elections made and terminations made after 12-31-2004.

P.L. 108-357, §238(a)(1):

Amended Code Sec. 1362(f)(1) by inserting ", section 1361(b)(3)(B)(ii)," after "subsection (a)". **Effective** for elections made and terminations made after 12-31-2004.

P.L. 108-357, §238(a)(2):

Amended Code Sec. 1362(f)(1)(B) by inserting ", section 1361(b)(3)(C)," after "subsection (d)". **Effective** for elections made and terminations made after 12-31-2004.

P.L. 108-357, §238(a)(3):

Amended Code Sec. 1362(f)(3)(A). **Effective** for elections made and terminations made after 12-31-2004. Prior to amendment, Code Sec. 1362(f)(3)(A) read as follows:

(A) so that the corporation is a small business corporation, or

P.L. 108-357, §238(a)(4):

Amended Code Sec. 1362(f)(4). **Effective** for elections made and terminations made after 12-31-2004. Prior to amendment, Code Sec. 1362(f)(4) read as follows:

(4) the corporation, and each person who was a shareholder in the corporation at any time during the period specified pursuant to this subsection, agrees to make such adjustments (consistent with the treatment of the corporation as an S corporation) as may be required by the Secretary with respect to such period,

P.L. 108-357, §238(a)(5):

Amended Code Sec. 1362(f) by inserting "or a qualified subchapter S subsidiary, as the case may be" after "S corporation" in the matter following paragraph (4). **Effective** for elections made and terminations made after 12-31-2004.

• **1996, Small Business Job Protection Act of 1996 (P.L. 104-188)**

P.L. 104-188, §1305(a):

Amended Code Sec. 1362(f). **Effective** with respect to elections for tax years beginning after 12-31-82. Prior to amendment, Code Sec. 1362(f) read as follows:

(f) INADVERTENT TERMINATIONS.—If—

(1) an election under subsection (a) by any corporation was terminated under paragraph (2) or (3) of subsection (d),

(2) the Secretary determines that the termination was inadvertent,

(3) no later than a reasonable period of time after discovery of the event resulting in such termination, steps were taken so that the corporation is once more a small business corporation, and

(4) the corporation, and each person who was a shareholder of the corporation at any time during the period specified pursuant to this subsection, agrees to make such adjustments (consistent with the treatment of the corporation as an S corporation) as may be required by the Secretary with respect to such period,

then, notwithstanding the terminating event, such corporation shall be treated as continuing to be an S corporation during the period specified by the Secretary.

[Sec. 1362(g)]

(g) ELECTION AFTER TERMINATION.—If a small business corporation has made an election under subsection (a) and if such election has been terminated under subsection (d), such corporation (and any successor corporation) shall not be eligible to make an election under subsection (a) for any taxable year before its 5th taxable year which begins after the 1st taxable year for which such termination is effective, unless the Secretary consents to such election.

Amendments

- **1996, Small Business Job Protection Act of 1996 (P.L. 104-188)**

P.L. 104-188, §1317(b), provides:

(b) TREATMENT OF CERTAIN ELECTIONS UNDER PRIOR LAW.—For purposes of section 1362(g) of the Internal Revenue Code of 1986 (relating to election after termination), any termination under section 1362(d) of such Code in a taxable year beginning before January 1, 1997, shall not be taken into account.

- **1982, Subchapter S Revision Act of 1982 (P.L. 97-354)**

P.L. 97-354, §2:

Added Code Sec. 1362. **Effective** for tax years beginning after 12-31-82, except that Code Sec. 1362(d)(3) applies to tax years beginning during 1982. See, however, the amendment note for Act Sec. 6(c)(2)-(4) following Code Sec. 1361 for special rules and exceptions concerning certain casualty insurance companies and qualified oil corporations.

P.L. 97-354, §6(b)(3), as amended by P.L. 98-369, §721(i) provides:

(3) NEW PASSIVE INCOME RULES APPLY TO TAXABLE YEARS BEGINNING DURING 1982—

(A) sections 1362(d)(3), 1366(f)(3), and 1375 of the Internal Revenue Code of 1954 (as amended by this Act) shall apply, and

(B) section 1372(e)(5) of such Code (as in effect on the day before the date of the enactment of this Act) shall not apply.

The preceding sentence shall not apply in the case of any corporation which elects (at such time and in such manner as the Secretary of the Treasury or his delegate shall prescribe) to have such sentence not apply. Subsection (e) shall not apply to any termination resulting from an election under the preceding sentence.

P.L. 97-354, §6(e), as amended by P.L. 98-369, §721(k), provides:

(e) TREATMENT OF CERTAIN ELECTIONS UNDER PRIOR LAW.—For purposes of section 1362(g) of the Internal Revenue Code of 1954, as amended by this Act (relating to no election permitted within 5 years after termination of prior election), any termination or revocation under section 1372(e) of such Code (as in effect on the day before the date of the enactment of this Act) shall not be taken into account.

[Sec. 1372]
SEC. 1372. PARTNERSHIP RULES TO APPLY FOR FRINGE BENEFIT PURPOSES.
[Sec. 1372(a)]
(a) GENERAL RULE.—For purposes of applying the provisions of this subtitle which relate to employee fringe benefits—

(1) the S corporation shall be treated as a partnership, and

(2) any 2-percent shareholder of the S corporation shall be treated as a partner of such partnership.

APPENDIX: Selected Code Sections Affected by the Tax Cuts and Jobs Act

[Sec. 1372(b)]

(b) 2-PERCENT SHAREHOLDER DEFINED.—For purposes of this section, the term "2-percent shareholder" means any person who owns (or is considered as owning within the meaning of section 318) on any day during the taxable year of the S corporation more than 2 percent of the outstanding stock of such corporation or stock possessing more than 2 percent of the total combined voting power of all stock of such corporation.

Amendments

- **1982, Subchapter S Revision Act of 1982 (P.L. 97-354)**

P.L. 97-354, § 2:

Amended Code Sec. 1372. **Effective**, generally, for tax years beginning after 12-31-82, except that:

(1) Code Sec. 1372(e)(5) as in effect on the day before the enactment of P.L. 97-354 shall not apply in the case of a tax year beginning during 1982.

(2) Special rules and exceptions apply to certain casualty insurance companies and qualified oil companies. See the amendment note for Act Sec. 6(c)(2)-(4) following Code Sec. 1361.

See, also, Act Sec. 6(b)(3), following Code Sec. 1362, for a special rule affecting Code Sec. 1372(e)(5).

(3) Regarding the treatment of existing fringe benefit plans, see Act Sec. 6(d), below.

P.L. 97-354, § 6(d) provides:

(d) TREATMENT OF EXISTING FRINGE BENEFIT PLANS.—

(1) IN GENERAL.—In the case of existing fringe benefits of a corporation which as of September 28, 1982, was an electing small business corporation, section 1372 of the Internal Revenue Code of 1954 (as added by this Act) shall apply only with respect to taxable years beginning after December 31, 1987.

(2) REQUIREMENTS.—This subsection shall cease to apply with respect to any corporation after whichever of the following first occurs:

(A) the first day of the first taxable year beginning after December 31, 1982, with respect to which the corporation does not meet the requirements of section 1372(e)(5) of such Code (as in effect on the day before the date of the enactment of this Act),

(B) any termination after December 31, 1982, of the election of the corporation under subchapter S of chapter 1 of such Code, or

(C) the first day on which more than 50 percent of the stock of the corporation is newly owned stock within the meaning of section 1378(c)(2) of such Code (as amended by this Act).

(3) EXISTING FRINGE BENEFIT.—For purposes of this subsection, the term "existing fringe benefit" means any employee fringe benefit of a type which the corporation provided to its employees as of September 28, 1982.

Prior to amendment, Code Sec. 1372 read as follows:

SEC. 1372. ELECTION BY SMALL BUSINESS CORPORATION.

[Sec. 1372(a)]

(a) ELIGIBILITY.—Except as provided in subsection (f), any small business corporation may elect, in accordance with the provisions of this section, not to be subject to the taxes imposed by this chapter.

Such election shall be valid only if all persons who are shareholders in such corporation on the day on which such election is made consent to such election.

Amendments

- **1978 (P.L. 95-628)**

P.L. 95-628, § 5(b)(2):

Amended Code Sec. 1372(a), apparently duplicating the amendment made to Code Sec. 1372(a) by P.L. 95-600, § 343(b)(1). **Effective** for elections made after 1-9-79, for tax years beginning after such date.

- **1978, Revenue Act of 1978 (P.L. 95-600)**

P.L. 95-600, § 343(b)(1):

Amended Code Sec. 1372(a), an amendment duplicated in P.L. 95-628, § 5(b)(2). **Effective** for tax years beginning after 12-31-78. Prior to amendment, Code Sec. 1372(a) read as follows:

(a) ELIGIBILITY.—Except as provided in subsection (f), any small business corporation may elect, in accordance with the provisions of this section, not to be subject to the taxes imposed by this chapter. Such election shall be valid only if all persons who are shareholders in such corporation—

(1) on the first day of the first taxable year for which such election is effective, if such election is made on or before such first day, or

(2) on the day on which the election is made, if the election is made after such first day, consent to such election.

[Sec. 1372(b)]

(b) EFFECT.—If a small business corporation makes an election under subsection (a), then—

(1) with respect to the taxable years of the corporation for which such election is in effect, such corporation shall not be subject to the taxes imposed by this chapter (other than as provided by section 58(d)(2) and by section 1378) and, with respect to such taxable years and all succeeding taxable years, the provisions of section 1377 shall apply to such corporation, and

(2) with respect to the taxable years of a shareholder of such corporation in which or with which the taxable years of the corporation for which such election is in effect end, the provisions of sections 1373, 1374, and 1375 shall apply to such shareholder, and with respect to such taxable years and all succeeding taxable years, the provisions of section 1376 shall apply to such shareholder.

Amendments

- **1976, Tax Reform Act of 1976 (P.L. 94-455)**

P.L. 94-455, § 1901(a)(149)(A):

Substituted "(other than as provided by section 58(d)(2) and by section 1378)" for "(other than the tax imposed by section 1378)" in Code Sec. 1372(b)(1). **Effective** with respect to tax years beginning after 12-31-76.

- **1966 (P.L. 89-389)**

P.L. 89-389, § 2(b):

Amended Code Sec. 1372(b)(1) by inserting "(other than the tax imposed by section 1378)" immediately after "this chapter." **Effective** with respect to tax years of electing small business corporations beginning after 4-14-66, but not with respect to sales or exchanges occurring before 2-24-66.

[Sec. 1372(c)]

(c) WHEN AND HOW MADE.—

(1) IN GENERAL.—An election under subsection (a) may be made by a small business corporation for any taxable year—

(A) at any time during the preceding taxable year, or

(B) at any time during the first 75 days of the taxable year.

(2) TREATMENT OF CERTAIN LATE ELECTIONS.—If—

(A) a small business corporation makes an election under subsection (a) for any taxable year, and

(B) such election is made after the first 75 days of the taxable year and on or before the last day of such taxable year,

then such election shall be treated as made for the following taxable year.

(3) MANNER OF MAKING ELECTION.—An election under subsection (a) shall be made in such manner as the Secretary shall prescribe by regulations.

Amendments

- **1978 (P.L. 95-628)**

P.L. 95-628, § 5(a):

Amended Code Sec. 1372(c), apparently duplicating the amendment made to Code Sec. 1372(c) by P.L. 95-600, § 343(a). **Effective** for elections made after 1-9-79, for tax years beginning after such date. The amendment has a retroactive application, as set forth in P.L. 95-628, § 5(d), below.

P.L. 95-628, § 5(d):

(d) RETROACTIVE APPLICATION OF "PRECEDING TAXABLE YEAR" AMENDMENT.—

(1) IN GENERAL.—If—

(A) a small business corporation has treated itself in its return as an electing small business corporation under subchapter S of chapter 1 of the Internal Revenue Code of 1954 for any taxable year beginning before the date 60 days after the date of the enactment of this Act (hereinafter in this subsection referred to as the "election year").

Code Sec. 1372

(B) such treatment was pursuant to an election which such corporation made during the taxable year immediately preceding the election year and which, but for this subsection, would not be effective, and

(C) at such time and in such manner as the Secretary of the Treasury or his delegate may prescribe by regulations—

(i) such corporation makes an election under this paragraph, and

(ii) all persons (or their personal representatives) who were shareholders of such corporation at any time beginning with the first day of the election year and ending on the date of the making of such election consent to such election, consent to the application of the amendment made by subsection (a), and consent to the application of paragraph (3) of this subsection,

then paragraph (1) of the first sentence of section 1372(c) of such Code (as amended by subsection (a)) shall apply with respect to the taxable years referred to in paragraph (2) of this subsection.

(2) YEARS TO WHICH AMENDMENT APPLIES.—In the case of an election under paragraph (1) by any corporation, the taxable years referred to in this paragraph are—

(A) the election year,

(B) all subsequent taxable years of such corporation, and

(C) in the case of each person who was a shareholder of such corporation at any time during any taxable year described in subparagraph (A) or (B)—

(i) the first taxable year of such person ending with or within a taxable year described in subparagraph (A) or (B), and

(ii) all subsequent taxable years of such person.

(3) STATUTE OF LIMITATIONS FOR ASSESSMENT OF DEFICIENCY.—If the assessment of any deficiency in income tax resulting from the filing of an election under paragraph (1) for a taxable year ending before the date of such filing would be prevented, but for the application of this paragraph, before the expiration of one year after the date of such filing by any law or rule of law, then such deficiency (to the extent attributable to such election) may be assessed at any time before the expiration of such one-year period notwithstanding any law or rule of law which would otherwise prevent such assessment.

- **1978, Revenue Act of 1978 (P.L. 95-600)**

P.L. 95-600, §343(a):

Amended Code Sec. 1372(c), an amendment duplicated in P.L. 95-628, §5(a). **Effective** for tax years beginning after 12-31-78. Prior to amendment, Code Sec. 1372(c) read as follows:

(c) WHERE AND HOW MADE.—An election under subsection (a) may be made by a small business corporation for any taxable year at any time during the first month of such taxable year, or at any time during the month preceding such first month. Such election shall be made in such manner as the Secretary shall prescribe by regulations.

- **1976, Tax Reform Act of 1976 (P.L. 94-455)**

P.L. 94-455, §1901(a)(149)(B):

Amended Code Sec. 1372(c). **Effective** with respect to tax years beginning after 12-31-76. Prior to amendment Code Sec. 1372(c) read as follows:

(c) WHERE AND HOW MADE.—

(1) IN GENERAL.—An election under subsection (a) may be made by a small business corporation for any taxable year at any time during the first month of such taxable year, or at any time during the month preceding such first month. Such election shall be made in such manner as the Secretary or his delegate shall prescribe by regulations.

(2) TAXABLE YEARS BEGINNING BEFORE DATE OF ENACTMENT.—An election may be made under subsection (a) by a small business corporation for its first taxable year which begins after December 31, 1957, and on or before the date of the enactment of this subchapter, and ends after such date at any time—

(A) within the 90-day period beginning on the day after the date of the enactment of this subchapter, or

(B) if its taxable year ends within such 90-day period, before the close of such taxable year.

An election may be made pursuant to this paragraph only if the small business corporation has been a small business corporation (as defined in section 1371(a)) on each day after the date of the enactment of this subchapter and before the day of such election.

[Sec. 1372(d)]

(d) YEARS FOR WHICH EFFECTIVE.—An election under subsection (a) shall be effective for the taxable year of the corporation for which it is made and for all succeeding taxable years of the corporation, unless it is terminated, with respect to any such taxable year, under subsection (e).

[Sec. 1372(e)]

(e) TERMINATION.—

(1) NEW SHAREHOLDERS.—

(A) An election under subsection (a) made by a small business corporation shall terminate if any person who was not a shareholder in such corporation on the day on which the election is made becomes a shareholder in such corporation and affirmatively refuses (in such manner as the Secretary may by regulations prescribe) to consent to such election on or before the 60th day after the day on which he acquires the stock.

(B) If the person acquiring the stock is the estate of a decedent, the period under subparagraph (A) for affirmatively refusing to consent to the election shall expire on the 60th day after whichever of the following is the earlier:

(i) The day on which the executor or administrator of the estate qualifies; or

(ii) The last day of the taxable year of the corporation in which the decedent died.

(C) Any termination of an election under subparagraph (A) by reason of the affirmative refusal of any person to consent to such election shall be effective for the taxable year of the corporation in which such person becomes a shareholder in the corporation (or, if later, the first taxable year for which such election would otherwise have been effective) and for all succeeding taxable years of the corporation.

(2) REVOCATION.—An election under subsection (a) made by a small business corporation may be revoked by it for any taxable year of the corporation after the first taxable year for which the election is effective. An election may be revoked only if all persons who are shareholders in the corporation on the day on which the revocation is made consent to the revocation. A revocation under this paragraph shall be effective—

(A) for the taxable year in which made, if made before the close of the first month of such taxable year,

(B) for the taxable year following the taxable year in which made, if made after the close of such first month,

and for all succeeding taxable years of the corporation. Such revocation shall be made in such manner as the Secretary shall prescribe by regulations.

(3) CEASES TO BE SMALL BUSINESS CORPORATION.—An election under subsection (a) made by a small business corporation shall terminate if at any time—

(A) after the first day of the first taxable year of the corporation for which the election is effective, if such election is made on or before such first day, or

(B) after the day on which the election is made, if such election is made after such first day,

the corporation ceases to be a small business corporation (as defined in section 1371(a)). Such termination shall be effective for the taxable year of the corporation in which the corporation ceases to be a small business corporation and for all succeeding taxable years of the corporation.

(4) FOREIGN INCOME.—An election under subsection (a) made by a small business corporation shall terminate if for any taxable year of the corporation for which the election is in effect, such corporation derives more than 80 percent of its gross receipts from sources outside the United States. Such termination shall be effective for the taxable year of the corporation in which it derives more than 80 percent of its gross receipts from sources outside the United States, and for all succeeding taxable years of the corporation.

(5) PASSIVE INVESTMENT INCOME.—

(A) Except as provided in subparagraph (B), an election under subsection (a) made by a small business corporation shall terminate if, for any taxable year of the corporation for which the election is in effect, such corporation has gross receipts more than 20 percent of which is passive investment income. Such termination shall be effective for the taxable year of the corporation in which it has gross receipts of such amount, and for all succeeding taxable years of the corporation.

(B) Subparagraph (A) shall not apply with respect to a taxable year in which a small business corporation has gross receipts more than 20 percent of which is passive investment income, if—

(i) such taxable year is the first taxable year in which the corporation commenced the active conduct of any trade or business or the next succeeding taxable year; and

(ii) the amount of passive investment income for such taxable year is less than $3,000.

APPENDIX: Selected Code Sections Affected by the Tax Cuts and Jobs Act   259

(C) For purposes of this paragraph, the term "passive investment income" means gross receipts derived from royalties, rents, dividends, interest, annuities, and sales or exchanges of stock or securities (gross receipts from such sales or exchanges being taken into account for purposes of this paragraph only to the extent of gains therefrom). Gross receipts derived from sales or exchanges of stock or securities for purposes of this paragraph shall not include amounts received by an electing small business corporation which are treated under section 331 (relating to corporate liquidations) as payments in exchange for stock where the electing small business corporation owned more than 50 percent of each class of the stock of the liquidating corporation.

Amendments

- **1978 (P.L. 95-628)**

P.L. 95-628, § 5(b)(1):

Amended Code Sec. 1372(e)(1)(A), apparently duplicating the amendment made to Code Sec. 1372 by P.L. 95-600, § 343(b)(2). **Effective** for elections made after 1-9-79, for tax years beginning after such date.

P.L. 95-628, § 5(b)(3):

Amended Code Sec. 1372(e)(1)(C) by inserting "(or, if later, the first taxable year for which such election would otherwise have been effective)" after "in the corporation". **Effective** for elections made after 1-9-79, for tax years beginning after such date. This amendment apparently duplicates the amendment made to Code Sec. 1372(e)(1)(C) by P.L. 95-600, § 343(b)(3).

- **1978, Revenue Act of 1978 (P.L. 95-600)**

P.L. 95-600, § 343(b)(2):

Amended Code Sec. 1372(e)(1)(A). **Effective** for tax years beginning after 12-31-78. Prior to amendment, Code Sec. 1372(e)(1)(A) read as follows:

(A) An election under subsection (a) made by a small business corporation shall terminate if any person who was not a shareholder in such corporation—

(i) on the first day of the first taxable year of the corporation for which the election is effective, if such election is made on or before such first day, or

(ii) on the day on which the election is made, if such election is made after such first day,

becomes a shareholder in such corporation and affirmatively refuses (in such manner as the Secretary shall by regulations prescribe) to consent to such election on or before the 60th day after the day on which he acquires the stock.

P.L. 95-600, § 343(b)(3):

Amended Code Sec. 1372(e)(1)(C) by inserting "(or, if later, the first taxable year for which such election would otherwise have been effective)" after "in the corporation". **Effective** for tax years beginning after 12-31-78.

- **1976, Tax Reform Act of 1976 (P.L. 94-455)**

P.L. 94-455, § 902(c)(3):

Amended Code Sec. 1372(e)(1). **Effective** for tax years beginning after 12-31-76. Prior to amendment, Code Sec. 1372(e)(1) read as follows:

(1) NEW SHAREHOLDERS.—An election under subsection (a) made by a small business corporation shall terminate if any person who was not a shareholder in such corporation—

(A) on the first day of the first taxable year of the corporation for which the election is effective, if such election is made on or before such first day, or

(B) on the day on which the election is made, if such election is made after such first day,

becomes a shareholder in such corporation and does not consent to such election within such time as the Secretary or his delegate shall prescribe by regulations. Such termination shall be effective for the taxable year of the corporation in which such person becomes a shareholder in the corporation and for all succeeding taxable years of the corporation.

P.L. 94-455, § 1906(b)(13)(A):

Amended the 1954 Code by substituting "Secretary" for "Secretary or his delegate" each place it appeared. **Effective** 2-1-77.

- **1971 (P.L. 91-683)**

P.L. 91-683, § 1(a):

Amended subsection 1372(e)(5) by adding the last sentence. For effective date, see Act Sec. 1(b)-(d), below.

P.L. 91-683, §§ 1(b)-(d), provides:

"(b) The amendment made by subsection (a) shall apply to taxable years of electing small business corporations ending after the date of the enactment of this Act [January 12, 1971]. Such amendment shall also apply with respect to any taxable year ending before October 7, 1970, but only if—

"(1) on such date the making of a refund or the allowance of a credit to the electing small business corporation is not prevented by any law or rule of law, and

"(2) within one year after the date of enactment of this Act and in such manner as the Secretary of the Treasury or his delegate prescribes by regulations—

"(A) the corporation elects to have such amendment so apply, and

"(B) all persons (or their personal representatives) who were shareholders of such corporation at any time during any taxable year beginning with the first taxable year to which this amendment applies and ending on or before the date of the enactment of this Act consent to such election and to the application of the amendment made by subsection (a).

"(c) If the assessment of any deficiency in income tax resulting from the filing of such election for a taxable year ending before the date of such filing is prevented before the expiration of one year after the date of such filing by any law or rule of law, such deficiency (to the extent attributable to such election) may be assessed at any time prior to the expiration of such one-year period notwithstanding any law or rule of law which would otherwise prevent such assessment.

"(d) If the election of a corporation under subsection (a) of section 1372 of the Internal Revenue Code of 1954 would have been terminated because of the application of subsection (e)(5) of such section (before the amendment made by subsection (a) of this section) but for the election by such corporation under paragraph (2) of subsection (b) (and the consent of shareholders under such paragraph), such election under section 1372(a) of such code shall not be treated as terminated for any year beginning before the date of the enactment of this Act as a result of—

"(1) such corporation filing its income tax return on a form 1120 (instead of a form 1120S), or

"(2) a new shareholder not consenting to such election of such corporation in accordance with the requirements of subsection (e)(1) of such section 1372."

- **1966 (P.L. 89-389)**

P.L. 89-389, § 3(a):

Amended Code Sec. 1372(e)(5). **Effective** for tax years of electing small business corporations ending after 4-14-66. The amendment also applies with respect to tax years beginning after 1962, and ending on or before 4-14-66, if (at such time and in such manner as the Secretary of the Treasury or his delegate prescribes by regulations)—(1) the corporation elects to have the amendment apply, and (2) all persons (or their personal representatives) who were shareholders of such corporation at any time during any tax year beginning after 1962, and ending on or before 4-14-66, consent to such election and to the application of the amendment. Prior to amendment, Sec. 1372(e)(5) read as follows:

"(5) Personal holding company income.—An election under subsection (a) made by a small business corporation shall terminate if, for any taxable year of the corporation for which the election is in effect, such corporation has gross receipts more than 20 percent of which is derived from royalties, rents, dividends, interest, annuities, and sales or exchanges of stock or securities (gross receipts from such sales or exchanges being taken into account for purposes of this paragraph only to the extent of gains therefrom). Such termination shall be effective for the taxable year of the corporation in which it has gross receipts of such amount, and for all succeeding taxable years of the corporation."

[Sec. 1372(f)]

(f) ELECTION AFTER TERMINATION.—If a small business corporation has made an election under subsection (a) and if such election has been terminated or revoked under subsection (e), such corporation (and any successor corporation) shall not be eligible to make an election under subsection (a) for any taxable year prior to its fifth taxable year which begins after the first taxable year for which such termination or revocation is effective, unless the Secretary consents to such election.

Amendments

- **1976, Tax Reform Act of 1976 (P.L. 94-455)**

P.L. 94-455, § 1906(b)(13)(A):

Amended 1954 Code by substituting "Secretary" for "Secretary or his delegate" each place it appeared. **Effective** 2-1-77.

Code Sec. 1372

- **1958, Technical Amendments Act of 1958 (P.L. 85-866)**

P.L. 85-866, §64(a):

Added Code Sec. 1372. **Effective** for tax years beginning after 12-31-57.

[Sec. 1372(g)—Repealed]

Amendments

- **1976, Tax Reform Act of 1976 (P.L. 94-455)**

P.L. 94-455, §1901(a)(149)(C):

Repealed Code Sec. 1372(g). **Effective** with respect to tax years beginning after 12-31-76. Prior to repeal, Code Sec. 1372(g) read as follows:

(g) CONSENT TO ELECTION BY CERTAIN SHAREHOLDERS OF STOCK HELD AS COMMUNITY PROPERTY.—If a husband and wife owned stock which was community property (or the income from which was community income) under the applicable community property law of a State, and if either spouse filed a timely consent to an election under subsection (a) for a taxable year beginning before January 1, 1961, the time for filing the consent of the other spouse to such election shall not expire prior to May 15, 1961.

- **1961 (P.L. 87-29)**

P.L. 87-29, §2:

Added Code Sec. 1372(g). **Effective** for tax years beginning before 1-1-61, the time for filing the consent not to expire prior to 5-15-61.

[Sec. 1374]

SEC. 1374. TAX IMPOSED ON CERTAIN BUILT-IN GAINS.

[Sec. 1374(a)]

(a) GENERAL RULE.—If for any taxable year beginning in the recognition period an S corporation has a net recognized built-in gain, there is hereby imposed a tax (computed under subsection (b)) on the income of such corporation for such taxable year.

Amendments

- **1988, Technical and Miscellaneous Revenue Act of 1988 (P.L. 100-647)**

P.L. 100-647, §1006(f)(1):

Amended Code Sec. 1374(a) by striking out "a recognized built-in gain" and inserting in lieu thereof "a net recognized built-in gain". **Effective** as if included in the provision of P.L. 99-514 to which it relates.

[Sec. 1374(b)]

(b) AMOUNT OF TAX.—

(1) IN GENERAL.—The amount of the tax imposed by subsection (a) shall be computed by applying the highest rate of tax specified in section 11(b) to the net recognized built-in gain of the S corporation for the taxable year.

(2) NET OPERATING LOSS CARRYFORWARDS FROM C YEARS ALLOWED.—Notwithstanding section 1371(b)(1), any net operating loss carryforward arising in a taxable year for which the corporation was a C corporation shall be allowed for purposes of this section as a deduction against the net recognized built-in gain of the S corporation for the taxable year. For purposes of determining the amount of any such loss which may be carried to subsequent taxable years, the amount of the net recognized built-in gain shall be treated as taxable income. Rules similar to the rules of the preceding sentences of this paragraph shall apply in the case of a capital loss carryforward arising in a taxable year for which the corporation was a C corporation.

(3) CREDITS.—

(A) IN GENERAL.—Except as provided in subparagraph (B), no credit shall be allowable under part IV of subchapter A of this chapter (other than under section 34) against the tax imposed by subsection (a).

⇛→ *Caution: Code Sec. 1374(b)(3)(B), below, prior to amendment by P.L. 115-97, applies to tax years beginning on or before December 31, 2021.*

(B) BUSINESS CREDIT CARRYFORWARDS FROM C YEARS ALLOWED.—Notwithstanding section 1371(b)(1), any business credit carryforward under section 39 arising in a taxable year for which the corporation was a C corporation shall be allowed as a credit against the tax imposed by subsection (a) in the same manner as if it were imposed by section 11.

A similar rule shall apply in the case of the minimum tax credit under section 53 to the extent attributable to taxable years for which the corporation was a C corporation.

⇛→ *Caution: Code Sec. 1374(b)(3)(B), below, as amended by P.L. 115-97, applies to tax years beginning after December 31, 2021.*

(B) BUSINESS CREDIT CARRYFORWARDS FROM C YEARS ALLOWED.—Notwithstanding section 1371(b)(1), any business credit carryforward under section 39 arising in a taxable year for which the corporation was a C corporation shall be allowed as a credit against the tax imposed by subsection (a) in the same manner as if it were imposed by section 11.

Amendments

- **2017, Tax Cuts and Jobs Act (P.L. 115-97)**

P.L. 115-97, §12002(c):

Amended Code Sec. 1374(b)(3)(B) by striking the last sentence. **Effective** for tax years beginning after 12-31-2021. Prior to being stricken, the last sentence of Code Sec. 1374(b)(3)(B) read as follows:

A similar rule shall apply in the case of the minimum tax credit under section 53 to the extent attributable to taxable years for which the corporation was a C corporation.

P.L. 115-97, §13001(b)(2)(N):

Amended Code Sec. 1374(b) by striking paragraph (4). **Effective** for tax years beginning after 12-31-2017. Prior to being stricken, Code Sec. 1374(b)(4) read as follows:

(4) COORDINATION WITH SECTION 1201(a).—For purposes of section 1201(a)—

(A) the tax imposed by subsection (a) shall be treated as if it were imposed by section 11, and

(B) the amount of the net recognized built-in gain shall be treated as the taxable income.

- **1989, Omnibus Budget Reconciliation Act of 1989 (P.L. 101-239)**

P.L. 101-239, §7811(c)(8):

Amended Code Sec. 1374(b)(3)(B) by adding at the end thereof a new sentence. **Effective** as if included in the provision of P.L. 100-647 to which it relates.

- **1988, Technical and Miscellaneous Revenue Act of 1988 (P.L. 100-647)**

P.L. 100-647, §1006(f)(2):

Amended Code Sec. 1374(b) by striking out paragraphs (1) and (2) and inserting new paragraphs (1) and (2). **Effective** as if included in the provision of P.L. 99-514 to which it relates. Prior to amendment, paragraphs (1) and (2) read as follows:

(1) IN GENERAL.—The tax imposed by subsection (a) shall be a tax computed by applying the highest rate of tax specified in section 11(b) to the lesser of—

(A) the recognized built-in gains of the S corporation for the taxable year, or

(B) the amount which would be the taxable income of the corporation for such taxable year if such corporation were not an S corporation.

(2) NET OPERATING LOSS CARRYFORWARDS FROM C YEARS ALLOWED.—Notwithstanding section 1371(b)(1), any net operating loss carryforward arising in a taxable year for which the corporation was a C corporation shall be allowed as a deduction against the lesser of the amounts referred to in subparagraph (A) or (B) of paragraph (1). For purposes of determining the amount of any such loss which may be carried to subsequent taxable years, the lesser of the amounts referred to in subparagraph (A) or (B) of paragraph (1) shall be treated as taxable income.

P.L. 100-647, §1006(f)(3):

Amended Code Sec. 1374(b)(4)(B). **Effective** as if included in the provision of P.L. 99-514 to which it relates. Prior to amendment, Code Sec. 1374(b)(4)(B) read as follows:

(B) the lower of the amounts specified in subparagraphs (A) and (B) of paragraph (1) shall be treated as the taxable income.

[Sec. 1374(c)]

(c) LIMITATIONS.—

(1) CORPORATIONS WHICH WERE ALWAYS S CORPORATIONS.—Subsection (a) shall not apply to any corporation if an election under section 1362(a) has been in effect with respect to such corporation for each of its taxable years. Except as provided in regulations, an S corporation and any predecessor corporation shall be treated as 1 corporation for purposes of the preceding sentence.

(2) LIMITATION ON AMOUNT OF NET RECOGNIZED BUILT-IN GAIN.—The amount of the net recognized built-in gain taken into account under this section for any taxable year shall not exceed the excess (if any) of—

(A) the net unrealized built-in gain, over

(B) the net recognized built-in gain for prior taxable years beginning in the recognition period.

Amendments

- **1988, Technical and Miscellaneous Revenue Act of 1988 (P.L. 100-647)**

P.L. 100-647, §1006(f)(4):

Amended Code Sec. 1374(c)(2) by striking out "recognized built-in gains" each place it appears and inserting in lieu thereof "net recognized built-in gain". **Effective** as if included in the provision of P.L. 99-514 to which it relates.

[Sec. 1374(d)]

(d) DEFINITIONS AND SPECIAL RULES.—For purposes of this section—

(1) NET UNREALIZED BUILT-IN GAIN.—The term "net unrealized built-in gain" means the amount (if any) by which—

(A) the fair market value of the assets of S corporation as of the beginning of its 1st taxable year for which an election under section 1362(a) is in effect, exceeds

(B) the aggregate adjusted bases of such assets at such time.

(2) NET RECOGNIZED BUILT-IN GAIN.—

(A) IN GENERAL.—The term "net recognized built-in gain" means, with respect to any taxable year in the recognition period, the lesser of—

(i) the amount which would be taxable income of the S corporation for such taxable year if only recognized built-in gains and recognized built-in losses were taken into account, or

(ii) such corporation's taxable income for such taxable year (determined as provided in section 1375(b)(1)(B)).

(B) CARRYOVER.—If, for any taxable year described in subparagraph (A), the amount referred to in clause (i) of subparagraph (A) exceeds the amount referred to in clause (ii) of subparagraph (A), such excess shall be treated as a recognized built-in gain in the succeeding taxable year.

(3) RECOGNIZED BUILT-IN GAIN.—The term "recognized built-in gain" means any gain recognized during the recognition period on the disposition of any asset except to the extent that the S corporation establishes that—

(A) such asset was not held by the S corporation as of the beginning of the 1st taxable year for which it was an S corporation, or

(B) such gain exceeds the excess (if any) of—

(i) the fair market value of such asset as of the beginning of such 1st taxable year, over

(ii) the adjusted basis of the asset as of such time.

(4) RECOGNIZED BUILT-IN LOSSES.—The term "recognized built-in loss" means any loss recognized during the recognition period on the disposition of any asset to the extent that the S corporation establishes that—

(A) such asset was held by the S corporation as of the beginning of the 1st taxable year referred to in paragraph (3), and

(B) such loss does not exceed the excess of—

(i) the adjusted basis of such asset as of the beginning of such 1st taxable year, over

(ii) the fair market value of such asset as of such time.

(5) TREATMENT OF CERTAIN BUILT-IN ITEMS.—

(A) INCOME ITEMS.—Any item of income which is properly taken into account during the recognition period but which is attributable to periods before the 1st taxable year for which the corporation was an S corporation shall be treated as a recognized built-in gain for the taxable year in which it is properly taken into account.

(B) DEDUCTION ITEMS.—Any amount which is allowable as a deduction during the recognition period (determined without regard to any carryover) but which is attributable to periods before the 1st taxable year referred to in subparagraph (A) shall be treated as a recognized built-in loss for the taxable year for which it is allowable as a deduction.

(C) ADJUSTMENT TO NET UNREALIZED BUILT-IN GAIN.—The amount of the net unrealized built-in gain shall be properly adjusted for amounts which would be treated as recognized built-in gains or losses under this paragraph if such amounts were properly taken into account (or allowable as a deduction) during the recognition period.

(6) TREATMENT OF CERTAIN PROPERTY.—If the adjusted basis of any asset is determined (in whole or in part) by reference to the adjusted basis of any other asset held by the S corporation as of the beginning of the 1st taxable year referred to in paragraph (3)—

(A) such asset shall be treated as held by the S corporation as of the beginning of such 1st taxable year, and

(B) any determination under paragraph (3)(B) or (4)(B) with respect to such asset shall be made by reference to the fair market value and adjusted basis of such other asset as of the beginning of such 1st taxable year.

(7) RECOGNITION PERIOD.—

(A) IN GENERAL.—The term "recognition period" means the 5-year period beginning with the 1st day of the 1st taxable year for which the corporation was an S corporation. For purposes of applying this section to any amount includible in income by reason of distributions to shareholders pursuant to section 593(e), the preceding sentence shall be applied without regard to the phrase "5-year".

(B) INSTALLMENT SALES.—If an S corporation sells an asset and reports the income from the sale using the installment method under section 453, the treatment of all payments received shall be governed by the provisions of this paragraph applicable to the taxable year in which such sale was made.

(8) TREATMENT OF TRANSFER OF ASSETS FROM C CORPORATION TO S CORPORATION.—

(A) IN GENERAL.—Except to the extent provided in regulations, if—

(i) an S corporation acquires any asset, and

(ii) the S corporation's basis in such asset is determined (in whole or in part) by reference to the basis of such asset (or any other property) in the hands of a C corporation,

then a tax is hereby imposed on any net recognized built-in gain attributable to any such assets for any taxable year beginning in the recognition period. The amount of such tax shall be determined under the rules of this section as modified by subparagraph (B).

(B) MODIFICATIONS.—For purposes of this paragraph, the modifications of this subparagraph are as follows:

(i) IN GENERAL.—The preceding paragraphs of this subsection shall be applied by taking into account the day on which the assets were acquired by the S corporation in lieu of the beginning of the 1st taxable year for which the corporation was an S corporation.

(ii) SUBSECTION (c)(1) NOT TO APPLY.—Subsection (c)(1) shall not apply.

(9) REFERENCE TO 1ST TAXABLE YEAR.—Any reference in this section to the 1st taxable year for which the corporation was an S corporation shall be treated as a reference to the 1st taxable year for which the corporation was an S corporation pursuant to its most recent election under section 1362.

Amendments

- **2018, Tax Technical Corrections Act of 2018 (P.L. 115-141)**

P.L. 115-141, §401(b)(33), Div. U:

Amended Code Sec. 1374(d)(2)(B) by striking the last sentence. **Effective** 3-23-2018. For a special rule, see Act Sec. 401(e), Div. U, below. Prior to being stricken, the last sentence of Code Sec. 1374(d)(2)(B) read as follows:

The preceding sentence shall apply only in the case of a corporation treated as an S corporation by reason of an election made on or after March 31, 1988.

P.L. 115-141, §401(e), Div. U, provides:

(e) GENERAL SAVINGS PROVISION WITH RESPECT TO DEADWOOD PROVISIONS.—If—

(1) any provision amended or repealed by the amendments made by subsection (b) or (d) applied to—

(A) any transaction occurring before the date of the enactment of this Act,

(B) any property acquired before such date of enactment, or

(C) any item of income, loss, deduction, or credit taken into account before such date of enactment, and

(2) the treatment of such transaction, property, or item under such provision would (without regard to the amendments or repeals made by such subsection) affect the liability for tax for periods ending after such date of enactment, nothing in the amendments or repeals made by this section shall be construed to affect the treatment of such transaction, property, or item for purposes of determining liability for tax for periods ending after such date of enactment.

- **2015, Protecting Americans from Tax Hikes Act of 2015 (P.L. 114-113)**

P.L. 114-113, §127(a), Div. Q:

Amended Code Sec. 1374(d)(7). **Effective** for tax years beginning after 12-31-2014. Prior to amendment, Code Sec. 1374(d)(7) read as follows:

(7) RECOGNITION PERIOD.—

(A) IN GENERAL.—The term "recognition period" means the 10-year period beginning with the 1st day of the 1st taxable year for which the corporation was an S corporation.

(B) SPECIAL RULES FOR 2009, 2010, AND 2011.—No tax shall be imposed on the net recognized built-in gain of an S corporation—

(i) in the case of any taxable year beginning in 2009 or 2010, if the 7th taxable year in the recognition period preceded such taxable year, or

(ii) in the case of any taxable year beginning in 2011, if the 5th year in the recognition period preceded such taxable year.

The preceding sentence shall be applied separately with respect to any asset to which paragraph (8) applies.

(C) SPECIAL RULE FOR 2012, 2013, AND 2014.—For purposes of determining the net recognized built-in gain for taxable years beginning in 2012, 2013, or 2014, subparagraphs (A) and (D) shall be applied by substituting "5-year" for "10-year".

(D) SPECIAL RULE FOR DISTRIBUTIONS TO SHAREHOLDERS.—For purposes of applying this section to any amount includible in income by reason of distributions to shareholders pursuant to section 593(e)—

(i) subparagraph (A) shall be applied without regard to the phrase "10-year", and

(ii) subparagraph (B) shall not apply.

(E) INSTALLMENT SALES.—If an S corporation sells an asset and reports the income from the sale using the installment method under section 453, the treatment of all payments received shall be governed by the provisions of this paragraph applicable to the taxable year in which such sale was made.

- **2014, Tax Increase Prevention Act of 2014 (P.L. 113-295)**

P.L. 113-295, §138(a)(1)-(2), Division A:

Amended Code Sec. 1374(d)(7)(C) by striking "2012 or 2013" and inserting "2012, 2013, or 2014", and by striking "2012 and 2013" in the heading and inserting "2012, 2013, AND 2014". **Effective** for tax years beginning after 12-31-2013.

- **2013, American Taxpayer Relief Act of 2012 (P.L. 112-240)**

P.L. 112-240, §326(a)(1)-(3):

Amended Code Sec. 1374(d)(7) by redesignating subparagraph (C) as subparagraph (D), and by inserting after subparagraph (B) a new subparagraph (C), and by adding at the end a new subparagraph (E). **Effective** for tax years beginning after 12-31-2011.

P.L. 112-240, §326(b):

Amended Code Sec. 1374(d)(2)(B) by inserting "described in subparagraph (A)" after ", for any taxable year". **Effective** for tax years beginning after 12-31-2011.

- **2010, Creating Small Business Jobs Act of 2010 (P.L. 111-240)**

P.L. 111-240, §2014(a):

Amended Code Sec. 1374(d)(7)(B). **Effective** for tax years beginning after 12-31-2010. Prior to amendment, Code Sec. 1374(d)(7)(B) read as follows:

(B) SPECIAL RULE FOR 2009 AND 2010.—In the case of any taxable year beginning in 2009 or 2010, no tax shall be imposed on the net recognized built-in gain of an S corporation if the 7th taxable year in the recognition period preceded such taxable year. The preceding sentence shall be applied separately with respect to any asset to which paragraph (8) applies.

- **2009, American Recovery and Reinvestment Tax Act of 2009 (P.L. 111-5)**

P.L. 111-5, § 1251(a):

Amended Code Sec. 1374(d)(7). **Effective** for tax years beginning after 12-31-2008. Prior to amendment, Code Sec. 1374(d)(7) read as follows:

(7) RECOGNITION PERIOD.—The term "recognition period" means the 10-year period beginning with the 1st day of the 1st taxable year for which the corporation was an S corporation. For purposes of applying this section to any amount includible in income by reason of section 593(e), the preceding sentence shall be applied without regard to the phrase "10-year".

- **1997, Taxpayer Relief Act of 1997 (P.L. 105-34)**

P.L. 105-34, § 1601(f)(5)(B):

Amended Code Sec. 1374(d)(7) by adding at the end a new sentence. **Effective** as if included in the provision of P.L. 104-188 to which it relates [effective for tax years beginning after 12-31-95.—CCH].

- **1989, Omnibus Budget Reconciliation Act of 1989 (P.L. 101-239)**

P.L. 101-239, § 7811(c)(4):

Amended Code Sec. 1374(d)(2)(A)(i) by striking "(except as provided in subsection (b)(2))" after "year if". **Effective** as if included in the provision of P.L. 100-647 to which it relates.

P.L. 101-239, § 7811(c)(5)(B)(i)-(ii):

Amended Code Sec. 1374(d)(5) by striking "during the recognition period" in subparagraph (B) and inserting "during the recognition period (determined without regard to any carryover)", and by striking "treated as recognized built-in gains or losses under this paragraph" in subparagraph (C) and inserting "which would be treated as recognized built-in gains or losses under this paragraph if such amounts were properly taken into account (or allowable as a deduction) during the recognition period". **Effective** as if included in the provision of P.L. 100-647 to which it relates.

- **1988, Technical and Miscellaneous Revenue Act of 1988 (P.L. 100-647)**

P.L. 100-647, § 1006(f)(5)(A):

Amended Code Sec. 1374(d) by striking out all that follows paragraph (1) and inserting in lieu thereof new paragraphs (2)-(9) and new subsection (e). **Effective** as if included in the provision of P.L. 99-514 to which it relates. Prior to amendment, all that followed Code Sec. 1374(d)(1) read as follows:

(2) RECOGNIZED BUILT-IN GAIN.—The term "recognized built-in gain" means any gain recognized during the recognition period on the disposition of any asset except to the extent that the S corporation establishes that—

(A) such asset was not held by the S corporation as of the beginning of the 1st taxable year referred to in paragraph (1), or

(B) such gain exceeds the excess (if any) of—

(i) the fair market value of such asset as of the beginning of such 1st taxable year, over

(ii) the adjusted basis of the asset as of such time.

(3) RECOGNITION PERIOD.—The term "recognition period" means the 10-year period beginning with the 1st day of the 1st taxable year for which the corporation was an S corporation.

(4) TAXABLE INCOME.—Taxable income of the corporation shall be determined under section 63(a)—

(A) without regard to the deductions allowed by part VIII of subchapter B (other than the deduction allowed by section 248, relating to organization expenditures), and

(B) without regard to the deduction under section 172.

- **1986, Tax Reform Act of 1986 (P.L. 99-514)**

P.L. 99-514, § 632(a):

Amended Code Sec. 1374. **Effective** to (1) any distribution in complete liquidation, and any sale or exchange, made by a corporation after 7-31-86, unless such corporation is completely liquidated before 1-1-87, (2) any transaction described in section 338 of the Internal Revenue Code of 1986 for which the acquisition date occurs after 12-31-86, and (3) any distribution (not in complete liquidation) made after 12-31-86. For special and transitional rules, see Act Sec. 633(b)-(f) following Code Sec. 26. Prior to amendment, Code Sec. 1374 read as follows:

SEC. 1374. TAX IMPOSED ON CERTAIN CAPITAL GAINS.

[Sec. 1374(a)]

(a) GENERAL RULE.—If for a taxable year of an S corporation—

(1) the net capital gain of such corporation exceeds $25,000, and exceeds 50 percent of its taxable income for such year, and

(2) the taxable income of such corporation for such year exceeds $25,000,

There is hereby imposed a tax (computed under subsection (b)) on the income of such corporation.

[Sec. 1374(b)]

(b) AMOUNT OF TAX.—The tax imposed by subsection (a) shall be the lower of—

(1) an amount equal to the tax, determined as provided in section 1201(a), on the amount by which the net capital gain of the corporation for the taxable year exceeds $25,000, or

(2) an amount equal to the tax which would be imposed by section 11 on the taxable income of the corporation for the taxable year if the corporation were not an S corporation.

No credit shall be allowable under part IV of subchapter A of this chapter (other than under section 34) against the tax imposed by subsection (a).

Amendments

- **1984, Deficit Reduction Act of 1984 (P.L. 98-369)**

P.L. 98-369, § 474(r)(27):

Amended Code Sec. 1374(b) by striking out "section 39" and inserting in lieu thereof "section 34". **Effective** for tax years beginning after 12-31-83, and to carrybacks from such years.

[Sec. 1374(c)]

(c) EXCEPTIONS.—

(1) IN GENERAL.—Subsection (a) shall not apply to an S corporation for any taxable year if the election under section 1362(a) which is in effect with respect to such corporation for such taxable year has been in effect for the 3 immediately preceding taxable years.

(2) NEW CORPORATIONS.—Subsection (a) shall not apply to an S corporation if—

(A) it has been in existence for less than 4 taxable years, and

(B) an election under section 1362(a) has been in effect with respect to such corporation for each of its taxable years.

To the extent provided in regulations, an S corporation and any predecessor corporation shall be treated as 1 corporation for purposes of this paragraph and paragraph (1).

(3) PROPERTY WITH SUBSTITUTED BASIS.—If—

(A) but for paragraph (1) or (2), subsection (a) would apply for the taxable year,

(B) any long-term capital gain is attributable to property acquired by the S corporation during the period beginning 3 years before the first day of the taxable year and ending on the last day of the taxable year, and

(C) the basis of such property is determined in whole or in part by reference to the basis of any property in the hands of another corporation which was not an S corporation throughout all of the period described in subparagraph (B) before the transfer by such other corporation and during which such other corporation was in existence,

then subsection (a) shall apply for the taxable year, but the amount of the tax determined under subsection (b) shall not exceed a tax, determined as provided in section 1201(a), on the net capital gain attributable to property acquired as provided in subparagraph (B) and having a basis described in subparagraph (C).

(4) TREATMENT OF CERTAIN GAINS OF OPTIONS AND COMMODITIES DEALERS.—

(A) EXCLUSION OF CERTAIN CAPITAL GAINS.—For purposes of this section, the net capital gain of any options dealer or commodities dealer shall be determined by not taking into account any gain or loss (in the normal course of the taxpayer's activity of dealing in or trading section 1256 contracts) from any section 1256 contract or property related to such a contract.

(B) DEFINITIONS.—For purposes of this paragraph—

(i) OPTIONS DEALER.—The term "options dealer" has the meaning given to such term by section 1256(g)(8).

(ii) COMMODITIES DEALER.—The term "commodities dealer" means a person who is actively engaged in trading section 1256 contracts and is registered with a domestic board of trade which is designated as a contract market by the Commodities Futures Trading Commission.

(iii) SECTION 1256 CONTRACTS.—The term "section 1256 contracts" has the meaning given to such term by section 1256(b).

Amendments

- **1984, Deficit Reduction Act of 1984 (P.L. 98-369)**

P.L. 98-369, §102(d)(1):
Amended Code Sec. 1374(c) by adding paragraph (4). **Effective** for positions established after 7-18-84, in tax years ending after such date.

P.L. 98-369, §721(u):
Amended Code Sec. 1374(c)(2) by striking out "(and any predecessor corporation)" in subparagraph (A) and by adding the sentence at the end thereof. **Effective** as if included in P.L. 97-354.

[Sec. 1374(d)]

(d) DETERMINATION OF TAXABLE INCOME.—For purposes of this section, taxable income of the corporation shall be determined under section 63(a) without regard to—

(1) the deduction allowed by section 172 (relating to net operating loss deduction), and

(2) the deductions allowed by part VIII of subchapter B (other than the deduction allowed by section 248, relating to organization expenditures).

Amendments

- **1983, Technical Corrections Act of 1982 (P.L. 97-448)**

P.L. 97-448, §305(d)(3):
Amended Code Sec. 1374(d) by striking out "subsections (a)(2) and (b)(2)" and inserting in lieu thereof "this section". **Effective** 10-19-82.

- **1982, Subchapter S Revision Act of 1982 (P.L. 97-354)**

P.L. 97-354, §2:
Amended Code Sec. 1374. **Effective**, generally, for tax years beginning after 12-31-82. See, however, the amendment note for Act Sec. 6(c)(2)-(4) following Code Sec. 1361 for special rules and exceptions applicable to certain casualty insurance companies and qualified oil corporations. Prior to amendment, Code Sec. 1374 read as follows:

SEC. 1374. CORPORATION NET OPERATING LOSS ALLOWED TO SHAREHOLDERS.

[Sec. 1374(a)]

(a) GENERAL RULE.—A net operating loss of an electing small business corporation for any taxable year shall be allowed as a deduction from gross income of the shareholders of such corporation in the manner and to the extent set forth in this section.

[Sec. 1374(b)]

(b) ALLOWANCE OF DEDUCTION.—Each person who is a shareholder of an electing small business corporation at any time during a taxable year of the corporation in which it has a net operating loss shall be allowed as a deduction from gross income, for his taxable year in which or with which the taxable year of the corporation ends (or for the final taxable year of a shareholder who dies before the end of the corporation's taxable year), an amount equal to his portion of the corporation's net operating loss (as determined under subsection (c)). The deduction allowed by this subsection shall, for purposes of this chapter, be considered as a deduction attributable to a trade or business carried on by the shareholder.

Amendments

- **1976, Tax Reform Act of 1976 (P.L. 94-455)**

P.L. 94-455, §1901(a)(150)(A):
Added the last sentence beginning "The deduction allowed by this subsection shall," to Code Sec. 1374(b). **Effective** with respect to tax years beginning after 12-31-76.

- **1962, Revenue Act of 1962 (P.L. 87-834)**

P.L. 87-834, §30:
Changed Code Sec. 1374(b) to apply retroactively to 9-2-58.

- **1959 (P.L. 86-376)**

P.L. 86-376, §2(b):
Inserted "(or for the final taxable year of a shareholder who dies before the end of the corporation's taxable year)"

after "the taxable year of the corporation ends" in Code Sec. 1374(b). **Effective** 9-24-59.

[Sec. 1374(c)]

(c) DETERMINATION OF SHAREHOLDER'S PORTION.—

(1) IN GENERAL.—For purposes of this section, a shareholder's portion of the net operating loss of an electing small business corporation is his pro rata share of the corporation's net operating loss (computed as provided in section 172(c), except that the deductions provided in part VIII (except section 248) of subchapter B shall not be allowed) for his taxable year in which or with which the taxable year of the corporation ends. For purposes of this paragraph, a shareholder's pro rata share of the corporation's net operating loss is the sum of the portions of the corporation's daily net operating loss attributable on a pro rata basis to the shares held by him on each day of the taxable year. For purposes of the preceding sentence, the corporation's daily net operating loss is the corporation's net operating loss divided by the number of days in the taxable year.

(2) LIMITATION.—A shareholder's portion of the net operating loss of an electing small business corporation for any taxable year shall not exceed the sum of—

(A) the adjusted basis (determined without regard to any adjustment under section 1376 for the taxable year) of the shareholder's stock in the electing small business corporation, determined as of the close of the taxable year of the corporation, (or, in respect of stock sold or otherwise disposed of during such taxable year, as of the day before the day of such sale or other disposition), and

(B) the adjusted basis (determined without regard to any adjustment under section 1376 for the taxable year) of any indebtedness of the corporation to the shareholder, determined as of the close of the taxable year of the corporation (or, if the shareholder is not a shareholder as of the close of such taxable year, as of the close of the last day in such taxable year on which the shareholder was a shareholder in the corporation).

[Sec. 1374(d)—Repealed]

- **1976, Tax Reform Act of 1976 (P.L. 94-455)**

P.L. 94-455, §1901(a)(150)(B):
Repealed Code Sec. 1374(d). **Effective** with respect to tax years beginning after 12-31-76. Prior to repeal, Code Sec. 1374(d) read as follows:

(d) APPLICATION WITH OTHER PROVISIONS.—

(1) IN GENERAL.—The deduction allowed by subsection (b) shall, for purposes of this chapter, be considered as a deduction attributable to a trade or business carried on by the shareholder.

(2) ADJUSTMENT OF NET OPERATING LOSS CARRYBACKS AND CARRYOVERS OF SHAREHOLDERS.—

For purposes of determining, under section 172, the net operating loss carrybacks to taxable years beginning before January 1, 1958, from a taxable year of the shareholder for which he is allowed a deduction under subsection (b), such deduction shall be disregarded in determining the net operating loss for such taxable year. In the case of a net operating loss for a taxable year in which a shareholder is allowed a deduction under subsection (b), the determination of the portion of such loss which may be carried to subsequent years shall be made without regard to the preceding sentence and in accordance with section 172(b)(2), but the sum of the taxable incomes for taxable years beginning before January 1, 1958, shall be deemed not to exceed the amount of the net operating loss determined with the application of the preceding sentence.

- **1958, Technical Amendments Act of 1958 (P.L. 85-866)**

P.L. 85-866, §64(a):
Added Code Sec. 1374. **Effective** for tax years beginning after 12-31-57.

[Sec. 1374(e)]

(e) REGULATIONS.—The Secretary shall prescribe such regulations as may be necessary to carry out the purposes of this section including regulations providing for the appropriate treatment of successor corporations.

Amendments
- **1988, Technical and Miscellaneous Revenue Act of 1988 (P.L. 100-647)**
P.L. 100-647, §1006(f)(5)(A):
Amended Code Sec. 1374 by adding at the end thereof new subsection (e). **Effective** as if included in the provision of P.L. 99-514 to which it relates.

[Sec. 1402]
SEC. 1402. DEFINITIONS.

[Sec. 1402(a)]
(a) NET EARNINGS FROM SELF-EMPLOYMENT.—The term "net earnings from self-employment" means the gross income derived by an individual from any trade or business carried on by such

individual, less the deductions allowed by this subtitle which are attributable to such trade or business, plus his distributive share (whether or not distributed) of income or loss described in section 702(a)(8) from any trade or business carried on by a partnership of which he is a member; except that in computing such gross income and deductions and such distributive share of partnership ordinary income or loss—

(1) there shall be excluded rentals from real estate and from personal property leased with the real estate (including such rentals paid in crop shares, and including payments under section 1233(a)(2) of the Food Security Act of 1985 (16 U.S.C. 3833(a)(2)) to individuals receiving benefits under section 202 or 223 of the Social Security Act) together with the deductions attributable thereto, unless such rentals are received in the course of a trade or business as a real estate dealer; except that the preceding provisions of this paragraph shall not apply to any income derived by the owner or tenant of land if (A) such income is derived under an arrangement, between the owner or tenant and another individual, which provides that such other individual shall produce agricultural or horticultural commodities (including livestock, bees, poultry, and fur-bearing animals and wildlife) on such land, and that there shall be material participation by the owner or tenant (as determined without regard to any activities of an agent of such owner or tenant) in the production or the management of the production of such agricultural or horticultural commodities, and (B) there is material participation by the owner or tenant (as determined without regard to any activities of an agent of such owner or tenant) with respect to any such agricultural or horticultural commodity;

(2) there shall be excluded dividends on any share of stock, and interest on any bond, debenture, note, or certificate, or other evidence of indebtedness, issued with interest coupons or in registered form by any corporation (including one issued by a government or political subdivision thereof), unless such dividends and interest are received in the course of a trade or business as a dealer in stocks or securities;

(3) there shall be excluded any gain or loss—

(A) which is considered as gain or loss from the sale or exchange of a capital asset,

(B) from the cutting of timber, or the disposal of timber, coal, or iron ore, if section 631 applies to such gain or loss, or

(C) from the sale, exchange, involuntary conversion, or other disposition of property if such property is neither—

(i) stock in trade or other property of a kind which would properly be includible in inventory if on hand at the close of the taxable year, nor

(ii) property held primarily for sale to customers in the ordinary course of the trade or business;

(4) the deduction for net operating losses provided in section 172 shall not be allowed;

(5) if—

(A) any of the income derived from a trade or business (other than a trade or business carried on by a partnership) is community income under community property laws applicable to such income, the gross income and deductions attributable to such trade or business shall be treated as the gross income and deductions of the spouse carrying on such trade or business or, if such trade or business is jointly operated, treated as the gross income and deductions of each spouse on the basis of their respective distributive share of the gross income and deductions; and

(B) any portion of a partner's distributive share of the ordinary income or loss from a trade or business carried on by a partnership is community income or loss under the community property laws applicable to such share, all of such distributive share shall be included in computing the net earnings from self-employment of such partner, and no part of such share shall be taken into account in computing the net earnings from self-employment of the spouse of such partner;

(6) a resident of Puerto Rico shall compute his net earnings from self-employment in the same manner as a citizen of the United States but without regard to section 933;

(7) the deduction for personal exemptions provided in section 151 shall not be allowed;

(8) an individual who is a duly ordained, commissioned, or licensed minister of a church or a member of a religious order shall compute his net earnings from self-employment derived from the performance of service described in subsection (c)(4) without regard to section 107 (relating to rental value of parsonages), section 119 (relating to meals and lodging furnished for the convenience of the employer), and section 911 (relating to citizens or residents of the United States living abroad), but shall not include in such net earnings from self-employment the rental value of any parsonage or any parsonage allowance (whether or not excludable under section 107) provided after the individual retires, or any other retirement benefit received by such individual from a church plan (as defined in section 414(e)) after the individual retires;

(9) the exclusion from gross income provided by section 931 shall not apply;

(10) there shall be excluded amounts received by a partner pursuant to a written plan of the partnership, which meets such requirements as are prescribed by the Secretary, and which provides for payments on account of retirement, on a periodic basis, to partners generally or to a class or classes of partners, such payments to continue at least until such partner's death, if—

(A) such partner rendered no services with respect to any trade or business carried on by such partnership (or its successors) during the taxable year of such partnership (or its successors), ending within or with his taxable year, in which such amounts were received, and

Code Sec. 1402

(B) no obligation exists (as of the close of the partnership's taxable year referred to in subparagraph (A)) from the other partners to such partner except with respect to retirement payments under such plan, and

(C) such partner's share, if any, of the capital of the partnership has been paid to him in full before the close of the partnership's taxable year referred to in subparagraph (A);

(11) the exclusion from gross income provided by section 911(a)(1) shall not apply;

(12) in lieu of the deduction provided by section 164(f) (relating to deduction for one-half of self-employment taxes), there shall be allowed a deduction equal to the product of—

(A) the taxpayer's net earnings from self-employment for the taxable year (determined without regard to this paragraph), and

(B) one-half of the sum of the rates imposed by subsections (a) and (b) of section 1401 for such year (determined without regard to the rate imposed under paragraph (2) of section 1401(b));

(13) there shall be excluded the distributive share of any item of income or loss of a limited partner, as such, other than guaranteed payments described in section 707(c) to that partner for services actually rendered to or on behalf of the partnership to the extent that those payments are established to be in the nature of remuneration for those services;

(14) in the case of church employee income, the special rules of subsection (j)(1) shall apply;

(15) in the case of a member of an Indian tribe, the special rules of section 7873 (relating to income derived by Indians from exercise of fishing rights) shall apply;

(16) the deduction provided by section 199 shall not be allowed; and

(17) notwithstanding the preceding provisions of this subsection, each spouse's share of income or loss from a qualified joint venture shall be taken into account as provided in section 761(f) in determining net earnings from self-employment of such spouse.

If the taxable year of a partner is different from that of the partnership, the distributive share which he is required to include in computing his net earnings from self-employment shall be based on the ordinary income or loss of the partnership for any taxable year of the partnership ending within or with his taxable year. In the case of any trade or business which is carried on by an individual or by a partnership and in which, if such trade or business were carried on exclusively by employees, the major portion of the services would constitute agricultural labor as defined in section 3121(g)—

(i) in the case of an individual, if the gross income derived by him from such trade or business is not more than the upper limit, the net earnings from self-employment derived by him from such trade or business may, at his option, be deemed to be 66²/₃ percent of such gross income; or

(ii) in the case of an individual, if the gross income derived by him from such trade or business is more than the upper limit and the net earnings from self-employment derived by him from such trade or business (computed under this subsection without regard to this sentence) are less than the lower limit, the net earnings from self-employment derived by him from such trade or business may, at his option, be deemed to be the lower limit; and

(iii) in the case of a member of a partnership, if his distributive share of the gross income of the partnership derived from such trade or business (after such gross income has been reduced by the sum of all payments to which section 707(c) applies) is not more than the upper limit, his distributive share of income described in section 702(a)(8) derived from such trade or business may, at his option, be deemed to be an amount equal to 66²/₃ percent of his distributive share of such gross income (after such gross income has been so reduced); or

(iv) in the case of a member of a partnership, if his distributive share of the gross income of the partnership derived from such trade or business (after such gross income has been reduced by the sum of all payments to which section 707(c) applies) is more than the upper limit and his distributive share (whether or not distributed) of income described in section 702(a)(8) derived from such trade or business (computed under this subsection without regard to this sentence) is less than the lower limit, his distributive share of income described in section 702(a)(8) derived from such trade or business may, at his option, be deemed to be the lower limit.

For purposes of the preceding sentence, gross income means—

(v) in the case of any such trade or business in which the income is computed under a cash receipts and disbursements method, the gross receipts from such trade or business reduced by the cost or other basis of property which was purchased and sold in carrying on such trade or business, adjusted (after such reduction) in accordance with the provisions of paragraphs (1) through (7) and paragraph (9) of this subsection; and

(vi) in the case of any such trade or business in which the income is computed under an accrual method, the gross income from such trade or business, adjusted in accordance with the provisions of paragraphs (1) through (7) and paragraph (9) of this subsection;

and, for purposes of such sentence, if an individual (including a member of a partnership) derives gross income from more than one such trade or business, such gross income (including his distributive share of the gross income of any partnership derived from any such trade or business) shall be deemed to have been derived from one trade or business.

The preceding sentence and clauses (i) through (iv) of the second preceding sentence shall also apply in the case of any trade or business (other than a trade or business specified in such second preceding sentence) which is carried on by an individual who is self-employed on a regular basis as defined in subsection (h), or by a partnership of which an individual is a member on a regular basis as defined in subsection (h), but only if such individual's net earnings from self-employment as

Code Sec. 1402

determined without regard to this sentence in the taxable year are less than the lower limit and less than 66⅔ percent of the sum (in such taxable year) of such individual's gross income derived from all trades or businesses carried on by him and his distributive share of the income or loss from all trades or businesses carried on by all the partnerships of which he is a member; except that this sentence shall not apply to more than 5 taxable years in the case of any individual, and in no case in which an individual elects to determine the amount of his net earnings from self-employment for a taxable year under the provisions of the two preceding sentences with respect to a trade or business to which the second preceding sentence applies and with respect to a trade or business to which this sentence applies shall such net earnings for such years exceed the lower limit.

Amendments

• **2018, Tax Technical Corrections Act of 2018 (P.L. 115-141)**

P.L. 115-141, §401(a)(197)(A)-(B), Div. U:

Amended Code Sec. 1402(a)(1) by striking "section 1233(2)" and inserting "section 1233(a)(2)", and by striking "16 U.S.C. 3833(2)" and inserting "16 U.S.C. 3833(a)(2)". **Effective** 3-23-2018.

• **2010, Tax Relief, Unemployment Insurance Reauthorization, and Job Creation Act of 2010 (P.L. 111-312)**

P.L. 111-312, §601(a)-(d), provides:

(a) IN GENERAL.—Notwithstanding any other provision of law—

(1) with respect to any taxable year which begins in the payroll tax holiday period, the rate of tax under section 1401(a) of the Internal Revenue Code of 1986 shall be 10.40 percent, and

(2) with respect to remuneration received during the payroll tax holiday period, the rate of tax under 3101(a) of such Code shall be 4.2 percent (including for purposes of determining the applicable percentage under section 3201(a) and 3211(a)(1) of such Code).

(b) COORDINATION WITH DEDUCTIONS FOR EMPLOYMENT TAXES.—

(1) DEDUCTION IN COMPUTING NET EARNINGS FROM SELFEMPLOYMENT.—For purposes of applying section 1402(a)(12) of the Internal Revenue Code of 1986, the rate of tax imposed by subsection 1401(a) of such Code shall be determined without regard to the reduction in such rate under this section.

(2) INDIVIDUAL DEDUCTION.—In the case of the taxes imposed by section 1401 of such Code for any taxable year which begins in the payroll tax holiday period, the deduction under section 164(f) with respect to such taxes shall be equal to the sum of—

(A) 59.6 percent of the portion of such taxes attributable to the tax imposed by section 1401(a) (determined after the application of this section), plus

(B) one-half of the portion of such taxes attributable to the tax imposed by section 1401(b).

(c) PAYROLL TAX HOLIDAY PERIOD.—The term "payroll tax holiday period" means calendar year 2011.

(d) EMPLOYER NOTIFICATION.—The Secretary of the Treasury shall notify employers of the payroll tax holiday period in any manner the Secretary deems appropriate.

• **2010, Patient Protection and Affordable Care Act (P.L. 111-148)**

P.L. 111-148, §9015(b)(2)(B):

Amended Code Sec. 1402(a)(12)(B) by inserting "(determined without regard to the rate imposed under paragraph (2) of section 1401(b))" after "for such year". **Effective** with respect to remuneration received, and for tax years beginning, after 12-31-2012.

• **2008, Heartland, Habitat, Harvest, and Horticulture Act of 2008 (P.L. 110-246)**

P.L. 110-246, §15301(a):

Amended Code Sec. 1402(a)(1) by inserting ", and including payments under section 1233(2) of the Food Security Act of 1985 (16 U.S.C. 3833(2)) to individuals receiving benefits under section 202 or 223 of the Social Security Act" after "crop shares". **Effective** for payments made after 12-31-2007.

P.L. 110-246, §15352(a)(1)(A)-(B):

Amended the matter following Code Sec. 1402(a)(17) by striking "$2,400" each place it appears and inserting "the upper limit", and by striking "$1,600" each place it appears and inserting "the lower limit". **Effective** for tax years beginning after 12-31-2007.

• **2007, Small Business and Work Opportunity Tax Act of 2007 (P.L. 110-28)**

P.L. 110-28, §8215(b)(1):

Amended Code Sec. 1402(a) by striking ", and" at the end of paragraph (15) and inserting a semicolon, by striking the period at the end of paragraph (16) and inserting "; and", and by inserting after paragraph (16) a new paragraph (17). **Effective** for tax years beginning after 12-31-2006.

• **2004, American Jobs Creation Act of 2004 (P.L. 108-357)**

P.L. 108-357, §102(d)(7):

Amended Code Sec. 1402(a) by striking "and" at the end of paragraph (14), by striking the period at the end of paragraph (15) and inserting ", and", and by inserting after paragraph (15) a new paragraph (16). **Effective** for tax years beginning after 12-31-2004.

• **2004, Social Security Protection Act of 2004 (P.L. 108-203)**

P.L. 108-203, §425(b):

Amended Code Sec. 1402(a)(5)(A) by striking "all of the gross income" and all that follows and inserting "the gross income and deductions attributable to such trade or business shall be treated as the gross income and deductions of the spouse carrying on such trade or business or, if such trade or business is jointly operated, treated as the gross income and deductions of each spouse on the basis of their respective distributive share of the gross income and deductions; and". **Effective** 3-2-2004. Prior to amendment, Code Sec. 1402(a)(5)(A) read as follows:

(A) any of the income derived from a trade or business (other than a trade or business carried on by a partnership) is community income under community property laws applicable to such income, all of the gross income and deductions attributable to such trade or business shall be treated as the gross income and deductions of the husband unless the wife exercises substantially all of the management and control of such trade or business, in which case all of such gross income and deductions shall be treated as the gross income and deductions of the wife; and

• **1997, Taxpayer Relief Act of 1997 (P.L. 105-34)**

P.L. 105-34, §935, provides:

No temporary or final regulation with respect to the definition of a limited partner under section 1402(a)(13) of the Internal Revenue Code of 1986 may be issued or made effective before July 1, 1998.

• **1996, Small Business Job Protection Act of 1996 (P.L. 104-188)**

P.L. 104-188, §1456(a):

Amended Code Sec. 1402(a)(8) by inserting ", but shall not include in such net earnings from self-employment the rental value of any parsonage or any parsonage allowance (whether or not excludable under section 107) provided after the individual retires, or any other retirement benefit received by such individual from a church plan (as defined in section 414(e)) after the individual retires" before the semicolon at the end. **Effective** for years beginning before, on, or after 12-31-94.

• **1990, Omnibus Budget Reconciliation Act of 1990 (P.L. 101-508)**

P.L. 101-508, §5123(a)(3):

Amended Code Sec. 1402(a) by repealing the last undesignated paragraph (as added by section 9022(h) of the Omnibus Budget Deconciliation Act of 1987). **Effective** with respect to income received for services performed in tax years beginning after 12-31-90. Prior to repeal, the last paragraph read as follows:

Any income of an individual which results from or is attributable to the performance of services by such indivdual as a director of a corporation during any taxable year shall be deemed to have been derived and received by such individual in that year at the time the services were performed regardless of when the income is actually paid to or received by such individual unless it was actually paid and recovered prior to that year.

- **1988, Technical and Miscellaneous Revenue Act of 1988 (P.L. 100-647)**

P.L. 100-647, §3043(c)(1):

Amended Code Sec. 1402(a) by striking out "and" at end of paragraph (13), by striking out the period at the end of paragraph (14) and inserting in lieu thereof "; and", and by inserting after paragraph (14) a new paragraph (15). **Effective** for all periods beginning before, on, or after 11-5-90. See, also, Act Sec. 3044(b), below.

P.L. 100-647, §3044(b), provides:

(b) NO INFERENCE CREATED.—Nothing in the amendments made by this subtitle shall create any inference as to the existence or non-existence or scope of any exemption from tax for income derived from fishing rights secured as of 3-17-88, by any treaty, law, or Executive Order.

- **1987, Revenue Act of 1987 (P.L. 100-203)**

P.L. 100-203, §9022(b):

Amended Code Sec. 1402(a) by adding at the end thereof a new paragraph. **Effective** for services performed in tax years beginning on or after 1-1-88.

- **1986, Tax Reform Act of 1986 (P.L. 99-514)**

P.L. 99-514, §1272(d)(8):

Amended Code Sec. 1402(a)(8) by striking out "and section 931 (relating to income from sources within possessions of the United States)"after "abroad)" and by inserting "and" after "of the employer),". **Effective**, generally, for tax years beginning after 12-31-86. However, for special rules and exceptions, see Act Sec. 1277(b)-(e) following Code Sec. 48. Prior to amendment, Code Sec. 1402(a)(8) read as follows:

(8) an individual who is a duly ordained, commissioned, or licensed minister of a church or a member of a religious order shall compute his net earnings from self-employment derived from the performance of service described in subsection (c)(4) without regard to section 107 (relating to rental value of parsonages), section 119 (relating to meals and lodging furnished for the convenience of the employer), section 911 (relating to citizens or residents of the United States living abroad) and section 931 (relating to income from sources within possessions of the United States);

P.L. 99-514, §1272(d)(9):

Amended Code Sec. 1402(a)(9). **Effective**, generally, for tax years beginning after 12-31-86. However, for special rules and exceptions, see Act Sec. 1277(b)-(e) following Code Sec. 48. Prior to amendment, Code Sec. 1402(a)(9) read as follows:

(9) the term "possession of the United States" as used in sections 931 (relating to income from sources within possessions of the United States) and 932 (relating to citizens of possessions of the United States) shall be deemed not to include the Virgin Islands, Guam, or American Samoa;

P.L. 99-514, §1882(b)(1)(B)(i):

Amended Code Sec. 1402(a)(14). **Effective** for remuneration paid or derived in tax years beginning after 12-31-85. Prior to amendment, Code Sec. 1402(a)(14) read as follows:

(14) with respect to remuneration for services which are treated as services in a trade or business under subsection (c)(2)(G)—

(A) no deduction for trade or business expenses provided under this Code (other than the deduction under paragraph (12)) shall apply;

(B) the provisions of subsection (b)(2) shall not apply; and

(C) if the amount of such remuneration from an employer for the taxable year is less than $100, such remuneration from that employer shall not be included in self-employment income.

- **1984, Deficit Reduction Act of 1984 (P.L. 98-369)**

P.L. 98-369, §2603(d)(2):

Amended Code Sec. 1402(a) by striking out "and" at the end of paragraph (12), by striking out the period at the end of paragraph (13) and inserting in lieu thereof "; and"; and by adding new paragraph (14). **Effective** for service performed after 12-31-83.

- **1983, Social Security Amendments of 1983 (P.L. 98-21)**

P.L. 98-21, §124(c)(2):

Amended Code Sec. 1402(a) by striking out "and" at the end of paragraph (11), by redesignating paragraph (12) as paragraph (13), and by inserting after paragraph (11) a new paragraph (12). **Effective** for tax years beginning after 1989.

P.L. 98-21, §323(b)(1):

Amended Code Sec. 1402(a)(11) by striking out "in the case of an individual described in section 911(d)(1)(B)," **Effective** for tax years beginning after 1983.

- **1981, Economic Recovery Tax Act of 1981 (P.L. 97-34)**

P.L. 97-34, §111(b)(3), (5):

Amended Code Sec. 1402(a)(8) by striking out "relating to income earned by employees in certain camps" and inserting in lieu thereof "relating to citizens or residents of the United States living abroad" and amended Code Sec. 1402(a)(11). **Effective** with respect to tax years beginning after 12-31-81. Prior to amendment, Code Sec. 1402(a)(11) read as follows:

(11) in the case of an individual who has been a resident of the United States during the entire taxable year, the exclusion from gross income provided by section 911(a)(2) shall not apply.

- **1978, Tax Treatment Extension Act of 1978 (P.L. 95-615)**

P.L. 95-615, §§202(f)(5), 209:

Amended Code Sec. 1402(a)(8) by striking out "relating to earned income from sources without the United States" and inserting in place thereof "relating to income earned by employees in certain camps". **Effective**, generally, for tax years beginning after 12-31-77, except as provided in Act Sec. 209(c), below.

P.L. 95-615, §209(c), provides:

(c) ELECTION OF PRIOR LAW.—

(1) A taxpayer may elect not to have the amendments made by this title apply with respect to any taxable year beginning after December 31, 1977, and before January 1, 1979.

(2) An election under this subsection shall be filed with a taxpayer's timely filed return for the first taxable year beginning after December 31, 1977.

- **1978, Revenue Act of 1978 (P.L. 95-600)**

P.L. 95-600, §§703(j)(8)(A), (r):

Amended the last paragraph of Code Sec. 1402(a) by striking out "subsection (i)" each place it appeared and inserting in place thereof "subsection (h)". **Effective** 10-4-76.

- **1977 (P.L. 95-216)**

P.L. 95-216, §313(b):

Amended Code Sec. 1402(a) by striking out "and" at the end of paragraph (10); by striking out the period at the end of paragraph (11) and inserting in lieu thereof "; and"; and by inserting after paragraph (11), a new paragraph (12). **Effective** for tax years beginning after 12-31-77.

- **1976, Tax Reform Act of 1976 (P.L. 94-455)**

P.L. 94-455, §1901(b)(1)(I)(iii):

Substituted "702(a)(8)" for "702(a)(9)" wherever it appeared in Code Sec. 1402(a). **Effective** with respect to tax years beginning after 12-31-76.

P.L. 94-455, §1901(b)(1)(X):

Struck out "(other than interest described in section 35)" following the words "unless such dividends and interest" in Code Sec. 1402(a)(2). **Effective** with respect to tax years beginning after 12-31-76.

P.L. 94-455, §1906(b)(13)(A):

Amended the 1954 Code by substituting "Secretary" for "Secretary or his delegate" each place it appeared. **Effective** 2-1-77.

- **1974 (P.L. 93-368)**

P.L. 93-368, §10(b):

Amended Code Sec. 1402(a)(1) by inserting after "material participation by the owner or tenant" in the two places it occurs the following: "(as determined without regard to any activities of an agent of such owner or tenant)". **Effective** for tax years beginning after 12-31-73.

- **1972, Social Security Amendments of 1972 (P.L. 92-603)**
P.L. 92-603, §121(b)(1):
Added the last sentence to paragraph (10). **Effective** for tax years beginning after 12-31-72.
P.L. 92-603, §124(b):
Added paragraph (11). **Effective** tax years beginning after 12-31-72.
P.L. 92-603, §140(b):
Amended paragraph (8) of Code Sec. 1402(a). **Effective** for tax years beginning after 12-31-72. Prior to amendment, paragraph (8) read as follows:
"(8) an individual who is a duly ordained, commissioned, or licensed minister of a church or a member of a religious order, shall compute his net earnings from self-employment derived from the performance of service described in subsection (c)(4) without regard to section 107 (relating to rental value of parsonages) and section 119 (relating to meals and lodging furnished for the convenience of the employer) and, in addition, if he is a citizen of the United States performing such service as an employee of an American employer (as defined in section 3121(h)) or as a minister in a foreign country who has a congregation which is composed predominantly of citizens of the United States, without regard to section 911 (relating to earned income from sources without the United States) and section 931 (relating to income from sources within possessions of the United States);"

- **1968, Social Security Amendments of 1967 (P.L. 90-248)**
P. L. 90-248, §118(a):
Amended Section 1402(a) by deleting "and" at the end of paragraph (8), by substituting "; and" for the period at the end of paragraph (9), and by adding new paragraph (10). **Effective** only with respect to tax years ending on or after 12-31-67.

- **1965, Social Security Amendments of 1965 (P.L. 89-97)**
P.L. 89-97, §312(b):
Amended the second sentence following Sec. 1402(a)(9) by substituting "$2,400" for "$1,800" each place it appears and by substituting "$1,600" for "$1,200" each place it appears. **Effective** with respect to tax years beginning after 12-31-65.

- **1964, Revenue Act of 1964 (P.L. 88-272)**
P.L. 88-272, §227(b)(6):
Amended Code Sec. 1402(a)(3)(B). **Effective** for tax years beginning after 12-31-63. Prior to amendment, Code Sec. 1402(a)(3)(B) read as follows:
"(B) from the cutting of timber, or the disposal of timber or coal, if section 631 applies to such gain or loss, or"

- **1960, Social Security Amendments of 1960 (P.L. 86-778)**
P.L. 86-778, §103(k):
Amended Code Sec. 1402(a) by adding paragraph (9) and by inserting "and paragraph (9)" in clause (v) and clause (vi) of the last sentence. **Effective** only in the case of tax years beginning after 1960, except that insofar as they involve the nonapplication of section 932 of the Internal Revenue Code of 1954 to the Virgin Islands for purposes of subchapter 2 of such Code, such amendments shall be effective in the case of all tax years with respect to which such chapter 2 (and corresponding provisions of prior law) are applicable.

- **1957 (P.L. 85-239)**
P.L. 85-239, §5:
Amended paragraph (8). **Effective** for tax years ending on or after 12-31-57, except, that, for purposes of the retirement test under old-age and survivors insurance, the amendment is effective for tax years beginning after August 1957. Prior to amendment, paragraph (8) read as follows:
"(8) an individual who is—
"(A) a duly ordained, commissioned, or licensed minister of a church or a member of a religious order; and
"(B) a citizen of the United States performing service described in subsection (c)(4) as an employee of an American employer (as defined in section 3121 (h)) or as a minister in a foreign country who has a congregation which is composed predominantly of citizens of the United States, shall compute his net earnings from self-employment derived from the performance of service described in subsection (c)(4) without regard to section 911 (relating to earned income from sources without the United States) and section 931 (relating to income from sources within possessions of the United States)."

- **1956, Social Security Amendments of 1956 (P.L. 880, 84th Cong.)**
P.L. 880, 84th Cong., §§201(e)(2), (g), (i):
Amended Sec. 1402(a)(1) by adding the provisions following the words "real estate dealer;". **Effective** for tax years ending after 1955.
P.L. 880, 84th Cong., §§201(e)(2), (g), (i):
Amended Sec. 1402(a)(8)(B) by adding: "or as a minister in a foreign country who has a congregation which is predominantly of citizens of the United States,". The **effective** date provision of §201(m)(2) provides:
"(2)(A) Except as provided in subparagraph (B), the amendment made by subsection (g) shall apply only with respect to taxable years ending after 1956.
"(B) Any individual who, for a taxable year ending after 1954 and prior to 1957, had income which by reason of the amendment made by subsection (g) would have been included within the meaning of "net earnings from self-employment" (as such term is defined in section 1402(a) of the Internal Revenue Code of 1954), if such income had been derived in a taxable year ending after 1956 by an individual who had filed a waiver certificate under section 1402(e) of such Code, may elect to have the amendment made by subsection (g) apply to his taxable years ending after 1954 and prior to 1957. No election made by any individual under this subparagraph shall be valid unless such individual has filed a waiver certificate under section 1402(e) of such Code prior to the making of such election or files a waiver certificate at the time he makes such election.
"(C) Any individual described in subparagraph (B) who has filed a waiver certificate under section 1402(e) of such Code prior to the date of enactment of this Act, or who files a waiver certificate under such section on or before the due date or his return (including any extension thereof) for his last taxable year ending prior to 1957, must make such election on or before the due date of his return (including any extension thereof) for his last taxable year ending prior to 1957, or before April 16, 1957, whichever is the later
"(D) Any individual described in subparagraph (B) who has not filed a waiver certificate under section 1402(e) of such Code on or before the due date of his return (including any extension thereof) for his last taxable year ending prior to 1957 must make such election on or before the due date of his return (including any extension thereof) for his first taxable year ending after 1956. Any individual described in this subparagraph whose period for filing a waiver certificate under section 1402(e) of such Code has expired at the time he makes such election may, notwithstanding the provisions of paragraph (2) of such section, file a waiver certificate at the time he makes such election.
"(E) An election under subparagraph (B) shall be made in such manner as the Secretary of the Treasury or his delegate shall prescribe by regulations. Notwithstanding the provisions of paragraph (3) of section 1402(e) of such Code, the waiver certificate filed by an individual who makes an election under subparagraph (B) (regardless of when filed) shall be effective for such individual's first taxable year ending after 1954 in which he had income which by reason of the amendment made by subsection (g) would have been included within the meaning of "net earnings from self-employment" (as such term is defined in section 1402(a) of such Code), if such income had been derived in a taxable year ending after 1956 by an individual who had filed a waiver certificate under section 1402(e) of such Code, or for the taxable year prescribed by such paragraph (3) of section 1402(e) if such taxable year is earlier, and for all succeeding taxable years.
"(F) No interest or penalty shall be assessed or collected for failure to file a return within the time prescribed by law, if such failure arises solely by reason of an election made by an individual under subparagraph (B), or for any underpayment of the tax imposed by section 1401 of such Code arising solely by reason of such election, for the period ending with the date such individual makes an election under subparagraph (B)."
P.L. 880, 84th Cong., §§201(e)(2), (g), (i):
Amended Sec. 1402(a) by striking out the last two sentences and inserting in their place the provisions containing the $1,800 and $1,200 optional provisions applicable to farmers. **Effective** for tax years ending on or after 12-31-56. Prior to the amendment, the deleted sentences read as follows:
"In the case of any trade or business which is carried on by an individual who reports his income on a cash receipts

and disbursements basis, and in which, if it were carried on exclusively by employees, the major portion of the services would constitute agricultural labor as defined in section 3121(g), (i) if the gross income derived from such trade or business by such individual is not more than $1,800, the net earnings from self-employment derived by him therefrom may, at his option, be deemed to be 50 percent of such gross income in lieu of his net earnings from self-employment from such trade or business computed as provided under the preceding provisions of this subsection, or (ii) if the gross income derived from such trade or business by such individual is more than $1,800 and the net earnings from self-employment derived by him therefrom, as computed under the preceding provisions of this subsection, are less than $900, such net earnings may instead, at the option of such individual, be deemed to be $900. For the purpose of the preceding sentence, gross income derived from such trade or business shall mean the gross receipts from such trade or business reduced by the cost or other basis of property which was purchased and sold in carrying on such trade or business, adjusted (after such reduction) in accordance with the preceding provisions of this subsection." Amendment made by § 201(i) is applicable for taxable years ending on or after 12-31-56.

• **1954, Social Security Amendments of 1954 (P.L. 761, 83rd Cong.)**
P.L. 761, 83rd Cong., § 201(a):
Amended paragraph (1) to read as prior to amendment by P.L. 880, deleted former paragraph (2), renumbered paragraphs (3) to (8), inclusive, as paragraphs (2) to (7), inclusive, and added the last two sentences of the subsection as they read prior to amendment by P.L. 880. **Effective** with respect to tax years ending after 1954. Prior to amendment by P.L. 761, paragraph (1) read as follows:
"(1) there shall be excluded rentals from real estate (including personal property leased with the real estate) and deductions attributable thereto, unless such rentals are received in the course of a trade or business as a real estate dealer;".

Prior to deletion, paragraph (2) read as follows:
"(2) there shall be excluded income derived from any trade or business in which, if the trade or business were carried on exclusively by employees, the major portion of the services would constitute agricultural labor as defined in section 3121(g); and there shall be excluded all deductions attributable to such income;".
P.L. 761, 83rd Cong., § 201(c):
Added new paragraph (8).

[Sec. 1402(b)]

(b) SELF-EMPLOYMENT INCOME.—The term "self-employment income" means the net earnings from self-employment derived by an individual (other than a nonresident alien individual, except as provided by an agreement under section 233 of the Social Security Act) during any taxable year; except that such term shall not include—

(1) in the case of the tax imposed by section 1401(a), that part of the net earnings from self-employment which is in excess of (i) an amount equal to the contribution and benefit base (as determined under section 230 of the Social Security Act) which is effective for the calendar year in which such taxable year begins, minus (ii) the amount of the wages paid to such individual during such taxable years; or

(2) the net earnings from self-employment, if such net earnings for the taxable year are less than $400.

For purposes of paragraph (1), the term "wages" (A) includes such remuneration paid to an employee for services included under an agreement entered into pursuant to the provisions of section 3121 (l) (relating to coverage of citizens of the United States who are employees of foreign affiliates of American employers), as would be wages under section 3121(a) if such services constituted employment under section 3121(b), and (B) includes compensation which is subject to the tax imposed by section 3201 or 3211. An individual who is not a citizen of the United States but who is a resident of the Commonwealth of Puerto Rico, the Virgin Islands, Guam, or American Samoa shall not, for purposes of this chapter be considered to be a nonresident alien individual. In the case of church employee income, the special rules of subsection (j)(2) shall apply for purposes of paragraph (2).

Amendments
• **2018, Tax Technical Corrections Act of 2018 (P.L. 115-141)**
P.L. 115-141, § 401(a)(198), Div. U:
Amended Code Sec. 1402(b) by striking "3211,." and inserting "3211.". **Effective** 3-23-2018.
• **1993, Omnibus Budget Reconciliation Act of 1993 (P.L. 103-66)**
P.L. 103-66, § 13207(b)(1)(A)-(D):
Amended Code Sec. 1402(b) by striking "that part of the net" in paragraph (1) and inserting "in the case of the tax imposed by section 1401(a), that part of the net", by striking "applicable contribution base (as determined under subsection (k))" in paragraph (1) and inserting "contribution and benefit base (as determined under section 230 of the Social Security Act)", by inserting "and" after "section 3121(b),", and by striking "and (C) includes" and all that follows through "3111(b)". **Effective** for 1994 and later calendar years. Prior to amendment, Code Sec. 1402(b) read as follows:
(b) SELF-EMPLOYMENT INCOME.—The term "self-employment income" means the net earnings from self-employment derived by an individual (other than a nonresident alien individual, except as provided by an agreement under section 233 of the Social Security Act) during any taxable year; except that such term shall not include—
(1) that part of the net earnings from self-employment which is in excess of (i) an amount equal to the applicable contribution base (as determined under subsection (k)) which is effective for the calendar year in which such taxable year begins, minus (ii) the amount of the wages paid to such individual during such taxable year; or
(2) the net earnings from self-employment, if such net earnings for the taxable year are less than $400.
For purposes of paragraph (1), the term "wages" (A) includes such remuneration paid to an employee for services included under an agreement entered into pursuant to the provisions of section 3121 (l) (relating to coverage of citizens of the United States who are employees of foreign affiliates of American employers), as would be wages under section 3121(a) if such services constituted employment under section 3121(b), (B) includes compensation which is subject to the tax imposed by section 3201 or 3211, and (C) includes, but only with respect to the tax imposed by section 1401(b), remuneration paid for medicare qualified government employment (as defined in section 3121(u)(3)) which is subject to the taxes imposed by sections 3101(b) and 3111(b). An individual who is not a citizen of the United States but who is a resident of the Commonwealth of Puerto Rico, the Virgin Islands, Guam, or American Samoa shall not, for purposes of this chapter be considered to be a nonresident alien individual. In the case of church employee income, the special rules of subsection (j)(2) shall apply for purposes of paragraph (2).
• **1990, Omnibus Budget Reconciliation Act of 1990 (P.L. 101-508)**
P.L. 101-508, § 11331(b)(1):
Amended Code Sec. 1402(b) by striking "the contribution and benefit base (as determined under section 230 of the Social Security Act)" and inserting "the applicable contribu-

tion base (as determined under subsection (k))". **Effective** for 1991 and later calendar years.

• **1986, Tax Reform Act of 1986 (P.L. 99-514)**

P.L. 99-514, § 1882(b)(1)(B)(ii):

Amended Code Sec. 1402(b) by adding at the end thereof a new sentence. **Effective** for remuneration paid or derived in tax years beginning after 12-31-85.

P.L. 99-514, § 1882(b)(1)(B)(iii):

Amended Code Sec. 1402(b) by striking out "clause (1)" and inserting in lieu thereof "paragraph (1)" in the second sentence. **Effective** for remuneration paid or derived in tax years beginning after 12-31-85.

• **1986, Omnibus Budget Reconciliation Act of 1986 (P.L. 99-509)**

P.L. 99-509, § 9002(b)(1)(B):

Amended Code Sec. 1402(b) in the flush sentence immediately following paragraph (2) by striking out "under agreement entered into pursuant to the provisions of section 218 of the Social Security Act (relating to coverage of State employees), or" following "for services included". For the **effective** date, see Act Sec. 9002(d), below.

P.L. 99-509, § 9002(d), provides:

(d) EFFECTIVE DATE.—The amendments made by this section are effective with respect to payments due with respect to wages paid after December 31, 1986, including wages paid after such date by a State (or political subdivision thereof) that modified its agreement pursuant to the provisions of section 218(e)(2) of the Social Security Act prior to the date of the enactment of this Act; except that in cases where, in accordance with the currently applicable schedule, deposits of taxes due under an agreement entered into pursuant to section 218 of the Social Security Act would be required within 3 days after the close of an eight-monthly period, such 3-day requirement shall be changed to a 7-day requirement for wages paid prior to October 1, 1987, and to a 5-day requirement for wages paid after september 30, 1987, and prior to October 1, 1988. For wages paid prior to October 1, 1988, the deposit schedule for taxes imposed under sections 3101 and 3111 shall be determined separately from the deposit schedule for taxes withheld under section 3402 if the taxes imposed under sections 3101 and 3111 are due with respect to service included under an agreement entered into pursuant to section 218 of the Social Security Act.

• **1986, Consolidated Omnibus Budget Reconciliation Act of 1985 (P.L. 99-272)**

P.L. 99-272, § 13205(a)(2)(B):

Amended Code Sec. 1402(b) by striking out "medicare qualified Federal employment (as defined in section 3121(u)(2))" and inserting in lieu thereof "medicare qualified government employment (as defined in section 3121(u)(3))". **Effective** for services performed after 3-31-86.

• **1983, Social Security Amendments of 1983 (P.L. 98-21)**

P.L. 98-21, § 321(e)(83):

Amended clause (A) of the second sentence of Code Sec. 1402(b) by striking out "employees of foreign subsidiaries of domestic corporations" and inserting in place thereof "employees of foreign affiliates of American employers". **Effective**, generally, for agreements entered into after 4-20-83. Under a special election provided in Act Sec. 321(f)(1)(B), such amendments may apply to agreements executed on or before 4-20-83. For the text of Act Sec. 321(f)(1)(B) see the amendment notes following Code Sec. 406(a). For the text of Code Sec. 1402(b) before amendment, see below.

P.L. 98-21, § 322(b)(2):

Amended the first sentence of Code Sec. 1402(b) by inserting after "nonresident alien individual": ", except as provided by an agreement under section 233 of the Social Security Act". **Effective** for tax years beginning on or after 4-20-83. Prior to amendment by Act Secs. 321(e)(3) and 322(b)(2), Code Sec. 1402(b) read as follows:

(b) SELF-EMPLOYMENT INCOME.—The term "self-employment income" means the net earnings from self-employment derived by an individual (other than a nonresident alien individual) during any taxable year; except that such term shall not include—

(1) that part of the net earnings from self-employment which is in excess of (i) an amount equal to the contribution and benefit base (as determined under section 230 of the Social Security Act) which is effective for the calendar year in which such taxable year begins, minus (ii) the amount of the wages paid to such individual during such taxable years; or

(2) the net earnings from self-employment, if such net earnings for the taxable year are less than $400.

For purposes of clause (1), the term "wages" (A) includes such remuneration paid to an employee for services included under an agreement entered into pursuant to the provisions of section 218 of the Social Security Act (relating to coverage of State employees), or under an agreement entered into pursuant to the provisions of section 3121(1) (relating to coverage of citizens of the United States who are employees of foreign subsidiaries of domestic corporations), as would be wages under section 3121(a) if such services constituted employment under section 3121(b), (B) includes compensation which is subject to the tax imposed by section 3201 or 3211, and (C) includes, but only with respect to the tax imposed by section 1401(b), remuneration paid for medicare qualified Federal employment (as defined in section 3121(u)(2)) which is subject to the taxes imposed by sections 3101(b) and 3111(b). An individual who is not a citizen of the United States but who is a resident of the Commonwealth of Puerto Rico, the Virgin Islands, Guam, or American Samoa shall not, for purposes of this chapter be considered to be a nonresident alien individual.

• **1982, Tax Equity and Fiscal Responsibility Act of 1982 (P.L. 97-248)**

P.L. 97-248, § 278(a)(2):

Amended Code Sec. 1402(b) by striking out "and" before "(B)" in the second sentence and by inserting ", and (C) includes, but only with respect to the tax imposed by section 1401(b), remuneration paid for medicare qualified Federal employment (as defined in section 3121(u)(2)) which is subject to the taxes imposed by sections 3101(b) and 3111(b)" before the period. **Effective** with respect to remuneration paid after 12-31-82.

• **1976, Tax Reform Act of 1976 (P.L. 94-455)**

P.L. 94-455, § 1901(a)(155)(A):

Amended Code Sec. 1402(b)(1). **Effective** with respect to tax years beginning after 12-31-76. Prior to amendment Code Sec. 1402(b)(1) read as follows:

(1) that part of the net earnings from self-employment which is in excess of—

(A) for any taxable year ending prior to 1955, (i) $3,600, minus (ii) the amount of the wages paid to such individual during the taxable year; and

(B) for any taxable year ending after 1954 and before 1959, (i) $4,200, minus (ii) the amount of the wages paid to such individual during the taxable year; and

(C) for any taxable year ending after 1958 and before 1966, (i) $4,800, minus (ii) the amount of the wages paid to such individual during the taxable year; and

(D) for any taxable year ending after 1965 and before 1968, (i) $6,600, minus (ii) the amount of wages paid to such individual during the taxable year; and

(E) for any taxable year ending after 1967 and beginning before 1972, (i) $7,800, minus (ii) the amount of the wages paid to such individual during the taxable year; and

(F) for any taxable year beginning after 1971 and before 1973, (i) $9,000, minus (ii) the amount of the wages paid to such individual during the taxable year; and

(G) for any taxable year beginning after 1972 and before 1974, (i) $10,800, minus (ii) the amount of wages paid to such individual during the taxable year; and

(H) for any taxable year beginning after 1973 and before 1975, (i) $13,200, minus (ii) the amount of the wages paid to such individual during the taxable year; and

(I) for any taxable year beginning in any calendar year after 1974, (i) an amount equal to the contribution and benefit base (as determined under section 230 of the Social Security Act) which is effective for such calendar year, minus (ii) the amount of the wages paid to such individual during such taxable year; or

• **1975 (P.L. 94-92)**

P.L. 94-92, § 203(a) and (c):

Amended the last paragraph of Code Sec. 1402(b) by striking out ", but solely with respect to the tax imposed by section 1401(b)," from item (B) of the second sentence thereof. **Effective** 1-1-75, and only with respect to compensation paid for services rendered on or after that date. Prior to amendment item (B) read as follows:

(B) includes, but solely with respect to the tax imposed by section 1401(b), compensation which is subject to the tax imposed by section 3201 or 3211.

Code Sec. 1402

- **1973 (P.L. 93-233)**
P.L. 93-233, § 5(b)(1):
Amended Code Sec. 1402(b)(1)(H) by substituting "$13,200" for "$12,600."
- **1973 (P.L. 93-66)**
P.L. 93-66, § 203(b)(1):
Amended Code Sec. 1402(b)(1)(H) by substituting "$12,600" for "$12,000." (But see P.L. 93-233, above.)
- **1972 (P.L. 92-336)**
P.L. 92-336, § 203(b)(1)(A) and (B):
Amended Code Sec. 1402(b)(1)(F) and added new subparagraphs (G) through (I). **Effective** only for tax years beginning after 1972. Prior to amendment Code Sec. 1402(b)(1)(F) read as follows:

(F) for any taxable year beginning after 1971, (i) $9,000, minus (ii) the amount of the wages paid to such individual during the taxable year; or
- **1971 (P.L. 92-5)**
P.L. 92-5, § 203(b)(1):
Amended Code Sec. 1402(b)(1) by inserting "and beginning before 1972" after "1967" in subparagraph (E) and by substituting "; and" for "; or" at the end, and by adding subparagraph (F). **Effective** only with respect to tax years beginning after 1971.
- **1968, Social Security Amendments of 1967 (P.L. 90-248)**
P.L. 90-248, § 108(b)(1):
Amended Code Sec. 1402(b)(1) by inserting "and before 1968" after "1965" in subparagraph (D), by substituting "and" for "or" at the end of said subparagraph, and by adding new subparagraph (E). **Effective** only with respect to tax years ending after 1967.

P.L. 90-248, § 502(b):
Amended the second sentence of Sec. 1402(b) by adding "(A)" after "wages" and by adding at the end thereof the material beginning with "and (B)". **Effective** only with respect to tax years ending on or after 12-31-68.
- **1965, Social Security Amendments of 1965 (P.L. 89-97)**
P.L. 89-97, § 320(b):
Amended Sec. 1402(b)(1)(C) by inserting "and before 1966" after "1958" and by striking out "; or" and inserting in lieu thereof "; and". **Effective** with respect to tax years ending after 1965.

P.L. 89-97, § 320(b):
Amended Sec. 1402(b)(1) by adding subparagraph (D). **Effective** with respect to tax years ending after 1965.
- **1960, Social Security Amendments of 1960 (P.L. 86-778)**
P.L. 86-778, § 103(1):
Amended Code Sec. 1402(b) by striking out "the Virgin Islands or a resident of Puerto Rico" and by substituting "the Commonwealth of Puerto Rico, the Virgin Islands, Guam, or American Samoa". **Effective** for tax years beginning after 1960.
- **1958, Social Security Amendments of 1958 (P.L. 85-840)**
P.L. 85-840, § 402(a):
Amended subparagraph (B) of Sec. 1402(b)(1) and added subparagraph (C). Prior to amendment, subparagraph (B) read as follows:

(B) for any taxable year ending after 1954, (i) $4,200, minus (ii) the amount of the wages paid to such individual during the taxable year; or.
- **1954, Social Security Amendments of 1954 (P.L. 761, 83rd Cong.)**
P.L. 761, 83rd Cong., § 201(b):
Amended subparagraph (A) of Sec. 1402(b)(1) and subparagraph (B) to read as reproduced in the amendment note for P.L. 85-840. Prior to amendment subparagraphs (A) and (B) read as follows:

(A) $3,600 minus

(B) the amount of the wages paid to such individual during the taxable year; or.

Added the comma and the language following the words "State employees)" in the second sentence.

[Sec. 1402(c)]

(c) TRADE OR BUSINESS.—The term "trade or business", when used with reference to self-employment income or net earnings from self-employment, shall have the same meaning as when used in section 162 (relating to trade or business expenses), except that such term shall not include—

(1) the performance of the functions of a public office, other than the functions of a public office of a State or a political subdivision thereof with respect to fees received in any period in which the functions are performed in a position compensated solely on a fee basis and in which such functions are not covered under an agreement entered into by such State and the Commissioner of Social Security pursuant to section 218 of the Social Security Act;

(2) the performance of service by an individual as an employee, other than—

(A) service described in section 3121(b)(14)(B) performed by an individual who has attained the age of 18,

(B) service described in section 3121(b)(16),

(C) service described in section 3121(b)(11), (12), or (15) performed in the United States (as defined in section 3121(e)(2)) by a citizen of the United States except service which constitutes "employment" under section 3121(y),

(D) service described in paragraph (4) of this subsection,

(E) service performed by an individual as an employee of a State or a political subdivision thereof in a position compensated solely on a fee basis with respect to fees received in any period in which such service is not covered under an agreement entered into by such State and the Commissioner of Social Security pursuant to section 218 of the Social Security Act,

(F) service described in section 3121(b)(20), and

(G) service described in section 3121(b)(8)(B);

(3) the performance of service by an individual as an employee or employee representative as defined in section 3231;

(4) the performance of service by a duly ordained, commissioned, or licensed minister of a church in the exercise of his ministry or by a member of a religious order in the exercise of duties required by such order;

(5) the performance of service by an individual in the exercise of his profession as a Christian Science practitioner; or

(6) the performance of service by an individual during the period for which an exemption under subsection (g) is effective with respect to him.

The provisions of paragraph (4) or (5) shall not apply to service (other than service performed by a member of a religious order who has taken a vow of poverty as a member of such order) performed by an individual unless an exemption under subsection (e) is effective with respect to him.

Amendments

- **1994, Social Security Independence and Program Improvements Act of 1994 (P.L. 103-296)**

P.L. 103-296, §108(h)(1):

Amended Code Sec. 1402(c)(1) and (c)(2)(E) by striking "Secretary of Health and Human Services" each place it appears and inserting "Commissioner of Social Security". **Effective** 3-31-95.

P.L. 103-296, §306 provides:

SEC. 306. LIMITED EXEMPTION FOR CANADIAN MINISTERS FROM CERTAIN SELF-EMPLOYMENT TAX LIABILITY.

(a) IN GENERAL.—Notwithstanding any other provision of law, if—

(1) an individual performed services described in section 1402(c)(4) of the Internal Revenue Code of 1986 which are subject to tax under section 1401 of such Code,

(2) such services were performed in Canada at a time when no agreement between the United States and Canada pursuant to section 233 of the Social Security Act was in effect, and

(3) such individual was required to pay contributions on the earnings from such services under the social insurance system of Canada,

then such individual may file a certificate under this section in such form and manner, and with such official, as may be prescribed in regulations issued under chapter 2 of such Code. Upon the filing of such certificate, notwithstanding any judgment which has been entered to the contrary, such individual shall be exempt from payment of such tax with respect to services described in paragraphs (1) and (2) and from any penalties or interest for failure to pay such tax or to file a self-employment tax return as required under section 6017 of such Code.

(b) PERIOD FOR FILING.—A certificate referred to in subsection (a) may be filed only during the 180-day period commencing with the date on which the regulations referred to in subsection (a) are issued.

(c) TAXABLE YEARS AFFECTED BY CERTIFICATE.—A certificate referred to in subsection (a) shall be effective for taxable years ending after December 31, 1978, and before January 1, 1985.

(d) RESTRICTION ON CREDITING OF EXEMPT SELF-EMPLOYMENT INCOME.—In any case in which an individual is exempt under this section from paying a tax imposed under section 1401 of the Internal Revenue Code of 1986, any income on which such tax would have been imposed but for such exemption shall not constitute self-employment income under section 211(b) of the Social Security Act (42 U.S.C. 411(b)), and, if such individual's primary insurance amount has been determined under section 215 of such Act (42 U.S.C. 415), notwithstanding section 215(f)(1) of such Act, the Secretary of Health and Human Services (prior to March 31, 1995) or the Commissioner of Social Security (after March 30, 1995) shall recompute such primary insurance amount so as to take into account the provisions of this subsection. The recomputation under this subsection shall be effective with respect to benefits for months following approval of the certificate of exemption.

P.L. 103-296, §319(a)(4):

Amended Code Sec. 1402(c)(2)(C) by adding at the end "except service which constitutes 'employment' under section 3121(y)". **Effective** with respect to service performed after the calendar quarter following the calendar quarter containing 8-15-94.

- **1986, Tax Reform Act of 1986 (P.L. 99-514)**

P.L. 99-514, §1883(a)(11)(A):

Amended Code Sec. 1402(c)(2) by indenting subparagraph (G) two additional ems so as to align its left margin with the margins of the other subparagraphs in such section. **Effective** 10-22-86.

- **1984, Deficit Reduction Act of 1984 (P.L. 98-369)**

P.L. 98-369, §2603(c)(2):

Amended Code Sec. 1402(c)(2) by striking out "and" at the end of subparagraph (E); by striking out the semicolon at the end of subparagraph (F) and inserting in lie thereof ", and" and by adding new subparagraph (G). **Effective** for service performed after 12-31-83. However, see Act Sec. 2603(f), below, for special rules.

P.L. 98-369, §2603(f), provides:

(f) In any case where a church or qualified church-controlled organization makes an election under section 3121(w) of the Internal Revenue Code of 1954, the Secretary of the Treasury shall refund (without interest) to such church or organization any taxes paid under sections 3101 and 3111 of such Code with respect to service performed after December 31, 1983, which is covered under such election. The refund shall be conditional upon the church or organization agreeing to pay to each employee (or former employee) the portion of the refund attributable to the tax imposed on such employee (or former employee) under section 3101, and such employee (or former employee) may not receive any other refund payment of such taxes.

P.L. 98-369, §2663(j)(5)(B):

Amended Code Sec. 1402(c)(1) and (c)(2)(E), by striking out "Health, Education, and Welfare" each place it appeared and inserting in lieu thereof "Health and Human Services". **Effective** as if included in P.L. 98-21.

- **1978, Revenue Act of 1978 (P.L. 95-600)**

P.L. 95-600, §§703(j)(8)(B), (r):

Amended Code Sec. 1402(c)(6) by striking out "subsection (h)" and inserting in place thereof "subsection (g)". **Effective** 10-4-76.

- **1976, Tax Reform Act of 1976 (P.L. 94-455)**

P.L. 94-455, §1207(e)(1)(B), (f)(4):

Added Code Sec. 1402(c)(2)(F). **Effective** for tax years ending after 12-31-54. But see Act Sec. 1207(f)(4), as amended by P.L. 95-600, Sec. 701(z)(1), (2), below, for special rules.

P.L. 94-455, §1207(f)(4)(B), as amended by P.L. 95-600, Sec. 701(z)(1), (2), provided:

(B) Notwithstanding subparagraph (A), if the owner or operator of any boat treated a share of the boat's catch of fish or other aquatic animal life (or a share of the proceeds therefrom) received by an individual after December 31, 1954, and before the date of the enactment of this Act for services performed by such individual after December 31, 1954, on such boat as being subject to the tax under chapter 21 of the Internal Revenue Code of 1954, then the amendments made by paragraphs (1)(A) and (B) and (2) of subsection (e) shall not apply with respect to such services performed by such individual (and the share of the catch, or proceeds therefrom, received by him for such services).

- **1968, Social Security Amendments of 1967 (P.L. 90-248)**

P.L. 90-248, §115(b)(1):

Amended Code Sec. 1402(c) in the last sentence by substituting "unless an exemption under subsection (e) is effective with respect to him" for "during the period for which a certificate filed by him under subsection (e) is in effect". **Effective** only with respect to tax years ending after 1967.

P.L. 90-248, §122(b):

Amended Sec. 1402(c)(1) and amended Code Sec. 1402(c)(2) by striking out "and" at the end of subparagraph (C), by substituting ", and" for a semicolon at the end of subparagraph (D) and by adding a new subparagraph (E). **Effective** with respect to fees received after 1967. But see, also Sec. 122(c), below. Prior to amendment Sec. 1402(c)(1) read as follows:

"(1) the performance of the functions of a public office;"

P.L. 90-248, §122(c), provides:

"Notwithstanding the provisions of subsections (a) and (b) of this section, any individual who in 1968 is in a position to which the amendments made by such subsections apply may make an irrevocable election not to have such amendments apply to the fees he receives in 1968 and every year thereafter, if on or before the due date of his income tax return for 1968 (including any extensions thereof) he files with the Secretary of the Treasury or his delegate, in such manner as the Secretary of the Treasury or his delegate shall by regulations prescribe, a certificate of election of exemption from such amendments."

Code Sec. 1402

- **1965, Social Security Amendments of 1965 (P.L. 89-97)**

P.L. 89-97, § 311:

Amended Sec. 1402(c)(5) by deleting "doctor of medicine or" and amended the last two sentences of Sec. 1402(c). **Effective** with respect to tax years ending on or after 12-31-65. Prior to amendment, the last two sentences read as follows:

"The provisions of paragraph (4) shall not apply to service (other than service performed by a member of a religious order who has taken a vow of poverty as a member of such order) performed by an individual during the period for which a certificate filed by such individual under subsection (e) is in effect. The provisions of paragraph (5) shall not apply to service performed by an individual in the exercise of his profession as a Christian Science practitioner during the period for which a certificate filed by him under subsection (e) is in effect."

P.L. 89-97, § 319(a):

Amended Sec. 1402(c) by striking out "or" at the end of paragraph (4), by striking out the period at the end of paragraph (5) and inserting in lieu thereof "; or", and by adding new paragraph (6). **Effective** with respect to tax years beginning after 12-31-50. If refund or credit of any overpayment resulting from enactment of this amendment is prevented on 7-30-65 or at any time on or before 4-15-66, by the operation of any law or rule of law, refund or credit may nevertheless be made or allowed if claim therefore is filed on or before 4-15-66. No interest shall be allowed or paid on any overpayment resulting from enactment of this amendment.

- **1960, Social Security Amendments of 1960 (P.L. 86-778)**

P.L. 86-778, § 106(b):

Amended Code Sec. 1402(c)(2). **Effective** for tax years ending on or after 12-31-60. Prior to amendment, it read as follows:

(2) the performance of service by an individual as an employee (other than service described in section 3121(b)(14)(B) performed by an individual who has attained the age of 18, service described in section 3121(b)(16), and service described in paragraph (4) of this subsection);.

- **1956, Social Security Amendments of 1956 (P.L. 880, 84th Cong.)**

P.L. 880, 84th Cong., § 201(e)(3), (f):

Amended Sec. 1402(c)(2) by adding after the words "age of 18": "service described in section 3121(b)(16)," and by deleting the words "other than" preceding the words "service described in paragraph (4)". **Effective** for tax years ending after 1954.

P.L. 880, 84th Cong., § 201(e)(3), (f):

Amended Sec. 1402(c)(5) by substituting the words "doctor of medicine" for "physician, lawyer, dentist, osteopath, veterinarian, chiropractor, naturopath, optometrist,". **Effective** for tax years ending after 1955.

- **1954, Social Security Amendments of 1954 (P.L. 761, 83rd Cong.)**

P.L. 761, 83rd Cong., § 201(c):

Added the words "and other than service described in paragraph (4) of this subsection" after "18" in paragraph (2). amended paragraph (5) by inserting "or" preceding "Christian Science practitioner" and deleting "architect, certified public accountant, accountant registered or licensed as an accountant under State or municipal law, full-time practicing public accountant, funeral director, or professional engineer" following "Christian Science practitioner.", and added the last two sentences to subsection (c). **Effective** only with respect to tax years ending after 1954.

[Sec. 1402(d)]

(d) EMPLOYEE AND WAGES.—The term "employee" and the term "wages" shall have the same meaning as when used in chapter 21 (sec. 3101 and following, relating to Federal Insurance Contributions Act).

[Sec. 1402(e)]

(e) MINISTERS, MEMBERS OF RELIGIOUS ORDERS, AND CHRISTIAN SCIENCE PRACTITIONERS.—

(1) EXEMPTION.—Subject to paragraph (2), any individual who is (A) a duly ordained, commissioned, or licensed minister of a church or a member of a religious order (other than a member of a religious order who has taken a vow of poverty as a member of such order) or (B) a Christian Science practitioner, upon filing an application (in such form and manner, and with such official, as may be prescribed by regulations made under this chapter) together with a statement that either he is conscientiously opposed to, or because of religious principles he is opposed to, the acceptance (with respect to services performed by him as such minister, member, or practitioner) of any public insurance which makes payments in the event of death, disability, old age, or retirement or makes payments toward the cost of, or provides services for, medical care (including the benefits of any insurance system established by the Social Security Act) and in the case of an individual described in subparagraph (A), that he has informed the ordaining, commissioning, or licensing body of the church or order that he is opposed to such insurance, shall receive an exemption from the tax imposed by this chapter with respect to services performed by him as such minister, member, or practitioner. Notwithstanding the preceding sentence, an exemption may not be granted to an individual under this subsection if he had filed an effective waiver certificate under this section as it was in effect before its amendment in 1967.

(2) VERIFICATION OF APPLICATION.—The Secretary may approve an application for an exemption filed pursuant to paragraph (1) only if the Secretary has verified that the individual applying for the exemption is aware of the grounds on which the individual may receive an exemption pursuant to this subsection and that the individual seeks exemption on such grounds. The Secretary (or the Commissioner of Social Security under an agreement with the Secretary) shall make such verification by such means as prescribed in regulations.

(3) TIME FOR FILING APPLICATION.—Any individual who desires to file an application pursuant to paragraph (1) must file such application on or before the due date of the return (including any extension thereof) for the second taxable year for which he has net earnings from self-employment (computed without regard to subsections (c)(4) and (c)(5)) of $400 or more, any part of which was derived from the performance of service described in subsection (c)(4) or (c)(5).

(4) EFFECTIVE DATE OF EXEMPTION.—An exemption received by an individual pursuant to this subsection shall be effective for the first taxable year for which he has net earnings from self-employment (computed without regard to subsections (c)(4) and (c)(5)) of $400 or more, any part of which was derived from the performance of service described in subsection (c)(4) or (c)(5), and for all succeeding taxable years. An exemption received pursuant to this subsection shall be irrevocable.

APPENDIX: Selected Code Sections Affected by the Tax Cuts and Jobs Act   277

Amendments

• **2014, Tax Technical Corrections Act of 2014 (P.L. 113-295)**

P.L. 113-295, §221(a)(91)(A)-(B), Division A:
Amended Code Sec. 1402(e)(3) by striking "whichever of the following dates is later: (A)" following "on or before", and by striking "; or (B)" and all that follows and inserting a period. **Effective** generally 12-19-2014. For a special rule, see Act Sec. 221(b)(2), Division A, below. Prior to being stricken, all that follows "; or (B)" read as follows:
the due date of the return (including any extension thereof) for his second taxable year ending after 1967.

P.L. 113-295, §221(b)(2), Division A, provides:
(2) SAVINGS PROVISION.—If—
(A) any provision amended or repealed by the amendments made by this section applied to—
(i) any transaction occurring before the date of the enactment of this Act,
(ii) any property acquired before such date of enactment, or
(iii) any item of income, loss, deduction, or credit taken into account before such date of enactment, and
(B) the treatment of such transaction, property, or item under such provision would (without regard to the amendments or repeals made by this section) affect the liability for tax for periods ending after date of enactment, nothing in the amendments or repeals made by this section shall be construed to affect the treatment of such transaction, property, or item for purposes of determining liability for tax for periods ending after such date of enactment.

• **1999, Tax Relief Extension Act of 1999 (P.L. 106-170)**

P.L. 106-170, §403, provides:
SEC. 403. REVOCATION BY MEMBERS OF THE CLERGY OF EXEMPTION FROM SOCIAL SECURITY COVERAGE.
(a) IN GENERAL.—Notwithstanding section 1402(e)(4) of the Internal Revenue Code of 1986, any exemption which has been received under section 1402(e)(1) of such Code by a duly ordained, commissioned, or licensed minister of a church, a member of a religious order, or a Christian Science practitioner, and which is effective for the taxable year in which this Act is enacted, may be revoked by filing an application therefor (in such form and manner, and with such official, as may be prescribed by the Commissioner of Internal Revenue), if such application is filed no later than the due date of the Federal income tax return (including any extension thereof) for the applicant's second taxable year beginning after December 31, 1999. Any such revocation shall be effective (for purposes of chapter 2 of the Internal Revenue Code of 1986 and title II of the Social Security Act (42 U.S.C. 401 et seq.)), as specified in the application, either with respect to the applicant's first taxable year beginning after December 31, 1999, or with respect to the applicant's second taxable year beginning after such date, and for all succeeding taxable years; and the applicant for any such revocation may not thereafter again file application for an exemption under such section 1402(e)(1). If the application is filed after the due date of the applicant's Federal income tax return for a taxable year and is effective with respect to that taxable year, it shall include or be accompanied by payment in full of an amount equal to the total of the taxes that would have been imposed by section 1401 of the Internal Revenue Code of 1986 with respect to all of the applicant's income derived in that taxable year which would have constituted net earnings from self-employment for purposes of chapter 2 of such Code (notwithstanding paragraphs (4) and (5) of section 1402(c)) except for the exemption under such section 1402(e)(1) of such Code.
(b) EFFECTIVE DATE.—Subsection (a) shall apply with respect to service performed (to the extent specified in such subsection) in taxable years beginning after December 31, 1999, and with respect to monthly insurance benefits payable under title II on the basis of the wages and self-employment income of any individual for months in or after the calendar year in which such individual's application for revocation (as described in such subsection) is effective (and lump-sum death payments payable under such title on the basis of such wages and self-employment income in the case of deaths occurring in or after such calendar year).

• **1994, Social Security Independence and Program Improvements Act of 1994 (P.L. 103-296)**

P.L. 103-296, §108(h)(1):
Amended Code Sec. 1402(e)(2) by striking "Secretary of Health and Human Services" each place it appears and inserting "Commissioner of Social Security". **Effective** 3-31-95.

• **1986, Tax Reform Act of 1986 (P.L. 99-514)**

P.L. 99-514, §1704(a)(1):
Amended Code Sec. 1402(e)(1) by inserting "and, in the case of an individual described in subparagraph (A), that he has informed the ordaining, commissioning, or licensing body of the church or order that he is opposed to such insurance" after "Act". **Effective** for applications filed after 12-31-86.

P.L. 99-514, §1704(a)(2):
Amended Code Sec. 1402(e), as amended by Act Sec. 1882A(a)(1), by striking out "Any individual" in paragraph (1) and inserting in lieu thereof "Subject to paragraph (2), any individual", and by redesignating paragraphs (2) and (3) as paragraphs (3) and (4), respectively, and by inserting after paragraph (1) new paragraph (2). **Effective** for applications filed after 12-31-86.

P.L. 99-514, §1704(b), provides:
(b) REVOCATION OF EXEMPTION.
(1) IN GENERAL.—Notwithstanding section 1402(e)(3) of the Internal Revenue Code of 1986, as redesignated by subsection (a)(2)(B) of this section, any exemption which has been received under section 1402(e)(1) of such Code by a duly ordained, commissioned, or licensed minister of a church, a member of a religious order, or a Christian Science practitioner, and which is effective for the taxable year in which this Act is enacted, may be revoked by filing an application therefor (in such form and manner, and with such official, as may be prescribed in regulations made under chapter 2 of subtitle A of such Code), if such application is filed—
(A) before the applicant becomes entitled to benefits under section 202(a) or 223 of the Social Security Act (without regard to section 202(j)(1) or 223(b) of such Act), and
(B) no later than the due date of the Federal income tax return (including any extension thereof) for the applicant's first taxable year beginning after the date of the enactment of this Act.
Any such revocation shall be effective (for purposes of chapter 2 of subtitle A of the Internal Revenue Code of 1986 and title II of the Social Security Act), as specified in the application, either with respect to the applicant's first taxable year ending on or after the date of the enactment of this Act or with respect to the applicant's first taxable year beginning after such date, and for all succeeding taxable years; and the applicant for any such revocation may not thereafter again file application for an exemption under such section 1402(e)(1). If the application is filed on or after the due date of the Federal income tax return for the applicant's first taxable year ending on or after the date of the enactment of this Act and is effective with respect to that taxable year, it shall include or be accompanied by payment in full of an amount equal to the total of the taxes that would have been imposed by section 1401 of the Internal Revenue Code of 1986 with respect to all of the applicant's income derived in that taxable year which would have constituted net earnings from self-employment for purposes of chapter 2 of subtitle A of such Code (notwithstanding paragraph (4) or (5) of section 1402(c) of such Code) but for the exemption under section 1402(e)(1) of such Code.
(2) EFFECTIVE DATE.—Paragraph (1) of this subsection shall apply with respect to service performed (to the extent specified in such paragraph) in taxable years ending on or after the date of the enactment of this Act and with respect to monthly insurance benefits payable under title II of the Social Security Act on the basis of the wages and self-employment income of any individual for months in or after the calendar year in which such individual's application for revocation (as described in such paragraph) is effective (and lump-sum death payments payable under such title on the basis of such wages and self-employment income in the case of deaths occurring in or after such calendar year).

• **1977 (P.L. 95-216)**

P.L. 95-216, §316, provides:
SEC. 316. (a) Notwithstanding section 1402(e)(3) of the Internal Revenue Code of 1954, any exemption which has been received under section 1402(e)(1) of such Code by a duly ordained, commissioned, or licensed minister of a church or a Christian Science practitioner, and which is effective for the taxable year in which this Act is enacted, may be revoked by filing an application therefor (in such form and manner, and with such official, as may be prescribed in regulations made under chapter 2 of such Code), if such application is filed—

Code Sec. 1402

(1) before the applicant becomes entitled to benefits under section 202(a) or 223 of the Social Security Act (without regard to section 202(j)(1) or 223(b) of such Act), and

(2) no later than the due date of the Federal income tax return (including any extension thereof) for the applicant's first taxable year beginning after the date of the enactment of this Act.

Any such revocation shall be effective (for purposes of chapter 2 of the Internal Revenue Code of 1954 and title II of the Social Security Act), as specified in the application, either with respect to the applicant's first taxable year ending on or after the date of the enactment of this Act or with respect to the applicant's first taxable year beginning after such date, and for all succeeding taxable years; and the applicant for any such revocation may not thereafter again file application for an exemption under such section 1402(e)(1). If the application is filed on or after the due date of the applicant's first taxable year ending on or after the date of the enactment of this Act and is effective with respect to that taxable year, it shall include or be accompanied by payment in full of an amount equal to the total of the taxes that would have been imposed by section 1401 of the Internal Revenue Code of 1954 with respect to all of the applicant's income derived in that taxable year which would have constituted net earnings from self-employment for purposes of chapter 2 of such Code (notwithstanding section 1402(c)(4) or (c)(5) of such Code) except for the exemption under section 1402(e)(1) of such Code.

(b) Subsection (a) shall apply with respect to service performed (to the extent specified in such subsection) in taxable years ending on or after the date of the enactment of this Act, and with respect to monthly insurance benefits payable under title II of the Social Security Act on the basis of the wages and self-employment income of any individual for months in or after the calendar year in which such individual's application for revocation (as described in such subsection) is filed (and lump-sum death payments payable under such title on the basis of such wages and slef-employment income in the case of deaths occurring in or after such calendar year).

Effective 12-20-77.

- **1968, Social Security Amendments of 1967 (P.L. 90-248)**

P.L. 90-248, §115(b)(2):

Amended Sec. 1402(e). **Effective** only with respect to tax years ending after 1967. Prior to amendment Sec. 1402(e) read as follows:

"(e) Ministers, Members of Religious Orders, and Christian Science Practitioners.—

"(1) Waiver certificate.—Any individual who is (A) a duly ordained, commissioned, or licensed minister of a church or a member of a religious order (other than a member of a religious order who has taken a vow of poverty as a member of such order) or (B) a Christian Science practitioner may file a certificate (in such form and manner, and with such official, as may be prescribed by regulations made under this chapter) certifying that he elects to have the insurance system established by title II of the Social Security Act extended to service described in subsection (c)(4) or (c)(5) performed by him.

"(2) Time for filing certificate.—Any individual who desires to file a certificate pursuant to paragraph (1) must file such certificate on or before whichever of the following dates is later: (A) the due date of the return (including any extension thereof) for his second taxable year ending after 1954 for which he has net earnings from self-employment (computed without regard to subsection (c)(4) and (c)(5)) of $400 or more, any part of which was derived from the performance of service described in subsection (c)(4) or (c)(5); or (B) the due date of the return (including any extension thereof) for his second taxable year ending after 1963.

"(3)(A) Effective date of certificate.—A certificate filed pursuant to this subsection shall be effective for the taxable year immediately preceding the earliest taxable year for which, at the time the certificate is filed, the period for filing a return (including any extension thereof) has not expired, and for all succeeding taxable years. An election made pursuant to this subsection shall be irrevocable.

"(B) Notwithstanding the first sentence of subparagraph (A), if an individual filed a certificate on or before the date of enactment of this subparagraph which (but for this subparagraph) is effective only for the first taxable year ending after 1956 and all succeeding taxable years, such certificate shall be effective for his first taxable year ending after 1955 and all succeeding taxable years if—

"(i) such individual files a supplemental certificate after the date of enactment of this subparagraph and on or before April 15, 1962,

"(ii) the tax under section 1401 in respect of all such individual's self-employment income (except for underpayments of tax attributable to errors made in good faith) for his first taxable year ending after 1955 is paid on or before April 15, 1962, and

"(iii) in any case where refund has been made of any such tax which (but for this subparagraph) is an overpayment, the amount refunded (including any interest paid under section 6611) is repaid on or before April 15, 1962.

The provisions of section 6401 shall not apply to any payment or repayment described in this subparagraph.

"(C) Notwithstanding the first sentence of subparagraph (A), if an individual files a certificate after the date of enactment of this subparagraph and on or before the due date of the return (including any extension thereof) for his second taxable year ending after 1962, such certificate shall be effective for his first taxable year ending after 1961 and all succeeding years.

"(D) Notwithstanding the first sentence of subparagraph (A), if an individual files a certificate after the date of the enactment of this subparagraph and on or before the due date of the return (including any extension thereof) for his second taxable year ending after 1963, such certificate shall be effective for his first taxable year ending after 1962 and all succeeding years.

"(E) For purposes of sections 6015 and 6654, a waiver certificate described in paragraph (1) shall be treated as taking effect on the first day of the first taxable year beginning after the date on which such certificate is filed.

"(4) Treatment of certain remuneration paid in 1955 and 1956 as wages.—If—

"(A) in 1955 or 1956 an individual was paid remuneration for service described in section 3121(b)(8)(A) which was erroneously treated by the organization employing him (under a certificate filed by such organization pursuant to section 3121(k) or the corresponding section of prior law) as employment (within the meaning of chapter 21), and

"(B) on or before the date of the enactment of this paragraph the taxes imposed by sections 3101 and 3111 were paid (in good faith and upon the assumption that the insurance system established by title II of the Social Security Act had been extended to such service) with respect to any part of the remuneration paid to such individual for such service,

then the remuneration with respect to which such taxes were paid, and with respect to which no credit or refund of such taxes (other than a credit or refund which would be allowable if such service had constituted employment) has been obtained on or before the date of the enactment of this paragraph, shall be deemed (for purposes of this chapter and chapter 21) to constitute remuneration paid for employment and not net earnings from self-employment.

"(5) Optional provision for certain certificates filed on or before April 15, 1967.—Notwithstanding any other provision of this section, in any case where an individual has derived earnings in any taxable year ending after 1954 from the performance of service described in subsection (c)(4), or in subsection (c)(5) insofar as it related to the performance of service by an individual in the exercise of his profession as a Christian Science practitioner, and has reported such earnings as self-employment income on a return filed on or before the due date prescribed for filing such return (including any extension thereof)—

"(A) a certificate filed by such individual on or before April 15, 1966, which (but for this subparagraph) is ineffective for the first taxable year ending after 1954 for which such a return was filed shall be effective for such first taxable year and for all succeeding taxable years, provided a supplemental certificate is filed by such individual (or a fiduciary acting for such individual or his estate, or his survivor within the meaning of section 205(c)(1)(C) of the Social Security Act) after the date of enactment of the Social Security Amendments of 1965 and on or before April 15, 1967, and

"(B) a certificate filed after the date of enactment of the Social Security Amendments of 1965 and on or before April 15, 1967, by a survivor (within the meaning of section 205(c)(1)(C) of the Social Security Act) of such an individual who died on or before April 15, 1966, may be effective, at the election of the person filing such a certificate, for the first taxable year ending after 1954 for which such a return was filed and for all succeeding years,

but only if—

"(i) the tax under section 1401 in respect to all such individual's self-employment income (except for underpayments of tax attributable to errors made in good faith), for each such year described in subparagraphs (A) and (B) ending before January 1, 1966, is paid on or before April 15, 1967, and

"(ii) in any case where refund has been made of any such tax which (but for this paragraph) is an overpayment, the amount refunded (including any interest paid under section 6611) is repaid on or before April 15, 1967.
The provisions of section 6401 shall not apply to any payment or repayment described in this paragraph."

- **1966, Tax Adjustment Act of 1966 (P.L. 89-368)**

P. L. 89-368, §102(c):
Added Code Sec. 1402(e)(3)(E). **Effective** 1-1-67.

- **1965, Social Security Amendments of 1965 (P.L. 89-97)**

P.L. 89-97, §311:
Amended Sec. 1402(e)(1) by striking out "extended to service" and all that follows and inserting in lieu thereof "extended to service described in subsection (c)(4) or (c)(5) performed by him"; amended Sec. 1402(e)(2)(A). **Effective** with respect to tax years ending on or after 12-31-65.

P.L. 89-97, §331(a):
Amended Sec. 1402(e) by striking out paragraphs (5) and (6) and inserting new paragraph (5). **Effective** with respect to (except as otherwise specifically provided in the subsections) only for certificates which supplemental certificates are filed pursuant to section 1402(e)(5)(A) after 7-30-65, and to certificates filed pursuant to section 1402(e)(5)(B) after such date; except that no monthly benefits under title II of the Social Security Act for the month in which this Act is enacted (July 1965) or any prior month shall be payable or increased by reason of such amendments, and no lump-sum death payment under such title shall be payable or increased by reason of such amendments in the case of any individual who died prior to 7-30-65. Prior Code Sec. 1402(e)(5) and (6) is applicable to any certificate filed pursuant thereto before such date if a supplemental certificate is not filed with respect to such certificate as provided in this section. Prior to amendment, Sec. 1402(e)(5) and (6) read as follows:

"(5) Optional provision for certain certificates filed on or before April 15, 1962.—In any case where an individual has derived earnings, in any taxable year ending after 1954 and before 1960, from the performance of service described in subsection (c)(4), or in subsection (c)(5) (as in effect prior to the enactment of this paragraph) insofar as it related to the performance of service by an individual in the exercise of his profession as a Christian Science practitioner, and has reported such earnings as self-employment income on a return filed on or before the date of the enactment of this paragraph and on or before the due date prescribed for filing such return (including any extension thereof)—

"(A) a certificate filed by such individual (or a fiduciary acting for such individual or his estate, or his survivor within the meaning of section 205(c)(1)(C) of the Social Security Act) after the date of the enactment of this paragraph and on or before April 15, 1962, may be effective, at the election of the person filing such certificate, for the first taxable year ending after 1954 and before 1960 for which such a return was filed, and for all succeeding taxable years, rather than for the period prescribed in paragraph (3), and

"(B) a certificate by such individual on or before the date of the enactment of this paragraph which (but for this subparagraph) is ineffective for the first taxable year ending after 1954 and before 1959 for which such a return was filed shall be effective for such first taxable year, and for all succeeding taxable years, provided a supplemental certificate is filed by such individual (or a fiduciary acting for such individual or his estate, or his survivor within the meaning of section 205(c)(1)(C) of the Social Security Act) after the date of the enactment of this paragraph and on or before April 15, 1962,
but only if—

"(i) the tax under section 1401 in respect of all such individual's self-employment income (except for underpayments of tax attributable to errors made in good faith), for each such year ending before 1960 in the case of a certificate described in subparagraph (A) or of each such year ending before 1959 in the case of a certificate described in subparagraph (B), is paid on or before April 15, 1962, and

"(ii) in any case where refund has been made of any such tax which (but for this paragraph) is an overpayment, the amount refunded (including any interest paid under section 6611) is repaid on or before April 15, 1962.
The provisions of section 6401 shall not apply to any payment or repayment described in this paragraph.

"(6) Certificate filed by fiduciaries or survivors on or before April 15, 1962.—In any case where an individual, whose death has occurred after September 12, 1960, and before April 16, 1962, derived earnings from the performance of services described in subsection (c)(4), or in subsection (c)(5) insofar as it relates to the performance of service by an individual in the exercise of his profession as a Christian Science practitioner, a certificate may be filed after the date of enactment of this paragraph, and on or before April 15, 1962, by a fiduciary acting for such individual's estate or by such individual's survivor within the meaning of section 205(c)(1)(C) of the Social Security Act. Such certificate shall be effective for the period prescribed in paragraph (3)(A) as if filed by the individual on the day of his death."

P.L. 89-97, §341(a)-(b):
Amended Sec. 1402(e)(2)(B) by substituting "1963" for "1962" and amended Sec. 1402(e)(3) by adding new subparagraph (D). **Effective** with respect to certificates filed pursuant to Sec. 1402(e) after 7-30-65, except that no monthly benefits under title II of the Social Security Act for the month in which this Act is enacted (July 1965) or any prior month shall be payable or increased by reason of such amendments.

- **1964 (P.L. 88-650)**

P.L. 88-650, §2:
Amended Code Sec. 1402(e)(2)(B) by substituting "1962" for "1959" and amended Code Sec. 1402(e)(3) by adding new subparagraph (C). **Effective** with respect to certificates filed after 10-13-64, the date of enactment, except that no monthly benefits under title II of the Social Security Act for the month in which this Act is enacted or any prior month shall be payable or increased by reason of such amendments.

- **1961, Social Security Amendments of 1961 (P.L. 87-64)**

P.L. 87-64, §202(a):
Added paragraph (6) to Code Sec. 1402(e). **Effective** as noted in Act Sec. 202(b), below.

P.L. 97-64, §202(b), provides:
"(b) The amendment made by subsection (a) shall take effect on the date of enactment of this Act (6-30-61—CCH.); except that no monthly benefits under title II of the Social Security Act for the month in which this Act is enacted or any prior month shall be payable or increased by reason of such amendment, and no lump-sum death payment under such title shall be payable or increased by reason of such amendment in the case of any individual who died prior to the date of enactment of this Act."

- **1960, Social Security Amendments of 1960 (P.L. 86-778)**

P.L. 86-778, §101(a):
Struck out "1956" at the end of paragraph (2) of Code Sec. 1402(e) and substituted "1959". **Effective** 9-14-60.

P.L. 86-778, §101(b):
Amended paragraph (3) of Code Sec. 1402(e). **Effective** 9-14-60. Prior to amendment, it read as follows:

"(3) Effective Date of Certificate.—A certificate filed pursuant to this subsection shall be effective for the first taxable year with respect to which it is filed (but in no case shall the certificate be effective for a taxable year with respect to which the period for filing a return has expired, or for a taxable year ending prior to 1955) and all succeeding taxable years. An election made pursuant to this subsection shall be irrevocable. Notwithstanding the first sentence of this paragraph:

"(A) A certificate filed by an individual after the date of the enactment of this subparagraph but on or before the due date of the return (including any extension thereof) for his second taxable year ending after 1956 shall be effective for the first taxable year ending after 1955 and all succeeding taxable years.

"(B) If an individual filed a certificate on or before the date of the enactment of this subparagraph which (but for this subparagraph) is effective only for the third or fourth taxable year ending after 1954 and all succeeding taxable years, such certificate shall be effective for his first taxable year ending after 1955 and all succeeding taxable years if such individual files a supplemental certificate after the date of the enactment of this subparagraph and on or before the due date of the return (including any extension thereof) for his second taxable year ending after 1956."

"(C) A certificate filed by an individual after the due date of the return (including any extension thereof) for his second taxable year ending after 1956 shall be effective for the taxable year immediately preceding the taxable year with respect to which it is filed and all succeeding taxable years."

P.L. 86-778, § 101(c):

§ 101(c) added a new paragraph (5) to Code Sec. 1402(e). **Effective** as noted in Act Sec. 101(d)-(f), below.

P.L. 86-778, § 101(d)-(f), provide:

"(d) In the case of a certificate or supplemental certificate filed pursuant to section 1402(e)(3)(B) or (5) of the Internal Revenue Code of 1954—

"(1) for purposes of computing interest, the due date for the payment of the tax under section 1401 which is due for any taxable year ending before 1959 solely by reason of the filing of a certificate which is effective under such section 1402(e)(3)(B) or (5) shall be April 15, 1962;

"(2) the statutory period for the assessment of any tax for any such year which is attributable to the filing of such certificate shall not expire before the expiration of 3 years from such due date; and

"(3) for purposes of section 6651 of such Code (relating to addition to tax for failure to file tax return), the amount of tax required to be shown on the return shall not include such tax under section 1401.

"(e) The provisions of section 205(c)(5)(F) of the Social Security Act, insofar as they prohibit inclusion in the records of the Secretary of Health, Education, and Welfare of self-employment income for a taxable year when the return or statement including such income is filed after the time limitation following such taxable year, shall not be applicable to earnings which are derived in any taxable year ending before 1960 and which constitute self-employment income solely by reason of the filing of a certificate which is effective under section 1402(e)(3)(B) or (5) of the Internal Revenue Code of 1954.

"(f) The amendments made by this section shall be applicable (except as otherwise specifically indicated therein) only with respect to certificates (and supplemental certificates) filed pursuant to section 1402(e) of the Internal Revenue Code of 1954 after the date of the enactment of this Act; except that no monthly benefits under title II of the Social Security Act for the month in which this Act is enacted or any prior month shall be payable or increased by reason of such amendments, and no lump-sum death payment under such title shall be payable or increased by reason of such amendments in the case of any individual who died prior to the date of the enactment of this Act."

- **1957 (P.L. 85-239)**

P.L. 85-239, §[1] and 2:

Amended paragraph (2) of Code Sec. 1402(e) by adding the words "whichever of the following dates is later: (A)" after the phrase "on or before" and by adding the phrase "; or (B) the due date of the return (including any extension thereof) for his second taxable year ending after 1956" after the phrase "as the case may be." Also added all of subparagraph (3) following the phrase "shall be irrevocable." Also added paragraph (4). **Effective** 8-30-57.

- **1954, Social Security Amendments of 1954 (P.L. 761, 83rd Cong.)**

P.L. 761, 83rd Cong., § 201(c):

Added subsection (e). **Effective** 1-1-55.

[Sec. 1402(f)]

(f) PARTNER'S TAXABLE YEAR ENDING AS THE RESULT OF DEATH.—In computing a partner's net earnings from self-employment for his taxable year which ends as a result of his death (but only if such taxable year ends within, and not with, the taxable year of the partnership), there shall be included so much of the deceased partner's distributive share of the partnership's ordinary income or loss for the partnership taxable year as is not attributable to an interest in the partnership during any period beginning on or after the first day of the first calendar month following the month in which such partner died. For purposes of this subsection—

(1) in determining the portion of the distributive share which is attributable to any period specified in the preceding sentence, the ordinary income or loss of the partnership shall be treated as having been realized or sustained ratably over the partnership taxable year; and

(2) the term "deceased partner's distributive share" includes the share of his estate or of any other person succeeding, by reason of his death, to rights with respect to his partnership interest.

Amendments

- **1958, Social Security Amendments of 1958 (P.L. 85-840)**

P.L. 85-840, § 403(a):

Added subsection (f) to Sec. 1402. For the **effective** date, see Act Sec. 403(b), below.

P.L. 85-840, § 403(b), provides:

(b)(1) Except as provided in paragraph (2), the amendment made by subsection (a) shall apply only with respect to individuals who die after the date of the enactment of this Act.

(2) In the case of an individual who died after 1955 and on or before the date of the enactment of this Act, the amendment made by subsection (a) shall apply only if—

(A) before January 1, 1960, there is filed a return (or amended return) of the tax imposed by chapter 2 of the Internal Revenue Code of 1954 for the taxable year ending as a result of his death, and

(B) in any case where the return is filed solely for the purpose of reporting net earnings from self-employment resulting from the amendment made by subsection (a), the return is accompanied by the amount of tax attributable to such net earnings.

In any case described in the preceding sentence, no interest or penalty shall be assessed or collected on the amount of any tax due under chapter 2 of such Code solely by reason of the operation of section 1402(f) of such Code.

[Sec. 1402(g)]

(g) MEMBERS OF CERTAIN RELIGIOUS FAITHS.—

(1) EXEMPTION.—Any individual may file an application (in such form and manner, and with such official, as may be prescribed by regulations under this chapter) for an exemption from the tax imposed by this chapter if he is a member of a recognized religious sect or division thereof and is an adherent of established tenets or teachings of such sect or division by reason of which he is conscientiously opposed to acceptance of the benefits of any private or public insurance which makes payments in the event of death, disability, old-age, or retirement or makes payments toward the cost of, or provides services for, medical care (including the benefits of any insurance system established by the Social Security Act). Such exemption may be granted only if the application contains or is accompanied by—

(A) such evidence of such individual's membership in, and adherence to the tenets or teachings of, the sect or division thereof as the Secretary may require for purposes of determining such individual's compliance with the preceding sentence, and

(B) his waiver of all benefits and other payments under titles II and XVIII of the Social Security Act on the basis of his wages and self-employment income as well as all such benefits and other payments to him on the basis of the wages and self-employment income of any other person, and only if the Commissioner of Social Security finds that—

(C) such sect or division thereof has the established tenets or teachings referred to in the preceding sentence,

(D) it is the practice, and has been for a period of time which he deems to be substantial, for members of such sect or division thereof to make provision for their dependent members which in his judgment is reasonable in view of their general level of living, and

(E) such sect or division thereof has been in existence at all times since December 31, 1950.

An exemption may not be granted to any individual if any benefit or other payment referred to in subparagraph (B) became payable (or, but for section 203 or 222(b) of the Social Security Act, would have become payable) at or before the time of the filing of such waiver.

(2) PERIOD FOR WHICH EXEMPTION EFFECTIVE.—An exemption granted to any individual pursuant to this subsection shall apply with respect to all taxable years beginning after December 31, 1950, except that such exemption shall not apply for any taxable year—

(A) beginning (i) before the taxable year in which such individual first met the requirements of the first sentence of paragraph (1), or (ii) before the time as of which the Commissioner of Social Security finds that the sect or division thereof of which such individual is a member met the requirements of subparagraphs (C) and (D), or

(B) ending (i) after the time such individual ceases to meet the requirements of the first sentence of paragraph (1), or (ii) after the time as of which the Commissioner of Social Security finds that the sect or division thereof of which he is a member ceases to meet the requirements of subparagraph (C) or (D).

(3) SUBSECTION TO APPLY TO CERTAIN CHURCH EMPLOYEES.—This subsection shall apply with respect to services which are described in subparagraph (B) of section 3121(b)(8) (and are not described in subparagraph (A) of such section).

Amendments

• **1994, Social Security Independence and Program Improvements Act of 1994 (P.L. 103-296)**

P.L. 103-296, § 108(h)(1):

Amended Code Sec. 1402(g)(1) and (g)(2)(A)-(B) by striking "Secretary of Health and Human Services" each place it appears and inserting "Commissioner of Social Security". **Effective** 3-31-95.

• **1989, Omnibus Budget Reconciliation Act of 1989 (P.L. 101-239)**

P.L. 101-239, § 10204(a)(1)(A)-(B):

Amended Code Sec. 1402(g)(3) by striking "not to apply" and inserting "to apply" in the heading, and by striking "shall not" and inserting "shall". **Effective** with respect to tax years beginning after 12-31-89.

• **1988, Technical and Miscellaneous Revenue Act of 1988 (P.L. 100-647)**

P.L. 100-647, § 8007(c)(1)-(2):

Amended Code Sec. 1402(g) by striking paragraphs (2) and (4); and by redesignating paragraphs (3) and (5) paragraphs (2) and (3), respectively. **Effective** for applications for exemptions filed on or after 11-10-88. Prior to amendment, Code Sec. 1402(g)(2) and (4) read as follows:

(2) TIME FOR FILING APPLICATION.—For purposes of this subsection, an application must be filed on or before the time prescribed for filing the return (including any extension thereof) for the first taxable year for which the individual has self-employment income (determined without regard to this subsection or subsection (c)(6)), except that an application filed after such date but on or before the last day of the third calendar month following the calendar month in which the taxpayer is first notified in writing by the Secretary that a timely application for an exemption from the tax imposed by this chapter has not been filed by him shall be deemed to be filed timely.

* * *

(4) APPLICATION BY FIDUCIARIES OR SURVIVORS.—In any case where an individual who has self-employment income dies before the expiration of the time prescribed by paragraph (2) for filing an application for exemption pursuant to this subsection, such an application may be filed with respect to such individual within such time by a fiduciary acting for such individual's estate or by such individual's survivor (within the meaning of section 205(c)(1)(C) of the Social Security Act).

• **1986, Tax Reform Act of 1986 (P.L. 99-514)**

P.L. 99-514, § 1882(a):

Amended Code Sec. 1402(g) by adding at the end thereof new paragraph (5). **Effective** 10-22-86.

• **1984, Deficit Reduction Act of 1984 (P.L. 98-369)**

P.L. 98-369, § 2663(j)(5)(B):

Amended Code Sec. 1402(g)(1), (g)(3)(A) and (g)(3)(B) by striking out "Health, Education, and Welfare" each place it appeared and inserting in lieu thereof "Health and Human Services". **Effective** as if included in P.L. 98-21.

• **1976, Tax Reform Act of 1976 (P.L. 94-455)**

P.L. 94-455, § 1901(a)(155)(B):

Repealed Code Sec. 1402(g) and redesignated subsection (h) as subsection (g). **Effective** with respect to tax years beginning after 12-31-76. Prior to repeal, Code Sec. 1402(g) read as follows:

(g) TREATMENT OF CERTAIN REMUNERATION ERRONEOUSLY REPORTED AS NET EARNINGS FROM SELF-EMPLOYMENT.—If—

(1) an amount is erroneously paid as tax under section 1401, for any taxable year ending after 1954 and before 1962, with respect to remuneration for service described in section 3121(b)(8) (other than service described in section 3121(b)(8)(A)), and such remuneration is reported as self-employment income on a return filed on or before the due date prescribed for filing such return (including any extension thereof),

(2) the individual who paid such amount (or a fiduciary acting for such individual or his estate, or his survivor (within the meaning of section 205(c)(1)(C) of the Social Security Act)) requests that such remuneration be deemed to constitute net earnings from self-employment,

(3) such request is filed after the date of the enactment of this paragraph and on or before April 15, 1962,

(4) such remuneration was paid to such individual for services performed in the employ of an organization which, on or before the date on which such request is filed, filed a certificate pursuant to section 3121(k), and

(5) no credit or refund of any portion of the amount erroneously paid for such taxable year as tax under section 1401 (other than a credit or refund which would be allowable if such tax were applicable with respect to such remuneration) has been obtained before the date on which such request is filed or, if obtained, the amount credited or refunded (including any interest under section 6611) is repaid on or before such date,

then, for purposes of this chapter and chapter 21, any amount of such remuneration which is paid to such individual before the calendar quarter in which such request is filed (or before the succeeding quarter if such certificate first becomes effective with respect to services performed by such individual in such succeeding quarter), and with respect to which no tax (other than an amount erroneously paid as tax) has been paid under chapter 21, shall be deemed to constitute net earnings from self-employment and not remuneration for employment. For purposes of section 3121(b)(8)(B)(ii) and (iii), if the certificate filed by such organization pursuant to section 3121(k) is not effective with respect to services performed by such individual on or before the first day of the calendar quarter in which the request is filed, such individual shall be deemed to have become an employee of such organization (or to have become a member of a group described in section 3121(k)(1)(E)) on the first day of the succeeding quarter.

P.L. 94-455, §1901(a)(155)(C):
Amended redesignated Code Sec. 1402(g)(2). **Effective** with respect to tax years beginning after 12-31-76. Prior to amendment Code Sec. 1402(g)(2) read as follows:
(2) TIME FOR FILING APPLICATION.—For purposes of this subsection, an application must be filed—
(A) In the case of an individual who has self-employment income (determined without regard to this subsection and subsection (c)(6)) for any taxable year ending before December 31, 1967, on or before December 31, 1968, and
(B) In any other case, on or before the time prescribed for filing the return (including any extension thereof) for the first taxable year ending on or after December 31, 1967, for which he has self-employment income (as so determined), except that an application filed after such date but on or before the last day of the third calendar month following the calendar month in which the taxpayer is first notified in writing by the Secretary or his delegate that a timely application for an exemption from the tax imposed by this chapter has not been filed by him shall be deemed to be filed timely.

P.L. 94-455, §1906(b)(13)(A):
Amended the 1954 Code by substituting "Secretary" for "Secretary or his delegate" each place it appeared. **Effective** 2-1-77.

- **1968, Social Security Amendments of 1967 (P.L. 90-248)**

P.L. 90-248, §501(a):
Amended Sec. 1402(h)(2). **Effective** with respect to tax years beginning after 12-31-50. For such purpose, chapter 2 of the Internal Revenue Code of 1954 shall be treated as applying to all tax years beginning after such date. See, also, §501(c), below. Prior to amendment, Sec. 1402(h)(2) read as follows:
"(2) Time for filing application.—For purposes of this subsection, an application must be filed—
"(A) In the case of an individual who has self-employment income (determined without regard to this subsection and subsection (c)(6)) for any taxable year ending before December 31, 1965, on or before April 15, 1966, and
"(B) In any other case, on or before the time prescribed for filing the return (including any extension thereof) for the first taxable year ending on or after December 31, 1965, for which he has self-employment income as so determined."

P.L. 90-248, §501(c), provides:
"(c) If refund or credit of any overpayment resulting from the enactment of this section is prevented on the date of the enactment of this Act or any time on or before December 31, 1968, by the operation of any law or rule of law, refund or credit of such overpayment may, nevertheless, be made or allowed if claim therefore is filed on or before December 31, 1968. No interest shall be allowed or paid on any overpayment resulting from the enactment of this section."

- **1965, Social Security Amendments of 1965 (P.L. 89-97)**

P.L. 89-97, §319(c):
Added Code Sec. 1402(h). **Effective** for tax years beginning after 12-31-50. If refund or credit of any overpayment resulting from the enactment of this provision is prevented on 7-30-65 or at any time on or before 4-15-66, by the operation of any law or rule of law, refund or credit of such overpayment may nevertheless be made or allowed if claim therefore is filed on or before 4-15-66. No interest shall be allowed or paid on any overpayment resulting from enactment of this provision.

- **1960, Social Security Amendments of 1960 (P.L. 86-778)**

P.L. 86-778, §105(c):
Added Code Sec. 1402(g).

[Sec. 1402(h)]

(h) REGULAR BASIS.—An individual shall be deemed to be self-employed on a regular basis in a taxable year, or to be a member of a partnership on a regular basis in such year, if he had net earnings from self-employment, as defined in the first sentence of subsection (a), of not less than $400 in at least two of the three consecutive taxable years immediately preceding such taxable year from trades or businesses carried on by such individual or such partnership.

Amendments
- **1976, Tax Reform Act of 1976 (P.L. 94-455)**

P.L. 94-455, §1901(a)(155)(B):
Redesignated former subsection (i) as Code Sec. 1402(h). **Effective** with respect to tax years beginning after 12-31-76.

- **1972, Social Security Amendments of 1972 (P.L. 92-603)**

P.L. 92-603, §121(b)(2):
Added Code Sec. 1402(i). **Effective** for tax years beginning after 12-31-72.

[Sec. 1402(i)]

(i) SPECIAL RULES FOR OPTIONS AND COMMODITIES DEALERS.—

(1) IN GENERAL.—Notwithstanding subsection (a)(3)(A), in determining the net earnings from self-employment of any options dealer or commodities dealer, there shall not be excluded any gain or loss (in the normal course of the taxpayer's activity of dealing in or trading section 1256 contracts) from section 1256 contracts or property related to such contracts.

(2) DEFINITIONS.—For purposes of this subsection—

(A) OPTIONS DEALER.—The term "options dealer" has the meaning given such term by section 1256(g)(8).

(B) COMMODITIES DEALER.—The term "commodities dealer" means a person who is actively engaged in trading section 1256 contracts and is registered with a domestic board of trade which is designated as a contract market by the Commodities Futures Trading Commission.

(C) SECTION 1256 CONTRACTS.—The term "section 1256 contract" has the meaning given to such term by section 1256(b).

Amendments
- **1986, Tax Reform Act of 1986 (P.L. 99-514)**

P.L. 99-514, §301(b)(12):
Amended Code Sec. 1402(i)(1). **Effective** for tax years beginning after 12-31-86. Prior to amendment, Code Sec. 1402(i)(1) read as follows:

(1) IN GENERAL.—In determining the net earnings from self-employment of any options dealer or commodities dealer—

(A) notwithstanding subsection (a)(3)(A), there shall not be excluded any gain or loss (in the normal course of the taxpayer's activity of dealing in or trading section 1256 contracts) from section 1256 contracts or property related to such contracts, and

(B) the deduction provided by section 1202 shall not apply.

- **1984, Deficit Reduction Act of 1984 (P.L. 98-369)**
P.L. 98-369, § 102(c)(1):
Amended Code Sec. 1402 by adding new subsection (i). **Effective** for tax years beginning after 7-18-84. However, see Act Sec. 102(g) under the amendment notes for Code Sec. 1256 for special rules.

[Sec. 1402(j)]

(j) SPECIAL RULES FOR CERTAIN CHURCH EMPLOYEE INCOME.—

(1) COMPUTATION OF NET EARNINGS.—In applying subsection (a)—

(A) church employee income shall not be reduced by any deduction;

(B) church employee income and deductions attributable to such income shall not be taken into account in determining the amount of other net earnings from self-employment.

(2) COMPUTATION OF SELF-EMPLOYMENT INCOME.—

(A) SEPARATE APPLICATION OF SUBSECTION (b)(2).—Paragraph (2) of subsection (b) shall be applied separately—

(i) to church employee income, and

(ii) to other net earnings from self-employment.

(B) $100 FLOOR.—In applying paragraph (2) of subsection (b) to church employee income, "$100" shall be substituted for "$400".

(3) COORDINATION WITH SUBSECTION (a)(12).—Paragraph (1) shall not apply to any amount allowable as a deduction under subsection (a)(12), and paragraph (1) shall be applied before determining the amount so allowable.

(4) CHURCH EMPLOYEE INCOME DEFINED.—For purposes of this section, the term "church employee income" means gross income for services which are described in section 3121(b)(8)(B) (and are not described in section 3121(b)(8)(A)).

Amendments

- **1986, Tax Reform Act of 1986 (P.L. 99-514)**
P.L. 99-514, § 1882(b)(1)(A):
Amended Code Sec. 1402 by adding at the end thereof new subsection (j). **Effective** for remuneration paid or derived in tax years beginning after 12-31-85.

[Sec. 1402(k)]

(k) CODIFICATION OF TREATMENT OF CERTAIN TERMINATION PAYMENTS RECEIVED BY FORMER INSURANCE SALESMEN.—Nothing in subsection (a) shall be construed as including in the net earnings from self-employment of an individual any amount received during the taxable year from an insurance company on account of services performed by such individual as an insurance salesman for such company if—

(1) such amount is received after termination of such individual's agreement to perform such services for such company,

(2) such individual performs no services for such company after such termination and before the close of such taxable year,

(3) such individual enters into a covenant not to compete against such company which applies to at least the 1-year period beginning on the date of such termination, and

(4) the amount of such payment—

(A) depends primarily on policies sold by or credited to the account of such individual during the last year of such agreement or the extent to which such policies remain in force for some period after such termination, or both, and

(B) does not depend to any extent on length of service or overall earnings from services performed for such company (without regard to whether eligibility for payment depends on length of service).

Amendments

- **1997, Taxpayer Relief Act of 1997 (P.L. 105-34)**
P.L. 105-34, § 922(a):
Amended Code Sec. 1402 by adding a new subsection (k). **Effective** for payments after 12-31-97.

- **1993, Omnibus Budget Reconciliation Act of 1993 (P.L. 103-66)**
P.L. 103-66, § 13207(b)(2):
Amended Code Sec. 1402 by striking subsection (k). **Effective** for 1994 and later calendar years. Prior to being stricken, Code Sec. 1402(k) read as follows:

(k) APPLICABLE CONTRIBUTION BASE.—For purposes of this chapter—

(1) OLD-AGE, SURVIVORS, AND DISABILITY INSURANCE.—For purposes of the tax imposed by section 1401(a), the applicable contribution base and benefit base determined under section 230 of the Social Security Act for such calendar year.

(2) HOSPITAL INSURANCE.—For purposes of the tax imposed by section 1401(b), the applicable contribution base for any calendar year is the applicable contribution base determined under section 3121(x)(2) for such calendar year.

- **1990, Omnibus Budget Reconciliation Act of 1990 (P.L. 101-508)**
P.L. 101-508, § 11331(b)(2):
Amended Code Sec. 1402 by adding at the end thereof a new subsection (k). **Effective** for 1991 and later calendar years.

[Sec. 1402(l)]

(l) UPPER AND LOWER LIMITS.—For purposes of subsection (a)—

(1) LOWER LIMIT.—The lower limit for any taxable year is the sum of the amounts required under section 213(d) of the Social Security Act for a quarter of coverage in effect with respect to each calendar quarter ending with or within such taxable year.

(2) Upper Limit.—The upper limit for any taxable year is the amount equal to 150 percent of the lower limit for such taxable year.

Amendments
- 2008, Heartland, Habitat, Harvest, and Horticulture Act of 2008 (P.L. 110-246)

P.L. 110-246, § 15352(a)(2):
Amended Code Sec. 1402 by adding at the end a new subsection (l). **Effective** for tax years beginning after 12-31-2007.

[Sec. 1411]
SEC. 1411. IMPOSITION OF TAX.
[Sec. 1411(a)]

(a) In General.—Except as provided in subsection (e)—

(1) Application to Individuals.—In the case of an individual, there is hereby imposed (in addition to any other tax imposed by this subtitle) for each taxable year a tax equal to 3.8 percent of the lesser of—

(A) net investment income for such taxable year, or

(B) the excess (if any) of—

(i) the modified adjusted gross income for such taxable year, over

(ii) the threshold amount.

(2) Application to Estates and Trusts.—In the case of an estate or trust, there is hereby imposed (in addition to any other tax imposed by this subtitle) for each taxable year a tax of 3.8 percent of the lesser of—

(A) the undistributed net investment income for such taxable year, or

(B) the excess (if any) of—

(i) the adjusted gross income (as defined in section 67(e)) for such taxable year, over

(ii) the dollar amount at which the highest tax bracket in section 1(e) begins for such taxable year.

[Sec. 1411(b)]

(b) Threshold Amount.—For purposes of this chapter, the term "threshold amount" means—

(1) in the case of a taxpayer making a joint return under section 6013 or a surviving spouse (as defined in section 2(a)), $250,000,

(2) in the case of a married taxpayer (as defined in section 7703) filing a separate return, ½ of the dollar amount determined under paragraph (1), and

(3) in any other case, $200,000.

[Sec. 1411(c)]

(c) Net Investment Income.—For purposes of this chapter—

(1) In General.—The term "net investment income" means the excess (if any) of—

(A) the sum of—
   (i) gross income from interest, dividends, annuities, royalties, and rents, other than such income which is derived in the ordinary course of a trade or business not described in paragraph (2),
   (ii) other gross income derived from a trade or business described in paragraph (2), and
   (iii) net gain (to the extent taken into account in computing taxable income) attributable to the disposition of property other than property held in a trade or business not described in paragraph (2), over
(B) the deductions allowed by this subtitle which are properly allocable to such gross income or net gain.

(2) TRADES AND BUSINESSES TO WHICH TAX APPLIES.—A trade or business is described in this paragraph if such trade or business is—
   (A) a passive activity (within the meaning of section 469) with respect to the taxpayer, or
   (B) a trade or business of trading in financial instruments or commodities (as defined in section 475(e)(2)).

(3) INCOME ON INVESTMENT OF WORKING CAPITAL SUBJECT TO TAX.—A rule similar to the rule of section 469(e)(1)(B) shall apply for purposes of this subsection.

(4) EXCEPTION FOR CERTAIN ACTIVE INTERESTS IN PARTNERSHIPS AND S CORPORATIONS.—In the case of a disposition of an interest in a partnership or S corporation—
   (A) gain from such disposition shall be taken into account under clause (iii) of paragraph (1)(A) only to the extent of the net gain which would be so taken into account by the transferor if all property of the partnership or S corporation were sold for fair market value immediately before the disposition of such interest, and
   (B) a rule similar to the rule of subparagraph (A) shall apply to a loss from such disposition.

(5) EXCEPTION FOR DISTRIBUTIONS FROM QUALIFIED PLANS.—The term "net investment income" shall not include any distribution from a plan or arrangement described in section 401(a), 403(a), 403(b), 408, 408A, or 457(b).

(6) SPECIAL RULE.—Net investment income shall not include any item taken into account in determining self-employment income for such taxable year on which a tax is imposed by section 1401(b).

[Sec. 1411(d)]
(d) MODIFIED ADJUSTED GROSS INCOME.—For purposes of this chapter, the term "modified adjusted gross income" means adjusted gross income increased by the excess of—
(1) the amount excluded from gross income under section 911(a)(1), over
(2) the amount of any deductions (taken into account in computing adjusted gross income) or exclusions disallowed under section 911(d)(6) with respect to the amounts described in paragraph (1).

[Sec. 1411(e)]
(e) NONAPPLICATION OF SECTION.—This section shall not apply to—
(1) a nonresident alien, or
(2) a trust all of the unexpired interests in which are devoted to one or more of the purposes described in section 170(c)(2)(B).

Amendments
• **2010, Health Care and Education Reconciliation Act of 2010 (P.L. 111-152)**
P.L. 111-152, §1402(a)(1):
Amended subtitle A by inserting after chapter 2 a new chapter 2A (Code Sec. 1411). **Effective** for tax years beginning after 12-31-2012.

[Sec. 3121]

SEC. 3121. DEFINITIONS.

[Sec. 3121(a)]

(a) WAGES.—For purposes of this chapter, the term "wages" means all remuneration for employment, including the cash value of all remuneration (including benefits) paid in any medium other than cash; except that such term shall not include—

(1) in the case of taxes imposed by sections 3101(a) and 3111(a) that part of the remuneration which, after remuneration (other than remuneration referred to in the succeeding paragraphs of this subsection) equal to the contribution and benefit base (as determined under section 230 of the Social Security Act) with respect to employment has been paid to an individual by an employer during the calendar year with respect to which such contribution and benefit base is effective, is paid to such individual by such employer during such calendar year. If an employer (hereinafter referred to as successor employer) during any calendar year acquires substantially all the property used in a trade or business of another employer (hereinafter referred to as a predecessor), or used in a separate unit of a trade or business of a predecessor, and immediately after the acquisition employs in his trade or business an individual who immediately prior to the acquisition was employed in the trade or business of such predecessor, then, for the purpose of determining whether the successor employer has paid remuneration (other than remuneration referred to in the succeeding paragraphs of this subsection) with respect to employment equal to the contribution and benefit base (as determined under section 230 of the Social Security Act) to such individual during such calendar year, any remuneration (other than remuneration referred to in the succeeding paragraph of this subsection) with respect to employment paid (or considered under this paragraph as having been paid) to such individual by such predecessor during such calendar year and prior to such acquisition shall be considered as having been paid by such successor employer;

(2) the amount of any payment (including any amount paid by an employer for insurance or annuities, or into a fund, to provide for any such payment) made to, or on behalf of, an employee or any of his dependents under a plan or system established by an employer which makes provision for his employees generally (or for his employees generally and their dependents) or for a class or classes of his employees (or for a class or classes of his employees and their dependents), on account of—

(A) sickness or accident disability (but, in the case of payments made to an employee or any of his dependents, this subparagraph shall exclude from the term "wages" only payments which are received under a workmen's compensation law), or

(B) medical or hospitalization expenses in connection with sickness or accident disability, or

(C) death, except that this paragraph does not apply to a payment for group-term life insurance to the extent that such payment is includible in the gross income of the employee,

(3) [Stricken.]

(4) any payment on account of sickness or accident disability, or medical or hospitalization expenses in connection with sickness or accident disability, made by an employer to, or on behalf of, an employee after the expiration of 6 calendar months following the last calendar month in which the employee worked for such employer;

(5) any payment made to, or on behalf of, an employee or his beneficiary—

(A) from or to a trust described in section 401(a) which is exempt from tax under section 501(a) at the time of such payment unless such payment is made to an employee of the trust as remuneration for services rendered as such employee and not as a beneficiary of the trust,

(B) under or to an annuity plan which, at the time of such payment, is a plan described in section 403(a),

(C) under a simplified employee pension (as defined in section 408(k)(1)), other than any contributions described in section 408(k)(6),

(D) under or to an annuity contract described in section 403(b), other than a payment for the purchase of such contract which is made by reason of a salary reduction agreement (whether evidenced by a written instrument or otherwise),

(E) under or to an exempt governmental deferred compensation plan (as defined in subsection (v)(3)),

(F) to supplement pension bnefits under a plan or trust described in any of the foregoing provisions of this paragraph to take into account some portion or all of the increase in the cost of living (as determined by the Secretary of Labor) since retirement but only if such supplemental payments are under a plan which is treated as a welfare plan under section 3(2)(B)(ii) of the Employee Retirement Income Security Act of 1974,

(G) under a cafeteria plan (within the meaning of section 125) if such payment would not be treated as wages without regard to such plan and it is reasonable to believe that (if section 125 applied for purposes of this section) section 125 would not treat any wages as constructively received,

(H) under an arrangement to which section 408(p) applies, other than any elective contributions under paragraph (2)(A)(i) thereof, or

(I) under a plan described in section 457(e)(11)(A)(ii) and maintained by an eligible employer (as defined in section 457(e)(1));

(6) the payment by an employer (without deduction from the remuneration of the employee)—

(A) of the tax imposed upon an employee under section 3101, or

(B) of any payment required from an employee under a State unemployment compensation law,

with respect to remuneration paid to an employee for domestic service in a private home of the employer or for agricultural labor;

(7)(A) remuneration paid in any medium other than cash to an employee for service not in the course of the employer's trade or business or for domestic service in a private home of the employer;

(B) cash remuneration paid by an employer in any calendar year to an employee for domestic service in a private home of the employer (including domestic service on a farm operated for profit), if the cash remuneration paid in such year by the employer to the employee for such service is less than the applicable dollar threshold (as defined in subsection (x)) for such year;

(C) cash remuneration paid by an employer in any calendar year to an employee for service not in the course of the employer's trade or business, if the cash remuneration paid in such year by the employer to the employee for such service is less than $100. As used in this subparagraph, the term "service not in the course of the employer's trade or business" does not include domestic service in a private home of the employer and does not include service described in subsection (g) (5);

(8)(A) remuneration paid in any medium other than cash for agricultural labor;

(B) cash remuneration paid by an employer in any calendar year to an employee for agricultural labor unless—

(i) the cash remuneration paid in such year by the employer to the employee for such labor is $150 or more, or

(ii) the employer's expenditures for agricultural labor in such year equal or exceed $2,500,

except that clause (ii) shall not apply in determining whether remuneration paid to an employee constitutes "wages" under this section if such employee (I) is employed as a hand harvest laborer and is paid on a piece rate basis in an operation which has been, and is customarily and generally recognized as having been, paid on a piece rate basis in the region of employment, (II) commutes daily from his permanent residence to the farm on which he

Code Sec. 3121

is so employed, and (III) has been employed in agriculture less than 13 weeks during the preceding calendar year;

(9) [Stricken.]

(10) remuneration paid by an employer in any calendar year to an employee for service described in subsection (d)(3)(C) (relating to home workers), if the cash remuneration paid in such year by the employer to the employee for such service is less than $100;

(11) remuneration paid to or on behalf of an employee if (and to the extent that) at the time of the payment of such remuneration it is reasonable to believe that a corresponding deduction is allowable under section 217 (determined without regard to section 274(n));

(12)(A) tips paid in any medium other than cash;

(B) cash tips received by an employee in any calendar month in the course of his employment by an employer unless the amount of such cash tips is $20 or more;

(13) any payment or series of payments by an employer to an employee or any of his dependents which is paid—

(A) upon or after the termination of an employee's employment relationship because of (i) death, or (ii) retirement for disability, and

(B) under a plan established by the employer which makes provision for his employees generally or a class or classes of his employees (or for such employees or class or classes of employees and their dependents),

other than such payment or series of payments which would have been paid if the employee's employment relationship had not been so terminated;

(14) any payment made by an employer to a survivor or the estate of a former employee after the calendar year in which such employee died;

(15) any payment made by an employer to an employee, if at the time such payment is made such employee is entitled to disability insurance benefits under section 223(a) of the Social Security Act and such entitlement commenced prior to the calendar year in which such payment is made, and if such employee did not perform any services for such employer during the period for which such payment is made;

(16) remuneration paid by an organization exempt from income tax under section 501(a) (other than an organization described in section 401(a)) or under section 521 in any calendar year to an employee for service rendered in the employ of such organization, if the remuneration paid in such year by the organization to the employee for such service is less than $100;

(17) [Stricken.]

(18) any payment made, or benefit furnished, to or for the benefit of an employee if at the time of such payment or such furnishing it is reasonable to believe that the employee will be able to exclude such payment or benefit from income under section 127, 129, 134(b)(4), or 134(b)(5);

(19) the value of any meals or lodging furnished by or on behalf of the employer if at the time of such furnishing it is reasonable to believe that the employee will be able to exclude such items from income under section 119;

(20) any benefit provided to or on behalf of an employee if at the time such benefit is provided it is reasonable to believe that the employee will be able to exclude such benefit from income under section 74(c), 108(f)(4), 117, or 132;

(21) in the case of a member of an Indian tribe, any remuneration on which no tax is imposed by this chapter by reason of section 7873 (relating to income derived by Indians from exercise of fishing rights);

(22) remuneration on account of—

(A) a transfer of a share of stock to any individual pursuant to an exercise of an incentive stock option (as defined in section 422(b)) or under an employee stock purchase plan (as defined in section 423(b)), or

(B) any disposition by the individual of such stock; or

(23) any benefit or payment which is excludable from the gross income of the employee under section 139B(b).

Nothing in the regulations prescribed for purposes of chapter 24 (relating to income tax withholding) which provides an exclusion from "wages" as used in such chapter shall be construed to require a similar exclusion from "wages" in the regulations prescribed for purposes of this chapter.

Except as otherwise provided in regulations prescribed by the Secretary, any third party which makes a payment included in wages solely by reason of the parenthetical matter contained in subparagraph (A) of paragraph (2) shall be treated for purposes of this chapter and chapter 22 as the employer with respect to such wages.

Amendments

• **2014, Tax Technical Corrections Act of 2014 (P.L. 113-295)**

P.L. 113-295, §221(a)(19)(B)(iv), Division A:

Amended Code Sec. 3121(a) by striking paragraph (17). **Effective** generally 12-19-2014. For a special rule, see Act Sec. 221(b)(2), Division A, below. Prior to being stricken, Code Sec. 3121(a)(17) read as follows:

(17) any contribution, payment, or service provided by an employer which may be excluded from the gross income of an employee, his spouse, or his dependents, under the provisions of section 120 (relating to amounts received under qualified group legal services plans);

P.L. 113-295, §221(b)(2), Division A, provides:

(2) SAVINGS PROVISION.—If—

(A) any provision amended or repealed by the amendments made by this section applied to—

(i) any transaction occurring before the date of the enactment of this Act,

(ii) any property acquired before such date of enactment, or

APPENDIX: Selected Code Sections Affected by the Tax Cuts and Jobs Act 289

(iii) any item of income, loss, deduction, or credit taken into account before such date of enactment, and

(B) the treatment of such transaction, property, or item under such provision would (without regard to the amendments or repeals made by this section) affect the liability for tax for periods ending after such date of enactment, nothing in the amendments or repeals made by this section shall be construed to affect the treatment of such transaction, property, or item for purposes of determining liability for tax for periods ending after such date of enactment.

- **2008, Heroes Earnings Assistance and Relief Tax Act of 2008 (P.L. 110-245)**

P.L. 110-245, §115(a)(1):

Amended Code Sec. 3121(a) by striking "or" at the end of paragraph (21), by striking the period at the end of paragraph (22) and inserting "; or", and by inserting after paragraph (22) a new paragraph (23). **Effective** as if included in section 5 of the Mortgage Forgiveness Debt Relief Act of 2007 (P.L. 110-142) [effective for tax years beginning after 12-31-2007.—CCH].

- **2004, Ronald W. Reagan National Defense Authorization Act for Fiscal Year 2005 (P.L. 108-375)**

P.L. 108-375, §585(b)(2)(B):

Amended Code Sec. 3121(a)(18) by striking "or 134(b)(4)" and inserting "134(b)(4), or 134(b)(5)". **Effective** for travel benefits provided after 10-28-2004.

- **2004, American Jobs Creation Act of 2004 (P.L. 108-357)**

P.L. 108-357, §251(a)(1)(A):

Amended Code Sec. 3121(a) by striking "or" at the end of paragraph (20), by striking the period at the end of paragraph (21) and inserting "; or", and by inserting after paragraph (21) a new paragraph (22). **Effective** for stock acquired pursuant to options exercised after 10-22-2004.

P.L. 108-357, §320(b)(1):

Amended Code Sec. 3121(a)(20) by inserting "108(f)(4)," after "74(c),". **Effective** for amounts received by an individual in tax years beginning after 12-31-2003.

- **2004, Social Security Protection Act of 2004 (P.L. 108-203)**

P.L. 108-203, §423(a):

Amended Code Sec. 3121(a)(7)(B) by striking "described in subsection (g)(5)" and inserting "on a farm operated for profit". **Effective** 3-2-2004.

- **2003, Military Family Tax Relief Act of 2003 (P.L. 108-121)**

P.L. 108-121, §106(b)(2):

Amended Code Sec. 3121(a)(18) by striking "or 129" and inserting ", 129, or 134(b)(4)". **Effective** for tax years beginning after 12-31-2002. For a special rule, see Act Sec. 106(d), below.

P.L. 108-121, §106(d), provides:

(d) NO INFERENCE.—No inference may be drawn from the amendments made by this section with respect to the tax treatment of any amounts under the program described in section 134(b)(4) of the Internal Revenue Code of 1986 (as added by this section) for any taxable year beginning before January 1, 2003.

- **2000, Community Renewal Tax Relief Act of 2000 (P.L. 106-554)**

P.L. 106-554, §319(15):

Amended Code Sec. 3121(a)(5) by striking the semicolon at the end of subparagraph (G) and inserting a comma. **Effective** 12-21-2000.

- **1998, IRS Restructuring and Reform Act of 1998 (P.L. 105-206)**

P.L. 105-206, §6023(13)(A)-(C):

Amended Code Sec. 3121(a)(5) by striking the semicolon at the end of subparagraph (F) and inserting a comma, by striking "or" at the end of subparagraph (G), and by striking the period at the end of subparagraph (I) and inserting a semicolon. **Effective** 7-22-98.

- **1996, Small Business Job Protection Act of 1996 (P.L. 104-188)**

P.L. 104-188, §1421(b)(8)(A):

Amended Code Sec. 3121(a)(5) by striking "or" at the end of subparagraph (F), by inserting "or" at the end of subparagraph (G), and by adding at the end a new subparagraph (H). **Effective** for tax years beginning after 12-31-96.

P.L. 104-188, §1458(b)(1):

Amended Code Sec. 3121(a)(5), as amended by Act Sec. 1421(b)(8)(A), by striking "(or)" ["or"] at the end of subparagraph (G), by inserting "or" at the end of subparagraph (H), and by adding at the end a new subparagraph (I). **Effective** for remuneration paid after 12-31-96. For a special rule, see Act Sec. 1802, below.

P.L. 104-188, §1802, provides:

ACT SEC. 1802. TREATMENT OF CERTAIN UNIVERSITY ACCOUNTS.

(a) IN GENERAL.—For purposes of subsection (s) of section 3121 of the Internal Revenue Code of 1986 (relating to concurrent employment by 2 or more employers)—

(1) the following entities shall be deemed to be related corporations that concurrently employ the same individual:

(A) a State university which employs health professionals as faculty members at a medical school, and

(B) an agency account of a State university which is described in subparagraph (A) and from which there is distributed to such faculty members payments forming a part of the compensation that the State, or such State university, as the case may be, agrees to pay to such faculty members, but only if—

(i) such agency account is authorized by State law and receives the funds for such payments from a faculty practice plan described in section 501(c)(3) of such Code and exempt from tax under section 501(a) of such Code,

(ii) such payments are distributed by such agency account to such faculty members who render patient care at such medical school, and

(iii) such faculty members comprise at least 30 percent of the membership of such faculty practice plan, and

(2) remuneration which is disbursed by such agency account to any such faculty member of the medical school described in paragraph (1)(A) shall be deemed to have been actually disbursed by the State, or such State university, as the case may be, as a common paymaster and not to have been actually disbursed by such agency account.

(b) EFFECTIVE DATE.—The provisions of subsection (a) shall apply to remuneration paid after December 31, 1996.

- **1994, Social Security Domestic Employment Reform Act of 1994 (P.L. 103-387)**

P.L. 103-387, §2(a)(1)(A):

Amended Code Sec. 3121(a)(7)(B). **Effective** for remuneration paid after 12-31-93. Prior to amendment, Code Sec. 3121(a)(7)(B) read as follows:

(B) Cash remuneration paid by an employer in any calendar quarter to an employee for domestic service in a private home of the employer, if the cash remuneration paid in such quarter by the employer to the employee for such service is less than $50. As used in this subparagraph, the term "domestic service in a private home of the employer" does not include service described in subsection (g)(5);

P.L. 103-387, §2(a)(4), provides:

(4) NO LOSS OF SOCIAL SECURITY COVERAGE FOR 1994: CONTINUATION OF W-2 FILING REQUIREMENT.—Notwithstanding the amendments made by this subsection, if the wages (as defined in section 3121(a) of the Internal Revenue Code of 1986) paid during 1994 to an employee for domestic service in a private home of the employer are less than $1,000—

(A) the employer shall file any return or statement required under section 6051 of such Code with respect to such wages (determined without regard to such amendments), and

(B) the employee shall be entitled to credit under section 209 of the Social Security Act with respect to any such wages required to be included on any such return or statement.

- **1993, Omnibus Budget Reconciliation Act of 1993 (P.L. 103-66)**

P.L. 103-66, §13207(a)(1)(A)-(C):

Amended Code Sec. 3121(a)(1) by inserting "in the case of taxes imposed by sections 3101(a) and 3111(a)" after "(1)", by striking "applicable contribution base (as determined under subsection (x))" each place it appears and inserting "contribution and benefit base (as determined under section 230 of the Social Security Act)", and by striking "such applicable contribution base" and inserting "such contribution and benefit base". **Effective** for 1994 and later calendar years.

Code Sec. 3121

- **1990, Omnibus Budget Reconciliation Act of 1990 (P.L. 101-508)**
  P.L. 101-508, §11331(a)(1)(A)(B):
  Amended Code Sec. 3121(a)(1) by striking "contribution and benefit base (as determined under section 230 of the Social Security Act)" each place it appears and inserting "applicable contribution base (as determined under subsection (x))", and by striking "such contribution and benefit base" and inserting "such applicable contribution base". **Effective** for 1991 and later calendar years.

- **1989 (P.L. 101-136)**
  P.L. 101-136, §528, provides:
  SEC. 528. No monies appropriated by this Act may be used to implement or enforce section 1151 of the Tax Reform Act of 1986 or the amendments made by such section.

- **1988, Technical and Miscellaneous Revenue Act of 1988 (P.L. 100-647)**
  P.L. 100-647, §1001(g)(4)(B)(i):
  Amended Code Sec. 3121(a)(11) by striking out "section 217" and inserting in lieu thereof "section 217 (determined without regard to section 274(n))". **Effective** as if included in the provision of P.L. 99-514 to which it relates.
  P.L. 100-647, §1011B(a)(23)(A):
  Amended Code Sec. 3121(a)(5)(G) by inserting "if such payment would not be treated as wages without regard to such plan and it is reasonable to believe that (if section 125 applied for purposes of this section) section 125 would not treat any wages as constructively received" after "section 125)". **Effective** as if included in the provision of P.L. 99-514 to which it relates.
  P.L. 100-647, §3043(c)(2):
  Amended Code Sec. 3121(a) by striking out "or" at the end of paragraph (19), by striking out the period at the end of paragraph (20) and inserting in lieu thereof "; or", and by inserting after paragraph (20) new paragraph (21). **Effective** for all periods beginning before, on, or after 11-10-88.
  P.L. 100-647, §3044(b), provides:
  (b) No INFERENCE CREATED.—Nothing in the amendments made by this subtitle shall create any inference as to the existence or non-existence or scope of any exemption from tax for income derived from fishing rights secured as of March 17, 1988, by any treaty, law, or Executive Order.
  P.L. 100-647, §8017(b):
  Amended Code Sec. 3121(a)(8)(B). **Effective** as if included in the provision of P.L. 100-203 to which it relates. Prior to amendment, Code Sec. 3121(a)(8)(B) read as follows:
  (B) cash remuneration paid by an employer in any calendar year to an employee for agricultural labor unless (i) the cash remuneration paid in such year by the employer to the employee for such labor is $150 or more, or (ii) the employer's expenditures for agricultural labor in such year equal or exceed $2,500;

- **1987, Revenue Act of 1987 (P.L. 100-203)**
  P.L. 100-203, §9002(b):
  Amended Code Sec. 3121(a)(8)(B) by striking out clause (ii) and inserting a new clause (ii). **Effective** with respect to remuneration for agricultural labor paid after 12-31-87. Prior to amendment, Code Sec. 3121(a)(8)(B)(ii) read as follows:
  (ii) the employee performs agricultural labor for the employer on 20 days or more during such year for cash remuneration computed on a time basis;
  P.L. 100-203, §9003(a)(2):
  Amended Code Sec. 3121(a)(2)(C) by striking out "death" and inserting "death, except that this paragraph does not apply to a payment for group term life insurance to the extent that such payment is includible in the gross income of the employee". **Effective** with respect to group term life insurance coverage in effect after 12-31-87, except that it shall not apply with respect to payments by the employer (or a successor of such employer) for group-term life insurance for such employer's former employees who separated from employment with the employer on or before 12-31-88, to the extent that such employee payments are not for coverage for any period for which such employee is employed by such employer (or a successor of such employer) after the date of such separation [**effective** date changed by P.L. 100-647, §8013(a)].

- **1986, Tax Reform Act of 1986 (P.L. 99-514)**
  P.L. 99-514, §122(e)(1):
  Amended Code Sec. 3121(a)(20) by striking out "117 or" and inserting in lieu thereof "74(c), 117, or". **Effective** for prizes and awards granted after 12-31-86.

P.L. 99-514, §1108(g)(7):
Amended Code Sec. 3121(a)(5) by striking out subparagraph (C) and inserting in lieu thereof new subparagraph (C). **Effective** for years beginning after 12-31-86. Prior to amendment, Code Sec. 3121(a)(5)(C) read as follows:
(C) under a simplified employee pension if, at the time of the payment, it is reasonable to believe that the employee will be entitled to a deduction under section 219(b)(2) for such payment,
P.L. 99-514, §1151(d)(2)(A):
Amended Code Sec. 3121(a)(5) by striking out"or" at the end of subparagraph (E), by inserting "or" at the end of subparagraph (F), and by inserting after subparagraph (F) new subparagraph (G). **Effective** for tax years beginning after 12-31-83.
P.L. 99-514, §1883(a)(11)(B):
Amended Code Sec. 3121(a)(8) by moving subparagraph (B) two ems to the left, so that its left margin is in flush alignment with the margin of subparagraph (A) of such section. **Effective** 10-22-86.

- **1984, Deficit Reduction Act of 1984 (P.L. 98-369)**
  P.L. 98-369, §491(d)(36):
  Amended Code Sec. 3121(a)(5) by striking out subparagraph (C) and by redesignating subparagraphs (D) through (G) as subparagraphs (C) through (F), respectively. **Effective** for obligations issued after 12-31-83. Prior to amendment, subparagraph (C) read as follows:
  (C) under or to a bond purchase plan which, at the time of such payment, is a qualified bond purchase plan described in section 405(a),
  P.L. 98-369, §531(d)(1)(A):
  Amended Code Sec. 3121(a) by striking out "all remuneration paid in any medium" in the material preceding paragraph (1) and inserting in lieu thereof "all remuneration (including benefits) paid in any medium", and by striking out "or" at the end of paragraph (18), by striking out the period at the end of paragraph (19) and inserting in lieu thereof "; or", and by inserting after paragraph (19) new paragraph (20). **Effective** 1-1-85.

- **1983, Social Security Amendments of 1983 (P.L. 98-21)**
  P.L. 98-21, §324(a)(2):
  Amended Code Sec. 3121(a)(5). **Effective** with respect to remuneration paid after 12-31-83. P.L. 98-21, §324(d)(1), as amended by P.L. 98-369, §2662(f)(2), provides that for purposes of applying such amendments to remuneration paid after 12-31-83, which would have been taken into account before 1-1-84, if such amendments had applied to periods before 1-1-84, such remuneration shall be taken into account when paid (or, at the election of the payor, at the time which would be appropriate if such amendments had applied). Prior to amendment, Code Sec. 3121(a)(5) read as follows:
  (5) any payment made to, or on behalf of, an employee or his beneficiary—
  (A) from or to a trust described in section 401(a) which is exempt from tax under section 501(a) at the time of such payment unless such payment is made to an employee of the trust as remuneration for services rendered as such employee and not as a beneficiary of the trust,
  (B) under or to an annuity plan which, at the time of such payment, is a plan described in section 403(a),
  (C) under or to a bond purchase plan which, at the time of such payment, is a qualified bond purchase plan described in section 405(a), or
  (D) under a simplified employee pension if, at the time of the payment, it is reasonable to believe that the employee will be entitled to a deduction under section 219 for such payment;
  P.L. 98-21, §324(d)(3)-(4), provides:
  (3) The amendments made by this section shall not apply to employer contributions made during 1984 and attributable to services performed during 1983 under a qualified cash or deferred arrangement (as defined in section 401(k) of the Internal Revenue Code of 1954) if, under the terms of such arrangement as in effect on March 24, 1983—
  (A) the employee makes an election with respect to such contribution before January 1, 1984, and
  (B) the employer identifies the amount of such contribution before January 1, 1984.

  * * *

  (4) In the case of an agreement in existence on March 24, 1983, between a nonqualified deferred compensation plan

(as defined in section 3121(v)(2)(C) of the Internal Revenue Code of 1954, as added by this section) and an individual—

(A) the amendments made by this section ***shall apply with respect to services performed by such individual after December 31, 1983, and ***

The preceding sentence shall not apply in the case of a plan to which section 457(a) of such Code applies. For purposes of this paragraph, any plan or agreement to make payments described in paragraph (2), (3), or (13)(A)(iii) of section 3121(a) of such Code (as in effect on the day before the date of the enactment of this Act) shall be treated as a nonqualified deferred compensation plan. [Last sentence added by P.L. 98-369, § 2662 (f)(2)(C).]

P.L. 98-21, § 324(a)(3):

Amended Code Sec. 3121(a) by: striking out in paragraph (2) subparagraph (A) and redesignating subparagraphs (B), (C), and (D) as subparagraphs (A), (B), and (C), respectively; by striking out paragraphs (3) and (9); by inserting in paragraph (13)(A) "or" after "death," and by striking out "or (iii) retirement after attaining an age specified in the plan referred to in subparagraph (B) or in a pension plan of the employer,"; and by striking out "subparagraph (B)" in the last sentence thereof and inserting in lieu thereof "subparagraph (A)". **Effective** with respect to remuneration paid after 12-31-83. But see § 324(d)(3) and (4) of P.L. 98-21. Prior to amendment, Code Sec. 3121(a)(2)(A), (3) and (9) read as follows:

(A) retirement, or

(3) any payment made to an employee (including any amount paid by an employer for insurance or annuities, or into a fund, to provide for any such payment) on account of retirement;

(9) any payment (other than vacation or sick pay) made to an employee after the month in which he attains age 62, if such employee did not work for the employer in the period for which such payment is made;

P.L. 98-21, § 327(a)(1):

Amended Code Sec. 3121(a) by striking out "or" at the end of paragraph (17), by striking out the period at the end of paragraph (18) and inserting in lieu thereof "; or", and by adding paragraph (19). **Effective** with respect to remuneration paid after 12-31-83.

P.L. 98-21, § 327(b)(1):

Amended Code Sec. 3121(a) by inserting the flush sentence after and below Code Sec. 3121(a)(19). **Effective** for remuneration (other than amounts excluded under Code Sec. 119) paid after 3-4-83, and to any such remuneration paid on or before such date which the employer treated as wages when paid. [**Effective** date changed by P.L. 98-369, § 2662(g).]

P.L. 98-21, § 328(a):

Amended Code Sec. 3121(a)(5)(D) by striking out "section 219" and inserting in lieu thereof "section 219(b)(2)". **Effective** with respect to remuneration paid after 12-31-83.

• **1981 (P.L. 97-123)**

P.L. 97-123, § 3(b)(1):

Amended Code Sec. 3121(a)(2)(B). **Effective** with respect to remuneration paid after 12-31-81. Prior to amendment, Code Sec. 3121(a)(2)(B) read as follows: "(B) sickness or accident disability, or".

P.L. 97-123, § 3(b)(2):

Amended Code Sec. 3121(a) by adding the last sentence at the end thereof. **Effective** with respect to remuneration paid after 12-31-81. But, see § 3(g)(2) of P.L. 97-123.

P.L. 97-123, § 3(d)-(f), provides:

(d)(1) The regulations prescribed under the last sentence of section 3121(a) of the Internal Revenue Code of 1954, and the regulations prescribed under subparagraph (D) of section 3231(e)(4) of such Code, shall provide procedures under which, if (with respect to any employee) the third party promptly—

(A) withholds the employee portion of the taxes involved,

(B) deposits such portion under section 6302 of such Code, and

(C) notifies the employer of the amount of the wages or compensation involved,

the employer (and not the third party) shall be liable for the employer portion of the taxes involved and for meeting the requirements of section 6041 of such Code (relating to receipts for employees) with respect to the wages or compensation involved.

(2) For purposes of paragraph (1)—

(A) the term "employer" means the employer for whom services are normally rendered,

(B) the term "taxes involved" means, in the case of any employee, the taxes under chapters 21 and 22 which are payable solely by reason of the parenthetical matter contained in subparagraph (B) of section 3121(a)(2) of such Code, or solely by reason of paragraph (4) of section 3231(e) of such Code, and

(C) the term "wages or compensation involved" means, in the case of any employee, wages or compensation with respect to which taxes described in subparagraph (B) are imposed.

(e) For purposes of applying section 209 of the Social Security Act, section 3121(a) of the Internal Revenue Code of 1954, and section 3231(e) of such Code with respect to the parenthetical matter contained in section 209(b)(2) of the Social Security Act or section 3121(a)(2)(B) of the Internal Revenue Code of 1954, or with respect to section 3231(e)(4) of such Code (as the case may be), payments under a State temporary disability law shall be treated as remuneration for service.

(f) Notwithstanding any other provision of law, no penalties or interest shall be assessed on account of any failure to make timely payment of taxes, imposed by section 3101, 3111, 3201(b), 3211, or 3221(b) of the Internal Revenue Code of 1954 with respect to payments made for the period beginning January 1, 1982, and ending June 30, 1982, to the extent that such taxes are attributable to this section (or the amendments made by this section) and that such failure is due to reasonable cause and not to willful neglect.

P.L. 97-123, § 3(g)(2), provides:

(2) This section (and the amendments made by this section) shall not apply with respect to any payment made by a third party to an employee pursuant to a contractual relationship of an employer with such third party entered into before December 14, 1981, if—

(A) coverage by such third party for the group in which such employee falls ceases before March 1, 1982, and

(B) no payment by such third party is made to such employee under such relationship after February 28, 1982.

• **1981, Economic Recovery Tax Act of 1981 (P.L. 97-34)**

P.L. 97-34, § 124(e)(2):

Amended Code Sec. 3121(a)(18) by striking out "section 127" and inserting in lieu thereof "section 127 or 129". **Effective** with respect to remuneration paid after 12-31-81.

• **1980, Omnibus Reconciliation Act of 1980 (P.L. 96-499)**

P.L. 96-499, § 1141(a)(1):

Amended Code Sec. 3121(a)(6). **Effective,** generally, for remuneration paid after 12-31-80, however, in the case of state and local governments, see P.L. 96-499, § 1141(c)(2), below. Prior to amendment, Code Sec. 3121(a)(6) provided:

(6) the payment by an employer (without deduction from the remuneration of the employee)—

(A) of the tax imposed upon an employee under section 3101 (or the corresponding section of prior law), or

(B) of any payment required from an employee under a State unemployment compensation law;

P.L. 96-499, § 1141(c)(2), provides:

(2) EXCEPTION FOR STATE AND LOCAL GOVERNMENTS.—

(A) the amendments made by this section (insofar as they affect the application of section 218 of the Social Security Act) shall not apply to any payment made before January 1, 1984, by any governmental unit for positions of a kind for which all or a substantial portion of the social security employee taxes were paid by such governmental unit (without deduction from the remuneration of the employee) under the practices of such governmental unit in effect on October 1, 1980.

(B) For purposes of subparagraph (A), the term 'social security employee taxes' means the amount required to be paid under section 218 of the Social Security Act as the equivalent of the taxes imposed by section 3101 of the Internal Revenue Code of 1954.

(C) For purposes of subparagraph (A), the term 'governmental unit' means a State or political subdivision thereof within the meaning of section 218 of the Social Security Act".

- **1980, Technical Corrections Act of 1979 (P.L. 96-222)**

  P.L. 96-222, §101(a)(10)(B)(i):

  Amended Code Sec. 3121(a)(5) by adding paragraph (5). **Effective** for payments made on or after 1-1-79.

- **1978, Revenue Act of 1978 (P.L. 95-600)**

  P.L. 95-600, §164(b)(3)(A), (B), (C), (d):

  Amended Code Sec. 3121(a). **Effective** for tax years beginning after 12-31-78, by: (A) striking out "or" at the end of paragraph (16); (B) striking out the period at the end of paragraph (17) and inserting in place thereof "; or"; and (C) adding paragraph (18).

- **1978 (P.L. 95-472)**

  P.L. 95-472, §3(b), (d):

  Added Code Sec. 3121(a)(17). **Effective** for tax years beginning after 1976.

- **1977 (P.L. 95-216)**

  P.L. 95-216, §356(a):

  Amended Code Sec. 3121(a)(7)(C). **Effective** for remuneration paid and services rendered after 12-31-77. Prior to amendment, Code Sec. 3121(a)(7)(C) read as follows:

  (C) cash remuneration paid by an employer in any calendar quarter to an employee for service not in the course of the employer's trade or business, if the cash remuneration paid in such quarter by the employer to the employee for such service is less than $50. As used in this subparagraph, the term "service not in the course of the employer's trade or business" does not include domestic service in a private home of the employer and does not include service described in subsection (g) (5);

  P.L. 95-216, §356(a):

  Amended Code Sec. 3121(a)(10). **Effective** for remuneration paid and services rendered after 12-31-77. Prior to amendment, Code Sec. 3121(a)(10) read as follows:

  (10) remuneration paid by an employer in any calendar quarter to an employee for service described in subsection (d)(3)(C) (relating to home workers), if the cash remuneration paid in such quarter by the employer to the employee for such service is less than $50;

  P.L. 95-216, §356(b):

  Amended Code Sec. 3121(a) by striking out "or" at the end of paragraph (14), by striking out the period at the end of paragraph (15) and inserting in lieu thereof "; or", and by adding paragraph (16). **Effective** for remuneration paid and services rendered after 12-31-77.

- **1973 (P.L. 93-233)**

  P.L. 93-233, §5(b)(2):

  Amended Code Sec. 3121(a)(1) by substituting "$13,200" for "$10,800." **Effective** with respect to remuneration paid after 1973.

- **1973 (P.L. 93-66)**

  P.L. 93-66, §203(b)(2):

  Amended Code Sec. 3121(a)(1) by substituting "$12,600" for "$12,000." **Effective** with respect to remuneration paid in 1974 (but see P.L. 93-233, above).

- **1972, Social Security Amendments of 1972 (P.L. 92-603)**

  P.L. 92-603, §104(i):

  Amended Code Sec. 3121(a)(9). **Effective** with respect to payments after 1974. Prior to amendment, Code Sec. 3121(a)(9) read as follows:

  "(9) any payment (other than vacation or sick pay) made to an employee after the month in which—

  "(A) in the case of a man, he attains the age of 65, or

  "(B) in the case of a woman, she attains the age of 62, if such employee did not work for the employer in the period for which such payment is made;".

  P.L. 92-603, §122(b):

  Added paragraph (14). **Effective** in the case of any payment made after 12-31-72.

  P.L. 92-603, §138(b):

  Added paragraph (15). **Effective** in the case of any payment made after 12-31-72.

- **1972 (P.L. 92-336)**

  P.L. 92-336, §203(b)(2)(A) (as amended by P.L. 93-233, §5(d)):

  Amended Code Sec. 3121(a)(1) by striking out $9,000 each place it appeared and inserting in lieu thereof $10,800 with respect to remuneration paid after December 1972. **Effective** with respect to remuneration paid after 1973, Sec. 3121(a)(1) is amended by striking out $10,800 each place it appears and inserting in lieu thereof "$12,000". (But see P.L. 93-66, above.) **Effective** with respect to remuneration paid after 1974, Sec. 3121 is amended: (i) by striking out $13,200 each place it appears and inserting in lieu thereof "the contribution and benefit base (as determined under section 230 of the Social Security Act)", and (ii) by striking out "by an employer during any calendar year", and inserting in lieu thereof "by an employer during the calendar year with respect to which such contribution and benefit base is effective".

- **1971 (P.L. 92-5)**

  P.L. 92-5, §203(b)(2):

  Amended Code Sec. 3121(a)(1). **Effective** with respect to remuneration paid after 12-31-71, by substituting "$9,000" for "$7,800" each place that such figure appears.

- **1968, Social Security Amendments of 1967 (P.L. 90-248)**

  P.L. 90-248, §108(b)(2):

  Amended Sec. 3121(a)(1) by substituting "$7,800" for "$6,600" in each place it appeared. **Effective** only with respect to remuneration paid after 12-31-67.

  P.L. 90-248, §504(a):

  Amended Sec. 3121(a) by deleting "or" at the end of paragraph (11), by substituting "; or" for the period at the end of paragraph (12), and by adding new paragraph (13). **Effective** with respect to remuneration paid after 1-2-68.

- **1965, Social Security Amendments of 1965 (P.L. 89-97)**

  P.L. 89-97, §313(c):

  Added Sec. 3121(a)(12). **Effective** with respect to tips received by employees after 1965.

  P.L. 89-97, §320(b):

  Amended Sec. 3121(a)(1) by substituting "$6,600" for "$4,800" in each place it appeared. **Effective** with respect to remuneration paid after 12-31-65.

- **1964 (P.L. 88-650)**

  P.L. 88-650, §4(b):

  Added Code Sec. 3121(a)(11). **Effective** with respect to remuneration paid on or after the first day of the first calendar month which begins more than 10 days after 10-13-64.

- **1964, Revenue Act of 1964 (P.L. 88-272)**

  P.L. 88-272, §220(c)(2):

  Amended subparagraph (B) of subsection (a)(5). **Effective** only with respect to remuneration paid after 1962. Prior to amendment, subparagraph (B) read as follows:

  "(B) under or to an annuity plan which, at the time of such payment, meets the requirements of section 401(a)(3), (4), (5), and (6);"

- **1958, Social Security Amendments of 1958 (P.L. 85-840)**

  P.L. 85-840, §402(b):

  Amended Sec. 3121(a) by substituting "$4,800" for "$4,200" wherever it appeared. **Effective** for remuneration paid after 1958.

- **1956, Social Security Amendments of 1956 (P.L. 880, 84th Cong.)**

  P.L. 880, 84th Cong., §201(b):

  Amended Sec. 3121(a)(9). **Effective** for remuneration paid after 10-31-56. Prior to the amendment Sec. 3121(a)(9) read as follows:

  "(9) any payment (other than vacation or sick pay) made to an employee after the month in which he attains the age of 65, if he did not work for the employer in the period for which such payment is made; or".

  P.L. 880, 84th Cong., 2d Sess., §201(h)(1):

  Amended Sec. 3121(a)(8)(B). **Effective** for remuneration paid after 1956. Prior to amendment, Sec. 3121(a)(8)(B) read as follows:

  "(B) cash remuneration paid by an employer in any calendar year to an employee for agricultural labor, if the cash remuneration paid in such year by the employer to the employee for such labor is less than $100;".

- **1954, Social Security Amendments of 1954 (P.L. 761, 83rd Cong.)**
P.L. 761, 83rd Cong., §204(a), (b):
Substituted "$4,200" wherever it appeared in paragraph (1) for "$3,600", added subparagraph (C) to paragraph (7), inserted "(A)" after "(8)" in paragraph (8), added subparagraph (B) to paragraph (8), and amended subparagraph (7)(B). **Effective** 1-1-55. Prior to amendment, subparagraph (7)(B) read as follows:

"(B) cash remuneration paid by an employer in any calendar quarter to an employee for domestic service in a private home of the employer, if the cash remuneration paid in the quarter for such service is less than $50 or the employee is not regularly employed by the employer in such quarter of payment. For purposes of this subparagraph, an employee shall be deemed to be regularly employed by an employer during a calendar quarter only if—

"(i) on each of some 24 days during the quarter the employee performs for the employer for some portion of the day domestic service in a private home of the employer, or

"(ii) the employee was regularly employed (as determined under clause (i)) by the employer in the performance of such service during the preceding calendar quarter.

"As used in this subparagraph, the term `domestic service in a private home of the employer' does not include service described in subsection (g)(5);".

[Sec. 3121(b)]

(b) EMPLOYMENT.—For purposes of this chapter, the term "employment" means any service, of whatever nature, performed (A) by an employee for the person employing him, irrespective of the citizenship or residence of either, (i) within the United States, or (ii) on or in connection with an American vessel or American aircraft under a contract of service which is entered into within the United States or during the performance of which and while the employee is employed on the vessel or aircraft it touches at a port in the United States, if the employee is employed on and in connection with such vessel or aircraft when outside the United States, or (B) outside the United States by a citizen of the United States [a citizen or resident of the United States (effective for remuneration paid after December 31, 1983)] as an employee for an American employer (as defined in subsection (h)), or (C) if it is service, regardless of where or by whom performed, which is designated as employment or recognized as equivalent to employment under an agreement entered into under section 233 of the Social Security Act; except that such term shall not include—

(1) service performed by foreign agricultural workers lawfully admitted to the United States from the Bahamas, Jamaica, and the other British West Indies, or from any other foreign country or possession thereof, on a temporary basis to perform agricultural labor;

(2) domestic service performed in a local college club, or local chapter of a college fraternity or sorority, by a student who is enrolled and is regularly attending classes at a school, college, or university;

(3)(A) service performed by a child under the age of 18 in the employ of his father or mother;

(B) service not in the course of the employer's trade or business, or domestic service in a private home of the employer, performed by an individual under the age of 21 in the employ of his father or mother, or performed by an individual in the employ of his spouse or son or daughter; except that the provisions of this subparagraph shall not be applicable to such domestic service performed by an individual in the employ of his son or daughter if—

(i) the employer is a surviving spouse or a divorced individual and has not remarried, or has a spouse living in the home who has a mental or physical condition which results in such spouse's being incapable of caring for a son, daughter, stepson, or stepdaughter (referred to in clause (ii)) for at least 4 continuous weeks in the calendar quarter in which the service is rendered, and

(ii) a son, daughter, stepson, or stepdaughter of such employer is living in the home, and

(iii) the son, daughter, stepson, or stepdaughter (referred to in clause (ii)) has not attained age 18 or has a mental or physical condition which requires the personal care and supervision of an adult for at least 4 continuous weeks in the calendar quarter in which the service is rendered;

(4) service performed by an individual on or in connection with a vessel not an American vessel, or on or in connection with an aircraft not an American aircraft, if (A) the individual is employed on and in connection with such vessel or aircraft when outside the United States and (B) (i) such individual is not a citizen of the United States or (ii) the employer is not an American employer;

(5) service performed in the employ of the United States or any instrumentality of the United States, if such service—

(A) would be excluded from the term "employment" for purposes of this title if the provisions of paragraphs (5) and (6) of this subsection as in effect in January 1983 had remained in effect, and

(B) is performed by an individual who—

(i) has been continuously performing service described in subparagraph (A) since December 31, 1983, and for purposes of this clause—

(I) if an individual performing service described in subparagraph (A) returns to the performance of such service after being separated therefrom for a period of less than 366 consecutive days, regardless of whether the period began before, on, or after December 31, 1983, then such service shall be considered continuous,

(II) if an individual performing service described in subparagraph (A) returns to the performance of such service after being detailed or transferred to an international organization as described under section 3343 of subchapter III of chapter 33 of title 5, United States Code, or under section 3581 of chapter 35 of such title, then the service performed for that organization shall be considered service described in subparagraph (A),

(III) if an individual performing service described in subparagraph (A) is reemployed or reinstated after being separated from such service for the purpose of accepting employment with the American Institute in Taiwan as provided under section 3310 of chapter 48 of title 22, United States Code, then the service performed for that Institute shall be considered service described in subparagraph (A),

(IV) if an individual performing service described in subparagraph (A) returns to the performance of such service after performing service as a member of a uniformed service (including, for purposes of this clause, service in the National Guard and temporary service in the Coast Guard Reserve) and after exercising restoration or reemployment rights as provided under chapter 43 of title 38, United States Code, then the service so performed as a member of a uniformed service shall be considered service described in subparagraph (A), and

(V) if an individual performing service described in subparagraph (A) returns to the performance of such service after employment (by a tribal organization) to which section 104(e)(2) of the Indian Self-Determination Act applies, then the service performed for that tribal organization shall be considered service described in subparagraph (A); or

(ii) is receiving an annuity from the Civil Service Retirement and Disability Fund, or benefits (for service as an employee) under another retirement system established by a law of the United States for employees of the Federal Government (other than for members of the uniformed service);

except that this paragraph shall not apply with respect to any such service performed on or after any date on which such individual performs—

(C) service performed as the President or Vice President of the United States,

(D) service performed—

(i) in a position placed in the Executive Schedule under Sections 5312 through 5317 of title 5, United States Code,

(ii) as a noncareer appointee in the Senior Executive Service or a noncareer member of the Senior Foreign Service, or

(iii) in a position to which the individual is appointed by the President (or his designee) or the Vice President under section 105(a)(1), 106(a)(1), or 107(a)(1) or (b)(1) of title 3, United States Code, if the maximum rate of basic pay for such position is at or above the rate for level V of the Executive Schedule,

(E) service performed as the Chief Justice of the United States, an Associate Justice of the Supreme Court, a judge of a United States court of appeals, a judge of a United States district court (including the district court of a territory), a judge of the United States Court of Federal Claims, a judge of the United States Court of International Trade, a judge of the United States Tax Court, a United States magistrate, or a referee in bankruptcy or United States bankruptcy judge,

(F) service performed as a Member, Delegate, or Resident Commissioner of or to the Congress,

(G) any other service in the legislative branch of the Federal Government if such service—

(i) is performed by an individual who was not subject to subchapter III of chapter 83 of title 5, United States Code, or to another retirement system established by a law of the United States for employees of the Federal Government (other than for members of the uniformed services), on December 31, 1983, or

(ii) is performed by an individual who has, at any time after December 31, 1983, received a lump-sum payment under section 8342(a) of title 5, United States Code, or under the corresponding provision of the law establishing the other retirement system described in clause (i), or

(iii) is performed by an individual after such individual has otherwise ceased to be subject to subchapter III of chapter 83 of title 5, United States Code (without having an application pending for coverage under such subchapter), while performing service in the legislative branch (determined without regard to the provisions of subparagraph (B) relating to continuity of employment), for any period of time after December 31, 1983, and for purposes of this subparagraph (G) an individual is subject to such subchapter III or to any such other retirement system at any time only if (a) such individual's pay is subject to deductions, contributions, or similar payments (concurrent with the service being performed at that time) under section 8334(a) of such title 5 or the corresponding provision of the law establishing such other system, or (in a case to which section 8332(k)(1) of such title applies) such individual is making payments of amounts equivalent to such deductions, contributions, or similar payments while on leave without pay, or (b) such individual is receiving an annuity from the Civil Service Retirement and Disability Fund, or is receiving benefits (for service as an employee) under another retirement system established by a law of the United States for employees of the Federal Government (other than for members of the uniformed services), or

(H) service performed by an individual—

(i) on or after the effective date of an election by such individual, under section 301 of the Federal Employees' Retirement System Act of 1986, section 307 of the Central Intelligence Agency Retirement Act (50 U.S.C. 2157), or the Federal Employees' Retirement System Open Enrollment Act of 1997, to become subject to the Federal Employees' Retirement System provided in chapter 84 of title 5, United States Code, or

(ii) on or after the effective date of an election by such individual, under regulations issued under section 860 of the Foreign Service Act of 1980, to become subject to the Foreign Service Pension System provided in subchapter II of chapter 8 of title I of such Act;

(6) service performed in the employ of the United States or any instrumentality of the United States if such service is performed—

(A) in a penal institution of the United States by an inmate thereof;

(B) by any individual as an employee included under section 5351(2) of title 5, United States Code (relating to certain interns, student nurses, and other student employees of hospitals of the Federal Government), other than as a medical or dental intern or a medical or dental resident in training; or

(C) by any individual as an employee serving on a temporary basis in case of fire, storm, earthquake, flood, or other similar emergency;

(7) service performed in the employ of a State, or any political subdivision thereof, or any instrumentality of any one or more of the foregoing which is wholly owned thereby, except that this paragraph shall not apply in the case of—

(A) service which, under subsection (j), constitutes covered transportation service,

(B) service in the employ of the Government of Guam or the Government of American Samoa or any political subdivision thereof, or of any instrumentality of any one or more of the foregoing which is wholly owned thereby, performed by an officer or employee thereof (including a member of the legislature of any such Government or political subdivision), and, for purposes of this title with respect to the taxes imposed by this chapter—

(i) any person whose service as such an officer or employee is not covered by a retirement system established by a law of the United States shall not, with respect to such service, be regarded as an employee of the United States or any agency or instrumentality thereof, and

(ii) the remuneration for service described in clause (i) (including fees paid to a public official) shall be deemed to have been paid by the Government of Guam or the Government of American Samoa or by a political subdivision thereof or an instrumentality of any one or more of the foregoing which is wholly owned thereby, whichever is appropriate,

(C) service performed in the employ of the District of Columbia or any instrumentality which is wholly owned thereby, if such service is not covered by a retirement system established by a law of the United States (other than the Federal Employees Retirement System provided in chapter 84 of title 5, United States Code); except that the provisions of this subparagraph shall not be applicable to service performed—

(i) in a hospital or penal institution by a patient or inmate thereof;

(ii) by any individual as an employee included under section 5351(2) of title 5, United States Code (relating to certain interns, student nurses, and other student employees of hospitals of the District of Columbia Government), other than as a medical or dental intern or as a medical or dental resident in training;

(iii) by any individual as an employee serving on a temporary basis in case of fire, storm, snow, earthquake, flood or other similar emergency; or

(iv) by a member of a board, committee, or council of the District of Columbia, paid on a per diem, meeting, or other fee basis,

(D) service performed in the employ of the Government of Guam (or any instrumentality which is wholly owned by such Government) by an employee properly classified as a temporary or intermittent employee, if such service is not covered by a retirement system established by a law of Guam; except that (i) the provisions of this subparagraph shall not be applicable to services performed by an elected official or a member of the legislature or in a hospital or penal institution by a patient or inmate thereof, and (ii) for purposes of this subparagraph, clauses (i) and (ii) of subparagraph (B) shall apply,

(E) service included under an agreement entered into pursuant to section 218 of the Social Security Act, or

(F) service in the employ of a State (other than the District of Columbia, Guam, or American Samoa), of any political subdivision thereof, or of any instrumentality of any one or more of the foregoing which is wholly owned thereby, by an individual who is not a member of a retirement system of such State, political subdivision, or instrumentality, except that the provisions of this subparagraph shall not be applicable to service performed—

(i) by an individual who is employed to relieve such individual from unemployment;

(ii) in a hospital, home, or other institution by a patient or inmate thereof;

(iii) by any individual as an employee serving on a temporary basis in case of fire, storm, snow, earthquake, flood, or other similar emergency;

(iv) by an election official or election worker if the remuneration paid in a calendar year for such service is less than $1,000 with respect to service performed during any calendar year commencing on or after January 1, 1995, ending on or before December 31, 1999, and the adjusted amount determined under section 218(c)(8)(B) of the Social Security Act for any calendar year commencing on or after January 1, 2000, with respect to service performed during such calendar year; or

(v) by an employee in a position compensated solely on a fee basis which is treated pursuant to section 1402(c)(2)(E) as a trade or business for purposes of inclusion of such fees in net earnings from self-employment; for purposes of this subparagraph, except as provided in regulations prescribed by the Secretary, the term "retirement system" has the meaning given such term by section 218(b)(4) of the Social Security Act;

(8)(A) service performed by a duly ordained, commissioned, or licensed minister of a church in the exercise of his ministry or by a member of a religious order in the exercise of duties required by such order, except that this subparagraph shall not apply to service performed by a member of such an order in the exercise of such duties, if an election of coverage under subsection (r) is in effect with respect to such order, or with respect to the autonomous subdivision thereof to which such member belongs;

(B) service performed in the employ of a church or qualified church-controlled organization if such church or organization has in effect an election under subsection (w), other than service in an unrelated trade or business (within the meaning of section 513(a));

(9) service performed by an individual as an employee or employee representative as defined in section 3231;

(10) service performed in the employ of—

(A) a school, college, or university, or

(B) an organization described in section 509(a)(3) if the organization is organized, and at all times thereafter is operated, exclusively for the benefit of, to perform the functions of, or to carry out the purposes of a school, college, or university and is operated, supervised, or controlled by or in connection with such school, college, or university unless it is a school, college, or university of a State or a political subdivision thereof and the services performed in its employ by a student referred to in section 218(c)(5) of the Social Security Act are covered under the agreement between the Commissioner of Social Security and such State entered into pursuant to section 218 of such Act;

if such service is performed by a student who is enrolled and regularly attending classes at such school, college, or university;

(11) service performed in the employ of a foreign government (including service as a consular or other officer or employee or a nondiplomatic representative);

(12) service performed in the employ of an instrumentality wholly owned by a foreign government—

(A) if the service is of a character similar to that performed in foreign countries by employees of the United States Government or of an instrumentality thereof; and

(B) if the Secretary of State shall certify to the Secretary of the Treasury that the foreign government, with respect to whose instrumentality and employees thereof exemption is claimed, grants an equivalent exemption with respect to similar service performed in the foreign country by employees of the United States Government and of instrumentalities thereof;

(13) service performed as a student nurse in the employ of a hospital or a nurses' training school by an individual who is enrolled and is regularly attending classes in a nurses' training school chartered or approved pursuant to State law;

(14)(A) service performed by an individual under the age of 18 in the delivery or distribution of newspapers or shopping news, not including delivery or distribution to any point for subsequent delivery or distribution;

(B) service performed by an individual in, and at the time of, the sale of newspapers or magazines to ultimate consumers, under an arrangement under which the newspapers or magazines are to be sold by him at a fixed price, his compensation being based on the retention of the excess of such price over the amount at which the newspapers or magazines are charged to him, whether or not he is guaranteed a minimum amount of compensation for such service, or is entitled to be credited with the unsold newspapers or magazines turned back;

(15) service performed in the employ of an international organization, except service which constitutes "employment" under subsection (y);

(16) service performed by an individual under an arrangement with the owner or tenant of land pursuant to which—

(A) such individual undertakes to produce agricultural or horticultural commodities (including livestock, bees, poultry, and fur-bearing animals and wildlife) on such land,

(B) the agricultural or horticultural commodities produced by such individual, or the proceeds therefrom, are to be divided between such individual and such owner or tenant, and

Code Sec. 3121

(C) the amount of such individual's share depends on the amount of the agricultural or horticultural commodities produced;

(17) [Stricken.]

(18) service performed in Guam by a resident of the Republic of the Philippines while in Guam on a temporary basis as a nonimmigrant alien admitted to Guam pursuant to section 101(a)(15)(H)(ii) of the Immigration and Nationality Act (8 U.S.C. 1101(a)(15)(H)(ii));

(19) service which is performed by a nonresident alien individual for the period he is temporarily present in the United States as a nonimmigrant under subparagraph (F), (J), (M), or (Q) of section 101(a)(15) of the Immigration and Nationality Act, as amended, and which is performed to carry out the purpose specified in subparagraph (F), (J), (M), or (Q), as the case may be;

(20) service (other than service described in paragraph (3)(A)) performed by an individual on a boat engaged in catching fish or other forms of aquatic animal life under an arrangement with the owner or operator of such boat pursuant to which—

(A) such individual does not receive any cash remuneration other than as provided in subparagraph (B) and other than cash remuneration—

(i) which does not exceed $100 per trip;

(ii) which is contingent on a minimum catch; and

(iii) which is paid solely for additional duties (such as mate, engineer, or cook) for which additional cash remuneration is traditional in the industry,

(B) such individual receives a share of the boat's (or the boats' in the case of a fishing operation involving more than one boat) catch of fish or other forms of aquatic animal life or a share of the proceeds from the sale of such catch, and

(C) the amount of such individual's share depends on the amount of the boat's (or the boats' in the case of a fishing operation involving more than one boat) catch of fish or other forms of aquatic animal life,

but only if the operating crew of such boat (or each boat from which the individual receives a share in the case of a fishing operation involving more than one boat) is normally made up of fewer than 10 individuals;

(21) domestic service in a private home of the employer which—

(A) is performed in any year by an individual under the age of 18 during any portion of such year; and

(B) is not the principal occupation of such employee; or

(22) service performed by members of Indian tribal councils as tribal council members in the employ of an Indian tribal government, except that this paragraph shall not apply in the case of service included under an agreement under section 218A of the Social Security Act.

For purposes of paragraph (20), the operating crew of a boat shall be treated as normally made up of fewer than 10 individuals if the average size of the operating crew on trips made during the preceding 4 calendar quarters consisted of fewer than 10 individuals.

Amendments

• **2018, Tribal Social Security Fairness Act of 2018 (P.L. 115-243)**

P.L. 115-243, §2(b)(2)(A)(i)-(iii):
Amended Code Sec. 3121(b) by striking "or" at the end in paragraph (20), by striking the period at the end in paragraph (21) and inserting "; or"; and by inserting after paragraph (21) a new paragraph (22). **Effective** 9-20-2018.

P.L. 115-243, §2(c), provides:
(c) RULE OF CONSTRUCTION.—Nothing in this Act or the amendments made by this Act shall be construed to affect application of any Federal income tax withholding requirements under the Internal Revenue Code of 1986.

• **2018, Tax Technical Corrections Act of 2018 (P.L. 115-141)**

P.L. 115-141, §401(a)(209), Div. U:
Amended Code Sec. 3121(b)(5)(B)(i)(V) by striking "section 105(e)(2)" and inserting "section 104(e)(2)". **Effective** 3-23-2018.

P.L. 115-141, §401(a)(210), Div. U:
Amended Code Sec. 3121(b)(5)(H)(i) by striking "1997" and inserting "1997,". **Effective** 3-23-2018.

P.L. 115-141, §401(a)(325)(A), Div. U:
Amended Code Sec. 3121(b)(5)(E) by striking "United States Claims Court" and inserting "United States Court of Federal Claims". [Note: Code Sec. 3121(b)(5)(E) does not contain the text "United States Claims Court". Therefore, this amendment cannot be made.—CCH] **Effective** 3-23-2018.

• **2014, Tax Technical Corrections Act of 2014 (P.L. 113-295)**

P.L. 113-295, §221(a)(99)(C)(i):
Amended Code Sec. 3121(b) by striking paragraph (17). **Effective** generally 12-19-2014. For a special rule, see Act Sec. 221(b)(2), Division A, below. Prior to being stricken, Code Sec. 3121(b)(17) read as follows:

(17) service in the employ of any organization which is performed (A) in any year during any part of which such organization is registered, or there is in effect a final order of the Subversive Activities Control Board requiring such organization to register, under the Internal Security Act of 1950, as amended, as a Communist-action organization, a Communist-front organization, or a Communist-infiltrated organization, and (B) after June 30, 1956;

P.L. 113-295, §221(b)(2), Division A, provides:
(2) SAVINGS PROVISION.—If—
(A) any provision amended or repealed by the amendments made by this section applied to—
(i) any transaction occurring before the date of the enactment of this Act,
(ii) any property acquired before such date of enactment, or
(iii) any item of income, loss, deduction, or credit taken into account before such date of enactment, and
(B) the treatment of such transaction, property, or item under such provision would (without regard to the amendments or repeals made by this section) affect the liability for tax for periods ending after date of enactment, nothing in the amendments or repeals made by this section shall be construed to affect the treatment of such transaction, property, or item for purposes of determining liability for tax for periods ending after such date of enactment.

• **2008, Worker, Retiree, and Employer Recovery Act of 2008 (P.L. 110-458)**

P.L. 110-458, §108(k)(1):
Amended Code Sec. 3121(b)(5)(E) by striking "or special trial judge" before "of the United States Tax Court". **Effective** as if included in the provision of the 2006 Act to which the amendment relates [effective 8-17-2006.—CCH].

- **2006, Pension Protection Act of 2006 (P.L. 109-280)**

P.L. 109-280, §854(c)(8):

Amended Code Sec. 3121(b)(5)(E) by inserting "or special trial judge" before "of the United States Tax Court". Effective 8-17-2006.

- **1997, Treasury and General Government Appropriations Act, 1998 (P.L. 105-61)**

P.L. 105-61, §642(d)(2)(A)-(B):

Amended Code Sec. 3121(b)(5)(H)(i) by striking "or" after "1986" and inserting a comma, and by inserting "or the Federal Employees' Retirement System Open Enrollment Act of 1997" after "(50 U.S.C. 2157),". **Effective** 10-10-97.

- **1997, Balanced Budget Act of 1997 (P.L. 105-33)**

P.L. 105-33, §11246(b)(2) (as amended by P.L. 105-277, Div. A, §802(a)(2)):

Amended Code Sec. 3121(b)(7)(C) by inserting "(other than the Federal Employees Retirement System provided in chapter 84 of title 5, United States Code)" after "law of the United States". **Effective** as if included in the enactment of title XI of P.L. 105-33.

- **1996, Small Business Job Protection Act of 1996 (P.L. 104-188)**

P.L. 104-188, §1116(a)(1)(A):

Amended Code Sec. 3121(b) by adding at the end a new sentence. For the **effective** date, see Act Sec. 1116(a)(3)(A), below.

P.L. 104-188, §1116(a)(1)(B):

Amended Code Sec. 3121(b)(20)(A). For the **effective** date, see Act Sec. 1116(a)(3)(A), below. Prior to amendment, Code Sec. 3121(b)(20)(A) read as follows:

(A) such individual does not receive any cash remuneration (other than as provided in subparagraph (B)),

P.L. 104-188, §1116(a)(3)(A), provides:

(A) IN GENERAL.—The amendments made by this subsection shall apply to remuneration paid—

(i) after December 31, 1994, and

(ii) after December 31, 1984, and before January 1, 1995, unless the payor treated such remuneration (when paid) as being subject to tax under chapter 21 of the Internal Revenue Code of 1986.

- **1994, Social Security Domestic Employment Reform Act of 1994 (P.L. 103-387)**

P.L. 103-387, §2(a)(1)(C)(i)-(iii):

Amended Code Sec. 3121(b) by striking "or" at the end of paragraph (19), by striking the period at the end of paragraph (20) and inserting "; or", and by adding at the end a new paragraph (21). **Effective** for services performed after 12-31-94.

- **1994, Social Security Independence and Program Improvements Act of 1994 (P.L. 103-296)**

P.L. 103-296, §108(b)(2):

Amended Code Sec. 3121(b)(10)(B) by striking "Secretary of Health and Human Services" each place it appears and inserting "Commissioner of Social Security". **Effective** 3-31-95.

P.L. 103-296, §303(a)(2):

Amended Code Sec. 3121(b)(7)(F)(iv) by striking "$100" and inserting "$1,000 with respect to service performed during any calendar year commencing on or after January 1, 1995, ending on or before December 31, 1999, and the adjusted amount determined under section 218(c)(8)(B) of the Social Security Act for any calendar year commencing on or after January 1, 2000, with respect to service performed during such calendar year". **Effective** with respect to service performed on or after 1-1-95.

P.L. 103-296, §319(a)(5):

Amended Code Sec. 3121(b)(15) by inserting ", except service which constitutes 'employment' under subsection (y)" after "organization". **Effective** with respect to service performed after the calendar quarter following the calendar quarter containing 8-15-94.

P.L. 103-296, §320(a)(1)(C):

Amended Code Sec. 3121(b)(19) by striking "(J), or (M)" each place it appears and inserting "(J), (M), or (Q)". **Effective** for the calendar quarter following 8-15-94.

- **1993, Intelligence Authorization Act for Fiscal Year 1994 (P.L. 103-178)**

P.L. 103-178, §204(c):

Amended Code Sec. 3121(b)(5)(H)(i) by striking "section 307 of the Central Intelligence Agency Retirement Act of 1964 for Certain Employees" and inserting in lieu thereof "section 307 of the Central Intelligence Agency Retirement Act (50 U.S.C. 2157)". **Effective** 12-3-93.

- **1992, Court of Federal Claims Technical and Procedural Improvements Act of 1992 (P.L. 102-572)**

P.L. 102-572, §902(b)(1):

Amended Code Sec. 3121(b)(5)(E) by striking "United States Claims Court" and inserting "United States Court of Federal Claims". **Effective** 10-29-92.

- **1990, Omnibus Budget Reconciliation Act of 1990 (P.L. 101-508)**

P.L. 101-508, §11332(b)(1):

Amended Code Sec. 3121(b)(7) by striking "or" at the end of subparagraph (D). **Effective** with respect to service performed after 7-1-91.

P.L. 101-508, §11332(b)(2):

Amended Code Sec. 3121(b)(7)(E) by striking the semicolon at the end thereof and inserting ", or". **Effective** with respect to service performed after 7-1-91.

P.L. 101-508, §11332(b)(3):

Amended Code Sec. 3121(b)(7) by adding at the end thereof a new subparagraph (F). **Effective** with respect to service performed after 7-1-91.

- **1988, Technical and Miscellaneous Revenue Act of 1988 (P.L. 100-647)**

P.L. 100-647, §1001(d)(2)(C)(i):

Amended Code Sec. 3121(b)(19) by striking out "(F) or (J)" each place it appears and inserting in lieu thereof "(F), (J), or (M)". **Effective** as if included in the provision of P.L. 99-514 to which it relates.

P.L. 100-647, §8015(b)(2):

Amended Code Sec. 3121(b)(5)(H). **Effective** as if included or reflected in section 304 of the Federal Employees' Retirement System Act of 1986 (100 Stat. 606) at the time of its enactment. Prior to amendment, Code Sec. 3121(b)(5)(H) read as follows:

(H) service performed by an individual on or after the effective date of an election by such individual under section 301(a) of the Federal Employees' Retirement System Act of 1986, or under regulations issued under section 860 of the Foreign Service Act of 1980 or section 307 of the Central Intelligence Agency Retirement Act of 1964 for Certain Employees, to become subject to chapter 84 of title 5, United States Code;

P.L. 100-647, §8015(c)(2):

Amended Code Sec. 3121(b)(5) in the matter following subparagraph (B)(ii), by inserting after "with respect to" "any such service performed on or after any date on which such individual performs". **Effective** for any individual only upon the performance by such individual of service described in subparagraph (C), (D), (E), (F), (G), or (H) of section 210(a)(5) of the Social Security Act (42 U.S.C. 410(a)(5)) on or after 11-10-88.

- **1987, Revenue Act of 1987 (P.L. 100-203)**

P.L. 100-203, §9004(b)(1):

Amended Code Sec. 3121(b)(3)(A) by striking "performed by an individual in the employ of his spouse, and service" before "performed". **Effective** with respect to remuneration paid after 12-31-87.

P.L. 100-203, §9004(b)(2):

Amended Code Sec. 3121(b)(3) by striking so much of subparagraph (B) as precedes clause (i) and inserting the new material that precedes clause (i). **Effective** with respect to remuneration paid after 12-31-87. Prior to amendment, the material preceding clause (i) read as follows:

(B) service not in the course of the employer's trade or business, or domestic service in a private home of the employer, performed by an individual in the employ of his son or daughter; except that the provisions of this subparagraph shall not be applicable to such domestic service if—

P.L. 100-203, § 9005(b)(1):
Amended Code Sec. 3121(b)(3)(A) by striking out "21" and inserting "18". **Effective** with respect to remuneration paid after 12-31-87.

P.L. 100-203, § 9005(b)(2):
Amended Code Sec. 3121(b)(3)(B) by inserting "under the age of 21 in the employ of his father or mother, or performed by an individual" after "individual" the first place it appears. **Effective** with respect to remuneration paid after 12-31-87.

- **1986, Omnibus Budget Reconciliation Act of 1986 (P.L. 99-509)**

P.L. 99-509, § 9002(b)(1)(A)(i)-(iii):
Amended Code Sec. 3121(b)(7) by striking out "; or" at the end of subparagraph (C) and inserting in lieu thereof a comma, by striking out the semicolon at the end of subparagraph (D) and inserting in lieu thereof ", or", and by adding after subparagraph (D) new subparagraph (E) For the **effective** date, see Act Sec. 9002(d), below.

P.L. 99-509, § 9002(d), provides:
(d) EFFECTIVE DATE.—The amendments made by this section are effective with respect to payments due with respect to wages paid after December 31, 1986, including wages paid after such date by a State (or political subdivision thereof) that modified its agreement pursuant to the provisions of section 218(e)(2) of the Social Security Act prior to the date of the enactment of this Act; except that in cases where, in accordance with the currently applicable schedule, deposits of taxes due under an agreement entered into pursuant to section 218 of the Social Security Act would be required within 3 days after the close of an eighth-monthly period, such 3-day requirement shall be changed to a 7-day requirement for wages paid prior to October 1, 1987, and to a 5-day requirement for wages paid after September 30, 1987, and prior to October 1, 1988. For wages paid prior to October 1, 1988, the deposit schedule for taxes imposed under sections 3101 and 3111 shall be determined separately from the deposit schedule for taxes withheld under section 3402 if the taxes imposed under sections 3101 and 3111 are due with respect to service included under an agreement entered into pursuant to section 218 of the Social Security Act.

- **1986 (P.L. 99-335)**

P.L. 99-335, § 304(b)(1)-(3):
Amended Code Sec. 3121(b)(5) by striking out "or" at the end of subparagraph (F); by striking out the semicolon at the end of subparagraph (G) and inserting in lieu thereof ", or"; and adding at the end new subparagraph. **Effective** 6-6-86.

- **1986, Consolidated Omnibus Budget Reconciliation Act of 1985 (P.L. 99-272)**

P.L. 99-272, § 13303(c)(2):
Amended Code Sec. 3121(b)(20) by inserting "(other than service described in paragraph (3)(A))" before "performed". **Effective** 4-7-86.

- **1985, Cherokee Leasing Act (P.L. 99-221)**

P.L. 99-221, § (3)(b)(1)-(3):
Amended Code Sec. 3121(b)(5)(B)(i) by striking out "and" at the end of subclause (III), by striking out "; or" at the end of the subclause (IV) and inserting in lieu thereof ", and", and by adding after subclause (IV) new subclause (V). **Effective** for any return to the performance of service in the employ of the United States, or of an instrumentality thereof, after 1983.

- **1984, Deficit Reduction Act of 1984 (P.L. 98-369)**

P.L. 98-369, § 2601(b)(1):
Amended Code Sec. 3121(b)(5)(B). **Effective** with respect to service performed after 12-31-83. Special rules appear in Act Sec. 2601(c)-(e), below. Prior to amendment, Code Sec. 3121(b)(5)(B) reads as follows:

(B) is performed by an individual who (i) has been continuously in the employ of the United States or an instrumentality thereof since December 31, 1983 (and for this purpose an individual who returns to the performance of such service after being separated therefrom following a previous period of such service shall nevertheless be considered upon such return as having been continuously in the employ of the United States or an instrumentality thereof, regardless of whether the period of such separation began before, on, or after December 31, 1983, if the period of such separation does not exceed 365 consecutive days), or (ii) is receiving an annuity from the Civil Service Retirement and Disability Fund, or benefits (for service as an employee) under another retirement system established by law of the United States for employees of the Federal Government other than for members of the uniformed services);

P.L. 98-369, § 2601(b)(2):
Further amended Code Sec. 3121(b)(5) (in the matter which follows "except that this paragraph shall not apply with respect to —") by striking out "(i)", "(ii)", "(iii)", "(iv)", and "(v)" and inserting in lieu thereof "(C)", "(D)", "(E)", "(F)", and "(G)", respectively; by striking out "(I)", "(II)", and "(III)", and inserting in lieu thereof "(i)", "(ii)", and "(iii)", respectively; and by striking out subparagraph (G) (as redesignated by subparagraph (A) of this paragraph) and inserting in lieu thereof new paragraph (G). **Effective** with respect to service performed after 12-31-83. Special rules appear in Act Sec. 2601(e), below. Prior to amendment, subparagraph (G) ((v), prior to redesignation) read as follows:

(v) any other service in the legislative branch of the Federal Government if such service is performed by an individual who, on December 31, 1983, is not subject to subchapter III of chapter 83 of title 5, United States Code;

P.L. 98-369, § 2601(c)-(e), provides:
(c) For purposes of section 210(a)(5)(G) of the Social Security Act and section 3121(b)(5)(G) of the Internal Revenue Code of 1954, an individual shall not be considered to be subject to subchapter III of chapter 83 of title 5, United States Code or to another retirement system established by a law of the United States for employees of the Federal Government (other than for members of the uniformed services), if he is contributing a reduced amount by reason of the Federal Employees' Retirement Contribution Temporary Adjustment Act of 1983.

(d)(1) Any individual who—

(A) was subject to subchapter III of chapter 83 of title 5, United States Code, or to another retirement system established by a law of the United States for employees of the Federal Government (other than for members of the uniformed services), on December 31, 1983 (as determined for purposes of section 210(a)(5)(G) of the Social Security Act), and

(B)(i) received a lump-sum payment under section 8342(a) of such title 5, or under the corresponding provision of the law establishing the other retirement system described in subparagraph (A), after December 31, 1983, and prior to June 15, 1984, or received such a payment on or after June 15, 1984, pursuant to an application which was filed in accordance with such section 8342(a) or the corresponding provision of the law establishing such other retirement system prior to that date, or

(ii) otherwise ceased to be subject to subchapter III of chapter 83 of title 5, United States Code, for a period after December 31, 1983, to which section 210(a)(5)(G)(iii) of the Social Security Act applies,

shall, if such individual again becomes subject to subchapter III of chapter 83 of title 5 (or effectively applies for coverage under such subchapter) after the date on which he last ceased to be subject to such subchapter but prior to, or within 30 days after, the date of the enactment of this Act, requalify for the exemption from social security coverage and taxes under section 210(a)(5) of the Social Security Act and section 3121(b)(5) of the Internal Revenue Code of 1954 as if the cessation of coverage under title 5 had not occurred.

(2) An individual meeting the requirements of subparagraphs (A) and (B) of paragraph (1) who is not in the employ of the United States or an instrumentality thereof on the date of the enactment of this Act may requalify for such exemptions in the same manner as under paragraph (1) if such individual again becomes subject to subchapter III of chapter 83 of title 5 (or effectively applies for coverage under such subchapter) within 30 days after the date on which he first returns to service in the legislative branch after such date of enactment, if such date (on which he returns to service) is within 365 days after he was last in the employ of the United States or an instrumentality thereof.

(3) If an individual meeting the requirements of subparagraphs (A) and (B) of paragraph (1) does not again become subject to subchapter III of chapter 83 of title 5 (or effectively apply for coverage under such subchapter) prior to the date of the enactment of this Act or within the relevant 30-day period as provided in paragraph (1) or (2), social security coverage and taxes by reason of section 210(a)(5)(G) of the Social Security Act and section 3121(b)(5)(G) of the Internal Revenue Code of 1954 shall, with respect to such individual's service in the legislative branch of the Federal Govern-

ment, become effective with the first month beginning after such 30-day period.

(4) The provisions of paragraphs (1) and (2) shall apply only for purposes of reestablishing an exemption from social security coverage and taxes, and do not affect the amount of service to be credited to an individual for purposes of title 5, United States Code.

(e)(1) For purposes of section 210(a)(5) of the Social Security Act (as in effect in January 1983 and as in effect on and after January 1, 1984) and section 3121(b)(5) of the Internal Revenue Code of 1954 (as so in effect), service performed in the employ of a non-profit organization described in section 501(c)(3) of the Internal Revenue Code of 1954 by an employee who is required by law to be subject to subchapter III of chapter 83 of title 5, United States Code, with respect to such service, shall be considered to be service performed in the employ of an instrumentality of the United States.

(2) For purposes of section 203 of the Federal Employees' Retirement Contribution Temporary Adjustment Act of 1983, service described in paragraph (1) which is also "employment" for purposes of title II of the Social Security Act, shall be considered to be "covered service".

P.L. 98-369, §2603(a)(2):

Amended Code Sec. 3121(b)(8) by inserting "(A)" after "(8)", by striking out "this paragraph" and inserting in lieu thereof "this subparagraph", and by adding at the end thereof new subparagraph (B). **Effective** for service performed after 12-31-83. A special rule appears in Act Sec. 2603(f), below.

P.L. 98-369, §2603(f), provides:

(f) In any case where a church or qualified church-controlled organization makes an election under section 3121(w) of the Internal Revenue Code of 1954, the Secretary of the Treasury shall refund (without interest) to such church or organization any taxes paid under sections 3101 and 3111 of such Code with respect to service performed after December 31, 1983, which is covered under such election. The refund shall be conditional upon the church or organization agreeing to pay to each employee (or former employee) the portion of the refund attributable to the tax imposed on such employee (or former employee) under section 3101, and such employee (or former employee) may not receive any other refund payment of such taxes.

P.L. 98-369, §2663(i)(1):

Amended Code Sec. 3121(b)(1) by striking out "(A)" and all that follows down through "or (B)". **Effective** on 7-18-84, but shall not be construed as changing or affecting any right, liability, status, or interpretation which existed (under the provisions of law involved) before that date. Prior to amendment, paragraph (1) of Code Sec. 3121(b) read as follows:

(1) service performed by foreign agricultural workers (A) under contracts entered into in accordance with title V of the Agricultural Act of 1949, as amended (7 U.S.C. 1461-1468), or (B) lawfully admitted to the United States from the Bahamas, Jamaica, and the other British West Indies, or from any other foreign country or possession thereof, on a temporary basis to perform agricultural labor;

P.L. 98-369, §2663(j)(5)(C):

Amended Code Sec. 3121(b)(10)(B) by striking out "Health, Education, and Welfare" and inserting in lieu thereof "Health and Human Services". **Effective** on 7-18-84, but shall not be construed as changing or affecting any right, liability, status, or interpretation which existed (under the provisions of law involved) before that date.

- **1983, Social Security Amendments of 1983 (P.L. 98-21)**

P.L. 98-21, §101(b)(1):

Amended Code Secs. 3121(b)(5) and (6). **Effective** with respect to service performed after 12-31-83. Prior to amendment, Code Sec. 3121(b)(5)-(6) read as follows:

(5) service performed in the employ of any instrumentality of the United States, if such instrumentality is exempt from the tax imposed by section 3111 by virtue of any provision of law which specifically refers to such section (or the corresponding section of prior law) in granting such exemption;

(6)(A) service performed in the employ of the United States or in the employ of any instrumentality of the United States, if such service is covered by a retirement system established by a law of the United States;

(B) service performed by an individual in the employ of an instrumentality of the United States if such instrumentality was exempt from the tax imposed by section 1410 of the Internal Revenue Code of 1939 on December 31, 1950, and if such service is covered by a retirement system established by such instrumentality; except that the provisions of this subparagraph shall not be applicable to—

(i) service performed in the employ of a corporation which is wholly owned by the United States;

(ii) service performed in the employ of a Federal land bank, a Federal intermediate credit bank, a bank for cooperatives, a Federal land bank association, a production credit association, a Federal Reserve Bank, a Federal Home Loan Bank, or a Federal Credit Union;

(iii) service performed in the employ of a State, county, or community committee under the Commodity Stabilization Service;

(iv) service performed by a civilian employee, not compensated from funds appropriated by the Congress, in the Army and Air Force Exchange Service, Army and Air Force Motion Picture Service, Navy Exchanges, Marine Corps Exchanges, or other activities, conducted by an instrumentality of the United States subject to the jurisdiction of the Secretary of Defense, at installations of the Department of Defense for the comfort, pleasure, contentment, and mental and physical improvement of personnel of such Department; or

(v) service performed by a civilian employee, not compensated from funds appropriated by the Congress, in the Coast Guard Exchanges or other activities, conducted by an instrumentality of the United States subject to the jurisdiction of the Secretary of Transportation, at installations of the Coast Guard for the comfort, pleasure, contentment, and mental and physical improvement of personnel of the Coast Guard;

(C) service performed in the employ of the United States or in the employ of any instrumentality of the United States, if such service is performed—

(i) as the President or Vice President of the United States or as a Member, Delegate, or Resident Commissioner of or to the Congress;

(ii) in the legislative branch;

(iii) in a penal institution of the United States by an inmate thereof;

(iv) by any individual as an employee included under section 5351(2) of title 5, United States Code (relating to certain interns, student nurses, and other student employees of hospitals of the Federal Government) other than as a medical or dental intern or a medical or dental resident in training;

(v) by any individual as an employee serving on a temporary basis in case of fire, storm, earthquake, flood, or other similar emergency; or

(vi) by any individual to whom subchapter III of chapter 83 of title 5, United States Code, does not apply because such individual is subject to another retirement system (other than the retirement system of the Tennessee Valley Authority);

P.L. 98-21, §102(b)(1):

Amended Code Sec. 3121(b)(8). **Effective** with respect to service performed after 12-31-83. Prior to amendment, Code Sec. 3121(b)(8) read as follows:

(8)(A) service performed by a duly ordained, commissioned, or licensed minister of a church in the exercise of his ministry or by a member of a religious order in the exercise of duties required by such order, except that this subparagraph shall not apply to service performed by a member of such an order in the exercise of such duties, if an election of coverage under subsection (r) is in effect with respect to such order, or with respect to the autonomous subdivision thereof to which such member belongs;

(B) service performed in the employ of a religious, charitable, educational, or other organization described in section 501(c)(3) which is exempt from income tax under section 501(a), but this subparagraph shall not apply to service performed during the period for which a certificate, filed pursuant to subsection (k) (or the corresponding subsection of prior law) or deemed to have been so filed under paragraph (4) or (5) of such subsection, is in effect if such service is performed by an employee—

(i) whose signature appears on the list filed (or deemed to have been filed) by such organization under subsection (k) (or the corresponding subsection of prior law),

(ii) who became an employee of such organization after the calendar quarter in which the certificate (other than a certificate referred to in clause (iii)) was filed (or deemed to have been filed), or

APPENDIX: Selected Code Sections Affected by the Tax Cuts and Jobs Act   301

(iii) who, after the calendar quarter in which the certificate was (or deemed to have been filed) filed with respect to a group described in section 3121(k)(1)(E), became a member of such group,

except that this subparagraph shall apply with respect to service performed by an employee as a member of a group described in section 3121(k)(1)(E) with respect to which no certificate is (or is deemed to be) in effect;

P.L. 98-21, §322(a)(2):

Amended the material preceding paragraph (1) in Code Sec. 3121(b) by striking out "either" before "(A)", and by inserting before "; except" the following: ", or (C) if it is service, regardless of where or by whom performed, which is designated as employment or recognized as equivalent to employment under an agreement entered into under section 233 of the Social Security Act". **Effective** with respect to tax years beginning on or after 4-20-83.

P.L. 98-21, §323(a)(1):

Amended the material preceding paragraph (1) in Code Sec. 3121(b) by striking out "a citizen of the United States" and inserting in lieu thereof "a citizen or resident of the United States". **Effective** for remuneration paid after 12-31-83.

- **1977 (P.L. 95-216)**

P.L. 95-216, §356(c):

Amended Code Sec. 3121(b)(10). **Effective** for remuneration paid and services rendered after 1977. Before amendment, paragraph (b)(10) read as follows:

(10)(A) service performed in any calendar quarter in the employ of any organization exempt from income tax under section 501(a) (other than an organization described in section 401(a)) or under section 521, if the remuneration for such service is less than $50;

(B) service performed in the employ of—

(i) a school, college, or university, or

(ii) an organization described in section 509(a)(3) if the organization is organized, and at all times thereafter is operated, exclusively for the benefit of, to perform the functions of, or to carry out the purposes of a school, college, or university and is operated, supervised, or controlled by or in connection with such school, college, or university unless it is a school, college, or university of a State or a political subdivision thereof and the services performed in its employ by a student referred to in section 218(c)(5) of the Social Security Act are covered under the agreement between the Secretary of Health, Education, and Welfare and such State entered into pursuant to section 218 of such Act;

if such service is performed by a student who is enrolled and regularly attending classes at such school, college, or university;

P.L. 95-216, §356(d):

Amended Code Sec. 3121(b)(17). **Effective** for remuneration paid and services rendered after 1977. Before amendment, paragraph (b)(17) read as follows:

(17) service in the employ of any organization which is performed (A) in any quarter during any part of which such organization is registered, or there is in effect a final order of the Subversive Activities Control Board requiring such organization to register, under the Internal Security Act of 1950, as amended, as a Communist-action organization, a Communist-front organization, or a Communist-infiltrated organization, and (B) after June 30, 1956;

- **1976 (P.L. 94-563)**

P.L. 94-563, §1b(,d):

Amended Code Sec. 3121(b)(8) by inserting after "filed pursuant to subsection (k) (or the corresponding subsection of prior law)" in the matter preceding clause (i): "or deemed to have been so filed under paragraph (4) or (5) of such subsection;" by inserting after "filed" in clauses (i), (ii), and (iii) the following: "(or deemed to have been filed)"; and by substituting "is (or is deemed to be) in effect" for "is in effect" in the matter following clause (iii). **Effective** for services performed after 1950, to the extent covered by waiver certificates filed or deemed to have been filed under section 3121(k)(4) or (5) of the Internal Revenue Code of 1954 (as added by such amendments).

- **1976, Tax Reform Act of 1976 (P.L. 94-455)**

P.L. 94-455, §1207(e)(1)(A):

Amended Code Sec. 3121(b) by striking out "or" at the end of paragraph (18); by striking out the period at the end of paragraph (19) and inserting in lieu thereof "; or"; and by adding a new paragraph (20).

P.L. 94-455, §1207(f)(4), as amended by P.L. 95-600, §701(z)(1), (2), provides:

(4) SUBSECTION (e).—

(A) The amendments made by paragraphs (1)(A) and (2)(A) of subsection (e) shall apply to services performed after December 31, 1954. The amendments made by paragraphs (1)(B), (1)(C), and (2)(B) of such subsection shall apply to taxable years ending after December 31, 1954. The amendments made by paragraph (3) of such subsection shall apply to calendar years beginning after the date of the enactment of this Act.

(B) Notwithstanding subparagraph (A), if the owner or operator of any boat treated a share of the boat's catch of fish or other aquatic animal life (or a share of the proceeds therefrom) received by an individual after December 31, 1954, and before the date of the enactment of this Act for services performed by such individual after December 31, 1954, on such boat as being subject to the tax under chapter 21 of the Internal Revenue Code of 1954, then the amendments made by paragraphs (1)(A) and (B) and (2) of subsection (e) shall not apply with respect to such services performed by such individual (and the share of the catch, or proceeds therefrom, received by him for such services).

P.L. 94-455, §1903(a)(3)(A):

Substituted ", of whatever nature, performed" for "performed after 1936 and prior to 1955 which was employment for purposes of subchapter A of chapter 9 of the Internal Revenue Code of 1939 under the law applicable to the period in which such service was performed, and any service, of whatever nature, performed after 1954"; and deleted ", in the case of service performed after 1954," in Code Sec. 3121(b). **Effective** for wages paid after 12-31-76.

P.L. 94-455, §1903(a)(3)(B):

Deleted "65 Stat. 119;" in Code Sec. 3121(b)(1). **Effective** for wages paid after 12-31-76.

P.L. 94-455, §1903(a)(3)(A)(C):

Substituted "Secretary of Transportation" for "Secretary of the Treasury" in Code Sec. 3121(b)(6)(B)(v). **Effective** for wages paid after 12-31-76.

P.L. 94-455, §1906(b)(13)(C):

Substituted "to the Secretary of the Treasury" for "to the Secretary" in Code Sec. 3121(b)(12)(B). **Effective** 2-1-77.

- **1972, Social Security Amendments of 1972 (P.L. 92-603)**

P.L. 92-603, §123(a)(2):

Added at the end of Code Sec. 3121(b)(8)(A): ", except that this subparagraph shall not apply to service performed by a member of such an order in the exercise of such duties, if an election of coverage under subsection (r) is in effect with respect to such order, or with respect to the autonomous subdivision thereof to which such member belongs". For **effective** date, see Code Sec. 3121(r).

P.L. 92-603, §125(a), provides:

"The provisions of section 210(a)(6)(B)(ii) of the Social Security Act and section 3121(b)(6)(B)(ii) of the Internal Revenue Code of 1954, insofar as they relate to service performed in the employ of a Federal home loan bank, shall be effective—

"(1) with respect to all service performed in the employ of a Federal home loan bank on and after the first day of the first calendar quarter which begins on or after the date of the enactment of this Act [October 30, 1972]; and

"(2) in the case of individuals who are in the employ of a Federal home loan bank on such first day, with respect to any service performed in the employ of a Federal home loan bank after the last day of the sixth calendar year preceding the year in which this Act is enacted: but this paragraph shall be effective only if an amount equal to the taxes imposed by sections 3101 and 3111 of such Code with respect to the services of all such individuals performed in the employ of Federal home loan banks after the last day of the sixth calendar year preceding the year in which this Act is enacted are paid under the provisions of section 3122 of such Code by July 1, 1973, or by such later date as may be provided in an agreement entered into before such date with the Secretary of the Treasury or his delegate for purposes of this paragraph."

P.L. 92-603, §128(b):

Added Code Sec. 3121(b)(7)(D). **Effective** for service performed on and after 1-1-73.

Code Sec. 3121

P.L. 92-603, § 129(a)(2):
Amended Code Sec. 3121(b)(10)(B). **Effective** for services performed after 12-31-72. Prior to amendment, said section read as follows:

"(B) service performed in the employ of a school, college, or university if such service is performed by a student who is enrolled and is regularly attending classes at such school, college, or university."

- **1968, Social Security Amendments of 1967 (P.L. 90-248)**

P.L. 90-248, § 123(b):
Amended Sec. 3121(b)(3)(B). **Effective** with respect to services performed after 12-31-67. Prior to amendment, Sec. 3121(b)(3)(B) read as follows:

"(B) service not in the course of the employer's trade or business, or domestic service in a private home of the employer, performed by an individual in the employ of his son or daughter;"

P.L. 90-248, § 403(i):
Amended Secs. 3121(b)(6)(C)(iv) and 3121(b)(7)(C)(ii) by substituting "under section 5351(2) of title 5, United States Code" for "under section 2 of the Act of August 4, 1947" and by deleting "; 5 U.S.C. 1052" which formerly appeared after the word "Government;" in both Code sections. Also amended Sec. 3121(b)(6)(C)(vi) by substituting "subchapter III of chapter 83 of title 5, United States Code" for "the Civil Service Retirement Act".

- **1965, Social Security Amendments of 1965 (P.L. 89-97)**

P.L. 89-97, § 103(o):
Amended Code Sec. 3121(b) by striking out "or" at the end of paragraph (16), by striking out the period at the end of paragraph (17) and substituting "; or", and by adding a new paragraph (18). **Effective** for service performed after 1960.

P.L. 89-97, § 104(b):
Amended paragraph (3) of Code Sec. 3121(b). **Effective** for services performed after 1960. Prior to amendment, it read as follows:

"(3) service performed by an individual in the employ of his son, daughter, or spouse, and service performed by a child under the age of 21 in the employ of his father or mother;".

P.L. 89-97, §§ 311, 317(b):
Amended Sec. 3121(b)(6)(C)(iv) by inserting before the semicolon at the end ", other than as a medical or dental intern or a medical or dental resident in training"; Amended Sec. 3121(b)(13) by striking out all that followed the first semicolon, "and thereof, or any instrumentality of any one or more of the foregoing wholly owned thereby, which is performed after 1960 and after the calendar quarter in which the Secretary of the Treasury receives a certification by the Governor of American Samoa that the Government of American Samoa desires to have the insurance system established by such title II extended to the officers and employees of such Government and such political subdivisions and instrumentalities."

- **1959, Farm Credit Act of 1959 (P.L. 86-168)**

P.L. 86-168, § 104(h):
Amended Code Sec. 3121(b)(6)(B)(ii) by substituting "Federal land bank association" for "national farm loan association". **Effective** 12-31-59.

P.L. 86-168, § 202(a):
Amended Code Sec. 3121(b)(6)(B)(ii) by adding "a Federal land bank, a Federal intermediate credit bank, a bank for cooperatives,". **Effective** 1-1-60.

- **1958, Social Security Amendments of 1958 (P.L. 85-840)**

P.L. 85-840, § 404(a):
Amended Sec. 3121(b)(1). **Effective** for service performed after 1958. Prior to amendment Sec. 3121(b)(1) read as follows:

"(1)(A) service performed in connection with the production or harvesting of any commodity defined as an agricultural commodity in section 15(g) of the Agricultural Marketing Act, as amended (46 Stat. 1550 § 3; 12 U. S. C. 1141j);

"(B) service performed by foreign agricultural workers (i) under contracts entered into in accordance with title V of the Agricultural Act of 1949, as amended (65 Stat. 119; 7 U. S. C. 1461-1468), or (ii) lawfully admitted to the United States from the Bahamas, Jamaica, and the other British West Indies, or from any other foreign country or possession thereof, on a temporary basis to perform agricultural labor;".

P.L. 85-840, § 405(b):
Amended Sec. 3121(b)(8)(B). **Effective** for certificates filed under Sec. 3121(k)(1) after 8-28-58 and requests filed under subparagraph (F) of that section after that date. Prior to amendment, Sec. 3121(b)(8)(B) read as follows:

"(B) service performed in the employ of a religious, charitable, educational, or other organization described in section 501(c)(3) which is exempt from income tax under section 501(a), but this subparagraph shall not apply to service performed during the period for which a certificate, filed pursuant to subsection (k) (or the corresponding subsection of prior law), is in effect if such service is performed by an employee—

"(i) whose signature appears on the list filed by such organization under subsection (k) (or the corresponding subsection of prior law), or

"(ii) who became an employee of such organization after the calendar quarter in which the certificate was filed;".

- **1956, Social Security Amendments of 1956 (P.L. 880, 84th Cong.)**

P.L. 880, 84th Cong., 2d Sess., § 201(c):
Amended Sec. 3121(b)(1). **Effective** for service performed after 1956. Prior to amendment Sec. 3121(b)(1) read as follows:

"(1)(A) service performed in connection with the production or harvesting of any commodity defined as an agricultural commodity in section 15(g) of the Agricultural Marketing Act, as amended (46 Stat. 1550 § 3; 12 U. S. C. 1141j);

"(B) service performed by foreign agricultural workers (i) under contracts entered into in accordance with title V of the Agricultural Act of 1949, as amended (65 Stat. 119; 7 U. S. C. 1461-1468), or (ii) lawfully admitted to the United States from the Bahamas, Jamaica, and the other British West Indies on a temporary basis to perform agricultural labor;".

P.L. 880, 84th Cong., 2d Sess., § 201(d)(1):
Amended Sec. 3121(b)(6)(B)(ii) by adding the following: "a Federal Home Loan Bank,". § 201(d)(2) amended Sec. 3121(b)(6)(C)(vi) by deleting "of 1930" following the words "Civil Service Retirement Act" and by adding the following: "(other than the retirement system of the Tennessee Valley Authority)". These amendments are identical with the amendments made by § 104(b) of P.L. 880 to Social Security Act Sec. 210 and the **effective** dates in § 104(i) of P.L. 880 apply. These provide as follows:

"(2)(A) Except as provided in subparagraphs (B) and (C), the amendments made by subsection (b) shall apply only with respect to service performed after June 30, 1957, and only if—

"(i) in the case of the amendment made by paragraph (1) of such subsection, the conditions prescribed in subparagraph (B) are met; and

"(ii) in the case of the amendment made by paragraph (2) of such subsection, the conditions prescribed in subparagraph (C) are met.

"(B) the amendment made by paragraph (1) of subsection (b) shall be effective only if—

"(i) the Federal Home Loan Bank Board submits to the Secretary of Health, Education, and Welfare, and the Secretary approves, before July 1, 1957, a plan, with respect to employees of Federal Home Loan Banks, for the coordination, on an equitable basis, of the benefits provided by the retirement system applicable to such employees with the benefits provided by title II of the Social Security Act; and

"(ii) such plan specifies, as the effective date of the plan July 1, 1957, or the first day of a prior calendar quarter beginning not earlier than January 1, 1956.

If the plan specifies as the effective date of the plan a day before July 1, 1957, the amendment made by paragraph (1) of subsection (b) shall apply with respect to service performed on or after such effective date; except that, if such effective date is prior to the day on which the Secretary approves the plan, such amendment shall not apply with respect to service performed, prior to the day on which the Secretary approves the plan, by an individual who is not an employee of a Federal Home Loan Bank on such day.

"(C) The amendment made by paragraph (2) of subsection (b) shall be effective only if—

"(i) the Board of Directors of the Tennessee Valley Authority submits to the Secretary of Health, Education, and Welfare, and the Secretary approves, before July 1, 1957, a plan, with respect to employees of the Tennessee Valley Authority, for the coordination, on an equitable basis, of the benefits provided by the retirement system applicable to such employees with the benefits provided by title II of the Social Security Act; and

"(ii) such plan specifies as the effective date of the plan July 1, 1957, or the first day of a prior calendar quarter beginning not earlier than January 1, 1956.

If the plan specifies as the effective date of the plan a day before July 1, 1957, the amendment made by paragraph (2) of subsection (b) shall apply with respect to service performed on or after such effective date; except that, if such effective date is prior to the day on which the Secretary approves the plan, such amendment shall not apply with respect to service performed, prior to the day on which the Secretary approves the plan, by an individual who is not an employee of the Tennessee Valley Authority on such day.

"(D) The Secretary of Health, Education, and Welfare shall, on or before July 31, 1957, submit a report to the Congress setting forth the details of any plan approved by him under subparagraph (B) or (C)."

P.L. 880, 84th Cong., 2d Sess., §201(e)(1):

Amended Sec. 3121(b) by deleting the "or" after paragraph (14); substituting a semicolon for the period after paragraph (15); and by adding paragraph (16). **Effective** for service performed after 1954.

P.L. 880, 84th Cong., 2d Sess., §121(d):

Amended Sec. 3121(b) by adding paragraph (17).

- **1954, Social Security Amendments of 1954 (P.L. 761, 83rd Cong.).**

P.L. 761, 83rd Cong., §205(a):

Amended paragraph (1). Prior to amendment, paragraph (1) read as follows:

"(1)(A) agricultural labor (as defined in subsection (g)) performed in any calendar quarter by an employee, unless the cash remuneration paid for such labor (other than service described in subparagraph (B)) is $50 or more and such labor is performed for an employer by an individual who is regularly employed by such employer to perform such agricultural labor. For purposes of this subparagraph, an individual shall be deemed to be regularly employed by an employer during a calendar quarter only if—

"(i) such individual performs agricultural labor (other than service described in subparagraph (B)) for such employer on a full-time basis on 60 days during such quarter, and

"(ii) the quarter was immediately preceded by a qualifying quarter.

For purposes of the preceding sentence, the term 'qualifying quarter' means—

"(I) any quarter during all of which such individual was continuously employed by such employer, or

"(II) any subsequent quarter which meets the test of clause (i) if, after the last quarter during all of which such individual was continuously employed by such employer, each intervening quarter met the test of clause (i).

Notwithstanding the preceding provisions of this subparagraph, an individual shall also be deemed to be regularly employed by an employer during a calendar quarter if such individual was regularly employed (upon application of clauses (i) and (ii)) by such employer during the preceding calendar quarter;

"(B) service performed in connection with the production or harvesting of any commodity defined as an agricultural commodity in section 15(g) of the Agricultural Marketing Act, as amended (46 Stat. 1550, §3; 12 U. S. C. 1141j), or in connection with the ginning of cotton;

"(C) service performed by foreign agricultural workers under contracts entered into in accordance with title V of the Agricultural Act of 1949, as amended (65 Stat. 119; 7 U. S. C. 1461-1468);".

P.L. 761, 83rd Cong., §205(b):

Deleted paragraph (3) and renumbered paragraphs (4), (5), (6), (7), (8), (9), (10), (11), (12), (13), and (14), as paragraphs (3), (4), (5), (6), (7), (8), (9), (10), (11), (12), and (13), respectively. Prior to deletion, former paragraph (3) read as follows:

"(3) service not in the course of the employer's trade or business performed in any calendar quarter by an employee, unless the cash remuneration paid for such service is $50 or more and such service is performed by an individual who is regularly employed by such employer to perform such service. For purposes of this paragraph, an individual shall be deemed to be regularly employed by an employer during a calendar quarter only if—

"(A) on each of some 24 days during such quarter such individual performs for such employer for some portion of the day service not in the course of the employer's trade or business, or

"(B) such individual was regularly employed (as determined under subparagraph (A)) by such employer in the performance of such service during the preceding calendar quarter.

As used in this paragraph, the term 'service not in the course of the employer's trade or business' does not include domestic service in a private home of the employer and does not include service described in subsection (g)(5);".

P.L. 761, 83rd Cong., §205(c):

Amended the redesignated paragraph (4) by substituting the language "if (A) the individual is employed on and in connection with such vessel or aircraft, when outside the United States and (B)(i) such individual is not a citizen of the United States or (ii) the employer is not an American employer" for the language "if the individual is employed on and in connection with such vessel or aircraft when outside the United States".

P.L. 761, 83rd Cong., §205(d)(1)(A):

Amended the redesignated subparagraph (6)(B) by inserting "by an individual" after "service performed", and by inserting "and if such service is covered by a retirement system established by such instrumentality;" after "December 31, 1950,".

P.L. 761, 83rd Cong., §205(d)(1)(B):

Amended the redesignated subparagraph (6)(B) by deleting "or" at the end of clause (iii), by adding "or" at the end of clause (iv), and by adding clause (v).

P.L. 761, 83rd Cong., §205(d)(2):

Amended subparagraph (6)(C). Prior to amendment, subparagraph (6)(C) read as follows:

"(C) service performed in the employ of the United States or in the employ of any instrumentality of the United States, if such service is performed—

"(i) as the President or Vice President of the United States or as a Member, Delegate, or Resident Commissioner, of or to the Congress;

"(ii) in the legislative branch;

"(iii) in the field service of the Post Office Department unless performed by any individual as an employee who is excluded by Executive order from the operation of the Civil Service Retirement Act of 1930 (46 Stat. 470; 5 U. S. C. 693) because he is serving under a temporary appointment pending final determination of eligibility for permanent or indefinite appointment;

"(iv) in or under the Bureau of the Census of the Department of Commerce by temporary employees employed for the taking of any census;

"(v) by any individual as an employee who is excluded by Executive order from the operation of the Civil Service Retirement Act of 1930 (46 Stat. 470; 5 U. S. C. 693) because he is paid on a contract or fee basis;

"(vi) by any individual as an employee receiving nominal compensation of $12 or less per annum;

"(vii) in a hospital, home, or other institution of the United States by a patient or inmate thereof;

"(viii) by any individual as a consular agent appointed under authority of section 551 of the Foreign Service Act of 1946 (60 Stat. 1011; 22 U. S. C. 951);

"(ix) by any individual as an employee included under section 2 of the Act of August 4, 1947 (relating to certain interns, student nurses, and other student employees of hospitals of the Federal Government) (61 Stat. 727; 5 U.S.C. 1052);

"(x) by any individual as an employee serving on a temporary basis in case of fire, storm, earthquake, flood, or other similar emergency;

"(xi) by any individual as an employee who is employed under a Federal relief program to relieve him from unemployment;

"(xii) as a member of a State, county, or community committee under the Commodity Stabilization Service or of any other board, council, committee, or other similar body, unless such board, council, committee, or other body is composed exclusively of individuals otherwise in the full-time employ of the United States; or

"(xiii) by an individual to whom the Civil Service Retirement Act of 1930 (46 Stat. 470; 5 U. S. C. 693) does not apply because such individual is subject to another retirement system;".

P.L. 761, 83rd Cong., § 205(e):

Deleted paragraph (15) and renumbered paragraphs (16) and (17) as paragraphs (15) and (16), respectively. Prior to deletion, former paragraph (15) read as follows:

"(15) service performed by an individual in (or as an officer or member of the crew of a vessel while it is engaged in) the catching, taking, harvesting, cultivating, or farming of any kind of fish, shellfish, crustacea, sponges, seaweeds, or other aquatic forms of animal and vegetable life (including service performed by any such individual as an ordinary incident to any such activity), except—

"(A) service performed in connection with the catching or taking of salmon or halibut, for commercial purposes, and

"(B) service performed on or in connection with a vessel of more than 10 net tons (determined in the manner provided for determining the register tonnage of merchant vessels under the laws of the United States);".

[Sec. 3121(c)]

(c) INCLUDED AND EXCLUDED SERVICE.—For purposes of this chapter, if the services performed during one-half or more of any pay period by an employee for the person employing him constitute employment, all the services of such employee for such period shall be deemed to be employment; but if the services performed during more than one-half of any such pay period by an employee for the person employing him do not constitute employment, then none of the services of such employee for such period shall be deemed to be employment. As used in this subsection, the term "pay period" means a period (of not more than 31 consecutive days) for which a payment of remuneration is ordinarily made to the employee by the person employing him. This subsection shall not be applicable with respect to services performed in a pay period by an employee for the person employing him, where any of such service is excepted by subsection (b)(9).

[Sec. 3121(d)]

(d) EMPLOYEE.—For purposes of this chapter, the term "employee" means—

(1) any officer of a corporation; or

(2) any individual who, under the usual common law rules applicable in determining the employer-employee relationship, has the status of an employee; or

(3) any individual (other than an individual who is an employee under paragraph (1) or (2)) who performs services for remuneration for any person—

(A) as an agent-driver or commission-driver engaged in distributing meat products, vegetable products, bakery products, beverages (other than milk), or laundry or dry-cleaning services, for his principal;

(B) as a full-time life insurance salesman;

(C) as a home worker performing work, according to specifications furnished by the person for whom the services are performed, on materials or goods furnished by such person which are required to be returned to such person or a person designated by him; or

(D) as a traveling or city salesman, other than as an agent-driver or commission-driver, engaged upon a full-time basis in the solicitation on behalf of, and the transmission to, his principal (except for side-line sales activities on behalf of some other person) of orders from wholesalers, retailers, contractors, or operators of hotels, restaurants, or other similar establishments for merchandise for resale or supplies for use in their business operations;

if the contract of service contemplates that substantially all of such services are to be performed personally by such individual; except that an individual shall not be included in the term "employee" under the provisions of this paragraph if such individual has a substantial investment in facilities used in connection with the performance of such services (other than in facilities for transportation), or if the services are in the nature of a single transaction not part of a continuing relationship with the person for whom the services are performed; or

(4) any individual who performs services that are included under an agreement entered into pursuant to section 218 or 218A of the Social Security Act.

Amendments

• **2018, Tribal Social Security Fairness Act of 2018 (P.L. 115-243)**

P.L. 115-243, § 2(b)(2)(B):

Amended Code Sec. 3121(d)(4) by inserting "or 218A" after "section 218". **Effective** 9-20-2018.

P.L. 115-243, § 2(c), provides:

(c) RULE OF CONSTRUCTION.—Nothing in this Act or the amendments made by this Act shall be construed to affect application of any Federal income tax withholding requirements under the Internal Revenue Code of 1986.

• **1997, Taxpayer Relief Act of 1997 (P.L. 105-34)**

P.L. 105-34, § 921, provides:

ACT SEC. 921. CLARIFICATION OF STANDARD TO BE USED IN DETERMINING EMPLOYMENT TAX STATUS OF SECURITIES BROKERS.

(a) IN GENERAL.—In determining for purposes of the Internal Revenue Code of 1986 whether a registered representative of a securities broker-dealer is an employee (as defined in section 3121(d) of the Internal Revenue Code of 1986), no weight shall be given to instructions from the service recipient which are imposed only in compliance with investor protection standards imposed by the Federal Government, any State government, or a governing body pursuant to a delegation by a Federal or State agency.

(b) EFFECTIVE DATE.—Subsection (a) shall apply to services performed after December 31, 1997.

• **1988, Technical and Miscellaneous Revenue Act of 1988 (P.L. 100-647)**

P.L. 100-647, § 8016(a)(3)(A)(i)-(ii):

Amended Code Sec. 3121(d) by redesignating paragraph (3) as paragraph (4), by striking "; or" at the end of such paragraph and inserting a period, and by moving such paragraph (as so redesignated and amended) to the end of the subsection; and by redesignating paragraph (4) as paragraph (3), and by striking the period at the end and inserting "; or". For the **effective** date, see Act Sec. 8016(b), below.

P.L. 100-647, § 8016(b), provides:

(b) EFFECTIVE DATE.—(1) Except as provided in paragraph (2), the amendments made by this section shall be effective on the date of the enactment of this Act.

(2) Any amendment made by this section to a provision of a particular Public Law which is referred to by its number, or to a provision of the Social Security Act or the Internal Revenue Code of 1986 as added or amended by a provision of a particular Public Law which is so referred to, shall be effective as though it had been included or reflected in the relevant provisions of that Public Law at the time of its enactment.

- **1986, Omnibus Budget Reconciliation Act of 1986 (P.L. 99-509)**

P.L. 99-509, §9002(b)(2)(A):

Amended Code Sec. 3121(d) by redesignating paragraph (3) as paragraph (4), and by inserting after paragraph (2) new paragraph (3). For the **effective** date, see Act Sec. 9002(d), below.

P.L. 99-509, §9002(d), provides:

(d) EFFECTIVE DATE.—The amendments made by this section are effective with respect to payments due with respect to wages paid after December 31, 1986, including wages paid after such date by a State (or political subdivision thereof) that modified its agreement pursuant to the provisions of section 218(e)(2) of the Social Security Act prior to the date of the enactment of this Act; except that in cases where, in accordance with the currently applicable schedule, deposits of taxes due under an agreement entered into pursuant to section 218 of the Social Security Act would be required within 3 days after the close of an eighth-monthly period, such 3-day requirement shall be changed to a 7-day requirement for wages paid prior to October 1, 1987, and to a 5-day requirement for wages paid after September 30, 1987, and prior to October 1, 1988. For wages paid prior to October 1, 1988, the deposit schedule for taxes imposed under sections 3101 and 3111 shall be determined separately from the deposit schedule for taxes withheld under section 3402 if the taxes imposed under sections 3101 and 3111 are due with respect to service included under an agreement entered into pursuant to section 218 of the Social Security Act.

- **1954, Social Security Amendments of 1954 (P.L. 761, 83rd Cong.)**

P.L. 761, 83rd Cong., §206(a):

Amended subparagraph (C) by deleting ", if the performance of such services is subject to licensing requirements under the laws of the State in which such services are performed" following "designated by him". **Effective** 1-1-55.

[Sec. 3121(e)]

(e) STATE, UNITED STATES, AND CITIZEN.—For purposes of this chapter—

(1) STATE.—The term "State" includes the District of Columbia, the Commonwealth of Puerto Rico, the Virgin Islands, Guam, and American Samoa.

(2) UNITED STATES.—The term "United States" when used in a geographical sense includes the Commonwealth of Puerto Rico, the Virgin Islands, Guam, and American Samoa.

An individual who is a citizen of the Commonwealth of Puerto Rico (but not otherwise a citizen of the United States) shall be considered, for purposes of this section, as a citizen of the United States.

Amendments

- **1960, Social Security Amendments of 1960 (P.L. 86-778)**

P.L. 86-778, §103(p):

Amended Code Sec. 3121(e). **Effective** for service performed after 1960. Prior to amendment it read as follows:

"(e) State, United States, and Citizen.—For purposes of this chapter—

"(1) State.—The term 'State' includes Hawaii, the District of Columbia, Puerto Rico, and the Virgin Islands.

"(2) United States.—The term 'United States' when used in a geographical sense includes Puerto Rico and the Virgin Islands.

An individual who is a citizen of Puerto Rico (but not otherwise a citizen of the United States) shall be considered, for purposes of this section, as a citizen of the United States."

- **1960, Hawaii Omnibus Act (P.L. 86-624)**

P.L. 86-624, §18(c):

Amended 1954 Code Sec. 3121(e)(1) by striking out "Hawaii," where it appeared following "includes". **Effective** 8-21-59.

- **1959, Alaska Omnibus Bill (P.L. 86-70)**

P.L. 86-70, §22(a):

Amended 1954 Code Sec. 3121(e)(1) by striking out "Alaska," where it appeared following "includes". **Effective** 1-3-59.

[Sec. 3121(f)]

(f) AMERICAN VESSEL AND AIRCRAFT.—For purposes of this chapter, the term "American vessel" means any vessel documented or numbered under the laws of the United States; and includes any vessel which is neither documented or numbered under the laws of the United States nor documented under the laws of any foreign country, if its crew is employed solely by one or more citizens or residents of the United States or corporations organized under the laws of the United States or of any State; and the term "American aircraft" means an aircraft registered under the laws of the United States.

[Sec. 3121(g)]

(g) AGRICULTURAL LABOR.—For purposes of this chapter, the term "agricultural labor" includes all service performed—

(1) on a farm, in the employ of any person, in connection with cultivating the soil, or in connection with raising or harvesting any agricultural or horticultural commodity, including the raising, shearing, feeding, caring for, training, and management of livestock, bees, poultry, and fur-bearing animals and wildlife;

(2) in the employ of the owner or tenant or other operator of a farm, in connection with the operation, management, conservation, improvement, or maintenance of such farm and its tools and equipment, or in salvaging timber or clearing land of brush and other debris left by a hurricane, if the major part of such service is performed on a farm;

(3) in connection with the production or harvesting of any commodity defined as an agricultural commodity in section 15(g) of the Agricultural Marketing Act, as amended (12 U.S.C. 1141(j), or in connection with the ginning of cotton, or in connection with the operation or maintenance of ditches, canals, reservoirs, or waterways, not owned or operated for profit, used exclusively for supplying and storing water for farming purposes;

(4)(A) in the employ of the operator of a farm in handling, planting, drying, packing, packaging, processing, freezing, grading, storing, or delivering to storage or to market or to a carrier for transportation to market, in its unmanufactured state, any agricultural or horticultural commodity; but only if such operator produced more than one-half of the commodity with respect to which such service is performed;

(B) in the employ of a group of operators of farms (other than a co-operative organization) in the performance of service described in subparagraph (A), but only if such operators produced all of the commodity with respect to which such service is performed. For purposes of this subparagraph, any unincorporated group of operators shall be deemed a cooperative organization if the number of operators comprising such group is more than 20 at any time during the calendar year in which such service is performed;

(C) the provisions of subparagraphs (A) and (B) shall not be deemed to be applicable with respect to service performed in connection with commercial canning or commercial freezing or in connection with any agricultural or horticultural commodity after its delivery to a terminal market for distribution for consumption; or

(5) on a farm operated for profit if such service is not in the course of the employer's trade or business.

As used in this subsection, the term "farm" includes stock, dairy, poultry, fruit, fur-bearing animal, and truck farms, plantations, ranches, nurseries, ranges, greenhouses or other similar structures used primarily for the raising of agricultural or horticultural commodities, and orchards.

Amendments

- **2004, Social Security Protection Act of 2004 (P.L. 108-203)**

P.L. 108-203, § 423(c):

Amended Code Sec. 3121(g)(5) by striking "or is domestic service in a private home of the employer" before the period. **Effective** 3-2-2004.

- **1977 (P.L. 95-216)**

P.L. 95-216, § 356(d):

Amended Code Sec. 3121(g)(4)(B). **Effective** for remuneration paid and services rendered after 1977. Before amendment, paragraph (g)(4)(B) read as follows:

(B) in the employ of a group of operators of farms (other than a co-operative organization) in the performance of service described in subparagraph (A), but only if such operators produced all of the commodity with respect to which such service is performed. For purposes of this subparagraph, any unincorporated group of operators shall be deemed a cooperative organization if the number of operators comprising such group is more than 20 at any time during the calendar quarter in which such service is performed;

- **1976, Tax Reform Act of 1976 (P.L. 94-455)**

P.L. 94-455, § 1903(a)(3)(D), (d):

Deleted "46 Stat. 1550, § 3;" in Code Sec. 3121(g)(3). **Effective** for wages paid after 12-31-76.

[Sec. 3121(h)]

(h) AMERICAN EMPLOYER.—For purposes of this chapter, the term "American employer" means an employer which is—

(1) the United States or any instrumentality thereof,

(2) an individual who is a resident of the United States,

(3) a partnership, if two-thirds or more of the partners are residents of the United States,

(4) a trust, if all of the trustees are residents of the United States, or

(5) a corporation organized under the laws of the United States or of any State.

[Sec. 3121(i)]

(i) COMPUTATION OF WAGES IN CERTAIN CASES.—

(1) DOMESTIC SERVICE.—For purposes of this chapter, in the case of domestic service described in subsection (a)(7)(B), any payment of cash remuneration for such service which is more or less than a whole-dollar amount shall, under such conditions and to such extent as may be prescribed by regulations made under this chapter, be computed to the nearest dollar. For the purpose of the computation to the nearest dollar, the payment of a fractional part of a dollar shall be disregarded unless it amounts to one-half dollar or more, in which case it shall be increased to $1. The amount of any payment of cash remuneration so computed to the nearest dollar shall, in lieu of the amount actually paid, be deemed to constitute the amount of cash remuneration for purposes of subsection (a)(7)(B).

(2) SERVICE IN THE UNIFORMED SERVICES.—For purposes of this chapter, in the case of an individual performing service, as a member of a uniformed service, to which the provisions of subsection (m)(1) are applicable, the term "wages" shall, subject to the provisions of subsection (a)(1) of this section, include as such individual's remuneration for such service only (A) his basic pay as described in chapter 3 and section 1009 of title 37, United States Code, in the case of an individual performing services to which subparagraph (A) of such subsection (m)(1) applies, or (B) his compensation for such service as determined under Section 206(a) of title 37, United States Code, in the case of an individual performing service to which subparagraph (B) of such subsection (m)(1) applies.

(3) PEACE CORPS VOLUNTEER SERVICE.—For purposes of this chapter, in the case of an individual performing service, as a volunteer or volunteer leader within the meaning of the Peace Corps Act, to which the provisions of section 3121(p) are applicable, the term "wages" shall, subject to the provisions of subsection (a)(1) of this section, include as such individual's remuneration for such service only amounts paid pursuant to section 5(c) or 6(1) of the Peace Corps Act.

(4) SERVICE PERFORMED BY CERTAIN MEMBERS OF RELIGIOUS ORDERS.—For purposes of this chapter, in any case where an individual is a member of a religious order (as defined in subsection (r)(2)) performing service in the exercise of duties required by such order, and an election of coverage under subsection (r) is in effect with respect to such order or with respect to the autonomous subdivision thereof to which such member belongs, the term "wages" shall, subject to the provisions of subsection (a)(1), include as such individual's remuneration for such service the fair market value of any board, lodging, clothing, and other perquisites furnished to such member by

such order or subdivision thereof or by any other person or organization pursuant to an agreement with such order or subdivision, except that the amount included as such individual's remuneration under this paragraph shall not be less than $100 a month.

(5) SERVICE PERFORMED BY CERTAIN RETIRED JUSTICES AND JUDGES.—For purposes of this chapter, in the case of an individual performing service under the provisions of section 294 of title 28, United States Code (relating to assignment of retired justices and judges to active duty), the term "wages" shall not include any payment under section 371(b) of such title 28 which is received during the period of such service.

Amendments

- **1987, Revenue Act of 1987 (P.L. 100-203)**

P.L. 100-203, §9001(b)(2):

Amended Code Sec. 3121(i)(2) by striking "only his basic pay" and all that follows and inserting "only (A) his basic pay as described in chapter 3 and section 1009 of title 37, United States Code, in the case of an individual performing service to which subparagraph (A) of such subsection (m)(1) applies, or (B) his compensation for such service as determined under section 206(a) of title 37, United States Code, in the case of an individual performing service to which subparagraph (B) of such subsection (m)(1) applies." **Effective** with respect to renumeration paid after 12-31-87.

- **1986, Consolidated Omnibus Budget Reconciliation Act of 1985 (P.L. 99-272)**

P.L. 99-272, §12112(b):

Amended Code Sec. 3121(i)(5) by striking out "shall, subject to the provisions of subsection (a)(1) of this section, include" and inserting in lieu thereof "shall not include". **Effective** with respect to service performed after 12-31-83.

- **1984, Deficit Reduction Act of 1984 (P.L. 98-369)**

P.L. 98-369, §2663(i)(2):

Amended Code Sec. 3121(i)(2) by striking out "section 102(10) of the Servicemen's and Veterans' Survivor Benefits Act" and inserting in lieu thereof "chapter 3 and section 1009 of title 37, United States Code". **Effective** 7-18-84, but it shall not be construed as changing or affecting any right, liability, status, or interpretation which existed (under the provisions of law involved) before that date.

- **1983, Social Security Act of 1983 (P.L. 98-21)**

P.L. 98-21, §101(c)(2):

Added paragraph (5) to Code Sec. 3121(i). **Effective** with respect to service performed after 12-31-83.

- **1972, Social Security Amendments of 1972 (P.L. 92-603)**

P.L. 92-603, §123(c)(2):

Added paragraph (4) to Code Sec. 3121(i). **Effective** 10-30-72.

- **1961, Peace Corps Act (P.L. 87-293)**

P.L. 87-293, §202(a)(1):

Added Code Sec. 1321(i)(3). **Effective** with respect to services performed after 9-22-61.

- **1956, Servicemen's and Veterans' Survivor Benefits Act (P.L. 881, 84th cong.)**

P.L. 881, 84th Cong., §410:

Amended Sec. 3121(i) by inserting "(1) Domestic Service.—" preceding the first sentence and by adding paragraph (2). **Effective** 1-1-57.

[Sec. 3121(j)]

(j) COVERED TRANSPORTATION SERVICE.—For purposes of this chapter—

(1) EXISTING TRANSPORTATION SYSTEMS—GENERAL RULE.—Except as provided in in paragraph (2), all service performed in the employ of a State or political subdivision in connection with its operation of a public transportation system shall constitute covered transportation service if any part of the transportation system was acquired from private ownership after 1936 and prior to 1951.

(2) EXISTING TRANSPORTATION SYSTEMS—CASES IN WHICH NO TRANSPORTATION EMPLOYEES, OR ONLY CERTAIN EMPLOYEES, ARE COVERED.—Service performed in the employ of a State or political subdivision in connection with the operation of its public transportation system shall not constitute covered transportation service if—

(A) any part of the transportation system was acquired from private ownership after 1936 and prior to 1951, and substantially all service in connection with the operation of the transportation system was, on December 31, 1950, covered under a general retirement system providing benefits which, by reason of a provision of the State constitution dealing specifically with retirement systems of the State or political subdivisions thereof, cannot be diminished or impaired; or

(B) no part of the transportation system operated by the State or political subdivision on December 31, 1950, was acquired from private ownership after 1936 and prior to 1951;

except that if such State or political subdivision makes an acquisition after 1950 from private ownership of any part of its transportation system, then, in the case of any employee who—

(C) became an employee of such State or political subdivision in connection with and at the time of its acquisition after 1950 of such part, and

(D) prior to such acquisition rendered service in employment (including as employment service covered by an agreement under section 218 of the Social Security Act) in connection with the operation of such part of the transportation system acquired by the State or political subdivision,

the service of such employee in connection with the operation of the transportation system shall constitute covered transportation service, commencing with the first day of the third calendar quarter following the calendar quarter in which the acquisition of such part took place, unless on such first day such service of such employee is covered by a general retirement system which does not, with respect to such employee, contain special provisions applicable only to employees described in subparagraph (C).

(3) TRANSPORTATION SYSTEMS ACQUIRED AFTER 1950.—All service performed in the employ of a State or political subdivision thereof in connection with its operation of a public transportation system shall constitute covered transportation service if the transportation system was not operated by the State or political subdivision prior to 1951 and, at the time of its first acquisition (after 1950) from private ownership of any part of its transportation system, the State or political

subdivision did not have a general retirement system covering substantially all service performed in connection with the operation of the transportation system.

(4) DEFINITIONS.—For purposes of this subsection—

(A) The term "general retirement system" means any pension, annuity, retirement, or similar fund or system established by a State or by a political subdivision thereof for employees of the State, political subdivision, or both; but such terms shall not include such a fund or system which covers only service performed in positions connected with the operation of its public transportation system.

(B) A transportation system or a part thereof shall be considered to have been acquired by a State or political subdivision from private ownership if prior to the acquisition service performed by employees in connection with the operation of the system or part thereof acquired constituted employment under this chapter or subchapter A of chapter 9 of the Internal Revenue Code of 1939 or was covered by an agreement made pursuant to section 218 of the Social Security Act and some of such employees became employees of the State or political subdivision in connection with and at the time of such acquisition.

(C) The term "political subdivision" includes an instrumentality of—

(i) a State,

(ii) one or more political subdivisions of a State, or

(iii) a State and one or more of its political subdivisions.

[Sec. 3121(k)—Repealed]

Amendments

- **1983, Social Security Act of 1983 (P.L. 98-21) P.L. 98-21, § 102(b)(2):**

Repealed Code Sec. 3121(k). **Effective** with respect to service performed after 12-31-83. The period for which a certificate is in effect under Code Sec. 3121(k) may not be terminated under paragraph (1)(D) or (2) of § 3121(k) on or after 3-31-83, but no such certificate shall be effective with respect to any service to which the amendments made by Act Sec. 102 apply.

If any individual, (1) on 1-1-84, is age 55 or over, and is an employee of an organization described in § 210(a)(8)(B) of the Social Security Act (a) which does not have in effect (on that date) a waiver certificate under Code Sec. 3121(k) and (b) to the employees of which social security coverage is extended on 1-1-84, solely by reason of enactment of this section, and (2) after 12-31-83, acquires the number of quarters of coverage (within the meaning of § 213 of the Social Security Act) which is required for purposes of this subparagraph under paragraph (2) then such individual shall be deemed to be a fully insured individual for all of the purposes of title II of such Act.

Prior to repeal, Code Sec. 3121(k) read as follows:

(k) EXEMPTION OF RELIGIOUS, CHARITABLE, AND CERTAIN OTHER ORGANIZATIONS.—

(1) WAIVER OF EXEMPTION BY ORGANIZATION.—

(A) An organization described in section 501(c)(3) which is exempt from income tax under section 501(a) may file a certificate (in such form and manner, and with such official, as may be prescribed by regulations made under this chapter) certifying that it desires to have the insurance system established by title II of the Social Security Act extended to service performed by its employees. Such certificate may be filed only if it is accompanied by a list containing the signature, address, and social security account number (if any) of each employee (if any) who concurs in the filing of the certificate. Such list may be amended at any time prior to the expiration of the twenty-fourth month following the calendar quarter in which the certificate is filed by filing with the prescribed official a supplemental list or lists containing the signature, address, and social security account number (if any) of each additional employee who concurs in the filing of the certificate. The list and any supplemental list shall be filed in such form and manner as may be prescribed by regulations made under this chapter.

(B) The certificate shall be in effect (for purposes of subsection (b)(8)(B) and for purposes of section 210(a)(8)(B) of the Social Security Act) for the period beginning with whichever of the following may be designated by the organization:

(i) the first day of the calendar quarter in which the certificate is filed,

(ii) the first day of the calendar quarter succeeding such quarter, or

(iii) the first day of any calendar quarter preceding the calendar quarter in which the certificate is filed, except that such date may not be earlier than the first day of the twentieth calendar quarter preceding the quarter in which such certificate is filed.

(C) In the case of service performed by an employee whose name appears on a supplemental list filed after the first month following the calendar quarter in which the certificate is filed, the certificate shall be in effect (for purposes of subsection (b)(8)(B) and for purposes of section 210(a)(8)(B) of the Social Security Act) only with respect to service performed by such individual for the period beginning with the first day of the calendar quarter in which such supplemental list is filed.

(D) The period for which a certificate filed pursuant to this subsection or the corresponding subsection of prior law is effective may be terminated by the organization, effective at the end of a calendar quarter, upon giving 2 years' advance notice in writing, but only if, at the time of the receipt of such notice, the certificate has been in effect for a period of not less than 8 years. The notice of termination may be revoked by the organization by giving, prior to the close of the calendar quarter specified in the notice of termination, a written notice of such revocation. Notice of termination or revocation thereof shall be filed in such form and manner, and with such official, as may be prescribed by regulations made under this chapter.

(E) If an organization described in subparagraph (A) employs both individuals who are in positions covered by a pension, annuity, retirement, or similar fund or system established by a State or by a political subdivision thereof and individuals who are not in such positions, the organization shall divide its employees into two separate groups. One group shall consist of all employees who are in positions covered by such a fund or system and (i) are members of such fund or system, or (ii) are not members of such fund or system but are eligible to become members thereof; and the other group shall consist of all remaining employees. An organization which has so divided its employees into two groups may file a certificate pursuant to subparagraph (A) with respect to the employees in either group, or may file a separate certificate pursuant to such subparagraph with respect to the employees in each group.

(F) If a certificate filed pursuant to this paragraph is effective for one or more calendar quarters prior to the quarter in which the certificate is filed, then—

(i) for purposes of computing interest and for purposes of section 6651 (relating to addition to tax for failure to file tax return or pay tax), the due date for the return and payment of the tax for such prior calendar quarters resulting from the filing of such certificate shall be the last day of the calendar month following the calendar quarter in which the certificate is filed; and

(ii) the statutory period for the assessment of such tax shall not expire before the expiration of 3 years from such due date.

(2) TERMINATION OF WAIVER PERIOD BY SECRETARY.—If the Secretary finds that any organization which filed a certificate pursuant to this subsection or the corresponding subsection of prior law has failed to comply substantially with the requirements applicable with respect to the taxes imposed by this chapter or the corresponding provisions of prior law or is no longer able to comply with the requirements applicable with respect to the taxes imposed by this

APPENDIX: Selected Code Sections Affected by the Tax Cuts and Jobs Act 309

chapter, the Secretary shall give such organization not less than 60 days' advance notice in writing that the period covered by such certificate will terminate at the end of the calendar quarter specified in such notice. Such notice of termination may be revoked by the Secretary by giving, prior to the close of the calendar quarter specified in the notice of termination, written notice of such revocation to the organization. No notice of termination or of revocation thereof shall be given under this paragraph to an organization without the prior concurrence of the Secretary of Health, Education, and Welfare.

(3) NO RENEWAL OF WAIVER.—In the event the period covered by a certificate filed pursuant to this subsection or the corresponding subsection of prior law is terminated by the organization, no certificate may again be filed by such organization pursuant to this subsection.

(4) CONSTRUCTIVE FILING OF CERTIFICATE WHERE NO REFUND OR CREDIT OF TAXES HAS BEEN MADE.—

(A) In any case where—

(i) an organization described in section 501(c)(3) which is exempt from income tax under section 501(a) has not filed a valid waiver certificate under paragraph (1) of this subsection (or under the corresponding provision of prior law) as of the date of the enactment of this paragraph or, if later, as of the earliest date on which it satisfies clause (ii of this subparagraph[.]), but

(ii) the taxes imposed by sections 3101 and 3111 have been paid with respect to the remuneration paid by such organization to its employees, as though such a certificate had been filed, during any period (subject to subparagraph (B)(i)) of not less than three consecutive calendar quarters,

such organization shall be deemed (except as provided in subparagraph (B) of this paragraph) for purposes of subsection (b)(8)(B) and section 210(a)(8)(B) of the Social Security Act, to have filed a valid waiver under paragraph (1) of this subsection (or under the corresponding provision of prior law) on the first day of the period described in clause (ii) of this subparagraph effective (subject to subparagraph (c)) on the first day of the calendar quarter in which such period began, and to have accompanied such certificate with a list containing the signature, address, and social security number (if any) of each employee with respect to whom the taxes described in such subparagraph were paid (and each such employee shall be deemed for such purposes to have concurred in the filing of the certificate). or

(B) Subparagraph (A) shall not apply with respect to any organization if—

(i) the period referred to in clause (ii) of such subparagraph (in the case of that organization) terminated before the end of the earliest calendar quarter falling wholly or partly within the time limitation (as defined in section 205(c)(1)(B) of the Social Security Act) immediately preceding the date of the enactment of this paragraph, or

(ii) a refund or credit of any part of the taxes which were paid as described in clause (ii) of such subparagraph with respect to remuneration for services performed on or after the first day of the earliest calendar quarter falling wholly or partly within the time limitation (as defined in section 205(c)(1)(B) of the Social Security Act) immediately preceding the first day of the calendar quarter other than a refund or credit which would have been allowed if a valid waiver certificate filed under paragraph (1) had been in effect) has been obtained by the organization or its employees prior to September 9, 1976, or

(iii) the organization, prior to the end of the period referred to in clause (ii) of such subparagraph (and, in the case of an organization organized on or before October 9, 1969, prior to October 19, 1976), had applied for a ruling or determination letter acknowledging it to be exempt from income tax under section 501(c)(3), and it subsequently received such ruling or determination letter and did not pay any taxes under sections 3101 and 3111 with respect to any employee with respect to any quarter ending after the twelfth month following the date of mailing or such ruling or determination letter and did not pay any such taxes with respect to any quarter beginning after the later of (I) December 31, 1975 or (II) the date on which such ruling or determination letter was issued.

(C) In the case of any organization which is deemed under this paragraph to have filed a valid waiver certificate under paragraph (1), if—

(i) the period with respect to which the taxes imposed by sections 3101 and 3111 were paid by such organization (as described in subparagraph (A)(ii)) terminated prior to October 1, 1976, or

(ii) the taxes imposed by sections 3101 and 3111 were not paid during the period referred to in clause (i) (whether such period has terminated or not) with respect to remuneration paid by such organization to individuals who became its employees after the close of the calendar quarter in which such period began,

taxes under sections 3101 and 3111—

(iii) in the case of an organization which meets the requirements of this subparagraph by reason of clause (i), with respect to remuneration paid by such organization after the termination of the period referred to in clause (i) and prior to July 1, 1977; or

(iv) in the case of an organization which meets the requirements of this subparagraph by reason of clause (ii), with respect to remuneration paid prior to July 1, 1977, to individuals who became its employees after the close of the calendar quarter in which the period referred to in clause (i) began,

which remain unpaid on the date of the enactment of this subparagraph, or which were paid after October 19, 1976, but prior to the date of the enactment of this subparagraph, shall not be due or payable (or, if paid, shall be refunded); and the certificate which such organization is deemed under this paragraph to have filed shall not apply to any service with respect to the remuneration for which the taxes imposed by sections 3101 and 3111 (which remain unpaid on the date of the enactment of this subparagraph, or were paid after October 19, 1976, but prior to the date of the enactment of this subparagraph) are not due and payable (or are refunded) by reason of the preceding provisions of this subparagraph. In applying this subparagraph for purposes of title II of the Social Security Act, the period during which reports of wages subject to the taxes imposed by section 3101 and 3111 were made by any organization may be conclusively treated as the period (described in subparagraph (A)(ii)) during which the taxes imposed by such sections were paid by such organization.

(5) CONSTRUCTIVE FILING OF CERTIFICATE WHERE REFUND OR CREDIT HAS BEEN MADE AND NEW CERTIFICATE IS NOT FILED.—In any case where—

(A) an organization described in section 501(c)(3) which is exempt from income tax under section 501(a) would be deemed under paragraph (4) of this subsection to have filed a valid waiver certificate under paragraph (1) if it were not excluded from such paragraph (4) (pursuant to subparagraph (B)(ii) thereof) because a refund or credit of all or a part of the taxes described in paragraph (4)(A)(ii) was obtained prior to September 9, 1976; and

(B) such organization has not, prior to April 1, 1978, filed a valid waiver certificate under paragraph (1) which is effective for a period beginning on or before the first day of the first calendar quarter with respect to which such refund or credit was made (or, if later, with the first day of the earliest calendar quarter for which such certificate may be in effect under paragraph (1)(B)(iii)) and which is accompanied by the list described in paragraph (1)(A),

such organization shall be deemed, for purposes of subsection (b)(8)(B) and section 210(a)(8)(B) of the Social Security Act, to have filed a valid waiver certificate under paragraph (1) of this subsection on April 1, 1978, effective for the period beginning on the first day of the first calendar quarter with respect to which the refund or credit referred to in subparagraph (A) of this paragraph was made (or, if later, with the first day of the earliest calendar quarter falling wholly or partly within the time limitation (as defined in section 205(c)(1)(B) of the Social Security Act) immediately preceding the date of the enactment of this paragraph), and to have accompanied such certificate with a list containing the signature, address, and social security number (if any) of each employee described in subparagraph (A) of paragraph (4) including any employee with respect to whom taxes were refunded or credited as described in subparagraph (A) of this paragraph (and each such employee shall be deemed for such purposes to have concurred in the filing of the certificate). A certificate which is deemed to have been filed by an organization on April 1, 1978, shall supersede any certificate which may have been actually filed by such organization prior to that day except to the extent prescribed by the Secretary.

(6) APPLICATION OF CERTAIN PROVISIONS TO CASES OF CONSTRUCTIVE FILING.—All of the provisions of this subsection (other than subparagraphs (B), (F), and (H) of paragraph (1)), including the provisions requiring payment of taxes under sections 3101 and 3111 with respect to the services involved (except as provided in paragraph (4)(c)) shall apply with

Code Sec. 3121

respect to any certificate which is deemed to have been filed by an organization on any day under paragraph (4) or (5), in the same way they would apply if the certificate had been actually filed on that day under paragraph (1); except that—

(A) the provisions relating to the filing of supplemental lists of concurring employees in the third sentence of paragraph (1)(A), and in paragraph (1)(C), shall apply to the extent prescribed by the Secretary;

(B) the provisions of paragraph (1)(E) shall not apply unless the taxes described in paragraph (4)(A)(ii) were paid by the organization as though a separate certificate had been filed with respect to one or both of the groups to which such provisions relate; and

(C) the action of the organization in obtaining the refund or credit described in paragraph (5)(A) shall not be considered a termination of such organization's coverage period for purposes of paragraph (3). Any organization which is deemed to have filed a waiver certificate under paragraph (4) or (5) shall be considered for purposes of section 3102(b) to have been required to deduct the taxes imposed by section 3101 with respect to the services involved.

(7) BOTH EMPLOYEE AND EMPLOYER TAXES PAYABLE BY ORGANIZATION FOR RETROACTIVE PERIOD IN CASES OF CONSTRUCTIVE FILING.—Notwithstanding any other provision of this chapter, in any case where an organization described in paragraph (5)(A) has not filed a valid waiver certificate under paragraph (1) prior to April 1, 1978, and is accordingly deemed under paragraph (5) to have filed such a certificate on April 1, 1978, the taxes due under section 3101, with respect to services constituting employment by reason of such certificate for any period prior to that date (along with the taxes due under section 3111 with respect to such services and the amount of any interest paid in connection with the refund or credit described in paragraph (5)(A)) shall be paid by such organization from its own funds and without any deduction from the wages of the individuals who performed such services; and those individuals shall have no liability for the payment of such taxes.

(8) EXTENDED PERIOD FOR PAYMENT OF TAXES FOR RETROACTIVE COVERAGE.—Notwithstanding any other provision of this title, in any case where—

(A) an organization is deemed under paragraph (4) to have filed a valid waiver certificate under paragraph (1), but the applicable period described in paragraph (4)(A)(ii) has terminated and part or all of the taxes imposed by sections 3101 and 3111 with respect to remuneration paid by such organization to its employees after the close of such period remains payable notwithstanding paragraph (4)(C), or

(B) an organization described in paragraph (5)(A) files a valid waiver certificate under paragraph (1) by March 31, 1978, as described in paragraph (5)(B), or (not having filed such a certificate by that date) is deemed under paragraph (5) to have filed such a certificate on April 1, 1978, or

(C) an individual files a request under section 3 of Public Law 94-563, or under section 312(c) of the Social Security Amendments of 1977, to have service treated as constituting remuneration for employment (as defined in section 3121(b) and in section 210(a) of the Social Security Act),

the taxes due under sections 3101 and 3111 with respect to services constituting employment by reason of such certificate for any period prior to the first day of the calendar quarter in which the date of such filing or constructive filing occurs, or with respect to service constituting employment by reason of such request, may be paid in installments over an appropriate period of time, as determined under regulations prescribed by the Secretary, rather than in a lump sum.

- 1977 (P.L. 95-216)

P.L. 95-216, §312(a)(1):

Amended Code Sec. 3121(k)(5). **Effective** as indicated in §312(h), below. Prior to amendment, paragraph (k)(5) read as follows:

(5) CONSTRUCTIVE FILING OF CERTIFICATE WHERE REFUND OR CREDIT HAS BEEN MADE AND NEW CERTIFICATE IS NOT FILED.—In any case where—

(A) an organization described in section 501(c)(3) which is exempt from income tax under section 501(a) would be deemed under paragraph (4) of this subsection to have filed a valid waiver certificate under paragraph (1) if it were not excluded from such paragraph (4) (pursuant to subparagraph (B)(ii) thereof) because a refund or credit of all or a part of the taxes described in paragraph (4)(A)(ii) was obtained prior to September 9, 1976; and

(B) such organization has not, prior to the expiration of 180 days after the date of the enactment of this paragraph, filed a valid waiver certificate under paragraph (1) which is effective for a period beginning on or before the first day of the first calendar quarter with respect to which such refund or credit was made (or, if later, with the first day of the earliest calendar quarter for which such certificate may be in effect under paragraph (1)(B)(iii)) and which is accompanied by the list described in paragraph (1)(A),

such organization shall be deemed, for purposes of subsection (b)(8)(B) and section 210(a)(8)(B) of the Social Security Act, to have filed a valid waiver certificate under paragraph (1) of this subsection on the 181st day after the date of the enactment of this paragraph, effective for the period beginning on the first day of the first calendar quarter with respect to which the refund or credit referred to in subparagraph (A) of this paragraph was made (or, if later, with the first day of the earliest calendar quarter falling wholly or partly within the time limitation (as defined in section 205(c)(1)(B) of the Social Security Act) immediately preceding the date of the enactment of this paragraph), and to have accompanied such certificate with a list containing the signature, address, and social security number (if any) of each employee described in subparagraph (A) of paragraph (4) including any employee with respect to whom taxes were refunded or credited as described in subparagraph (A) of this paragraph (and each such employee shall be deemed for such purposes to have concurred in the filing of the certificate). A certificate which is deemed to have been filed by an organization on such 181st day shall supersede any certificate which may have been actually filed by such organization prior to that day except to the extent prescribed by the Secretary.

P.L. 95-216, §312(a)(2)(A), (B), and (C):

Amended Code Sec. 3121(k)(7) by striking out "prior to the expiration of 180 days after the date of the enactment of this paragraph" and inserting in lieu thereof "prior to April 1, 1978,"; by striking out "the 181st day after such date," and inserting in lieu thereof "April 1, 1978,"; and by striking out "prior to the first day of the calendar quarter in which such 181st day occurs" and inserting in lieu thereof "prior to that date". **Effective** as indicated in §312(h), below. Prior to amendment, paragraph (k)(7) read as follows:

(7) BOTH EMPLOYEE AND EMPLOYER TAXES PAYABLE BY ORGANIZATION FOR RETROACTIVE PERIOD IN CASES OF CONSTRUCTIVE FILING.—Notwithstanding any other provision of this chapter, in any case where an organization described in paragraph (5)(A) has not filed a valid waiver certificate under paragraph (1) prior to the expiration of 180 days after the date of the enactment of this paragraph and is accordingly deemed under paragraph (5) to have filed such a certificate on the 181st day after such date, the taxes due under section 3101 with respect to services constituting employment by reason of such certificate for any period prior to the first day of the calendar quarter in which such 181st day occurs (along with the taxes due under section 3111 with respect to such services and the amount of any interest paid in connection with the refund or credit described in paragraph (5)(A)) shall be paid by such organization from its own funds and without any deduction from the wages of the individuals who performed such services; and those individuals shall have no liability for the payment of such taxes.

P.L. 95-216, §312(a)(3):

Amended paragraph (k)(8) by striking out "by the end of the 180-day period following the date of the enactment of this paragraph" and inserting in lieu thereof "prior to April 1, 1978,"; by striking out "within that period" and inserting in lieu thereof "prior to April 1, 1978"; and by striking out "on the 181st day following that date" and inserting in lieu thereof "on that date". **Effective** as indicated in §312(h), below. Prior to amendment, paragraph (k)(8) read as follows:

(8) EXTENDED PERIOD FOR PAYMENT OF TAXES FOR RETROACTIVE COVERAGE.—Notwithstanding any other provision of this title, in any case where an organization described in paragraph (5)(A) files a valid waiver certificate under paragraph (1) by the end of the 180-day period following the date of the enactment of this paragraph as described in paragraph (5)(B), or (not having filed such a certificate within that period) is deemed under paragraph (5) to have filed such a certificate on the 181st day following that date, the taxes due under sections 3101 and 3111 with respect to services constituting employment by reason of such certificate for any period prior to the first day of the calendar quarter in which the date of such filing or constructive filing occurs may be paid in installments over an appropriate period of time, as determined under regulations prescribed by the Secretary, rather than in a lump sum.

APPENDIX: Selected Code Sections Affected by the Tax Cuts and Jobs Act 311

P.L. 95-216, § 312(b)(1):
Added a new subparagraph (k)(4)(C). **Effective** as indicated in § 312(h), below.

P.L. 95-216, § 312(b)(2):
Amended subparagraph (k)(4)(A) by inserting "(subject to subparagraph (C))" after "effective" in the matter following clause (ii). **Effective** as indicated in § 312(h), below.

P.L. 95-216, § 312(b)(3):
Amended Code Sec. 3121(k)(6) by inserting "(except as provided in paragraph (4)(C))" after "services involved" in the matter preceding subparagraph (A). **Effective** as indicated in § 312(h), below.

P.L. 95-216, § 312(b)(4):
Amended paragraph (k)(4) by striking out "date of enactment of this paragraph" in subparagraph (B)(ii) and inserting in lieu thereof "first day of the calendar quarter". **Effective** as indicated in § 312(h), below.

P.L. 95-216, § 312(d):
Amended paragraph (k)(8), as amended by § 312(a)(3). **Effective** as indicated in § 312(h), below.

P.L. 95-216 § 312(e):
Amended the first sentence of Section 3 of P.L. 94-563 (in the matter following paragraph(3)) by inserting "on or before April 15, 1980," after "filed"; and by inserting "(or by satisfactory evidence that appropriate arrangements have been made for the repayment of such taxes in installments as provided in section 3121(k)(8) of such Code)" after "so refunded or credited". **Effective** as indicated in § 312(h), below.

P.L. 95-216, § 312(f):
Amended paragraph (k)(4)(A)(i) by striking out "or any subsequent date" and inserting in lieu thereof "(or, if later, as of the earliest date on which it satisfies clause (ii) of this subparagraph [.])". **Effective** as indicated in § 312(h), below.

P.L. 95-216, § 312(g)(1)-(2):
Amended subparagraph (k)(4)(B) by striking out the period at the end of clause (ii) and inserting in lieu thereof ", or"; and by adding after clause (ii) a clause (iii). **Effective** as indicated in § 312(h), below. Prior to amendment, paragraph (k)(4) read as follows:

(4) CONSTRUCTIVE FILING OF CERTIFICATE WHERE NO REFUND OR CREDIT OF TAXES HAS BEEN MADE.—

(A) In any case where—

(i) an organization described in section 501(c)(3) which is exempt from income tax under section 501(a) has not filed a valid waiver certificate under paragraph (1) of this subsection (or under the corresponding provision of prior law) as of the date of the enactment of this paragraph or any subsequent date, but

(ii) the taxes imposed by sections 3101 and 3111 have been paid with respect to the remuneration paid by such organization to its employees, as though such a certificate had been filed, during any period (subject to subparagraph (B)(ii)) of not less than three consecutive calendar quarters, such organization shall be deemed (except as provided in subparagraph (B) of this paragraph) for purposes of subsection (b)(8)(B) and section 210(a)(8)(B) of the Social Security Act, to have filed a valid waiver certificate under paragraph (1) of this subsection (or under the corresponding provision of prior law) on the first day of the period described in clause (ii) of this subparagraph effective on the first day of the calendar quarter in which such period began, and to have accompanied such certificate with a list containing the signature, address, and social security number (if any) of each employee with respect to whom the taxes described in such subparagraph were paid (and each such employee shall be deemed for such purposes to have concurred in the filing of the certificate).

(B) Subparagraph (A) shall not apply with respect to any organization if—

(i) the period referred to in clause (ii) of such subparagraph (in the case of that organization) terminated before the end of the earliest calendar quarter falling wholly or partly within the time limitation (as defined in section 205(c)(1)(B) of the Social Security Act) immediately preceding the date of the enactment of this paragraph, or

(ii) a refund or credit of any part of the taxes which were paid as described in clause (ii) of such subparagraph with respect to remuneration for services performed on or after the first day of the earliest calendar quarter falling wholly or partly within the time limitation (as defined in section 205(c)(1)(B) of the Social Security Act) immediately preceding the date of enactment of this paragraph (other than a refund or credit which would have been allowed if a valid waiver certificate filed under paragraph (1) had been in effect) has been obtained by the organization or its employees prior to September 9, 1976.

P.L. 95-216, § 312(h), provides:
The amendments made by subsections (a), (b), (d), (e), (f), and (g) of this section shall be effective as though they had been included as a part of the amendments made to section 3121(k) of the Internal Revenue Code of 1954 by the first section of Public Law 94-563 (or, in the case of the amendments made by subsection (e), as a part of section 3 of such Public Law).

- **1976 (P.L. 94-563)**

P.L. 94-563, § 1(c):
Added paragraphs (4), (5), (6), (7), and (8) at the end of Code Sec. 3121(k). **Effective** for services performed after 1950, to the extent covered by waiver certificates filed or deemed to have been filed under section 3121(k)(4) or (5) of the Internal Revenue Code of 1954 (as added by such amendments).

P.L. 94-563, § 2, provides:
SEC. 2. Notwithstanding any other provision of law, no refund or credit of any tax paid under section 3101 or 3111 of the Internal Revenue Code of 1954 by an organization described in section 501(c)(3) of such Code which is exempt from income tax under section 501(a) of such Code shall be made on or after September 9, 1976, by reason of such organization's failure to file a waiver certificate under section 3121(k)(1) of such Code (or the corresponding provision of prior law), if such organization is deemed to have filed such a certificate under section 3121(k)(4) of such Code (as added by the first section of this Act).

P.L. 94-563, § 3 (as amended by P.L. 95-216), provides:
SEC. 3. In any case where—

(1) an individual performed service, as an employee of an organization which is deemed under section 3121(k)(5) of the Internal Revenue Code of 1954 to have filed a waiver certificate under section 3121(k)(1) of such Code, at any time prior to the period for which such certificate is effective;

(2) the taxes imposed by sections 3101 and 3111 of such Code were paid with respect to remuneration paid for such service, but such service (or any part thereof) does not constitute employment (as defined in section 210(a) of the Social Security Act and section 3121(b) of such Code) because the applicable taxes so paid were not refunded or credited (otherwise than through a refund or credit which would have been allowed if a valid waiver certificate filed under section 3121(k)(1) of such Code had been in effect) prior to September 9, 1976; and

(3) any portion of such service (with respect to which taxes were paid and refunded or credited as described in paragraph (2)) would constitute employment (as so defined) if the organization had actually filed under section 3121(k)(1) of such Code a valid waiver certificate effective as provided in section 3121(k)(5)(B) thereof (with such individual's signature appearing on the accompanying list),

the remuneration paid for the portion of such service described in paragraph (3) shall, upon the request of such individual (filed on or before April 15, 1980, in such manner and form, and with such official, as may be prescribed by regulations made under title II of the Social Security Act) accompanied by full repayment of the taxes which were paid under section 3101 of such Code with respect to such remuneration and so refunded or credited (or by satisfactory evidence that appropriate arrangements have been made for repayment of such taxes in installments as provided in section 3121 (k)(8) of such Code), be deemed to constitute remuneration for employment as so defined. In any case where remuneration paid by an organization to an individual is deemed under the preceding sentence to constitute remuneration for employment, such organization shall be liable (notwithstanding any other provision of such Code) for repayment of any taxes which it paid under section 3111 of such Code with respect to such remuneration and which were refunded or credited to it.

- **1976, Tax Reform Act of 1976 (P.L. 94-455)**

P.L. 94-455, § 1903(a)(3)(E):
Deleted subparagraphs (F) and (H) of Code Sec. 3121(k)(1) and redesignated subparagraph (G) as subparagraph (F). **Effective** for wages paid after 12-31-76. Prior to amendment, subparagraphs (F) and (H) read as follows:

(F) An organization which filed a certificate under this subsection after 1955 but prior to the enactment of this subparagraph may file a request at any time before 1960 to have such certificate effective, with respect to the service of

Code Sec. 3121

individuals who concurred in the filing of such certificate (initially or through the filing of a supplemental list) prior to enactment of this subparagraph and who concur in the filing of such new request, for the period beginning with the first day of any calendar quarter preceding the first calendar quarter for which it was effective and following the last calendar quarter of 1955. Such request shall be filed with such official and in such form and manner as may be prescribed by regulations made under this chapter. If a request is filed pursuant to this subparagraph—

(i) for purposes of computing interest and for purposes of section 6651 (relating to addition to tax for failure to file tax return or pay tax), the due date for the return and payment of the tax for any calendar quarter resulting from the filing of such request shall be the last day of the calendar month following the calendar quarter in which the request is filed; and

(ii) the statutory period for the assessment of such tax shall not expire before the expiration of 3 years from such due date.

* * *

(H) An organization which files a certificate under subparagraph (A) before 1966 may amend such certificate during 1965 or 1966 to make the certificate effective with the first day of any calendar quarter preceding the quarter for which such certificate originally became effective, except that such date may not be earlier than the first day of the twentieth calendar quarter preceding the quarter in which such certificate is so amended. If an organization amends its certificate pursuant to the preceding sentence, such amendment shall be effective with respect to the service of individuals who concurred in the filing of such certificate (initially or through the filing of a supplemental list) and who concur in the filing of such amendment. An amendment to a certificate filed pursuant to this subparagraph shall be filed with such official and in such form and manner as may be prescribed by regulations made under this chapter. If an amendment is filed pursuant to this subparagraph—

(i) for purposes of computing interest and for purposes of section 6651 (relating to addition to tax for failure to file tax return or pay tax), the due date for the return and payment of the tax for any calendar quarter resulting from the filing of such an amendment shall be the last day of the calendar month following the calendar quarter in which the amendment is filed; and

(ii) the statutory period for the assessment of such tax shall not expire before the expiration of three years from such due date.

P.L. 94-455, §1906(b)(13)(A):

Amended 1954 Code by substituting "Secretary" for "Secretary or his delegate" each place it appeared. **Effective** 2-1-77.

- **1969, Tax Reform Act of 1969 (P.L. 91-172)**

P.L. 91-172, §943(c)(1)-(3):

Amended subparagraphs (k)(1)(F)(i), (G)(i) and (H)(i) by inserting "or pay tax" immediately after "tax return" in each instance. **Effective** with respect to returns the date prescribed by law (without regard to any extension of time) for filing of which is after 12-31-69, and with respect to notices and demands for payment of tax made after 12-31-69.

- **1965, Social Security Amendments of 1965 (P.L. 89-97)**

P.L. 89-97, §316(a), (b):

Amended Sec. 3121(k)(1)(B)(iii) and amended Sec. 3121(k)(l) by adding subparagraph (H). **Effective** with respect to certificates filed under Sec. 3121(k)(1)(A) after 7-30-65.

- **1960, Social Security Amendments of 1960 (P.L. 86-778)**

P.L. 86-778, §105(a):

Amended Code Sec. 3121(k) by: (1) striking out, in the first sentence of paragraph (1)(A), the phrase "and that at least two-thirds of its employees concur in the filing of the certificate" where it appeared at the end of that sentence; (2) inserting "(if any)" following "each employee" in the second sentence of paragraph (1)(A); and (3) striking out the last two sentences of paragraph (1)(E) and substituting the present last sentence of that paragraph. **Effective** with respect to certificates filed under Code Sec. 3121(k)(1) after 9-13-60. Prior to deletion, the last two sentences read as follows: "An organization which has so divided its employees into two groups may file a certificate pursuant to subparagraph (A) with respect to the employees in one of the groups if at least two-thirds of the employees in such groups concur in the filing of the certificate. The organization may also file such a certificate with respect to the employees in the other group if at least two-thirds of the employees in such other group concur in the filing of such certificate."

- **1958, Social Security Amendments of 1958 (P.L. 85-840)**

P.L. 85-840, §405(a):

Amended Sec. 3121(k)(1), except for the amendments added by P.L. 86-778. **Effective** for certificates filed under Sec. 3121(k)(1) after 8-28-58 and requests filed under subparagraph (F) on or after that date. Prior to amendment, Sec. 3121(k)(1) read as follows:

"(1) Waiver of exemption by organization.—An organization described in section 501(c)(3) which is exempt from income tax under section 501(a) may file a certificate (in such form and manner, and with such official, as may be prescribed by regulations made under this chapter) certifying that it desires to have the insurance system established by title II of the Social Security Act extended to service performed by its employees and that at least two-thirds of its employees concur in the filing of the certificate. Such certificate may be filed only if it is accompanied by a list containing the signature, address, and social security account number (if any) of each employee who concurs in the filing of the certificate. Such list may be amended at any time prior to the expiration of the twenty-fourth month following the first calendar quarter for which the certificate is in effect, or at any time prior to January 1, 1959, whichever is the later, by filing with the prescribed official a supplemental list or lists containing the signature, address, and social security number (if any) of each additional employee who concurs in the filing of the certificate. The list and any supplemental list shall be filed in such form and manner as may be prescribed by regulations made under this chapter. The certificate shall be in effect (for purposes of subsection (b)(8)(B) and for purposes of section 210(a)(8)(B) of the Social Security Act) for the period beginning with the first day of the calendar quarter in which such certificate is filed or the first day of the succeeding calendar quarter, as may be specified in the certificate, except that, in the case of service performed by an individual whose name appears on a supplemental list filed after the first month following the first calendar quarter for which the certificate is in effect, the certificate shall be in effect, for purposes of such subsection (b)(8) and for purposes of section 210(a)(8) of the Social Security Act, only with respect to service performed by such individual after the calendar quarter in which such supplemental list is filed. The period for which a certificate filed pursuant to this subsection or the corresponding subsection of prior law is effective may be terminated by the organization, effective at the end of a calendar quarter, upon giving 2 years' advance notice in writing, but only if, at the time of the receipt of such notice, the certificate has been in effect for a period of not less than 8 years. The notice of termination may be revoked by the organization by giving, prior to the close of the calendar quarter specified in the notice of termination, a written notice of such revocation. Notice of termination or revocation thereof shall be filed in such form and manner, and with such official, as may be prescribed by regulations made under this chapter."

- **1956, Social Security Amendments of 1956 (P.L. 880, 84th Cong.)**

P.L. 880, 84th Cong., 2d Sess., §201(k), (l):

Amended Sec. 3121(k)(1). **Effective** for certificates filed after 1956 under Sec. 3121(k). Prior to amendment, Sec. 3121(k)(1) read as follows:

"(1) Waiver of exemption by organization.—An organization described in section 501(c)(3) which is exempt from income tax under section 501(a) may file a certificate (in such form and manner, and with such official, as may be prescribed by regulations made under this chapter) certifying that it desires to have the insurance system established by title II of the Social Security Act extended to service performed by its employees and that at least two-thirds of its employees concur in the filing of the certificate. Such certificate may be filed only if it is accompanied by a list containing the signature, address, and social security account number (if any) of each employee who concurs in the filing of the certificate. Such list may be amended at any time prior to the expiration of the twenty-fourth month following the first calendar quarter for which the certificate is in effect by filing with the prescribed official a supplemental list or lists containing the signature, address, and social security account number (if any) of each additional employee who concurs in the filing of the certificate. The list

APPENDIX: Selected Code Sections Affected by the Tax Cuts and Jobs Act

and any supplemental list shall be filed in such form and manner as may be prescribed by regulations made under this chapter. The certificate shall be in effect (for purposes of subsection (b)(8)(B) and for purposes of section 210(a)(8)(B) of the Social Security Act) for the period beginning with the first day following the close of the calendar quarter in which such certificate is filed, except that, in the case of service performed by an individual whose name appears on a supplemental list filed after the first month following the first calendar quarter for which the certificate is in effect, the certificate shall be in effect, for purposes of such subsection (b)(8) and for purposes of section 210(a)(8) of the Social Security Act, only with respect to service performed by such individual after the calendar quarter in which such supplemental list is filed. The period for which a certificate filed pursuant to this subsection or the corresponding subsection of prior law is effective may be terminated by the organization, effective at the end of a calendar quarter, upon giving 2 years' advance notice in writing, but only if, at the time of the receipt of such notice, the certificate has been in effect for a period of not less than 8 years. The notice of termination may be revoked by the organization by giving, prior to the close of the calendar quarter specified in the notice of termination, a written notice of such revocation. Notice of termination or revocation thereof shall be filed in such form and manner, and with such official, as may be prescribed by the regulations made under this chapter."

- **1954, Social Security Amendments of 1954 (P.L. 761, 83rd Cong.)**

P.L. 761, 83rd Cong., § 207(a), (b):

Amended Sec. 3121(k)(1). **Effective** 9-1-54. Prior to amendment Sec. 3121(k)(1) read as follows:

"(1) Waiver of exemption by organization.—An organization described in section 501(c)(3) which is exempt from income tax under section 501(a) may file a certificate (in such form and manner, and with such official, as may be prescribed by regulations made under this chapter) certifying that it desires to have the insurance system established by title II of the Social Security Act extended to service performed by its employees and that at least two-thirds of its employees concur in the filing of the certificate. Such certificate may be filed only if it is accompanied by a list containing the signature, address, and social security account number (if any) of each employee who concurs in the filing of the certificate. Such list may be amended at any time prior to the expiration of the first month following the first calendar quarter for which the certificate is in effect, by filing with such official a supplemental list or lists containing the signature, address, and social security account number (if any) of each additional employee who concurs in the filing of the certificate. The list and any supplemental list shall be filed in such form and manner as may be prescribed by regulations made under this chapter. The certificate shall be in effect (for purposes of subsection (b)(8)(B) and for purposes of section 210(a)(8)(B) of the Social Security Act) for the period beginning with the first day of the calendar quarter in which such certificate is filed. The period for which a certificate filed pursuant to this subsection or the corresponding subsection of prior law is effective may be terminated by the organization, effective at the end of a calendar quarter, upon giving 2 years' advance notice in writing, but only if, at the time of the receipt of such notice, the certificate has been in effect for a period of not less than 8 years. The notice of termination may be revoked by the organization by giving, prior to the close of the calendar quarter specified in the notice of termination, a written notice of such revocation. Notice of termination or revocation thereof shall be filed in such form and manner, and with such official, as may be prescribed by regulations made under this chapter."

[Sec. 3121(l)]

(l) AGREEMENTS ENTERED INTO BY AMERICAN EMPLOYERS WITH RESPECT TO FOREIGN AFFILIATES.—

(1) AGREEMENT WITH RESPECT TO CERTAIN EMPLOYEES OF FOREIGN AFFILIATE.—The Secretary shall, at the American employer's request, enter into an agreement (in such manner and form as may be prescribed by the Secretary) with any American employer (as defined in subsection (h)) who desires to have the insurance system established by title II of the Social Security Act extended to service performed outside the United States in the employ of any 1 or more of such employer's foreign affiliates (as defined in paragraph (6)) by all employees who are citizens or residents of the United States, except that the agreement shall not apply to any service performed by, or remuneration paid to, an employee if such service or remuneration would be excluded from the term "employment" or "wages", as defined in this section, had the service been performed in the United States. Such agreement may be amended at any time so as to be made applicable, in the same manner and under the same conditions, with respect to any other foreign affiliate of such American employer. Such agreement shall be applicable with respect to citizens or residents of the United States who, on or after the effective date of the agreement, are employees of and perform services outside the United States for any foreign affiliate specified in the agreement. Such agreement shall provide—

(A) that the American employer shall pay to the Secretary, at such time or times as the Secretary may by regulations prescribe, amounts equivalent to the sum of the taxes which would be imposed by sections 3101 and 3111 (including amounts equivalent to the interest, additions to the taxes, additional amounts, and penalties which would be applicable) with respect to the remuneration which would be wages if the services covered by the agreement constituted employment as defined in this section; and

(B) that the American employer will comply with such regulations relating to payments and reports as the Secretary may prescribe to carry out the purposes of this subsection.

(2) EFFECTIVE PERIOD OF AGREEMENT.—An agreement entered into pursuant to paragraph (1) shall be in effect for the period beginning with the first day of the calendar quarter in which such agreement is entered into or the first day of the succeeding calendar quarter, as may be specified in the agreement; except that in case such agreement is amended to include the services performed for any other affiliate and such amendment is executed after the first month following the first calendar quarter for which the agreement is in effect, the agreement shall be in effect with respect to service performed for such other affiliate only after the calendar quarter in which such amendment is executed. Notwithstanding any other provision of this subsection, the period for which any such agreement is effective with respect to any foreign entity shall terminate at the end of any calendar quarter in which the foreign entity, at any time in such quarter, ceases to be a foreign affiliate as defined in paragraph (6).

(3) NO TERMINATION OF AGREEMENT.—No agreement under this subsection may be terminated, either in its entirety or with respect to any foreign affiliate, on or after June 15, 1989.

Code Sec. 3121

(4) DEPOSITS IN TRUST FUNDS.—For purposes of section 201 of the Social Security Act, relating to appropriations to the Federal Old-Age and Survivors Insurance Trust Fund and the Federal Disability Insurance Trust Fund, such remuneration—

(A) paid for services covered by an agreement entered into pursuant to paragraph (1) as would be wages if the services constituted employment, and

(B) as is reported to the Secretary pursuant to the provisions of such agreement or of the regulations issued under this subsection,

shall be considered wages subject to the taxes imposed by this chapter.

(5) OVERPAYMENTS AND UNDERPAYMENTS.—

(A) If more or less than the correct amount due under an agreement entered into pursuant to this subsection is paid with respect to any payment of remuneration, proper adjustments with respect to the amounts due under such agreement shall be made, without interest, in such manner and at such times as may be required by regulations prescribed by the Secretary.

(B) If an overpayment cannot be adjusted under subparagraph (A), the amount thereof shall be paid by the Secretary, through the Fiscal Service of the Treasury Department, but only if a claim for such overpayment is filed with the Secretary within two years from the time such overpayment was made.

(6) FOREIGN AFFILIATE DEFINED.—For purposes of this subsection and section 210(a) of the Social Security Act—

(A) IN GENERAL.—A foreign affiliate of an American employer is any foreign entity in which such American employer has not less than a 10-percent interest.

(B) DETERMINATION OF 10-PERCENT INTEREST.—For purposes of subparagraph (A), an American employer has a 10-percent interest in any entity if such employer has such an interest directly (or through one or more entities)—

(i) in the case of a corporation, in the voting stock thereof, and

(ii) in the case of any other entity, in the profits thereof.

(7) AMERICAN EMPLOYER AS SEPARATE ENTITY.—Each American employer which enters into an agreement pursuant to paragraph (1) of this subsection shall, for purposes of this subsection and section 6413(c)(2)(C), relating to special refunds in the case of employees of certain foreign entities, be considered an employer in its capacity as a party to such agreement separate and distinct from its identity as a person employing individuals on its own account.

(8) REGULATIONS.—Regulations of the Secretary to carry out the purposes of this subsection shall be designed to make the requirements imposed on American employers with respect to services covered by an agreement entered into pursuant to this subsection the same, so far as practicable, as those imposed upon employers pursuant to this title with respect to the taxes imposed by this chapter.

Amendments

• 1989, Omnibus Budget Reconciliation Act of 1989 (P.L. 101-239)

P.L. 101-239, § 10201(a)(1)-(4):

Amended Code Sec. 3121(l) by adding at the end of paragraph (2) a new sentence, by striking paragraphs (3), (4), and (5), by inserting after paragraph (2) a new paragraph (3), and by redesignating paragraphs (6) through (10) as paragraphs (4) through (8) respectively. **Effective** with respect to any agreement in effect under section 3121(l) of the Internal Revenue Code of 1986 on or after 6-15-89, with respect to which no notice of termination is in effect on such date. Prior to amendment, Code Sec. 3121(l)(3)-(5) read as follows:

(3) TERMINATION OF PERIOD BY AN AMERICAN EMPLOYER.—The period for which an agreement entered into pursuant to paragraph (1) of this subsection is effective may be terminated with respect to any one or more of its foreign affiliates by the American employer, effective at the end of a calendar quarter, upon giving two years' advance notice in writing, but only if, at the time of the receipt of such notice, the agreement has been in effect for a period of not less than eight years. The notice of termination may be revoked by the American employer by giving, prior to the close of the calendar quarter specified in the notice of termination, a written notice of such revocation. Notice of termination or revocation thereof shall be filed in such form and manner as may be prescribed by regulations. Notwithstanding any other provision of this subsection, the period for which any such agreement is effective with respect to any foreign entity shall terminate at the end of any calendar quarter in which the foreign entity, at any time in such quarter, ceases to be a foreign affiliate as defined in paragraph (8).

(4) TERMINATION OF PERIOD BY SECRETARY.—If the Secretary finds that any American employer which entered into an agreement pursuant to this subsection has failed to comply substantially with the terms of such agreement, the Secretary shall give such American employer not less than sixty days' advance notice in writing and the period covered by such agreement will terminate at the end of the calendar quarter specified in such notice. Such notice of termination may be revoked by the Secretary by giving, prior to the close of the calendar quarter specified in the notice of termination, written notice of such revocation to the American employer. No notice of termination or of revocation thereof shall be given under this paragraph to an American employer without the prior concurrence of the Secretary of Health, Education, and Welfare.

(5) NO RENEWAL OF AGREEMENT.—If any agreement entered into pursuant to paragraph (1) of this subsection is terminated in its entirety (A) by a notice of termination filed by the American employer pursuant to paragraph (3), or (B) by a notice of termination given by the Secretary pursuant to paragraph (4), the American employer may not again enter into an agreement pursuant to paragraph (1). If any such agreement is terminated with respect to any foreign affiliate, such agreement may not thereafter be amended so as again to make it applicable with respect to such affiliate.

P.L. 101-239, § 10201(b)(3):

Amended Code Sec. 3121(l)(1) by striking "paragraph (8)" and inserting "paragraph (6)" in the matter preceding subparagraph (A). **Effective** with respect to any agreement in effect under section 3121(l) of the Internal Revenue Code of 1986 on or after 6-15-89, with respect to which no notice of termination is in effect on such date.

• 1983, Social Security Act of 1983 (P.L. 98-21)

P.L. 98-21, § 321(a)(1):

Amended that part of Code Sec. 3121(l) which preceded the second sentence of paragraph (1). **Effective** with respect to agreements entered into after 4-20-83. Prior to amendment, the material read as follows:

"(l) AGREEMENTS ENTERED INTO BY DOMESTIC CORPORATIONS WITH RESPECT TO FOREIGN SUBSIDIARIES.—

(1) AGREEMENT WITH RESPECT TO CERTAIN EMPLOYEES OF FOREIGN SUBSIDIARIES.—The Secretary shall, at the request of any domestic corporation, enter into an agreement (in such form and manner as may be prescribed by the Secretary) with any

such corporation which desires to have the insurance system established by title II of the Social Security Act extended to service performed outside the United States in the employ of any one or more of its foreign subsidiaries (as defined in paragraph (8)) by all employees who are citizens of the United States, except that the agreement shall not be applicable to any service performed by, or remuneration paid to, an employee if such service or remuneration would be excluded from the term 'employment' or 'wages', as defined in this section, had the service been performed in the United States."

P.L. 98-21, § 321(a)(2):

Amended Code Sec. 3121(l)(8). **Effective** with respect to agreements entered into after 4-20-83. Prior to amendment, Code Sec. 3121(l)(8) read as follows:

"(8) DEFINITION OF FOREIGN SUBSIDIARY.—For purposes of this subsection and section 210(a) of the Social Security Act, a foreign subsidiary of a domestic corporation is—

(A) a foreign corporation not less than 20 percent of the voting stock of which is owned by such domestic corporation; or

(B) a foreign corporation more than 50 percent of the voting stock of which is owned by the foreign corporation described in subparagraph (A)."

P.L. 98-21, § 321(e)(1):

Amended Code Sec. 3121(l) (not otherwise amended by P.L. 98-21) by striking out "domestic corporation" and inserting in lieu thereof "American employer"; by striking out "domestic corporations" and inserting in lieu thereof "American employers"; by striking out "subsidiary" and inserting in lieu thereof "affiliate"; by striking out "subsidiaries" and inserting in lieu thereof "affiliates"; by striking out "foreign corporation" and inserting in lieu thereof "foreign entity"; by striking out "foreign corporations" and inserting in lieu thereof "foreign entities"; by striking out "citizens" and inserting in lieu thereof "citizens or residents" and by striking out "a" where it appeared before "domestic" and inserting in lieu thereof "an". **Effective** for agreements entered into after 4-20-83.

• **1976, Tax Reform Act of 1976 (P.L. 94-455)**

P.L. 94-455, § 1903(a)(3)(F):

Deleted ", but in no case prior to January 1, 1955" in Code Sec. 3121(l)(2). **Effective** for wages paid after 12-31-76.

P.L. 94-455, § 1906(b)(13)(A):

Amended 1954 Code by substituting "Secretary" for "Secretary or his delegate" each place it appeared. **Effective** 2-1-77.

• **1958, Technical Amendments Act of 1958 (P.L. 85-866)**

P.L. 85-866, § 69:

Amended the heading of Sec. 3121(l)(3) by striking out "BE" and substituting "BY". Prior to amendment the heading read: "TERMINATION OF PERIOD BE A DOMESTIC CORPORATION". **Effective** 1-1-54.

• **1956, Social Security Amendments of 1956 (P.L. 880, 84th Cong.)**

P.L. 880, 84th Cong., § 103(j), 201(j):

Amended Sec. 3121(l)(6) by striking "Fund" in the heading and inserting in its place "Funds"; by inserting after "Federal Old-Age and Survivors Insurance Trust Fund" the following: "and the Federal Disability Insurance Trust Fund". Sec. 3121(l)(8)(A) was amended by substituting the phrase "not less than 20" for "more than 50". **Effective** 8-1-56.

• **1954, Social Security Amendments of 1954 (P.L. 761, 83rd Cong.)**

P.L. 761, 83rd Cong., § 209:

Amended Sec. 3121 by adding subsection (l). **Effective** 9-1-54.

[Sec. 3121(m)]

(m) SERVICE IN THE UNIFORMED SERVICES.—For purposes of this chapter—

(1) INCLUSION OF SERVICE.—The term "employment" shall, notwithstanding the provisions of subsection (b) of this section, include—

(A) service performed by an individual as a member of a uniformed service on active duty, but such term shall not include any such service which is performed while on leave without pay, and

(B) service performed by an individual as a member of a uniformed service on inactive duty training.

(2) ACTIVE DUTY.—The term "active duty" means "active duty" as described in paragraph (21) of section 101 of title 38, United States Code and, except that it shall also include "active duty for training" as described in paragraph (22) of such section.

(3) INACTIVE DUTY TRAINING.—The term "inactive duty training" means "inactive duty training" as described in paragraph (23) of such section 101.

Amendments

• **1987, Revenue Act of 1987 (P.L. 100-203)**

P.L. 100-203, § 9001(b)(1):

Amended Code Sec. 3121(m)(1). **Effective** with respect to remuneration paid after 12-31-87. Prior to amendment, Code Sec. 3121(m)(1) read as follows:

(1) INCLUSION OF SERVICE.—The term "employment" shall, notwithstanding the provisions of subsection (b) of this section, include service performed by an individual as a member of a uniformed service on active duty; but such term shall not include any such service which is performed while on leave without pay.

• **1984, Deficit Reduction Act of 1984 (P.L. 98-369)**

P.L. 98-369, § 2663(i)(3):

Amended Sec. 3121(m)(2) by striking out "section 102 of the Servicemen's and Veterans' Survivor Benefits Act" and inserting in lieu thereof "paragraph (21) of section 101 of title 38, United States Code"; and by striking out "such section" and inserting in lieu thereof "paragraph (22) of such section". **Effective** 7-18-84, but shall not be construed as changing or affecting any right, liability, status, or interpretation which existed (under the provisions of law involved) before that date.

P.L. 98-369, § 2663(i)(4):

Amended Code Section 3121(m)(3) by striking out "such section 102" and inserting in lieu thereof "paragraph (23) of such section 101". **Effective** 7-18-84, but shall not be construed as changing or affecting any right, liability, status, or interpretation which existed (under the provisions of law involved) before that date.

• **1976, Tax Reform Act of 1976 (P.L. 94-455)**

P.L. 94-455, § 1903(a)(3)(G), (d):

Deleted "after December 1956" in Code Sec. 3121(m)(1). **Effective** for wages paid after 12-31-76.

• **1956, Servicemen's and Veterans' Survivor Benefits Act (P.L. 881, 84th Cong.)**

P.L. 881, 84th Cong., § 411(a):

Amended Sec. 3121 by adding subsection (m). **Effective** under § 603(a) of P.L. 881.

[Sec. 3121(n)]

(n) MEMBER OF A UNIFORMED SERVICE.—For purposes of this chapter, the term "member of a uniformed service" means any person appointed, enlisted, or inducted in a component of the Army, Navy, Air Force, Marine Corps, or Coast Guard (including a reserve component as defined in section 101(27) of title 38, United States Code), or in one of those services without specification of component, or as a commissioned officer of the Coast and Geodetic Survey, the National Oceanic and Atmospheric Administration Corps, or the Regular or Reserve Corps of the Public Health Service, and any person serving in the Army or Air Force under call or conscription. The term includes—

(1) a retired member of any of those services;

(2) a member of the Fleet Reserve or Fleet Marine Corps Reserve;

(3) a cadet at the United States Military Academy, a midshipman at the United States Naval Academy, and a cadet at the United States Coast Guard Academy or United States Air Force Academy;

(4) a member of the Reserve Officers' Training Corps, the Naval Reserve Officers' Training Corps, or the Air Force Reserve Officers' Training Corps, when ordered to annual training duty for fourteen days or more, and while performing authorized travel to and from that duty; and

(5) any person while en route to or from, or at, a place for final acceptance or for entry upon active duty in the military, naval, or air service—

(A) who has been provisionally accepted for such duty; or

(B) who, under the Military Selective Service Act, has been selected for active military, naval, or air service;

and has been ordered or directed to proceed to such place.

The term does not include a temporary member of the Coast Guard Reserve.

Amendments

• **1984, Deficit Reduction Act of 1984 (P.L. 98-369)**

P.L. 98-369, §2663(i)(5):

Amended Code Sec. 3121(n) by striking out "a reserve component of a uniformed service as defined in section 102(3) of the Servicemen's and Veterans' Survivor Benefits Act" in the first sentence and inserting in lieu thereof "a reserve component as defined in section 101(27) of title 38, United States Code"; by inserting ", the National Oceanic and Atmospheric Administration Corps," after "Coast and Geodetic Survey" in the first sentence; by striking out "military or naval" each place it appears in paragraph (5) and inserting in lieu thereof "military, naval, or air"; and by striking out "Universal Military Training and Service Act" in paragraph (5)(B) and inserting in lieu thereof "Military Selective Service Act". **Effective** 7-18-84, but shall not be construed as changing or affecting any right, liability, status, or interpretation which existed (under the provisions of law involved) before that date.

• **1956, Servicemen's and Veterans' Survivor Benefits Act (P.L. 881, 84th Cong.)**

P.L. 881, 84th Cong., §411(a):

Amended Sec. 3121 by adding subsection (n). **Effective** under §603(a) of P.L. 881.

[Sec. 3121(o)]

(o) CREW LEADER.—For purposes of this chapter, the term "crew leader" means an individual who furnishes individuals to perform agricultural labor for another person, if such individual pays (either on his own behalf or on behalf of such person) the individuals so furnished by him for the agricultural labor performed by them and if such individual has not entered into an agreement with such person whereby such individual has been designated as an employee of such person; and such individuals furnished by the crew leader to perform agricultural labor for another person shall be deemed to be the employees of such crew leader. For purposes of this chapter and chapter 2, a crew leader shall, with respect to service performed in furnishing individuals to perform agricultural labor for another person and service performed as a member of the crew, be deemed not to be an employee of such other person.

Amendments

• **1956, Social Security Amendments of 1956 (P.L. 880, 84th Cong.)**

P.L. 880, 84th Cong., 2d Sess., §201(h)(2):

Amended Sec. 3121 by adding subsection (o). **Effective** for service performed after 1956.

[Sec. 3121(p)]

(p) PEACE CORPS VOLUNTEER SERVICE.—For purposes of this chapter, the term "employment" shall, notwithstanding the provisions of subsection (b) of this section, include service performed by an individual as a volunteer or volunteer leader within the meaning of the Peace Corps Act.

Amendments

• **1961, Peace Corps Act (P.L. 87-293)**

P.L. 87-293, §202(a)(2):

Added Code Sec. 3121(p). **Effective** for services performed after 9-22-61.

[Sec. 3121(q)]

(q) TIPS INCLUDED FOR BOTH EMPLOYEE AND EMPLOYER TAXES.—For purposes of this chapter, tips received by an employee in the course of his employment shall be considered remuneration for such employment (and deemed to have been paid by the employer for purposes of subsections (a) and (b) of section 3111). Such remuneration shall be deemed to be paid at the time a written statement including such tips is furnished to the employer pursuant to section 6053(a) or (if no statement including such tips is so furnished) at the time received; except that, in determining the employer's liability in connection with the taxes imposed by section 3111 with respect to such tips in any case where no statement including such tips was so furnished (or to the extent that the statement so furnished was inaccurate or incomplete), such remuneration shall be deemed for purposes of subtitle F to be paid on the date on which notice and demand for such taxes is made to the employer by the Secretary.

Amendments

• **1987, Revenue Act of 1987 (P.L. 100-203)**
P.L. 100-203, § 9006(a)(1)-(4):
Amended Code Sec. 3121(q) by striking out "Employee Taxes" in the heading and inserting "Both Employee and Employer Taxes", by striking out "other than for purposes of the taxes imposed by section 3111" after "this chapter", by striking out "remuneration for employment" and inserting "remuneration for such employment (and deemed to have been paid by the employer for purposes of subsections (a) and (b) of section 3111)", and by inserting after "at the time received" the following "; except that, in determining the employer's liability in connection with the taxes imposed by section 3111 with respect to such tips in any case where no statement including such tips was so furnished (or to the extent that the statement so furnished was inaccurate or incomplete), such remuneration shall be deemed for purposes of subtitle F to be paid on the date on which notice and demand for such taxes is made to the employer by the Secretary." **Effective** with respect to tips received (and wages paid) on and after 1-1-88.

• **1965, Social Security Amendments of 1965 (P.L. 89-97)**
P.L. 89-97, § 313(c):
Added Sec. 3121(q). **Effective** with respect to tips received by employees after 1965.

[Sec. 3121(r)]

(r) ELECTION OF COVERAGE BY RELIGIOUS ORDERS.—

(1) CERTIFICATE OF ELECTION BY ORDER.—A religious order whose members are required to take a vow of poverty, or any autonomous subdivision of such order, may file a certificate (in such form and manner, and with such official, as may be prescribed by regulations under this chapter) electing to have the insurance system established by title II of the Social Security Act extended to services performed by its members in the exercise of duties required by such order or such subdivision thereof. Such certificate of election shall provide that—

(A) such election of coverage by such order or subdivision shall be irrevocable;

(B) such election shall apply to all current and future members of such order, or in the case of a subdivision thereof to all current and future members of such order who belong to such subdivision;

(C) all services performed by a member of such an order or subdivision in the exercise of duties required by such order or subdivision shall be deemed to have been performed by such member as an employee of such order or subdivision; and

(D) the wages of each member, upon which such order or subdivision shall pay the taxes imposed by sections 3101 and 3111, will be determined as provided in subsection (i)(4).

(2) DEFINITION OF MEMBER.—For purposes of this subsection, a member of a religious order means any individual who is subject to a vow of poverty as a member of such order and who performs tasks usually required (and to the extent usually required) of an active member of such order and who is not considered retired because of old age or total disability.

(3) EFFECTIVE DATE FOR ELECTION.—

(A) A certificate of election of coverage shall be in effect, for purposes of subsection (b)(8) and for purposes of section 210(a)(8) of the Social Security Act, for the period beginning with whichever of the following may be designated by the order or subdivision thereof:

(i) the first day of the calendar quarter in which the certificate is filed,

(ii) the first day of the calendar quarter succeeding such quarter, or

(iii) the first day of any calendar quarter preceding the calendar quarter in which the certificate is filed, except that such date may not be earlier than the first day of the twentieth calendar quarter preceding the quarter in which such certificate is filed.

Whenever a date is designated under clause (iii), the election shall apply to services performed before the quarter in which the certificate is filed only if the member performing such services was a member at the time such services were performed and is living on the first day of the quarter in which such certificate is filed.

(B) If a certificate of election filed pursuant to this subsection is effective for one or more calendar quarters prior to the quarter in which such certificate is filed, then—

(i) for purposes of computing interest and for purposes of section 6651 (relating to addition to tax for failure to file tax return), the due date for the return and payment of the tax for such prior calendar quarters resulting from the filing of such certificate shall be the last day of the calendar month following the calendar quarter in which the certificate is filed; and

(ii) the statutory period for the assessment of such tax shall not expire before the expiration of 3 years from such due date.

Amendments

• **1983, Social Security Act of 1983 (P.L. 98-21)**
P.L. 98-21, § 102(b)(3):
Amended Code Sec. 3121(r) by striking out "subsection (b)(8)(A)" and "section 210(a)(8)(A) in paragraph (3) and inserting in lieu thereof "subsection (b)(8)" and "section 210(a)(8)", respectively; and by striking out paragraph (4). **Effective** with respect to service performed after 12-31-83. The period for which a certificate is in effect under Code Sec. 3121(k) may not be terminated under § 3121(k)(1)(D) or 3121(k)(2) on or after 3-31-83, but no such certificate shall be effective to any service to which the amendments made by § 102 of P.L. 98-21 apply. If any individual, (1) on 1-1-84, is age 55 or over, and is an employee of an organization described in § 210(a)(8)(B) of the Social Security Act (a) which does not have in effect (on that date) a waiver certificate under Code Sec. 3121(k) and (b) to the employees of which social security coverage is extended on 1-1-84, solely by reason of enactment of this section, and (2) after 12-31-83, acquires the number of quarters of coverage (within the meaning of § 213 of the Social Security Act) which is required for purposes of this subparagraph under paragraph (2), then such individual shall be deemed to be a fully insured individual for all of the purposes of title II of such act. Prior to amendment, Code Sec. 3121(r)(4) read as follows:

(4) COORDINATION WITH COVERAGE OF LAY EMPLOYEES.—Notwithstanding the preceding provisions of this subsection, no certificate of election shall become effective with respect to an order or subdivision thereof, unless—

(A) if at the time the certificate of election is filed a certificate of waiver of exemption under subsection (k) is in effect with respect to such order or subdivision, such order or subdivision amends such certificate of waiver of exemption (in such form and manner as may be prescribed by regulations made under this chapter) to provide that it may not be revoked, or

(B) if at the time the certificate of election is filed a certificate of waiver of exemption under such subsection is not in effect with respect to such order or subdivision, such order or subdivision files such certificate of waiver of exemption under the provisions of such subsection except that such certificate of waiver of exemption cannot become effective at a later date than the certificate of election and such certificate of waiver of exemption must specify that such certificate of waiver of exemption may not be revoked. The certificate of waiver of exemption required under this subparagraph shall be filed notwithstanding the provisions of subsection (k)(3).

• **1972, Social Security Amendments of 1972 (P.L. 92-603)**

P.L. 92-603, §123(b):

Added Code Sec. 3121(r). **Effective** 10-30-72.

[Sec. 3121(s)]

(s) CONCURRENT EMPLOYMENT BY TWO OR MORE EMPLOYERS.—For purposes of sections 3102, 3111 and 3121(a)(1), if two or more related corporations concurrently employ the same individual and compensate such individual through a common paymaster which is one of such corporations, each such corporation shall be considered to have paid as remuneration to such individual only the amounts actually disbursed by it to such individual and shall not be considered to have paid as remuneration to such individual amounts actually disbursed to such individual by another of such corporations.

Amendments

• **1983, Social Security Act of 1983 (P.L. 98-21)**

P.L. 98-21, §125, provides:

SEC. 125. TREATMENT OF CERTAIN FACULTY PRACTICE PLANS.

(a) GENERAL RULE.—For purposes of subsection (s) of section 3121 of the Internal Revenue Code of 1954 (relating to concurrent employment by 2 or more employers)—

(1) the following entities shall be deemed to be related corporations:

(A) a State university which employs health professionals as faculty members at a medical school, and

(B) a faculty practice plan described in section 501(c)(3) of such Code and exempt from tax under section 501(a) of such Code—

(i) which employs faculty members of such medical school, and

(ii) 30 percent or more of the employees of which are concurrently employed by such medical school; and

(2) remuneration which is disbursed by such faculty practice plan to a health professional employed by both such entities shall be deemed to have been actually disbursed by such university as a common paymaster and not to have been actually disbursed by such faculty practice plan.

(b) EFFECTIVE DATE.—The provisions of subsection (a) shall apply to remuneration paid after December 31, 1983.

• **1977 (P.L. 95-216)**

P.L. 95-216, §314(a), (c):

Added Code Sec. 3121(s). **Effective** for wages paid after 12-31-78.

[Sec. 3121(t)—Repealed]

Amendments

• **1987, Revenue Act of 1987 (P.L. 100-203)**

P.L. 100-203, §9006(b)(2):

Repealed Code Sec. 3121(t). **Effective** with respect to tips received (and wages paid) on and after 1-1-88. Prior to repeal, Code Sec. 3121(t) read as follows:

(t) SPECIAL RULE FOR DETERMINING WAGES SUBJECT TO EMPLOYER TAX IN CASE OF CERTAIN EMPLOYEES WHOSE EMPLOYEES RECEIVE INCOME FROM TIPS.—If the wages paid by an employer with respect to the employment during any month of an individual who (for services performed in connection with such employment) receives tips which constitute wages, and to which section 3102(a) applies, are less than the total amount which would be payable (with respect to such employment) at the minimum wage rate applicable to such individual under section 6(a)(1) of the Fair Labor Standards Act of 1938 (determined without regard to section 3(m) of such Act), the wages so paid shall be deemed for purposes of section 3111 to be equal to such total amount.

• **1977 (P.L. 95-216)**

P.L. 95-216, §315(a):

Added Code Sec. 3121(t). **Effective** for wages paid for employment performed after 1977.

[Sec. 3121(u)]

(u) APPLICATION OF HOSPITAL INSURANCE TAX TO FEDERAL, STATE, AND LOCAL EMPLOYMENT.—

(1) FEDERAL EMPLOYMENT.—For purposes of the taxes imposed by sections 3101(b) and 3111(b), subsection (b) shall be applied without regard to paragraph (5) thereof.

(2) STATE AND LOCAL EMPLOYMENT.—For purposes of the taxes imposed by sections 3101(b) and 3111(b)—

(A) IN GENERAL.—Except as provided in subparagraphs (B) and (C), subsection (b) shall be applied without regard to paragraph (7) thereof.

(B) EXCEPTION FOR CERTAIN SERVICES.—Service shall not be treated as employment by reason of subparagraph (A) if—

(i) the service is included under an agreement under section 218 of the Social Security Act, or

(ii) the service is performed—

(I) by an individual who is employed by a State or political subdivision thereof to relieve him from unemployment,

(II) in a hospital, home, or other institution by a patient or inmate thereof as an employee of a State or political subdivision thereof or of the District of Columbia,

(III) by an individual, as an employee of a State or political subdivision thereof or of the District of Columbia, serving on a temporary basis in case of fire, storm, snow, earthquake, flood or other similar emergency,

(IV) by any individual as an employee included under section 5351(2) of title 5, United States Code (relating to certain interns, student nurses, and other student employees of hospitals of the District of Columbia Government), other than as a medical or dental intern or a medical or dental resident in training,

(V) by an election official or election worker if the remuneration paid in a calendar year for such service is less than $1,000 with respect to service performed during any calendar year commencing on or after January 1, 1995, ending on or before December 31, 1999, and the adjusted amount determined under section 218(c)(8)(B) of the Social Security Act for any calendar year commencing on or after January 1, 2000, with respect to service performed during such calendar year, or

(VI) by an individual in a position described in section 1402(c)(2)(E).

As used in this subparagraph, the terms "State" and "political subdivision" have the meanings given those terms in section 218(b) of the Social Security Act.

(C) EXCEPTION FOR CURRENT EMPLOYMENT WHICH CONTINUES.—Service performed for an employer shall not be treated as employment by reason of subparagraph (A) if—

(i) such service would be excluded from the term "employment" for purposes of this chapter if subparagraph (A) did not apply;

(ii) such service is performed by an individual—

(I) who was performing substantial and regular service for remuneration for that employer before April 1, 1986,

(II) who is a bona fide employee of that employer on March 31, 1986, and

(III) whose employment relationship with that employer was not entered into for purposes of meeting the requirements of this subparagraph; and

(iii) the employment relationship with that employer has not been terminated after March 31, 1986.

(D) TREATMENT OF AGENCIES AND INSTRUMENTALITIES.—For purposes of subparagraph (C), under regulations—

(i) All agencies and instrumentalities of a State (as defined in section 218(b) of the Social Security Act) or of the District of Columbia shall be treated as a single employer.

(ii) All agencies and instrumentalities of a political subdivision of a State (as so defined) shall be treated as a single employer and shall not be treated as described in clause (i).

(3) MEDICARE QUALIFIED GOVERNMENT EMPLOYMENT.—For purposes of this chapter, the term "medicare qualified government employment" means service which—

(A) is employment (as defined in subsection (b)) with the application of paragraphs (1) and (2), but

(B) would not be employment (as so defined) without the application of such paragraphs.

Amendments

- **1994, Social Security Independence and Program Improvements Act of 1994 (P.L. 103-296)**

P.L. 103-296, §303(b)(2):

Amended Code Sec. 3121(u)(2)(B)(ii)(V) by striking "$100" and inserting "$1,000 with respect to service performed during any calendar year commencing on or after January 1, 1995, ending on or before December 31, 1999, and the adjusted amount determined under section 218(c)(8)(B) of the Social Security Act for any calendar year commencing on or after January 1, 2000, with respect to service performed during such calendar year". **Effective** with respect to service performed on or after 1-1-95.

- **1988, Technical and Miscellaneous Revenue Act of 1988 (P.L. 100-647)**

P.L. 100-647, §1018(r)(2)(A):

Amended Code Sec. 3121(u)(2)(B)(ii) by striking out "or" at the end of subclause (IV), by striking out the period at the end of subclause (V) and inserting in lieu thereof ", or", and by inserting after subclause (V) new subclause (VI). **Effective** for services performed after 3-31-86.

- **1986, Tax Reform Act of 1986 (P.L. 99-514)**

P.L. 99-514, §1895(b)(18)(A):

Amended Code Sec. 3121(u)(2)(B)(ii) by striking out "or" at the end of subclause (III), by striking out the period at the end of subclause (IV) and inserting in lieu thereof ", or", and by adding at the end thereof new subclause (V). **Effective** as if included in the enactment of P.L. 99-272.

- **1986, Consolidated Omnibus Budget Reconciliation Act of 1985 (P.L. 99-272)**

P.L. 99-272, §13205(a)(1):

Amended Code Sec. 3121(u). **Effective** for services performed after 3-31-86. Prior to amendment, Code Sec. 3121(u) read as follows:

(u) APPLICATION OF HOSPITAL INSURANCE TAX TO FEDERAL EMPLOYMENT.—

(1) IN GENERAL.—For purposes of the taxes imposed by sections 3101(b) and 3111(b), subsection (b) shall be applied without regard to paragraph (5) thereof.

(2) MEDICARE QUALIFIED FEDERAL EMPLOYMENT.—For purposes of this chapter, the term "medicare qualified Federal employment" means service which—

(A) is employment (as defined in subsection (b)) with the application of paragraph (1), but

(B) would not be employment (as so defined) without the application of paragraph (1).

- **1983, Social Security Act of 1983 (P.L. 98-21)**

P.L. 98-21, §101(b)(2):

Amended Code Sec. 3121(u)(1). **Effective** with respect to service performed after 12-31-83. Prior to amendment Code Sec. 3121(u)(1) read as follows:

(1) IN GENERAL.—For purposes of the taxes imposed by sections 3101(b) and 3111(b)—

(A) paragraph (6) of subsection (b) shall be applied without regard to subparagraphs (A), (B), and (C)(i), (ii), and (vi) thereof, and

(B) paragraph (5) of subsection (b) (and the provisions of law referred to therein) shall not apply.

- **1982, Tax Equity and Fiscal Responsibility Act of 1982 (P.L. 97-248)**

P.L. 97-248, §278(a)(1):

Added Code Sec. 3121(u). **Effective** for remuneration paid after 12-31-82.

[Sec. 3121(v)]

(v) TREATMENT OF CERTAIN DEFERRED COMPENSATION AND SALARY REDUCTION ARRANGEMENTS.—

(1) CERTAIN EMPLOYER CONTRIBUTIONS TREATED AS WAGES.—Nothing in any paragraph of subsection (a) (other than paragraph (1)) shall exclude from the term "wages"—

(A) any employer contribution under a qualified cash or deferred arrangement (as defined in section 401(k)) to the extent not included in gross income by reason of section 402(e)(3) or consisting of designated Roth contributions (as defined in section 402A(c)), or

(B) any amount treated as an employer contribution under section 414(h)(2) where the pickup referred to in such section is pursuant to a salary reduction agreement (whether evidenced by a written instrument or otherwise).

(2) TREATMENT OF CERTAIN NONQUALIFIED DEFERRED COMPENSATION PLANS.—

(A) IN GENERAL.—Any amount deferred under a nonqualified deferred compensation plan shall be taken into account for purposes of this chapter as of the later of—

(i) when the services are performed, or

(ii) when there is no substantial risk of forfeiture of the rights to such amount.

The preceding sentence shall not apply to any excess parachute payment (as defined in section 280G(b)) or to any specified stock compensation (as defined in section 4985) on which tax is imposed by section 4985.

(B) TAXED ONLY ONCE.—Any amount taken into account as wages by reason of subparagraph (A) (and the income attributable thereto) shall not thereafter be treated as wages for purposes of this chapter.

(C) NONQUALIFIED DEFERRED COMPENSATION PLAN.—For purposes of this paragraph, the term "nonqualified deferred compensation plan" means any plan or other arrangement for deferral of compensation other than a plan described in subsection (a)(5).

(3) EXEMPT GOVERNMENTAL DEFERRED COMPENSATION PLAN.—For purposes of subsection (a)(5), the term "exempt governmental deferred compensation plan" means any plan providing for deferral of compensation established and maintained for its employees by the United States, by a State or political subdivision thereof, or by an agency or instrumentality of any of the foregoing. Such term shall not include—

(A) any plan to which section 83, 402(b), 403(c), 457(a), or 457(f)(1) applies,

(B) any annuity contract described in section 403(b), and

(C) the Thrift Savings Fund (within the meaning of subchapter III of chapter 84 of title 5, United States Code).

Amendments

• **2007, Tax Technical Corrections Act of 2007 (P.L. 110-172)**

P.L. 110-172, §8(a)(2):

Amended Code Sec. 3121(v)(1)(A) by inserting "or consisting of designated Roth contributions (as defined in section 402A(c)" before the comma at the end. **Effective** as if included in the provision of the Economic Growth and Tax Relief Reconciliation Act of 2001 (P.L. 107-16) to which it relates [**effective** for tax years beginning after 12-31-2005.—CCH].

• **2004, American Jobs Creation Act of 2004 (P.L. 108-357)**

P.L. 108-357, §802(c)(1):

Amended the last sentence of Code Sec. 3121(v)(2)(A) by inserting before the period "or to any specified stock compensation (as defined in section 4985) on which tax is imposed by section 4985". For the **effective** date, see Act Sec. 802(d), below.

P.L. 108-357, §802(d), provides:

(d) EFFECTIVE DATE.—The amendments made by this section shall take effect on March 4, 2003; except that periods before such date shall not be taken into account in applying the periods in subsections (a) and (e)(1) of section 4985 of the Internal Revenue Code of 1986, as added by this section.

• **1992, Unemployment Compensation Amendments of 1992 (P.L. 102-318)**

P.L. 102-318, §521(b)(34):

Amended Code Sec. 3121(v)(1)(A) by striking "section 402(a)(8)" and inserting "section 402(e)(3)". **Effective** for distributions after 12-31-92.

• **1988, Technical and Miscellaneous Revenue Act of 1988 (P.L. 100-647)**

P.L. 100-647, §1011(e)(8):

Amended Code Sec. 3121(v)(3)(A) by striking out "457(e)(1)" and inserting in lieu thereof "457(f)(1)". **Effective** as if included in the provision of P.L. 99-514 to which it relates.

P.L. 100-647, §1018(u)(35):

Amended Code Sec. 3121(v)(3)(C) by striking out "Saving" and inserting in lieu thereof "Savings". **Effective** as if included in the provision of P.L. 99-514 to which it relates.

• **1986, Tax Reform Act of 1986 (P.L. 99-514)**

P.L. 99-514, §1147(b):

Amended Code Sec. 3121(v)(3) by striking out "and" at the end of subparagraph (A), by striking out the period at the end of subparagraph (B), and inserting in lieu thereof ", and", and by inserting after subparagraph (B) the new subparagraph (C). **Effective** 10-22-86.

P.L. 99-514, §1899A(38):

Amended Code Sec. 3121(v)(2)(A)(ii) by striking out "forfeiture" and inserting in lieu thereof "forfeiture". **Effective** 10-22-86.

• **1984, Deficit Reduction Act of 1984 (P.L. 98-369)**

P.L. 98-369, §67(c):

Amended Code Sec. 3121(v)(2)(A) by adding the sentence at the end thereof. **Effective** for payments under agreements entered into or renewed after 6-14-84, in tax years ending after such date. A special rule appears below.

P.L. 98-369, §67(e)(2), provides:

(2) Special Rule for Contract Amendments.—In the case of any contract entered into before June 15, 1984, any amendment to such contract after June 14, 1984, which amends such contract in any significant relevant aspect shall be treated as a new contract.

P.L. 98-369, §2661(o)(3):

Amended Code Sec. 3121(v)(1)(B). **Effective** 1-1-84. Prior to amendment, subparagraph (B) read as follows:

(B) any amount treated as an employer contribution under section 414(h)(2).

• **1983, Social Security Act of 1983 (P.L. 98-21)**

P.L. 98-21, §324(a)(1):

Added Code Sec. 3121(v). **Effective**, generally, for remuneration paid after 12-31-83; it shall not apply, however, to employer contributions made during 1984 and attributable to services performed during 1983 under a qualified cash or deferred arrangement (as defined in Code Sec. 401(k)) if, under the terms of such arrangement as in effect on 3-24-83, (A) the employee makes an election with respect to such contribution before 1-1-84, and (B) the employer identifies the amount of such contribution before 1-1-84. In the case of an agreement in existence on 3-24-83, between a nonqualified deferred compensation plan (as defined in Code Sec. 3121(v)(2)(C), as added by P.L. 98-21), and an individual, (A) the amendments made by Act Sec. 324(a) (which includes new Code Sec. 3121(v)) and (c) shall apply with respect to services performed by such individual after 12-31-83. The preceding sentence shall not apply in the case of a plan to which Code Sec. 457(a) applies. P.L. 98-21, §324(d)(1), as amended by P.L.98-369, §2662(f)(2), provides that for purposes of applying such amendments to remuneration paid after 12-31-83, which would have been taken into account before 1-1-84, if such amendments had applied to periods before 1-1-84, such remuneration shall be taken into account when paid (or, at the election of the payor, at the time which would be appropriate if such amendments had applied). P.L. 98-21, §324(d)(4), as amended by P.L. 98-369, §2662(f)(2)(C), provides that for, purposes of this paragraph, any plan or agreement to make payments described in paragraph (2), (3), or (13)(A)(iii) of section 3121(a) of such Code (as in effect on the day before the date of the enactment of this Act) shall be treated as a nonqualified deferred compensation plan.

[Sec. 3121(w)]

(w) EXEMPTION OF CHURCHES AND QUALIFIED CHURCH-CONTROLLED ORGANIZATIONS.—

(1) GENERAL RULE.—Any church or qualified church-controlled organization (as defined in paragraph (3)) may make an election within the time period described in paragraph (2), in accordance with such procedures as the Secretary determines to be appropriate, that services performed in the employ of such church or organization shall be excluded from employment for purposes of title II of the Social Security Act and this chapter. An election may be made under this subsection only if the church or qualified church-controlled organization states that such church or organization is opposed for religious reasons to the payment of the tax imposed under section 3111.

(2) TIMING AND DURATION OF ELECTION.—An election under this subsection must be made prior to the first date, more than 90 days after July 18, 1984, on which a quarterly employment tax return for the tax imposed under section 3111 is due, or would be due but for the election, from such church or organization. An election under this subsection shall apply to current and future employees, and shall apply to service performed after December 31, 1983. The election may be revoked by the church or organization under regulations prescribed by the Secretary. The election shall be revoked by the Secretary if such church or organization fails to furnish the information required under section 6051 to the Secretary for a period of 2 years or more with respect to remuneration paid for such services by such church or organization, and, upon request by the Secretary, fails to furnish all such previously unfurnished information for the period covered by the election. Any revocation under the preceding sentence shall apply retroactively to the beginning of the 2-year period for which the information was not furnished.

(3) DEFINITIONS—

(A) For purposes of this subsection, the term "church" means a church, a convention or association of churches, or an elementary or secondary school which is controlled, operated, or principally supported by a church or by a convention or association of churches.

(B) For purposes of this subsection, the term "qualified church-controlled organization" means any church-controlled tax-exempt organization described in section 501(c)(3), other than an organization which—

(i) offers goods, services, or facilities for sale, other than on an incidental basis, to the general public, other than goods, services, or facilities which are sold at a nominal charge which is substantially less than the cost of providing such goods, services, or facilities; and

(ii) normally receives more than 25 percent of its support from either (I) governmental sources, or (II) receipts from admissions, sales of merchandise, performance of services, or furnishing of facilities, in activities which are not unrelated trades or businesses, or both.

Amendments

- **1986, Tax Reform Act of 1986 (P.L. 99-514)**

P.L. 99-514, §1882(c):

Amended Code Sec. 3121(w)(2) by striking out the last two sentences and inserting in lieu thereof three new sentences. **Effective** 10-22-86. Prior to amendment, the last two sentences read as follows:

The election may not be revoked by the church or organization, but shall be permanently revoked by the Secretary if such church or organization fails to furnish the information required under section 6051 to the Secretary for a period of 2 years or more with respect to remuneration paid for such services by such church or organization, and, upon request by the Secretary, fails to furnish all such previously unfurnished information for the period covered by the election. Such revocation shall apply retroactively to the beginning of the 2-year period for which the information was not furnished.

P.L. 99-514, §1899A(39):

Amended the first sentence of paragraph (1) of Code Sec. 3121(w) by striking out "chapter 21 of this Code" and inserting in lieu thereof "this chapter". **Effective** 10-22-86.

P.L. 99-514, §1899A(40):

Amended Code Sec. 3121(w)(2) by striking out "the date of the enactment of this subsection" and inserting in lieu thereof "July 18, 1984". **Effective** 10-22-86.

- **1984, Deficit Reduction Act of 1984 (P.L. 98-369)**

P.L. 98-369, §2603(b):

Amended Code Sec. 3121 by adding at the end thereof new subsection (w). **Effective** for service performed after 12-31-83. A special rule appears below.

P.L. 98-369, §2603(f), provides:

(f) In any case where a church or qualified church controlled organization makes an election under section 3121(w) of the Internal Revenue Code of 1954, the Secretary of the Treasury shall refund (without interest) to such church or organization any taxes paid under sections 3101 and 3111 of such Code with respect to service performed after December 31, 1983, which is covered under such election. The refund shall be conditional upon the church or organization agreeing to pay to each employee (or former employee) the portion of the refund attributable to the tax imposed on such employee (or former employee) under section 3101, and such employee (or former employee) may not receive any other refund payment of such taxes.

[Sec. 3121(x)]

(x) APPLICABLE DOLLAR THRESHOLD.—For purposes of subsection (a)(7)(B), the term "applicable dollar threshold" means $1,000. In the case of calendar years after 1995, the Commissioner of Social Security shall adjust such $1,000 amount at the same time and in the same manner as under section 215(a)(1)(B)(ii) of the Social Security Act with respect to the amounts referred to in section 215(a)(1)(B)(i) of such Act, except that, for purposes of this paragraph, 1993 shall be substituted for the calendar year referred to in section 215(a)(1)(B)(ii)(II) of such Act. If any amount as adjusted under the preceding sentence is not a multiple of $100, such amount shall be rounded to the next lowest multiple of $100.

Amendments

- **1994, Social Security Domestic Employment Reform Act of 1994 (P.L. 103-387)**

P.L. 103-387, §2(a)(1)(B):

Amended Code Sec. 3121 by adding at the end thereof [sic] a new subsection (x). **Effective** for remuneration paid after 12-31-93.

[Sec. 3121(x)—Stricken]

Amendments

- **1993, Omnibus Budget Reconciliation Act of 1993 (P.L. 103-66)**

P.L. 103-66, §13207(a)(2):

Amended Code Sec. 3121 by striking subsection (x). **Effective** for 1994 and later calendar years. Prior to amendment, Code Sec. 3121(x) read as follows:

(x) APPLICABLE CONTRIBUTION BASE.—For purposes of this chapter—

(1) OLD-AGE, SURVIVORS, AND DISABILITY INSURANCE.—For purposes of the taxes imposed by sections 3101(a) and 3111(a), the applicable contribution base for any calendar year is the contribution and benefit base determined under section 230 of the Social Security Act for such calendar year.

(2) HOSPITAL INSURANCE.—For purposes of the taxes imposed by section 3101(b) and 3111(b), the applicable contribution base is—

(A) $125,000 for calendar year 1991, and

(B) for any calendar year after 1991, the applicable contribution base for the preceding year adjusted in the same manner as is used in adjusting the contribution and benefit base under section 230(b) of the Social Security Act.

- **1990, Omnibus Budget Reconciliation Act of 1990 (P.L. 101-508)**

P.L. 101-508, §11331(a)(2):

Amended Code Sec. 3121 by adding at the end thereof a new subsection (x). **Effective** for 1991 and later calendar years.

- **1989 (P.L. 101-140)**

P.L. 101-140, §203(a)(2), provides:

Code Sec. 3121(x) as added by Section 1011B(a)(22)(A) of the Technical and Miscellaneous Revenue Act of 1988 (P.L. 100-647) shall be applied as if the amendment made by such section has not been enacted. Code Sec. 3121(x), as added by Act Sec. 1011B(a)(22)(A) of P.L. 100-647, read as follows:

(x) Benefits Provided Under Certain Employee Benefit Plans.—Notwithstanding any paragraph of subsection (a) (other than paragraph (1)), the term "wages" shall include any amount which is includible in gross income by reason of section 89. **Effective** as if included in section 1151 of P.L. 99-514.

- **1988, Technical and Miscellaneous Revenue Act of 1988 (P.L. 100-647)**

P.L. 100-647, §1011B(a)(22)(A):

Amended Code Sec. 3121 by adding at the end thereof new subsection (x). Not **effective** for any individual who separated from service with the employer before 1-1-89.

[Sec. 3121(y)]

(y) SERVICE IN THE EMPLOY OF INTERNATIONAL ORGANIZATIONS BY CERTAIN TRANSFERRED FEDERAL EMPLOYEES.—

(1) IN GENERAL.—For purposes of this chapter, service performed in the employ of an international organization by an individual pursuant to a transfer of such individual to such international organization pursuant to section 3582 of title 5, United States Code, shall constitute "employment" if—

(A) immediately before such transfer, such individual performed service with a Federal agency which constituted "employment" under subsection (b) for purposes of the taxes imposed by sections 3101(a) and 3111(a), and

(B) such individual would be entitled, upon separation from such international organization and proper application, to reemployment with such Federal agency under such section 3582.

(2) DEFINITIONS.—For purposes of this subsection—

(A) FEDERAL AGENCY.—The term "Federal agency" means an agency, as defined in section 3581(1) of title 5, United States Code.

(B) INTERNATIONAL ORGANIZATION.—The term "international organization" has the meaning provided such term by section 3581(3) of title 5, United States Code.

Amendments

- **1994, Social Security Independence and Program Improvements Act of 1994 (P.L. 103-296)**

P.L. 103-296, §319(a)(1):

Amended Code Sec. 3121 by adding at the end thereof a new subsection (y). **Effective** with respect to service performed after the calendar quarter following the calendar quarter containing 8-15-94.

[Sec. 3121(z)]

(z) Treatment of Certain Foreign Persons as American Employers.—

(1) In General.—If any employee of a foreign person is performing services in connection with a contract between the United States Government (or any instrumentality thereof) and any member of any domestically controlled group of entities which includes such foreign person, such foreign person shall be treated for purposes of this chapter as an American employer with respect to such services performed by such employee.

(2) Domestically Controlled Group of Entities.—For purposes of this subsection—

(A) In General.—The term "domestically controlled group of entities" means a controlled group of entities the common parent of which is a domestic corporation.

(B) Controlled Group of Entities.—The term "controlled group of entities" means a controlled group of corporations as defined in section 1563(a)(1), except that—

(i) "more than 50 percent" shall be substituted for "at least 80 percent" each place it appears therein, and

(ii) the determination shall be made without regard to subsections (a)(4) and (b)(2) of section 1563.

A partnership or any other entity (other than a corporation) shall be treated as a member of a controlled group of entities if such entity is controlled (within the meaning of section 954(d)(3)) by members of such group (including any entity treated as a member of such group by reason of this sentence).

(3) Liability of Common Parent.—In the case of a foreign person who is a member of any domestically controlled group of entities, the common parent of such group shall be jointly and severally liable for any tax under this chapter for which such foreign person is liable by reason of this subsection, and for any penalty imposed on such person by this title with respect to any failure to pay such tax or to file any return or statement with respect to such tax or wages subject to such tax. No deduction shall be allowed under this title for any liability imposed by the preceding sentence.

(4) Provisions Preventing Double Taxation.—

(A) Agreements.—Paragraph (1) shall not apply to any services which are covered by an agreement under subsection (l).

(B) Equivalent Foreign Taxation.—Paragraph (1) shall not apply to any services if the employer establishes to the satisfaction of the Secretary that the remuneration paid by such employer for such services is subject to a tax imposed by a foreign country which is substantially equivalent to the taxes imposed by this chapter.

(5) Cross Reference.—For relief from taxes in cases covered by certain international agreements, see sections 3101(c) and 3111(c).

Amendments

• **2008, Heroes Earnings Assistance and Relief Tax Act of 2008 (P.L. 110-245)**
P.L. 110-245, §302(a):

Amended Code Sec. 3121 by adding at the end a new subsection (z). **Effective** for services performed in calendar months beginning more than 30 days after 6-17-2008.